FACT-FINDING WITHOUT FACTS

Fact-Finding Without Facts explores international criminal fact-finding – empirically, conceptually, and normatively. After reviewing thousands of pages of transcripts from various international criminal tribunals, the author reveals that international criminal trials are beset by numerous and severe fact-finding impediments that substantially impair the tribunals' ability to determine who did what to whom. These fact-finding impediments have heretofore received virtually no publicity, let alone scholarly treatment, and they are deeply troubling not only because they raise grave concerns about the accuracy of the judgments currently being issued but because they can be expected to similarly impair the next generation of international trials that will be held at the International Criminal Court. After setting forth her empirical findings, the author considers their conceptual and normative implications. The author concludes that international criminal tribunals purport a fact-finding competence that they do not possess and, as a consequence, base their judgments on a less precise, more amorphous method of fact-finding than they publicly acknowledge. The book ends with an exploration of various normative questions, including the most foundational: whether the international tribunals' fact-finding impediments fatally undermine the international criminal justice project.

Nancy Amoury Combs is a Professor of Law at the William and Mary Law School, where she is the 2009–2011 Cabell Research Professor and a 2008 recipient of William and Mary's Alumni Fellowship Award for teaching excellence. She earned her PhD from Leiden University and her JD from the University of California at Berkeley School of Law. She has served as a law clerk to Judge Diarmuid O'Scannlain on the Ninth Circuit Court of Appeals and to Justice Anthony Kennedy on the U.S. Supreme Court.

Prior to joining the faculty at William and Mary Law School, Professor Combs served as legal advisor at the Iran–United States Claims Tribunal in The Hague. She has written extensively on topics in international law and international criminal justice, publishing two books and numerous articles and essays appearing in the *University of Pennsylvania Law Review*, the *Vanderbilt Law Review*, the *Hastings Law Journal*, the *American Journal of International Law*, the *Harvard International Law Journal*, and the *Chicago Journal of International Law*, among others. She currently serves as member of the International Expert Framework, an international working group that is developing general rules and principles of international criminal procedure.

Fact-Finding Without Facts

THE UNCERTAIN EVIDENTIARY FOUNDATIONS OF INTERNATIONAL CRIMINAL CONVICTIONS

NANCY AMOURY COMBS
William and Mary Law School

CAMBRIDGE
UNIVERSITY PRESS

CAMBRIDGE
UNIVERSITY PRESS

University Printing House, Cambridge CB2 8BS, United Kingdom

One Liberty Plaza, 20th Floor, New York, NY 10006, USA

477 Williamstown Road, Port Melbourne, VIC 3207, Australia

314-321, 3rd Floor, Plot 3, Splendor Forum, Jasola District Centre, New Delhi - 110025, India

103 Penang Road, #05-06/07, Visioncrest Commercial, Singapore 238467

Cambridge University Press is part of the University of Cambridge.

It furthers the University's mission by disseminating knowledge in the pursuit of education, learning and research at the highest international levels of excellence.

www.cambridge.org
Information on this title: www.cambridge.org/9780521111157

First published 2010

A catalogue record for this publication is available from the British Library

Library of Congress Cataloging in Publication data
Combs, Nancy A., 1965–
Fact-finding in international criminal law / Nancy A. Combs.
p. cm.
Includes bibliographical references and index.
ISBN 978-0-521-11115-7 (hardback)
1. International criminal courts. 2. Evidence, Criminal. I. Title.
KZ6304.5.E94C66 2010
345′.06–dc22 2009043282

ISBN 978-0-521-11115-7 Hardback

For Dadu

Contents

Acknowledgments

This book has benefited immeasurably from the comments of those who read previous drafts as well as those who provided comments during the conferences and workshops where I presented portions of this book. In particular, I'm grateful to Lan Cao, Douglass Cassel, Bruce Combs, Mirjan Damaška, Mark Drumbl, Kevin Heller, Máximo Langer, Erik Lillquist, Linda Malone, Paul Marcus, Larry May, John Murphy, and those who attended Harvard Law School's Global Governance Workshop; George Washington University's Global Law Workshop; Washington & Lee's Transnational Law Institute Workshop; UCLA's Symposium on Trends and Tensions in International Criminal Procedure; the 2008 Annual Meeting of the International Society for the Reform of Criminal Law; University of Wisconsin's Law, War and Human Security Workshop; University of Illinois College of Law's Symposium on International Criminal Processes and Human Rights; and the 2007 IVR Conference on Law and Legal Cultures in the 21st Century.

I am also grateful for the research assistance of Karen Anslinger, Philip Fijalkovich, Noah Foreman, Andrew Gore, Kevin Grady, Kristina Hofmann, Michele Slachetka, Mary Thibadeau, Rebecca Wharton, and Michael Willems.

Introduction

After decades of inactivity, international criminal law has lately emerged as one of the most rapidly developing and influential subjects of international law and global politics. Sixty years after Nazi offenders were prosecuted at Nuremberg, the international community established an international criminal tribunal to prosecute those responsible for international crimes in the former Yugoslavia (ICTY). The ICTY spawned a number of progeny, including the International Criminal Tribunal for Rwanda (ICTR), the Special Court for Sierra Leone (SCSL), the Special Panels in the Dili District Court in East Timor (Special Panels), the Extraordinary Chambers in the Courts of Cambodia, the Special Tribunal for Lebanon and, most importantly, a permanent International Criminal Court (ICC). The establishment of these institutions constitutes, in Mark Drumbl's words, "one of the more extensive waves of institution-building in modern international relations."[1]

Most international law scholars warmly greeted the establishment of these tribunals.[2] Although large-scale atrocities have been committed since the dawn of humanity, for most of human history these atrocities have not elicited

[1] Mark A. Drumbl, Atrocity, Punishment, and International Law 10 (2007).

[2] Richard Goldstone called the new international tribunals "a tremendous and exciting step forward," Richard Goldstone, *Conference Luncheon Address*, 7 Transnat'l L. & Contemp. Probs. 1, 2 (1997), while Payam Akhavan hailed them as "an unprecedented institutional expression of the indivisibility of peace and respect for human rights" that represented "a radical departure from the traditional realpolitik paradigm which has so often and for so long ignored the victims of mass murder and legitimized the rule of tyrants in the name of promoting the purported *summum bonum* of stability," Payam Akhavan, *Justice and Reconciliation in the Great Lakes Region of Africa: The Contribution of the International Criminal Tribunal for Rwanda*, 7 Duke J. Comp. & Int'l L. 325, 327 (1997).

At least that was the view of commentators with an internationalist perspective. Scholars of a realist bent have questioned the wisdom and viability of international trials. *See, e.g.*, Jack Goldsmith & Stephen Krasner, *The Limits of Idealism*, Dædalus, Winter 2003, at 47, 47–53; Anthony D'Amato, *Peace vs. Accountability in Bosnia*, 88 Am. J. Int'l L. 500, 500–02 (1994). For a brief discussion of the realist critique of international criminal law, see Drumbl, note 1, at 10.

criminal sanctions. So, the move to impose accountability on brutal dictators who were responsible for widespread death, suffering, and destruction was considered a tremendous advance, and early commentators credited international criminal prosecutions with promoting a host of praiseworthy purposes. International criminal prosecutions were said to affirm the rule of law in previously lawless societies,[3] to promote peace building and transition to democracy in war-torn lands,[4] to assist in reconciling former enemies,[5] to deter future megalomaniacs from committing similar crimes,[6] to create a historical record of the conflict,[7] and to diminish the victims' propensity to blame collectively all those in the offenders' group.[8] International criminal justice was, in sum, the subject of a great deal of soaring and inspirational rhetoric.

In recent years, the glow surrounding international criminal justice has begun to fade. The scandalous length and cost of international criminal trials have driven some critiques,[9] while inadequate outreach efforts have formed

[3] MARTHA MINOW, BETWEEN VENGEANCE AND FORGIVENESS: FACING HISTORY AFTER GENOCIDE AND MASS VIOLENCE 25 (1998); RUTI G. TEITEL, TRANSITIONAL JUSTICE 56 (2000); Stephan Landsman, *Alternative Responses to Serious Human Rights Abuses: Of Prosecution and Truth Commissions*, 59 L. & CONTEMP. PROBS. 81, 83 (1996); The Secretary General, *The Rule of Law and Transitional Justice in Conflict and Post-Conflict Societies, delivered to the Security Council*, para. 39, U.N. Doc. S/2004/616 (Aug. 23, 2004).

[4] Antonio Cassese, *On the Current Trends Towards Criminal Prosecution and Punishment of Breaches of International Humanitarian Law*, 9 EUR. J. INT'L L. 2, 9–10 (1998).

[5] For a discussion of this literature, *see* Harvey M. Weinstein & Eric Stover, *Introduction: Conflict, Justice and Reclamation, in* MY NEIGHBOR, MY ENEMY: JUSTICE AND COMMUNITY IN THE AFTERMATH OF MASS ATROCITY 1, 3–4 (2004).

[6] Diane F. Orentlicher, *Settling Accounts: The Duty to Prosecute Human Rights Violations of a Prior Regime*, 100 YALE L.J. 2537, 2542 (1991); Alejandro Miguel Garro & Enrique Dahl, *Legal Accountability for Human Rights Violations in Argentina: One Step Forward and Two Steps Backward*, 8 HUM. RTS. L.J. 283, 343 (1987); Jaime Malamud-Goti, *Transitional Governments in the Breach: Why Punish State Criminals?* 12 HUM. RTS. Q. 1, 12 (1990); M. Cherif Bassiouni, *Justice and Peace: The Importance of Choosing Accountability over Realpolitik*, 35 CASE W. RES. J. INT'L L. 191, 192 (2003). Indeed, the Security Council established the ICTY while the Yugoslavian conflict was still underway with the express goal of deterring international crimes. *See Report of the International Tribunal for the Prosecution of Persons Responsible for Serious Violations of International Humanitarian Law Committed in the Territory of the Former Yugoslavia Since 1991*, para. 13, 49th Sess., U.N. Doc. A/49/150 (Aug. 29, 1994).

[7] Richard May & Marieke Wierda, *Evidence Before the ICTY, in* ESSAYS ON ICTY PROCEDURE AND EVIDENCE IN HONOUR OF GABRIELLE KIRK MCDONALD 249, 252–53 (Richard May et al. eds., 2001); Cassese, *On the Current Trends*, note 4, at 9–10; Antonio Cassese, *Reflections on International Criminal Justice*, 61 MOD. L. REV. 1, 6–9 (1998).

[8] Cassese, *On the Current Trends*, note 4, at 9; *see also* MINOW, note 3, at 40; Richard J. Goldstone, *50 Years after Nuremberg: A New International Criminal Tribunal for Human Rights Criminals, in* CONTEMPORARY GENOCIDES: CAUSES, CASES, CONSEQUENCES 215, 215–16 (Albert J. Jongman ed., 1996).

[9] *See, e.g.*, John E. Ackerman, *Assignment of Defense Counsel at the ICTY, in* ESSAYS ON ICTY PROCEDURE AND EVIDENCE IN HONOUR OF GABRIELLE KIRK MCDONALD 167, 170 (Richard May et al. eds., 2001); Mark A. Drumbl, *Rule of Law Amid Lawlessness: Counseling the Accused*

the basis for others.[10] On a much broader scale, Larry May, in his trilogy on crimes against humanity, war crimes, and aggression,[11] has carefully scrutinized and explicated the normative foundations of international criminal law, rejecting much that does not conform to his moral minimalist account. Other scholars have begun questioning the ability of international criminal tribunals to achieve many of the goals that previously had been reflexively attributed to them. Thus, whereas early commentators unquestioningly assumed that international criminal prosecutions would serve to deter the next generation of genocidal maniacs, more recently scholars have questioned that assumption.[12] Recent empirical research also has called into question the ability of international criminal tribunals to advance reconciliation and peace-building efforts following large-scale violence.[13] And Mark Drumbl, for his part, has offered a comprehensive and sophisticated critique of international criminal justice, concluding that there exists a palpable disconnect between the effects of sentencing and the penological theories that are expected to justify the imposition of criminal punishment.[14]

These are impressive studies because they scrutinize many of the foundational beliefs that drove the establishment of the international criminal tribunals, but, as impressive as they are, they assume the question that forms the

in Rwanda's Domestic Genocide Trials, 29 COLUM. HUM. RTS. L. REV. 545, 623 (1998); Daryl A. Mundis, *Improving the Operation and Functioning of the International Criminal Tribunals*, 94 AM. J. INT'L L. 759, 759 (2000); Mary Margaret Penrose, *Lest We Fail: The Importance of Enforcement in International Criminal Law*, 15 AM. U. INT'L L. REV. 321, 367–69 (1999); Patrick L. Robinson, *Ensuring Fair and Expeditious Trials at the International Criminal Tribunal for the Former Yugoslavia*, 11 EUR. J. INT'L L. 569, 584 (2000); Patricia M. Wald, *To "Establish Incredible Events by Credible Evidence": The Use of Affidavit Testimony in Yugoslavia War Crimes Tribunal Proceedings*, 42 HARV. INT'L L.J. 535, 536 (2001); International Crisis Group, *The International Criminal Tribunal for Rwanda: Justice Delayed* ii (June 7, 2001).

[10] *See, e.g.*, Geoffrey Nice & Philippe Vallières-Roland, *Procedural Innovations in War Crime Trials*, 3 J. INT'L CRIM. JUST. 354, 355 (2005); Samantha Power, *Rwanda: The Two Faces of Justice*, 50 N.Y. REVIEW OF BOOKS, Jan. 16, 2003; Ivan Simonović, *Dealing with the Legacy of Past War Crimes and Human Rights Abuses*, 2 J. INT'L CRIM. JUST. 701, 706–07 (2004); Christopher M. Gosnell, *A Court Too Far*, INT'L HERALD TRIB., Mar. 28, 2008.

[11] *See generally* LARRY MAY, CRIMES AGAINST HUMANITY: A NORMATIVE ACCOUNT (2005); LARRY MAY, WAR CRIMES AND JUST WAR (2007); LARRY MAY, AGGRESSION AND CRIMES AGAINST PEACE (2008).

[12] *See, e.g.*, Julian Ku & Jide Nzelibe, *Do International Criminal Tribunals Deter or Exacerbate Humanitarian Atrocities?*, 84 WASH. U. L. REV. 777 (2007); Martti Koskenniemi, *Between Impunity and Show Trials*, 6 MAX PLANCK Y.B. U.N. L. 1, 8–11 (2002).

[13] ERIC STOVER, THE WITNESSES: WAR CRIMES AND THE PROMISE OF JUSTICE IN THE HAGUE (2005); Laurel Fletcher & Harvey Weinstein, *Violence and Social Repair: Rethinking the Contribution of Justice to Reconciliation*, 24 HUM. RTS. Q. 573 (2002); Marie-Benedicte Dembour & Emily Haslan, *Silencing Hearings? Victim-Witnesses at War Crimes Trials*, 15 EUR. J. INT'L L. 151 (2004).

[14] DRUMBL, note 1, at 149–80.

basis for this work. The scholars I have mentioned might question whether the prosecution of certain international crimes can be justified given their infringement on state sovereignty,[15] or they might conclude that international criminal trials impair the prospects for reconciliation rather than advance them,[16] but their critiques presuppose that international trials – even if they can do nothing else – can determine with some measure of certainty whether a defendant engaged in the acts alleged in the indictment.[17] That is, even if international trials have uncertain philosophical foundations, even if they regularly fail to deter, rehabilitate, or reconcile, international criminal trials have at least been considered useful mechanisms for determining who did what to whom during a mass atrocity.

It is that assumption that I will challenge. My study will reveal that international criminal trials confront severe impediments to accurate fact-finding, impediments that should give rise to serious doubts about the accuracy of the Trial Chambers' factual determinations. The basis for my study is a large-scale review of transcripts from the ICTR, the SCSL, and the Special Panels. From this review, I conclude that much eyewitness testimony at the international tribunals is of highly questionable reliability. In particular, many international witnesses are unable to convey the information that court personnel expect – and need – to receive, if they are to have confidence in the factual determinations they make. Sometimes witnesses claim not to know the sought-after information, whereas in other cases the communication breaks down as a result of the questioning process. Chapter 2 details these testimonial deficiencies while Chapter 3 considers some of their causes. Chapter 3 reports, for instance, that many witnesses lack the education and life experiences to be able to read maps, tell time, or answer questions concerning distances and dates. Cultural norms and taboos create additional communication difficulties, as some witnesses are reluctant to speak directly or at all about certain events and as international judges inappropriately assess witnesses' demeanor and willingness to answer questions by Western norms. The need for language interpretation for virtually every fact witness – sometimes through multiple interpreters – and the unfamiliarity of most witnesses with the predominantly

[15] *See, e.g.*, MAY, CRIMES AGAINST HUMANITY, note 11, at 83 (contending that "international prosecutions require a showing that harm that is group-based has occurred").

[16] *See, e.g.*, STOVER, note 13, at 15.

[17] When Larry May, for instance, proposed a series of reforms designed to reduce the appearance of political influence over international trials, he acknowledged that accepting his proposals would make "the pursuit of the truth of the causes of the larger atrocity harder to ascertain by means of trials." He consoled readers, however, that "There will be truths nonetheless that will emerge . . . namely that truth concerning whether a given defendant did participate in an atrocity and to what extent." MAY, AGGRESSION, note 11, at 337.

adversarial trial procedures used at the international tribunals only compound these problems.

My review does not encompass ICTY proceedings because the ICTY is an outlier amongst the tribunals that have prosecuted international crimes and that will be doing so in the future. Although a cursory review of ICTY transcripts reveals that those proceedings do feature some of the problems that will be described in the following pages, because the ICTY prosecutes crimes that took place in Europe, the educational, cultural, and linguistic divergences between witnesses and courtroom staff that so impair communication at the ICTR, the SCSL, and the Special Panels do not prove as distortive. That in itself would not be reason to exclude the ICTY from my study, but the fact that the ICC is currently focused exclusively on African conflicts suggests that the fact-finding impediments that I have identified in ICTR, SCSL, and Special Panels proceedings constitute a continuing concern for international criminal justice despite the fact that the ICTY does not feature them in the same number or severity.

As a consequence of the fact-finding impediments that I will describe, the testimony of international witnesses often is vague, unclear, and lacking in the information necessary for fact finders to make reasoned factual assessments. Moreover, what clear information witnesses do provide in court often conflicts with the information that the witnesses previously provided in their pre-trial statements. Chapter 4 canvases such inconsistencies and reveals that they both pervade international criminal testimony and frequently pertain to core features of that testimony. In particular, my review of all of the completed SCSL cases and a handful of ICTR cases shows that more than 50 percent of the prosecution witnesses appearing in these trials testified in a way that was seriously inconsistent with their pretrial statements. Sometimes the inconsistencies related to such details as the date, time, or place of the crime, but as frequently they related to such fundamental matters as the nature of the crime and the nature of the defendant's involvement in the crime.

The inconsistencies that pervade international criminal transcripts can be explained by the educational, cultural, and linguistic factors described in Chapter 3, but they, along with other problematic features of witness testimony, also can be explained by witness mendacity. Indeed, many of the other testimonial difficulties chronicled in Chapter 2 – from the failure to answer date, time, and distance questions to the circuitous responses that so lengthen and complicate communication – could also stem from a witness's desire to evade. Although every criminal justice system in the world has its share of lying witnesses, Chapter 5 suggests that some international tribunals have more than their share. The group-based loyalty and ethnic divisions that gave rise to the international crimes in the first place can create powerful incentives to put enemies in prison, whether they belong there or not, and the international tribunals offer additional incentives – perhaps unwittingly – through the financial assistance that they provide to testifying witnesses. Whatever the causes of the false testimony, Chapter 5 reveals that some international criminal tribunals hear a lot of it. Indeed, my review of ICTR cases shows that more than 90 percent of them featured an alibi or another example of diametrically opposing testimony from defense and prosecution witnesses. Although some of these witnesses may be honestly mistaken, the use of alibis and the incidence of contradictory testimony so vastly exceeds that which is common to domestic trials that it would be naïve to dismiss a substantial portion of it as arising from honest mistakes.

These fact-finding impediments might not be worthy of significant concern if most convictions were supported by a substantial quantity of documentary or forensic evidence, but that simply is not the case for today's international trials. Whereas prosecutors at the Nuremberg Tribunal could rely on a colossal cache of documents to establish the guilt of the Nazi defendants before them, today's international criminals no longer leave a clear paper trail of their offenses. Orders are issued orally, and lines of command are blurred through the use of parallel structures of authority. Even forensic proof that a particular massacre took place is often lacking. As a consequence, prosecutors at today's international tribunals rely almost exclusively on eyewitness testimony. The substantial reliance on eyewitness testimony in itself would be worrisome because recent psychological research, as well as advances in DNA testing, has shown eyewitness testimony to be unreliable in numerous regards. The fact-finding impediments detailed in Chapters 2 through 5 serve only to increase the uncertainty of international criminal fact-finding based on such eyewitness testimony.

Although the factors just described should raise grave concerns about the reliability and credibility of the testimony presented to the international tribunals and the concomitant accuracy of the judgments that are based on that testimony, these problems heretofore have received virtually no publicity, let alone scholarly treatment or remedial legislation. Although occasional nongovernmental organization (NGO) reports have commented on a dearth of interpreters at one tribunal or judicial insensitivity at another, no comprehensive efforts have been undertaken to examine the significant impediments to accurate fact-finding that exist at the international tribunals. Such an examination is vitally important to the legitimacy of the international criminal justice project. Concededly, trials involve multiple layers of knowing. They encompass a normative spectrum that, in Robert Burns' words, features at one end "'[d]id he do it?' kinds of questions (brutally elementary data) to questions involving the interpretation of the meaning of circumstantial evidence and then to the provisional acceptance of morally and politically charged narratives."[18] I focus here only on the "brutally elementary data" question of "[d]id he do it?," but that is a crucial question, for it is arguably the question on which all other questions are based.

In considering that question, I conclude that international criminal trials purport a fact-finding competence that they do not possess. International criminal trials are conducted as Western-style proceedings, which embody certain fact-finding expectations. Chapter 6 considers these expectations and assesses the capacity of international criminal trials to meet them. As a result of this assessment, I conclude that, by using the Western trial form, international criminal proceedings cloak themselves in a garb of fact-finding competence, but it is only a cloak, for many of the key expectations and assumptions that underlie the Western trial form do not exist in the international context. Chapter 6 also highlights the ways in which international tribunals obscure the uncertain foundations of their factual determinations.

That international criminal trials are less reliable adjudicatory mechanisms than they appear does not mean that the judgments reached after those trials are of questionable legal accuracy. Certainly, the fact-finding impediments that I will describe render assessing prosecutorial allegations a challenging task. Prosecution testimony is frequently vague, lacking in detail, and contradicted by defense testimony. Fact finders are typically presented no documentary or forensic evidence on which they can anchor their findings, and they have little ability to assess the witnesses' demeanor because the witnesses speak a different language and adhere to different cultural norms than the fact finders. Consequently, if the tribunals were asked to determine the defendant's guilt on a preponderance-of-the-evidence standard, we might expect them to reach inaccurate conclusions a substantial proportion of the time. But the tribunals are not asked whether it is more likely than not that the defendant committed the crime; they are asked whether the prosecution has proven beyond a reasonable doubt that the defendant committed the crime. That is a much easier question to answer correctly, and while I cannot say whether the tribunals do answer it correctly in any particular case – let alone in a whole body of them – I can assess whether their treatment of fact-finding impediments generally comports with the beyond-a-reasonable-doubt standard that ostensibly applies to international criminal prosecutions.

This assessment takes place in Chapter 7. Through a comparison between witness testimony and the Trial Chambers' description and treatment of that testimony, I discovered that, as a general matter, the tribunals take a cavalier

[18] Robert P. Burns, *How Law Knows in the American Trial Court, in* How Law Knows 126, 127 (Austin Sarat et al. eds., 2007).

approach to fact-finding impediments. Many testimonial deficiencies are never mentioned in the Trial Chambers' judgments, and most of those that are, are reflexively attributed to innocent causes that do not impact the witnesses' credibility. Even severe inconsistencies between a witness's testimony and pre-trial statement are sometimes overlooked, though a particularly large number of particularly substantial inconsistencies typically does garner judicial attention. Chapter 7 begins by describing the Trial Chambers' general approach to fact-finding impediments, and then it illustrates those general conclusions with a comprehensive and careful examination of the *CDF* case at the SCSL. The two sections together show that the Trial Chambers frequently are willing to base their factual findings on deeply flawed witness testimony. Indeed, considering that vague, inconsistent testimony is the standard fare of the international criminal trials, that perjury is prevalent, and that even the most basic facts cannot be verified, one might have thought that Trial Chambers would rarely be able to find that the prosecution has proven its allegations beyond a reasonable doubt. But as a result of the lackadaisical attitude that most Trial Chambers bring to fact-finding impediments, the very opposite is true: The international tribunals under study convict the vast majority of defendants who come before them of at least one of the crimes for which they are charged.

So, why do the Trial Chambers seem so unconcerned about fact-finding impediments? Chapter 8 considers this question, beginning with a discussion of politics. International criminal tribunals are intensely political institutions, and although we have no reason to believe that political considerations directly influence the disposition of particular cases, they may well operate indirectly to bias the Trial Chambers in favor of conviction. Next, the chapter briefly considers the backgrounds of the judges as a factor that might also incline them toward conviction. Whereas these factors may play a small role in the Trial Chambers' cavalier treatment of testimonial deficiencies, I believe that the attitude derives more directly and fundamentally from principles of organizational liability that appeared in the Nuremberg Charter. These organizational liability principles were ostensibly discredited during the Nuremberg Trial, but I maintain that they continue to exert a powerful influence over fact-finding at today's international tribunals.

I argue indeed that, if the Trial Chambers appear largely unconcerned about testimonial deficiencies, it is because the testimony itself is not the exclusive basis for the Trial Chambers' factual determinations. Although the Trial Chambers appear to be convicting defendants on the basis of the acts charged in the indictments and basing their factual findings about those acts solely on the testimony that has been presented to them, I contend that the Trial Chambers in fact supplement that testimony with inferences that they draw from the defendants' official position or institutional affiliation in the context of the international crimes that have been committed. Chapter 8 carefully examines these inferences and shows why they can prove particularly compelling and how they can explain and justify both the Trial Chambers' casual treatment of most fact-finding impediments as well as certain otherwise inexplicable acquittals. I suggest in particular that, because objective or reliable evidence is so difficult to come by in the international realm, Trial Chambers rely on official position or institutional affiliation as a proxy of sorts for the defendant's involvement in the crimes. Prosecutors must still present some evidence to support the specific allegations appearing in the indictment; however, the stronger the inferences that can reasonably be drawn from official position, the more that Trial Chambers are willing to overlook problematic features of prosecution witness testimony or attribute those problems to innocent causes. Further, just as a defendant's official position or institutional affiliation can point to a defendant's involvement in the atrocities and thereby encourage a Trial Chamber to disregard testimonial deficiencies, other proxies can suggest the defendant's innocence and thereby incline a Trial Chamber to scrutinize testimonial deficiencies more carefully. These I discuss through an analysis of the ICTR's six acquittals.

The conclusions reached in the first eight chapters of the book give rise to a series of normative questions that I address in Chapters 9 and 10. The most obvious explores improvements that might be made to enhance the accuracy of international criminal fact-finding. Two paths present themselves. The more attractive of the two seeks to improve testimonial quality so that it will provide a more solid foundation for the judgments that the Trial Chambers will eventually reach. To that end, I begin Chapter 9 by advocating various adaptations to the pretrial, trial, and posttrial processes that currently exist at the international tribunals. I go on, in section B of Chapter 9, to explore more radical reforms; in particular, I consider whether international trial procedures should be fundamentally reformulated, as a means of improving testimonial quality. The second, less desirable, path to improving fact-finding accuracy focuses not on improving the quality of the testimony offered in support of the Trial Chambers' judgments but rather on adapting the charges that the prosecution alleges so that they better fit the (problematic) evidence that the Trial Chambers will receive. The second approach, then, assumes suboptimal testimony and considers how we might use certain existing but controversial liability doctrines to create a better alignment between the evidence that is received and the convictions that are entered. Improving that alignment, I argue, requires prosecutors to focus less on an individual defendant's particular actions and more on the defendant's role in the group criminality that characterized the atrocity as a whole.

Finally, Chapter 10 addresses the broadest and most pressing normative question: Will the fact-finding impediments that I have identified, if they persist, fatally undermine the work of the international tribunals? To explore that question, I first consider the adequacy of drawing inferences from official position and institutional affiliation. Although these proxies can provide useful information in many cases, they do so only when prosecutors target the "right" individuals and when the Trial Chambers have a sophisticated and nuanced understanding of the way the violence was carried out in the region in question. Assuming that these requirements are not always met, I evaluate the fact-finding approach adopted by the SCSL's Appeals Chamber in the *AFRC* case because it would reduce the impact of the testimonial deficiencies. Concluding that this approach is also deficient in some regards, I consider in the book's final chapter the way in which the evidence presented at the international tribunals interacts with the applicable standard of proof. In particular, I explore the views of modern scholars and researchers who view the beyond-a-reasonable-doubt standard as variable standard that signifies (and should signify) different levels of certainty in different cases. This understanding of the standard of proof in international criminal cases not only affords us an alternative explanation for international criminal fact-finding but it provides us a solid and satisfying justification for it.

1

The Evidence Supporting International Criminal Convictions

1.A. THE PREVALENCE OF EYEWITNESS TESTIMONY

Although the Nuremberg trial provides the legal, theoretical, and normative underpinnings for today's international criminal proceedings, it does not stand as their evidentiary model. The high-level Nazi officials who were prosecuted at the Nuremberg Tribunal were convicted on the strength of their own documentation. Nazi leaders kept meticulous written records;[19] as one Nuremberg prosecutor put it: "These Nazis had a mania for writing things down. It is an amazing psychological phenomenon that not one of these men could have a minor political conversation without recording it."[20] Recognizing that witnesses had fallible memories and might collapse under cross-examination, lead prosecutor Robert Jackson decided to use witnesses sparingly and instead to base his prosecution of the Nazis almost exclusively on their own documents.[21] Nuremberg prosecutors reviewed approximately one hundred thousand documents,[22] and they presented a substantial proportion of these to the Tribunal: The prosecution put 331 documents into the record during the first four hours of the Nuremberg trial,[23] and it submitted many thousands of documents during the trial as a whole.[24]

[19] Telford Taylor, The Anatomy of the Nuremberg Trials 57 (1992); Ann Tusa & John Tusa, The Nuremberg Trial 97 (1983).

[20] Tusa, note 19, at 100–01.

[21] Robert Jackson, The Nurnberg Case viii (1947); Tusa, note 19, at 101. Jackson wished also to create a historical record of Nazi atrocities. Tusa, note 19, at 101;. Telford Taylor, *The Nuremberg Trials*, 55 Colum. L. Rev. 488, 521 (1955).

[22] Jackson, note 21, at viii; Tusa, note 19, at 101; Harold Leventhal et al., *The Nuernberg Verdict*, 60 Harv. L. Rev. 857, 860 (1947). The documents of the SS alone filled six freight cars. Eugene Davidson, the Trial of the Germans 33 (1994).

[23] Taylor, note 19, at 174.

[24] 1 Trial of the Major War Criminals before the International Military Tribunal 172 (1947).

Unlike the leaders of Nazi Germany, who meticulously documented their illegal acts, the architects of more recent atrocities have left few written records,[25] and what written records they did leave often are not made available to prosecutors.[26] Consequently, the vast bulk of the evidence presented to the current international tribunals comes in the form of witness testimony. Moreover, virtually all of this testimony is provided by fact witnesses; only a tiny percentage of prosecution witnesses at the international tribunals are experts,[27] and their testimony rarely bears directly on the guilt of the defendants. In early ICTR cases, for instance, expert testimony was introduced primarily to establish that a genocide had taken place against the Tutsi.[28] Now, that fact is so well established that the Trial Chambers take judicial notice of it.[29] In more recent ICTR trials and in SCSL trials, the prosecution will occasionally introduce experts to testify about the command structure of a particular military force[30] or the powers wielded by a particular defendant,[31] or those who held the same

[25] *See* Prosecutor v. Kayishema & Ruzindana, Case No. ICTR-95-1-T, Judgement, para. 65 (May 21, 1999) [hereinafter Kayishema & Ruzindana Judgement]. Occasionally, modern-day prosecutions for international crimes will feature substantial documentary evidence, but problems can still arise. For instance, the vast bulk of the evidence in the first Iraqi Special Tribunal case – against Saddam Hussein – was documentary. But Human Rights Watch criticized the Tribunal for basing its conviction of Hussein on these documents because there was "no indication that the investigative judge took any steps to verify any of the documents, or sought out information that would be relevant to determining the authenticity of the documents." Human Rights Watch, *Judging Dujail: The First Trial before the Iraqi High Tribunal* 55 (Nov. 2006).

[26] The initial efforts of ICTY prosecutors to obtain highly relevant official documents from Croatia in relation to the charges against General Tihomir Blaškić, for instance, failed when Croatia declined to produce the documents. *See* Prosecutor v. Blaškić, Case No. IT-94-14-AR108*bis*, Judgement on the Request of the Republic of Croatia for Review of the Decision of Trial Chamber II of 18 July 1997 (Oct. 29, 1997).

[27] In each of the SCSL's first two trials, the prosecution presented only three expert witnesses out of seventy-five and fifty-nine prosecution witnesses, respectively. Prosecutor v. Fofana & Kondewa, Case No. SCSL-04-14-T, Judgement, Annex F, para. 21 (Aug. 2, 2007) [hereinafter CDF Judgement]; Prosecutor v. Brima et al., Case No. SCSL-2004-16-T, Judgement, paras. 10, 149 (June 20, 2007) [hereinafter AFRC Judgement]. Some early ICTR cases similarly featured a few expert witnesses, but many of the more recent cases have featured only one or none at all.

[28] In the *Akayesu* case, for instance, Dr. Alison Des Forges testified for five days about the history and contours of the Rwandan conflict, among other background issues. Prosecutor v. Akayesu, Case No. ICTR-96-4, Transcript [hereinafter Akayesu Transcript] (Feb. 11, 12, 13, 18, 21, 1997); *see also* Kayishema & Ruzindana Judgement, note 25, at paras. 34–54.

[29] Prosecutor v. Karemera et al., Case No. ICTR-98-44-AR73(C), Decision on Prosecutor's Interlocutory Appeal of Decision on Judicial Notice (June 16, 2006).

[30] *See, e.g.*, Prosecutor v. Sam Hinga Norman et al., Case No. SCSL-2004-14-T, Transcript, June 14, 2005 [hereinafter CDF Transcript]; Prosecutor v. Brima et al., Case No. SCSL-2004-16, Transcript, Oct. 14, 2005 [hereinafter AFRC Transcript].

[31] Prosecutor v. Semanza, Case No. ICTR-97-20-T, Judgement, paras. 295–298 (May 15, 2003) [hereinafter Semanza Judgement]; Prosecutor v. Ntagerura et al., Case No. ICTR-99-46-T, Transcript, Sept. 19, 2001 [hereinafter Ntagerura Transcript].

position as that of the defendant,[32] but these experts often base their decisions on information provided to them by the same eyewitnesses whose questionable testimony I will be discussing below.[33] Besides, the defense frequently counters with competing experts,[34] and rarely does any of the expert testimony relate directly to the specific actions or omissions of the defendant.

Of the three tribunals under study, only the Special Panels have regularly received forensic evidence relevant to the charges in the indictments. Because the violence in East Timor was short lived, and U.N. forces entered and controlled the territory immediately after the violence ended, forensic experts were able to perform some autopsies and exhumations.[35] As a consequence, the Special Panels could determine with some certainty that the alleged victims of the defendants' crimes had in fact been killed and had been killed in the way that the indictment alleged.[36] ICTR and SCSL Trial Chambers can have no such confidence. The magnitude of the atrocities in Rwanda and the long length of the war in Sierra Leone made similar forensic investigations impractical in those locations. Virtually the only forensic evidence that the ICTR has received has been introduced to prove the occurrence of the genocide: That is, it has proven only that certain large-scale massacres did take place and that the victims of those massacres were Tutsi.[37] Some of this evidence bore so little relationship to the allegations in the indictment that ICTR Trial Chambers have refused to admit it,[38] and the SCSL has rarely received even this sort of evidence.[39] Indeed, the very occurrence of a crime has sometimes been the

[32] Prosecutor v. Akayesu, Case No. ICTR-96-4-T, Judgement, para. 73 (Sept. 2, 1998) [hereinafter Akayesu Judgement].

[33] *See, e.g.*, AFRC Judgement, note 27, at para. 549.

[34] *See, e.g.*, Semanza Judgement, note 31, at paras. 300–302; AFRC Judgement, note 27, at para. 548.

[35] MOHAMED C. OTHMAN, ACCOUNTABILITY FOR INTERNATIONAL HUMANITARIAN LAW VIOLATIONS: THE CASE OF RWANDA AND EAST TIMOR 106–07 (2005).

[36] *See* Prosecution v. Tacaqui, Case No. 20/2001, Judgement, at 6 (Dec. 9, 2004) [hereinafter Tacaqui Judgement]; Prosecution v. Correia, Case No. 27/2003, Judgement, at 7 (Apr. 25, 2005); Prosecution v. Mesquita et al., Case No. 28/2003, Judgement, at 10 (Dec. 6, 2004).

[37] *See, e.g.*, Kayishema & Ruzindana Judgement, note 25, at paras. 325–326, 432. *But see* Prosecutor v. Ntagerura et al., Case No. ICTR-99-46-T, Judgement and Sentence, paras. 245, 252, 259, 260 (Feb. 25, 2004) (noting testimony by eyewitnesses and medical examiners that several exhumed bodies were identifiable as the remains of specific individuals) [hereinafter Ntagerura Judgement]. Alison Des Forges and Timothy Longman maintain that "investigators made no systematic effort to gather documentary and forensic evidence linking alleged suspects to specific crimes." Alison Des Forges and Timothy Longman, *Legal Responses to Genocide in Rwanda, in* MY NEIGHBOR, MY ENEMY: JUSTICE AND COMMUNITY IN THE AFTERMATH OF MASS ATROCITY 49, 53 (Eric Stover & Harvey Weinstein eds., 2004).

[38] *See, e.g.*, Prosecutor v. Rutaganda, Case No. ICTR-96-3, Judgement, para. 258 (Dec. 6, 1999) [hereinafter Rutaganda Judgement]; Prosecutor v. Kamuhanda, Case No. ICTR-95-54A-T, Judgement, para. 222 (Jan. 22, 2004) [hereinafter Kamuhanda Judgement].

[39] One exception was the testimony of forensic anthropologist William Haglund who testified in the *CDF* case. After examining the remains of four victims, Haglund determined that they

subject of conflicting claims, as I discuss in more detail in Chapter 5.[40] Even if the ICTR and SCSL had access to forensic evidence that would more conclusively establish the existence and nature of the crimes, such evidence would not assist the fact finders in determining the key question in any criminal trial: What role, if any, did the defendant play in the crime? Even the Special Panels have not received forensic evidence that would bear on that question. Thus, for the key determinations on which the defendants' guilt or innocence is based, the international tribunals have had to rely virtually exclusively on eyewitness testimony.

1.B. THE LIMITATIONS OF EYEWITNESS TESTIMONY

That the international tribunals base their factual determinations virtually exclusively on eyewitness testimony is a worry because recent research suggests that, even under the best of circumstances, eyewitness testimony frequently is inaccurate. Chapters 2 through 5 detail why trials at the international tribunals feature anything but the best of circumstances, but before we even begin to delve into that material, the remainder of this chapter details the problems generally associated with eyewitness testimony in criminal cases and the international tribunals' failure to take these problems seriously.

Although in centuries past, eyewitness testimony was considered among the most reliable forms of evidence, it has recently fallen into disrepute. Numerous studies have shown the fallibility of eyewitness perception, and the advent of DNA testing has borne out these studies by showing that nearly 80 percent of wrongful convictions in the United States involved eyewitness error.[41] Certain factors increase the likelihood of inaccurate testimony, and unfortunately many of these factors are at work in international criminal trials. Studies show, for instance, that memory of faces fades over time.[42] The first ICTR trial began

had died from injuries that were consistent with their relatives' descriptions of events. *See* CDF Transcript, June 20, 2005, at 39–47.

[40] *See* text accompanying notes 656 to 662.

[41] *See* Brandon L. Garrett, *Judging Innocence*, 108 COLUM. L. REV. 55, 78–79 (2008); The Innocence Project, *2006 Annual Report* 13, *available at* www.innocenceproject.org/Images/437/ip_annual_report_06_final.pdf. Field experiments on eyewitness identification in which the accuracy of the identifications is known also produce substantial error rates. *See* BRIAN L. CUTLER & STEVEN D. PENROD, MISTAKEN IDENTIFICATION: THE EYEWITNESS, PSYCHOLOGY, AND THE LAW 8-13 (1995); Douglas J. Narby et al., *The Effects of Witness, Target, and Situational Factors on Eyewitness Identifications, in* PSYCHOLOGICAL ISSUES IN EYEWITNESS IDENTIFICATION 23, 24–48 (Siegfried L. Sporer et al. eds., 1996); Brian L. Cutler et al. *Conceptual, Practical, and Empirical Issues Associated with Eyewitness Identification Test Media, in* ADULT EYEWITNESS TESTIMONY: CURRENT TRENDS AND DEVELOPMENTS 163, 166–181 (DAVID F. ROSS et al. eds., 1994).

[42] *See* JOHN W. SHEPHERD ET AL., IDENTIFICATION EVIDENCE: A PSYCHOLOGICAL EVALUATION 80–86 (1982) (describing authors' study showing that memory remained relatively constant

nearly three years after the events in question,[43] and trials continue to this day, with witnesses describing events that took place more than fifteen years ago. The fact, then, that international witnesses frequently claim that they cannot remember certain details of the events they witnessed thus should not come as a surprise.

Research also shows that individuals who witness (or are victims of) violent events are more likely to misperceive than individuals who witness nonviolent events[44] because the ability to perceive declines when an individual is experiencing stress.[45] Researchers led by Charles Morgan III, for instance, found that American military personnel who had just experienced a highly stressful mock interrogation session misidentified their interrogators as much as 68 percent of the time, even though each subject had had forty minutes to observe his interrogator. By contrast, the error rates for military personnel who were interrogated under low-stress conditions were markedly lower.[46] These studies bode poorly for the accuracy of international tribunal testimony because the events described therein are the most violent imaginable. Indeed, if the heightened stress levels caused by a vigorous mock interrogation is sufficient to induce perception errors in nearly seven out of ten individuals, it is frightening to consider the inaccuracies that are apt to be contained in international tribunal testimony, during which witnesses describe amputations, decapitations, gang rapes, and large-scale massacres of which the witness was either a victim or an intended victim.

Courts prosecuting international crimes have not always recognized the negative impact of stress on memory and perception. In the Israeli prosecution of the man alleged to be "Ivan the Terrible" – a brutal and infamous guard at the Nazi's Treblinka concentration camp – the Israeli trial court implied that the horror of the events witnessed *enhanced* the witnesses' memory and perception. In discussing the accuracy of witness testimony, the court asked

for a few months after an event but declined sharply after eleven months); Hadyn D. Ellis, *Practical Aspects of Face Memory, in* EYEWITNESS TESTIMONY: PSYCHOLOGICAL PERSPECTIVES 12, 23–25 (Gary L. Wells & Elizabeth F. Loftus eds., 1984) (summarizing research).

43 Akayesu Judgement, note 32, at para. 17.

44 ELIZABETH LOFTUS ET AL., EYEWITNESS TESTIMONY: CIVIL AND CRIMINAL 25 (2007).

45 *See, e.g.*, John C. Brigham et al., *The Effect of Arousal on Facial Recognition*, 4 BAS. APPLIED SOC. PSYCHOL. 279, 291 (1983); Sven-Ake Christianson & Elizabeth F. Loftus, *Memory for Traumatic Events*, 1 APPLIED COGN. PSYCHOL. 225, 227 (1987); Brian R. Clifford & Clive R. Hollin, *Effects of Type of Incident and the Number of Perpetrators on Eyewitness Memory*, 66 J. APPLIED PSYCHOL. 364, 369 (1981); Saul M. Kassin, *Eyewitness Identification: Victims Versus Bystanders*, 14 J. APPLIED SOC. PSYCHOL. 519, 520 (1984); Douglas P. Peters, *Eyewitness Memory and Arousal in a Natural Setting, in* 1 PRACTICAL ASPECTS OF MEMORY: CURRENT RESEARCH AND ISSUES: MEMORY IN EVERYDAY LIFE 89, 94 (Michael M. Gruneberg et al. eds., 1988).

46 Charles A. Morgan III et al., *Accuracy of Eyewitness Memory for Persons Encountered During Exposure to Highly Intense Stress*, 27 INT'L J. L. & PSYCHIATRY 265, 268, 272 (2004).

rhetorically: "[I]s it at all possible to forget? Can people who were in the vale of slaughter and experienced its horror, who lived in an atmosphere of oppression, terror, fear, and persecution within the narrow confines of the extermination camp; people who saw day after day, the killing, the humiliation, the brutality, the abuse by German oppressors and their Ukrainian vassals in the Treblinka camp, forget all this?"[47] Certainly not, the court concluded, stating: "No, it is not possible to forget the scenes of horror, the atmosphere of terror, all that took place in the extermination camp. It is impossible to forget Ivan the Terrible and his atrocities."[48]

More recently, an ICTR Trial Chamber, in the *Rutaganda* case, observed that

> [m]any of the witnesses who testified before the Chamber in this case have seen atrocities committed against members of their families and close friends and/or have themselves been the victims of such atrocities. Some of these witnesses became very emotional and cried in the witness box, when they were questioned about certain events. A few witnesses displayed physical signs of fear and pain when they were asked about certain atrocities of which they were victims.[49]

The Trial Chamber went on to assure the public that it had "taken into consideration these factors in assessing the evidence of such witnesses,"[50] but – worryingly – it did not say *how* it had taken those factors into consideration.

Distortion caused by the introduction of postevent information is also likely to impair testimonial accuracy at the international tribunals. Research shows that a witness's memory of an event can be substantially altered by information that person later learns about the event.[51] In some studies, subjects who were merely asked about a particular item inaccurately incorporated that item into their memory of the events.[52] As a consequence, studies show that postcrime police questioning can substantially distort a witness's recollection of the crime; indeed, psychologist David Hall and his coauthors conclude that "fairly subtle aspects of the way in which questions are worded can have profound effects on a subject's recollection of details of an event."[53] These studies give cause for concern because we can expect international witnesses to receive a great deal of potentially distortive postcrime information. First, because so much

[47] The Demjanjuk Trial 10 (Alex Felix Landau ed., 1991).
[48] *Id.* at 93.
[49] Rutaganda Judgement, note 38, at para. 22.
[50] *Id.*
[51] David F. Hall, et al., *Postevent Information and Changes in Recollection for a Natural Event, in* Eyewitness Testimony: Psychological Perspectives 124 (Gary L. Wells & Elizabeth F. Loftus eds., 1984).
[52] Loftus et al., note 44, at 58–63.
[53] Hall, et al., note 51, at 131.

time elapses between the crimes and the trials, international witnesses are usually interviewed numerous times before trial, and each set of interview questions has the potential to introduce inaccurate information. Second, the fact that international crimes are typically widespread means that they are likely to give rise to a great deal of postcrime discussion. An American assault victim may wish to talk about her assault with friends and family, but she is not apt to receive any information from them or from any other sources about the crime. The same is not true for a Sierra Leonean assault victim. Because her assault took place during a long-lasting, large-scale armed conflict, the entire community has information to share about the crimes, about the direct perpetrators of those crimes, and about the high-level architects who initiated the conflict.[54] Consequently, the memories of international witnesses are apt be continually revised as witnesses receive information about related crimes, related prosecutions, and the overarching aspects of the conflict as a whole.

Admittedly, the accuracy prospects of some international witness identifications are enhanced because some international defendants were well-known personages who were already recognizable to witnesses and other members of the community before the crimes took place. But the potential for error remains high even in these cases as a result of the utter chaos surrounding most of the crimes. Many Rwandan witnesses testify about massacres in which thousands of people were hacked to death in the course of hours. We cannot expect an individual who has been the target of this sort of one-on-one, brutal violence to have formed a clear and accurate memory of who precisely was leading the attack and what exactly that person was doing, even if the perpetrator is recognizable.

Given the existence of widespread perception impediments that are apt to impair the accuracy of international tribunal testimony, we might have expected that the international tribunals would take special care both in their own identification processes and in their assessment of identifications. My cursory research on the topic does not bear out this expectation, however. The ICTY has drawn attention "to the need for 'extreme caution' in relation to visual identification evidence" and has acknowledged "the frailties of human perceptions and the very serious risk that a miscarriage of justice might result from reliance upon even the most confident witnesses who purport to identify an accused without an adequate opportunity to verify their observations."[55]

[54] *See, e.g.*, Prosecutor v. Karera, Case No. ICTR-01-74-T, Judgement, para. 134 (Dec. 7, 2007) ("Witness BMH testified that she discussed the events of the war with Witness BMF on a daily basis, up to the time of her testimony.") [hereinafter Karera Judgement].

[55] Prosecutor v. Kupreškić et al., Case No. IT-95-16-A, Appeals Judgement, para. 34 (Oct. 23, 2001).

Although the tribunals under study occasionally repeat those admonitions,[56] it is not clear that they incorporate them into their decision-making processes. Indeed, in some cases, the Trial Chambers not only fail to exercise "extreme caution" in relation to eyewitness identifications, they also use discredited identification techniques that increase the likelihood of misidentifications.

Although the ICTY has, on occasion, received expert reports critiquing some of their identification methods,[57] and ICTY Trial Chambers themselves have refused to credit identifications that were made from inappropriate photo arrays,[58] the tribunals under study have not received such useful expert testimony,[59] and they have at times disregarded the potential impact of identification procedures that were so obviously distortive that no expert was needed to point out their flaws. In *Kamuhanda*, for instance, the prosecution used improper identification processes both for its in-court and its out-of-court identifications. For the out-of-court identification, the prosecution presented witnesses with a picture from which they were asked to identify the defendant. The problem was, the defendant was the only man in the picture; all of the other pictured individuals were women. The defendant also had a red mark on his shirt, intended to make his identification even easier. The in-court identification of the defendant was equally problematic because the defendant was flanked by armed guards, and the only other people on the defense side of the room were women.[60] The Trial Chamber seemed unperturbed by these obviously inappropriate procedures and gave the back of its hand to defense objections, saying:

> 63. The Chamber notes that in Court the Witnesses were not asked to look at a specific part of the Courtroom to identify the Accused. The Chamber is mindful of the fact that the Witnesses were asked to look in the Courtroom

[56] CDF Judgement, note 27, at para. 259 & n.363; Prosecutor v. Sesay et al., Case No. SCSL-04-15-T, Judgement, para. 492 (Mar. 2, 2009) [hereinafter RUF Judgement]; Prosecutor v. Ndindabahizi, Case No. ICTR-2001-71-I, Judgement and Sentence, para. 24 (July 15, 2004) [hereinafter Ndindabahizi Judgement]; Prosecutor v. Niyitegeka, Case No. 96-14-T, Judgement, para. 49 (May 16, 2003) [hereinafter Niyitegeka Judgement].

[57] *See, e.g.*, Prosecutor v. Limaj, Case No. IT-03-66-T, Judgement and Sentence, para. 19 (Nov. 30, 2005) [hereinafter Limaj Judgement].

[58] *See, e.g.*, Prosecutor v. Vasiljević, Case No. IT-98-32-T, Judgement, para. 18 (Nov. 29, 2002). Sometimes, investigators themselves will acknowledge that they failed to follow ICTY procedures. *See* Prosecutor v. Haradinaj et al., Case No IT-04-84, Transcript, June 25, 2007, at 6098–99.

[59] In *Kayishema & Ruzindana*, a French psychiatrist, Regis Pouget, provided the ICTR a report and testimony regarding the general problems afflicting eyewitness testimony. Pouget, however, did not call into question any of the ICTR's specific practices. Prosecutor v. Kayishema & Ruzindana, Case No. ICTR-95-1-T, Transcript, July 1, 1998, at 29–66 [hereinafter Kayishema & Ruzindana Transcript].

[60] Kamuhanda Judgement, note 38, at paras. 61–62.

> as a whole and see if they could identify the Accused. The Chamber notes further that the process of the identification of the Accused in the Courtroom does not stand in isolation: it is rather part of a process, the culmination of which is the identification of the Accused in the Courtroom.
>
> 64. The Chamber has also noted the Defence submission on the issue of the identification through the use of photographs.
>
> 65. All these issues have been considered in the assessment of the evidence in the case. The Chamber has assessed the credibility of each Witness, bearing in mind all the factors argued in favour and against each Witness.

The *Ndindabahizi* Trial Chamber similarly failed to respond to defense counsel who objected to the prosecution's in-court identification on the grounds that the defendant "was the only black male in the courtroom not wearing a lawyer's robe or a security officer's uniform, and that a guide given to all witnesses contains a sketch which indicates the location of the Accused in the courtroom."[61] And when Media Case defendant Hassan Ngeze asked to be shielded from the view of witnesses who, he claimed, had misidentified him, the Trial Chamber rejected Ngeze's motion, observing that defense counsel could "test the witnesses' knowledge of the suspect and his physical appearance" during cross-examination.[62] The Trial Chamber's ruling effectively disregarded the main thrust of the defense motion: that once the witnesses saw Ngeze in the courtroom, they would know how to accurately describe him. The *Rwamakuba* case suggests that such knowledge can be crucial. Andre Rwamakuba refused to attend his trial,[63] and a number of witnesses consequently misidentified him in photographs.[64] These misidentifications substantially impaired the witnesses' credibility, and it is not coincidental that Rwamakuba is one of the few ICTR defendants to have been acquitted. At the same time, Trial Chambers are not necessarily fazed by misidentifications. Although *Ntakirutimana* witness II claimed that he had known defendant Elizaphan Ntakirutimana since he was a child because Ntakirutimana was the witness's pastor,[65] when the witness was

[61] Ndindabahizi Judgement, note 56, at para. 157; *see also* Prosecutor v. Ndindabahizi, Case No. ICTR-01-71-T, Transcript, Sept. 16, 2003, at 39 [hereinafter Ndindabahizi Transcript]; Ndindabahizi Transcript, Sept. 22, 2003, at 14; Ndindabahizi Transcript, Sept. 29, 2003, at 36. The Trial Chamber's judgment noted when witnesses made such in-court identifications, thus indicating that the Trial Chamber placed some weight on the identifications. *See, e.g.*, Ndindabahizi Judgement, note 56, at paras. 117, 133, 153.

[62] Prosecutor v. Ngeze, Case No. ICTR-97-27-I, Decision on the Defence's Motion to Suppress the Identification of Hassan Ngeze (Oct. 12, 2000).

[63] Prosecutor v. Rwamakuba, Case No. ICTR-98-44C-T, Judgement, para. 9 & n.16 (Sept. 20, 2006) [hereinafter Rwamakuba Judgement].

[64] *Id.* at paras. 62, 94, 174, 176.

[65] Prosecutor v. Elizaphan and Gerald Ntakirutimana, Case No. ICTR-96-17-T, Transcript, Oct. 22, 2001, at 107 [hereinafter Ntakirutimana Transcript].

asked to identify the defendant in the courtroom, he was not able to do so, even though the defendant was quite old and one of the few nonuniformed African men in the courtroom. The witness sought to explain his failure by observing that "[i]t's maybe due to the fact that I haven't seen him for a long time."[66] The next morning, the witness had a different explanation, asserting: "When I speak a lot, I do not see very well." Thus, the witness went on: "When I was asked... whether I could see [Ntakirutimana], I wasn't able to see him because at that time I had problem [sic] with my eyes."[67] Later in the day, the witness was given another opportunity to identify the pastor. This time he was able to and offered yet another explanation for his initial failure to do so: According to witness II, he not only had "a problem of sight" but the defendant had "tried to hide his head, [but], when we all stood up [to leave the courtroom], I recognised him."[68] The Trial Chamber accepted these explanations, stating: "Having observed the witness the Chamber does not consider that the episode on the first day of his testimony affects his credibility."[69]

The following chapters detail the fact-finding challenges that are revealed by my large-scale review of trial testimony. But this chapter suggests that, before we take even our first glance at the transcripts, we have reason to worry about the accuracy of international tribunal factual determinations. For one thing, factual determinations at the international tribunals are based almost exclusively on eyewitness testimony, which is notoriously unreliable. Moreover, various factors, such as the brutality of the events witnessed and the time lag between those events and the witness's testimony, increase the likelihood that international tribunal testimony in particular will be inaccurate. Finally, the tribunals do not appear to carefully scrutinize identification procedures to ensure that best practices are followed and mistakes thereby minimized; indeed, the tribunals sometimes are willing to rely on identifications produced by obviously distortive methods. These facts would give us reason to worry about the accuracy of international criminal tribunal factual findings even if these trials did not feature other, serious impediments to factual accuracy. They do, however, and it is to these impediments that I now turn.

66 Ntakirutimana Transcript, Oct. 22, 2001, at 132.
67 Ntakirutimana Transcript, Oct. 23, 2001, at 2.
68 Ntakirutimana Transcript, Oct. 25, 2001, at 39.
69 Prosecutor v. Elizaphan & Gérard Ntakirutimana, Case No. ICTR-96-17-T, Judgement and Sentence, para. 647 (Feb. 21, 2003) [hereinafter Ntakirutimana Judgement].

2

Questions Unanswered

International Witnesses and the Information Unconveyed

The defense witness Celestino Dasibere appeared to the Court to be completely confused and unreliable: the transcript of the hearing is a cold medium and can not convey the sense of displacement and incapability to express intelligible concepts that affected the witness. Mr. Dasibere looked as a source of inextricable untrustworthiness and smoky ideas. Apart from the confession of the unreliability of his memory, the witness repeatedly showed to base his recollection of the facts on the quick sands of a fragile memory, ready to affirm one concept and to negate it immediately after. There's a sense of consternation left after hearing such witness: the Court doesn't want to base any factual finding on his words.

– Prosecutor v. Francisco Perreira, Special Panel for Serious Crimes, Case No. 34/2003, Judgement at 25 (Apr. 27, 2005)

International criminal trials employ Western-style criminal procedures that presuppose a smooth flow of questions and answers between counsel and witnesses. In particular, it is expected that, in response to counsel's questioning, eyewitnesses will convey the details of the events they witnessed in a form that the fact finder can both understand and critically evaluate. To be sure, clear communication between witnesses and fact finders is not always realized, even in domestic cases. Trials involving medical malpractice, product liability, and patent claims – to provide only a few examples – frequently feature testimony about scientific or technological issues that are difficult for witnesses to clearly explain and for fact finders to satisfactorily grasp. But the ordinary domestic criminal trial rarely presents these problems. Eyewitnesses have a story to tell about certain events relevant to the defendant's criminal culpability, and, through counsel's questioning, they are able to tell that story in a way that not only is comprehensible to the fact finder but that provides the fact finder sufficient information to draw reasonable conclusions about the defendant's liability. Witnesses in domestic criminal trials may not answer counsel's questions accurately – a problem I describe in Chapter 1 – but they do answer the questions, and they do answer them intelligibly.

The same is frequently not true at the ICTR, SCSL, and Special Panels. Indeed, the smooth flow of questions and answers that is the norm in domestic criminal trials often is unattainable at those tribunals. International witnesses frequently are unable or unwilling to relate whole categories of information that are crucial to accurate fact-finding. Sometimes, witnesses claim not to know the sought-after information, a phenomenon that I discuss in Section A. At other times, the difficulties seem to stem from the mode of courtroom questioning. Some witnesses claim not to understand counsel's questions, for instance, while others respond evasively or otherwise unresponsively, and still others testify in a manner that is almost entirely unintelligible to courtroom personnel. Section 2.B explores these difficulties. Make no mistake: Many of these difficulties stem from factors beyond the witnesses' control. Chapter 3, indeed, considers various educational, cultural, and linguistic causes for the testimonial deficiencies that I describe in this chapter. But whatever their causes, these difficulties create tremendous uncertainty about even the most basic aspects of the criminal activities at issue in international trials.

2.A. INTERNATIONAL WITNESSES AND THEIR INABILITY TO ANSWER WHO, WHAT, WHERE, OR WHEN QUESTIONS

Q. Do you know whether it was in the year 1999 or the year 2000? 1999 or 2000?

A. These things, Pa, I do not understand these things. When you tell me 1990 I don't understand. I don't even say months, I only understand [inaudible] numbers. I really don't understand anything.

– Prosecutor v. Brima et al., Case No. SCSL-2004-16-PT, Transcript, Apr. 8, 2005, at 20

International witnesses frequently maintain that they are unable to answer the questions posed to them, even questions concerning basic facts about the witnesses themselves. Some witnesses are unable to tell the court how old they are,[70] for instance, and others who do are sometimes

[70] CDF Transcript, Sept. 27, 2006, at 22; AFRC Transcript, Mar. 8, 2005, at 17–18; AFRC Transcript, July 5, 2005, at 64; AFRC Transcript, July 7, 2005, at 28; AFRC Transcript, July 13, 2005, at 48; Prosecution v. Sesay et al., Case No. SCSL-04-15-T, Transcript, July 27, 2004, at 56 [hereinafter RUF Transcript]; Prosecutor v. Joao Franca da Silva et al., Judicial System Monitoring Programme, Case Notes, Oct. 22, 2002 (on file with author) [hereinafter Lolotoe Case Notes]. Sometimes witnesses will know their approximate age, but not their birthdates. Lolotoe Case Notes, May 8, 2002, at 6; RUF Transcript, July 28, 2004, at 4; AFRC Transcript, July 26, 2005, at 87. And efforts to help *Lolotoe* witness Amelia Belo approximate her date of birth by tying it to significant world events such as World War II or the Japanese invasion revealed only that the witness knew nothing of World War II or the Japanese

mistaken.[71] Sierra Leonean witness TF1-085 told the court that she was nineteen years old, but, according to claims she made in her pretrial statement, she was in fact twenty-two. Similarly, the pretrial statements of Sierra Leonean witness TF1-199 indicated that he was twenty-two at the time he testified; but, when on the stand, he maintained that he was only eighteen.[72] More startling still, Timorese witness 18 testified that he was forty-eight years old in 2001, but a courtroom monitor observed he looked much older than this, and the witness himself claimed to have been born before World War II.[73] At least Sierra Leonean witness TF1-085 once had a birth certificate, unlike many international witnesses, but it did not help her to answer counsel's questions because it had been "eaten by rats."[74] Age is not the only personal detail that international witnesses sometimes have trouble providing. Sierra Leonean witness TF1-214 could not tell the Trial Chamber where she had been born[75] or how long she had been married;[76] Sierra Leonean witness TF1-024 did not know how long he had been a mechanic;[77] and although Rwandan witness ACM identified herself as a Tutsi-Bagogwe, when she was asked the meaning of Bagogwe, she was able to say only that the Bagogwe are a subgroup of the Tutsi ethnic group. She went on: "[W]hen I was born, I found this word in existence. I am unable to provide further explanation of it."[78]

International witnesses profess ignorance not only about details of their own personal histories but also about events in the world around them. Rwandan witness ACM was unfamiliar with any of Rwanda's more than 1,500 *secteurs* except her own,[79] while Sierra Leonean witness TF2-157 had no idea how the

invasion. Lolotoe Case Notes, Oct. 22, 2002, at 6. *See also* CDF Transcript, Nov. 4, 2004, at 23–24 (witness unable to estimate the age of another); Prosecutor v. Kajelijeli, Case No. ICTR-98–44A-T, Transcript, Dec. 7, 2001, at 43 (witness appeared unable to do the subtraction necessary to ascertain how old her daughter was) [hereinafter Kajelijeli Transcript]; AFRC Transcript, July 13, 2005, at 48 (witness unable to say how old she was when she was captured); AFRC Transcript, July 14, 2005, at 51 (witness unable to say how old she was when rebels attacked in 1997); Prosecutor v. Taylor, Case No. SCSL-2003–01-T, Transcript, May 12, 2008, at 9533–34 (witness unable to say how old he was when he started school) [hereinafter Taylor Transcript].

[71] RUF Transcript, July 22, 2004, at 6.

[72] Kyra Sanin, U.C. Berkeley War Crimes Studies Center, Special Court Monitoring Program, Update No. 57, Oct. 5, 2005, at 4.

[73] Prosecutor v. Joni Marques et al., Judicial System Monitoring Programme, Case Notes, Sept. 19, 2001, at 213 (on file with author) [hereinafter Los Palos Case Notes].

[74] AFRC Transcript, Apr. 7, 2005, at 123–25.

[75] RUF Transcript, July 13, 2004, at 37. *See also* RUF Transcript, July 22, 2004, at 44 (Witness TF1-331 not able to say in what District or Chiefdom she was born).

[76] RUF Transcript, July 14, 2004, at 2.

[77] AFRC Transcript, Mar. 8, 2005, at 18.

[78] Kajelijeli Transcript, Dec. 11, 2001, at 38.

[79] *Id.* at 61.

Sierra Leonean government had come into being – whether by election or otherwise.[80] Even governmental affairs close to home may escape the notice of some witnesses. East Timorese witness Benedito da Costa was unable to state who was in charge of appointing village heads, and although he said he wanted East Timor to be independent, he did not know from which country East Timor sought independence.[81] Most international witnesses are called to testify about the particular atrocities they witnessed, and it frequently becomes clear that they have little awareness of the larger conflict. Sierra Leonean witness TF1-021, for instance, seemed to know virtually nothing about the conflict between the government and rebel forces during the early years of the Sierra Leonean war,[82] and witness TF1-214 did not know what the term "AFRC" referred to.[83]

Although witnesses' inability to answer such basic questions about themselves or the world around them can be startling to court personnel, it rarely impairs the tribunals' fact-finding in any significant way. However, questions about a witness's personal history form only a small fraction of the questions that go unanswered during international trials, and most of the unanswered questions *are* of vital importance – to the Trial Chamber's ability to assess the witness's credibility, to the defendant's ability to present a defense, and most globally, to the Trial Chamber's ability to determine whether the charges in the indictment have been proven. In this section, I focus on questions that seek dates, times, distances, numerical estimations, and other specific details about the crime, because these are the crucial questions that are most likely to go unanswered.

2.A.i. *Dates*

International witnesses tend to have considerable trouble dating the events they witnessed. Admittedly, some events have proven easier to date than others. The Rwandan genocide began immediately after the April 6, 1994 assassination of President Habyarimana. Similarly, most of the Timorese violence followed directly upon East Timor's August 30, 1999 independence vote. Because those events were so cataclysmic and so clearly set off the ensuing violence, most Rwandan and Timorese witnesses have been able to date the crimes they witnessed with reasonable specificity. They have not been able to precisely

[80] CDF Transcript, June 16, 2004, at 25; *see also* AFRC Transcript, Apr. 15, 2005, at 36 (witness does not know who ruled Sierra Leone before President Kabbah came into power); RUF Transcript, July 27, 2004, at 54 (witness knew that Kabbah had been elected at some point but not whether he was in power during the relevant time).

[81] Lolotoe Case Notes, Apr. 9, 2002, at 4–5.

[82] AFRC Transcript, Apr. 15, 2005, at 36–38.

[83] RUF Transcript, July 15, 2004, at 15–16.

date much of anything else, however, and most Sierra Leonean witnesses have had difficulty even dating the crimes they witnessed because those crimes did not follow upon any particularly memorable event. Sometimes witnesses are able to say that the event in question occurred during the dry season or the rainy season[84] or, better yet, during a particular month,[85] but that often is as precise as the dating gets, and many witnesses cannot provide even that much information. Sierra Leonean witness TF1-157 could not recall even the year in which rebels attacked Bonoya and, when questioned further on this point, revealed that he did not know how many days there were in a month.[86] Similarly, Sierra Leonean witness TF1-085, who could not say in what year she was captured, revealed that she did not know how long a year was.[87] Some witnesses generalize their ignorance. Rwandan witness VAR observed that "it is difficult to remember dates. We can only remember years."[88] Even well-educated witnesses can have difficulty answering date questions. Sierra Leonean priest Father Garrick, who held two bachelor's degrees, could say only that defendant Kondewa came to Bonthe sometime in 1998.[89] Indeed, dates proved such a problematic realm for questioning in the SCSL's *CDF* case that when defense counsel Dr. Jabbi asked a witness, "on what day did the Kamajors enter Kenema?" the presiding judge remarked sarcastically, "Dr. Jabbi, I wish you luck."[90] Other examples of witnesses' inability to date events appear in the notes.[91]

[84] RUF Transcript, July 21, 2004, at 2–3, 11; RUF Transcript, Oct. 21, 2004, at 8, 21–22; RUF Transcript, Jan. 13, 2005, at 94–97; RUF Transcript, Mar. 17, 2006, at 79; CDF Transcript, June 21, 2004, at 54–55; Taylor Transcript, Apr. 8, 2008, at 6966; Taylor Transcript, Apr. 9, 2008, at 7017, 7052; Taylor Transcript, Apr. 14, 2008, at 7388; CDF Transcript, Sept. 14, 2004, at 160; CDF Transcript, Nov. 8, 2004, at 17, 24–25, 44; CDF Transcript, Nov. 12, 2004, at 4; CDF Transcript, Nov. 16, 2004, at 46; AFRC Transcript, Apr. 8, 2005, at 20; AFRC Transcript, June 30, 2005, at 82–83, 97–99; AFRC Transcript, July 7, 2005, at 102, 112–13; AFRC Transcript, July 14, 2005, at 41–42, 49; AFRC Transcript, Sept. 15, 2005, at 68; AFRC Transcript, Sept. 19, 2005, at 62.

[85] Ndindabahizi Transcript, Sept. 3, 2003, at 36; Ntakirutimana Transcript, Sept. 24, 2001, at 8, 29; Ntakirutimana Transcript, Sept. 26, 2001, at 43–46, 58; AFRC Transcript, Apr. 6, 2005, at 61; AFRC Transcript, Apr. 11, 2005, at 86; AFRC Transcript, June 27, 2005, at 96; AFRC Transcript, June 30, 2005, at 100; AFRC Transcript, July 1, 2005, at 8; AFRC Transcript, July 7, 2005, at 44; AFRC Transcript, July 11, 2005, at 56, 74–75; AFRC Transcript, July 12, 2005, at 25; AFRC Transcript, July 13, 2005, at 26, 49; RUF Transcript, Oct. 4, 2004, at 80–81; RUF Transcript, Oct. 8, 2004, at 182; RUF Transcript, Oct. 14, 2004, at 50, 57, 78; RUF Transcript, Oct. 18, 2004, at 31, 92; RUF Transcript, Oct. 25, 2004, at 96; RUF Transcript, Oct. 27, 2004, at 13–14.

[86] AFRC Transcript, July 25, 2005, at 30.

[87] AFRC Transcript, Apr. 7, 2005, at 73–74.

[88] Prosecution v. Semanza, Case No. ICTR-97–20-T, Transcript, Mar. 12, 2001, at 24 [hereinafter Semanza Transcript].

[89] CDF Transcript, Nov. 11, 2004, at 20. *See also* RUF Transcript, Oct. 11, 2004, at 3–4.

[90] CDF Transcript, Sept. 21, 2004, at 37.

[91] Los Palos Case Notes, July 16, 2001, at 26; Lolotoe Case Notes, May 9, 2002, at 2; Lolotoe Case Notes, Oct. 23, 2002, at 1; Lolotoe Case Notes, Mar. 17, 2003, at 18–20; CDF Transcript,

Sometimes when witnesses do provide dates for the events they witnessed, these dates are proven to be erroneous. Rwandan witness CGM, for instance, testified that a particular event occurred "last month" and proceeded to place it at the beginning of June because he believed "we are in the month of June right now." The presiding judge had to inform the witness that it was in fact September.[92] Sierra Leonean witness TF1-277 expressed absolute certainty that the events in question had occurred on Monday, December 22, 1998. He remained unshaken in his conviction even after counsel informed him that December 22, 1998 fell on a Tuesday.[93] Similarly, Sierra Leonean witness TF1-085 remained convinced that rebels came to her house on Thursday, January 5, 1999 despite being informed that January 5, 1999 was a Tuesday.[94] And although Sierra Leonean witness TF2-032 initially maintained that an important meeting had been held in 1999, he revised the date of the meeting to 1998 when he was reminded that the relevant attack had occurred in 1998.[95]

June 16, 2004, at 5, 26–28; CDF Transcript, June 18, 2004, at 34–36; CDF Transcript, June 21, 2004, at 29; CDF Transcript, Sept. 9, 2004, at 119; CDF Transcript, Sept. 20, 2004, at 58–59; CDF Transcript, Sept. 21, 2004, at 17–20, 37–38, 40, 74–80; CDF Transcript, Sept. 23, 2004, at 20–21; CDF Transcript, Sept. 29, 2004, at 25–28; CDF Transcript, Nov. 2, 2004, at 88, 131; CDF Transcript, Nov. 8, 2004, at 111–12; CDF Transcript, Nov. 9, 2004, at 39; CDF Transcript, Nov. 12, 2004, at 26; CDF Transcript, Nov. 16, 2004, at 95; CDF Transcript, Feb. 9, 2005, at 7–8; CDF Transcript, Mar. 10, 2005, at 37–38; CDF Transcript, Mar. 14, 2005, at 46; CDF Transcript, June 1, 2006, at 19–20, 59–60; AFRC Transcript, Apr. 6, 2005, at 16; AFRC Transcript, Apr. 7, 2005, at 61; AFRC Transcript, June 24, 2005, at 115–16; AFRC Transcript, June 27, 2005, at 41, 95–96; AFRC Transcript, June 28, 2005, at 9; AFRC Transcript, June 29, 2005, at 6, 24; AFRC Transcript, June 30, 2005, at 96; AFRC Transcript, July 7, 2005, at 46; AFRC Transcript, July 8, 2005, at 18–19; 34–35; AFRC Transcript, Sept. 29, 2005, at 18; AFRC Transcript, Sept. 21, 2005, at 19, 31; Taylor Transcript, Apr. 2, 2008, at 6440–6441; Taylor Transcript, Apr. 4, 2008, at 6686; Taylor Transcript, Apr. 11, 2008, at 7307–7308; Taylor Transcript, Apr. 24, 2008, at 8548–49; Taylor Transcript, May 20, 2008, at 10277; Taylor Transcript, May 22, 2008, at 10592, 10615; Taylor Transcript, Aug. 21, 2008, at 14235–36, 14303; Taylor Transcript, Sept. 5, 2008, at 15603–04; Taylor Transcript, Sept. 10, 2008, at 15889; Taylor Transcript, Sept. 11, 2008, at 16028; Taylor Transcript, Sept. 16, 2008, at 16374–75, 16355–57; Taylor Transcript, Sept. 17, 2008, at 16431–32; RUF Transcript, July 19, 2004, at 47, 74; RUF Transcript, Oct. 14, 2004, at 34, 54, 60, 101, 110; RUF Transcript, Oct. 18, 2004, at 70, 95–96; RUF Transcript, Oct. 19, 2004, at 30–31, 42–43, 45, 104, 107; RUF Transcript, Oct. 22, 2004, at 18, 31–32; RUF Transcript, Oct. 28, 2004, at 27–28, 86–88, 89–90; RUF Transcript, Apr. 15, 2005, at 24; RUF Transcript, Dec. 8, 2005, at 44; Prosecutor v. Karera, Case No. ICTR-01–74-T, Transcript, Jan. 9, 2006, at 27 [hereinafter Karera Transcript]; Kajelijeli Transcript, July 18, 2001, at 83; Ntakirutimana Transcript, Sept. 28, 2001, at 62–63; Ndindabahizi Transcript, Sept. 3, 2003, at 41; Ndindabahizi Transcript, Sept. 8, 2003, at 2; Ndindabahizi Transcript, Sept. 15, 2003, at 28; Ndindabahizi Transcript, Sept. 16, 2003, at 47; Ndindabahizi Transcript, Sept. 29, 2003, at 42; Prosecutor v. Kamuhanda, Case No. ICTR-99–54A-T, Transcript, Jan. 28, 2002, at 115 [hereinafter Kamuhanda Transcript]; Kamuhanda Transcript, Feb. 5, 2002, at 11.

[92] Ndindabahizi Transcript, Sept. 15, 2003, at 22–24.

[93] AFRC Transcript, Mar. 8, 2005, at 75–76.

[94] AFRC Transcript, Apr. 7, 2005, at 116–17.

[95] CDF Transcript, Sept. 13, 2004, at 56–57.

Finally, ICTR Media Trial witness Omar Serushago testified that a certain Colonel Rwendeye had attended two death-squad meetings in 1993 and 1994. Confronted with evidence that Rwendeye had died in 1990, Serushago rejected that evidence and instead maintained that Rwendeye had died at the end of 1992. When it was pointed out that Serushago's revision nonetheless made Rwendeye "the only dead man at the meeting,"[96] Serushago claimed that he had testified that the meetings had taken place at the end of 1992 and 1993.[97]

Dates are of key significance to a tribunal's ability to find facts. For one thing, a witness's failure to date events can conceal inconsistencies between witness accounts that would otherwise come to light. More importantly, a witness's failure to date events impairs a defendant's ability to present an alibi, which is often the most powerful defense that a defendant can put forward. That is, it is obviously more factually compelling to assert, "I did not make a speech calling for the extermination of the Tutsi at a rally in Cyangugu on February 12, 1994, and I can prove it because I was attending a meeting of government ministers in Kigali on that day" than it is to say "I did not make a speech calling for the extermination of the Tutsi at a rally in Cyangugu." Plenty of convicted defendants assert the latter, to no effect. By contrast, three of the ICTR's six acquittals occurred in the *Cyangugu* and *Military I* cases, in which witnesses LAI, LAJ, and LAB were proven to have perjured themselves. The perjury came to light only because the witnesses dated the events they allegedly witnessed reasonably precisely; thus when the defendants submitted their passports, they could prove that they were not even in Rwanda on the days in question. The defendants' passport stamps would have been probative of nothing, however, if all the witnesses had said was that the events had occurred during the rainy season. Alfred Musema is but one ICTR defendant who learned this lesson firsthand. Musema was accused of participating in an attack at the Nyakumumu cave. Musema had an airtight alibi from May 30, 1994 to June 10, 1994, but because the witnesses could say only that the attack had occurred sometime "around the end of May or early June," Musema's alibi did him no good; the Trial Chamber found that Musema had participated in the attack.

2.A.ii. *Duration*

Questions seeking to ascertain the duration of an event also are questions that frequently go unanswered at the international tribunals under study. Many

[96] Lars Waldorf, *Silent Partner*, Diplomatie Judiciaire, Nov. 27, 2001.

[97] Prosecutor v. Nahimana et al., Case No. ICTR-99-52-T, Judgement and Sentence, para. 735 (Dec. 3, 2003) [hereinafter Nahimana Judgement].

international witnesses cannot tell time[98] and either do not know the duration of various units of time, such as months or years,[99] or see no reason for such precision. As a consequence, witnesses frequently can estimate neither relatively long periods of time – such as for how long a certain East Timorese man had been village chief[100] or for how long the AFRC held control of a certain region[101] – nor short periods of time, such as how long it took for an injured victim to die once she was brought indoors[102] or how long bombing lasted in a particular town.[103] Other examples appear in the notes,[104] but suffice it to say that questioning about the duration of events often proceeds as it did in this excerpt from the SCSL's *AFRC* trial:

Q. Do you remember how long it took you to go to (inaudible) the people who captured you?
A. No.
Q. Do you remember how long it took you to go up the hills and on to Waterloo?
A. I cannot remember.
Q. From Waterloo to Masiaka, do you remember how long it took?
A. I cannot remember.[105]

[98] *See, e.g.*, CDF Transcript, June 17, 2004, at 53–54; Prosecutor v. Gaspar Leki, Judicial System Monitoring Programme, Case Notes, Apr. 4, 2002 (on file with author).
[99] *See, e.g.*, AFRC Transcript, Apr. 8, 2005, at 19–20; AFRC Transcript, July 7, 2005, at 53; AFRC Transcript, July 25, 2005, at 30; AFRC Transcript, Apr. 7, 2005, at 73–74.
[100] Lolotoe Case Notes, Apr. 9, 2002, at 4.
[101] CDF Transcript, Sept. 23, 2004, at 20–21.
[102] AFRC Transcript, Mar. 8, 2005, at 58–59.
[103] AFRC Transcript, Apr. 7, 2005, at 112. Studies show that Western witnesses tend to exaggerate the duration of the events they witnessed. But unlike many international witnesses, they can make some estimation of the duration, and their exaggerations are generally minor. *See* LOFTUS ET AL., note 44, at 19–21.
[104] Prosecutor v. Nyiramasuhuko et al., Case No. ICTR-98–42-T, Transcript, Mar. 19, 2003, at 15 [hereinafter Nyiramasuhuko Transcript]; Ndindabahizi Transcript, Sept. 16, 2003, at 8–9; Kamuhanda Transcript, Feb. 12, 2002, at 61, 64; Taylor Transcript, Apr. 4, 2008, at 6684–86; Taylor Transcript, Aug. 28, 2008, at 14869; RUF Transcript, July 19, 2004, at 77; RUF Transcript, July 15, 2004, at 6; RUF Transcript, July 21, 2004, at 2–3; RUF Transcript, July 27, 2004, at 52–53, 57; RUF Transcript, Oct. 21, 2004, at 80, 84; RUF Transcript, Apr. 12, 2005, at 39–40; RUF Transcript, Nov. 4, 2005, at 32; CDF Transcript, Sept. 23, 2004, at 127–29; CDF Transcript, Sept. 27, 2004, at 106; CDF Transcript, Nov. 3, 2004, at 3–4; CDF Transcript, Mar. 14, 2005, at 46; AFRC Transcript, Mar. 8, 2005, at 58; AFRC Transcript, Apr. 7, 2005, at 46, 106; AFRC Transcript, Apr. 8, 2005, at 24–25; AFRC Transcript, June 27, 2005, at 7; AFRC Transcript, June 29, 2005, at 6; AFRC Transcript, June 30, 2005, at 96; AFRC Transcript, July 7, 2005, at 110; AFRC Transcript, July 11, 2005, at 74, 80–81, 109, 117; AFRC Transcript, Sept. 20, 2005, at 36; AFRC Transcript, Sept. 21, 2005, at 19; AFRC Transcript, Sept. 26, 2005, at 29–30; AFRC Transcript, Sept. 29, 2005, at 18; Los Palos Case Notes, July 18, 2001, at 34; Los Palos Case Notes, Sept. 28, 2001, at 306.
[105] AFRC Transcript, Apr. 7, 2005, at 61.

As with the date misestimations described previously, sometimes international witnesses do estimate the duration of events but do so erroneously. Sierra Leonean witness TF1-024, for instance, claimed to have traversed twelve miles on foot in forty-five minutes. The witness adhered to his estimate even after counsel suggested that it would be difficult to drive that distance in forty-five minutes, let alone to walk it.[106] Similarly, Sierra Leonean witness TF1-074 estimated that he was with his abductors for three years – from 1998 to 2002.[107] And the Special Panels had this to say about Augustus Perreira's duration estimate:

> The only part of the testimony of Augustus Perreira which appears frankly untenable and that casts a doubt on the reliability and on the capacity of the witness to assess not only measures in time and in space but, in the end, the logic of his own words, can be found in the passage where the witness described a one hour period between the infliction of the first blow to the victim delivered by the accused and the shooting of victim by Lino Barreto. The distance between the two incident location [sic] is very short, the river being adjacent to the school. According to the witness, the victim is supposed to have run or at least walked continuously (the witness was specifically questioned on this point by Judge Rapoza). The witness asserted that between the said two places the victim Alvaro Tilman moved in continuous motion, without any stop or interruption on the way. It appears frankly incredible and unreasonable that it took one hour to cover the distance of 400 hundreds [sic] meters. Once the witness was made aware of the unlikelihood of his account he modified his account maintaining that the victim covered the distance in 40 minutes.[108]

2.A.iii. *Distance*

Distance estimations often prove similarly confounding to international witnesses. Some witnesses state flat out that they do not know the lengths of Western units of measurement, such as miles or kilometers.[109] Others convey the same ignorance indirectly, as Rwandan witness CGC did when he said, "I cannot give the distance in terms of kilometers because I haven't been to

[106] AFRC Transcript, Mar. 7, 2005, at 81.

[107] AFRC Transcript, July 5, 2005, at 29.

[108] Prosecutor v. Francisco Perreira, Case No. 34/2003, Judgement, at 11 (Apr. 27, 2005) [hereinafter Perreira Judgement].

[109] AFRC Transcript, Mar. 8, 2005, at 31; Karera Judgement, note 54, at para. 296 (witness maintains that he does not understand the metric system and can estimate only by "paces."); Los Palos Case Notes, July 27, 2001, at 84 ("I don't know what 100 meters is, I only found out when a journalist told me."); Los Palos Case Notes, July 30, 2001, at 94 ("I really don't know about meters."); *see also* Taylor Transcript, Apr. 15, 2008, at 7620; Taylor Transcript, Apr. 16, 2008, at 7738–39 (witness unable to estimate by means of football fields).

school."[110] And although Sierra Leonean witness TF1-024 claimed to know how long a mile was, he was not able to say how long it took him to walk one mile – maintaining that he had never done such a thing – and he did not know what one would reach if one walked out the doors of the SCSL and continued walking for a mile.[111] Even some well-educated witnesses have difficulty with distance estimations.[112] Sierra Leonean witness Father Garrick, who, as mentioned above, has two university degrees, was unable to estimate the distance between Bonthe Town and Talia Yobehko,[113] while Sierra Leonean witness Albert Nallo, who was educated to the fifth form, was unable to estimate the distance between the town of Koribondo and the CDF headquarters at Base Zero.[114] Rwandan witness CGV attested that he could not measure distances because he was not an "agronomist."[115]

Some witnesses who are unable to measure distances in Western units of measurement are able to estimate how long it would take to traverse the distance on foot.[116] But some witnesses cannot do even that.[117] Sierra Leonean witness Joseph Lansana responded to the question, "how far is [Baoma Kpengeh] to Sorgia?" by stating, "I wouldn't know the number of miles, but it is a little bit

[110] Ndindabahizi Transcript, Sept. 29, 2003, at 22. *See also* Akayesu Transcript, Oct. 24, 1997, at 25; Kajelijeli Transcript, July 19, 2001, at 29.

[111] AFRC Transcript, Mar. 8, 2005, at 31.

[112] In addition to the examples provided in the text, see, for example, Prosecutor v. Musema, Case No. ICTR-96–13-A, Judgement and Sentence, para. 436 (Jan. 27, 2000) ("When pressed as to details on distances and the numbers of vehicles and people that he saw while hidden in a bush in Kucyapa, the witness stated that he was unable to give such details, even though he was an educated man.") [hereinafter Musema Judgement]; CDF Transcript, Sept. 27, 2004, at 88–89; AFRC Transcript, July 11, 2005, at 94, 104–05 (High school-educated witness who was a journalist could not say whether Yaya was north, south, east, or west from Tombodo or whether "Rosos was further north from Freetown than Gbinti.").

[113] CDF Transcript, Nov. 11, 2004, at 29.

[114] CDF Transcript, Mar. 11, 2005, at 104.

[115] Ndindabahizi Transcript, Sept. 16, 2003, at 22–23.

[116] Ndindabahizi Transcript, Sept. 22, 2003, at 21; Ndindabahizi Transcript, Sept. 29, 2003, at 28; Semanza Transcript, Dec. 6, 2000, at 95–96; Semanza Transcript, Mar. 12, 2001, at 82–83; Prosecutor v. Karemera et al., Case No. ICTR-98–44-T, Transcript, Dec. 5, 2003, at 15 [hereinafter Karemera Transcript]; Akayesu Transcript, Oct. 27, 1997, at 51; CDF Transcript, Nov. 11, 2004, at 29; CDF Transcript, Sept. 28, 2006, at 52; AFRC Transcript, July 5, 2005, at 25–26; Taylor Transcript, Apr. 14, 2008, at 7417–18; Taylor Transcript, Apr. 16, 2008, at 7739–40.

[117] *See, e.g.*, CDF Transcript, June 15, 2004, at 42–43; CDF Transcript, June 17, 2004, at 10; CDF Transcript, Nov. 2, 2004, at 132; CDF Transcript, Nov. 4, 2004, at 16–17; AFRC Transcript, June 27, 2005, at 90; AFRC Transcript, July 11, 2005, at 104; Prosecutor v. Muhimana Case No. ICTR-95–1B-T, Transcript, Apr. 29, 2004, at 24 [hereinafter Muhimana Transcript]; Prosecutor v. Rutaganda, Case No. ICTR-96–3-T, Transcript, Mar. 20, 1997, at 87 [hereinafter Rutaganda Transcript]; Ntakirutimana Transcript, Sept. 20, 2001, at 149–50; Ntakirutimana Transcript, Sept. 24, 2001, at 11, 12, 29–30, 134–35; Ndindabahizi Transcript, Sept. 16, 2003, at 27; Los Palos Case Notes, Aug. 2, 2001, at 120; Los Palos Case Notes, Aug. 21, 2001, at 177.

far."[118] Sierra Leonean witness TF2-154 similarly had no ability to estimate the distance between her house and the police station in Kenema, as the following exchange demonstrates:

Q: [H]ow far is it from your house to the police station in Kenema?
A: The distance is a bit far from where we are.
Q. How many minutes would it take you walking from your house to the police station?
A. I have never set a time to walk – to time myself, so I don't know.
Q. Could you please give us an estimate to assist this Court? I know Kenema, some of the judges don't know. So please try and assist us. You've tried so far. If you were to walk from your house to the police station, how long would it take you; ten minutes, 20 minutes, 30 minutes, one hour?
A. The distance is a – it is far from our house to the police station. I have never set a time to know – to walk from my house to the police station.[119]

Smaller units of measurement often prove no easier for international witnesses, although the most frequent question posed to them – which seeks to ascertain how far the witnesses were from the events that they witnessed – can often be answered by reference to people or objects in the courtroom.[120] So, for instance, Sierra Leonean witness TF2-039 was able to say that the relevant distance was "like from that table to where I am sitting."[121] Some witnesses have difficulty making even those sorts of comparisons, however, as is evident from the following excerpt from the *AFRC* trial in the SCSL:

Q. At one time, you have told this Court that he stood before you and pointed a gun at you, telling you to eat the flesh of the cooked Kamajor; is that not so?
A. Yes.

[118] CDF Transcript, Sept. 28, 2006, at 69.

[119] CDF Transcript, Sept. 27, 2004, at 88. Another defense counsel finally interjected to ask whether the distance would be about the same as from the courthouse to Pademba Road Prisons. The witness agreed that it was, and it was thereby determined that the distance was about one quarter of a mile. *Id.* at 89.

[120] Ntakirutimana Transcript, Sept. 24, 2001, at 16, 23–24; Ntakirutimana Transcript, Sept. 25, 2001, at 26; Ntakirutimana Transcript, Oct. 23, 2001, at 119; Ndindabahizi Transcript, Sept. 29, 2003, at 53; Taylor Transcript, Sept. 12, 2008, at 16122; AFRC Transcript, July 18, 2005, at 89; AFRC Transcript, June 28, 2005, at 116–17, 118; AFRC Transcript, July 20, 2005, at 47–48; CDF Transcript, Dec. 6, 2004, at 80–81; RUF Transcript, July 22, 2004, at 13; RUF Transcript, July 29, 2004, at 6; RUF Transcript, Oct. 21, 2004, at 11–12; Los Palos Case Notes, July 18, 2001, at 40; Los Palos Case Notes, July 30, 2001, at 94; Los Palos Case Notes, Sept. 25, 2001, at 271, 272; Los Palos Case Notes, Sept. 26, 2001, at 286–87, 288; Los Palos Case Notes, Sept. 29, 2001, at 312; Lolotoe Case Notes, Nov. 4, 2002, at 5. *See also* Ntakirutimana Transcript, Sept. 24, 2001, at 6 (witness estimating the size of an exit to the side of the technician's booth in the courtroom).

[121] CDF Transcript, Sept. 23, 2004, at 104; *see also id.* at 108.

Q. Just demonstrate again how close he was to you.
A. Well, we were standing in a queue and he was standing, calling us to him one after the other, to meet him where he was standing.
Q. How close did you get to him?
A. The distance was long.
Q. I do not understand that. Just show us, how close was he to you?
A. It was like he was standing there and we were down in the queue. When someone goes and meets him, then the other would go and meet him where he was standing, one after the other.
Q. What I'm asking you, if you would be patient, is when you went to meet him, how close were you to him?
A. Well as he was standing, I came close to him. When he was standing, I came close to him and he was – he held the meat in his hand and he gave it to me to take.
Q. Was it like one yard away from him?
A. Well, I wouldn't know that.
Q. I take it you were very close to him?
A. Well, I was nearer to him. He was standing there and I was nearer to him.[122]

In the above exchange, counsel pressed the witness to come up with some sort of estimate, but the witness effectively refused. On other occasions, witnesses will accede, but the answers they provide may be no more useful. In the following excerpt, for instance, Sierra Leonean witness TF1-024 was happy to assent to just about anything counsel put forward:

Q. I appreciate that you cannot precisely say the size, but if you look at the size of this courtroom, can you say that the kitchen was as big as this courtroom?
A. No, it's long. It's not wide. It's longer than in here. It's squared.
Q. You say that the kitchen was the same area, maybe half the size of this courtroom?
A. This courtroom is bigger than the kitchen a little bit.
Q. How much smaller than this courtroom was the kitchen? Was it half as big as this courtroom?
A. Half, just half.
Q. Was it a quarter of this courtroom?
A. About a quarter, yes.[123]

[122] AFRC Transcript, Apr. 7, 2005, at 72–73. For other examples, see Prosecutor v. Bagilishema, Case No. ICTR-95–1A-T, Judgement, para. 642 (June 7, 2001) [hereinafter Bagilishema Judgement]; Akayesu Transcript, Jan. 27, 1997, at 128–29; AFRC Transcript, June 30, 2005, at 112, 113.
[123] AFRC Transcript, Mar. 8, 2005, at 32; *cf.* RUF Transcript, July 22, 2004, at 53, 55 (witness repeatedly answered "yes" before counsel had even finished asking questions).

And this excerpt from the Special Panels shows that pressing a witness to estimate in meters can backfire:

DEFENSE COUNSEL: How wide was the road?

WITNESS: I'm not an expert in measuring things, because you are forcing me – I feel the question is not appropriate but I'll try – maybe 100 meters wide – don't blame me if it's wrong.

DEFENSE COUNSEL: Nobody's blaming you, but that's maybe a bit much.

WITNESS: It was enough for only one car to pass.

DEFENSE COUNSEL: So maybe 3 or 4 meters?

WITNESS: Wide enough for only one car to pass.[124]

Accurate answers to distance questions are crucial to accurate fact-finding. How much weight a Trial Chamber can justifiably place on a witness's identification of a defendant at a particular scene will depend in large part on how far the witness was from the defendant. A Trial Chamber that hears only that "the distance wasn't great"[125] is making factual findings in the dark. Distance estimates also enhance a Trial Chamber's ability to assess witness credibility. For one thing, the plausibility of a witness's account may depend to some degree on the distances between the locations that the witness describes. Witness TF1-024 was mistaken about walking twelve miles in forty-five minutes, but that became clear only because we knew that the distance was twelve miles. Further, although witnesses who are able to estimate distances by analogies to objects in the courtroom appear to provide the Trial Chambers some useful information, it is not clear how useful that information is because the Trial Chambers cannot assess the witnesses' ability to make these estimations. In domestic courtrooms, defense counsel routinely test witnesses' ability to estimate distances outside the courtroom by testing their ability to estimate distances inside the courtroom. So, if a witness seriously misjudges a courtroom distance, the fact finder is not so likely to credit that witness's out-of-courtroom distance estimations. But when a witness cannot measure distances by means of objective units in the first place, no such testing can take place.

2.A.iv. *Numerical Estimations*

Numerical estimations often prove just as difficult for international witnesses as date, duration, and distance estimations.[126] Knowing approximately how many

[124] Los Palos Case Notes, July 31, 2001, at 103.

[125] Prosecutor v. Bagilishema, Case No. ICTR-95–1A-T, Transcript, Jan. 26, 2000, at 16 [hereinafter Bagilishema Transcript].

[126] *See, e.g.*, Musema Judgement, note 112, at para. 436; Niyitegeka Judgement, note 56, at para. 102; Muhimana Transcript, Apr. 30, 2004, at 67–68; Ndindabahizi Transcript, Sept. 16, 2003, at

attackers were at a particular massacre site, for instance, or approximately how many civilians were illegally detained helps the Trial Chamber to fulfill its truth-telling functions and in some cases is relevant to the legal characterization of the defendant's actions. But international witnesses are frequently unable to provide such estimations. When Sierra Leonean witness TF2-152 was asked how many Kamajors were with him, he could answer only that "there were many."[127] When Rwandan witness VN was asked to approximate the number of attackers, he responded, "I cannot give you an idea of their numbers. They were as many as ants."[128] And when Sierra Leonean witness TF1-064 was asked how many rebels there were, her initial response was that "[t]here were lots of them, I can't even tell the number." Later she was asked whether she could give "some idea of the number of people who were there," to which she replied, "I have told you I don't know the number." When pressed further as to whether "there was more than the number of people in this room or less than," she replied, "[t]here were many of them. I don't know whether there were 8 of them, or 10 or 20, but I knew that there were a lot of them."[129]

Even estimating smaller numbers can prove difficult for international witnesses. Sierra Leonean witness TF2-012 was unable to estimate how often in an average year he would travel to Koribondo,[130] and many Sierra Leonean and Rwandan witnesses are unable to estimate how many times they have met with the prosecution.[131] Witness TF2-157 was unable to estimate whether the number

35; Ntakirutimana Transcript, Sept. 28, 2001, at 29, 39, 70–72; CDF Transcript, June 21, 2004, at 50; CDF Transcript, Feb. 9, 2005, at 18; CDF Transcript, June 3, 2005, at 35; AFRC Transcript, Mar. 8, 2005, at 43; AFRC Transcript, June 27, 2005, at 79, 80, 87–88, 90; AFRC Transcript, July 1, 2005, at 14; AFRC Transcript, July 7, 2005, at 108; AFRC Transcript, July 11, 2005, at 17, 76–77; AFRC Transcript, July 12, 2005, at 5, 12; AFRC Transcript, July 14, 2005, at 34; AFRC Transcript, July 18, 2005, at 106; AFRC Transcript, Sept. 19, 2005, at 53–54; RUF Transcript, July 22, 2004, at 11, 46; RUF Transcript, July 27, 2004, at 17; RUF Transcript, Oct. 5, 2004, at 32; RUF Transcript, Oct. 18, 2004, at 53, 67, 72, 73, 74; RUF Transcript, Oct. 21, 2004, at 94–95; Taylor Transcript, Apr. 4, 2008, at 6667; Los Palos Case Notes, Aug. 2, 2001, at 119.

[127] CDF Transcript, Sept. 27, 2004, at 114.

[128] Semanza Transcript, Nov. 14, 2000, at 44.

[129] RUF Transcript, July 19, 2004, at 50, 78. *See also* RUF Transcript, July 15, 2004, at 35 (witness unable to estimate the number of people in the mosque for prayers); AFRC Transcript, Apr. 7, 2005, at 104–05 (witness unable to estimate how many were in her group, moving to Masiaka).

[130] CDF Transcript, June 21, 2004, at 32; *see also* CDF Transcript, Sept. 23, 2004, at 22 (witness had difficulty estimating how often he went out of Kenema).

[131] *See, e.g.*, CDF Transcript, Sept. 8, 2004, at 67–68; CDF Transcript, Sept. 9, 2004, at 118–19; CDF Transcript, Sept. 14, 2004, at 110–13; CDF Transcript, Nov. 23, 2004, at 40; CDF Transcript, Dec. 1, 2004, at 31; CDF Transcript, Feb. 9, 2005, at 23; AFRC Transcript, June 27, 2005, at 38–39, 108–10; RUF Transcript, July 27, 2004, at 73; RUF Transcript, Apr. 19, 2005, at 46–47; Prosecutor v. Seromba, Case No. ICTR-01–66-T, Transcript, Sept. 30, 2004, at 58 [hereinafter Seromba Transcript]; Seromba Transcript, Oct. 15, 2004, at 43; Prosecutor v. Niyitegeka, Case No. ICTR-96–14-T, Transcript, Aug. 19, 2002, at 32–34 [hereinafter Niyitegeka Transcript]; Niyitegeka Transcript, Aug. 20, 2002, at 68; Niyitegeka Transcript, Aug. 28, 2002, at 119–20.

of civilians in a particular town "exceeded 10, 20, 30, [or] 40,"[132] and witness TF2-033 – a police officer at the Kenema police station – was initially unwilling to estimate the number of police personnel employed at that station.[133] The following excerpt provides an example of the kinds of exchanges that can take place over numerical estimations:

Q. Mr. Witness, you testified that after you left the kitchen several people tried to run away; is that correct?
A. Yes, sir.
Q. Can you recall how many people tried to run away?
A. There are many who wanted to run away.
Q. My first question is can you describe what you mean "with plenty"?
A. There were a large number who wanted to go away.
Q. What is a large number?
A. I mean there were a lot of people.
Q. How many?

PRESIDING JUDGE: You have asked that twice, Mr. Knoops.
MR. KNOOPS: But I'm not getting any answer, Your Honour. I'm sorry.
JUDGE LUSSICK: Witness, when you say a lot of people, was it more than five people?
THE WITNESS: Yes, there were more than five.
JUDGE LUSSICK: Was it more than ten people?
THE WITNESS: There are more than five to ten people that run away.
JUDGE LUSSICK: How many would you say ran away?
THE WITNESS: Some wanted to run away – they wanted to go away, but they were not able to go away because the rebels stopped them from going.
JUDGE LUSSICK: Yes, but I didn't ask you that. You said it was more than five or ten people that ran away. How many would you say ran away?
THE WITNESS: I cannot tell the amount. There are many. I cannot tell you a direct figure.[134]

Sometimes, when witnesses do provide numerical estimates, the estimates prove obviously inaccurate. The ICTR's *Kamuhanda* Trial Chamber discredited witness GEM's testimony in part because she estimated that there were one million Tutsi taking refuge at the Gikomero Parish, while other witnesses placed the number of Tutsi refugees in the thousands.[135] East Timorese witness

[132] CDF Transcript, June 17, 2004, at 36.
[133] CDF Transcript, Sept. 20, 2004, at 123.
[134] AFRC Transcript, Mar. 8, 2005, at 8.
[135] Kamuhanda Transcript, Feb. 11, 2002, at 106.

Benedito da Costa said that he and thirteen others were detained together, yet he named only ten detainees besides himself and said that five of the detainees were held in one location and six in another.[136] Sometimes, the witnesses find it so difficult to provide an accurate numerical estimate that they seem simply to guess at the answers. In her written statement, *Akayesu* witness JJ estimated that five hundred Tutsi had been beaten by the *Interahamwe*, whereas in testimony, she placed the number at sixty.[137] Going in the other direction, *Kamuhanda* witness GEM reported in his pretrial statement that he hid in a sorghum field with fifty others, whereas he testified that he hid with five thousand others.[138] *Niyitegeka* witness HR similarly could not make up his mind about approximately how many Tutsi took refuge on Muyira Hill. In his statement, he put the number at fifteen thousand, whereas during direct testimony, he placed it at five thousand, and in cross-examination, he said that there were more than five thousand.[139]

Inadequate or inappropriate responses to numerical questions can sometimes lead counsel to challenge the witness's ability to count. When that occurred during the testimony of East Timorese witness Alfred Paku, the Special Panel recounted, "[t]he witness was able to count, one-by-one, the people in the courtroom but didn't know how many months there are in a year. He knows there are seven days in a week though."[140] And after Sierra Leonean witness TF1-024 testified that thirty people had been killed in a certain attack, it was revealed that the witness did not know how to count; the witness then testified that he nonetheless knew that thirty people had been killed because the rebels had said they had killed that many.[141]

2.A.v. *Two-Dimensional Representations*

Sometimes counsel try to elucidate or test a witness's account by means of maps, photographs, sketches, and other two-dimensional representations, but the witnesses often cannot make heads or tails out of them. Counsel at the Special Panels and SCSL rarely even attempted to facilitate testimony with such two-dimensional representations,[142] presumably recognizing that witnesses would be unable to answer questions about them. Early on in the *CDF* trial, the

[136] Lolotoe Case Notes, Apr. 8, 2002, at 5. In later questioning, the witness was made aware of the discrepancy and named three other detainees. Lolotoe Case Notes, Apr. 12, 2002, at 3.
[137] Akayesu Transcript, Oct. 23, 1997, at 102–03.
[138] Kamuhanda Transcript, Feb. 11, 2002, at 106.
[139] Niyitegeka Judgement, note 56, at para. 102.
[140] Tacaqui Judgement, note 36, at 34.
[141] AFRC Transcript, Mar. 7, 2005, at 102–03.
[142] *See* Tim Kelsall, Culture Under Cross-Examination: International Justice and the Special Court for Sierra Leone 119 (2009).

prosecution asked witness TF2-021 one question on reexamination: "If I were to show you a map of Sierra Leone, would you be able to understand this map?" The witness answered "no," and that was the end of the reexamination.[143] Special Panels defendant Hilario da Silva responded similarly when he was given a sketch of the crime scene, saying, "[i]f we go to Lautem I'll show you, but I don't understand this paper."[144] Similarly, when ICTR prosecution investigator Tony Lucassen was asked why he had not shown maps to Rwandan witnesses, he replied that in his experience "local Rwandese witnesses . . . are not very experienced in map use."[145] ICTR defense counsel do frequently show witnesses photographs and other two-dimensional representations as a means of testing the witnesses' accounts, but in many instances the witnesses maintain that they are unable to make sense of the map or photograph.[146] In refusing even to look at the photographs presented to him, Rwandan witness GEL, for instance, exclaimed, "[p]lease, don't drag me on to photographs. I didn't undergo studies on photography, on how to sketch matters, photographs are for people who are intellectuals."[147] And, as with date and distance questions, even well-educated witnesses can assert difficulty with map reading. Rwandan witness GEK was sufficiently educated to know how to read some English[148] but maintained that she was unable to understand the map that was presented to her.[149]

As I discuss in Chapter 5, perjury is widespread at some international tribunals, particularly at the ICTR. Witnesses have been known to fabricate their presence at massacre sites and other locations, so it is not surprising that defense counsel would attempt to use maps and photographs as a means of determining whether the witness really was where she said she was. But it rarely works. Perjuring witnesses can maintain that they do not understand the map or photograph, and their assertion will be plausible because plenty of honest international witnesses *are* unaccustomed to viewing three-dimensional objects in two-dimensional representations. The *Niyitegeka* Trial Chamber, for

[143] CDF Transcript, Nov. 4, 2004, at 38. *AFRC* witness TF1-157 similarly testified that he had never seen a map or a chart. AFRC Transcript, July 25, 2005, at 29.

[144] Los Palos Case Notes, July 26, 2001, at 78.

[145] Ntakirutimana Transcript, Sept. 19, 2001, at 9–10.

[146] *See, e.g.*, Ntakirutimana Transcript, Sept. 24, 2001, at 126–27; Ntakirutimana Transcript, Sept. 25, 2001, at 8–11; Kamuhanda Transcript, Sept. 12, 2001, at 88–90; Kamuhanda Transcript, Sept. 19, 2001, at 32; Kamuhanda Transcript, Sept. 24, 2001, at 29–31; Kamuhanda Transcript, Feb. 14, 2002, at 4–7, 10, 26; Kamuhanda Transcript, Sept. 11, 2002, at 84; Kajelijeli Transcript, Dec. 12, 2001, at 58; Musema Judgement, note 112, at paras. 380, 436, 838; Niyitegeka Judgement, note 56, at para. 151; Akayesu Transcript, Oct. 27, 1997, at 40.

[147] Kamuhanda Transcript, Feb. 13, 2002, at 130.

[148] Kamuhanda Transcript, Sept. 4, 2001, at 17–18.

[149] *Id.* at 108–09.

instance, acknowledged that "the witness's inability to identify Muyira Hill in a photograph in court undermines his evidence relating to this attack" but nonetheless concluded that "the witness's difficulty with reading photographs does not affect the witness's credibility."[150]

As was true with date and distance estimations, a witness's inability to understand maps and photographs can also impair the Trial Chambers' capacity to assess the reliability of a witness's account. Even if the Trial Chamber has every reason to believe that the witness was indeed at the crime scene, the Trial Chamber can find it useful to know where exactly the witness was at the scene. In *Bagilishema*, for instance, witness G claimed to have seen the defendant at the Gatwaro Stadium, and because the witness was able to mark her position on a photograph of the stadium, the Trial Chamber was able to determine that the witness's "line of sight would have had to travel at a gentle upward angle through the low-roofed and presumably crowded porch and its supporting columns, out over a 50-metre stretch of equally crowded field, before it reached the steep verdant (and thus dark coloured) backdrop of Gatwaro, 55 to 65 metres away, where hundreds of attackers were said to have assembled."[151] As a result of these suboptimal visual conditions, the Trial Chamber declined to rely on witness G's testimony, a decision that the Trial Chamber probably would not have reached had witness G been unable to understand the photograph she was presented.

2.A.vi. *Important Details*

I began this section by discussing certain unimportant personal details that international witnesses sometimes have difficulty providing, such as the witness's age or the length of time that he has been married. As I noted, a witness's inability to provide these details is of little consequence because the details are not relevant to the events that form the basis of the witness's testimony. Not surprisingly, however, international witnesses are also frequently unable to provide the court with details that *are* relevant to their testimony. So, for instance, witnesses who testify that the defendant arrived at a location in a vehicle might be asked about the make or model of the vehicle. Rwandan witness CGM's response to such a question was typical. He said:

> It was a beautiful car but I do not know the model or type of vehicle it was. It was a white car. It's one of those vehicles used by the authorities. You know, I am a peasant, I'm a farmer, so in my conditions I wouldn't be able to give

[150] Niyitegeka Judgement, note 56, at para. 151.
[151] Bagilishema Judgement, note 122, at paras. 648–649.

you the models of or makes of cars. We talk about lorries or pick-ups and so on and so forth, but we don't really speak about makes of cars.[152]

In similar vein, Special Panels' witness 3 stated that he was completely unable to describe the guns that the militia members were carrying,[153] and a Special Panels prosecutor asked another witness to draw a sketch of the kind of weapons he saw because no one could understand from his testimony whether he was referring to some type of gun or "arrows and bows."[154] Other examples appear in the notes.[155]

2.A.vii. *Court Procedures*

International witnesses not only have difficulty providing the details of the events they witnessed but also frequently misunderstand key features of the judicial system in which they are participating, and these misunderstandings can impede a witness's ability to answer questions or provide clear testimony. Many international witnesses, for instance, are unfamiliar with the sorts of adversarial procedures that govern international trials, and they feel aggrieved and insulted when their testimony is challenged during cross-examination.[156]

[152] Ndindabahizi Transcript, Sept. 15, 2003, at 10.

[153] Los Palos Case Notes, Aug. 2, 2001, at 124.

[154] Los Palos Case Notes, Aug. 22, 2001, at 187.

[155] *See, e.g.*, Los Palos Case Notes, Aug. 22, 2001, at 192 ("I don't know what type of car it was, I'm illiterate, that's all."); Ndindabahizi Transcript, Sept. 16, 2003, at 51–52 ("The make of the car? Well, I don't know it. . . . I know it was a saloon car and I know its colour, but I don't know its make"); Ndindabahizi Transcript, Sept. 29, 2003, at 29 ("I am unable to tell the different makes of vehicles, but it was a vehicle with a long chassis. It was the kind of vehicle on which one normally mounts antennae."); Kamuhanda Transcript, Feb. 12, 2002, at 48 ("I am not that experienced, that qualified in determining the make or type of vehicle."); Ntakirutimana Transcript, Sept. 24, 2001, at 9–10; Ntakirutimana Transcript, Sept. 25, 2001, at 30–32; Ntakirutimana Transcript, Sept. 26, 2001, at 38–39; AFRC Transcript, June 27, 2005, at 44–45; AFRC Transcript, June 28, 2005, at 106; RUF Transcript, July 21, 2004, at 11–14; RUF Transcript, July 27, 2004, at 61; RUF Transcript, Oct. 7, 2004, at 23–24.

[156] *See, e.g.*, RUF Transcript, July 19, 2004, at 66; RUF Transcript, July 21, 2004, at 12, 19; RUF Transcript, Oct. 5, 2004, at 191; RUF Transcript, Oct. 6, 2004, at 63, 67–68, 72–76; RUF Transcript, Oct. 7, 2004, at 23–24, 119, 153, 191, 201; AFRC Transcript, Apr. 6, 2005, at 47–48, 50–52; AFRC Transcript, April 18, 2005, at 47–48; AFRC Transcript, June 28, 2005, at 48–49, 50–52; AFRC Transcript, June 30, 2005, at 116–17; AFRC Transcript, July 1, 2005, at 24; AFRC Transcript, July 18, 2005, at 98, 106–08; CDF Transcript, May 22, 2006, at 45, 46, 52, 68; Ndindabahizi Transcript, Sept. 8, 2003, at 16; Ndindabahizi Transcript, Sept. 15, 2003, at 28, 36, 51; Kamuhanda Transcript, Sept. 13, 2001, at 91; Kamuhanda Transcript, Sept. 19, 2001, at 61–62; Kamuhanda Transcript, Feb. 5, 2002, at 26, 28, 31; Kamuhanda Transcript, Feb. 6, 2002, at 87; Ntakirutimana Transcript, Sept. 20, 2001, at 57–58; Ntakirutimana Transcript, Sept. 24, 2001, at 100–01; Ntakirutimana Transcript, Sept. 27, 2001, at 125–27; Alison Thompson, U.C. Berkeley War Crimes Studies Center, Special Court Monitoring Program, Update No. 72,

Rwandan witness GGD described his cross-examination as "torture,"[157] and Sierra Leonean witness TF2-006 fell to sobbing because he believed defense counsel was accusing him of lying.[158] Rwandan witness GKJ objected to questions that probed inconsistencies between her testimony and her statements, and she finally exhorted counsel to "stop harassing me," accusing counsel of "insisting on making me go crazy."[159] Rwandan witness GDO became even more agitated, and announced to the Trial Chamber:

> [L]et me tell you very frankly that I am tired. I thought I was coming to give testimony as I was asked to. I have done that, but I realise now that it is as if I were being tried. I have no intention to submit myself to any trial because, in any case, that will not resuscitate my children who died. If you want to spare me this difficulty, if you don't want me to fall sick before you, please stop there, because if I speak too much, if I get annoyed, I fall sick.[160]

A few moments later, the witness fainted.[161] GDO was not the only witness to fall ill upon cross-examination,[162] and witness GDD was so unwilling to answer questions on cross-examination that the Trial Chamber was unable to rely on his testimony, determining that the defense had been unable to conduct an effective cross-examination.[163]

International witnesses not only frequently fail to understand the adversarial nature of the questioning they receive at the international tribunals; they also frequently lack awareness of who the criminal justice players are, what roles they can be expected to play, and how investigations and court cases proceed. Rwandan witness ACM, for instance, did not know that she was speaking with the ICTR when they initially contacted her for information.[164] Sierra Leonean witness TF1-074 thought that the people who took his statement were judges,[165] while witnesses TF2-096, TF1-054, and TF1-305 described the prosecutor as "my lawyer."[166] When asked whether he had spoken to the

Mar. 10, 2006, at 3; Los Palos Case Notes, July 30, 2001, at 95; Los Palos Case Notes, July 31, 2001, at 105.

[157] Niyitegeka Transcript, Aug. 29, 2002, at 145.

[158] CDF Transcript, Feb. 9, 2005, at 61–63.

[159] Kamuhanda Transcript, May 7, 2002, at 82, 105.

[160] Kajelijeli Transcript, July 18, 2001, at 109–10.

[161] *Id.* at 114.

[162] Prosecutor v. Bagosora et al., Case No. ICTR-98-41-T, Transcript, Dec. 1, 2003, at 62 (French version) [hereinafter Military I Transcript]; Military I Transcript, Mar. 31, 2004, at 55; Los Palos Case Notes, Aug. 13, 2001, at 153; AFRC Transcript, July 8, 2005, at 49; Taylor Transcript, Sept. 10, 2008, at 15961–62; Taylor Transcript, Sept. 11, 2008, at 15968.

[163] Niyitegeka Judgement, note 56, at paras. 90–91.

[164] Kajelijeli Transcript, Dec. 11, 2001, at 83.

[165] RUF Transcript, July 12, 2004, at 56.

[166] CDF Transcript, Nov. 8, 2004, at 44; AFRC Transcript, Apr. 20, 2005, at 26; RUF Transcript, July 27, 2004, at 63–64.

prosecutor about what had happened to him, witness TF1-217 asked, "[w]hich one is the Prosecutor?"[167] Witness TF1-064 likewise did not know the meaning of "prosecutor" and seemed also not to comprehend the difference between the prosecution and defense.[168]

Defense counsel questions often center on the statements witnesses made before trial, and this topic too poses challenges because many witnesses do not entirely understand what they are doing when they provide the prosecution with a statement. One Sierra Leonean witness believed that when he provided more information to the prosecution during a second interview, he was not in fact giving them another statement but was just verifying what was in the first statement.[169] Witness TF2-140 likewise had difficulty understanding the purpose of the second interview and conceived of the second statement as "a cross-examination which is drawn from the original statement I gave my original investigator."[170] The witnesses' confusion about these matters can have serious implications both for the witnesses and for the accuracy of the tribunals' fact-finding. As a general matter, studies of child witnesses have shown that children with a greater understanding of the court system provided more accurate answers to questions than did children with less understanding of the court system, even when age was controlled statistically.[171] In a more particular example from the international tribunals, *Karera* witness BMH explained the substantial inconsistencies between her pretrial statement and her testimony by claiming that she had "lied in her statement because she wanted the interviewers to leave quickly as she believed them to represent [the defendant]." The Trial Chamber accepted this explanation,[172] which may have been truthful, but the Trial Chamber's on-site visit had already proven the witness to have lied or been mistaken about a different issue, so it is just as plausible that the witness invoked this explanation to cover up another mistake or instance of false testimony.

Exchanges with East Timorese defendants were even more unnerving because they demonstrated so clearly the defendants' failure to understand the proceedings against them and their options in those proceedings. The following excerpt from the *Umbertus Ena* case shows, for instance, the difficulty

[167] RUF Transcript, July 22, 2004, at 36.

[168] RUF Transcript, July 19, 2004, at 69, 72; *see also* RUF Transcript, July 27, 2004, at 63–65 (witness does not know the difference between prosecution and defense).

[169] CDF Transcript, Sept. 17, 2004, at 116.

[170] CDF Transcript, Sept. 14, 2004, at 110; *see also* AFRC Transcript, July 14, 2005, at 32–33.

[171] Gail S. Goodman et al., *Face-to Face Confrontation: Effects of Closed-Circuit Technology on Children's Eyewitness Testimony and Juror's Decisions*, 22 L. & Human Behavior 165, 198–200 (1998).

[172] Karera Judgement, note 54, at para. 164.

that can attend even a Panel's relatively straightforward efforts to ascertain whether a defendant understands the nature of the charges against him:

JUDGE: Can you understand the nature of the accusation against you? Did you read indictments or someone read it for you?

DEFENDANT: I'm saying like this, I will speak about, I said that I'm only a small man and there is people who would like to kill myself, and I defend myself so I could leave.

JUDGE: You will have time to make declaration, but now the tribunal would like to ask you whether you have read the indictments and that if you understand the nature of the indictments. Last time we read for you about the right that you have to access your legal defense and that you have opportunity to discuss about the accusation against you with your defense. Did you read the indictments submitted by the prosecutor against you?

DEFENDANT: Can I speak?

JUDGE: Yes please.

DEFENDANT: Would you want me to speak loudly or to answer your question?

DEFENSE COUNSEL: Your honor, my client does not understand. If you can give me time 5 minutes to speak to him about what is happening now. I have spoken to him last time, but it seems that he still not understand.

JUDGE: The court gives five minutes for the defense to talk to his client about this, but first let's try again.

JUDGE: Umbertus Ena, do you know why you are here?

DEFENDANT: Because of what happened in 1999.

DEFENSE COUNSEL: I'm worrying that he may mitigated himself and I worry because he is very unsophisticated man.

JUDGE: This court gives five minutes to both defense counsels to talk to their clients. This court is postponed to 5 minutes.

AFTER 5-MINUTE BREAK

JUDGE: After the consult with the defense counsel, I think that I can ask the question, Umbertus Ena, can you please stand up? Do you understand the accusation against you?

DEFENDANT: I know.
JUDGE: Do you know the nature of the accusation?
DEFENDANT: I know.[173]

Guilty-plea colloquies proceeded similarly and suggested that many Special Panels defendants pled guilty without any real awareness of the nature or consequences of doing so. When Special Panels judges asked Benjamin Sarmento if he wanted to plead guilty, for instance, he seemed to indicate that he did, but he repeatedly asserted that he had been ordered to commit the crimes, making such statements as: "People send us to kill. That's why we did it. That is like we accept our guilty" and "[t]his charge, I accept, because they told me to do it. That's why I accept. But the problem is that for me to think about doing it, I wouldn't have done it. That is because I was told to do it."[174] Despite the obvious ambiguities in Sarmento's admissions, the Panel accepted his guilty plea. A few minutes later, Sarmento's codefendant, Romeiro Tilman, also attempted to plead guilty, and his responses were even more equivocal. Tilman apparently held the victim down while someone else killed him. When asked if he was prepared to plead guilty, Tilman responded:

> I agree. This is not because of what I wanted, but because those in charge forced me. I did it. It is not that I used a knife, or a machete to kill. I didn't. The commander of militia forced me. I was scared of death. My colleague did it. And I have been in jail for over 3 years. This wrong is not mine. The person who did this is not here. And I, have come to accept my wrong.... I feel that I am wrong because I held with my hands.[175]

Because Tilman claimed to have been forced to commit the crime, the court adjourned to allow him to consult with his lawyer. Returning from his consultation, Tilman said simply: "I am guilty."[176]

2.A.viii. *Summary*

This section has examined the many categories of information that international witnesses frequently fail to provide. Not answering a cross-examiner's question is not in itself unusual. What is unusual is the frequency with which

[173] Prosecutor v. Ena, Case No. 05/2002, Judicial System Monitoring Programme, Preliminary Hearing Case Notes, Feb. 14, 2003, at 2 (on file with author).
[174] Public Prosecutor v. Sarmento, Special Panel for Serious Crimes, Court Record, at 10 (June 30, 2003) (on file with author).
[175] *Id.* at 15.
[176] *Id.* at 16.

questions go unanswered at the international tribunals and the types of questions that the witnesses fail to answer. What is notable about international witnesses, indeed, is their frequent inability to convey the sort of information that is crucial to the Trial Chamber's ability to find facts and assess credibility. A vague account devoid of details is an account that cannot be effectively challenged. When a witness cannot date the events she witnessed, the witness prevents the defendant from presenting an alibi. When a witness cannot name the make of the defendant's car, then the witness's account cannot be undermined by evidence showing that the defendant drove a car of a different make. When a witness is unable to say for how long the rebels occupied his village, then the witness's testimony cannot be inconsistent with that of another witness who might estimate a shorter or longer occupation. And when a witness professes not to understand maps or photographs, the witness renders the defense unable to prove that she was never even at the scene of the crime. In other words, all manner of innocent inaccuracies as well as deliberate lies can be concealed through a witness's plausible claim that he is unable to answer a question.

Questioning at the international tribunals sometimes fails to elicit useful information, not because the witness does not have the information that counsel seeks but because the witness fails to understand counsel's question or does not provide an answer that is intelligible to courtroom personnel. It is these phenomena that the following section addresses.

2.B. QUESTIONS AND ANSWERS: A DIFFERENT SORT OF COMMUNICATION BREAKDOWN

Summarizing the testimonies has turned out to be a complex task, because the declarations of each witness extended for many pages and they almost never followed a logic or intelligible structure.

– Prosecution v. Tacaqui, Dili District Court, Special Panel for Serious Crimes, Case No. 20/2001, Judgement at 30 (Dec. 9, 2004)

Witness questioning is rarely a smooth, straightforward affair at the international tribunals, even when the witnesses apparently have the information that counsel seeks. Sometimes witnesses do not understand the questions they are asked, sometimes counsel and judges do not understand the answers they are given, and each of these communications breakdowns can take a variety of forms. Sometimes the problem is a simple one of terminology; that is, the witness does not understand one or more of the words that counsel has used in a question. When asked if there had been any military attacks, for instance,

Sierra Leonean witness TF2-198 answered, "I don't understand that language; military attack, what do you mean?"[177] Similarly, when asked to "tell this Court the period over which the rebels that came attacked Koribundo," witness TF2-157 responded, "[w]hat do you mean by period?"[178] Witness TF2-109 did not understand the word "additional" when asked if she had made two "additional statements,"[179] and Witness TF1-085 did not understand a reference to the defendant's rank.[180] Witness TF1-278, meanwhile, could not understand what counsel meant when she asked whether the witness's statement had been "read over" to him.[181] Other examples appear in the notes.[182]

Such terminological difficulties are usually easily remedied. For instance, when Witness TF1-085 failed to understand the question: Did the investigators "ask you to clarify previous statements?," the judge advised counsel to "put it in another form. It was very technical words." When counsel subsequently asked, "[d]id you at any time tell the Prosecution that you wanted to clear certain points in your previous statements?" the witness understood.[183] Similarly, although witness TF1-024 could not understand the question "did you observe him doing anything else?" he did understand when the question was changed to "was he doing anything else aside from what you said?"[184] The same witness showed that he misunderstood the question "[h]ow were they killed?" when he answered, "[t]hey killed them through their chests, some their legs." It was only when counsel specifically asked if the victims had been shot that the witness confirmed that they had.[185] Finally, when witness TF1-012 gave confused responses to counsel's question whether "Gullit was in control of Number 11," one of the judges opined that the witness may not have understood the term "in control" and suggested that counsel ask him if Gullit was "the big man for the area." That phrasing seemed to do the trick.[186]

[177] CDF Transcript, June 15, 2004, at 60.

[178] CDF Transcript, June 16, 2004, at 26–27. *See also* CDF Transcript, June 18, 2004, at 16–17 (witness unable to understand when asked whether he had had any interaction with the Kamajors).

[179] CDF Transcript, Nov. 8, 2004, at 65.

[180] AFRC Transcript, Apr. 7, 2005, at 67.

[181] AFRC Transcript, Apr. 6, 2005, at 21–22.

[182] *See, e.g.*, Taylor Transcript, Aug. 21, 2008, at 14278; Taylor Transcript, Sept. 16, 2008, at 16328–31; CDF Transcript, Feb. 9, 2005, at 19; AFRC Transcript, June 30, 2005, at 111–12; AFRC Transcript, Sept. 29, 2005, at 60–61; RUF Transcript, July 28, 2004, at 20–21; RUF Transcript, Oct 6, 2004, at 79–80; RUF Transcript, Oct 8, 2004, at 199; RUF Transcript, Oct. 11, 2004, at 58–59, 113–14, 142.

[183] AFRC Transcript, Apr. 7, 2005, at 59.

[184] AFRC Transcript, Mar. 7, 2005, at 51.

[185] *Id.* at 47.

[186] RUF Transcript, Feb. 3, 2005, at 74.

Sometimes witness confusion stems not from the terminology used in the question but from the form of the question. Compound or multipart questions have proven particularly vexing to SCSL witnesses.[187] Studies have shown that multipart questions are confusing both to adult and child witnesses in Western countries,[188] and these have proven virtually impossible for some international witnesses to comprehend. Time and again, judges at the SCSL urged counsel to divide a question into a series of questions.[189] For example, when a witness seemed unable to answer the defense counsel's question "when ... the Kamajors told you that Chief Norman was coming to talk to them were you eager to go and hear Chief Norman?," Judge Itoe reformulated the question into the following series of questions:

PRESIDENT: You know [Chief Norman] very well, huh? ...
WITNESS: Yes, sir.
PRESIDENT: Right. He is your chief?
WITNESS: Yes, sir.
PRESIDENT: He was coming to hold a meeting with you.
WITNESS: Yes, sir.
PRESIDENT: Were you happy to go to the meeting?
WITNESS: Yes, I was glad.[190]

Defense counsel seemed to learn little from the above interchange, however, for in the very next breath, he asked: "Whom did you find speaking [at the meeting] when you arrived?" Again, concluding that the witness was unable to comprehend the question, Judge Boutet broke it down into two questions that the witness was able to answer: "[W]hen you got to that meeting ... was there anybody speaking?" and "who was speaking?" Among many

[187] Some Rwandan witnesses have also had trouble with compound questions. *See, e.g.*, Ndindabahizi Transcript, Sept. 8, 2003, at 5; Kajelijeli Transcript, Nov. 27, 2001, at 39–40.

[188] Louise Ellison, The Adversarial Process and the Vulnerable Witness 95 (2001); Ingrid M. Cordon et al., *Children in Court, in* Adversarial Versus Inquisitorial Justice: Psychological Perspectives on Criminal Justice Systems 167, 171 (Peter J. van Koppen & Steven D. Penrod eds., 2003).

[189] *See, e.g.*, CDF Transcript, June 17, 2004, at 5; CDF Transcript, June 17, 2004, at 38–39 (Judge advised counsel to break up the question, "Did you vote in the election that brought Tejan Kabbah to power?"); CDF Transcript, Sept. 10, 2004, at 36–37; AFRC Transcript, Apr. 11, 2005, at 80; AFRC Transcript, June 27, 2005, at 53; AFRC Transcript, July 12, 2005, at 35; RUF Transcript, Oct. 7, 2004, at 11; Taylor Transcript, Aug. 21, 2008, at 14269–70; Taylor Transcript, Sept. 11, 2008, at 16052–54. Sometimes ICTR judges give the same advice. *See* Ndindabahizi Transcript, Sept. 3, 2003, at 52. And sometimes the witness himself asks counsel to "break ... up" the question. *See* RUF Transcript, Oct. 18, 2004, at 104; RUF Transcript, Oct. 19, 2004, at 10–11, 57–58, 60–61; *see also* Taylor Transcript, Aug. 28, 2008, at 14898–99.

[190] CDF Transcript, June 18, 2004, at 18–19.

other examples, counsel likewise had to disaggregate such questions as the following:

- "When the Kamajors took over Bo in February 1998 they were later chased out by the junta in that same February. Am I correct?"[191]
- "Did the Prosecution or anyone else of the Special Court ever ask you whether you would be willing to talk to any of the Defence teams?"[192]
- "[W]ould I be correct to suggest to you that you did not carry out the instructions as well because you had a discretion to choose between orders that were bad and orders that were good?"[193]
- "[I]t took such a long time [to elect a successor paramount chief] because of the bitterness that had existed from this amalgamation?"[194]
- "[I]t is fair to say, madam, that the only thing that you know about what happened in Kono is from what you heard from the people living there. Is that right?"[195]

Sometimes the SCSL judges have seemed excessively concerned about witnesses' ability to make sense of compound questions. Even the prosecution's very straightforward request to "describe to this Court a typical day at that time in Kondembaia" led the judge to admonish him: "Is that question not complicated? It's complicated. It's a very complicated question." The prosecutor thereafter abandoned the question.[196] Similarly, the presiding judge chastised counsel for asking the question "you are able to speak English and to understand spoken English?," noting "you have two questions there. Are you able to speak English, one question; are you able to understand English, second question. You should separate them." The presiding judge delivered this advice despite the fact that the witness seemed to answer the question perfectly well, stating: "[Y]es sir. There are some bits of English that I do not understand."[197] Other examples of judicial concern appear in the notes.[198] But despite the fact that judges may overreact in certain instances, there is no question that the format of questioning must be carefully monitored. Indeed, compound questions

[191] CDF Transcript, Mar. 14, 2005, at 59.
[192] CDF Transcript, Sept. 9, 2004, at 121.
[193] CDF Transcript, Mar. 14, 2005, at 35.
[194] CDF Transcript, Sept. 14, 2004, at 32.
[195] RUF Transcript, July 15, 2004, at 16.
[196] RUF Transcript, July 14, 2004, at 3.
[197] AFRC Transcript, Mar. 7, 2005, at 64.
[198] RUF Transcript, Oct. 6, 2004, at 48; RUF Transcript, Oct. 7, 2004, at 11; RUF Transcript, Oct. 8, 2004, at 68–69; RUF Transcript, Oct. 21, 2004, at 40–41; RUF Transcript, Jan. 28, 2005, at 19; CDF Transcript, Dec. 2, 2004, at 83–84; AFRC Transcript, July 21, 2005, at 36; AFRC Transcript, Sept. 23, 2005, at 102; Ntakirutimana Transcript, Sept. 24, 2001, at 42–43; Ntakirutimana Transcript, Sept. 27, 2001, at 13–14.

can lead witnesses to provide inaccurate answers. Witness TF2-157 answered negatively to the question "[b]ut you agree with me that the SLPP government was overthrown in 1997?" It was only when the president of the Trial Chamber divided up the question that it became clear that the witness answered negatively because he did not know the date of the SLPP's overthrow.[199]

It is not only compound questions that can prove problematic to international witnesses but also questions that are phrased with any sort of complexity, as the following exchange shows:

DEFENSE COUNSEL: Did you feel you could refuse to have sexual intercourse with him?

WITNESS: Yes.

JUDGE SEBUTINDE: Sorry, Madam Prosecutor. Listen to your question: "Did you feel you could refuse." What kind of a question is that?

DEFENSE COUNSEL: Perhaps I –

JUDGE SEBUTINDE: I have not understood. I, for one, do not understand, "Did you feel you could refuse?" Maybe you need to re-phrase that.

DEFENSE COUNSEL: I will do so, Your Honour.

JUDGE SEBUTINDE: I am not even sure what she has answered to.

DEFENSE COUNSEL: Witness, did the colonel who captured you ask you for your consent to have sexual intercourse with him?

WITNESS: Yes, he told me.

DEFENSE COUNSEL: Did you agree to have sexual intercourse with him?

WITNESS: No.[200]

Other examples of questions that proved troublingly complex appear in the notes,[201] but sometimes open-ended questions can be just as problematic as complex ones.[202] Sierra Leonean witness TF1-024 was not able to answer the question "what else did you see?" or follow the instruction to "tell the court exactly what you saw." Counsel consequently had to ask specific questions about the events the witness saw in order to lead the witness through the exchange.[203] Similarly, a Special Panels' translator reported to an NGO monitor

[199] CDF Transcript, June 17, 2004, at 40.

[200] AFRC Transcript, Apr. 7, 2005, at 36.

[201] AFRC Transcript, June 30, 2005, at 107–08; AFRC Transcript, July 1, 2005, at 35–36; RUF Transcript, July 27, 2004, at 69; Ntakirutimana Transcript, Sept. 24, 2001, at 130–31.

[202] *See, e.g.*, RUF Transcript, July 27, 2004, at 53; RUF Transcript, Oct. 25, 2004, at 54–55; AFRC Transcript, Sept. 23, 2005, at 13–16; Taylor Transcript, Aug. 28, 2008, at 14883–84.

[203] AFRC Transcript, Mar. 7, 2005, at 45–46.

that open-ended questions, such as "what happened next?" or "in what part of the house?" had no meaning for a particular witness.[204]

Sometimes a witness will not expressly state that he fails to understand the question, but it becomes clear that there exists some confusion because the witness's response to the question is not in fact responsive. In some instances, the answer will bear no relationship to the question. For instance, one East Timorese witness was asked, "by what means did you travel from Osaide to Lolotoe?," and he answered, "I was wearing my pants and my shirt."[205] Another East Timorese witness was twice asked how many times the defendant hit the victim, and twice the witness answered, "about 11:00."[206] And when East Timorese witness Orlando Ati was asked in what condition were the machetes, he replied, "I don't know the type of machete."[207] Such exchanges were particularly prevalent at the Special Panels, but other examples – from the SCSL and ICTR as well as the Special Panels – appear in the notes.[208]

[204] Lolotoe Case Notes, Oct. 25, 2002, at 1.

[205] Lolotoe Case Notes, Nov. 4, 2002, at 4.

[206] Los Palos Case Notes, Aug. 14, 2001, at 156.

[207] Lolotoe Case Notes, Feb. 3, 2003, at 8.

[208] When asked why he left Pendembu, the place where he was born, witness TF2-021 said "There I was born. There I stayed with my mother." CDF Transcript, Nov. 2, 2004, at 28. When asked "how were you taken to Lolotoe?," an East Timorese witness answered "because the militia couldn't get my son . . . [I]f the militia got my son . . . then they would not have taken us." The question "who took you to the army's house?" was answered, "I didn't recognize the army." Lolotoe Case Notes, Oct. 23, 2002, at 4; *see also* Lolotoe Case Notes, Apr. 9, 2002, at 4; Lolotoe Case Notes, Oct. 22, 2002, at 10; Lolotoe Case Notes, Oct. 23, 2002, at 7; Lolotoe Case Notes, Nov. 14, 2002, at 5; Lolotoe Case Notes, Nov. 14, 2002, at 7–8; Lolotoe Case Notes, Mar. 17, 2003, at 11; Lolotoe Case Notes, Mar. 18, 2003, at 4–5; Lolotoe Case Notes, Mar. 19, 2003, at 8; Lolotoe Case Notes, Mar. 19, 2003, at 10; AFRC Transcript, Mar. 8, 2005, at 22, 43–44; AFRC Transcript, Apr. 7, 2005, at 46; AFRC Transcript, June 27, 2005, at 4; AFRC Transcript, July 20, 2005, at 46; AFRC Transcript, Sept. 22, 2005, at 29–30; AFRC Transcript, Sept. 23, 2005, at 11–12, 20; RUF Transcript, July 21, 2004, at 15; RUF Transcript, July 22, 2004, at 6, 8, 47, 48, 50; RUF Transcript, July 27, 2004, at 52; RUF Transcript, July 28, 2004, at 29; RUF Transcript, Oct. 6, 2004, at 89; RUF Transcript, Oct. 21, 2004, at 56, 57–58; RUF Transcript, Oct. 22, 2004, at 2–3; Taylor Transcript, Apr. 14, 2008, at 7423, 7533–34; Taylor Transcript, Apr. 14, 2008, at 7423; Taylor Transcript, Apr. 24, 2008, at 8536; Taylor Transcript, Aug. 21, 2008, at 14257; Taylor Transcript, Sept. 4, 2008, at 15441–42; Taylor Transcript, Sept. 8, 2008, at 15708; Kamuhanda Transcript, Jan. 21, 2003, at 12; Ntakirutimana Transcript, Sept. 24, 2001, at 15.

A number of additional examples can be found in the pages of the *Ndindabahizi* case. Witness CGB was asked "did you do your interview at your home or after the visit by the investigators did you go to the Kibuye guesthouse in order to provide your statement?" to which he responded "yes." Ndindabahizi Transcript, Sept. 22, 2003, at 32. When asked what Ndindabahizi looked like, witness CGY reported what Ndindabahizi was doing. Ndindabahizi Transcript, Sept. 8, 2003, at 36. When the prosecution asked witness CGV how much time had elapsed between the time Ndindabahizi disembarked from the white Toyota until the time he threw a grenade to the attackers, the witness failed to answer that question and reported instead what people did after the grenade was thrown. Ndindabahizi Transcript, Sept. 16, 2003, at 26. *See also* Ndindabahizi Transcript, Sept. 8, 2003, at 50.

In other instances, the witness's answer is unresponsive, but it is "off" in a slightly less jarring way. For instance, Sierra Leonean witness TF2-040 had testified that "[w]e saw them in the morning," but when defense counsel asked the witness "[w]ho is we?" the witness responded, "[w]e saw Kamajors."[209] Witness TF1-277 was injured during the conflict and had asserted in a written statement that he bled for three hours. When defense counsel asked whether the bleeding had been continuous during the three hours, the witness replied, "[n]ot for three hours, because I had picnic in my bag and that helped to sustain me."[210] Another example derives from the testimony of witness TF1-085, who described *RUF* defendant Issa Sesay as "not too much tall" but taller than [*AFRC* defendant] Five-Five. The witness then went on to describe Five-Five as "huge and tall" but stated that Issa Sesay, who is "not too much tall" is actually taller than the "huge and tall" Five-Five.[211] And witness TF1-084 testified that rebels were taking "old people" and putting them in vehicles. When asked how old the people were, he said, "I was able to recognize a small girl that was 14 years of age."[212] Other examples appear in the notes.[213]

In some cases, the confusion – or some sort of communication difficulty – becomes apparent because counsel must ask a question multiple times in order to get a responsive answer from the witness. Indeed, obtaining information about the simplest details can be a frustrating and time-consuming endeavor at the international tribunals. Defense counsel in *Ndindabahizi*, for instance, had to ask the witness three times how many times the witness saw Ndindabahizi between 1980 and 1985 before receiving an answer because the witness kept focusing on the number of times he saw Ndindabahizi *after* 1985.[214] It likewise took three questions to get an answer from *AFRC* witness TF1-084 about whether a man named Akim had been with the rebels.[215] It took three questions before *RUF* witness TF1-214 would say that she did not hear the rebels say

[209] CDF Transcript, Sept. 21, 2004, at 22.
[210] AFRC Transcript, Mar. 8, 2005, at 102.
[211] AFRC Transcript, Apr. 7, 2005, at 96–97.
[212] AFRC Transcript, Apr. 6, 2005, at 40.
[213] The response to "[d]id he say what would happen to you if you didn't give . . . sandalwood?" was "[o]ld man – if you have some sandalwood, give it to me." Lolotoe Case Notes, Apr. 8, 2002, at 8. *Ndindabahizi* witness CGM testified that he knew Ndindabahizi because the latter had been the educational inspectorate in the witness's region. When asked "can you explain further as to what you mean by the educational inspectorate in your region," witness CGM responded, "I saw him in that educational unit on so many occasions, and that is why I'm saying that I know him there." Ndindabahizi Transcript, Sept. 15, 2003, at 3. *See also* Los Palos Case Notes, July 12, 2001, at 21; Taylor Transcript, Aug. 21, 2008, at 14269, 14300; Taylor Transcript, Sept. 1, 2008, at 15010; Taylor Transcript, Sept. 8, 2008, at 15664, 15736; RUF Transcript, Oct. 8, 2004, at 4; AFRC Transcript, June 28, 2005, at 37; AFRC Transcript, June 27, 2005, at 64; AFRC Transcript, July 7, 2005, at 81; Ntakirutimana Transcript, Sept. 24, 2001, at 82.
[214] Ndindabahizi Transcript, Sept. 16, 2003, at 16–18.
[215] AFRC Transcript, Apr. 6, 2005, at 46.

anything about what they were going to do next,[216] and it took three questions before Special Panels' defendant Joni Marques would answer why he thought a certain victim had been beaten.[217] And those were examples of the brief exchanges. It took pages of testimony from *CDF* witness TF2-040 – who is a policeman in Kenema – before judges learned that there are four different categories of police in Kenema and that he was unable to see who was shooting when he was hiding in his home.[218] Similarly lengthy exchanges had to be conducted with *CDF* witness TF2-176 only to learn that he did not in fact know whether the Kamajors had come to town before 1998.[219] And an exchange in which Special Panels' Judge Dolzany da Costa sought to ascertain whether witness 23 and the victim were related was so convoluted that the judge finally exclaimed: "I give up, this is impossible to get a straight answer."[220] Other examples appear in the notes.[221]

A few excerpts will give the flavor of such interactions. In the following exchange, Special Panels counsel asked whether investigators had asked the witness one question or a series of questions:

COUNSEL: Was it several questions or just one question?
WITNESS 1: I know about when they hit me, that is what I told.

[216] RUF Transcript, July 14, 2004, at 38.
[217] Los Palos Case Notes, July 11, 2001, at 12.
[218] CDF Transcript, Sept. 21, 2004, at 49–51, 55–57.
[219] CDF Transcript, June 18. 2004, at 4–10.
[220] Los Palos Case Notes, Sept. 24, 2001, at 263.
[221] Taylor Transcript, Jan. 9, 2008, at 767–74; Taylor Transcript, Apr. 7, 2008, at 6765–66; Taylor Transcript, Apr. 14, 2008, at 7543–44; Taylor Transcript, Apr. 25, 2008, at 8616–18; Taylor Transcript, May 12, 2008, at 9563, 10100–05; Taylor Transcript, May 19, 2008, at 10212–15; Taylor Transcript, May 20, 2008, at 10246–10247; Taylor Transcript, Aug. 28, 2008, at 14888–90, 14892–95, 14900–02; Taylor Transcript, Sept. 9, 2008, at 15835–36; Taylor Transcript, Sept. 10, 2008, at 15905–06; CDF Transcript, Nov. 26, 2004, at 106–07; CDF Transcript, Feb. 15, 2005, at 5–8; CDF Transcript, Feb. 17, 2005, at 137–42; CDF Transcript, Mar. 1, 2005, at 49–54; AFRC Transcript, Apr. 6, 2005, at 47; AFRC Transcript, Apr. 8, 2005, at 21, 26, 73–75; AFRC Transcript, June 27, 2005, at 108–10; AFRC Transcript, June 28, 2005, at 110–12, 119–20; AFRC Transcript, July 5, 2005, at 22–23; AFRC Transcript, July 7, 2005, at 62; AFRC Transcript, July 11, 2005, at 113, 134–35, 145–46; AFRC Transcript, Sept. 22, 2005, at 14, 40–42, 67; AFRC Transcript, Sept. 23, 2005, at 13–17, 23–24, 39–41; RUF Transcript, July 21, 2004, at 31–32; RUF Transcript, July 27, 2004, at 66, 68–69; RUF Transcript, Oct. 5, 2004, at 48–50; RUF Transcript, Oct. 6, 2004, at 82–91; RUF Transcript, Oct. 7, 2004, at 58–60; RUF Transcript, Oct. 11, 2004, at 23–24, 121–25; RUF Transcript, Oct. 20, 2004, at 34–35; RUF Transcript, Apr. 8, 2005, at 16–17, 23–28; RUF Transcript, Apr. 15, 2005, at 24, 41; RUF Transcript, July 7, 2005, at 40–42; Lolotoe Case Notes, Apr. 8, 2002, at 4, 5; Lolotoe Case Notes, Oct. 28, 2002, at 3; Karera Transcript, Feb. 1, 2006, at 49–50; Ndindabahizi Transcript, Sept. 15, 2003, at 16–17; Kamuhanda Transcript, May 6, 2002, at 8–10; Ntakirutimana Transcript, Sept. 24, 2001, at 132–33; Ntakirutimana Transcript, Sept. 25, 2001, at 7–8; Ntakirutimana Transcript, Sept. 27, 2001, at 30–31; Ntakirutimana Transcript, Oct. 23, 2001, at 3–4, 7–8; Ntakirutimana Transcript, Oct. 25, 2001, at 20–21; Los Palos Case Notes, July 18, 2001, at 39. Arnold Brackman recounts numerous instances in which Japanese defendants and witnesses before the International Military Tribunal for the Far East "circled" questions without answering them. *See, e.g.*, ARNOLD C. BRACKMAN, THE OTHER NUREMBERG 287, 294–95 (1987).

COUNSEL: Was it a series of questions, or one question with a long answer?
WITNESS 1: Not in relation to other matters, just in relation to my arrest.
JUDGE: If you don't understand the question, please let us know and we will try to explain. Was it one question and a response or many questions and response?
WITNESS 1: That's correct. They asked me about my suffering.
COUNSEL: Can you remember if it was one question?
WITNESS 1: In Lolotoe?
COUNSEL: Were you questioned more than once?
WITNESS 1: Just once.[222]

In the next excerpt, *CDF* defense counsel had to press witness TF2-198 repeatedly just to learn where and with whom the witness lived:

Q. Sir, with whom do you live in Koribundu?
A. I live in my father's house in Koribundu.
Q. Now, you say your father's house; is that his house or is it a house that your father has left you?
A. It's my father's house, therein I live.
Q. Who lives there with you, sir?
A. It's my father – my father, my own father that left me there.
Q. Yes, your father left you the house; is that what you are telling us?
A. Yes.
Q. Now, at this time – at this time, who lives in that house with you?
A. Right now the house is not there, it has been burnt.
Q. That's the house that your father left you has been burnt?
A. Yes, it is.
Q. Where do you live now? . . .
Q. Where do you live now, sir, what house do you live in presently?
A. In one man's house at Blama Road.
Q. And who lives there with you, sir?
A. I and the house owner and my family.[223]

Most witnesses do eventually answer the question posed if only to say that they do not know the answer. But it is not infrequent that counsel, like Judge Dolzany da Costa, simply give up without receiving an answer. Sometimes counsel give up relatively quickly,[224] but in other instances they give up only

[222] Lolotoe Case Notes, Apr. 11, 2002, at 1.
[223] CDF Transcript, June 15, 2004, at 10.
[224] *See, e.g.*, Lolotoe Case Notes, Apr. 8, 2002, at 7; Lolotoe Case Notes, Nov. 4, 2001, at 5; Lolotoe Case Notes, Feb. 3, 2003, at 8; AFRC Transcript, July 11, 2005, at 113; RUF Transcript, July 27, 2004, at 69; Ntakirutimana Transcript, Oct. 23, 2001, at 7–8.

when it becomes patently clear that no clear answers will be forthcoming.[225] The following lengthy exchange provides an example of the latter phenomenon:

Q. I just want to ask you about your visit to see the Prosecution in February of this year; okay? Do you remember that visit?
A. Where?
Q. In Koinadugu.
A. Was I the one that I saw him?
Q. That's yes, I'm suggesting you saw the Prosecution or somebody from the Prosecution in Koinadugu February 2004?

MR. PRESIDENT: The word Prosecution.
MR. JORDASH: I beg your pardon.
MR. PRESIDENT: She doesn't appear to understand the word Prosecution.
THE WITNESS: I don't understand the word pros – I don't understand the word Prosecutor.

MR. JORDASH:

Q. Do you remember seeing somebody from the Special Court in Koinadugu in February of this year?
A. From the time that I was here, inside Kabala town?
Q. Do you recall going to Kabala town to see somebody from the Special Court?
A. Yes.
Q. Now, at that time were you living in the Koinadugu area, just the area, or were you living in Freetown area?
A. Who?
Q. You.
A. What do you mean by that, staying where? Staying, what does that mean?
Q. Let me ask a different question. Did you travel to Kabala by – well, how did you travel to Kabala?
A. If I travelled to Kabala?
Q. Yes.
A. What travelling do you mean?
Q. Did you walk to Kabala to see the person from the Special Court?
A. That – I don't know how to understand that question.
Q. You understand what walking is, do you?
A. Yes.

[225] *See, e.g.*, Taylor Transcript, May 22, 2008, at 10621–23; Taylor Transcript, Aug. 28, 2008, at 14888–90; AFRC Transcript, June 27, 2005, at 108–10; RUF Transcript, July 27, 2004, at 66; RUF Transcript, Oct. 5, 2004, at 187–92; RUF Transcript, Oct. 6, 2004, at 58–60; RUF Transcript, Oct. 7, 2004, at 149–50; Lolotoe Case Notes, May 7, 2002, at 5.

Q. So did you walk to Kabala to see the person from the Special Court or –
A. What you are talking about, going to see – going to see the Special Court, is it Kabala special court or where?
Q. Just take – listen to the questions. You have told us that you went to Kabala in February to see somebody from the Special Court. Is that true?
A. To go and see somebody who came from the Special Court?
Q. Yes.
A. No, I did not leave here to go there to see somebody who came from the Special Court. Somebody went there and met me but I did not leave here to go and see somebody that came from the Special Court.
Q. Okay, let me try this: In Kabala in February you saw somebody from the Special Court; is that correct?
A. Who left here to go to Kabala?
Q. Just listen to the question. You saw somebody from the Special Court in Kabala – you saw somebody from the Special Court in Kabala – you saw somebody from the Special Court in Kabala in February of this year. You told us that; is that correct?
A. I don't understand that question and I cannot answer that question.
Q. Well, just listen to the question. You know Kabala?
A. Mmm.
Q. You know the Special Court?
A. Yes.
Q. You know February?
A. Yes, because there is no special court in Kabala.
Q. You know people from the Special Court? You have seen people from the Special Court; is that correct?
A. In Kabala?
Q. Yes.
A. No, Kabala special court, me? I did not see anybody there.

JUDGE BOUTET: I think her evidence was she saw somebody in Koinadugu not Kabala. So there might be some confusion. That may be the reason why you are getting this kind of answer, so –
MR. JORDASH: Okay, I'll try again. Thank you, Your Honour.
MR. JORDASH:

Q. Let's just try this again. Did you see somebody in Koinadugu in February and that person being from the Special Court?
A. In Kabala?
Q. Just listen to the question. Did you see somebody in Koinadugu – did you see somebody from the Special Court in Koinadugu in February of last year?
A. Yes.

Q. Where in Koinadugu did that take place?
A. What?
Q. Where in Koinadugu did that take place?
A. I – if it's inside Koinadugu town, we don't have any special court there. That is to say the person came from the town, Koinadugu? No.
Q. Okay.
A. If it's from Freetown here –
Q. Let me remind you. In February of this year you were given 25,000 Leones from somebody from the Special Court. Do you remember that?
A. 25?
Q. 25,000 Leones. Do you remember that?
A. In Koinadugu?
Q. Well, do you remember being given 25,000 Leones in February?
A. I don't understand that month that you are talking about.
Q. Well, just concentrate on the money then. Do you remember being given 25,000 Leones by somebody from the Special Court?
A. I do remember somebody came from the Special Court but – I do remember that somebody came from the Special Court and went there, but to say that somebody from Koinadugu town, no.
Q. If you will just forget locations for a minute, do you remember being given 25,000 Leones by somebody from the Special Court?
A. That question, I cannot answer it.
Q. Okay. Are you unemployed at the moment?
A. I?
Q. You. Do you work at the moment?
A. Except the job that I learnt, this is what I'm doing.
Q. And how much do you earn in a week?
A. The job that I do?
Q. Yes, how much do you earn with the job that you do in one week?
A. The facts – what I do is that I give debts to people and I do not make cash sales. I give debts to people and at the end of the week I collect. Okay, sorry, that is for one month. I give them – what I sell in debts and I collect at the end of the month – I collect the money at the end of the month.
Q. How much money do you make through your job in one week?
A. Well, that's – the brillion that I make, these are things that I buy in rolls with the ink. I buy the brillion that I dye in rolls and the ink too. All these things are bought.
Q. Let me just stop you there. I'm asking you a very specific question, not what you do, but how much money you make from doing it. Could you answer that question, please?
A. The money that I earn, you know, from that job that I learnt?

Q. Yes.
A. The money – the money is just – sometimes I go, if it's brillion, buy them in rolls with some other things.
Q. How many Leones in a week do you take to your home?
A. Well, because it's a – it's a little bit difficult for me to tell you the profit because by the time I finish selling the profit would have finished.
Q. Much less than 25,000 Leones, is it?
A. The profit?
Q. The profit.
A. It's more than that.
Q. Just finally, do you really not remember receiving 25,000 Leones from the Prosecution – from the people from the Special Court, is that true?
A. Mmm.
Q. Was that – is it true you don't remember or you don't want to answer?
A. 25,000, I cannot remember.
Q. Thank you.[226]

Sometimes the witness's failure to answer a question is of little significance because the question seeks merely to make a rhetorical point, such as when an ICTR prosecutor repeatedly asked *Kamuhanda* defense witness GPI, "you do not want Kamuhanda to be convicted?"[227] In other instances, however, counsel do seem intent on obtaining relevant information through their questioning yet fail to do so.[228]

Cultural issues and traditional patterns of speech and assumptions about the world may account for some of the communication difficulties described above. These issues are discussed in more detail in Chapter 3, but I will touch on the subject here by providing a few examples. Communication can break down, for instance, when a witness assumes a piece of information or background knowledge that is not shared by her courtroom listeners. Sierra Leonean witness TF1-085, for instance, had earlier testified that she had been forced to marry a certain colonel. As the following excerpt shows, a lengthy exchange ensued when she later seemed to suggest that she was married to one of the defendants, who was nicknamed "Five-Five":

Q. Do you remember a ceremony taking place in Masiaka?
A. Yes.

[226] RUF Transcript, July 15, 2004, at 9–12.
[227] Kamuhanda Transcript, Jan. 29, 2003, at 41.
[228] *See, e.g.*, CDF Transcript, June 17, 2004, at 43; CDF Transcript, June 18, 2004, at 45–46; CDF Transcript, Sept. 8, 2004, at 56–58; AFRC Transcript, Mar. 8, 2005, at 96.

Q. What ceremony?
A. Captain married me to Five-Five, he said because I was his wife.

Ms. Thompson: Your Honours, I didn't understand the answer to that. So perhaps my learned friend might repeat the question.
Presiding Judge: The question was answered and we will ask – I think we should allow counsel to clarify it in the normal way.
Ms. Pack:

Q. Who did the colonel ask you to marry?
A. The colonel that captured me, he married me to Five-Five, he said because I was his wife.
Q. Whose wife were you?
A. The colonel.
Q. Did you marry anyone else apart from the colonel?
A. No.
Q. So when you say he married you to Five-Five, what do you mean by that?
A. Five-Five was the overall boss, so he went there as a father-in-law with money.
Q. Who went where with money?
A. The colonel went with money to Five-Five.
Q. To do what?
A. Saying that he was going to marry me.
Q. Who was going to marry you? Who was going to be your husband?
A. The colonel himself.[229]

In the following example, the witness seemed to assume that he could not answer counsel's question unless counsel provided the witness with certain information:

Q. Mr. Witness, can you recall that you, prior to your testimony in this Court, spoke with members of the Prosecution in Freetown?
A. Asked me where?
Q. In Freetown.
A. It's just my lawyer. I met him here, but he did not ask me anything. Except with the – except now that I am testifying, but prior to that, no.
Q. Can you recall any meetings with members of the Prosecution, say, a few weeks ago?
A. Will you tell me the place where we met with these Prosecution people? If it is true I will answer. If it is not true I will also answer to that question.

[229] AFRC Transcript, Apr. 7, 2005, at 37–38.

Q. In Freetown?
A. Where exactly in Freetown?
Q. Mr. Witness, this is a question we would like to ask you to answer. Do you recall any meetings with the Office of the Prosecution in Freetown a few weeks ago. Somewhere in Freetown.
A. That's what I am saying. You show me the place and I don't know any place here. If you tell me exactly where the question may – if it is true, I will answer.
Q. You don't recall any place in Freetown where you met people of the Prosecution prior to your testimony this week?
A. Together with whom? If you tell me those who I was involved, I will answer yes if it is true.
Q. Mr. Witness, I have to remind you that we are now in a position to ask you questions and I respectfully ask you to answer the questions and not to answer me questions [sic]. Could you please think whether you had a meeting with any member of the Prosecution a few weeks ago somewhere in Freetown prior to your –
A. You asked me to remember – remember whom? I don't know the individual. How can I think about somebody whom I don't know.
Q. Mr. Witness, can you recall any meetings with the Prosecution of the Special Court outside Freetown prior to your testimony this week, the last few months?
A. Where else? If you show me the place that you want I will tell you. But I don't know the place. What do you want me to tell you? I cannot tell you anything.
Q. Mr. Witness –

PRESIDING JUDGE: Just a minute, Mr. Knoops. We seem to have come to an impasse on this. Mr. Witness, do you understand the questions that the lawyer is asking you?
THE WITNESS: I understand, but I am asking you to tell me the place. If you don't tell me the place, how can I give you an answer?
PRESIDING JUDGE: Mr. Knoops, are you unwilling or would you like to clarify this with the witness?
MR. KNOOPS: I would like to ask a question in a different line if Your Honours –
PRESIDING JUDGE: Very well.
MR. KNOOPS:

Q. Mr. Witness, how many times before your statement this week in court did you speak with members of the Prosecution of the Special Court? Can you recall whether you have spoken to them at all?

A. With whom?
Q. My question is in general.
A. If you tell me the individual that spoke to me and the name of the individual I will answer if that is the name.
Q. Does that mean, Mr. Witness, that you recall having spoken to somebody of the Prosecution? Is that a yes or no?
A. I have told you, you tell me the name so that I can remember with the individual that I spoke with and if you don't give me the name of an individual, how can I remember.

PRESIDING JUDGE: Mr. Witness, the lawyer is not asking you – he is saying do you remember talking to anyone in the Prosecution office. Anyone at all.
THE WITNESS: Your question has doubted me. Put it well so that I can understand it.[230]

The exchange continued in the same fashion for several more pages, and other examples of similar exchanges appear in the notes.[231]

Sometimes it is the witness's pattern of speech that leads to the communication breakdown. In an astounding seven-page exchange from the SCSL's *CDF* case, witness TF2-162 drove courtroom personnel to distraction by answering all of counsel's questions in the conditional tense.[232] Other times, communication breaks down when the witness seems to lack the vocabulary necessary to explain himself clearly. As the following exchange shows, witness TF1-083 was simply unable to state with any sort of clarity or precision where he went when rebels came to his house:

Q. And where did you go?
A. When they kicked at the door, I ran out. I ran out, because when we came out, starting from the pharmacy all the other houses in that lane when they kicked at our doors – well, everybody ran out.
Q. Where did you go, Mr. Witness?
A. When they kicked our doors, we ran out. This house it was in – they have just roofed it. It was almost between 8.00 to 9.00. The house was newly roofed. We entered into the house, me and my brother together with our younger sister. That is where we took refuge that night.
Q. Can you tell us where this house with the new roof was located?

[230] AFRC Transcript, July 25, 2005, at 34–36.
[231] For instance, when witness TF1-282 was asked, "[d]o you have to buy food to eat?" she responded "[l]ike which type of food?" AFRC Transcript, Apr. 14, 2005, at 21.
[232] CDF Transcript, Sept. 8, 2004, at 71–78.

A. Well, it was around the area, it was back of – like where I'm sitting here. Like if you look at the other lane at the back.
Q. So it was very close to your house; is that correct?
A. It was before our house. It was – it is just the same area. You see, when we talk about an area, you go there. It is not that it is opposite my house, but it is the same area.[233]

Witness TF2-198 was asked to describe the change that took place in Koribondo as a result of the war, and his response was equally uninformative.

Q. Describe to us, please, what those changes were.
A. In fact, we used to see different, different people that we were not used to seeing, and that is one of the changes.
Q. Why was that, do you know?
A. Yes, in fact, that was the time that we started experiencing war, you know, coming from Liberia.
Q. Describe to us, please, what you mean by war coming from Liberia, who was involved in what occurred?
A. We were sitting and when we saw people coming, you know, coming and calling them RUF, and people coming, staying with some other people, you know, people running and coming to us and people staying with us in Koribundu and some passing. These are the experiences that we had, you know, when I refer – which I refer to as war.

Other times, communication is impeded because the witness will go off on tangents or insist on recounting minute aspects of the event in question rather than focusing on the particular issues of interest to counsel.[234] Marie-Benedicte Dembour and Emily Haslan have observed that "[e]ven witnesses who can tell a clear, direct story often wish to provide more detail than is warranted in a criminal trial."[235] And in other instances, it is simply hard to follow the witness's testimony. Judges and counsel repeatedly interrupted the testimony of *AFRC* witness TF1-184, for instance, so as to clarify who was doing what to whom.[236]

Sometimes, although it is clear that there is a communication difficulty, the nature of the difficulty remains entirely unclear. The Special Panels had exceptional problems with language interpretation, as I discuss in Chapter 3, and misinterpretations likely caused many of their communication breakdowns.

[233] AFRC Transcript, Apr. 8, 2005, at 51.
[234] *See, e.g.*, AFRC Transcript, Sept. 23, 2005, at 13–17, 39–41; AFRC Transcript, Sept. 27, 2005, at 17–18.
[235] Dembour & Haslan, note 13, at 158–59.
[236] AFRC Transcript, Sept. 27, 2005, at 23–24, 31–33, 37–38, 43, 46; *see also* AFRC Transcript, Sept. 22, 2005, at 20.

Whatever the reason, many Special Panels' exchanges verge on the incoherent. It was impossible to tell during one exchange in the *Los Palos* case, for instance, whether the witness was testifying that a beating lasted fifteen seconds or fifteen minutes,[237] and at one point during the *Lolotoe* case defense counsel insisted that the court "order this witness to answer the questions directly [because] his answers have no relations to the questions."[238] Other examples abound.[239] As one Special Panel put it:

> The transcripts of the hearings amounted to a conspicuous volume of hundreds of pages; each witness spoke at length ... yet it can hardly be said that many of the witnesses gave a crystal-clear version of the facts upon which they were asked to testify.... Most of the people who came before the judges to say what they saw of the facts and to give their contribution to the trial, were basically illiterate and scarcely able to narrate events in a congruent and exhaustive manner. Their ways to refer things appeared very often (also due to difficulties of translation from English or Portuguese to Tetum and then to Baikeno and back, sometimes answers didn't match with the questions asked) obscure and numb, like a piece of wood or of stone in the process of being worked by the artisan to become an utensil or a decoration. However, in the inherent conflict and contraposition of Parties that the trial is, with Parties trying to see their own truth confirmed, the shape of things to come sometimes was dispersed with the result that the testimony came not neat and sometimes almost unreadable.
>
> It has sometime happened that this exposure of some witnesses to the cross-examination and to the rules and customs of inquiry by the Parties ... has brought confusion and contradiction, instead of clarity, with witnesses unable to come out from the bundle of contradictions created from their own words. In many cases the original version of a fact or of a detail regardless of relevance was modified during the course of testimony and the attempt to clarify the facts lead to renewed sources of confusion.[240]

The communication difficulties that appear during witness questioning always lengthen proceedings and frustrate court personnel, but in many cases they do not substantially impair fact-finding. For instance, although it took a couple of pages of testimony to clarify matters, it did eventually become clear that witness TF1-085 was married to the colonel and not to Five-Five.

[237] Los Palos Case Notes, July 31, 2001, at 104.
[238] Lolotoe Case Notes, May 9, 2002, at 4.
[239] *See* David Cohen, *Indifference and Accountability: The United Nations and the Politics of International Justice in East Timor*, East – West Center Special Reports, No. 9, at 51 (June 2006); Los Palos Case Notes, July 11, 2001, at 12; Los Palos Case Notes, July 18, 2001, at 32; Los Palos Case Notes, July 26, 2001, at 79–80; Los Palos Case Notes, Aug. 8, 2001, at 132; Lolotoe Case Notes, Apr. 8, 2002, at 5, 8; Lolotoe Case Notes, Mar. 17, 2003, at 18–20.
[240] Tacaqui Judgement, note 36, at 5.

Likewise, although certain exchanges in the testimony of *Kajelijeli* witness GDT indicated that her parents had been killed during the 1994 genocide, subsequent questioning revealed that her father was still alive and her mother had died in 1998.[241] In other cases, however, fact-finding is impaired. One has to assume, for instance, that some misunderstandings are never identified – and thus never cleared up. Fact-finding is also impaired when counsel simply abandon a line of questioning without having received a responsive reply. But even when the witness does eventually answer the question, fact-finding can be impaired because it is often not clear *why* the witness did not answer initially, and the answer to that question may be key to the fact finder's assessment of the accuracy of the testimony or the credibility of the witness. Chapter 3 takes up this "why" question and explores the factors that may account for the fact-finding impediments described in this chapter.

[241] Kajelijeli Transcript, Dec. 6, 2001, at 95–96.

3

The Educational, Linguistic, and Cultural Impediments to Accurate Fact-Finding at the International Tribunals

Chapter 2 amply demonstrates that many witnesses at the ICTR, SCSL, and Special Panels fail to answer basic questions that are central to the witness's account of the events witnessed. This chapter considers why those questions do not get answered. The most obvious explanation, and the one the witnesses themselves most frequently invoke, is the witnesses' lack of education. Cultural factors provide another plausible reason for many communication difficulties, as do interpretation errors. The following sections will discuss each of these causes.

3.A. EDUCATION, LITERACY, AND LIFE EXPERIENCES

Fact witnesses are expected to recount their firsthand experiences that are relevant to the charges brought against the defendant. In the Western countries from which international criminal procedures derive, it goes without saying that fact witnesses have the ability to convey such information. Indeed, while a great deal of Western scholarship focuses on perjuring witnesses or witnesses whose testimony is impaired by errors of perception or memory, it is taken for granted that witnesses have the education and skills necessary to convey what they witnessed in a reasonably clear and coherent way. Indeed, it is only in the context of children's testimony that one generally finds any discussion of the assumptions on which witness testimony is based. Speaking in relation to child witnesses, for instance, Ingrid Cordon and her coauthors observe that adversarial legal systems in particular hold many implicit expectations of witnesses, including that witnesses have "some knowledge of judicial processes [and] can understand the language of the courtroom, particularly attorneys' questions."[242] Whereas those expectations pose little or no difficulties for

[242] Cordon et al., note 188, at 168.

educated witnesses, they can constitute severe challenges for the uneducated, the illiterate, and those lacking in certain life experiences.

It is certainly reasonable to assume that illiteracy and lack of education substantially impair the ability of many international witnesses to answer the questions posed to them. Sierra Leone has perhaps the lowest literacy rate in the world, at 35 percent.[243] Timor-Leste's is not much better, at 43 percent,[244] and even in somewhat more developed Rwanda, less than two-thirds of the population can read and write.[245] These low literacy rates reflect low levels of school attendance. Only 41 percent of Sierra Leonean children attend primary school,[246] and although Timor-Leste's school attendance rate has been improving, historically it has been very low.[247]

Because SCSL prosecutors and defense counsel asked virtually all SCSL witnesses about their literacy and schooling, I was able to determine that the education and literacy rates of SCSL witnesses roughly mirror the education and literacy rates of the general population of Sierra Leone.[248] For instance, education and/or literacy information is available for forty-five prosecution fact witnesses in the *AFRC* case, and it reveals that twenty-one of these witnesses (or 47 percent) were illiterate and/or had never attended school,[249] while three more witnesses (or 7 percent) had attended school only for a very short

[243] UNICEF, *At a Glance: Sierra Leone, available at* www.unicef.org/infobycountry/sierraleone_statistics.html. Other sets of statistics place the male literacy rate at 36 percent and the female literacy rate at 23 percent. Mikako Nishimuko, *Access to Primary Education in Sierra Leone, The Perceived Gap Between Policy and Practice and the Role of Religious Affiliation and British Aid*, 6 EDUCATE 32, 32 (2006).

[244] U.S. Department of State, *Background Note: East Timor, available at* www.state.gov/r/pa/ei/bgn/35878.htm.

[245] Rwanda has a 65 percent literacy rate. *See* UNICEF, *Rwanda, available at* www.unicef.org/infobycountry/rwanda_1717.html.

[246] Nishimuko, note 243, at 32 (reporting that 41 percent of Sierra Leonean males attend primary school while 39 percent of Sierra Leonean females do).

[247] The U.N. Development Programme reports that although gains in education have been made in recent years, between 10 and 30 percent of Timorese children still do not attend school. U.N. Development Programme, *Timor-Leste Faces Development Challenges, available at* http://content.undp.org/go/newsroom/march-2006/timor-leste-hdr20060309.en?g11n.enc=ISO-8859–1.

[248] Many Rwandan and East Timorese witnesses asserted in passing that they were illiterate or had no formal schooling, but no useful statistics can be presented because counsel failed to ask most witnesses about their literacy or schooling.

[249] TF1-278, AFRC Transcript, Apr. 6, 2005, at 22–23; TF1-084, *id.*, Apr. 6, 2005, at 37; TF1-085, *id.*, Apr. 7, 2005, at 9, 53, 114; TF1-320, *id.*, Apr. 8, 2005, at 12; TF1-083, *id.*, Apr. 8, 2005, at 45; TF1-282, *id.*, Apr. 13, 2005, at 5; TF1-256, *id.*, Apr. 15, 2005, at 18; TF1-253, *id.*, Apr. 18, 2005, at 82; TF1-053, *id.*, Apr. 19, 2005, at 7, 72; TF1-076, *id.*, June 27, 2005, at 101; TF1-198, *id.*, June 28, 2005, at 4, 46; TF1-310, *id.*, July 5, 2005, at 64–65; TF1-209, *id.*, July 7, 2005, at 44; TF1-133, *id.*, July 7, 2005, at 81; TF1-055, *id.*, July 12, 2005, at 131; TF1-299, *id.*, July 14, 2005, at 51; TF1-113, *id.*, July 18, 2005, at 116–18; TF1-157, *id.*, July 25, 2005, at 29, 46; TF1-267, *id.*, July 26, 2005, at 101; TF1-156, *id.*, Sept. 26, 2005, at 64; TF1-184, *id.*, Sept. 29, 2005, at 105.

time.[250] Similarly, education and/or literacy information is available for forty prosecution fact witnesses in the *RUF* case, and it showed that nineteen of these (or 48 percent) were illiterate and/or had never attended school,[251] while three more (or 8 percent) had attended school for only a very short time.[252] The education/literacy level of *CDF* witnesses was slightly higher. Information was available for fifty-five prosecution fact witnesses, showing that eighteen (or 33 percent) were illiterate and/or had never attended any school,[253] while seven more (or 13 percent) had attended school for only a few years.[254]

Given these statistics, it should come as no surprise that witnesses frequently invoke their lack of education and literacy when they are unable to answer a question.[255] The witness might point out that he is just "a primitive man from the bush,"[256] for instance, or assert that if he had gone to school, then he "might have known the right words."[257] These explanations are plausible. It

[250] TF1-094, AFRC Transcript, July 13, 2005, at 28; TF1-074, *id.*, July 5, 2005, at 39; TF1-062, *id.*, June 27, 2005, at 3–4, 60.

[251] TF1-074, RUF Transcript, July 12, 2004, at 66; TF1-196, *id.*, July 13, 2004, at 9, 18–19; TF1-214, *id.*, July 14, 2004, at 3; TF1-064, *id.*, July 19, 2004, at 46; TF1-077, *id.*, July 21, 2004, at 35; TF1-331, *id.*, July 22, 2004, at 44; TF1-305, *id.*, July 27, 2004, at 51–52; TF1-016, *id.*, Oct. 21, 2004, at 4; TF1-197, *id.* Oct. 21, 2004, at 54; TF1-195, *id.*, Feb. 1, 2005, at 2; TF1-218, *id.*, Feb. 1, 2005, at 79; TF1-172, *id.*, May 17, 2005, at 4; TF1-097, *id.*, Nov. 28, 2005, at 103; TF1-022, *id.*, Nov. 29, 2005, at 22; TF1-008, *id.*, Dec. 8, 2005, at 40; TF1-343, *id.*, Mar. 17, 2006, at 57–58; TF1-031, *id.*, Mar. 17, 2006, at 94; TF1-028, *id.*, Mar. 17, 2006, at 107; TF1-159, *id.*, Apr. 5, 2006, at 3–4.

[252] TF1-253, RUF Transcript, July 28, 2004, at 4–5; TF1-263, *id.*, Apr. 6, 2005, at 5, 13; TF1-215, *id.*, Aug. 2, 2005, at 62.

[253] The following *CDF* prosecution witnesses testified that they never attended school: TF2-198, CDF Transcript, June 15, 2004, at 11; TF2-176, *id.*, June 17, 2004, at 75; TF2-012, *id.*, June 21, 2004, at 21; TF2-162, *id.*, Sept. 8, 2004, at 7; TF2-159, Sept. 9, 2004, at 98; TF2-040, *id.*, Sept. 21, 2004, at 14; TF2-039, *id.*, Sept. 23, 2004, at 116–17; TF2-012, *id.*, Nov. 3, 2004, at 5; TF2-201, *id.*, Nov. 5, 2004, at 18; TF2-004, *id.*, Nov. 9, 2004, at 97–98; TF2-007, *id.*, Dec. 2, 2004, at 82; TF2-058, *id.*, Dec. 3, 2004, at 48–49; TF2-056, *id.*, Dec. 6, 2004, at 64; TF2-006, *id.*, Feb. 9, 2005, at 21–22; TF2-035, *id.*, Feb. 14, 2005, at 3–4; TF2-048, *id.*, Feb. 23, 2005, at 3–4; TF2-144, *id.*, Feb. 24, 2005, at 56; TF2-189, *id.*, June 3, 2005, at 3–4.

[254] TF2-157, CDF Transcript, June 16, 2004, at 2–3; TF2-015, *id.*, Feb. 11, 2005, at 2 (witness attended Arabic school for eight years but there is no indication that he learned anything except Arabic); TF2-013, *id.*, Feb. 24, 2005, at 7; TF2-173, *id.*, Mar. 4, 2005, at 54; TF2-187, *id.*, June 1, 2005, at 7–8; TF2-134, *id.*, June 3, 2005, at 22; TF2-080, *id.*, June 6, 2005, at 18–20.

[255] *See, e.g.*, Lolotoe Case Notes, Apr. 9, 2002, at 4; Los Palos Case Notes, July 12, 2001, at 18; Los Palos Case Notes, July 23, 2001, at 55; Los Palos Case Notes, July 27, 2001, at 83; Los Palos Case Notes, July 16, 2001, at 25; Los Palos Case Notes, Aug. 9, 2001, at 142, 143; Los Palos Case Notes, Aug. 21, 2001, at 179; Los Palos Case Notes, Aug. 22, 2001, at 192; Los Palos Case Notes, Jan. 10, 2001, at 319; Taylor Transcript, Mar. 13, 2008, at 5976; CDF Transcript, June 16, 2004, at 25; CDF Transcript, June 21, 2004, at 47; AFRC Transcript, Apr. 8, 2005, at 34; AFRC Transcript, June 2, 2005, at 35; AFRC Transcript, June 28, 2005, at 21, 36; AFRC Transcript, July 14, 2005, at 51; Ndindabahizi Transcript, Sept. 15, 2003, at 10.

[256] CDF Transcript, June 16, 2004, at 25; *see also* AFRC Transcript, Apr. 15, 2005, at 36 (witness does not know who ruled Sierra Leone before President Kabbah came into power).

[257] Los Palos Case Notes, July 27, 2001, at 83.

is reasonable to suppose that a witness who has never been to school will not know how long a mile or a month is. A witness who has never learned to read or write probably will not know how to read a map. And many international witnesses not only lack the formal education by which they would learn how to measure or tell time, they also lack the kinds of life experiences for which that sort of knowledge would be useful. Witnesses who spend their lives engaged in subsistence farming need to keep track of the rainy and dry seasons but have far less need to know specific months and days. Witnesses who virtually never leave their villages have little reason to look at a map and have even less need to know that it is 6.5 miles to the nearest village. The witness may rarely go there anyway, and when he does, he knows it will take about an hour and a half to walk, and that is all the information he needs. And it should come as no surprise that a witness who has only rarely ever seen an automobile would be unable to describe the automobile that she witnessed by means of the specific terms that Westerners would use.

Although lack of education and life experiences are among the more obvious explanations for the difficulties witnesses frequently experience in answering the questions posed to them, other factors such as interpretation errors and cultural divergences also play a role, as the following two sections describe.

3.B. INTERPRETATION ERRORS

I know of no judge in [an international] tribunal who does not acknowledge that he or she is totally at the mercy of the translator in the courtroom.

– Patricia M. Wald, *Running the Trial of the Century: The Nuremberg Legacy*, 7 CARDOZO L. REV. 1559, 1570–71 (2006)

The need for language translation provides another obvious explanation for many of the communication difficulties that I describe in Chapter 2. Language interpretation is not unique to international courtrooms; as populations have become more diverse, language interpreters have become commonplace participants in the legal proceedings of most Western nations. Interpreters are used primarily to keep immigrant defendants informed of the proceedings, but they also occasionally interpret witness testimony. Although interpretation is obviously necessary when courtroom participants do not speak the same language, interpretation also unquestionably impedes communication and impairs the fact finder's ability to assess the credibility and veracity of the witness's testimony.

The most obvious problem is that interpreters sometimes make mistakes. A six-month investigation of Michigan trials, for instance, revealed that interpreters frequently omitted phrases and changed key words. In one case, the word "shoot" was translated as "kill," whereas in another case, the word "car" was translated as "couch."[258] In a California case, an interpreter translated "as for the Vietnamese, I never associate with them" as "no,"[259] and a Washington interpreter translated "I will aim at you" as "I will kill you."[260] Even the highly publicized O. J. Simpson murder trial featured some interpretation inaccuracies.[261] Many of the interpretation problems in American courtrooms can be traced to inconsistent training, inadequate standards,[262] and just plain ignorance. For instance, an Oregon jury convicted Mixtec Santiago Ventura Morales of murder after the court provided him and his witnesses with Spanish interpreters when they had little comprehension of Spanish. The officer who initially questioned Ventura was unaware of the differences between Mixtec and Spanish,[263] and the trial judge apparently knew no better as he permitted the trial to continue despite the fact that the Spanish interpreters were frequently unable to translate the witnesses' testimony because the witnesses were not responding in Spanish.[264]

As training requirements and standards have improved in the United States,[265] instances of blatantly inaccurate translations have declined,[266] but more subtle inaccuracies remain, and they too can be distortive. Susan Berk-Seligson's research has shown, for instance, that even technically accurate translations can be phrased in a variety of ways, and each of them might produce a different impression on the fact finder. Interpreters, for instance, frequently change the grammatical case of a question or answer; so, for instance,

[258] Ken Kolker, *Trial and Errors*, GRAND RAPIDS PRESS, Feb. 21, 1993.

[259] Joanne I. Moore & Ron A. Mamiya, *Interpreters in Court Proceedings, in* IMMIGRANTS IN COURTS 29, 39 (Joanne I. Moore ed., 1999).

[260] Washington State Court Interpreter Task Force, *Evaluation of Spanish Interpreters in Washington Courts*, FINAL REPORT, 1988, *Annex to* FINAL REPORT OF THE COURT INTERPRETER TASK FORCE (1989).

[261] In examining 482 questions posed to Rosa López, Azucena Rigney found interpretation mistakes in 3.1 percent of them. Azucena C. Rigney, *Questioning in Interpreted Testimony*, 6 FORENSIC LINGUISTICS 83, 92–93 (1999).

[262] Holly Mikkelson & Hanne Mintz, *Orientation Workshops for Interpreters of All Languages: How to Strike a Balance Between the Ideal World and Reality, in* THE CRITICAL LINK: INTERPRETERS IN THE COMMUNITY 55, 55–56 (Silvana E. Carr et al. eds., 1995). Only in recent years have states begun to test and certify interpreters. As recently as the late 1980s, almost all American jurisdictions utilized the services of untrained, untested court reporters. Moore & Mamiya, note 259, at 30.

[263] The officer opined: "They go hand-in-hand in Mexican country down there." Peter Carlin, *What Becomes of the Resurrected?*, LOS ANGELES TIMES MAGAZINE, Mar. 8, 1992, at 22.

[264] Lourdes De León, *The Mixtecs' Annual 3000-mile Journey, in* NOSOTROS, THE HISPANIC PEOPLE OF OREGON, ESSAYS AND RECOLLECTIONS 119, 119 (Erasmo Gamboa & Carolyn M. Buan eds., 1995).

[265] *See* Holly Mikkelson, *Towards a Redefinition of the Role of the Court Interpreter*, 3 INTERPRETING 21, 21–22 (1998) (discussing the rise of standards to guide interpreters' conduct) [hereinafter Mikkelson, *Towards a Redefinition*].

[266] *But see* Peter Finn, *Lawyers Criticize Quality of Guantanamo Interpreters*, WASH. POST, Oct. 14, 2008.

an answer phrased in an active voice might be translated in a passive voice, which serves to deemphasize the role of the subject.[267] Interpreters also insert or omit meaningless particles – expressions such as "you know," or "well," or "so you see" – which serve a politeness function in discourse. Although seemingly unimportant, inserting these "hedges" can make a witness's certain-sounding answers seem hesitant, whereas omitting them can have the opposite effect. Interpreters also may either include or omit politeness forms, such as "sir" or "ma'am," that can influence a fact finder's view of the testimony.[268] Berk-Seligson concludes that "the interpreter has the powerful capability of changing the intent of what [a] non-English-speaking witness wishes to say in the way he or she would like to say it."[269]

I have briefly mentioned the interpretation difficulties that arise in American courtrooms to show that even under generally good circumstances, language interpretation impedes a fact finder's ability to assess witness testimony. The circumstances prevailing at the international tribunals, by contrast, are not even close to "generally good." Not only is more interpretation required at the international tribunals because in most cases every word must be translated into one or more languages but, as I discuss below, cultural divergences between witnesses and courtroom personnel, along with linguistic and conceptual divergences, magnify the distortion wrought by language interpretation.[270] As the ICTY's prosecutor acknowledged in that tribunal's first case, a "great deal of accuracy is bound to be lost in the translation process."[271]

The very first international criminal trials at Nuremberg and Tokyo saw a number of these difficulties. At Nuremberg, for instance, German witnesses and defendants frequently began their sentences with "ja," which was typically translated as "yes." Although "ja" does literally mean "yes," the Germans used it as a filler word, such as "well" or "um." Consequently, translating

[267] *See* Susan Berk-Seligson, The Bilingual Courtroom: Court Interpreters in the Judicial Process 97–118 (2002). Berk-Seligson's quantitative analysis of the interpretation of verbs in two trials showed that in more than 20 percent of the instances, interpreters translated an active verb phrase as passive or vice versa. *Id.* at 116–17.

[268] *Id.* at 137–42. In sum, without even being aware of it, an interpreter can, "make the tone of a witness's testimony or an attorney's question more harsh and antagonistic than it was when it was originally uttered, or, conversely, she can make its effect softer, more cooperative, and less challenging than the original." *Id.* at 2.

[269] *Id.* at 196–97.

[270] Joshua Karton, *Lost in Translation: International Criminal Tribunals and the Legal Implications of Interpreted Testimony*, 41 Vand. J. Transnat'l L. 1 (2008).

[271] Prosecutor v. Tadić, Case No. IT-94-I-T, Transcript, May 7, 1996, at 47. *See also* Prosecutor v. Mucić et al., Case No. IT-96–21, Transcript, Sept. 4, 1997, at 6797–6798 ("The attorneys who speak both English and Bosnian have noticed many errors in the translation which change the meaning. . . . The answer given on several occasions changed not only the names of people and places but also the very substance of what the witness was saying.").

"ja" as "yes" in those instances completely altered the meaning of the witness's answer.[272] Translation at the Tokyo Tribunal proved even more prone to error, in part because Japanese is one of the most difficult languages to translate to English.[273] Simultaneous interpretation proved highly problematic, so counsel were limited to posing short, simple questions to witnesses.[274] And even then mistakes occurred. "Little Glass Eye" sometimes became "Big Glass Eye" and even appeared once as "Big Glass Tooth."[275] Some of the interpretation inaccuracies stemmed from "the Westerners' utter ignorance of basic Far Eastern history,"[276] whereas even more problems were borne from the different styles of Japanese and English speech. Because "the Japanese language [is] less direct than English," Japanese defendants might have appeared to be circumventing questions when their speech merely conformed to the norms of Japanese indirectness. The interpreters at times sought to remedy this problem by interpreting Japanese answers in the direct way that the English-speaking lawyers expected, but they may have distorted the testimony they were conveying in the process.[277] And as is always the case, the personality and style of the interpreters also colored their interpretations and the fact finders' impressions of the testimony. As Francesca Gaiba put it: "Young women with 'chirpy little voices' translating rough generals... diminished the power of testimony."[278]

More recent international criminal tribunals have experienced even more serious interpretation difficulties. Indeed, colossal interpretation problems impaired every aspect of Special Panels' proceedings. The Special Panels, particularly at their outset, were severely understaffed in interpreters. As a result of this understaffing, hearings had to be postponed,[279] judgments were issued in

[272] *See* Joseph E. Persico, Nuremberg: Infamy on Trial 263 (1994). Once the chief interpreter, Peter Uiberall, became aware of this problem, he instructed his staff to wait before translating "ja" as "yes" in order to confirm that that was in fact the correct meaning. Eyewitnesses at Nuremberg 47 (Hilary Gaskin ed., 1990).

[273] Brackman, note 221, at 23; John L. Ginn, Sugamo Prison, Tokyo: An Account of the Trial and Sentencing of Japanese War Criminals in 1948, by a U.S. Participant 50 (1992).

[274] Brackman, note 221, at 23; Philip R. Piccigallo, The Japanese on Trial: Allied War Crimes Operations in the East 1945–1951 (1980).

[275] Mistakes such as these frequently drew outbursts of laughter from Japanese or American spectators. Tim Maga, Judgment at Tokyo: the Japanese War Crimes Trial 15–16 (2001).

[276] As just one example, Brackman reports that while the Chinese refer to themselves as the "Han" race, that phrase was interpreted as the "Hun" race. Brackman, note 221, at 299.

[277] Maga, note 275, at 57.

[278] Francesca Gaiba, The Origins of Simultaneous Interpretation: The Nuremberg Trial 107 (1998).

[279] Suzanne Katzenstein, Note, *Hybrid Tribunals: Searching for Justice in East Timor*, 16 Harv. Hum. Rts. J. 245, 251–52 (2003); Judicial System Monitoring Programme, *Special Panels for*

only one of the Panels' official languages, even though judges on that very Panel were unable to read the judgments,[280] and the defendants' rights were violated. Defendants were frequently unable to communicate with their lawyers during their trials because they spoke different languages, and no interpreters were provided.[281] Defendants also had difficulty following the proceedings because overworked interpreters frequently failed to translate exchanges between judges and counsel.[282]

Because the Special Panels did not have a sufficient number of interpreters with the appropriate linguistic competencies, witness questioning frequently proceeded through multiple translations. That is, the Special Panels often had no interpreters who could translate directly from the witness's language to one of the court's official languages, so two or three interpreters had to be used. Thus, from the point at which a question was asked until counsel received a reply, it was not uncommon for six interpretations to have been made,[283] and the risk for inaccuracies and distortions increased with each one of them. The dearth of interpreters also led the Special Panels to require interpreters to translate for hours at a time and to continue to do so over a full trial day,[284] despite the negative impact that such a grueling schedule would have for the quality of interpretations. It should come as no surprise, then, that interpretation difficulties significantly impaired the ability of Special Panels' judges to assess witness testimony. Indeed, sometimes the judges could not even understand witness testimony. Judge Antonio Helder Viana do Carmo does not speak English, and he reported that he was often "not able to follow his trials properly."[285] And at various times during the *Los Palos* trial, an NGO courtroom monitor who was transcribing the proceedings wrote simply: "chaos with translations."[286]

Serious Cases–Weekly Report 27–31 January 2003 (Jan. 27–31, 2003) *available at* www.jsmp.minihub.org/Reports/spscweeksumm/SPSC27–31Jan03jr10feb03.pdf.

[280] *See* Lino de Carvalho v. Prosecutor General, Court of Appeal of East Timor, Criminal Appeal No. 25 of 2001, Judgement of Fredrick Egonda-Ntende, para. 1 (Oct. 29, 2001); Julio Fernandes v. Prosecutor General, Court of Appeal of East Timor, Criminal Appeal No. 7 of 2001, Judgement of Fredrick Egonda-Ntende, para. 36 (June 29, 2001).

[281] Judicial System Monitoring Programme, *The General Prosecutor v. Joni Marques and 9 Others (The Los Palos Case): A JSMP Trial Report*, at § 3.2.4.5 (Mar. 2002) [hereinafter *The Los Palos Case Report*].

[282] Lolotoe Case Notes, Oct. 23, 2002, at 3; Judicial System Monitoring Programme, *The Lolotoe Case: A Small Step Forward* § 3.4 (July 2004), *available at* www.jsmp.minihub.org/Reports/jsmpreports/Lolotoe%20Reports/Lolotoe%20report%20-%20FINAL.pdf [hereinafter *The Lolotoe Case: A Small Step Forward*].

[283] *The Los Palos Case Report*, note 281, at §§ 3.2.4.2, 3.2.4.3.

[284] *The Lolotoe Case: A Small Step Forward*, note 282, at § 3.4; Lolotoe Case Notes, Apr. 8, 2002, at 8; Lolotoe Case Notes, Oct. 31, 2002, at 7.

[285] Cohen, *Indifference*, note 239, at 23.

[286] Los Palos Case Notes, July 18, 2001, at 31; Los Palos Case Notes, July 24, 2001, at 70.

As time went on, the Special Panels hired more interpreters, but inadequate training and standards persisted as significant problems. All of the Special Panels' interpreters were appointed at the U.N. volunteer level; that is, none were professional translators,[287] so it came as no surprise when even Special Panels judges described the interpretation as "not very competent."[288] In addition, even when the Special Panels hired more interpreters, they hired interpreters only for the Panels' four official languages – English, Portuguese, Bahasa Indonesia, and Tetum. Thus, when a witness testified in a tribal language, no official interpreter was available, and the Special Panels had to "just look around and see who [they could] find."[289] The interpreters they could find often had no legal training and frequently were entirely ill equipped for the task: One Bunak translator, for instance, repeatedly summarized the witnesses' testimony in the third person, despite the Panels' repeated instructions to translate the witness's actual words.[290] Another Bunak translator had never before translated Bunak in a courtroom, and he translated a judge's statement to a witness, "you have come to testify in the case against the three accused," as "you have come here to testify against the three accused who murdered people."[291] And in some instances, the only available interpreter was the interpreter who worked for the prosecution, who would have to be used despite conflict-of-interest concerns.[292] The Panels did occasionally take appropriate measures to address particularly egregious problems. The *Lolotoe* Panel, for instance, disqualified a translator who had engaged in a shouting match with judges and had refused to obey court orders.[293] But earlier in the trial, the prosecution had become so fed up with mistranslations that it had asked to stop the trial to seek better interpretation; yet the Panel denied the request.[294]

A few examples from Special Panels' proceedings should give a flavor of the kinds of inaccuracies that resulted from the conditions described in the

[287] Cohen, *Indifference*, note 239, at 27.

[288] *Id.*

[289] *Id.* at 28.

[290] Lolotoe Case Notes, Oct. 22, 2003, at 6–8. For another instance of this, see Lolotoe Case Notes, Nov. 14, 2002, at 12. Judges at the SCSL have also had to repeatedly instruct interpreters not to add words to the witness's answers to make them more coherent. *See, e.g.*, AFRC Transcript, Mar. 7, 2005, at 94–95; AFRC Transcript, Mar. 8, 2005, at 14–15; RUF Transcript, July 13, 2004, at 28–29.

[291] *The Lolotoe Case: A Small Step Forward*, note 282, at § 3.4; Lolotoe Case Notes, May 8, 2002, at 6–7.

[292] *The Los Palos Case Report*, note 281, at § 3.2.1.2; Lolotoe Case Notes, Oct. 24, 2002; Los Palos Case Notes, Aug. 8, 2001, at 137.

[293] Judicial System Monitoring Programme, *Major Issues to Arise in Lolotoe*, Nov. 4–19, 2002, at 8. And the Panel agreed to dismiss a Bunak interpreter who made a serious translation error and asked to be excused. Lolotoe Case Notes, May 8, 2002, at 6–7.

[294] *See* Lolotoe Case Notes, Oct. 22, 2002.

preceding paragraphs. Defendant Manuel da Costa was interpreted as testifying that codefendant Joni Marques had been ordered by two youths to set up a roadblock, when in fact he had testified that Marques had ordered the youths to set up the roadblock[295] – an error that had clear implications for the prosecution's theory of Marques' command responsibility. In another instance, a Portuguese defense counsel asked a question in English about the "hitting of Evaristo Lopez." When speaking in English, this defense counsel did not pronounce the "h" at the beginnings of words, and the interpreter translated the "eating of Evaristo Lopez" into Bahasa Indonesia.[296] And in the *Lolotoe* trial, a Bunak-speaking witness testified that certain people wanted to arrest and kill her husband. The Bunak interpreter accurately translated the witness's answer into Bahasa Indonesia, but the interpreter translating from Bahasa Indonesia to English stated only that people wanted to arrest the witness's husband. This discrepancy might not have been revealed except that the defense counsel, who was listening to the English translation, objected when the prosecutor – who had been listening to the Bahasa interpretation – referred to the people who wanted the witness's husband killed. Prosecutors and defense counsel also questioned or corrected the interpretation at other times, and it was sometimes difficult even to understand what a witness or even a defense counsel was saying,[297] let alone to assess the witness's credibility.

Resource constraints accounted for many of the Special Panels' interpretation deficiencies,[298] but even the better-resourced tribunals have encountered similar problems. Despite its much more generous budget, the ICTR has had to use chain translations because it simply cannot obtain the services of a sufficient number of Kinyarwanda–English interpreters. Thus, Kinyarwandan testimony is typically translated first to French and then from French to English.[299] Likewise, at the SCSL, Mende testimony is sometimes translated first to Krio and then to English.[300] Even when only one translation is made, mistakes are common. For instance, *CDF* witness TF2-201 was asked if he had reported the murder that he had committed to his commander. Although the transcript reports that the witness said "no," the Sierra Leonean judge was convinced

[295] Los Palos Case Notes, July 19, 2001, at 49.
[296] *The Los Palos Case Report*, note 281, at §3.2.4.4.
[297] *See, e.g.*, Lolotoe Case Notes, Oct. 22, 2002, at 3–4; Lolotoe Case Notes, Oct. 23, 2002, at 4, 7, 9.
[298] *See* Cohen, *Indifference*, note 239, at 23.
[299] Stephen J. Rapp, *Achieving Accountability for the Greatest Crimes: The Legacy of the International Tribunals*, 55 DRAKE L. REV. 259, 277 (2007); *see also* Akayesu Judgement, note 32, at para. 145; Kamuhanda Transcript, Sept. 19, 2001, at 99; Alexander Zahar, *The ICTR's Media Judgement and the Reinvention of Direct and Public Incitement to Genocide*, 16 CRIM. L. FORUM 33, 41 n.26 (2005).
[300] Michelle Staggs & Sara Kendall, U.C. Berkeley War Crimes Studies Center, Special Court Monitoring Program, Update No. 4, Sept. 17, 2004, at 3.

that he had said yes. When asked a second time, the witness's ostensible answer again was no, but the Sierra Leonean judge persisted, convinced that the witness had in fact said yes. After the question was asked a third time, it became clear that the witness had indeed reported the killing to his commander.[301] Also in the *CDF* case, witness Albert Nallo was interpreted as saying that "we beat him," when he had actually said "we tabbied" him, which meant that they had tied him neatly.[302] The only reason that these and other mistakes came to light was that SCSL trials feature a Sierra Leonean judge and some Sierra Leonean defense counsel. ICTR defense counsel sometimes catch mistranslations between English and French,[303] but because no Rwandans are serving as ICTR prosecutors, defense counsel, or judges, mistranslations of Kinyarwanda go unnoticed.

Although being aware of an interpretation problem is better than not being aware of it, it is not the same as remedying it. Indeed, in one instance, the SCSL found itself so unable to deal with an interpretation challenge that it abandoned verbatim interpretation. Witness TF2-162 was repeatedly asked to speak more slowly so that the interpreters could translate his testimony. He refused, saying "that is the only way I can speak." The Trial Chamber capitulated and ordered the interpreter to summarize his testimony rather than translating it verbatim, saying: "It is not at his age that you can change him, if he speaks in a particular fashion. Let's just go ahead and bear with him, please. Let the interpreters do everything to summarise him very faithfully, not necessarily getting into what they consider a verbatim report. Please understand the way he speaks and adapt yourself to him."[304]

I have mentioned the resource constraints that exacerbated interpretation difficulties at the Special Panels, but even in their absence interpretation would

[301] CDF Transcript, Nov. 3, 2004, at 38–39.

[302] CDF Transcript, Mar. 10, 2005, at 48–49.

[303] In the ICTR's *Bisengimana* case, the Prosecution's English witness list contained thirty-three witnesses, while its French witness list contained only thirty-one names. Prosecutor v. Bisengimana, Case No. ICTR-2002–60-I, Decision on Bisengimana's Motion for Complete and Accurate Translation into Working Languages of the Tribunal and Respect for the Rights of the Accused (Mar. 7, 2003). It was only because French defense counsel was also proficient in English that she noticed the discrepancy. She otherwise would have been unprepared for two of the witnesses that the prosecution would have called. Similarly, defense counsel in *Rutaganda* brought to light that French transcripts reported that the prosecutor spoke of an "incident involving *six* people," whereas English transcripts (accurately) reported the prosecutor as having spoken of "an incident involving these *three* people." Prosecutor v. Rutaganda, Case No. ICTR-96–3-T, Defence Motion to Direct the Prosecutor to Investigate a Case of False Testimony, at 2 n.1 (Mar. 2, 1998); *see also* Nyiramasuhuko Transcript, Mar. 20, 2003, at 28; Prosecutor v. Kajelijeli, Case No. ICTR-98–44A-T, Judgement and Sentence, para. 296 (Dec. 1, 2003) [hereinafter Kajelijeli Judgement].

[304] CDF Transcript, Sept. 8, 2004, at 17–18.

prove a fact-finding challenge. For one thing, interpretation at the international tribunals must be conducted between radically different languages, and, as David Henige notes, verbatim translations are virtually impossible under those circumstances.[305] Even Spanish to English translations suffer distortions when English tag questions and declarative questions are translated literally;[306] interpreting less similar languages is ever more problematic. The ICTR observed in its very first case that the "interpretation of oral testimony of witnesses from Kinyarwanda into one of the official languages of the Tribunal has been a particularly great challenge due to the fact that the syntax and everyday modes of expression in the Kinyarwanda language are complex and difficult to translate into French or English."[307] Even more difficulties were experienced at the Special Panels, where some witnesses could testify only in simple tribal languages that featured few rules of grammar.[308]

The cultural divergences that I will describe in the next section also disrupt interpretation. At the microlevel, cultural understandings will color the interpretations of various words or phrases. In the ICTR's *Akayesu* case, for instance, the Trial Chamber discussed the various terms and phrases that could be used to signify the English term "rape." Although the dictionary definitions of many of these terms did not seem to convey the force inherent in a rape, the interpreters translated each of the terms as "rape," and the Trial Chamber determined that it was correct to do so in light of the contextual circumstances.[309]

Cultural taboos can hinder the witnesses from testifying clearly and directly about sexual matters or other delicate issues, as I discuss in the next section. The same taboos can also inhibit interpreters so that fact finders fail to receive a clear picture of events even when witnesses have testified clearly. Distortions wrought by interpreter inhibitions appeared at Nuremberg when some of the interpreters proved reluctant to accurately translate vulgar language. One female interpreter refused to interpret "brothel,"[310] while another female interpreter rendered the sentence "you just had to piss on the Jews" as "you just had to ignore the Jews."[311] More recently, in the SCSL's *RUF* trial, the interpreter translated a witness as stating that a rebel had said to a girl, "let me have sex with you." Hearing this, a linguist in the translation booth shouted "no" and insisted that the interpreter correct the translation of the rebel's

[305] David Henige, *Oral Tradition as a Means of Constructing the Past, in* Writing African History 176 (John Edward Philips ed., 2005).
[306] Rigney, note 261, at 96–101.
[307] Akayesu Judgement, note 32, at para. 145.
[308] *See, e.g.*, Lolotoe Case Notes, Oct. 25, 2002.
[309] Akayesu Judgement, note 32, at paras. 152–154.
[310] Tusa, note 19, at 434.
[311] Gaiba, note 278, at 107–08.

statement to "I want to fuck you."[312] The interpreter had been too embarrassed to use the obscenity.[313]

Even more problematic than the cultural taboos that give rise to sporadic interpretation inaccuracies is the fact that translations of specific terms presuppose a shared cultural knowledge between speaker and listener. This body of shared assumptions allows some of the steps in a sequence of statements to be omitted. Because these steps are presumed to be obvious or understood, it is not considered necessary to state them expressly. An example of this is provided by Michael Cooke, who was required to translate from English to Djambarrpuyngu the findings of an Australian coronial inquiry that examined the death of an Aboriginal man at the hands of Australian police. The police officer chose to remain silent and declined to give sworn testimony to the coroner. The coroner's findings mentioned the officer's decision to remain silent, and a purely literal translation would have stopped there. Cooke knew, however, that, in the Aboriginal culture, it would be a sign of shame or guilt to be silent about a killing in which you are implicated,[314] so he chose to add several sentences to the translation explaining that the officer's decision not to speak "does not mean that he was guilty or innocent. It means that he is worried that his words might make serious trouble for him."[315] In similar vein, the question "[w]here did you sleep?" during a direct examination gave rise to considerable confusion when addressed to an Australian Aboriginal. For a Westerner, the question implies the sleep of night but for Aboriginals, who often attend all-night ceremonies and whose high unemployment rate means that they are not required to sleep only at night, the question contains no such implication.[316]

As a consequence of the need to make explicit the implicit steps in a logical argument, Cooke argues that in-court interpreters might also need to provide explication and explanation as an integral part of the process of translation

[312] RUF Transcript, July 14, 2004, at 26–27.

[313] The same problem can arise in domestic trials that feature witnesses from different cultures than the court personnel. In a Minnesota criminal case, Hmong interpreters repeatedly substituted English euphemisms for vulgar and obscene Hmong terms, some of which were uttered by the alleged crime victim. Timothy Dunnigan & Bruce T. Downing, *Legal Interpreting on Trial: A Case Study, in* TRANSLATION AND THE LAW 93, 98 (Marshall Morris ed., 1996). In that case, the inaccuracies may have had a significant effect in reinforcing the prosecution's cultural stereotypes of the victim as a "shy, naïve and innocent Asian woman." *Id.*

[314] Michael Cooke, *Understood by All Concerned?: Anglo/Aboriginal Legal Translation, in* TRANSLATION AND THE LAW 37, 51–52 (Marshall Morris ed., 1995).

[315] *Id.* at 53.

[316] *Michael Cooke, Interpreting in a Cross-Cultural Examination: An Aboriginal Case Study,* 113 INT'L J. OF THE SOC. OF LANGUAGE 99, 105 (1995) [hereinafter Cooke, *Interpreting in a Cross-Cultural Examination*].

across divergent cultures. Interpretation codes typically do not permit this,[317] but that did not stop one Bunak interpreter from providing such explanations. The interpreter subsequently informed an NGO trial monitor that such prosecution questions as "what happened next?" or "in what part of the house?" had no meaning for a particular witness. Because the interpreter believed that the witness "had no concept of what they were getting at," he often offered her examples, such as asking, "did you go home or did they beat you?"[318] It is by no means clear, however, that the judges or lawyers were aware of the interpreter's interventions.

A final impediment to accurate translation stems from the fact that some of the languages in need of translation at the international tribunals simply do not have the vocabulary to convey the concepts in question. Similar problems can arise when interpreting between languages used in countries with common-law and civil law traditions. As Holly Mikkelson observes:

> A concept in one culture may simply not exist in another culture, and the interpreter must use a descriptive phrase to convey the idea adequately. An example of this is the term "arraignment," which refers to a proceeding unique to the common-law system. To render this concept faithfully in another language, the interpreter would have to use a phrase like "initial appearance at which charges are read and a plea is entered." This is impossibly long for simultaneous interpretation, so most interpreters use a phrase such as "reading of charges" or "initial proceeding."[319]

Sometimes, the target language not only does not contain terms of art used in a particular legal system but also does not contain simple words used in everyday conversation. For instance, Special Panels counsel had great difficulty in obtaining an answer to the question "[d]o you know the difference between soldier and militia?" The prosecutor maintained that the word "difference" does not exist in Tetum, and the East Timorese judge advised counsel to ask the question in a way that did not use that word.[320] Another Timorese

[317] *See, e.g.*, Code of Ethics for Interpreters and Translators Employed by the Special Court for Sierra Leone, art. 7(c) (May 25, 2004).

[318] Lolotoe Case Notes, Oct. 25, 2002, at 1.

[319] Holly Mikkelson, *Verbatim Interpretation: An Oxymoron*, *available at* www.acebo.com/papers/verbatim.htm. Cole and Maslow-Armand likewise note the difficulty of interpreting/explaining the right to a jury trial to a defendant whose home country does not provide jury trials. Richard W. Cole & Laura Maslow-Armand, *The Role of Counsel and the Courts in Addressing Foreign Language and Cultural Barriers at Different Stages of a Criminal Proceeding*, 19 W. New Eng. L. Rev. 193, 195 (1997).

[320] Lolotoe Case Notes, Apr. 11, 2002, at 2.

interpreter had to interrupt the *Los Palos* trial to clear up confusion resulting from the fact that "the word for lighter and match is the same."[321] And at the SCSL, pages of testimony centered on what the witness meant by the word "usually" as it was used in her statement until the interpreter interjected that "[t]here is no word for 'usually' in the Mende language."[322]

An even larger problem for a tribunal such as the Special Panels is not that the target language does not contain a precise analogue to the term or the legal concept under translation such that a longer, descriptive phrase must be used, but the far more severe problem that Tetum and other more obscure East Timorese languages have never been languages of law or government so that they may not contain many of the words necessary even to construct the descriptive phrasing.[323] East Timor, for instance, had been a Portuguese colony for more than 450 years[324] when Indonesia invaded the island in December 1975 and formally annexed the territory, proclaiming it to be Indonesia's twenty-seventh province.[325] During the twenty-four years of Indonesia's occupation, East Timor's judicial system was run entirely by Indonesians. Because East Timorese were excluded from the judicial processes, they have had "no experience of a functional criminal justice system."[326] So, even when the words exist in East Timorese languages to convey the relevant concepts, the concepts themselves may not be understood. As David Mearns said in relation to the East Timorese: "The abstract notion of justice and the concept of equality before the law are principles that do not easily fit with the experience of a people

[321] Los Palos Case Notes, Aug. 16, 2001, at 167.

[322] AFRC Transcript, July 18, 2005, at 106–11.

[323] Holly Mikkelson notes this problem arising in relation to interpretations of Hmong and Tigrinyan immigrants to the United States. Mikkelson, *Towards a Redefinition*, note 265, at 32. Similarly, the words contained or not contained in Aboriginal languages frequently reflect the Aboriginal people's radically different conception of justice which emphasizes reparation and reconciliation over retribution. The Cree language, for instance, has no word for "guilty." The closest Cree word to "guilty" means "doing some act," but the Cree word does not connote any illegality. ALVIN C. HAMILTON, A FEATHER AND NOT A GAVEL: WORKING TOWARDS ABORIGINAL JUSTICE 53 (2001).

[324] For a discussion of the Timorese colonial period, see James J. Fox, *Tracing the Path, Recounting the Path: Historical Perspectives on Timor, in* OUT OF THE ASHES: DESTRUCTION AND RECONSTRUCTION OF EAST TIMOR 8–23 (James J. Fox & Dionísio Babo-Soares eds., 2003).

[325] *See Report of the International Commission of Inquiry on East Timor to the Secretary-General*, para. 5, U.N. Doc. A/54/726-S/2000/59 (Jan. 31, 2000); Phillip J. Curtin, Comment, *Genocide in East Timor? Calling for an International Criminal Tribunal for East Timor in Light of* Akayesu, 19 DICK. J. INT'L L. 181, 184–85 (2000); Sylvia de Bertodano, *Current Developments in Internationalized Courts*, 1 J. INT'L CRIM. JUST. 226, 228–29 (2003).

[326] U.N. Development Programme, Report, *The Community Reconciliation Process of the Commission for Reception, Truth and Reconciliation*, at 28 (April 2004), *available at* www.undp.east-timor.org/documentsreports/governance_capacitydevelopment/Piers%20report%20Final.pdf [hereinafter *UNDP Report on the Community Reconciliation Process*].

who have never lived in a democratic society."[327] The torturous exchanges reproduced in Chapter 2 – that resulted when the Special Panels sought to ascertain whether defendants understood the charges against them or were pleading guilty knowingly and voluntarily – prove Mearns's point, as does the testimony of witness Benedito da Costa in the *Lolotoe* case. After testifying that one of the defendants had arrested him, da Costa was asked whether he had been taken before a judge to evaluate the legality of the arrest. Even after the prosecutor asked the question in several different ways, da Costa could answer only: "I don't know about that."[328]

The foregoing discussion makes clear that the distortions wrought by language interpretation negatively impact fact-finding at the international tribunals in a variety of ways. In addition, even when the interpretations are accurate, they impede a fact finder's ability to assess demeanor.[329] The next section will explore the ways in which cultural divergences between witnesses and Western court personnel impair the fact finder's ability to "read" certain demeanor cues, but the need for language interpretation means additionally that some cues will be entirely obscured. That is, Western court personnel may have difficulty evaluating the significance of a witness's hesitancy in answering questions because such hesitancy can have different connotations in different cultures, but the introduction of language interpretation may obscure even that the witness's answers were hesitant. Language interpretation also impairs counsel's ability to test a witness's veracity, as will become especially clear during Chapter 4's discussion of witness inconsistencies. Suffice it to say here that witness testimony frequently diverges from the pretrial statements that the witnesses have provided to prosecutors, and when witnesses are confronted with such inconsistencies they frequently blame the interpreters who participated in the statement taking.

Most importantly, there is every reason to believe that many of the most frustrating and incoherent exchanges appearing in international tribunal transcripts result at least in part from misinterpretations. As Chapter 2 describes, international tribunal transcripts often feature questions and answers that bear no relationship to one another, and we must assume that many of these stem from inaccurate language interpretation. For instance, an NGO trial monitor reported that a *Lolotoe* witness responded inappropriately to the question "who moved you to the house of Johni?" because the question was interpreted

[327] David Mearns, *Looking Both Ways: Models for Justice in East Timor*, Australian Legal Resources International Publication at 49 (Nov. 2002) (on file with author).
[328] Lolotoe Case Notes, Apr. 8, 2002, at 5.
[329] *See* Steve Norman, *Assessing the Credibility of Refugee Applicants: A Judicial Perspective*, 19 Int'l J. Refugee L. 273, 289–90 (2007); Karton, note 270, at 29.

as "who was with you in the kitchen of Johni's house?"[330] And although we rarely have that sort of independent confirmation of interpretation mistakes, some of the more divergent questions and answers seem as though they could not be anything but misinterpretations. When, for instance, the ICTR's *Ndindabahizi* prosecutor asked if an event occurred on the "6th or 7th of April," and the witness responded, "[i]t was the 6th, not the 4th,"[331] we can be virtually certain that a mistranslation has occurred. Likewise when the response to the question "how many times did the defendant hit the victim?" is "about 11:00," it is hard not to blame the interpreters.[332]

Chapter 2 also describes numerous instances in which questions had to be asked repeatedly before the witness provided a responsive answer, and misinterpretations likely also played a role in many of those exchanges. A Special Panels trial monitor reported, for instance, that the question "how long were you in Johni's kitchen?" had to be put a number of times because, although the witness answered, "I don't know for certain how long we were there exactly in hours or minutes but we were not there a day," the interpreter failed initially to translate "no more than a day."[333] And when the prosecution in the SCSL's *AFRC* case had difficulty controlling a witness "who tended to give long or tangential responses, sometimes clearly misunderstanding or ignoring the question," it three times alluded to possible interpretation errors, suggesting that they might have caused the communication difficulties.[334] Finally, Chapter 2 cites and reproduces some lengthy Special Panels exchanges that bordered on the incoherent, and it seems reasonable to believe that the intermittent "chaos with interpretation," as reported by trial monitors, played a role in the confusion.

3.C. CULTURAL DIVERGENCES

Cultural influences affect the methods by which people communicate and the subjects that they consider appropriate for discussion. Even in a homogenous

[330] Lolotoe Case Notes, Oct. 23, 2002, at 9.

[331] Ndindabahizi Transcript, Sept. 2, 2003, at 33.

[332] Los Palos Case Notes, Aug. 14, 2001, at 156. Moore & Mamiya observe that confusing answers or the need to keep repeating questions often stems from inadequate interpretation. Moore & Mamiya, note 259, at 37. DeMuniz likewise notes that, in the Santiago Ventura trial, Mixtec witnesses who were bewildered by the questions that were being translated from English to Spanish gave seemingly inappropriate or nonsensical answers. Paul J. DeMuniz, *Introduction to* IMMIGRANTS IN COURTS 3, 4 (Joanne I. Moore ed., 1999).

[333] Lolotoe Case Notes, Oct. 23, 2002, at 9. For another mistranslation caught by the trial monitor, see Lolotoe Case Notes, Oct. 31, 2002, at 4.

[334] Kyra Sanin, U.C. Berkeley War Crimes Studies Center, Special Court Monitoring Program Update No. 56, Sept. 23, 2005, at 3.

society, men and women communicate differently, as do people of higher and lower social standing. Research shows that these differences can lead juries to differentially evaluate the testimony of men and women and different classes of persons.[335] Cultural differences among nonhomogenous groups lead to even greater divergences in manner of speech and demeanor. These issues have been the subject of recent research in countries with diverse populations as well as large native and Aboriginal populations.

Studies have shown, for instance, that Western fact finders can easily misinterpret the cultural norms of immigrant witnesses. In many cultures, for instance, making eye contact with another is a sign of disrespect, so immigrants from such cultures will avert their eyes while testifying. Western fact finders, by contrast, typically consider maintaining eye contact to indicate forthrightness and trustworthiness, so they may view immigrants who fail to do so as deceptive or shifty.[336] Exaggerated hand gestures common to certain cultures likewise may be incorrectly interpreted as a sign of peculiar or aggressive behavior rather than as a customary means of accentuating a point.[337] Some cultures value stoicism and disdain public demonstrations of emotion. Criminal defendants from such cultures may appear to lack remorse for their crimes when their demeanor in fact reflects only adherence to their cultural values.[338] As problematic as these cultural divergences can prove during a

[335] Research indicates, for instance, that female witnesses and witnesses of low social status more frequently engage in what has been termed "powerless" speech. That is, they use more "hedges," such as "I think" or "it seems as though"; they use more modifiers, such as "kind of" or "sort of," and they use more appended phrases such as "you know." They also use more hesitation forms, such as "well" and "um," and they more frequently state their declarations with a rising inflection, which makes the declarations sound more like questions. Robin Tolmach Lakoff, *Women's Language*, 10 Language & Style 222, 225–28 (1977); Robin Lakoff, Language and Women's Place 14–17 (1975); John M. Conley et al., *The Power of Language: Presentation Style in the Courtroom*, 1978 Duke L. J. 1375, 1380 (1978). Research indicates that fact finders are less favorably disposed to witnesses who use a "powerless" style of testimony. *See* Conley et al., *supra* at 1385–86; *see generally*, Monica Hersh Khetarpal Sholar, *Jurors' Perceptions of Gender-Based Linguistic Differences*, 10 Wm & Mary J. of Women & L. 91 (2003).

[336] *See* Joanna Ruppel, *The Need for a Benefit of the Doubt Standard in Credibility Evaluation of Asylum Applicants*, 23 Colum. Hum. Rts. L. Rev. 1, 12–13, 13 n.44 (1992); Paul R. Tremblay, *Interviewing and Counseling Across Cultures: Heuristics and Biases*, 9 Clinical L. Rev. 373, 394 (2002); William Y. Chin, *Multiple Cultures, One Criminal Justice System: The Need for a "Cultural Ombudsman" in the Courtroom*, 53 Drake L. Rev. 651, 659 (2005); Juan-Vicente Palerm et al., *Mexican Immigrants in Courts, in* Immigrants in Courts 73, 92 (Joanne I. Moore ed., 1999) (discussing rural Mexicans); Tai Van Ta, *Vietnamese Immigrants in American Courts, in* Immigrants in Courts 140, 155 (Joanne I. Moore ed., 1999) (discussing Vietnamese); DeMuniz, note 332, at 4–5.

[337] Cole & Maslow-Armand, note 319, at 195; Chin, note 336, at 659.

[338] *See* People v. Superior Court (Soon Ja Du), 7 Cal. Rptr. 2d 177, 181 (Cal. Dist. Ct. App. 1992); In Kwan Fai Mak v. Blodgett, 754 F. Supp. 1490, 1499 (W.D. Wash. 1991, *aff'd per curiam and remanded* 970 F.2d 614 (9th Cir. 1992)) (discussing the cultural expectations of Chinese males).

domestic criminal trial, they at least have become the subject of considerable research. That research has educated the legal professionals who interact with immigrants and native populations and has spurred efforts to bridge the cultural divides. Murder convictions have been reversed following sociolinguistic expert testimony,[339] and educational efforts have sought to prevent wrongful convictions in the first place. Training sessions on intercultural communication for judges and lawyers have been conducted,[340] and proposals have been advanced to provide jury instructions that would explain intercultural communication and to develop programs that would enhance communication between Western court personnel and immigrant or Aboriginal populations.[341]

The kind of intercultural communication difficulties that appear in the odd domestic case are not only part and parcel of every case at the international tribunals but are apt to be more severe and more distortive, as I will describe in the pages below. Yet there has been little effort to systematically investigate what cultural divergences exist at a given tribunal and how those divergences might impede the fact finders' ability to understand witness testimony or assess its credibility. What is abundantly clear, however, is that witnesses at the ICTR, SCSL, and the Special Panels live very different lives and frequently subscribe to very different worldviews than the Western court personnel who hear their testimony. Those differences create numerous barriers to understanding and assessing witness testimony.

To begin, although educational deficiencies may play the primary role in explaining the difficulty that many international witnesses have in answering the who, what, where, and when questions that I describe in Chapter 2, cultural factors also play a part. Certainly, an inability or unwillingness to divide space into certain identifiable units has cultural roots and connotations. Anthropologist James Littlejohn's research, for instance, suggests that Sierra Leonean and Western notions of space differ radically. Littlejohn determined that the Temne people (who make up the largest tribe in Sierra Leone) do not view space as either "arithmetically measured or geometrically analysed" but instead break it up into units such as "a day's journey" or, for shorter distances, "the earshot."

339 *See* Diana Eades, *Legal Recognition of Cultural Differences in Communication: The Case of Robyn Kina*, 16 LANGUAGE & COMMUNICATION 215, 225 (1996); John J. Gumperz, *Contextualization and Ideology in Intercultural Communication*, *in* CULTURE OF COMMUNICATION: ANALYSES OF INTERCULTURAL SITUATIONS 35, 50 (Aldo Di Luzio et al. eds., 2001).

340 *See, e.g.*, Eades, note 339, at 225; Courts Administration Authority, South Australia District Court Judicial Officers, *available at* www.courts.sa.gov.au/courts/district/judicial_officers.html.

341 Kathy Mack, *An Australian Perspective on Feminism, Race and Evidence*, 28 S.W. U. L. REV. 367, 382 (1999); Michael Cooke, *Aboriginal Evidence in the Cross-Cultural Courtroom*, *in* LANGUAGE IN EVIDENCE: ISSUES CONFRONTING ABORIGINAL AND MULTICULTURAL AUSTRALIA 55, 95 (Diana Eades ed., 1995); Chin, note 336, at 653.

Littlejohn observes that although Westerners have become so accustomed to organizing space through geometrical analysis and arithmetical measurement that it has come to seem the natural thing to do, Temne space is ordered otherwise. "The size of a farm for example is arrived at by estimating the number of bags of rice it ought to produce, . . . [and when] men hire themselves out to hoe for a farmer, the farmer and the labourer agree on an area which the labourer should complete in a day's work. The day's work, however, consists of completing the area."[342] Sometimes precise units of measurement are desired – for instance, when sticks of equal length are needed for constructing a house. In that case, the Temne will use a stick of the desired length as a model. That there exist differing conceptions of space across cultures helps to explain why even some well-educated international witnesses cannot provide distance estimations, and it helps to explain certain otherwise inexplicable witness responses. Rwandan witness VN, for instance, was not only unable to answer questions regarding the distance separating him from his attacker, but he admonished counsel: "Do not ask me questions about distances. To give an approximate distance would not be to tell the truth."[343]

Different cultures not only view such measures differently but may also attach radically different levels of importance to them. Linguist and interpreter Michael Cooke has observed that Aboriginal peoples frequently become confused when asked about details of time and place. "They cannot understand the importance of such things. They think, 'Why are they asking me all this?'"[344] Likewise, witnesses at the international tribunals under discussion frequently express impatience when questioned on such details,[345] and some make clear that they consider it unimportant to provide truly accurate answers. Rwandan witness J, for instance, testified that the man who raped her remained on top of her for four hours. When an ICTR judge expressed skepticism that it was so long, witness J responded in a way that made clear the unabashedly subjective nature of her estimate. She said: "For me, it was about four hours or maybe one year because the suffering was too much."[346] Similarly, Sierra Leonean witness TF1-012 initially testified that a rebel named Mosquito returned after "a week."

[342] James Littlejohn, *Temne Space*, 36 ANTHROPOLOGICAL Q. 1, 4 (1963).

[343] Semanza Transcript, Nov. 14, 2000, at 46–48.

[344] Cooke, *Interpreting in a Cross-Cultural Examination*, note 316.

[345] *See, e.g.*, Ndindabahizi Transcript, Sept. 8, 2003, at 16–17; Ndindabahizi Transcript, Sept. 15, 2003, at 28–29, 36–38; Kajelijeli Transcript, July 19, 2001, at 29; Kamuhanda Transcript, Sept. 13, 2001, at 91–92; Kamuhanda Transcript, Feb. 5, 2002, at 31; Kamuhanda Transcript, Feb. 6, 2002, at 87–88; RUF Transcript, July 19, 2004, at 74; RUF Transcript, July 21, 2004, at 12. *Cf.* AFRC Transcript, Sept. 27, 2005, at 11, 58, 77 (witness TF1-184 repeatedly expressing impatience when asked to spell place names).

[346] Prosecutor v. Musema, Case No. ICTR-96-13-T, Transcript, Mar. 11, 1999, at 48 [hereinafter Musema Transcript].

When the witness later suggested that Mosquito returned after several weeks, counsel pointed out the inconsistency. TF1-012 replied offhandedly: "We are native people. That which is not up to a month, we call it a week."[347]

Cultural divergences between witnesses and Western court personnel also impede communication on other key topics. At the most global level, researchers in some African regions that have suffered widespread conflict have identified a reluctance to speak of the violence for fear that such discussions would cause the violence to return. Fiona Ross reports that "in some societies, talk about past violence is considered suspicious,"[348] and Rosalind Shaw's ethnographic research in Sierra Leone reveals the existence of similar views. Shaw reports that almost without exception the Sierra Leoneans she talked to wanted to forget the conflict:

> Speaking of the violence – especially in public – was (and is) viewed as encouraging its return, calling it forth when it is still very close, and might at any moment erupt again. People in the northern Sierra Leonean communities in which I conducted research discussed the war within their families and inside their houses but often reminded each other not to "pull it outside" and thereby risk endowing it with reality. Some were concerned that "pulling it outside" would exacerbate social tensions and make it more likely that violence would resume, while others felt that doing so could also summon forth the violence in a more spiritual sense.[349]

Many Rwandans feel similarly.[350] Witnesses who have agreed to testify at the international tribunals have obviously overcome to some degree any reluctance they may have had to speak about the violence; however, snippets of such views occasionally make their way into the transcripts. A tribal chief testifying in the *CDF* case, for instance, expressed a reluctance to answer certain questions for fear that the answers would "open old wounds."[351] And even when such views are not expressly articulated, they may nonetheless be contributing to some of

[347] RUF Transcript, Feb. 3, 2005, at 70.

[348] Fiona C. Ross, Bearing Witness: Women and the Truth and Reconciliation Commission in South Africa 178 n.18 (2003).

[349] Rosalind Shaw, *Rethinking Truth and Reconciliation Commissions: Lessons from Sierra Leone*, United States Institute of Peace Special Report 130, at 8–9 (Feb. 2005), *available at* http://www.usip.org/files/resources/sr130.pdf.

[350] Timothy Longman & Théonèste Rutagengwa, *Memory, Identity and Community in Rwanda*, *in* My Neighbor, My Enemy: Justice and Community in the Aftermath of Mass Atrocity 162, 174–75 (Eric Stover & Harvey Weinstein eds., 2004); *see also* Priscilla B. Hayner, Unspeakable Truths 189 (2001) (describing "a palpable sense in Mozambique that if you talked about the war, it might come back; if the war was mentioned, Mozambicans were likely to change the subject").

[351] CDF Transcript, Sept. 13, 2004, at 81.

the many frustrating exchanges in which witnesses seem intent on evading the questions posed to them.

I will turn now to some specific issues that have been the subject of cultural divergences. Special Panels judges, for instance, had tremendous difficulty ascertaining whether witnesses were related – in the Western sense of the term – to defendants. After marriage, an East Timorese individual belongs not only to a certain, specified family but also to a "sacred house" that traces the individual's lineage to the common ancestor who founded the house.[352] As a result of these cultural norms, the Timorese conception of family relationships is much broader than that of Westerners, and it caused considerable confusion among Western court personnel. The witness in the following exchange, for example, had just identified one of the defendants and another person as the witness's brothers:

JUDGE: So you have two younger brothers?
WITNESS 13: Yes.
JUDGE: Do your brothers come from the same mother?
WITNESS 13: No we are just from the same tribe.
JUDGE: We in court want to know if they are family – same mother and father.
WITNESS 13: No, we are from the same tribe, same traditions, and same ancestors, but different fathers.
JUDGE: And different mothers also?
WITNESS 13: Yes.[353]

When witness 20 was asked, "[are] you related to any of the accused?" he identified six of the ten defendants as his "sons." The judge then pointed out that the defendants could not be the witness's son because the witness was younger than or the same age as the defendants, to which the witness responded: "Of course, some of them are older, but considering our *adat* laws of our family ties, and I originated from the first great-grandmother and so I consider them my children."[354] Sometimes, the family relationship remains unclear even after several questions are posed and answered. In the *Januario Da Costa & Punef* case, for instance, the witness stated that the defendant was his "brother-in-law." Asked if the defendant was married to his sister, the witness responded that the defendant's mother was his father's older sister.

[352] Tanja Hohe & Rod Nixon, *Reconciling Justice: 'Traditional' Law and State Judiciary in East Timor*. Paper prepared for the U.S. Institute of Peace and delivered at the workshop on the Working of Non-State Justice Systems, held at the Development Institute, Brighton United Kingdom, at 14 (Mar. 6–7, 2003).
[353] Los Palos Case Notes, Aug. 22, 2001, at 189.
[354] Los Palos Case Notes, Sept. 20, 2001, at 235.

He was then asked, "so, you are cousins?" and the witness responded, "we have the same surname."[355] The familial relationship between a potential witness and one of the *Los Palos* defendants – Gonsalo dos Santos – was left similarly murky, as the following exchange demonstrates:

JUDGE: Are you married to Gonsalo dos Santos's sister or is he married to your sister?

WITNESS: No he's my uncle, so it's not like that. My younger sister married Gonsalo dos Santos's father. She is not my real younger sister, she has close family relations with my family.

JUDGE: So you don't have real family ties with Gonsalo dos Santos?

WITNESS: I'm not that close with Gonsalo dos Santos but my family relationship with his mother is quite close.[356]

Although questions pertaining to familial relationships are not as prevalent at the ICTR and SCSL, they too can cause confusion when they do arise. For instance, Sierra Leonean witness TF2-096 began describing a woman as "her sister" but later had to clarify that the woman was only her friend.[357] Similarly, when witness TF2-071 was asked whether he was a brother-in-law to a certain set of persons, the presiding judge – a Cameroonian – saw fit to inform the courtroom that "when you marry a woman in Africa, you marry the whole village."[358] And sometimes the familial relationship never gets clarified: Although prosecutors alleged that a *Ndindabahizi* witness was related to the defendant, the witness denied that the relations "would be described as kinship in the Rwandan culture,"[359] and the matter was dropped.

I have recounted the above exchanges to provide examples in which differing cultural understandings impede communication, but it is also notable that the Special Panels showed no interest in adapting their Western-based rules and procedures to the East Timorese context in which they operated. Special Panels' witnesses were asked about their family ties to defendants and victims in order to identify potential biases and to give effect to section 35(2) of the Transitional Rules of Criminal Procedure, which provides that the spouse, parents, children, or relatives of the defendant within the second degree are not required to testify.[360] Special Panels judges satisfied the literal terms of section 35(2),

[355] Prosecutor v. Da Costa & Punef, Case No. 22/2003, Judgement, at 5 (Apr. 25, 2005) [hereinafter Da Costa & Punef Judgement]; Los Palos Case Notes, Sept. 24, 2001, at 263.

[356] Los Palos Case Notes, Sept. 24, 2001, at 263.

[357] CDF Transcript, Nov. 8, 2004, at 28.

[358] CDF Transcript, Nov. 11, 2004, at 110.

[359] Ndindabahizi Judgement, note 56, at para. 321.

[360] *See* UNTAET Regulation No. 2000/30 on Transitional Rules of Criminal Procedure, UNTAET/REG/2000/30 (as amended by Regulation 2001/25 of September 14, 2001).

and they probed for Western conceptions of bias; but, because their questioning sought to identify only Western-style familial relationships and took no account of the broader Timorese conception of family, the questioning failed to identify serious biases that could have distorted witness testimony. Consider, for instance, that although the six defendants that witness 20 identified as his sons were not his offspring in the Western sense, the witness obviously felt a strong familial bond to them, which might have influenced his testimony. However, there is no evidence that the Special Panels took any account of these broader familial relationships in assessing witness testimony.

Cultural taboos surrounding sexual violence have also given rise to communication difficulties at the international tribunals. Even Western victims of sexual violence are often reluctant to testify in detail about the crimes committed against them,[361] and that reluctance is all the more pronounced in societies such as in Rwanda, Sierra Leone, and East Timor, where the mere reporting of rape can leave victims vulnerable to rejection, ridicule, and stigmatization.[362] Not surprisingly, then, many East Timorese, Rwandan, and Sierra Leonean rape victims have declined to come forward at all,[363] and some of those who have come forward did not immediately report their rapes – they rather spoke initially only about the other kinds of violence done to them or their family members.[364] That is, these witnesses waited until they were giving their second

[361] ELLISON, note 188, at 16–17.

[362] *See, e.g.*, Human Rights Watch, *Struggling to Survive: Barriers to Justice for Rape Victims in Rwanda* 29–30 (Sept. 29, 2004); Amnesty International, *Sierra Leone: Getting Reparations Rights for Survivors of Sexual Violence*, AFR 51/005/2007, at 7 (Nov. 1, 2007); Shana Eaton, *Sierra Leone: The Proving Ground for Prosecuting Rape as a War Crime*, 35 GEO. J. INT'L L. 873, 916–17 (2004); Commission for Reception Truth and Reconciliation in East Timor, *Chega! The Report of the Commission for Reception Truth and Reconciliation in Timor-Leste*, chs. 7.7, 7.71, (2005); *Indonesia Colluded with Timor Militia Terror: Gusmao Wife*, AGENCE FRANCE-PRESSE, Nov. 9, 2000; Seth Mydans, *Sexual Violence as Tool of War: Pattern Emerging in East Timor*, N.Y. TIMES, Mar. 1, 2001.

[363] *See* Lars Waldorf, *Mass Justice for Mass Atrocity: Rethinking Local Justice as Transitional Justice*, 79 TEMPLE L. REV. 1, 62 (2006); HUMAN RIGHTS WATCH, SHATTERED LIVES: SEXUAL VIOLENCE DURING THE RWANDAN GENOCIDE AND ITS AFTERMATH (1996); Human Rights Watch, *"We'll Kill You If You Cry": Sexual Violence in the Sierra Leone Conflict*, Vol. 15, No. 1(A) 52 (Jan. 15, 2003); Kati Bambrick, *Silent Victims, Young Girls at Risk: An Evaluation of Post-War Rape and Response to Rape in the Provinces of Sierra Leone* 26–28 (Campaign for Good Governance, 2004), *available at* www.peacewomen.org/resources/Sierra_Leone/GoodGovernanceSilentVictims.pdf; Susan Harris Rimmer, *"Orphans" or Veterans?: Justice for Children Born of War in East Timor*, 42 TEX. INT'L L.J. 323, 330–31 (2007).

Because rape victims frequently do not come forward, prosecutors sometimes rely on hearsay testimony to prove their rape charges. *See* Prosecutor v. Muhimana, Case No. ICTR-95–1B-T, Judgement and Sentence, para. 224 (Apr. 28, 2005) [hereinafter Muhimana Judgement].

[364] *See, e.g.*, Musema Judgement, note 112, at para. 836; Prosecutor v. Gacumbitsi, Case No. ICTR-2001–64-T, Judgement, para. 219 (June 17, 2004) [hereinafter Gacumbitsi Judgement]; Nyiramasuhuko Transcript, Mar. 24, 2003, at 16–17; Akayesu Transcript, Mar. 13, 1998, at 191;

or third statement to mention their rapes – because it was only then that they felt comfortable with the investigators to whom they were speaking. But such a practice leaves a witness vulnerable to the obvious question from the defense: Why did you not mention the rape initially, when you were describing all of the other violence you suffered or witnessed?[365] A Western victim's credibility would be in shreds if she failed to mention that she had been raped until a late stage of the investigation. The tribunals, by contrast, seem to take little notice of such omissions.[366] That stance may well be appropriate given the widespread taboo against discussing sexual matters that prevails in the regions in question, but it likewise could have the effect of encouraging witnesses to embellish or to lie outright about their experiences.

When rape victims are willing to come forward, they find themselves having to speak in public about things that are rarely said even in private in their home countries. Kinyarwanda has no one certain word for "rape," and victims will frequently use phrases that might be considered euphemisms to Western ears but that clearly signify rape to Rwandans.[367] Tribunal prosecutors, seeking to make out their best case, cannot be satisfied with euphemisms, though, so they typically require witnesses to describe their rapes in more graphic detail.[368] Tribunal personnel do what they can to ameliorate the witnesses' discomfort. Sometimes defense counsel waive their right to cross-examine victims of sexual violence if the crimes do not directly implicate their clients.[369] Even providing direct testimony can be excruciating, though, so *Gacumbitsi* witness TAP was

Muhimana Transcript, Apr. 15, 2004, at 61; Kajelijeli Transcript, Dec. 12, 2001, at 16–17; RUF Transcript, July 19, 2004, at 73; *see also* Taylor Transcript, May 8, 2008, at 9288 (witness did not initially tell investigators of her niece's rape).

[365] One witness responded that the rape was too "painful and shameful" to discuss, *see* RUF Transcript, July 19, 2004, at 73, whereas another brushed it off as something "I did not find the need to discuss," Kajelijeli Transcript, Dec. 12, 2001, at 16. An expert witness called by the defense in the ICTR's *Akayesu* case noted this problem, acknowledging that there is a cultural reluctance to discuss rape but also maintaining that women began to allege rape after the genocide for purposes of blackmail. Akayesu Judgement, note 32, at para. 442.

[366] In the *Kajelijeli* Judgment, the Trial Chamber deemed witness ACM's testimony "reliable" and did not mention her initial failure to report the rape or the discrepancies that appeared in her various accounts about where the rape took place. Kajelijeli Judgement, note 303, at para. 679. In discussing witness J's omissions in the *Musema* case, the Trial Chamber "recognize[d] that it is especially difficult to testify about rape and sexual violence, moreover in a public forum." Musema Judgement, note 112, at para. 842.

[367] Akayesu Judgement, note 32, at paras. 152–154. Similarly, in *Musema*, witness J was asked by the prosecution, "[w]ould I be correct in saying that, you are no longer able to have sex, following this incident.?" The witness replied euphemistically: "Because of what happened to me, I cannot get married again." Musema Transcript, Mar. 11, 1999, at 50.

[368] *See, e.g.*, Semanza Transcript, Mar. 19, 2001, at 47–48.

[369] *See, e.g.*, Michele Staggs, U.C. Berkeley War Crimes Studies Center, Special Court Monitoring Program, Update No. 20, Feb. 4, 2005, at 3.

permitted to describe her rape in writing after she told the court: "It is very painful.... Things of that nature are not spoken of. Our parents never taught us to speak like that; it was a taboo."[370] And language interpreters, recognizing that witnesses may feel as though they are being insulted or ridiculed when asked explicit questions, seek to phrase the questions in ways less likely to offend.[371] But they must be careful not to cause or facilitate confusion. Several pages of SCSL transcripts centered on an apparent inconsistency between witness TF1-198's statement and her testimony. Her statement reported that a soldier had inserted a big stick into her vagina, but she testified that the stick had been inserted into her "anus." During questioning about this inconsistency, the interpreter finally interjected to observe that women from the witness's region "are usually very inhibited in calling vagina; they usually don't say they stuck something in my vagina. They will say it is stuck in my anus. But the word anus in Kono has an ambiguity when you talking about women. It may mean the vagina and it can actually mean the anus."[372]

Even male witnesses can be reluctant to speak plainly about rape. In the *Seromba* case, a lengthy exchange took place between the prosecution and a male witness to clarify that, by using the term "forced marriage," the witness actually meant "rape."[373] Similarly, when asked what had happened to some young women who had been captured by the Kamajors, Sierra Leonean witness TF2-021 stated euphemistically that "Papay Konde took them." When then asked, "[a]nd what did he do with them?" the witness responded, "[t]hey were with him at his house."[374] In *Akayesu*, the defendant was willing to acknowledge that mass killings had occurred in his *commune*, but he vehemently denied that even a single rape had occurred at the Taba Bureau Communal – even when he was not there.[375] And even the Trial Chambers occasionally take up sexual euphemisms. The SCSL's Trial Chamber I, which has two African judges, described the efficacy of the Kamajor's initiation process in a judgment by stating that it "was widely believed that little boys were more effectively immunized because they *had not had any time with women*."[376]

Taboos regarding sexual violence are sufficiently well known that Western court personnel expect them to distort or impede communication about rape and other forms of sexual assault, but many international witnesses subscribe

370 Prosecutor v. Gacumbitsi, Case No. ICTR-01–64-T, Transcript, Aug. 6, 2003, at 9–10 [hereinafter Gacumbitsi Transcript].

371 Interview with Leopold Furufuru, ICTR Translator, Mar. 13, 2006 (by telephone).

372 AFRC Transcript, June 28, 2005, at 24–25.

373 Seromba Transcript, Apr. 4, 2006, at 44–46.

374 CDF Transcript, Nov. 2, 2004, at 48.

375 Akayesu Judgement, note 32, at para. 32.

376 CDF Judgement, note 27, at para. 670.

to other, less well-known taboos as well as to magical and mystical happenings that are unfamiliar to Western court personnel. East Timorese defendant Carlos Soares proved how persuasive these beliefs can be when he killed a man because he believed that the man had used magic on his children.[377] Indeed, the vast majority of East Timorese survive by means of subsistence farming and believe that they must maintain excellent relations with their ancestors so as to ensure appropriate weather conditions, soil fertility, and the like.[378] Maintaining these relations requires East Timorese to perform certain rituals, maintain certain hierarchical social relationships, and adhere to certain taboos. If these practices are not followed, East Timorese believe, misfortune will result.[379] One of these taboos came to light in the Special Panels *Los Palos* case when one of the defendants was questioned about who had been on a bus during an ambush. After the defendant named seven people, the prosecutor asked whether an individual named Harasio, who subsequently had been killed, also had been on the bus. The defendant refused to give a clear answer to this question, and a frustrating exchange between the prosecutor and the defendant ensued during which the defendant appeared befuddled at best and uncooperative at worst. The defendant's reluctance to answer the prosecutor's question was finally explained by East Timorese defense counsel, who informed the court of a "cultural tradition where you cannot mention dead people."[380] The cause of this frustrating exchange was thus revealed, but Special Panels testimony is filled with frustrating – sometimes incoherent – exchanges, as detailed in Chapter 2, and one has wonder whether unarticulated taboos play a role in many of them.

Taboos, superstitions, and magic similarly pervade the lives of many Sierra Leoneans. Belief in spirits and witchcraft is prevalent,[381] and taboos and other ritualistic practices guide and constrain behavior in numerous aspects of Sierra

[377] Prosecutor v. Carlos Soares Carmona, Case No. 03C.G.2000, Judgement, at 3–5 (Apr. 25, 2001) [hereinafter Carmona Judgement].

[378] Hohe & Nixon, note 352, at 11.

[379] *Id.* "The idea that mystical sanctions are likely to be imposed by the ancestors or the spirits remains a very strong force" in East Timor. Mearns, note 327, at 44–45; *see also* Dionísio Babo-Soares, Nahe Biti: *The Philosophy and Process of Grassroots Reconciliation (and Justice) in East Timor,* 5 Asia Pacific J. Anthropology 15, 22 (2004).

[380] Los Palos Case Notes, July 18, 2001, at 33. For a discussion of the ways in which taboos also can complicate Aboriginal witness testimony, see Michael Walsh, *Interactional Styles in the Courtroom: An Example from Northern Australia, in* Language and the Law 217, 229–30 (John Gibbons ed., 1994).

[381] *See generally* Anthony J. Gittins, Mende Religion (1987). *See also* Rosalind Shaw, Memories of the Slave Trade: Ritual and the Historical Imagination in Sierra Leone 201–25 (2002); Mariane Ferme, The Underneath of Things: Violence, History, and the Everyday in Sierra Leone 175–78 (2001); Beryl L. Bellman, The Language of Secrecy: Symbols and Metaphors in Poro Ritual 56, 83–84 (1984); Rosalind Shaw, "Tok

Leonean life.[382] Not surprisingly, then, omens, superstitions, and taboos frequently appear in the transcripts of SCSL cases as well. Witness TF1-184, for instance, presented confusing testimony regarding allegations of witchcraft. The defendant's alleged desire for a chameleon's egg featured prominently in this account but in an incomprehensible way.[383] Witness TF1-064, for her part, testified that her mother went to greet someone but stopped after she hit her left foot. Nothing further was said then, but it later became clear that defense counsel misunderstood the witness's statement and believed that the person whom the witness's mother-in-law was greeting had stepped on the mother-in-law's foot. It was only then that the Sierra Leonean and Cameroonian judges explained that hitting one's left foot was considered a bad omen for a journey. As Cameroonian Judge Itoe explained: "It's generally the conception . . . in most African societies, if you are going somewhere and you hit your left leg, the immediate reflect is 'I'm not going, I may run into problems.'"[384] The same witness also testified that when she returned to her village, her aunt was afraid to come near her because her aunt assumed that the witness was a ghost.[385]

The SCSL's *CDF* case featured considerable testimony regarding magical powers that could be bestowed on fighters.[386] One former CDF battalion commander, for instance, testified with admiration about the Tamaboros, a "supernatural-powered people" who used "magical powers" to disappear so that "nobody can see them" and "no bullet can go through them."[387] Similarly, numerous former CDF combatants testified about Kamajor society initiation ceremonies, which were understood to protect initiates from bullets.[388] The

Af, Lef Af": *A Political Economy of Temne Techniques of Secrecy and Self, in* AFRICAN PHILOSOPHY AS CULTURAL INQUIRY 25, 43 (Ivan Karp & D.A. Masolo eds., 2000) [hereinafter Shaw, Tok Af]; Rosalind Shaw, *Cannibal Transformations: Colonialism and Commodification in the Sierra Leone Hinterland, in* MAGICAL INTERPRETATIONS, MATERIAL REALITIES: MODERNITY, WITCHCRAFT AND THE OCCULT IN POST-COLONIAL AFRICA 50, 62–65 (Henrietta L. Moore & Todd Sanders eds., 2001); Michael D. Jackson, *Structure and Event: Witchcraft Confession Among the Kuranko*, 10 J. ROYAL ANTHROPOL. INST. (MAN) 387 (1975).

382 SHAW, note 381, 170–200; FERME, note 381, at 184–86; GITTINS, note 381, at 137–55; C. Magbaily Fyle & Isabella Heroe, *Krio Traditional Beliefs*, 7 AFRICANA RESEARCH BULL. 3 (1977).

383 AFRC Transcript, Sept. 27, 2005, at 31–35.

384 RUF Transcript, July 19, 2004, at 77, 80.

385 *Id.* at 68. *See also* AFRC Transcript, July 14, 2005, at 56–57 (witness describing pains that Temne get at the end of every month).

386 Anthropologist Rosalind Shaw similarly describes belief in "medicine that will produce Darkness, thereby allowing them to see enemy soldiers before they themselves are seen." Shaw, Tok Af, note 381, at 36; *see also* Rosalind Shaw, *Robert Kaplan and "Juju Journalism" in Sierra Leone's Rebel War: The Primitivizing of an African Conflict, in* MAGIC AND MODERNITY: INTERFACES OF REVELATION AND CONCEALMENT 81, 87, 89 (Birgit Meyer & Peter Pels eds., 2003).

387 CDF Transcript, June 1, 2006, at 45–46.

388 CDF Transcript, Nov. 16, 2004, at 49–50, 56; CDF Transcript, May 18, 2006, at 69–70; CDF Transcript, May 25, 2006, at 7; CDF Transcript, May 23, 2006, at 22–23; CDF Transcript, June 1, 2006, at 56–57.

same CDF battalion commander, for instance, testified that when fighting became intense in a certain region, everyone sought immunization via the "mystical power" of the Kamajors, even women and children.[389] Likewise village elder M. T. Collier testified that people came "from far and wide" to be initiated. Collier reported that if you were initiated, then "even if you were shot at, the bullet cannot go through you.... Even if you are shot at with a bow, it cannot pierce you.... If somebody had a cutlass and he wanted to inflict an injury on you, no, he wouldn't be able to do that."[390] In similar vein, defense witness Mohamed Kineh Swaray testified that the Kamajors used no weapons to defend themselves during their attack on the SS camp, but rather relied on the powers conferred on them during the initiation process.[391]

Witness TF2-140, a former child soldier, recounted the requirements for initiation, mentioning in particular that only virgins could receive immunity because the magic would not work unless a soldier was "pure" and free from "contamination" from a woman.[392] To retain protection against bullets, witness TF2-140 reported, the soldier had to maintain his virginity, refrain from looting, and avoid certain foods.[393] Other witnesses testified that the protective powers of the immunization process would evaporate if a Kamajor touched a corpse,[394] whereas still other witnesses cited additional rules, which prohibited urinating or defecating in a graveyard, sitting on a chair after a woman experiencing her menstrual period had sat on it, and stepping on a banana peel.[395] The witnesses who testified as to the initiations wholeheartedly believed in their efficacy.[396] Indeed, *CDF* defendant Sam Hinga Norman described the immunization as functioning like a "iron shield" and was so sure of its protective powers that he offered to stage a demonstration for the SCSL judges during which he would "catch the gunshot."[397]

[389] CDF Transcript, June 1, 2006, at 56–57.

[390] CDF Transcript, Feb. 16, 2006, at 66–67. Prosecution witness Albert Nallo testified that he "joined the society as a Kamajor fighter for the supernatural powers that the Kamajors had." CDF Transcript, Mar. 14, 2004, at 66.

[391] CDF Transcript, May 25, 2006, at 104.

[392] CDF Transcript, Sept. 14, 2004, at 131–32. According to this witness, any deaths among the CDF soldiers resulted from those soldiers breaking this rule. *Id. See also id.* at 161.

[393] CDF Transcript, Sept. 14, 2004, at 161–62. Witness TF2-021 reported that initiated Kamajors could not eat nut oil or see the peel of a banana. CDF Transcript, Nov. 3, 2004, at 50.

[394] Alison Thompson, U.C. Berkeley War Crimes Studies Center, Special Court Monitoring Program, Update No. 70, Feb. 24, 2006, at 6 n.5; CDF Transcript, Feb. 23, 2006, at 66.

[395] CDF Transcript, March 11, 2005, at 49.

[396] *See, e.g.*, CDF Transcript, Sept. 14, 2004, at 163; CDF Transcript, June 6, 2005, at 38–39.

[397] CDF Transcript, Jan. 27, 2006, at 46. The Trial Chamber declined Norman's offer. In a similar vein, a Kamajor soldier offered journalist Jeffrey Goldberg the opportunity to wear the Kamajor's war vest "which made him impervious to bullets." The Kamajor would then fire bullets from an AK-47 into the journalist's chest. When the journalist declined, the Kamajor

Because the taboos and mystical beliefs that I have just described were discussed openly, they likely impaired fact-finding very little, even if they did lengthen proceedings as certain concepts had to be explained to Western court personnel who were unfamiliar with them. In a similar example from the ICTR, numerous Rwandan witnesses refused to identify a defendant by pointing at him, asserting that pointing is prohibited in Rwandan culture. That taboo, like those described in the preceding paragraphs, posed no fact-finding impediment because the witnesses were easily able to identify defendants by such other means as describing their location in the courtroom, touching them, or describing their dress.[398]

Other cultural issues have a greater propensity to impair fact-finding, however. The threat of mystical sanctions forms a central aspect of the East Timorese understanding of crime and its appropriate punishment,[399] and it consequently has had a significant effect on proceedings at the Special Panels. East Timorese view crimes and other transgressions of the social order as disruptions of the cosmic flow of values. Because crime creates an imbalance of values, the appropriate response to crime must aim to restore that balance, which will in turn reinforce the sociocosmic order.[400] Such a restoration requires reconciliation between affected individuals and their communities; and, to achieve that reconciliation, offenders are typically required to acknowledge their wrongdoing publicly, to apologize, and to obtain the victim's forgiveness.[401] A successful reconciliation signifies that the conflict has been resolved and that both sides are again engaged in a peaceful relationship; if reconciliation fails to occur, by contrast, East Timorese believe that the social order will remain imbalanced and that the entire community will be subject to mystical sanctions.

became "dangerously upset." Jeffrey Goldberg, *A Continent's Chaos: Why do Americans Find it Intolerable in Europe but Inevitable in Africa?*, N.Y. TIMES MAG., May 21, 2000, at 13–14.

[398] The contours of the prohibition on pointing was subject to some dispute among witnesses. Some witnesses maintained that it is considered improper to point at someone for whom one has respect. Semanza Transcript, Nov. 27, 2001, at 65. Other witnesses suggested that the prohibition applies only to girls and women, Semanza Transcript, Nov. 26, 2001, at 10; Semanza Transcript, Nov. 12, 2001, at 16, while still others stated simply that pointing is prohibited, Semanza Transcript, Oct. 8, 2001, at 112–13; Semanza Transcript, Oct. 4, 2001, at 42; Semanza Transcript, Mar. 7, 2001, at 90–91. In later cases, witnesses were no longer asked to point at defendants but rather were asked to describe their dress. *See, e.g.*, Ndindabahizi Transcript, Sept. 1, 2003, at 56; Ndindabahizi Transcript, Sept. 16, 2003, at 8.

[399] Indeed, "[a]ll socio-cultural aspects of 'traditional' society are interdependent. Any one aspect, such as law, kinship or the belief system cannot be extracted from the entire socio-cosmic system without taking it out of context." Hohe & Nixon, note 352, at 12.

[400] *Id.* at 18.

[401] *UNDP Report on the Community Reconciliation Process*, note 326, at 26–27; *see also* Babo-Soares, note 379, at 15–16.

Special Panels defendants wanted to return to their original communities after suffering whatever punishment the Special Panels chose to mete out, but they knew that they would not be welcomed back unless they had reconciled with their victims. As a consequence of their desire for reconciliation, virtually all Special Panels defendants admitted their wrongdoing immediately upon apprehension.[402] Most of the Special Panels early defendants did not formally plead guilty; sometimes their admissions failed to precisely match the charges in the indictments, and sometimes they maintained that they had been forced – or at least ordered – to commit the crimes.[403] However, the defendant's admissions did vastly simplify the prosecution's task; and, as time wore on, more and more Special Panels defendants did formally plead guilty. By the time the Special Panels proceedings ended, more than 50 percent of its defendants had pled guilty,[404] a far higher guilty plea rate than at the other international tribunals.

A cultural proclivity to acknowledge wrongdoing may be laudable, if the acknowledgment is informed and accurate, but Special Panels confessions were frequently neither. Virtually all of the Special Panels defendants were illiterate farmers, who were largely unaware of the consequences of their confessions or of the guilty pleas that frequently followed them. The guilty plea colloquies that I reproduce in Chapter 2 highlight this point. Worse still, the defendants sometimes confessed to more wrongdoing than they were responsible for. In the *Francisco Pereirra* case, for instance, the defendant confessed to having killed the victim. Luckily, the case went to trial because two eyewitnesses *for the prosecution* maintained that, although the defendant did cut the victim with his sword, the victim died only after another assailant had shot him in the head. In confessing to the crime, however, the defendant never even mentioned

[402] *See, e.g.*, Prosecutor v. Julio Fernandez, Case No. 02 C.G.2000, Judgement, at 4 (Mar. 1, 2000); Carmona Judgement, note 377, at 3–4; Prosecutor v. Gonçalves Leto Bere, Case No. 10/2000, Judgement at 5 (May 15, 2001) [hereinafter Gonçalves Leto Bere Judgement]; Prosecutor v. Carlos Soares, Case No. 12/2000, Judgement, at 4 (May 31, 2001) [hereinafter Carlos Soares Judgement]; Prosecutor v. Joseph Leki, Case No. 5/2000, Judgement, at 2 (June 11, 2001) [hereinafter Joseph Leki Judgement]; Prosecutor v. Jose Valente, Case No. 3/2001, Judgement, at 2 (June 19, 2001) [hereinafter Valente Judgement]; Prosecutor v. Agustinho da Costa, Case No. 07/2000, Judgement, at 8 (Oct. 11, 2001).

[403] *See, e.g.*, Valente Judgement, note 402, at 2; Los Palos Case Notes, Sept. 9, 2001, at 4–6; Suzannah Linton & Caitlin Reiger, *The Evolving Jurisprudence and Practice of East Timor's Special Panels for Serious Crimes on Admissions of Guilt, Duress and Superior Orders*, 4 Y.B. INT'L HUM. L. 1, 20 (2001). In the *Gaspar Leki* case, for instance, the defendant pled guilty to murder because he shot and killed a man who had been hiding in the bushes. The Panel initially accepted the guilty plea, and only as a result of further questioning did it learn that, although the defendant had been ordered to shoot anything that moved, he believed that he was shooting a wild pig in the bush. Since the element of deliberate intent to commit murder was called into question, the Panel reversed its decision to accept the guilty plea and proceeded to trial. *Id.* at 17–18.

[404] Telephone interview with Nicholas Koumjian, deputy prosecutor for serious crimes, Special Panels for Serious Crimes (July 29, 2004).

the other assailant or the gunshot.[405] Some of the distortions described above might have been ameliorated if the Special Panels had had a sufficient number of adequately trained defense counsel, but they did not. Consequently, once a defendant did make an incriminating statement, a conviction was virtually assured.

Other features of the cultures in question also have the potential to significantly impair fact-finding. For instance, because Rwandans, Sierra Leoneans, and East Timorese live in an oral tradition, they frequently report events that were recounted to them as though they personally saw them. The ICTR heard expert testimony on this point,[406] and it has arisen repeatedly in all three tribunals. Although, if asked to do so, the witnesses can distinguish between what they saw "with their own eyes" and what they were told, the distinction does not hold the significance for them that Westerners place on it. That is, although Westerners would substantially discount a report that had merely been recounted to a witness, most international witnesses consider that if they were told of the event by someone who personally witnessed it or by someone who is in a position of authority, then that is as good as having seen it themselves. As *Kamuhanda* witness GPC informed counsel, "traditionally in Rwanda we can know what is happening somewhere without going there." He explained that "[w]e come to know because in Rwanda when people witness something, they speak of it to other people, helping the other people to inform themselves. . . . So everyone knows about events where they were not present."[407] Or, as the ICTR's *Musema* Trial Chamber put it: Rwandans adhere to a "tradition that the perceived knowledge of one becomes the knowledge of all."[408] The following excerpt from the ICTR's *Ndindabahizi* case shows a witness's impatience with a defense counsel who is seeking to draw a distinction between what one personally sees and what one hears from another:

DEFENSE COUNSEL: Were you a direct witness of the death of Mr. Charles Munyanhindi?

WITNESS CGB: Vuguziga himself came to brag about it and, furthermore, that is why he is presently in detention.

DEFENSE COUNSEL: Were you an eyewitness? Did you see, with your very own eyes, Vuguziga strike Charles Munyanhindi?

WITNESS CGB: I have told you that Vuguziga himself was boasting about having killed him and today he has confessed to having killed him.

[405] Perreira Judgement, note 108, at 13–16.
[406] Akayesu Judgement, note 32, at para. 155.
[407] Kamuhanda Transcript, Jan. 22, 2003, at 41.
[408] Musema Judgement, note 112, at para. 103.

MR. PRESIDENT: But all we are interested in now is to find out whether you saw the event, and that implies either a yes or no answer.

WITNESS CGB: I did not see it with my own eyes, but I know that he is the one who killed him.

Defense counsel subsequently asked the witness: "Would it be correct to say, Mr. Witness, that when you hear mention being made of an incident, that you imagine yourself to have been an eyewitness of that incident, generally speaking?" The witness responded: "When someone asserts that that is a true fact, you yourself will take it to be the truth."[409]

Tribunal transcripts contain numerous examples of this phenomenon.[410] ICTR witness GAA, for instance, testified that he saw the defendant Kamuhanda arrive at the Gikomero massacre site in his vehicle, get out of his vehicle, and then later get back into his vehicle and drive away.[411] The prosecution further asked GAA to tell the Court "how many people *you saw* shot that day by the Hutus." GAA responded that "an approximate number would be 3000 persons." The prosecution then asked "[h]ow long did the shooting go on for? How long did you *hear or see* it continue?" GAA responded "[t]he shooting went on for between four to five hours."[412] During cross-examination, however, the witness revealed that he had run away as soon as the first shots were fired. Consequently, when defense counsel asked him how he was able to know that the shooting had continued for four to five hours, he had to acknowledge that "some of my family members... told me that the shooting went on for the amount of time that I have mentioned." Likewise, he admitted that he had not actually seen the three thousand people killed but learned it only months later when he returned from exile and prepared a report in his capacity as a local government official.[413] Finally, GAA also had described the event in his written statement, in which he asserted that "Kamuhanda... headed for his native village in his pick-up truck." When asked how GAA was able to tell the direction in which Kamuhanda had traveled when GAA had already left the scene, GAA responded that others had told him.[414]

[409] Ndindabahizi Transcript, Sept. 22, 2003, at 19–20. *See also* Seromba Transcript, Nov. 8, 2005, at 24–25 (witness expressing impatience with counsel's efforts to ascertain whether the witness personally saw the defendant).

[410] In addition to the examples appearing in the text, see Bagilishema Judgement, note 122, at paras. 611, 693; CDF Transcript, June 15, 2004, at 36; AFRC Transcript, July 20, 2005, at 19–20; AFRC Transcript, July 21, 2005, at 51.

[411] Kamuhanda Transcript, Sept. 19, 2001, at 111–15.

[412] *Id.* at 118.

[413] Kamuhanda Transcript, Sept. 20, 2001, at 33–37.

[414] *Id.* at 41–42.

Although one SCSL investigator testified that she always asked potential witnesses how they came to know the events that they were recounting so as to ascertain "whether or not the witness had actually seen what they were talking about with their own eyes or whether somebody else had told them,"[415] a review of SCSL and ICTR transcripts makes clear that not every investigator adheres to that sensible practice.[416] Witness TF2-016, for instance, testified that he was present when two people were killed. Only when presented with an earlier, inconsistent statement did the witness acknowledge that he was not in fact present when the individuals were killed but arrived at the scene only later.[417] And, as the following exchange from the Special Panels' *Los Palos* case shows, even after repeated questioning, it can remain unclear whether or not the witness personally witnessed an event or merely was told about it:

PROSECUTOR: Who did you see stabbing [Antonio]?
WITNESS 9: Carolino
PROSECUTOR: Was he by himself?
WITNESS 9: He was alone there.
PROSECUTOR: Where was Antonio then?
WITNESS 9: His wife came and hugged me and said "your brother is dead, he was stabbed by Carolino," that's how I know.
PROSECUTOR: Was he dead?
WITNESS 9: He was stabbed and bleeding but not dead.
PROSECUTOR: Did you see with your eyes him being stabbed?
WITNESS 9: I truly saw it.
PROSECUTOR: Where was Antonio when being stabbed?
WITNESS 9: His house was up on a hill and they stabbed him there, his wife ran and reported to me because I was village chief.
PROSECUTOR: Who were they?
WITNESS 9: I said they because at the time there were a lot of people, maybe 20 people.
PROSECUTOR: Did you recognize them?
WITNESS 9: Yes, but none of them are here now.
PROSECUTOR: What did Carolino use to stab?
WITNESS 9: A bayonette from the command.

[415] CDF Transcript, Mar. 2, 2005, at 9.
[416] Taylor Transcript, May 6, 2008, at 9078, 9086–87; RUF Transcript, Apr. 15, 2005, at 35–36; RUF Transcript, Nov. 24, 2005, at 51–52; CDF Transcript, Feb. 15, 2005, at 26–27; CDF Transcript, Sept. 9, 2004, at 99–103; CDF Transcript, Mar. 8, 2005, at 45; AFRC Transcript, July 5, 2005, at 50–51; Lolotoe Case Notes, Mar. 18, 2003, at 6–7, 16–17; Karera Transcript, Jan. 9, 2006, at 9, 13–14, 17, 36–37; Muhimana Transcript, Apr. 6, 2004, at 15; Gacumbitsi Transcript, Aug. 4, 2003, at 18; Ndindabahizi Transcript, Sept. 22, 2003, at 10–11, 30–31.
[417] CDF Transcript, Mar. 1, 2005, at 49–54.

PROSECUTOR: How far away were you when he got stabbed?
WITNESS 9: From here to there.
PROSECUTOR: 30 meters?
WITNESS 9: 30 to 50 meters.
PROSECUTOR: And she said "your brother is dead?"
WITNESS 9: Yes.
PROSECUTOR: So he had already been stabbed when she said that to you?
WITNESS 9: Yes, and she came and reported it.
PROSECUTOR: But where were you?
WITNESS 9: On my way back from Los Palos.
PROSECUTOR: So how could you see him being stabbed?
WITNESS 9: His wife embraced me and cried.
PROSECUTOR: So, did you see him stabbed or were you told by his wife?
WITNESS 9: I didn't see it at first, but his wife came and I saw him bleeding.
PROSECUTOR: Thank you.[418]

Some tribunal counsel have sought to ameliorate the distortive effect of witnesses' failure to distinguish between events witnessed and events recounted by specifically asking witnesses whether they had witnessed the events with "their own eyes."[419] We can easily imagine that such questions were not always asked, however, and consequently judges may have placed unwarranted weight on a witness's testimony. Moreover, the propensity of witnesses to blur what they saw with what they only heard about also can impair a Trial Chamber's ability to assess the significance of witness inconsistencies. It is common, for instance, that a witness will testify to seeing an event, although the previous written statement will report only that the witness heard about it, or vice versa. Although such an inconsistency might discredit a witness's testimony in other courtrooms, international tribunals typically ignore it. The *Ndindabahizi* Trial Chamber, for instance, dismissed concerns about this sort of discrepancy, saying: "Rwandans do not always express clearly the difference between what they have seen with their own eyes and what they have heard."[420] The *Musema*

[418] Los Palos Case Notes, Aug. 16, 2001, at 168–69.

[419] *See, e.g.*, Karemera Transcript, Dec. 3, 2003, at 16; Karemera Transcript, Dec. 8, 2003, at 53; Lolotoe Case Notes, Feb. 3, 2003, at 8. Sometimes counsel asks if the witness heard something with his own ears. Lolotoe Case Notes, Nov. 5, 2002, at 16; Los Palos Case Notes, Aug. 14, 2001, at 160; Los Palos Case Notes, Aug. 16, 2001, at 169; Los Palos Case Notes, Aug. 23, 2001, at 198.

Concern about this problem led the ICTY to include a provision in its witness statement form which requires witnesses to attest: "I understand that I am requested to describe things I know because I observed them and I will clearly indicate in my statement facts I learned from others." *See, e.g.*, Prosecutor v. Milošević, Case No. IT-02–54-T, Prosecution Exhibit 212a.

[420] Ndindabahizi Judgement, note 56, at para. 216.

Trial Chamber likewise ignored similar discrepancies: Witness I had testified about the rape and killing of one Annunciata Mujawayezu. Whereas the witness had written in her statement that Musema had undressed Mujawayezu, the witness testified that she saw nothing of the kind. Whereas the witness reported in her statement that Mujawayezu's hands, ears, and breast were cut off and given to her hungry five-year-old son to eat, the witness testified that only Mujawayezu's breast was cut off. Finally, the witness's statement reported that some men in the crowd had ordered some Twas to rape Mujawayezu, but she testified that it was Musema who ordered the Twas to rape Mujawayezu. Witness I explained these inconsistencies by invoking the cultural norm just described. When she wrote her statement, the witness explained, she wrote down everything she knew, both through her own witnessing and through that of others.[421] The Trial Chamber accepted the witness's explanation,[422] and although it may have been appropriate to do so, there is little way to tell.

A final arena in which cultural norms can impede communication between international witnesses and their Western listeners relates to patterns of speech and modes of communication. As noted in Chapter 2, international witnesses frequently fail to answer questions in the clear and direct way that Western court personnel are expecting. Sometimes witness answers fail to match the questions, and sometimes witness testimony veers off to seemingly irrelevant topics. A frustrated Special Panels prosecutor summarized the problem when he complained to the bench: "Your Honor, this witness does not want to answer questions, he just wants to tell a story."[423] This tendency to just "tell a story" may be culturally based.

Anthropologist James Gee reports that "oral-strategy narratives," which are prevalent in Sierra Leone, "typically involve a series of associated segments that may seem anecdotal in character, with focus on time, person, or place often shifting across segments, and with major parts of the narrative having to be inferred by the listener. To non-initiates, the stories may give the impression of 'having no beginning, no middle, no end – thus no point.'"[424] Anthropologist Michael Jackson similarly asserts that in societies "where cyclical models of both human life and social time predominate," the idea that both stories and lives consist in "sequences of events aligned along a continuum from a beginning, through a middle, toward an end . . . may lose its analytical usefulness."[425]

[421] Musema Judgement, note 112, at paras. 811–813.
[422] *Id.* at para. 823.
[423] Lolotoe Case Notes, March 24, 2003, at 7–8.
[424] James Paul Gee, *The Narrativization of Experience in the Oral Style*, 167 J. Educ. 9, 13 (1985).
[425] Michael Jackson, The politics of Storytelling: Violence, Transgression and Intersubjectivity 31 (2002).

Sierra Leoneans also value secrecy, as is discussed in Chapter 5, and consequently they use a variety of indirect communication forms that facilitate the concealment of information. These include parables, gnomic expressions, exaggerated descriptions, allegorical accounts, and ritual metaphors. Anthropologist Mariane Ferme has observed that Sierra Leoneans consider "a person who communicates directly what she or he desires or thinks . . . to be an idiot or no better than a child."[426] Kelsall, indeed, shows how certain exchanges in the *CDF* case – of the sort that I described in Chapter 2 – reflect these indirect communications forms.[427]

Research suggests that Rwandans employ similarly indirect modes of communication, and the ICTR has even received expert witness testimony on the subject. Dr. Mathias Ruzindana testified in the *Akayesu* case that "it is a particular feature of the Rwandan culture that people are not always direct in answering questions, especially if the question is delicate." Consequently, answers to delicate questions often must be "decoded" to be understood correctly. The *Akayesu* Trial Chamber observed this phenomenon when witnesses were asked the ordinary meaning of the term *Inyenzi*. According to the Trial Chamber, witnesses were reluctant or unwilling to state that the word meant cockroach, although it became clear to the Chamber during the course of the proceedings that any Rwandan would know the ordinary meaning of the word.[428]

It is vital for Trial Chambers to receive the sort of information provided by Dr. Ruzindana so that they do not inappropriately assess the credibility of non-Western witnesses by Western cultural norms. A Western witness who provides indirect, circuitous answers may be judged either to lack confidence in her perceptions or even to be lying. But that is because ordinary Western speech patterns tend to be relatively direct. If the ordinary speech patterns for those in the witness's group feature indirectness and circularity, then the witness's indirect answers should not be held against her. The problem is that most trial judges are not sufficiently familiar with the cultures in question to know what, if any, speech signals or demeanor cues should legitimately give rise to concern. Admittedly, recent empirical research suggests that fact finders have only limited ability to detect lying through the observation of demeanor,[429] but whatever ability they do possess is sharply diminished when

[426] FERME, note 381, at 6–7.

[427] KELSALL, note 142, at 180-84.

[428] Akayesu Judgement, note 32, at para. 156.

[429] Olin Guy Wellborn III, *Demeanor*, 76 CORNELL L. REV. 1075, 1075, 1078–91 (1991); *see also* Paul Ekman & Maureen O'Sullivan, *Who Can Catch a Liar?*, 46 AM. PSYCHOLOGIST 913 (1991); Joseph W. Rand, *The Demeanor Gap: Race, Lie Detection, and the Jury*, 33 CONN. L. REV. 1, 1–4,

they are evaluating a witness whose speech and demeanor norms differ sharply from those of the fact finder.

3.D. EDUCATION, INTERPRETATION, AND CULTURE: INNOCENT EXPLANATIONS OR CONCEALMENT TECHNIQUES?

The previous sections have considered three of the most likely explanations for the testimonial deficiencies described in Chapter 2. Lack of education stands as the most prominent. There is no question that international witnesses fail to answer many of the questions posed to them because they simply do not know the answers. They do not know how to measure, they cannot read a map, and they pay no attention to Western-style dates. There is likewise no question that interpretation distorts communication at the international tribunals. Although this distortion can be reduced if international tribunals devote more resources to interpretation, it cannot be eliminated. The cultural divergences between international witnesses and their Western interlocutors stand as a final, compelling explanation for many of the international tribunals' communication difficulties. Taboos, mystical beliefs, and other unfamiliar cultural practices impede communication between witnesses and court personnel, and divergent modes of speech make understanding only harder to achieve.

In many cases, it is difficult, if not impossible, to determine which of the above three explanations is muddying the waters at any given time. A witness's failure to provide a clear and direct response to a question might result from the witness's indirect speech pattern, it might reflect a cultural reluctance to speak publicly about the violence, or it might instead reflect an interpretation error in which counsel asked one question and the witness answered another. A witness's failure to answer a specific question might stem from the witness's ignorance about the matter in question or it might reflect a taboo discouraging discussion of the matter. Although being able to pinpoint the precise cause of the communication difficulty may be useful in some instances, typically it does not matter a great deal which of the above three explanations is at work because none of them call into question the witness's credibility.

But the very fact that questioning at the international tribunals is so frequently bedeviled by educational deficits, interpretation errors, and cultural

14 (2000). *But see* Mark A. deTurck & Gerald R Miller, *Training Observers to Detect Deception: Effects of Self-Monitoring and Rehearsal*, 16 HUM. COMM. Q. 420 (1990) (finding that training can improve a person's ability to detect deception).

divergences means that witnesses can invoke these communication impediments even when they are not at play as a means of concealing lying, inconsistencies, or other weaknesses in witness testimony. International witnesses who are falsely accusing a defendant, for instance, may find it most profitable to provide a vague account that is devoid of meaningful details. Dating events permits a defendant to contradict the witness's testimony, as *Cyangugu* witnesses LAI and LAP learned, so it may prove a safer bet for the witness to claim not to know the relevant dates. Making distance and numerical estimates can likewise leave a witness vulnerable to contradiction, so they too are better left unstated. Even feigned ignorance about adversarial procedures can benefit a perjuring witness. Contrived indignation about the tenor of a cross-examination may lead counsel to abandon a line of questioning, and even if the questioning persists, the witness will at least have bought some time to consider a response. Some defense counsel go so far as to accuse witnesses of feigning illness whenever they are vigorously cross-examined.[430]

It is not only lack of education that witnesses can invoke to conceal misleading or perjurious testimony but also cultural practices. That is, witnesses can point to taboos, mystical beliefs, or other cultural tendencies that are unfamiliar to Westerners as a concealment mechanism. For instance, as discussed above, international witnesses often conceive of family in broader terms than most Westerners do, but it is difficult to know whether any particular invocation of that broad conception is genuine. *Niyitegeka* witness GGV, for instance, testified that the defendant and the defendant's brother named Elam once visited the witness's house. Defense counsel subsequently confronted the witness with the fact that the defendant had no brothers named Elam. The prosecution, on redirect, then suggested to the witness that "in African culture, and certainly in East African culture, the term brother is used to refer not only to the other children of one's parents, but might also be used to refer to other members or the children of one's uncles or cousins." The witness eagerly assented and stated that he had no idea whether the defendant and Elam had the same parents; all he knew was they had a sufficiently close relationship that Elam referred to the defendant as his "brother."[431] In a similar vein, witness TF2-096 invoked the gender discrimination that is so prevalent in Sierra Leone to explain why she had not reported to the authorities a murder that she had witnessed. She said: "No, I wouldn't be able to make that complaint, because I am a

[430] Interview with Howard Morrison, former ICTY and ICTR defense counsel, May 22, 2006 (by telephone).

[431] Niyitegeka Transcript, Aug. 28, 2002, at 78–84.

woman."[432] The presiding judge's remarks directly after the witness's statement made clear that he found her explanation persuasive.[433]

Cultural invocations are very common and very difficult to evaluate. For instance, at the ICTR, three *Ndindabahizi* witnesses invoked culture to withstand defense questioning about their identification of the defendant. Although Ndindabahizi did not know any of the witnesses, the three witnesses had maintained that they had seen him on several occasions before the massacres. Witnesses CTK and CGC were asked whether they had ever spoken to Ndindabahizi. Witness CTK replied that she could not have done so because she was not in his age group.[434] Witness CGC, who had testified that he was about fourteen or fifteen years old when he had seen Ndindabahizi, responded similarly: "Do you think there could be any conversation between a young man, a child, and somebody the standing – of that standing?"[435] And when witness CGN was asked if Ndindabahizi had ever spoken to him, the witness appeared shocked by the suggestion: "Speak to me?" the witness exclaimed. "We were not of the same social standing. He is somebody who attended university. And what interests would he have to speak to a farmer? . . . When you don't belong to the same social class you do not know each other."[436]

In an even more worrisome example, two other *Ndindabahizi* witnesses – CGV and CGM – testified respectively about Ndindabahizi's presence and participation in attacks that occurred on Gitwa Hill and at a roadblock. Both witnesses had previously testified in genocide trials in Rwanda about the same events but had failed to mention Ndindabahizi's presence in their earlier testimony. When defense counsel asked why they failed to note the presence and active involvement of a person as important as a former government minister, the witnesses invoked culture. Witness CGM asserted:

> I have a reason. You know when somebody has fled and you don't know where he is, you cannot talk about him when you cannot see him. You only talk about people you see. Why talk about people you cannot see when you don't know where those people are? And why will I testify against the Accused when he is not there? I brought charges against only people I could see and whose location I knew.

When defense counsel pressed the witness, asking, "[d]id you not think that it was necessary to mention the presence of a former minister at the roadblock, a minister who besides made anti-Tutsi statements and distributed weapons?"

432 CDF Transcript, Nov. 8, 2004, at 74.
433 *Id.*
434 Ndindabahizi Transcript, Sept. 3, 2003, at 47.
435 Ndindabahizi Transcript, Sept. 29, 2003, at 44–45.
436 Ndindabahizi Transcript, Sept. 8, 2003, at 24.

the witness asserted additionally that Rwandan law prohibits a person from accusing someone who is not present.[437] Witness CGV responded similarly to defense questioning: "Do you think I will testify against somebody that I cannot see? I can't do that. If I had seen him, I would have testified against him, because he killed members of my family. I could not accuse him, because he was not there.... You cannot bring a complaint against someone who is not present."[438]

The witnesses' explanations seemed to invoke both cultural and legal norms, although the legal aspects of their explanations were not responsive to the defense counsel's questions because counsel did not ask why the witnesses failed to bring charges against the defendant but only why they failed even to mention the involvement of such a high-ranking person when describing the events to the Rwandan court. Indeed, in a Western court, the witnesses' failure to mention the defendant during their earlier testimony would call into question their subsequent accusations, but at the ICTR the invocation of the cultural norm seemed to eliminate any damage that otherwise might have been done to their credibility. The Trial Chamber expressly accepted the witnesses' explanation for failing to mention Ndindabahizi in their earlier testimony.[439] Although that explanation may have been accurate, the witnesses could well have fabricated the norms they invoked; the Trial Chamber certainly gave no indication that it researched the matter.

Finally, consider the numerous examples of frustrating exchanges and unresponsive responses that are cited and described in Chapter 2. Although these may reflect a cultural proclivity toward circuitous answers and generally indirect speech, they may also reflect a witness's desire to evade the question at hand or at least to buy some time to consider the answer that witness wishes to give. It certainly seems to be the case that witnesses have more difficulty understanding questions that challenge their testimony or that highlight their potentially self-interested motivations.[440] For instance, questions involving witnesses' dealings with the prosecution – particularly the financial support they receive as a result of being called as witnesses – are especially likely to be the subject of lengthy and confused exchanges,[441] as are questions probing inconsistencies in the

[437] Ndindabahizi Transcript, Sept. 15, 2003, at 29–30.

[438] Ndindabahizi Transcript, Sept. 16, 2003, at 16.

[439] Ndindabahizi Judgement, note 56, at paras. 123, 253. The Trial Chamber declined to credit witness CGV's testimony on other grounds, finding that it was uncorroborated, internally inconsistent, and contradicted by the testimony of other witnesses. *Id.* at para. 128.

[440] Kamuhanda Transcript, Jan. 28, 2002, at 104–05; RUF Transcript, Oct. 5, 2004, at 184–85; RUF Transcript, Oct. 7, 2004, at 39–41.

[441] *See, e.g.*, Taylor Transcript, Jan. 9, 2008, at 780–89; RUF Transcript, July 15, 2004, at 9–13; RUF Transcript, July 13, 2004, at 11–12; AFRC Transcript, July 25, 2005, at 33–40; Los Palos Case Notes, Sept. 26, 2001, at 284. Some witnesses even complain of feeling ill when cross-examined

witness's account.[442] Indeed, more than one defense counsel has observed that witnesses sail through direct examination but on cross-examination become "non-understanding, non-educated."[443] A particularly blatant example of this phenomenon can be found in General Tarnue's testimony in the SCSL's *RUF* case. Tarnue was college educated,[444] so we might have expected him to be able to answer basic time, date, and distance questions and to provide the court with a coherent and detailed account of events. On direct examination, he did. General Tarnue was comfortable and competent in relating his military training experience in the United States and Liberia,[445] his meeting with Charles Taylor in Gbarnga,[446] and his training of civilians, adults, and children while under Charles Taylor's command.[447] However, on cross-examination, General Tarnue suddenly seemed perplexed by simple, straightforward questions and either gave nonresponsive answers[448] or simply delayed responding by restating the question that counsel had posed.[449]

Even Special Panels judges have suggested that witnesses might be seeking to exploit their lack of education. As the *Tacaqui* Panel put it:

> What's more, it should be noted that a pattern of behavior was noticed in many witnesses: the paucity of their culture was used by them as a defense. In other words, when a contradiction emerged, the excuse of the limited capacity to understand or remember was readily used by the same interviewed

on such topics. *See* Taylor Transcript, Sept. 10, 2008, at 15961–62; Taylor Transcript, Sept. 11, 2008, at 15968.

442 *See, e.g.*, Nyiramasuhuko Transcript, Mar. 20, 2003, at 2; Ntakirutimana Transcript, Sept. 20, 2001, at 78–81; Ntakirutimana Transcript, Sept. 24, 2001, at 111–13; AFRC Transcript, Mar. 7, 2005, at 99–100; AFRC Transcript, Mar. 8, 2005, at 109–19; AFRC Transcript, Apr. 11, 2005, at 80–86; AFRC Transcript, Apr. 18, 2005, at 38–43, 60–64; AFRC Transcript, July 21, 2005, at 43–47; CDF Transcript, Nov. 9, 2004, at 91–93; RUF Transcript, July 21, 2004, at 18–19; RUF Transcript, July 27, 2004, at 24–31; RUF Transcript, Oct. 7, 2004, at 154–62; RUF Transcript, Oct. 11, 2004, at 46–48; Taylor Transcript, Sept. 1, 2008, at 15016–19, 15026–29. *Taylor* witness TF1-585 complained of feeling ill when questioned about inconsistencies between her statement and subsequent testimony. *See* Taylor Transcript, Sept. 11, 2008, at 15976–79.

443 CDF Transcript, Sept. 9, 2004, at 79. Defense counsel Charles Margai, who is himself Sierra Leonean, accused a witness of being more intelligent than he wanted the court to believe. CDF Transcript, June 17, 2004, at 48–49. *See also ICTR/Zigiranyirazo* – Bagaragaza *Witness Gives the Defence a Hard Time*, Hirondelle News Agency, June 15, 2006 (observing that although, on direct examination, the witness gave detailed testimony, on cross-examination, he eluded defense counsel's questions and "said as little as possible").

444 RUF Transcript, Oct. 4, 2004, at 45.

445 *Id.* at 49–51.

446 *Id.* at 56–61.

447 *Id.* at 62–64. When the witness was asked whom he was training, the witness provided comprehensive details regarding the "Small Boys Unit" and the "Yellow Jackets," various aspects of the training program, and his frequent interactions with Charles Taylor.

448 RUF Transcript, Oct. 5, 2004, at 193.

449 *Id.* at 192.

> to justify even the most macroscopic of contradictions. Facing a request for clarification, or being asked which were the correct of two versions, the answer was often: "I don't know: we are simple people; we didn't go to school; we are illiterate; we are not like big people; we are son of God, what we know we say, what we don't know, we don't say." Sometimes, when the contradiction was made clear to the witness and he was asked why, for example, he hadn't added the name of the suspect to the list of aggressors, at the time of the investigation, the reply was: "I made the name, if they wrote it or not, I don't know." The same pattern of behaviour was repeated for several times, in different testimonies and appeared to be a pattern of formulaic excuse, as an easy escape from the pressure of the examination.[450]

3.E. SUMMARY

This chapter has canvassed a series of possible explanations for the testimonial deficiencies described in Chapter 2. There is no question that educational, linguistic, and cultural factors play a role in a substantial proportion of the problems I identify. But it is equally true that those same factors may be plausibly invoked to conceal evasiveness, inconsistencies, or outright perjury. Whether the testimonial problems are caused by "innocent" educational, linguistic, and cultural factors or rather signify unreliable or even perjurious testimony cannot be conclusively known in most cases, and that fact underlies many of the concerns I raise about international criminal fact-finding in subsequent chapters. The topic of the next chapter – inconsistencies between witnesses' pretrial statements and their testimony – exemplifies this uncertainty. Inconsistencies are probably the most prevalent testimonial problem at the international tribunals and perhaps the most worrisome, for although inconsistencies are particularly easy to explain by means of the "innocent" explanations canvassed in this chapter, they are also particularly likely to reflect perjury.

[450] Tacaqui Judgement, note 36, at 5.

4

Of Inconsistencies and Their Explanations

Educational deficiencies, cultural divergences, and translation errors stand as significant fact-finding impediments that certainly account for many of the confused exchanges and nonresponsive responses that pervade international criminal trials. They also stand to explain another key problem bedeviling testimony at the international tribunals: inconsistencies. Investigators interview witnesses before they come to court, and they draft written statements purporting to contain the information that the witnesses conveyed to them. The problem is that a substantial proportion of witnesses testify inconsistently with their written statements or with their in-court testimony in previous cases. Although some of these inconsistencies are trivial, many are not. Indeed, this section will provide a great many examples in the text and considerably more in the footnotes to give a sense of just how prevalent the discrepancies between statements and testimony are and just how substantial. In short, a large proportion of international witnesses testify inconsistently about core features of the events that they ostensibly witnessed. These inconsistencies, if attributable to the witnesses, should call their testimony into considerable doubt. Section 4.A examines the kinds of inconsistencies that appear, Section B considers their prevalence, and Section C explores the causes of the inconsistencies.

4.A. THE NATURE OF THE INCONSISTENCIES

Discrepancies between statements and testimony cover a wide range of topics and are particularly apt to concern dates, distances, duration, numbers, and the other sorts of key details that international witnesses so often have trouble providing. For instance, *Los Palos* witness 13(a) testified that the victim was driving a Mikrolet, whereas his statement says that it was a yellow truck;[451] similarly, witness 16's statement reports that twenty-one houses were burned

[451] Los Palos Case Notes, Aug. 22, 2001, at 192.

in his village, although he testified that only two were burned.[452] *Muhimana* witness AP testified inconsistently about the name of a rape victim, whom she apparently knew well – identifying her as Goretti Mukashyaka in her statement but as Immaculée Mukakayiro in testimony.[453] Even a witness's capacity to provide such details can be contested. After *AFRC* witness TF1-133 testified that 131 children were with her in Makeni, counsel asked her if she could count. She responded that she could. Her statement reports, however, that she did not know how to count.[454] As observed in Chapter 2, these details can prove vitally important. It matters a great deal whether a defendant was fifty yards from a crime scene or 250, and it matters when an event occurred. Witnesses who fail to date events leave defendants less able to prove that they were not involved in those events, and witnesses who do date events in their statements but later change those dates when testifying might be attempting to change their story once it becomes clear that the date the witness initially provided would not implicate the defendant in the crimes. Many other examples of discrepancies about details appear in the notes.[455]

[452] Los Palos Case Notes, Aug. 23, 2001, at 206.

[453] Muhimana Judgement, note 363, at para. 27.

[454] AFRC Transcript, July 7, 2005, at 116–17.

[455] Akayesu Judgement, note 32, at para. 236; Muhimana Judgement, note 363, at paras. 269–270; Prosecution v. Simba, Case No. ICTR-01-76-T, Judgement and Sentence, paras. 167, 169, 382 (Dec. 13, 2005) [hereinafter Simba Judgement]; Karera Judgement, note 54, at paras. 116, 164, 226–228, 299; Niyitegeka Judgement, note 56, at paras. 59, 60, 65, 99, 102, 167, 277, 278, 306; Kajelijeli Judgement, note 303, at para. 680; Prosecutor v. Muvunyi, Case No. ICTR-2000–55A-T, Judgement and Sentence, para. 171 (Sept. 12, 2006) [hereinafter Muvunyi Judgement]; Musema Judgement, note 112, at paras. 385–387; Kamuhanda Judgement, note 38, at paras. 327, 339; Gacumbitsi Judgement, note 364, at para. 123; Bagilishema Judgement, note 122, at paras. 403, 412–413; Semanza Judgement, note 31, at para. 171; Military I Transcript, July 2, 2003, at 9, 22, 30; Military I Transcript, July 3, 2003, at 56, 59–60, Nyiramasuhuko Transcript, Mar. 20, 2003, at 25–35, 60–61; Ndindabahizi Transcript, Sept. 22, 2003, at 12, 22–23; Muhimana Transcript, Mar. 31, 2004, at 4, 18–19; Muhimana Transcript, Apr. 19, 2004, at 43–45; Karemera Transcript, Dec. 5, 2003, at 17–18, 20; Kamuhanda Transcript, Sept. 19, 2001, at 62–65; Kamuhanda Transcript, Sept. 4, 2002, at 29–31; Gacumbitsi Transcript, Aug. 6, 2003, at 43, 44, 46; Karera Transcript, Jan. 31, 2006, at 9–10;Taylor Transcript, Jan. 8, 2008, at 758–59; Taylor Transcript, Feb. 12, 2008, at 3622–24; Taylor Transcript, Mar. 13, 2008, at 6079; Taylor Transcript, May 12, 2008, at 9544; CDF Transcript, June 21, 2004, at 54–55; CDF Transcript, Sept. 9, 2004, at 85–87; CDF Transcript, Sept. 13, 2004, at 101–03; CDF Transcript, Dec. 6, 2004, at 80–81; CDF Transcript, Feb. 9, 2005, at 18; CDF Transcript, Feb. 22, 2005, at 73–74, 91–104; CDF Transcript, Mar. 4, 2005, at 14–19, 24–28; CDF Transcript, Mar. 8, 2005, at 45; RUF Transcript, July 21, 2004, at 25–26; RUF Transcript, Oct. 8, 2004, at 138–40; RUF Transcript, Apr. 14, 2005, at 27–33, 38–40; RUF Transcript, Apr. 15, 2005, at 91, 100; RUF Transcript, May 12, 2005, at 66–67; RUF Transcript, Nov. 22, 2005, at 29–30; RUF Transcript, Mar. 31, 2005, at 3–4; AFRC Transcript, Apr. 6, 2005, at 24–27; AFRC Transcript, Apr. 8, 2005, at 79; AFRC Transcript, Apr. 12, 2005, at 34–38, 38–39, 53–60, 63–65, 67–69; AFRC Transcript, Apr. 19, 2005, at 52–59; AFRC Transcript, Apr. 20, 2005, at 21–25; AFRC Transcript, June 21, 2005, at 53–64; AFRC Transcript, June 22, 2005, at 26–27, 47–48; AFRC Transcript, June 23, 2005, at 132–35; AFRC Transcript, June 30,

Witnesses also testify inconsistently about the events that they witnessed. Sometimes the inconsistencies pertain to relatively minor points. *Muhimana* witness BJ's statement, for instance, reported that an *Interahamwe* member had broken down a door, whereas in testimony she denied that he even came through the door.[456] These sorts of inconsistencies we can expect; it is well documented that high levels of stress can "direct attention to the central features of the arousing event at the expense of the peripheral features. Accordingly, an extremely stressed person will encode and remember central aspects of the experience while failing to encode trivial details."[457] Frequently, however, the inconsistencies that appear at the international tribunals under study pertain to fundamental aspects of the witness's account. I have included numerous examples in the following paragraphs (and many, many more in the notes) to convey just how serious the inconsistencies can be. For instance, *AFRC* witness TF1-209's statement said that she had fled with her two-year-old son, later lost him, and has never seen him again. She testified, by contrast, that the boy was six and that he was shot and killed in her presence.[458] The statement of *AFRC* witness TF1-158 reports that he did not witness any killings in a particular town, but at trial he testified that he saw a boy and girl killed there.[459] *Ndindabahizi* witness CGC's inconsistency goes in the other direction: His statement reports that he witnessed a killing of a half-caste, but he denied doing so in his testimony.[460] *CDF* witness TF2-144 testified that he witnessed the Kamajors amputate a man's arm, whereas the witness's statement reports that it was a woman whose arm was amputated.[461] *Kamuhanda* witness GEL's statement says that the attack occurred at the Bureau communal, whereas he testified that it occurred at the Parish.[462] Witness TF1-004 testified that two of his three houses had been burned, although his statement said that one of his two houses had been burned.[463] *RUF* witness TF1-122 testified that a rebel named Mosquito killed one farmer during a particular incident, whereas his statement says that

2005, at 122–23; AFRC Transcript, July 11, 2005, at 151–52; AFRC Transcript, July 12, 2005, at 85; AFRC Transcript, July 21, 2005, at 82–83, 96; AFRC Transcript, July 26, 2005, at 96; AFRC Transcript, Sept. 19, 2005, at 45–46; Los Palos Case Notes, Aug. 1, 2001, at 109; Los Palos Case Notes, Aug. 2, 2001, at 120; Los Palos Case Notes, Aug. 21, 2001, at 179; Los Palos Case Notes, Sept. 28, 2001, at 306; Prosecutor v. Paulino de Jesus, Case No. 6/2002, Judgement, at 10–11 (Jan. 28, 2004) [hereinafter Paulino de Jesus Judgement].

456 Muhimana Transcript, Apr. 6, 2004, at 50.

457 Richard J. McNally, Remembering Trauma 49–50 (2003).

458 AFRC Transcript, July 7, 2005, at 50.

459 AFRC Transcript, July 26, 2005, at 97–98.

460 Ndindabahizi Transcript, Sept. 29, 2003, at 48.

461 CDF Transcript, Feb. 25, 2005, at 7–9.

462 Kamuhanda Transcript, Feb. 14, 2002, at 31–40.

463 AFRC Transcript, June 23, 2005, at 103–04.

Mosquito killed two young boys.[464] Also speaking of Mosquito, *RUF* witness TF1-129's statement reported that Mosquito had shot RUF combatants in the legs, but he testified that it was rebel soldiers who had shot the combatants.[465] Meanwhile, *Taylor* witness Varmuyan Sherif testified that he saw Mosquito execute five soldiers at Kailahun, whereas his statement reported that Mosquito had left Kailahun just before the witness arrived.[466]

Sometimes, the witness's entire account changes between her statement and her testimony. *CDF* witness TF2-154 attested in her statement that one victim died after a tire had been placed around his head and then set on fire. In testimony, however, she denied that there had been a tire placed on the victim's head and insisted that he ran away, was shot, and was then thrown into the flames of a burning house. With respect to a second victim, TF2-154's statement stated that he had been thrown into a fire, but she testified that he had been set on fire.[467] *Ntakirutimana* witness MM testified that a certain pastor had been shot, but his statement reports that the pastor was killed with a machete.[468] Witness TF2-006's statement reports that he was the only one injured in a certain incident, whereas he testified that five others were also injured.[469] Sometimes the facts of the crimes are so grotesque that one does not know what to make of the inconsistencies. For instance, *CDF* witness TF2-152 testified that the Kamajors cut out his friend's heart and gave it to the witness, whereas his statement says that it was the victim's liver that had been cut out and given to the witness.[470] Many other examples appear in the notes.[471]

464 AFRC Transcript, June 24, 2005, at 111–14.
465 RUF Transcript, May 12, 2005, at 61–66.
466 Taylor Transcript, Jan. 11, 2008, at 1089–91.
467 CDF Transcript, Sept. 27, 2004, at 63–72.
468 Ntakirutimana Transcript, Sept. 20, 2001, at 75–81.
469 CDF Transcript, Feb. 9, 2005, at 28.
470 CDF Transcript, Sept. 27, 2004, at 152–54.
471 Semanza Judgement, note 31, at paras. 93, 171; Prosecutor v. Mpambara, Case No. ICTR-01-65-T, Judgement, para. 151 (Sept. 11, 2006) [hereinafter Mpambara Judgement]; Musema Judgement, note 112, at para. 811; Gacumbitsi Judgement, note 364, at para. 192; Ntakirutimana Judgement, note 69, at paras. 366–370; Kamuhanda Judgement, note 38, at para. 440; Rwamakuba Judgement, note 63, at para. 113; Akayesu Judgement, note 32, at para. 407; Military I Transcript, July 4, 2003, at 24–25, 39–40, 54; Ntakirutimana Transcript, Sept. 24, 2001, at 109–21, 140–43; Ntakirutimana Transcript, Sept. 26, 2001, at 80–81; Ntakirutimana Transcript, Sept. 27, 2001, at 69–71; Nyiramasuhuko Transcript, Mar. 20, 2003, at 43; Gacumbitsi Transcript, Aug. 6, 2003, at 41; Kajelijeli Transcript, Dec. 11, 2001, at 97–107; Karemera Transcript, Dec. 8, 2003, at 65; Kamuhanda Transcript, Sept. 4, 2001, at 46; Kamuhanda Transcript, Sept. 19, 2001, at 75–76; Kamuhanda Transcript, Jan. 31, 2002, at 77–79; Kamuhanda Transcript, Feb. 7, 2002, at 92–94; Seromba Transcript, Oct. 4, 2004, at 23–24; Seromba Transcript, Oct. 7, 2004, at 11–12; Seromba Transcript, Oct. 11, 2004, at 3; Muhimana Transcript, Apr. 1, 2004, at 29–31; Muhimana Transcript, Apr. 7, 2004, at 32, 34–36; Muhimana Transcript, Apr. 8, 2004, at 26–29, 36, 48–50 (French version); Muhimana Transcript, Apr. 20, 2004, at 20; Muhimana Transcript, Apr. 30, 2004, at 47–49, 54–55; Taylor Transcript, Jan. 11, 2008, at 1098–1105; Taylor Transcript,

If discrepancies concerning the crimes themselves were not worrisome enough, witnesses also frequently testify inconsistently about the defendant's involvement in the crimes. Sometimes the witness's testimony will inculpate the defendant when the statement did not. *Akayesu* witness Karangwa testified, for instance, that the defendant shot and killed all three of Karangwa's brothers, but his statement says that the defendant shot and killed only one of the witness's brothers and that the other two brothers were chopped to death by men who were with the defendant.[472] The statement of *Ndindabahizi* witness CGV says that Ndindabahizi only watched a particular massacre, whereas CGV testified that Ndindabahizi himself participated in the massacre, throwing grenades and the like. Similarly, whereas the statement of *Los Palos* witness 7 reports that

Jan. 12, 2008, at 1109–14; Taylor Transcript, Jan. 24, 2008, at 2118–24, 2130–32, 2134–36; Taylor Transcript, Mar. 14, 2008, at 6096–97, 6100–01, 6133–36; CDF Transcript, June 18, 2004, at 11–12; CDF Transcript, Sept. 9, 2004, at 108; CDF Transcript, Nov. 2, 2004, at 123–30; CDF Transcript, Nov. 3, 2004, at 52–59; CDF Transcript, Nov. 4, 2004, at 4–8, 12, 13–14; CDF Transcript, Feb. 14, 2005, at 32–34; CDF Transcript, Feb. 22, 2005, at 108–10; CDF Transcript, Feb. 25, 2005, at 25–32; CDF Transcript, Mar. 4, 2005, at 94; RUF Transcript, July 15, 2004, at 1–3; RUF Transcript, July 19, 2004, at 77, 86–87; RUF Transcript, July 21, 2004, at 27, 30–32; RUF Transcript, July 22, 2004, at 37–38; RUF Transcript, Oct. 7, 2004, at 154–70; RUF Transcript, Oct. 11, 2004, at 156–63; RUF Transcript, Jan. 13, 2005, at 86–87; RUF Transcript, Feb. 3, 2005, at 66–67, 68–73; RUF Transcript, Apr. 7, 2005, at 101–02; RUF Transcript, Apr. 8, 2005, at 40–41, 46–62, 79; RUF Transcript, Apr. 15, 2005, at 8–9, 15, 22, 40–41, 56, 60–61, 101; RUF Transcript, Apr. 18, 2005, at 22, 24; RUF Transcript, July 7, 2005, at 12–16, 30–32; RUF Transcript, July 8, 2005, at 40–42, 43–46; RUF Transcript, July 27, 2005, at 19–20, 70–72; RUF Transcript, Aug. 2, 2005, at 48; RUF Transcript, Nov. 4, 2005, at 32–51; RUF Transcript, Nov. 7, 2005, at 11–13; RUF Transcript, Nov. 22, 2005, at 90–95; RUF Transcript, Nov. 23, 2005, at 42–57; RUF Transcript, Dec. 5, 2005, at 79, 83–93; RUF Transcript, Dec. 8, 2005, at 43; AFRC Transcript, Apr. 7, 2005, at 121; AFRC Transcript, Apr. 8, 2005, at 40–43, 43–44, 79–80; AFRC Transcript, Apr. 12, 2005, at 3–4; AFRC Transcript, Apr. 19, 2005, at 47–48; AFRC Transcript, Apr. 20, 2005, at 47–49, 51–52; AFRC Transcript, June 21, 2005, at 33–35; AFRC Transcript, June 24, 2005, at 110; AFRC Transcript, June 28, 2005, at 47–49; AFRC Transcript, June 29, 2005, at 13–16, 18–19; AFRC Transcript, July 1, 2005, at 34–35; AFRC Transcript, July 7, 2005, at 57–58; AFRC Transcript, July 11, 2005, at 150–51; AFRC Transcript, July 12, 2005, at 13–14, 20–21, 76–77, 78; AFRC Transcript, July 14, 2005, at 38–39; AFRC Transcript, July 18, 2005, at 27, 31, 102–05; AFRC Transcript, July 12, 2005, at 13–14; AFRC Transcript, Sept. 26, 2005, at 12–14; AFRC Transcript, Oct. 17, 2005, at 36, 41–47; Lolotoe Case Notes, Apr. 11, 2002, at 4–5; Lolotoe Case Notes, Apr. 12, 2002, at 6; Lolotoe Case Notes, May 7, 2002, at 4; Lolotoe Case Notes, Nov. 14, 2002, at 24–25; Los Palos Case Notes, July 23, 2001, at 57; Los Palos Case Notes, July 24, 2001, at 59, 60, 62, 66; Los Palos Case Notes, July 27, 2001, at 83, 90; Los Palos Case Notes, July 26, 2001, at 75, 78; Los Palos Case Notes, Aug. 2, 2001, at 120, 122, 125; Los Palos Case Notes, Aug. 8, 2001, at 145; Los Palos Case Notes, Aug. 21, 2001, at 173; Los Palos Case Notes, Aug. 22, 2001, at 190; Los Palos Case Notes, Aug. 21, 2001, at 173; Los Palos Case Notes, Sept. 20, 2001, at 226, 229; Los Palos Case Notes, Sept. 25, 2001, at 273; Los Palos Case Notes, Sept. 26, 2001, at 287; Los Palos Case Notes, Sept. 29, 2001, at 309; Alison Thompson, U.C. Berkeley War Crimes Studies Center, Special Court Monitoring Program, Update No. 71, Mar. 3, 2006, at 4–5; Prosecutor v. Sesay et al., Decision on Sesay Defense Motion to Direct the Prosecutor to Investigate the Matter of False Testimony by Witness TF1-366, paras. 43–44 (July 26, 2006).

[472] Akayesu Judgement, note 32, at para. 237.

a man named Syaful ordered the witness to beat the victim, he testified that it was Cesar and defendant Joao da Costa who ordered him to commit the crime.[473] And although *AFRC* witness Gibril Massaquoi's statement reports that defendants Five-Five and Gullit ordered executions but did not personally kill anyone, Massaquoi testified that Five-Five had shot and killed a man.[474] Relatedly, SCSL trials have involved substantial testimony about the command responsibility of defendants, and some witnesses will name the defendants as commanders during their testimony, even though their statements name other individuals as commanding those same battles.[475] *CDF* witness TF2-134 went further and disavowed all of the portions of her statement that reported that defendant Kondewa had threatened the Kamajors with punishment if they continued to commit crimes.[476] Other examples appear in the notes.[477]

Sometimes the later testimony seeks to exculpate, not inculpate. The statement of Joao Amaral, a witness in the Special Panels' *Aparicio Guterres* case, for instance, reported that Amaral had seen the defendant stabbing the victim, but at trial he insisted that another individual had stabbed the victim and that the defendant had only waved a bloody knife around.[478] The statement of *Los Palos* witness 10 reported that defendant Paolo da Costa participated in a beating whereas the witness testified that the defendant just stood there.[479] *Gacumbitsi* witness TAC's statement says that the defendant was armed and personally killed the two victims, whereas at trial the witness reported that the victims were killed by two policemen.[480] *AFRC* witness TF1-277's statement says that the witness saw one of the defendants kill a twenty-year-old woman, whereas on the stand he denied saying that.[481] Finally, *CDF* witness TF2-012 said in his statement that defendant Fofana was at a key meeting, yet he testified that he did not know who Fofana was.[482] Other examples in which the witnesses'

[473] Los Palos Case Notes, Aug. 14, 2001, at 158.
[474] AFRC Judgement, note 27, at para. 907.
[475] *See* RUF Transcript, Apr. 7, 2005, at 91–93, 109–17.
[476] CDF Transcript, June 3, 2005, at 35–47.
[477] Akayesu Judgement, note 32, at para. 185; Military I Transcript, July 2, 2003, at 32–35; Ntakirutimana Transcript, Sept. 26, 2001, at 108–11; Taylor Transcript, Jan. 8, 2008, at 755–58; Taylor Transcript, Feb. 7, 2008, at 3348–51; Taylor Transcript, Mar. 13, 2008, at 5974–76; AFRC Transcript, July 11, 2005, at 145–46; Prosecutor v. Sesay et al., Decision on Sesay Defense Motion to Direct the Prosecutor to Investigate the Matter of False Testimony by Witness TF1-366, paras. 45–48 (July 26, 2006).
[478] Prosecution v. Aparicio Guterres, Case No. 18a/2003, Judgement, at 3 (Feb. 28, 2005) [hereinafter Guterres Judgement].
[479] Los Palos Case Notes, Aug. 21, 2001, at 177.
[480] Gacumbitsi Judgement, note 364, at para. 192.
[481] AFRC Transcript, Mar. 9, 2005, at 6–7.
[482] CDF Transcript, June 21, 2004, at 48–50.

statements and testimony diverge regarding the defendant's role in the crimes appear in the notes.[483]

Most worryingly of all perhaps, witnesses will sometimes testify that the defendant played a key role in the crime, but the witness's statement, which may feature a detailed description of the crime and surrounding scenes, fails even to mention the defendant.[484] In other instances, equally significant facts sometimes fail to make their way into the statements. Witness TF1-077, for instance, testified that her three children were killed, yet those deaths were not included in her statement.[485] Witness TF2-198 testified that he saw his brother being been killed and his body taken away to be cooked and eaten. Although that fact would certainly seem worthy of mention, the witness apparently said nothing about it to investigators.[486] Similarly, although a key portion of the testimony of witness TF1-074 concerned an attack at Efin, that event did not appear in either of his two statements.[487] Numerous other examples appear in the notes.[488]

[483] Bagilishema Judgement, note 122, at paras. 403, 415; Mpambara Judgement, note 471, at para. 107; Karera Transcript, Feb. 1, 2006, at 24; Muhimana Transcript, Apr. 15, 2004, at 63; Muhimana Transcript, Apr. 19, 2004, at 55; Muhimana Transcript, Apr. 30, 2004, at 68–69; Los Palos Case Notes, Sept. 20, 2001, at 223; Los Palos Case Notes, July 31, 2001, at 103; Los Palos Case Notes, Aug. 7, 2001, at 129; Los Palos Case Notes, Aug. 8, 2001, at 141; Los Palos Case Notes, Aug. 16, 2001, at 164, 167; Los Palos Case Notes, Sept. 24, 2001, at 265–66; Los Palos Case Notes, Sept. 25, 2001, at 272; CDF Transcript, Feb. 11, 2005, at 78–79; CDF Transcript, Feb. 24, 2005, at 90–91; RUF Transcript, Mar. 23, 2006, at 18–27; RUF Transcript, Jan. 25, 2005, at 52–57; RUF Transcript, Apr. 8, 2005, at 32–35, 80, 99–101, 104–06; RUF Transcript, Nov. 7, 2005, at 17–18; AFRC Transcript, Mar. 8, 2005, at 109–19; AFRC Transcript, July 21, 2005, at 43–51.

[484] *See, e.g.*, Akayesu Judgement, note 32, at paras. 248, 266; Simba Judgement, note 455, at paras. 108, 195; Gacumbitsi Judgement, note 364, at para. 54; Rwamakuba Judgement, note 63, at paras. 114, 145, 192; Kajelijeli Judgement, note 303, at para. 467; Ntakirutimana Judgement, note 69, at para. 255; Musema Judgement, note 112, at para. 440; Karera Judgement, note 54, at para. 53; Niyitegeka Judgement, note 56, at paras. 101, 154, 158; Da Costa & Punef Judgement, note 355, at 5; Paulino de Jesus Judgement, note 455, at 9; Tacaqui Judgement, note 36, at 26–27; Gacumbitsi Transcript, Aug. 19, 2003, at 22; Kajelijeli Transcript, Dec. 7, 2001, at 27–28; Kajelijeli Transcript, Dec. 5, 2001 (in French), at 85–96; Muhimana Transcript, Mar. 30, 2004, at 55–56; Muhimana Transcript, Apr. 29, 2004, at 22–24; Ntakirutimana Transcript, Sept. 20, 2001, at 32–33; Niyitegeka Transcript, Aug. 13, 2002, at 24–25; Prosecutor v. Bagosora et al., Case No. ICTR-98-41-T, Judgement and Sentence, para. 269 (Dec. 18, 2008) [hereinafter Bagosora et al. Judgement]; RUF Transcript, Nov. 25, 2004, at 30; RUF Transcript, Oct. 19, 2004, at 18–20; RUF Transcript, Jan. 24, 2005, at 95–111; RUF Transcript, Feb. 3, 2005, at 36–40; RUF Transcript, Mar. 23, 2006, at 77–80, 141–45; AFRC Transcript, July 11, 2005, at 140–50; Kamuhanda Transcript, Sept. 19, 2001, at 72–73; Los Palos Case Notes, Sept. 18, 2001, at 255–56.

[485] RUF Transcript, July 21, 2004, at 17.

[486] CDF Transcript, June 15, 2004, at 25–31.

[487] RUF Transcript, July 12, 2004, at 41.

[488] Muhimana Judgement, note 363, at paras. 269–270; Ntakirutimana Judgement, note 69, at para. 255; Kamuhanda Judgement, note 38, at para. 352; Kamuhanda Transcript, Sept. 4, 2001, at 80; Kamuhanda Transcript, Sept. 19, 2001, at 61, 72–75; Kamuhanda Transcript, Sept. 24, 2001, at 111–12; Kamuhanda Transcript, Jan. 31, 2002, at 76–77; Kamuhanda Transcript, Feb. 11,

Witnesses testify inconsistently not only about the defendant's role in the crime but also about the role of other perpetrators. In his statement, *RUF* witness TF1-097 said it was an SLA soldier who cut off his hand. He testified, however, that it was an RUF soldier who cut off his hand.[489] The statement of another *RUF* witness, TF1-343, reports that the burns on her foot were caused by bombs that ECOMOG jets had dropped on her village. The witness testified, however, that rebels had burned her foot.[490] Other examples appear in the notes.[491] Sometimes witnesses change their minds about their own involvement in the crimes. *Muvunyi* witness CCP, for instance, admitted to investigators that he had turned Tutsi victims over to their killers, but on the stand he denied participating in the killings.[492] Similarly, the statement of *Gacumbitsi* witness NG2 reports that the witness was armed during the attack, but at trial he testified that he carried no weapons.[493] Conversely, the statement of *Karera* witness BMR reports that he never manned a roadblock, but in testimony BMR admitted to having done so.[494]

Some inconsistencies relate to the reliability of the witness's testimony. For instance, Niyitegeka witness GGH testified that he was able to recognize a particular leader because he knew the man before the war. In his statement, however, he said that he had not known the man before the war.[495] Other discrepancies call into question the witness's actual witnessing of the events in question. For instance, *Kajelijeli* witness GAO testified that he personally witnessed the killing of two Tutsi, but his statement reported that he only heard about the murders after they occurred.[496] Similarly, in his statement,

2002, at 113–14; Ntakirutimana Transcript, Sept. 27, 2001, at 78–81, 112–13; RUF Transcript, July 27, 2004, at 24–31, 69; RUF Transcript, Oct. 7, 2004, at 144–48; RUF Transcript, Oct. 19, 2004, at 16–26; RUF Transcript, Feb. 3, 2005, at 36–40; RUF Transcript, Apr. 28, 2005, at 108–09; RUF Transcript, July 8, 2005, at 35–39; RUF Transcript, Mar. 17, 2006, at 6–7, 18–19, 95; AFRC Transcript, Mar. 8, 2005, at 101–08; AFRC Transcript, Apr. 12, 2005, at 9; AFRC Transcript, Apr. 19, 2005, at 61–68; AFRC Transcript, Apr. 20, 2005, at 25–26; AFRC Transcript, Apr. 22, 2005, at 32–33; AFRC Transcript, Apr. 18, 2005, at 60–63; AFRC Transcript, Apr. 19, 2005, at 61–68; AFRC Transcript, June 22, 2005, at 53–54; AFRC Transcript, July 12, 2005, at 27–31; AFRC Transcript, July 20, 2005, at 54–56; AFRC Transcript, July 26, 2005, at 82–86; AFRC Transcript, Sept. 30, 2005, at 65–67; Taylor Transcript, Jan. 15, 2008, at 1330–32; Taylor Transcript, May 8, 2008, at 9265; Los Palos Case Notes, July 18, 2001, at 32.

489 RUF Transcript, Nov. 28, 2005, at 108–09.

490 RUF Transcript, Mar. 17, 2006, at 100–01.

491 AFRC Transcript, July 5, 2005, at 37–39; AFRC Transcript, July 18, 2005, at 114–17; AFRC Transcript, Oct. 17, 2005, at 36, 41–47; AFRC Transcript, Sept. 29, 2005, at 68–72; Karera Transcript, Jan. 30, 2006, at 5–6; Karera Transcript, Jan. 31, 2006, at 19–20.

492 Muvunyi Judgement, note 455, at para. 201.

493 *See, e.g.*, Gacumbitsi Judgement, note 364, at para. 128.

494 Karera Transcript, Feb. 1, 2006, at 28.

495 Niyitegeka Judgement, note 56, at para. 165.

496 Kajelijeli Judgement, note 303, at para. 522.

RUF witness TF1-074 said, "I never saw him actually performing the amputations," yet he testified that he had seen it "with [his] own naked eye," claiming: "I was not drunk. I saw all that happened."[497] And witness Sagahutu testified in *Zigiranyirazo* that he heard the defendant Zigiranyirazo describe the incriminating details of a certain meeting, yet when testifying in *Bagosora et al.*, the same witness indicated that he heard about the meeting not from Zigiranyirazo himself but from someone to whom Zigiranyirazo told.[498]

Other inconsistencies go in the other direction; that is, the statement reports an eyewitness accounting, whereas the testimony denies one. So, for instance, the statement of Sierra Leonean witness TF2-144 placed him and the victim's wife at the scene of the victim's death, but TF2-144 testified that neither he nor the victim's wife personally witnessed the killing.[499] Similarly, *Ntakirutimana* witness GG's statement reports that the witness watched the events through a window, yet he testified that he had hidden after the crimes began and thus did not see anything.[500] And sometimes witnesses are inconsistent not about whether they were in hiding but about where.[501] Witness TF1-157 testified that he hid in a graveyard, for instance, although his statement has him hiding in his house.[502] Witness BMJ testified that he was hiding in a ditch thirty-two paces away from Karera, whereas his statement reported that he was hiding in bushes 150 meters away.[503] Other examples appear in the notes.[504]

Finally, some discrepancies have little relevance to the prosecution's overall case but are startling nonetheless. *CDF* witness TF2-006, for instance, apparently told investigators that his occupation was that of a welder, and when asked in court if he was a welder, he initially said that he was. But soon thereafter, he denied that he was a welder and denied having said that he was either to investigators or in court a few minutes earlier.[505] Similarly strange, *RUF* witness TF1-314 told investigators that she was pregnant while living in Makeni, whereas

[497] RUF Transcript, July 12, 2004, at 41–42.

[498] Prosecutor v. Zigiranyirazo, Case No. ICTR-01-73-T, Judgement, para. 116 (Dec. 18, 2008) [hereinafter Zigiranyirazo Judgement].

[499] CDF Transcript, Feb. 25, 2005, at 13–14.

[500] Ntakirutimana Transcript, Sept. 24, 2001, at 144–45.

[501] *See, e.g.*, Ntakirutimana Judgement, note 69, at para. 369; Karera Judgement, note 54, at para. 304; CDF Transcript, Dec. 1, 2004, at 30–40.

[502] AFRC Transcript, Sept. 26, 2005, at 54–55. *See also* Muhimana Transcript, Apr. 5, 2004, at 22.

[503] Karera Judgement, note 54, at para. 296.

[504] Kajelijeli Judgement, note 303, at para. 296; Karera Judgement, note 54, at para. 302; Ntakirutimana Transcript, Sept. 27, 2001, at 20–23; Karera Transcript, Jan. 31, 2006, at 9–10; CDF Transcript, Mar. 8, 2005, at 45; AFRC Transcript, July 21, 2005, at 72–73; RUF Transcript, Apr. 8, 2005, at 14–16 (inconsistency regarding whether the witness knew the defendant before he saw him at a particular event); AFRC Transcript, July 11, 2005, at 140–41 (discrepancy regarding witness's affiliation with the AFRC); AFRC Transcript, July 12, 2005, at 7–8; AFRC Transcript, July 26, 2005, at 93–94; Taylor Transcript, Feb. 25, 2008, at 4628–34.

[505] CDF Transcript, Feb. 9, 2005, at 42–43.

she testified that she was pregnant while living in Buedu.[506] In *Kajelijeli*, witness GDO stated that she was hiding with her two children, whereas she testified that she was hiding with her four children.[507] *AFRC* witness TF1-282 apparently told investigators that she cooked, cleaned, and did laundry for the rebel who had forced her to marry him, but on the stand she denied doing any of those things.[508] The statement of *Akayesu* witness Karangwa reports that he buried the bodies of his three murdered brothers, but at trial Karangwa denied having done so.[509] Similarly irrelevant but bizarre is that *CDF* witness TF2-006's statement apparently contained the wrong names for the witness's wife and mother.[510] Other examples appear in the notes.[511]

Sometimes a witness's proclivity to be confused – or to appear confused – intersects with his or her proclivity to testify inconsistently. Several pages of transcripts in the *Muhimana* case, for instance, were devoted to defense counsel's efforts to pin down an apparent inconsistency in witness AU's testimony,[512] and it was equally unclear whether *AFRC* witness TF1-209 modified her initial statement to change the name of an individual.[513] In *Los Palos*, witness 6 at first denied the assertions appearing in his statement, only to accept that they were true a few minutes later, saying that he had "forgotten."[514] And witness CTG seemed to testify inconsistently about the number of people in defendant Ndindabahizi's car, but it may have been confusion or an interpretation error.[515]

It is sometimes difficult to categorize the nature of the inconsistency because on the stand the witness tells an entirely different story from the one that appears in his statement. For instance, witness TF2-159's statement and testimony diverge in numerous respects. First, the statement reports that he witnessed the killing of five people, whereas he testified that he saw eight people killed. Next, the statement says that he was severely beaten "on two occasions," but he testified that he was beaten only once. Finally, the witness denied telling investigators that he had been taken to Joe Tamidey to be killed and that his brother had intervened on his behalf, as his statement reports.[516]

[506] RUF Transcript, Nov. 7, 2005, at 38–39.
[507] Kajelijeli Transcript, July 19, 2001, at 34–35.
[508] AFRC Transcript, Apr. 14, 2005, at 37–41.
[509] Akayesu Judgement, note 32, at para. 238.
[510] CDF Transcript, Feb. 9, 2005, at 46–47.
[511] Kamuhanda Transcript, Sept. 19, 2001, at 67–69; Kamuhanda Transcript, Sept. 25, 2001, at 43–44; Kamuhanda Transcript, Jan. 29, 2002, at 23–24; Kamuhanda Transcript, Jan. 31, 2002, at 77–79; Muhimana Transcript, Apr. 30, 2004, at 50–51; CDF Transcript, Sept. 14, 2004, at 146–48; RUF Transcript, Apr. 7, 2005, at 46–47; RUF Transcript, Nov. 4, 2005, at 13–19.
[512] Muhimana Transcript, Apr. 7, 2004, at 27–30.
[513] AFRC Transcript, July 7, 2005, at 55–56.
[514] Los Palos Case Notes, Aug. 13, 2001, at 149.
[515] Ndindabahizi Transcript, Sept. 3, 2003, at 55.
[516] CDF Transcript, Sept. 9, 2004, at 159–60.

The witness statement further reports that he saw ten houses burned, but he testified that twenty-five houses were burned.[517] Finally, the witness denied providing investigators all sorts of additional information that appeared in his statement, including that he was present when his three grandparents were locked in his house and set on fire.[518] In a similar vein, although witness TF2-004's statement reports that his father had him and his brother initiated into the Kamajor society after rebels had killed his mother, stepmother, and grandmother, he testified that he did not even have a brother and that his stepmother had not been killed but that his sister – who had not appeared in the statement – had been killed.[519] The witness also disavowed other key aspects of his statement.[520] Sometimes the witness's story changes once and then back again. The initial statement of *RUF* witness TF1-012 reported that he saw defendant Gullit murder a hunchback. Two weeks before trial, TF1-012 disavowed that statement and said that he never saw Gullit murder anyone. On the stand, however, he maintained that he was in fact an eyewitness to Gullit's murder of the hunchback.[521] Other examples appear in the notes.[522]

Finally, witnesses sometimes deny that they even made the statement in question.[523] Such an allegation gives rise to particularly serious questions. If the witness truly did not make the statement, then that means that the investigator fabricated evidence out of whole cloth. If the witness did in fact make the statement, then he either forgot that he did so or perjured himself by denying that he did. Either explanation calls the witness's testimony into serious question. In particular, even if the denial stemmed from a memory lapse, that means that the witness has trouble remembering events that took place much more recently than the crimes he witnessed.

Inconsistencies appear not only between a witness's statement and testimony but also between different statements given by the same witness and different sets of testimony. Prosecutors often take more than one statement from a given witness, and a witness's subsequent statement(s) can conflict with her initial

[517] *Id.* at 97–98.
[518] CDF Transcript, Sept. 10, 2004, at 5–13.
[519] CDF Transcript, Nov. 9, 2004, at 88–92.
[520] *Id.* at 92, 103, 105–11, 116–18.
[521] RUF Transcript, Feb. 3, 2005, at 75–78.
[522] RUF Transcript, Apr. 15, 2005, at 15–18 and *passim*; RUF Transcript, Feb. 3, 2005, at 48–56; AFRC Transcript, July 12, 2005, at 101–18; *see also* Ntakirutimana Transcript, Oct. 25, 2001, at 7–13 (witness denied the entire substance of an interview that he allegedly gave to African Rights).
[523] *See, e.g.*, Simba Judgement, note 455, at paras. 108, 166; Kajelijeli Transcript, Nov. 27, 2001, at 10; Prosecutor v. Bizimungu et al., Case No. ICTR-99-50-I, Transcript, Jan. 21, 2004, at 29–34 (witness denied making a confession to the *Gacaca* courts); Lolotoe Case Notes, Apr. 12, 2002, at 3; Lolotoe Case Notes, May 15, 2002, at 4; RUF Transcript, Apr. 28, 2005, at 87; AFRC Transcript, Apr. 11, 2005, at 85–86.

statement on key points.[524] For instance, in a subsequent statement, *AFRC* witness TF1-062 reported that any references to the CDF that appeared in his initial statement were meant to be references to the AFRC/RUF.[525] In another example, *CDF* witness TF2-096 denied in a later statement having stated in an earlier statement that two *CDF* defendants had continued killing civilians after a third defendant had arrived.[526] Similarly, in his later statement *RUF* witness TF1-035 denied saying that defendant Kallon had participated in the killing of twenty people.[527] In some cases, the subsequent statements are taken only days or weeks before the witness testifies,[528] so the inconsistencies between the two statements very much resemble the inconsistencies between statements and testimony.

Witnesses also have been known to testify inconsistently in the same case. *Los Palos* witness 14 testified on direct examination, for instance, that he saw one of the defendants burning houses, but during cross-examination he said that the defendant was only jumping around.[529] *CDF* witness TF2-016 testified at one point that he personally witnessed a murder and at another point that he did not see the murder but only saw the dead body after the killing.[530] And *RUF* witness TF1-141 identified "Master" as the alias for defendant Morris Kallon, despite having said earlier at trial that "Master" was the alias for another RUF leader, Sam Bockarie.[531] More examples appear in the notes.[532] And sometimes witnesses testify inconsistently in different cases.[533] Witness TF1-253 testified in the *AFRC* case that 300,000 leones had been stolen from him, but less than a year before, in the *RUF* case, he testified that only 140,000 to 150,000 leones had been stolen from him.[534] Rwandan witness XV testified that ESO soldiers under

[524] Muvunyi Judgement, note 455, at para. 171; CDF Transcript, Sept. 10, 2004, at 35; CDF Transcript, Nov. 8, 2004, at 44–47; RUF Transcript, Nov. 28, 2005, at 103; AFRC Transcript, Apr. 11, 2005, at 80; AFRC Transcript, July 12, 2005, at 8–9.

[525] AFRC Transcript, June 27, 2005, at 55–56.

[526] CDF Transcript, Nov. 8, 2004, at 44–47, 61–68.

[527] RUF Transcript, July 7, 2005, at 45–48.

[528] *See* Muvunyi Judgement, note 455, at para. 171; CDF Transcript, Nov. 8, 2004, at 44–47, 61–68; RUF Transcript, Dec. 8, 2005, at 46–48.

[529] Los Palos Case Notes, Aug. 23, 2001, at 199.

[530] CDF Transcript, Mar. 1, 2005, at 49–54.

[531] Michele Staggs, U.C. Berkeley War Crimes Studies Center, Special Court Monitoring Program Update No. 28, Mar. 25, 2005, at 3.

[532] Karera Judgement, note 54, at para. 306; Ndindabahizi Transcript, Sept. 16, 2003, at 51–52; CDF Transcript, June 15, 2004, at 31–32; AFRC Transcript, June 21, 2005, at 56–58; AFRC Transcript, Sept. 19, 2005, at 72–74; Lolotoe Case Notes, Mar. 20, 2003, at 3–4; Lolotoe Case Notes, Apr. 12, 2002, at 3; Los Palos Case Notes, Aug. 13, 2001, at 153; Los Palos Case Notes, Aug. 8, 2001, at 135; Los Palos Case Notes, July 11, 2001, at 9–10; Los Palos Case Notes, July 12, 2001, at 16–17; Los Palos Case Notes, July 26, 2001, at 79.

[533] Musema Judgement, note 112, at paras. 417, 450; Taylor Transcript, Jan. 16, 2008, at 1343–45.

[534] AFRC Transcript, Apr. 18, 2005, at 38–43.

the command of the defendant had abducted his sister who was never seen again, but during cross-examination it emerged that, in judicial proceedings in Rwandan courts, XV had sought compensation from a certain medical doctor for the death of his sister.[535] And *Ntakirutimana* witness OO provided three conflicting versions of events: one during his *Ntakirutimana* testimony, one during his *Musema* testimony, and one in his statement.[536]

4.B. THE PREVALENCE OF THE INCONSISTENCIES

Inconsistencies and omissions such as the ones I have described would be troubling if they occurred only once in a while, but in fact they are commonplace at the international tribunals. I reviewed the testimony of prosecution witnesses in three of the four SCSL cases and in a number of Special Panels and ICTR cases. In some of these cases, the testimony of virtually every witness featured some inconsistencies or omissions between the witnesses' statements and testimony.[537] More importantly in all of these cases, a large proportion of witnesses testified in a way that was *seriously* inconsistent with their previous statements.[538] At the SCSL, for instance, 54 percent of *AFRC* prosecution fact witnesses testified in a way that I considered

[535] Muvunyi Judgement, note 455, at para. 252.

[536] Ntakirutimana Judgement, note 69, at para. 168.

[537] In *Seromba*, of the eleven prosecution fact witnesses whose cross-examinations were public, the testimony of only one (witness YAT) featured no inconsistencies. Similarly, of the thirteen *Karera* prosecution witnesses whose cross-examination could be reviewed, the testimony of only one (witness BMM) featured no inconsistencies, whereas in *Kajelijeli*, only two of the eleven prosecution witnesses whose testimony could be evaluated had no inconsistencies.

[538] In calculating the proportion of witnesses who testified seriously inconsistently, I removed from my sample witnesses whose entire cross-examination could not be reviewed because it was conducted in closed session. The cross-examinations of some witnesses were conducted partially in closed sessions, and so I weighted these witnesses accordingly. That is, if one-half of the total number of pages of cross-examination for a particular witness was unavailable, then I counted that witness as one-half of a witness. So far as I know, there is no reason to think that inconsistencies would be unevenly distributed between closed and open sessions, but just in case they were, I also calculated the proportion of witnesses testifying seriously inconsistently without weighting. For these calculations, therefore, I counted each witness as a whole witness even if the vast majority of the witness's cross-examination was held in closed session. Consequently, these calculations should understate the proportion of witnesses who testify seriously inconsistently because some witnesses who did testify seriously inconsistently did so in closed session and thus were mistakenly placed in the "no-serious-inconsistency" category. Even using this overly generous calculation method, my review shows that a large proportion of international witnesses testify in a way that is seriously inconsistent with their pretrial statements. Using this method, the percentages of SCSL prosecution fact witnesses who testify seriously inconsistently was 53 percent in the *AFRC* case, 51 percent in the *RUF* case, and 29 percent in the *CDF* case. At the ICTR, the nonweighted percentages of witnesses who testified seriously inconsistently was 62 percent in *Karera*, 47 percent in *Muhimana*, 45 percent in *Kajelijeli*, 45 percent in *Niyitegeka*, 36 percent in *Seromba*, and 33 percent in *Gacumbitsi*.

seriously inconsistent with those witnesses' pretrial statements.[539] The proportion was 53 percent in the *RUF* case[540] and 35 percent in the *CDF*

[539] The *AFRC* case featured fifty-seven prosecution witnesses, two of whom were not fact witnesses and six of whom were cross-examined entirely in closed session. Taking account of testimony that was partially in closed session, I was able to evaluate the testimony of 48.5 witnesses and 26 of these testified seriously inconsistently. *See* AFRC Transcript, Mar. 7, 2005, at 97–107 (witness TF1-024); AFRC Transcript, Mar. 8 2005, at 109–11 (witness TF1-277); AFRC Transcript, Apr. 7, 2005, at 78–82 (witness TF1-085); AFRC Transcript, Apr. 8, 2005, at 29–30, 34–38, 40–43, 43–44 (witness TF1-320); AFRC Transcript, Apr. 8, 2005, at 79–83 (witness TF1-083); AFRC Transcript, Apr. 11, 2005, at 80–86; Apr. 12, 2005, at 3–5, 7–9 (witness TF1-227); AFRC Transcript, Apr. 14, 2005, at 38–40 (witness TF1-282); AFRC Transcript, Apr. 18, 2005, at 38–43, 60–67 (witness TF1-253); AFRC Transcript, Apr. 19, 2005, at 47–48, 61–68 (witness TF1-053); AFRC Transcript, June 22, 2005, at 22–25 (witness TF1-334); AFRC Transcript, June 23, 2005, at 103–04, 106–08 (witness TF1-004); AFRC Transcript, June 24, 2005, at 110–15 (witness TF1-122); AFRC Transcript, June 27, 2005, at 55–60 (witness TF1-062); AFRC Transcript, June 28, 2005, at 47–49 (witness TF1-198); AFRC Transcript, July 5, 2005, at 37–39, 50–51 (witness TF1-074); AFRC Transcript, July 7, 2005, at 49–51, 57–62 (witness TF1-209); AFRC Transcript, July 7, 2005, at 116–17 (witness TF1-133); AFRC Transcript, July 11, 2005, at 140–52, July 12, 2005, at 13–14, 27–30 (witness TF1-033); AFRC Transcript, July 14, 2005, at 38–39 (witness TF1-094); AFRC Transcript, July 18, 2005, at 114–17 (witness TF1-113); AFRC Transcript, July 21, 2005, at 43–51, 82–83 (witness TF1-045); AFRC Transcript, July 26, 2005, at 73–76, 93–94, 97–98 (witness TF1-158); AFRC Transcript, Sept. 21, 2005, at 4–9 (witness TF1-167); AFRC Transcript, Sept. 23, 2005, at 33–38 (witness TF1-153); AFRC Transcript, Sept. 26, 2005, at 54–55 (witness TF1-156); AFRC Transcript, Oct. 17, 2005, at 40–45 (witness TF1-217).

[540] The SCSL failed to post many of its most recent *RUF* transcripts, so I was not able to evaluate these. I was able to evaluate the testimony of fifty-three witnesses, however, and of these twenty-eight testified seriously inconsistently. *See* RUF Transcript, July 12, 2004, at 41–42, 49–52 (witness TF1-074); RUF Transcript, July 15, 2004, at 1–3 (witness TF1-214); RUF Transcript, July 19, 2004, at 73, 86–87 (witness TF1-064); RUF Transcript, July 21, 2004, at 17–20, 30–32 (witness TF1-077); RUF Transcript, July 22, 2004, at 35–38 (witness TF1-217); RUF Transcript, July 27, 2004, at 24–31 (witness TF1-199); RUF Transcript, July 27, 2004, at 65–70, 74 (witness TF1-305); RUF Transcript, Oct. 11, 2004, at 156–63 (witness TF1-314); RUF Transcript, Oct. 19, 2004, at 16–26 (witness TF1-167); RUF Transcript, Jan. 24, 2005, at 95–111; Jan. 25, 2005, at 52–57 (witness TF1-071); RUF Transcript, Feb. 1, 2005, at 29–51; Michele Staggs, U.C. Berkeley War Crimes Studies Center, Special Court Monitoring Program, Update No. 20, Feb. 4, 2005, at 4 (witness TF1-195); RUF Transcript, Feb. 3, 2005, at 36–40, 48–56 (witness TF1-012); RUF Transcript, Apr. 7, 2005, at 91–117; RUF Transcript, Apr. 8, 2005, 40–41, 80, 99–101, 104–06 (witness TF1-263); RUF Transcript, Apr. 14, 2005, at 23–26, 63–64; RUF Transcript, Apr. 15, 2005, at 8–9, 15–18, 22, 40, 56, 101; RUF Transcript, Apr. 18, 2005, at 22 (witness TF1-141); RUF Transcript, Apr. 28, 2005, at 86–87, 108–13 (witness TF1-114); RUF Transcript, May 12, 2005, at 61–67 (witness TF1-129); RUF Transcript, July 7, 2005, at 3–17, 30–51 (witness TF1-035); RUF Transcript, July 7, 2005, at 142–43; RUF Transcript, July 8, 2005, at 23–28 (witness TF1-122); RUF Transcript, Nov. 4, 2005, at 32–51; RUF Transcript, Nov. 7, 2005, at 17–18, 33–41 (witness TF1-314); RUF Transcript, Nov. 22, 2005, at 29–33, 42–57, 90–95; RUF Transcript, Nov. 25, 2005, at 30 (witness TF1-045); RUF Transcript, Nov. 28, 2005, at 103–11 (witness TF1-097); RUF Transcript, Dec. 5, 2005, at 79 (witness TF1-184); RUF Transcript, Dec. 8, 2005, at 43–50 (witness TF1-008); Alison Thompson, U.C. Berkeley War Crimes Studies Center, Special Court Monitoring Program, Update No. 71, Mar. 3, 2006, at 4–5 (witness TF1-113); RUF Transcript, Mar. 17, 2006, at 7–11 (witness TF1-330); RUF Transcript, Mar. 17, 2006, at 100–01 (witness TF1-343); RUF Transcript, Mar. 23, 2006, at 18–27, 77–80, 141–45 (witness TF1-288); Alison

case.[541] The percentage of witnesses whose testimony and statements featured serious discrepancies averaged about 50 percent through the ICTR cases that I reviewed. Sixty-seven percent of *Karera* witnesses testified in a way that was seriously inconsistent with those witnesses' pretrial statements,[542] whereas 51 percent of *Muhimana* witnesses did,[543] 49 percent of *Gacumbitsi* witnesses did,[544]

Thompson, U.C. Berkeley War Crimes Studies Center, Special Court Monitoring Program, Update No. 80A, June 23, 2006, at 2 (witness TF1-367).

541 The *CDF* case featured seventy-five prosecution witnesses, four of whom were non-fact witnesses and seven of whose cross-examination testimony was held entirely in closed session. After taking account of cross-examination testimony in closed sessions, sixty-two witnesses remained and, twenty-two testified seriously inconsistently. *See* CDF Transcript, June 15, 2004, at 25–32 (witness TF2-198); CDF Transcript, June 18, 2004, at 11–12 (witness TF2-176); CDF Transcript, June 21, 2004, at 48–50; CDF Transcript, June 22, 2004, at 18–19, 34–35 (witness TF2-012); CDF Transcript, Sept. 9, 2004, at 37–38, 104, 107–08, 126–27, 159–60; CDF Transcript, Sept. 10, 2004, at 5–13 (witness TF2-159); CDF Transcript, Sept. 13, 2004, at 52, 102–04 (witness TF2-032); CDF Transcript, Sept. 14, 2004, at 146–49 (witness TF2-140); CDF Transcript, Sept. 27, 2004, at 53–76 (witness TF2-154); CDF Transcript, Sept. 27, 2004, at 146–55 (witness TF2-152); CDF Transcript, Nov. 2, 2004, at 123–30; CDF Transcript, Nov. 3, 2004, at 52–59; CDF Transcript, Nov. 4, 2004, at 4–8, 12–14 (witness TF2-021); CDF Transcript, Nov. 8, 2004, at 61–68 (witness TF2-096); CDF Transcript, Nov. 9, 2004, at 88–92, 103, 105–11, 116–18 (witness TF2-004); CDF Transcript, Feb. 9, 2005, at 28, 42–43, 46–47 (witness TF2-006); CDF Transcript, Feb. 10, 2005, at 78–80 (witness TF2-190); CDF Transcript, Feb. 11, 2005, at 78–79 (witness TF2-022); CDF Transcript, Feb. 17, 2005, at 137–41 (witness TF2-222); CDF Transcript, Feb. 22, 2005, at 73–75 (witness TF2-047); CDF Transcript, Feb. 25, 2005, at 4–9, 13–14, 24–29 (witness TF2-144); CDF Transcript, Mar. 4, 2005, at 11–23 (witness TF2-168); CDF Transcript, Mar. 4, 2005, at 94 (witness TF2-173); CDF Transcript, Mar. 8, 2005, at 45 (witness TF2-167); CDF Transcript, Mar. 15, 2005, at 13–14, 17–27, 62–63 (witness TF2-014); CDF Transcript, June 3, 2005, at 36–47 (witness TF2-134).

542 *Karera* featured eighteen prosecution witnesses, one of whom was a non-fact witness and four of whose cross-examination testimony was entirely in closed session. After taking account of cross-examination testimony in closed sessions, 11.87 witnesses remained, and eight testified seriously inconsistently. See Karera Judgement, note 54, at para. 53 (witness BMA); para. 116 (witness BMU); para. 164 (witness BMH); para. 296 (witness BMJ); paras. 299, 302; Karera Transcript, Jan. 30, 2006, at 5–6 (witness BML); Karera Transcript, Jan. 31, 2006, at 9–10, 19–20; Karera Judgement, note 54, at para. 226 (witness BMI); Karera Transcript, Jan. 9, 2006, at 36 (witness BMG); Karera Transcript, Feb. 1, 2006, at 24 (witness BMR).

543 *Muhimana* featured nineteen prosecution witnesses, one of whom was a non-fact witness. After taking account of cross-examination testimony in closed sessions, 17.61 witnesses remained and nine of those witnesses testified seriously inconsistently. *See* Muhimana Judgement, note 363, at paras. 27–29 (witness AP); Muhimana Transcript, Mar. 30, 2004, at 55–56 (witness AP); Muhimana Transcript, Apr. 15, 2004, at 60–62 (witness AQ); Muhimana Transcript, Apr. 29, 2004, at 23–24 (witness AF); Muhimana Transcript, Apr. 30, 2004, at 47–49, 68–69 (witness B1); Muhimana Transcript, Apr. 19, 2004, at 43–45, 55 (witness AT); Muhimana Transcript, Apr. 7, 2004, at 32, 34–35, 36 (witness AU); Muhimana Transcript, Apr. 6, 2004, at 50 (witness BJ); Muhimana Transcript, Apr. 1, 2004, at 29–31 (witness AX); Muhimana Transcript, Apr. 8, 2004, at 30, 38, 52–53 (French version) (witness BH).

544 *Gacumbitsi* featured fifteen prosecution witnesses. Two of the fifteen were non-fact witnesses, the cross-examinations of four more were held entirely in closed session, and substantial portions of the cross-examination testimony of the remaining nine witnesses were also held in closed session. Three witnesses testified seriously inconsistently. *See* Gacumbitsi Transcript,

46 percent of *Kajelijeli* witnesses did,[545] 45 percent of *Niyitegeka* witnesses did,[546] and 41 percent of *Seromba* witnesses did.[547]

Determining whether an inconsistency or omission is serious is necessarily subjective, but I have little doubt that the inconsistencies that I considered serious (and indeed many of those that I did not so consider) are sufficiently grave that they would substantially impair the credibility of a witness who was appearing in a domestic court. In particular, I considered an inconsistency or omission to be serious either if it pertained to a key issue in the trial or if it pertained to the kind of fact that one is unlikely to forget. In the former category, then, were details that directly related to the defendant's actions or overall liability or to the witness's credibility or the weight the Trial Chamber should place on the witness's testimony. So, I considered it serious, for instance, if a witness's statement failed to mention the defendant's participation in a crime when the witness testified about that crime or if the witness's statement described a different sort of participation than that which the witness described in his testimony. I also considered it a serious inconsistency if the witness's statement and testimony diverged significantly regarding the witness's ability to observe the events she described. So, if the witness's statement placed the witness one hundred meters from the massacre site, and the witness's testimony placed the witness much closer, I considered that a serious inconsistency.

I also considered serious inconsistencies about facts that may not have directly pertained to the defendant's guilt but that called the witness's credibility

Aug. 5, 2003, at 45 (witness TAS); Gacumbitsi Transcript, Aug. 6, 2003, at 41, 43 (witness TAP); Gacumbitsi Judgement, note 364, at para. 192 (witness TAC).

545 *Kajelijeli* featured thirteen prosecution witnesses, three of whom were non-fact witnesses and one of whose cross-examination testimony was entirely in closed session. After taking account of cross-examination testimony in closed sessions, 10.91 witnesses remained and five testified seriously inconsistently. *See* Kajelijeli Transcript, July 19, 2001, at 34–35 (witness GDO); Kajelijeli Transcript, Dec. 5, 2001, at 85–96 (French version) (witness GDQ); Kajelijeli Transcript, Dec. 12, 2001, at 15–16, 83–90 (witness ACM); Prosecutor v. Kajelijeli, Case No. ICTR-99-44A-T, Decision on Kajelijeli's Request to Admit Into Evidence the Statements of GAO, July 1, 2003 (witness GAO); Kajelijeli Judgement, note 303, at paras. 296, 467 (witness GDD).

546 *Niyitegeka* featured fourteen prosecution witnesses, one of whom was a non-fact witnesses and two of whose cross-examination testimony was entirely in closed session. Of the remaining eleven prosecution witnesses, five testified seriously inconsistently. *See* Niyitegeka Judgement, note 56, at paras. 60, 61 (witness GGH); para. 101 (witness HR); para. 165 (witness DAF); para. 306 (witness GGO); Niyitegeka Transcript, Aug. 13, 2002, at 24–25, 44 (witness GHA).

547 *Seromba* featured fifteen prosecution witnesses, three of whom were non-fact witnesses and one of whose cross-examination testimony was entirely in closed session. After taking account of cross-examination testimony in closed sessions, 9.82 witnesses remained, and four testified seriously inconsistently. *See* Prosecutor v. Seromba, Case No. ICTR-2001-66-I, Judgement, para. 93 (witness CBN), 216, 237 (witness CNJ) (Dec. 13, 2006) [hereinafter Seromba Judgement]; Seromba Transcript, Oct. 7, 2004, at 11–12 (witness CBT); Seromba Transcript, Oct. 11, 2004, at 3 (witness CDK).

and reliability into question because they are not the sort of facts that one would expect to be mistaken about at one time or another. I considered it serious, for instance, if a defendant testified inconsistently about where he hid because one would expect that he'd remember whether he hid in the parish church, say, or in the bushes behind his house. Similarly, I considered it a serious inconsistency if a witness testified that she hid with one of her children when her statement reported that she hid with three of her children. Divergences regarding certain kinds of details might be considered serious inconsistencies in one case and not another. So, for instance, although I would consider a ten-day date discrepancy to be absolutely trivial in an SCSL case, I would consider it serious in an ICTR case if it pertained to the period immediately following President Habyarimana's assassination because virtually all Rwandans were keenly aware of the events that occurred directly after that event.

4.C. THE CAUSES OF THE INCONSISTENCIES

The same factors that I identify to explain the testimonial deficiencies discussed in Chapter 2 also provide plausible explanations for the inconsistencies that pervade international witness testimony. Turning first to educational deficiencies, the many international witnesses who are illiterate cannot read their statements,[548] so they cannot verify that the investigator accurately recorded the content of their interview.[549] Investigators are supposed to read the statement back to the witness, but witnesses frequently cannot remember whether their statements were read back to them, and, even if they were, neither the witnesses nor we can know whether they were read back accurately.

Cultural divergences also may play a role in a significant proportion of inconsistencies. The fact that Western space and time measurements have little meaning for some witnesses likely explains the many inconsistencies that arise over those details. One easily can imagine witnesses estimating one figure at one time and another figure at another time and not considering either to be particularly meaningful. Chapter 3 also notes that witnesses from certain cultures may be reluctant to discuss certain sensitive matters, particularly during

[548] RUF Transcript, July 27, 2004, at 74; AFRC Transcript, July 18, 2005, at 116, 118. Often counsel seek to show witnesses their statements to facilitate questioning, but they are unable to do so because the witnesses cannot read the statements. *See, e.g.*, CDF Transcript, June 18, 2004, at 12; CDF Transcript, June 21, 2004, at 49; CDF Transcript, Feb. 14, 2005, at 31; CDF Transcript, Feb. 22, 2005, at 87.

[549] Investigators typically have witnesses sign their statements, but these signatures have little probative value in the case of illiterate witnesses because the witness will not have read the statement.

an initial interview. Witnesses may become more comfortable discussing such issues in later statements or in their courtroom testimony, but doing so will create a discrepancy with the initial statement that did not mention the issue. Finally, cultural divergences often impair a fact finder's ability to determine whether a given inconsistency resulted from an innocent mistake or rather seriously undermines the witness's credibility. In particular, witnesses frequently invoke cultural norms to explain inconsistencies, but it is nearly impossible for fact finders who are not well versed in the relevant culture to ascertain whether those explanations hold water.

Some of the explanations, indeed, would appear patently ridiculous if proffered by a Western witness. For example, the statement of Sierra Leonean witness TF1-004 reports that a boy came from Bo road to inform the witness and some other members of the community about approaching soldiers. The witness testified, by contrast, that it was a "tall man" who brought the warning. When confronted with the inconsistency, the witness observed that although the messenger was a boy at the time, he was a tall man now.[550] Sierra Leonean witness, TF1-305, reported that when her statement was read back to her, she did not recognize a term that was used. So, defense counsel asked: "Did you ask them to change that word?" The witness answered: "How can I tell them to change it? I mean, I didn't say it, so it's not my business to tell them to change it. I don't know anything about the word."[551] And a *Muhimana* witness testified that he spent four years in primary school. When confronted with his previous statement in which he said that he had spent only one year in school, the witness asserted that he might as well have said that he spent no years in primary school because he did not learn anything there.[552]

A witness's invocation of cultural norms can even leave fact finders in doubt as to whether an apparent inconsistency truly constitutes an inconsistency. For instance, the statement of *Niyitegeka* witness GGO reports that the witness saw a man named Kabanda "captured and taken to Gitwa Hill" to certain leaders, including Niyitegeka. In court, however, GGO testified that, from his hiding spot in the pine forests of Kazirandimwe, he saw Kabanda being decapitated. When questioned about the apparent inconsistency, GGO denied that there was one. He claimed that when he told investigators that Kabanda had been taken to the leaders on Gitwa Hill, he had meant that Kabanda's head had been taken. As he put it: "It was the head of the victim which was brought to the leaders, including the defendant Niyitegeka.... [W]hen someone is decapitated and

[550] AFRC Transcript, June 23, 2005, at 106–08.
[551] RUF Transcript, July 27, 2004, at 65.
[552] Muhimana Transcript, Apr. 19, 2004, at 43–44.

is emasculated, for us, it's the individual as a whole who has passed on, who has disappeared."[553] In similar vein, *CDF* witness TF2-108 told investigators that Joe Koi killed Baggie Vaiey. The witness testified, however, that Kamajors had killed Vaiey after Koi refused to identify Vaiey as his relative. In a Western court, this would be a significant discrepancy, but the witness maintained that his statement and testimony were consistent. As he put it:

> I am still saying that [Koi] killed him because he disowned him and because if they captured somebody who was a relative and he was taken to Talia Yawbeko and he had no relative and you are called to identify him and you say he is not your relative, you would have been able to save him, but no, he didn't save him. You denied him. You disowned him and you were there when they killed him then that would show that it was you who gave evidence for him to be killed.[554]

Errors introduced through language translation also are unquestionably to blame for a portion of the inconsistencies that I have described. Witnesses rarely speak the same languages as the investigators, so the investigators' questions and the witnesses' answers must be translated. And if interpretation mistakes are prevalent in the highly publicized and well-regulated trial arena, one can only imagine how much more prevalent they must be in the unregulated realm of statement taking in the field. It came to light, for instance, that one SCSL investigator had used unlicensed interpreters who were connected in some fashion to the witnesses whose statements they were interpreting.[555] And when the Special Panels once called an interpreter to the stand to testify about a statement that diverged markedly from the witness's testimony, the judges found out that even though much time had passed since the translation, the interpreter was still in the "very early stages of learning English."[556] Occasionally, we can be certain, or relatively certain at least, that an interpretation error has occurred. The English version of the statement of *Muhimana* witness BI, for instance, reported that there were four thousand refugees in the church, whereas the French version put the number of refugees at one thousand.[557] Similarly, *CDF* witness TF2-012's statement said that, during a large meeting, the people thanked Chief Norman who was addressing the

553 Niyitegeka Transcript, Aug. 29, 2002, at 48.

554 CDF Transcript, May 30, 2005, at 21–22; *see also* Karera Transcript, Feb. 1, 2006, at 24 (witness claiming that there was no inconsistency between his statement – which reported that Karera had ordered a Tutsi sent to the cell in Rushashi *commune* – and his testimony that Karera had ordered the Tutsi killed because, by sending a person to the communal gaol, Karera was really sending him to his death).

555 CDF Transcript, Mar. 2, 2005, at 17.

556 Cohen, *Indifference*, note 239, at 27.

557 Muhimana Transcript, Apr. 30, 2004, at 46.

crowd, but this too was probably an interpretation error. At trial, the witness maintained that in fact he had said the reverse: that Chief Norman had thanked the people,[558] which is a far more plausible account. How many other inconsistencies are attributable to translation errors cannot be known. What can be known is that witnesses often blame the interpreters for the inconsistencies,[559] and their attributions may well be accurate in a large percentage of cases.

In addition to the three factors discussed here and in Chapter 3 – lack of education, cultural divergences, and translation errors – that are likely implicated in many testimonial deficiencies including inconsistencies, another factor emerges to explain inconsistencies alone: investigator errors. Witnesses are particularly keen to blame the investigators when their testimony fails to match their pretrial statements.[560] Most frequently, witnesses claim that the investigators omitted information from the witnesses' statements,[561] but sometimes

[558] CDF Transcript, June 21, 2004, at 52.

[559] *See, e.g.*, RUF Transcript, July 7, 2005, at 45; AFRC Transcript, Mar. 7, 2005, at 100–02; AFRC Transcript, June 27, 2005, at 59; RUF Transcript, Apr. 11, 2002, at 6; Kamuhanda Transcript, Sept. 19, 2001, at 61; Los Palos Case Notes, July 24, 2001, at 62, 87; Los Palos Case Notes, Aug. 2, 2001, at 119–20; Los Palos Case Notes, Aug. 21, 2001, at 177; Los Palos Case Notes, Sept. 25, 2001, at 273.

[560] *See, e.g.*, Ntakirutimana Judgement, note 69, at paras. 168, 169, 255, 369; Niyitegeka Judgement, note 56, at paras. 59, 165; Gacumbitsi Judgement, note 364, at para. 160; Semanza Judgement, note 31, at para. 171; Military I Transcript, July 2, 2003, at 22; Military I Transcript, July 3, 2003, at 60; Military I Transcript, July 4, 2003, at 24–25, 55; Military I Transcript, Feb. 17, 2004, at 23, 25; Nyiramasuhuko Transcript, Mar. 20, 2003, at 44; Karemera Transcript, Dec. 5, 2003, at 17; Akayesu Transcript, Jan. 29, 1997, at 16–18; Akayesu Transcript, Oct. 23, 1997, at 103–04; Kajelijeli Transcript, July 19, 2001, at 33–34; Seromba Transcript, Oct. 4, 2004, at 11–12; Seromba Transcript, Oct. 6, 2004, at 24–25; Seromba Transcript, Oct. 11, 2004, at 3; Seromba Transcript, Oct. 13, 2004, at 11; Muhimana Transcript, Apr. 19, 2004, at 55; Ndindabahizi Transcript, Sept. 16, 2003, at 12, 15; Ndindabahizi Transcript, Sept. 29, 2003, at 48; Kamuhanda Transcript, Sept. 17, 2001, at 47; Kamuhanda Transcript, Sept. 25, 2001, at 51–53; Kamuhanda Transcript, Sept. 19, 2001, at 61, 75–76; Kamuhanda Transcript, Jan. 29, 2002, at 23, 25; Kamuhanda Transcript, Jan. 30, 2002, at 87–88; Kamuhanda Transcript, Feb. 6, 2002, at 103–05; Kamuhanda Transcript, Feb. 7, 2002, at 92–94; Kamuhanda Transcript, Feb. 11, 2002, at 44–46;. Ntakirutimana Transcript, Sept. 20, 2001, at 145–46; Ntakirutimana Transcript, Sept. 24, 2001, at 110–11, 141; Taylor Transcript, Mar. 13, 2008, at 5976; CDF Transcript, Sept. 9, 2004, at 108; CDF Transcript, Feb. 22, 2005, at 83; RUF Transcript, Oct. 7, 2004, at 175–81; RUF Transcript, Feb. 3, 2005, at 36, 51; RUF Transcript, Mar. 17, 2006, at 7; Alison Thompson, U.C. Berkeley War Crimes Studies Center, Special Court Monitoring Program, Update No. 71, Mar. 3, 2006, at 5; AFRC Transcript, Apr. 19, 2005, at 45; AFRC Transcript, July 20, 2005, at 39; Los Palos Case Notes, July 23, 2001, at 57; Los Palos Case Notes, July 24, 2001, at 89–90.

[561] *See, e.g.*, Akayesu Judgement, note 32, at para. 248; Ntakirutimana Judgement, note 69, at paras. 168, 255, 369; Semanza Judgement, note 31, at para. 171; Niyitegeka Transcript, Aug. 13, 2002, at 44; Kajelijeli Transcript, Dec. 7, 2001, at 27–28; Taylor Transcript, Jan. 9, 2008, at 777–80; Taylor Transcript, Mar. 13, 2008, at 6028–29; Akayesu Transcript, Jan. 29, 1997, at 16–18; Muhimana Transcript, Apr. 19, 2004, at 55; Kamuhanda Transcript, Sept. 17, 2001, at 47; Kamuhanda Transcript, Sept. 19, 2001, at 61, 75–76; Kamuhanda Transcript, Sept. 24, 2001, at

witnesses accuse the investigators of inserting fabricated information.[562] It is unlikely that investigators err as often as witnesses claim that they err, but there is no question that errors do occur and that the quality of the investigators' work product is uneven. Interviews with ICTR and SCSL investigators generate off-the-record stories of investigators who at best lack an adequate understanding of the conflict that they are investigating and the culture and habits of the people who are to be witnesses,[563] and who at worst are lazy and/or incompetent. Occasionally, evidence of such poor performance makes its way into a case's transcripts or judgment. For instance, a prosecution investigator in the Special Panels' *Ena* case and a defense investigator in the ICTR's *Akayesu* case each submitted statements for two or more witnesses that were identical.[564] As the *Ena* Panel described it:

> The Court expresses its concern that two of the statements (the statement of Laurinda Oki and Maria Lafu Ulan, both dated 20 March 2002) are identical. Other than the name, age and time of interview, the text of the statements are identical – even the spacing and punctuation marks are replicated. The first five paragraphs of the statement of Terezinha Punef (also taken on 20 March 2002) are identical to these two statements, while the remaining paragraphs of the statement display striking similarities in terms of words, phrasing and contents. In addition, the statement of Olinda Cono (taken on 22 March 2002) shows striking similarities in terms of words, phrasing and contents to these statements.[565]

111–12; Kamuhanda Transcript, Sept. 25, 2001, at 51–53; Kamuhanda Transcript, Jan. 30, 2002, at 87–88; Kamuhanda Transcript, Feb. 6, 2002, at 103–05; RUF Transcript, Mar. 17, 2006, at 7; AFRC Transcript, Apr. 19, 2005, at 45.

562 Gacumbitsi Judgement, note 364, at para. 160; Niyitegeka Judgement, note 56, at paras. 59, 165; Kajelijeli Transcript, July 19, 2001, at 34–35; Kajelijeli Transcript, Dec. 12, 2001, at 83–90; Military I Transcript, July 2, 2003, at 22; Military I Transcript, July 3, 2003, at 60; Military I Transcript, July 4, 2003, at 24–25, 55; Military I Transcript, Feb. 17, 2004, at 23, 25; Nyiramasuhuko Transcript, Mar. 20, 2003, at 44; Ndindabahizi Transcript, Sept. 16, 2003, at 12, 15; Ndindabahizi Transcript, Sept. 29, 2003, at 48; Kamuhanda Transcript, Sept. 24, 2001, at 24–25; Kamuhanda Transcript, Jan. 29, 2002, at 23, 25; Kamuhanda Transcript, Feb. 7, 2002, at 92–94; Kamuhanda Transcript, Feb. 11, 2002, at 44–46; Ntakirutimana Transcript, Sept. 20, 2001, at 145–46; Ntakirutimana Transcript, Sept. 24, 2001, at 110–11, 141; Ntakirutimana Transcript, Oct. 23, 2001, at 6–7, 17; Taylor Transcript, Mar. 13, 2008, at 5976; CDF Transcript, Sept. 9, 2004, at 108; CDF Transcript, Feb. 22, 2005, at 83; RUF Transcript, Oct. 7, 2004, at 175–81; RUF Transcript, Feb. 3, 2005, at 36, 51; Los Palos Case Notes, July 23, 2001, at 57. RUF witness TF1-305 believed that investigators must have added the term "AFRC" to her statement because the witness said that she had never heard of the word. RUF Transcript, July 27, 2004, at 65–70.

563 Penelope van Tuyl, U.C. Berkeley War Crimes Studies Center, *Effective, Efficient, and Fair?: An Inquiry into the Investigative Practices of the Office of the Prosecutor at the Special Court for Sierra Leone* 43 (Sept. 2008).

564 Akayesu Judgement, note 32, at para. 443; Prosecution v. Ena & Ena, Case No. 5/2002, Judgement, para. 67 (Mar. 23, 2004) [hereinafter Ena Judgement].

565 Ena Judgement, note 564, at para. 67.

Similarly, an investigator's failure to accurately identify the witness whose statement was being taken caused widespread confusion during the *Ndindabahizi* trial as prosecutors believed that it had statements from two witnesses with the same name, defense counsel believed that one witness had provided two statements, and the truth was that investigators had simply misidentified a witness providing one of the statements.[566]

Occasionally, when inconsistencies have proven too dramatic to ignore, the Trial Chambers have called the investigator to the stand to testify about the procedures the investigator followed during the statement taking. Although some investigators apparently adhere to routine practices that include reading the statements back to witnesses and having witnesses sign their statements,[567] other investigators, even in the same institution, dispensed with such practices.[568] And although good practices are to be prized, the tribunals did not always encourage them with their incentive structure. According to one ICTR investigator, in the ICTR's early days, an investigator's performance review – which determined whether his contract would be renewed – was based on the number of statements he took. The ICTR was roundly condemned in those days for its slow pace, so one can understand why it would adopt a performance review policy that stressed productivity, but there is little question that it also encouraged investigators to prize quantity over quality.

Questions regarding investigators are apt to loom particularly large when the witness testifies at trial about a key fact that he failed to mention in his pretrial interview. When asked on the stand, "[w]hy didn't you mention this crucial fact in your statement?," witnesses virtually always maintain that it was "because the investigators never asked about it."[569] That explanation may

[566] Ndindabahizi Transcript, Sept. 29, 2003, at 1–17.

[567] CDF Transcript, Mar. 2, 2005, at 8. Some witnesses also attested to this procedure. *See, e.g.*, CDF Transcript, Dec. 1, 2004, at 32; CDF Transcript, Feb. 15, 2005, at 7; CDF Transcript, Mar. 4, 2005, at 90–91.

[568] RUF Transcript, Apr. 28, 2005, at 16–17. In addition, witnesses frequently maintain that their statements were not read back to them. *See, e.g.*, Ntakirutimana Transcript, Sept. 24, 2001, at 113; CDF Transcript, June 22, 2004, at 21; CDF Transcript, Sept. 9, 2004, at 159–61; CDF Transcript, Mar. 4, 2005, at 12; RUF Transcript, Oct. 19, 2004, at 20–21. The ICTY has also had its share of investigators who fail to follow procedures. *See, e.g.*, *"Intuitive" Identification*, Sense News Agency, June 25, 2007.

[569] *See, e.g.*, Karera Judgement, note 54, at para. 115; Niyitegeka Judgement, note 56, at para. 101; Musema Judgement, note 112, at para. 706; Muhimana Judgement, note 363, at paras. 269–270; Akayesu Judgement, note 32, at para. 266; Ntakirutimana Judgement, note 69, at para. 255; Kajelijeli Judgement, note 303, at para. 467; Rwamakuba Judgement, note 63, at para. 114; Kajelijeli Transcript, Dec. 5, 2001 (French version), at 79–80; Kamuhanda Transcript, Sept. 4, 2001, at 80; Kamuhanda Transcript, Sept. 24, 2001, at 26; Kamuhanda Transcript, Jan. 31, 2002, at 76–77; Ntakirutimana Transcript, Sept. 20, 2001, at 33; Niyitegeka Transcript, Aug. 13, 2002, at 47–48; Taylor Transcript, May 12, 2008, at 9570; RUF Transcript, July 27, 2004, at 27, 69; RUF Transcript, Jan. 24, 2005, at 104; RUF Transcript, Mar. 17, 2005, at 95; AFRC Transcript, Apr. 18,

seem suspect when the omitted fact is central to the prosecution's case, but even then, the witness may be speaking the truth. By all accounts, investigators frequently are sent to a region to gather evidence about one defendant or about a particular type of offense, such as sexual assaults or the forced recruitment of child soldiers. In those situations, investigators may focus their questions on that which is specifically relevant to their particular inquiry, thereby giving the witness little opportunity to provide information about other crimes and other perpetrators.[570] Ideally, if a witness does mention another offender or another crime that is outside the scope of that investigator's original inquiry, the investigator would delve further into that matter or at least send a new investigations team to follow up with the witness and take a more comprehensive statement about the additional matter, but often that does not occur.[571] *RUF* witness TF1-199, for instance, testified about the kidnapping of U.N. officials. Because the crime was not mentioned in the witness's pretrial statement, the investigator who took the statement was called to the stand. Although the judges opined that the investigator "must have known of the importance of the abduction of UN peacekeepers in relation to this trial; that it was a serious allegation on the indictment," the investigator nonetheless asserted that she may not have written it down because it fell outside the scope of her focus, which was child soldiers.[572]

Inconsistencies are a prevalent feature of international trials, and because they result from one or more of several causes it is difficult to know what to make of them. They may arise in consequence of the educational, cultural, and linguistic factors described in Chapter 3, or they may stem from investigators' errors. It is reasonable to think that many of them do. But inconsistencies, even more than the testimonial deficiencies identified in Chapter 2, are equally likely to indicate that the witness lied – either while giving a statement or while testifying. Defense counsel typically probe inconsistencies vigorously during cross-examination in order to suggest just that – that the witness has changed her story and thus should not be believed. The foregoing chapters show, indeed, that international trials suffer from a variety of severe

2005, at 62; AFRC Transcript, July 20, 2005, at 54–55; AFRC Transcript, Sept. 21, 2005, at 4–5; AFRC Transcript, Sept. 30, 2005, at 66. *Muhimana* witness AF invoked this explanation, but defense counsel later showed that the witness had been asked about the defendant. Muhimana Transcript, Apr. 29, 2004, at 22–24. *See also* Rwamakuba Judgement, note 63, at para. 150 (noting that the assertion that the witness was not previously asked a particular question "is a fairly common explanation provided by both Prosecution and Defence Witnesses").

570 Even the ICC investigations tend to focus on one crime or type of crime so that questions about matters outside of that focus are often not asked. Katy Glassborow, *ICC Investigative Strategy Under Fire*, INT'L WAR AND PEACE REPORTING, Oct. 17, 2008.

571 Interview with KJ, former ICTR investigator, July 7, 2006 (by telephone).

572 RUF Transcript, Apr. 28, 2005, at 18–20.

fact-finding impediments. Witnesses fail to answer whole categories of questions that are crucial to accurate decision making, and the questions that they do answer are frequently answered differently over time. These problems would impair fact-finding even if we were confident that they were attributable to one or more of the "innocent" explanations. But perjury looms large as a plausible, alternative explanation. The following chapter explores perjury at the international tribunals as a means of considering just how plausible an alternative explanation it is.

5

Perjury

The Counternarrative

Perjury stands as a compelling counternarrative to explain the testimonial problems heretofore identified. I have described already the ways in which a witness might feign ignorance or lack of understanding in order to make his accounts more plausible, more incriminating, and less likely to contradict the accounts of other witnesses or that same witness's previous account. Long, drawn-out exchanges in which the witness fails to answer the questions directly can similarly buy the witness time to consider which answers he wishes to provide and can even frustrate the interrogating counsel to such a degree that the counsel just abandons the line of questioning entirely. Finally, the potential of perjury to explain the inconsistencies just described is even more straightforward. Successive witness accounts may vary because the witness has forgotten the perjured details he earlier provided to investigators. Or a witness may not know the identity of the defendant at the time he provides his statement, so it is only later that he inserts the defendant into his account. Or the converse may be true. The witness may accurately inculpate the defendant during his pretrial interview but later find it in his interest to exculpate the defendant at trial.

As earlier noted, there is little way of ascertaining whether any given testimonial deficiency does in fact result from perjury, but what we can explore is whether other indications suggest that perjury is a considerable problem for the international tribunals. To explore this question, this chapter first considers perjury as a cultural phenomenon. It then explores the incentives for perjury that the international tribunals provide. Finally, the chapter ends by examining the general prevalence of perjury in international criminal proceedings. In sum, the inquiry conducted in this chapter shows that, although we cannot know whether any particular testimonial problem reflects perjury, we can know that there is a great deal of lying taking place at (some) international tribunals.

5.A. A CULTURAL COMPONENT TO PERJURY?

Particularly at the outset of my study, I conducted numerous interviews with international tribunal personnel. Most were Western, but some were African, and Rwandan in particular. My questions focused on communication difficulties, and virtually every interviewee volunteered that Rwandans and Sierra Leoneans viewed truth and deception differently from Westerners. Some interviewees contended only that Rwandan and Sierra Leonean witnesses were inclined to tailor their testimony to convey what they believed the Western investigator, lawyer, or judge questioning them wished to hear.[573] Thus, one defense counsel maintained that witnesses frequently will speak well of his clients when he is interviewing them but will convey all manner of incriminating information about the clients when the witnesses are interviewed by the prosecution.[574] Indeed, when another defense counsel made this observation, I asked if I might speak to the counsel's Sierra Leonean investigator. The defense counsel readily gave me permission to interview the investigator but cautioned that the investigator would likely tell me what he thought *I* wanted to hear for my research purposes.[575] Other interviewees went further and alleged that lying is more accepted in Rwandan and Sierra Leonean cultures and does not carry the same negative connotations that Westerners would place on it.[576] Even the ICTR's former chief of prosecutions described Rwandans in a newspaper interview as having "a demure culture with deep ethnic roots and tensions, where lying is not only tolerated but sometimes encouraged."[577]

Perhaps these assertions stem only from Western prejudice, as David Cohen has contended,[578] but they have received a certain amount of scholarly

[573] Interview with DD, former SCSL prosecution investigator, Sept. 26, 2006 (by telephone); Interview with Michiel Pestman, SCSL defense counsel, May 19, 2006 (by telephone); Interview with SS, SCSL defense section, May 24, 2006 (by telephone).

[574] Interview with Peter Robinson, ICTR defense counsel, May 9, 2006 (by telephone). One example of this phenomenon was provided by alleged Rwandan génocidaire Juvenal Uwilingiyimana. Prior to his mysterious death, Uwilingiyimana had been providing information to both the prosecution and the defense. Because both sides were keen to have him testify, one can surmise that he provided different information to the different sides. *See It's a Lying Shame*, South China Morning Post, Mar. 22, 2006.

[575] Interview with Michiel Pestman, SCSL defense counsel, May 19, 2006 (by telephone).

[576] Interview with FL, former ICTR prosecutor, July 10, 2006 (by telephone); Interview with Peter Robinson, ICTR defense counsel, May 9, 2006 (by telephone); Interview with Michiel Pestman, SCSL defense counsel, May 19, 2006 (by telephone); Interview with Howard Morrison, former ICTY and ICTR defense counsel, May 22, 2006 (by telephone); Interview with NE, ICTR defense investigator, May 31, 2006.

[577] *It's a Lying Shame*, South China Morning Post, Mar. 22, 2006.

[578] Cohen, *Indifference*, note 239, at 61.

support. An expert witness for the defense in the *Semanza* case, Professor Pascal Ndengejeho, testified that lying is an integral aspect of intelligence in Rwandan culture. According to Professor Ndengejeho, "[h]e who knows how to manipulate lies is considered more intelligent than the others in Rwandan culture."[579] Although the testimony of Professor Ndengejeho might be dismissed as biased by the adversarial nature of the proceeding, other Rwandan and non-Rwandan scholars have described Rwandan views about veracity in similar terms. Rwandan scholar Aloys Rukebesha, for instance, traces current Rwandan views about communication to precolonial times and maintains that "throughout history, [Rwanda] always meticulously maintained a system of communication that contradicted what people actually thought."[580] According to Rukebesha, when discussing daily affairs, precolonial Rwandans felt free to "retract or add to, color and even invent none or all [of the account]" such that one really did not know what in fact happened.[581] When it came to discussing more important matters, Rwandans followed a basic rule: "[S]ay only what c[ould] be repeated before any authority."[582] Adherence to this rule formed part of a survival strategy; indeed, the nature and content of the information that an individual would convey depended on the relationship between the speaker and the recipient of the information.[583] In particular, when speaking to a superior, the speaker's goal was not necessarily to provide information that was objectively accurate but to consolidate his own social position and make a positive impression on the superior.[584] As Rukebesha put it, "[t]ruth was not spoken for itself.... [I]nstead of telling one's superiors the truth, one hid it and distorted it to gain favor with important people."[585]

This cultural disposition has persisted to the present day, according to Rukebesha and other scholars. Rukebesha notes the importance of secrecy in Rwandan communications, opining that secrecy "is a dominant theme in Rwandan society."[586] Danielle de Lame has likewise given secrecy considerable thought and has contended that "[c]irculation and holding back information are cultural facts" in Rwanda.[587] Other scholars address directly the role of

579 Semanza Transcript, Jan. 31, 2002, at 116.

580 Aloys Rukebesha, *Esotérisme et Communication Sociale au Rwanda: Rukebesha nous parle de son ouvrage*, 35 LA RELÈVE 3, 3 (Michele Slachetka trans., 1985).

581 ALOYS RUKEBESHA, ÉSOTÉRISME ET COMMUNICATION SOCIALE 167 (Michele Slachetka trans., 1985).

582 RUKEBESHA, note 581, at 168.

583 C.M. Overdulve, *Fonction de la langue et de la communication au Rwanda*, 53 NOUVELLE REVUE DE SCIENCE MISSIONNAIRE, 271, 274 (Michele Slachetka trans., 1997).

584 *Id.* at 275.

585 RUKEBESHA, note 581, at 169.

586 Rukebesha, note 580, at 3.

587 DANIELLE DE LAME, A HILL AMONG A THOUSAND 14 (2005).

accuracy in current Rwandan speech. For instance, according to C. M. Overdulve, a Dutch pastor and scholar who resided in Rwanda for many years, even today what matters to the Rwandan is not in the first place the agreement between his speech and reality but rather the relationship between the two speaking parties.[588] Overdulve notes that when a European seeks information from a Rwandan through an interpreter, a complex set of considerations come into play for both the interpreter and the Rwandan from whom the information is sought. The interpreter likely wishes to maintain a good relationship with the European because there are advantages in that. So, he must consider:

> What does this European want to hear? What would please him? What does he not want to hear? What is he thinking by asking these questions? What idea does he want to confirm? But there is more: What is he going to do with this information? Can this have, either for me or for the [Rwandan who is being questioned] unfortunate consequences?

The interpreter must also consider the Rwandan and ask himself: "Who is he? What is his position? Does he have connections in the political realm? What do I have to fear from his possible misfortune? Or can I expect to reap certain benefits, if I please him?"[589] Pierre Crépeau describes it similarly in his study of Rwandan proverbs: "[T]he moral value of speech is not a function of [the degree to which the speech] corresponds to reality . . . above all, it is a function of utility. Morally good speech is that which is beneficial; morally bad speech is that which is harmful."[590]

Although a lack of concern for accuracy sounds negative to Western ears, scholars maintain that truth and lies do not carry the same moral connotations in Rwanda.[591] Indeed, Pierre Erny maintains that a fundamental aspect of the Rwandan conception of intelligence is the art of lying.[592] In similar vein, Overdulve writes that although one can speak of "hypocrisy" or "deceit" in English, there are no equivalent Kinyarwandan words because the Kinyarwandan concepts have positive connotations. Concepts such as hypocrisy are positive values in Rwanda because they are necessary to survive, and a person using them shows his wisdom, prudence, and ability to support himself in that society.[593] Erny asked several students at the National University of

[588] Overdulve, note 583, at 276.
[589] *Id.* at 279.
[590] PIERRE CRÉPEAU, PAROLE ET SAGESSE: VALEURS SOCIALES DANS LES PROVERBES DU RWANDA 224 (Michele Slachetka trans., 1985).
[591] *Id.* at 224; Overdulve, note 583, at 281–82.
[592] Pierre Erny, *L'esprit de l'éducation au Rwanda ou le "caractère national" décrit par un groupe d'étudiants*, GENÈVE-AFRIQUE, vol. XXI no.1, 25, 49 (Michele Slachetka trans., 1983).
[593] Overdulve, note 583, at 282.

Rwanda to give a brief description of the national character of a Rwandan, and their answers mirror the above descriptions. As one student put it: "The Rwandan is fundamentally careful and cautious. He rarely answers in a definite manner.... [B]efore answering, [a Rwandan] wants to know the objective of the question."[594] Another student remarked, "[d]iscretion is so sought after and practiced, that, in exceeding the limits, it devolves into a sort of social hypocrisy. It is possible that a person will say yes while meaning no, and no while meaning yes, in order to avoid compromising himself."[595] As another student put it: "Because nobody says what he thinks or thinks what he says, because nobody believes right off the bat what another says, empty talk is interminable and proceeds according to preestablished formulas."[596] This circumspection, according to scholars and ordinary Rwandans, is all the more prevalent when Rwandans are dealing with foreigners.[597]

Anthropologists similarly note the prevalence of secret societies and the numerous strategies of concealment that permeate the everyday in Sierra Leone.[598] As noted in Chapter 3, these strategies of concealment play out most obviously in the kind of indirect, ambiguous exchanges that characterize so much testimony at the SCSL, but they may also suggest a higher tolerance for lying or, at the least, for purposefully evasive responses. Tim Kelsall notes, for instance, that

> anthropological knowledge of the Sierra Leone culture area would lead us to expect many witnesses not to give the full story, or the full truth in their initial encounters with Prosecutors. The Krio saying *Tok Af Lef Af* encapsulates the idea that only a foolish, untrustworthy or downright reprehensible person will divulge everything they know in a first encounter, meaning that many people will withhold some portion of the truth, taking half, leaving half not least because the person they are dealing with might constitute a threat.[599]

Both Sierra Leonean and Rwandan witnesses have invoked just this sort of reasoning when confronted with their lies or evasions. For instance, when

[594] Erny, note 592, at 46.

[595] *Id.*

[596] *Id.* at 51–52.

[597] Overdulve, note 583, at 280.

[598] KELSALL, note 142, at 171-76. Angered by defense counsel's suggestion that he was never close to Charles Taylor, prosecution witness Joseph "Zigzag" Marzah revealed that he and Taylor were in the same secret religious society and "had eaten human hearts" together on "multiple occasions." Following this revelation, "Marzah appeared shaken and crossed himself, explaining that he had broken the laws of his [secret] society." The Trial of Charles Taylor, *Prosecution Witness "Zigzag" Marzah Finishes Testimony, says Taylor Ate Human Hearts*, Mar. 14, 2008, *available at* http://charlestaylortrial.org/.

[599] KELSALL, note 142, at 214–15.

Sierra Leonean witness TF1-141 admitted to lying in the statement he provided investigators, he explained it thus:

> The first time I met with this woman [investigator], I never knew what would happen after I have spoken to this woman. I had that fear in me. So I didn't have any confidence to talk to her. I decided to be putting things indirectly. But now that I've developed this confidence I've got – I had the confidence to talk to Sharan . . . and I spoke to her all I knew and what happened exactly.[600]

Similarly, Sierra Leonean witness Varmuyan Sherif admitted that he had initially withheld information from investigators until he satisfied himself that he could trust them.[601] Witness TF1-017 likewise admitted that he did not tell prosecutors everything he knew during his first interview. When it was revealed that he not only withheld information but had provided false information, he opined that "it is okay to make up facts if you are hesitant about the facts."[602] And, although it became clear that Sierra Leonean witness TF2-190 had provided false statements to investigators, the witness denied that he had "lied," stating "I was not telling lies. I was really afraid and when you are scared you do not know how to position yourself."[603] Some Rwandan witnesses invoke similar reasoning. For instance, when it was pointed out to *Karera* witness BMA that he had not mentioned the defendant in his previous statement, he stated that he either forgot certain details or he "did not wish to reveal the entire truth at that time."[604]

Whether or not certain sets of international witnesses have a somewhat flexible view of the truth as a cultural matter is a controversial question. What is not controversial is that international witnesses have a variety of incentives to lie, a topic I turn to next.

5.B. PERJURY INCENTIVES

International witnesses face a variety of pressures that – separately or in combination – encourage them to lie on the stand. Group-based loyalties stand as one. In the *Limaj* case, for instance, an ICTY Trial Chamber observed that "notions of honour and other group values have a particular relevance to the cultural background of witnesses with Albanian roots in Kosovo" and consequently "had a bearing upon the willingness of some witnesses to speak the

[600] RUF Transcript, Apr. 14, 2005, at 23; *see also id.* at 10–11, 32.
[601] Taylor Transcript, Jan. 11, 2008, at 1098–1101.
[602] CDF Transcript, Nov. 22, 2004, at 39, 44 (on file with author).
[603] CDF Transcript, Feb. 10, 2005, at 79.
[604] Karera Judgement, note 54, at para. 53.

truth in court."[605] The *Limaj* Trial Chamber indicated that the "notions of honour and other group values" impeding truthful testimony in that case predated the conflict; but, even if such group-based loyalties do not have "particular relevance to the cultural background" of other sets of international witnesses before the crimes in question took place, the fact that these witnesses were the subject of an international crime will make those values relevant by the time that the witnesses are testifying. International crimes virtually always target whole peoples, whether for religious, ethnic, political, or similar reasons; thus, victims of such crimes are not randomly chosen, as they typically are in one-off domestic crimes, but rather become victims as a result of their membership in the group in question. In other words, international criminal trials necessarily will feature many fact witnesses who have reason to be biased because these witnesses are members of the group that was targeted while the defendant is a member of the offenders' group. Certainly, every Tutsi witness has a reason to want revenge from the Hutu, and even conflicts such as Sierra Leone's, which did not target ethnic groups per se, had ethnic and tribal components to them.

Additionally, international tribunals hear not only the testimony of victims but also that of insiders, and they, like insider witnesses in domestic trials, often have many reasons to lie. First, as a result of their incriminating testimony, insider witnesses may receive de facto immunity from prosecution[606] or significant sentence reductions if they themselves are being prosecuted.[607]

[605] Limaj Judgement, note 57, at para. 13.

[606] *See* Thijs Bouwknegt, *Rwanda's Genocide Tribunal's Witness 'Hiding,'* Radio Netherlands Worldwide, Oct. 2, 2008. ICTR prosecutors, for instance, issued a sealed indictment and an arrest warrant against Juvénal Uwilingiyimana, a former minister of Commerce and director of Rwanda's Office of Tourism and National Parks during the genocide, charging him with helping to plan and implement the genocide by allowing militia members to train in Rwanda's dense forests and by ordering executions at roadblocks once the genocide had begun. Uwilingiyimana reportedly had valuable information implicating high-ranking ICTR defendants, so when he indicated a willingness to reveal that information, prosecutors agreed to hold the arrest warrant in abeyance. We cannot know whether the ICTR eventually would have prosecuted Uwilingiyimana; as it happened, he went missing a few days after one of his interview sessions with ICTR prosecutors, and his badly decomposed body was found in a Belgian canal nearly a month later. *See Prosecutor's Statement Regarding the Death of ICTR Indictee Juvénal Uwilingiyimana*, ICTR Newsletter, December 2005-January 2006, at 7, *available at* http://69.94.11.53/ENGLISH/newsletter/dec05-jan06/dec05-jan06.pdf. Defense counsel in the SCSL's *AFRC* cases alleged that insider witness Gibril Massaquoi had been informed by SCSL investigators that he was a suspect, and he agreed to testify in order to escape an indictment, Kara Sanin, U.C. Berkeley War Crimes Studies Center, Special Court Monitoring Program, Update No. 58, Oct. 10, 2005, at 4, and *RUF* defense counsel leveled similar allegations regarding insider witness John Tarnue, RUF Transcript, Oct. 7, 2004, at 10.

[607] Substantial cooperation with the prosecution is considered a mitigating factor in sentencing at the ICTR and SCSL, SCSL Rules of Procedure and Evidence, Rule 101(b)(ii) (2008), *available at* http://www.sc-sl.org/LinkClick.aspx?fileticket=1YNrqhd4L5s%3d&tabid=176 [hereinafter SCSL RPE]; ICTR Rules of Procedure and Evidence, Rule 101(b)(ii) (2008), *available at*

Personal animosity may also motivate insider witnesses to falsely accuse the defendant. *Taylor* insider witness TF1-406 admitted that he "hated" Charles Taylor,[608] for instance, and *AFRC* insider witness TF1-184 may have sought defendant Brima's conviction because TF1-184 had been a close associate of a man Brima was alleged to have killed.[609] Similarly, *CDF* insider witness Albert Nallo had reason to hate defendant Norman because Norman had removed Nallo from his position in the CDF.[610] And another insider witness in the *CDF* case – TF2-021 – had been an RUF rebel before the CDF captured him, so his testimony against the *CDF* defendants may have been colored by loyalty to the RUF. In their study of the psychology of proof, experimental psychologist Willem Wagenaar and his coauthors caution against relying on the testimony of witnesses whose independence is known to be compromised.[611] If the international tribunals followed that advice, however, their trials would have no witnesses.[612]

When ideological commitments and personal animosity do not motivate false testimony, fear sometimes does. Although most witnesses testify under pseudonyms, many still have reason to fear retaliation following their testimony.[613] A key insider witness in the SCSL's *AFRC* trial was beaten nearly

http://69.94.11.53/ENGLISH/rules/080314/080314.pdf [hereinafter ICTR RPE.], and a number of insiders have received sentencing concessions as a result of their testimony in other cases. Prosecutor v. Serushago, Case No. ICTR-98–39-S, Sentence, paras. 31–33, 41–42 (Feb. 5, 1999) [hereinafter Serushago Judgement]; Prosecutor v. Ruggiu, Case No. ICTR-97–32-I, Judgement and Sentence, paras. 56–58 (June 1, 2000). Several ICTY defendants, including Milan Babić, Miroslav Deronjić, Momir Nikolić, and Dragan Obrenović were able to negotiate very favorable plea agreements in part because they testified in a series of subsequent cases. One SCSL insider, who had been imprisoned in Sierra Leone on unrelated charges was led to believe that he would not receive the death penalty for his Sierra Leonean crimes if he cooperated with the SCSL. van Tuyl, note 563, at 39.

[608] Taylor Transcript, Jan. 10, 2008, at 955–56. *See also* Taylor Transcript, Jan. 10, 2008, at 1047–48 (witness admitting that his whole family hated Taylor in part because Taylor's forces had burned to death his father's two wives).

[609] AFRC Judgement, note 27, at para. 362.

[610] CDF Transcript, Mar. 11, 2005, at 30.

[611] Willem A. Wagenaar et al., Anchored Narratives: The Psychology of Criminal Evidence 169 (1993).

[612] The *CDF* Trial Chamber asserted that it treated the testimony of insider witnesses "with particular caution," CDF Judgement, note 27, at para. 278; *see also* CDF Judgement, Annex C, Separate Concurring and Partially Dissenting Opinion of Hon. Justice Bankole Thompson Filed Pursuant to Article 18 of the Statute, para. 47 [hereinafter Justice Thompson's Dissent], but my examination of the *CDF* case in Chapter 7 calls that assertion into question.

[613] The identity of witnesses frequently becomes known despite the use of pseudonyms. *See, e.g.* Stover, note 13, at 1–2, 47–48, 74, 99; *Kosovo Journalist Indicted by UN Court*, Balkan Insight, May 20, 2008; Karemera Transcript, Apr. 10, 2008, at 22–23; Ndindabahizi Transcript, Sept. 1, 2003, at 56–57; Ndindabahizi Transcript, Sept. 3, 2003, at 35–36, 48; Ndindabahizi Transcript, Sept. 8, 2003, at 27–28; Ndindabahizi Transcript, Sept. 9, 2003, at 9, 16–18; Ndindabahizi Transcript, Sept. 15, 2003, at 13, 36, 39–40; Ndindabahizi Transcript, Sept. 22, 2003, at 14–18.

to death after he testified,[614] and a passel of Rwandan witnesses in both ICTR trials and Rwanda's domestic trials have been threatened, injured, or killed following their testimony.[615] Most frequently, witnesses who fear retaliation simply refuse to testify at all,[616] but threats and intimidation can also motivate witnesses to lie on the stand. A witness in the ICTR's Media Case, for instance, testified that members of a victims' survivors group threatened him after he refused their request to testify falsely,[617] and similar threats seemed to have succeeded in the notorious *Victor Manuel Alves* case at the Special Panels. There, all six prosecution eyewitnesses provided initial statements attesting that the defendant had intentionally shot at close range and killed a pro-Indonesian militia member, but all of them later changed their stories and testified either that they had not seen the killing at all or that the defendant had placed the rifle over his shoulder and had shot backward as he walked in the other direction.[618] Similarly, a number of witnesses in the Special Panels' *Tacaqui* case implicated the defendant in their written statements but then renounced those statements on the stand,[619] suggesting thereby that they were afraid to testify against him. But one witness maintained that he falsely implicated Tacaqui initially because he feared that he would otherwise be accused of the crime.[620] Other examples of apparent intimidation motivating false testimony appear in the notes.[621]

Financial incentives provided by the international tribunals stand as another, especially compelling inducement to lie. The international tribunals provide witnesses stipends and services that enable the witnesses to travel to the tribunal and to maintain themselves and their families while the witnesses are away from home. SCSL stipends come to 16,000 leones per day (or approximately US$5.25)[622] and the ICTR provides stipends of $22 per day for

614 Human Rights Watch, *Bringing Justice: the Special Court for Sierra Leone Accomplishments, Shortcomings, and Needed Support*, Vol. 16, No. 8A, at 31 (Sept. 2004).

615 *Genocide Survivors in Danger, Says IBUKA*, Hirondelle News Agency, Nov. 16, 2005; Power, note 10; *Prosecution Witness Assassinated in Rwanda*, Hirondelle News Agency, Oct. 20, 2004; Modestus Kessy, *Genocide Witness Killed After Testifying*, The Guardian (Dar es Salam), Oct. 22, 2004; Nasser Ega-Musa, *Another Failure of Justice in Africa*, Wash. Post, Mar. 6, 1997, at A21.

616 The *Simba* judgment, for instance, discusses allegations that the government of Rwanda sought to prevent defense witnesses from testifying. Simba Judgement, note 455, at paras. 41–53.

617 Prosecutor v. Nahimana et al., Case No. ICTR-99–52-T, Transcript, Mar. 13, 2003, at 61 [hereinafter Nahimana Transcript].

618 Cohen, *Indifference*, note 239, at 63.

619 *See* Tacaqui Judgement, note 36, at 30–32.

620 *See id.* at 33.

621 Niyitegeka Judgement, note 56, at paras. 222, 398; Michele Staggs, U.C. Berkeley War Crimes Studies Center, Special Court Monitoring Program, Update No. 20, Feb. 4, 2005, at 4.

622 Kyra Sanin & Anna Stirnemann, U.C. Berkeley War Crimes Study Center, *Child Witnesses at the Special Court for Sierra Leone* 23–24 (March 2006), *available at* http://socrates.berkeley.edu/~warcrime/ChildWitnessReport_000.pdf.pdf.

protected witnesses and $110 per day for nonprotected witnesses.[623] These sums are intended as compensation for "wages, earnings and time lost as a result of testifying." The daily allowances accrue for all of the time the witness is in the service of the tribunal, which frequently runs into weeks or months.[624] In addition to this allowance, the SCSL also reimburses witnesses for food, accommodation, transportation, and clothing, and witnesses may in addition travel with one support person, who also receives reimbursement for food, lodging, and transportation while the witness is in Freetown.[625] Finally, the tribunals provide witnesses with medical care for certain conditions.[626] The ICTR, for instance, has set up its own clinic and treats witnesses on a long-term basis, including by providing some HIV treatment. The clinic provides care to more than two hundred witnesses, some of whom are seen weekly. Some witnesses who testified as far back as 1997 are still receiving care.[627]

There is no question that the tribunals must provide witnesses with sufficient financial support to enable them to travel to the tribunals and sustain themselves and their families while they are there, but it is also true that the sums that witnesses receive may make witnessing an attractive endeavor. Some

[623] E-mail from Sylvie Becky, ICTR Victims and Witness Support, May 20, 2008 (on file with author).

[624] Similarly, the SCSL provided witness TF1-334, who testified in *AFRC*, *RUF*, and *Taylor*, a home for more than two years and spent more than $30,000 on him. *See* Taylor Transcript, Apr. 24, 2008, at 8537.

[625] Sanin and Stirnemann, note 622, at 23–24 (citing Special Court Practice Direction on Allowances for Witnesses and Expert Witnesses, adopted 16 July 2004). For references to the provision of food to witnesses, see Taylor Transcript, Jan. 9, 2008, at 781; AFRC Transcript, Sept. 19, 2005, at 32; AFRC Transcript, Apr. 20, 2005, at 6–7; AFRC Transcript, Apr. 18, 2005, at 49; RUF Transcript, Jan. 13, 2005, at 60; RUF Transcript, Oct. 7, 2004, at 28; CDF Transcript, Sept. 14, 2004, at 126; CDF Transcript, Sept. 9, 2004, at 3; CDF Transcript, Nov. 2, 2004, at 110; CDF Transcript, June 22, 2004, at 1–2, 3; CDF Transcript, Sept. 8, 2004, at 69.

For references to the provision of lodging to witnesses, see Taylor Transcript, Jan. 24, 2008, at 2159; AFRC Transcript, Sept. 19, 2005, at 31; RUF Transcript, Oct. 7, 2004, at 30; CDF Transcript, Sept. 8, 2004, at 69.

For references to the provision of transportation to witnesses, see Taylor Transcript, Jan. 9, 2008, at 781; Taylor Transcript, Jan. 14, 2008, at 1122–24; Taylor Transcript, Jan. 24, 2008, at 2159–60; AFRC Transcript, June 17, 2005, at 29; AFRC Transcript, Apr. 20, 2005, at 6–7; RUF Transcript, Jan. 13, 2005, at 58.

For references to the provision of clothing to witnesses, see RUF Transcript, Jan. 13, 2005, at 58; CDF Transcript, Sept. 9, 2004, at 115; CDF Transcript, Nov. 2, 2004, at 110; CDF Transcript, Sept. 8, 2004, at 70.

[626] *Second Annual Report of the President of the Special Court for Sierra Leone for the Period 1 January 2004 – 17 January 2005*, at 32, *available at* http://www.sc-sl.org/Documents/specialcourtannualreport2004–2005.pdf; *see also* AFRC Transcript, Sept. 19, 2005, at 33; AFRC Transcript, June 16, 2005, at 13; AFRC Transcript, Apr. 20, 2005, at 12; RUF Transcript, Jan. 13, 2005, at 58; CDF Transcript, Sept. 14, 2004, at 126–27; CDF Transcript, Sept. 9, 2004, at 3, 115–16; CDF Transcript, Sept. 8, 2004, at 71–78; Taylor Transcript, Jan. 16, 2008, at 1391.

[627] *See Helping Hand to ICTR Witnesses*, Internews, *available at* http://www.internews.org.rw/articles5.htm#helping.

tribunal testimony suggests that the reimbursements may exceed the cost of the items or services that the witnesses and their companions receive,[628] and defense counsel frequently observe that the daily allowances that the tribunals provide to witnesses far exceed what those witnesses would earn in their usual occupations.[629] The ICTR's US$22 daily allowance may not seem like a windfall, but to a population with a per capita income of US$250 per year,[630] it is good money indeed. Even the US$5.25 daily allowance that the SCSL provides witnesses vastly exceeds the average Sierra Leonean income, which is less than US$1 per day.[631] The medical services provided by the tribunals also stand as substantial incentives given the dearth of doctors in Sierra Leone and Rwanda and the low life expectancies in those countries.[632] Finally, payments are sometimes made for questionable activities. *Taylor* witness Varmuyan Sherif, for instance, seems to have been paid for locating prosecution witnesses.[633] Whether the stipends and services provided to witnesses motivate individuals to fabricate testimony in order to become witnesses cannot be known, but we do know of some isolated instances of financially motivated lying. For instance, at least one Sierra Leonean witness lied about his age because he believed that older witnesses would obtain more benefits than younger ones.[634] And an East Timorese witness explained an inconsistency between her statement and her testimony

[628] AFRC Transcript, Apr. 20, 2005, at 7–8; AFRC Transcript, Sept. 19, 2005, at 32–33; Nahimana Transcript, Nov. 19, 2001, at 20–26.

[629] Witness TF2-012 received the equivalent of nearly $39 per week during most of the 4 months that he was in Freetown. He acknowledged that the sums provided by the SCSL were far in excess of what he would ordinarily earn. CDF Transcript, Nov. 2, 2004, at 108–09, 111–12. *See also* AFRC Transcript, Apr. 14, 2005, at 24–26; RUF Transcript, Jan. 13, 2005, at 61–66; CDF Transcript, Sept. 8, 2004, at 46–47. Defense counsel also frequently have difficulty ascertaining just what has been paid. See Prosecutor v. Nzirorera, Case No. ICTR-98-44-T, Motion to Compel Full Disclosure of ICTR Payments for the Benefit of Witnesses G and T (Apr. 21, 2006), where defense counsel maintained that witnesses had received additional payments that prosecutors had not disclosed; *see also* CDF Transcript, Nov. 2, 2004, at 106.

[630] US AID Country Profile, *Rwanda*, *available at* http://www.usaid.gov/locations/sub-saharan_africa/countries/rwanda/rwanda_profile.pdf.

[631] Sierra Leone's yearly per capita income is US$200. US AID Country Profile, Sierra Leone, *available at* http://www.usaid.gov/locations/sub-saharan_africa/countries/sierraleone/sierraleone_profile.pdf.

[632] Sierra Leone has 0.03 doctors per one thousand people, UN Office for the Coordination of Humanitarian Affairs, *Sierra Leone Humanitarian Country Profile*, *available at* http://www.irinnews.org/country.aspx?CountryCode=SL&RegionCode=WA, while Rwanda has 0.05 doctors per one thousand people, UN Office for the Coordination of Humanitarian Affairs, *Rwanda Humanitarian Country Profile*, *available at* http://www.irinnews.org/country.aspx?CountryCode=RW&RegionCode=GL. Life expectancy for Sierra Leoneans is between thirty-seven and forty years of age, World Health Organization Statistics, *available at* http://www.who.int/countries/sle/en/, and the life expectancy for Rwandans is between forty-four and forty-seven years of age, World Health Organization Statistics, *available at* http://www.who.int/countries/rwa/en/.

[633] Taylor Transcript, Jan. 14, 2008, at 1125–26.

[634] RUF Transcript, Apr. 14, 2005, at 23–26.

by stating that she confirmed the contents of her statement only because she wished to get a sink and some building materials that the U.N. administration was providing.[635]

Insider witnesses stand to benefit even more because the tribunals often spend large sums to relocate and provide security for insider witnesses and their families when the witness's testimony is considered to place them in danger.[636] As the ICTR Prosecutor Hassan Jallow has observed, high-level insiders will not testify unless the tribunal provides them and their families adequate security, which usually includes relocation.[637] Consequently, several ICTR defendants who ultimately pled guilty and testified against other ICTR defendants negotiated in their plea agreements for the prosecution to relocate their families and provide them security.[638] The ICTR and the SCSL also have relocated and provided security for a number of insider witnesses who have testified against their former associates, and these benefits provide witnesses a crucial incentive to testify.[639] Former Brigadier General John Tarnue, for instance, testified that he was relieved when the SCSL made contact with him after he found himself in Ghana, having fled Liberia in fear of his life. He testified that he was desperate to get out of Ghana and would have done anything to help his wife and children.[640] The SCSL did in fact relocate Tarnue and his family and indeed spent more than $90,000 in relocation and support costs during the eighteen months before Tarnue testified.[641] *AFRC* prosecution witness George Johnson similarly admitted that he hoped that SCSL would see fit to relocate him.[642] And relocation has been so desired by ICTY witnesses that prosecutors frequently neglect to tell witnesses that relocation is even possible. As one

[635] Los Palos Case Notes, Aug. 21, 2001, at 181.

[636] *See* SCSL, *Second Annual Report*, note 626, at 32.

[637] Jallow also has noted that few countries are willing to receive high-level génocidaires. Consequently, "[p]rotection, relocation and support has turned out to be very expensive" for the ICTR's prosecution. Hassan B. Jallow, *The OTP-ICTR: Ongoing Challenges of Completion*, Guest Lecture Series of the Office of the Prosecutor, Nov. 1, 2004, at 6, *available at* http://69.94.11.53/ENGLISH/colloquium06/ictr_completion.pdf.

[638] Prosecutor v. Kambanda, Case No. ICTR-97–23-1, Joint Motion for Consideration of Plea Agreement Between Jean Kambanda and the Office of the Prosecutor, Annexure A Plea Agreement Between Jean Kambanda and the Office of the Prosecutor, para. 45 (Apr. 30, 1998); Prosecutor v. Serushago, Case No. ICTR-98–37, Plea Agreement Between Omar Serushago and the Office of the Prosecutor, para. 45 (Dec. 4, 1998); Prosecutor v. Ruggiu, Case No. ICTR-97–32-DP, Plea Agreement Between Georges Ruggiu and the Office of the Prosecutor, para. 226 (Apr. 11, 2000).

[639] *See, e.g.*, Muvunyi Judgement, note 455, at para. 56; AFRC Transcript, Sept. 19, 2005, at 31; AFRC Transcript, June 17, 2005, at 31. SCSL Prosecutor Stephen Rapp reported in June 2007 that the SCSL had by then relocated fifteen witnesses. *See* Jessica Bennett, *Not Above the Law*, Newsweek, June 12, 2007.

[640] RUF Transcript, Oct. 7, 2004, at 46–48.

[641] *Id.* at 29–30.

[642] AFRC Transcript, Sept. 19, 2005, at 30–31.

ICTY prosecutor revealed, "we often fudge on telling a potential witness about the full range of protective measures. I mean, if you did that, the system would be clogged with witnesses demanding to be relocated to another country."[643]

Witnesses may reap financial and other benefits from false testimony beyond that which the tribunals provide them. Indeed, false accusations have proven a serious problem in Rwanda's own domestic genocide trials, although Rwandan courts do not pay witnesses any stipends. There, other incentives provide the motivation for the perjury. Rwanda expert Alison Des Forges has observed, for instance, that it is not uncommon in Rwanda's genocide trials for defendants to be "falsely accused by those who seek their posts or property or who wish retribution for some current or past wrong, real or imagined."[644] Belgian Professor Filip Reyntjens has likewise testified that defendants in Rwandan courts have been falsely accused by those who seek "to get their property."[645] Even Rwandan prosecutors have acknowledged that a substantial percentage of genocide defendants in Rwandan courts were innocent,[646] with many of those innocent defendants having been falsely accused. The same sorts of incentives can also give rise to false testimony at the ICTR. In the *Karemera* case, for instance, witness HH admitted to providing false evidence about ICTR defendant François Karera at the request of one Mutabazi. According to witness HH, Mutabazi wanted Karera to remain in prison so that Mutabazi would not have to pay Karera the money Mutabazi owed him. And witness HH expected some recompense from Mutabazi for his false testimony.[647] In a similar vein, *Seromba* witness FE27 asserted that he testified falsely against Seromba because he was told that if he did so, he would be "released," presumably from a Rwandan prison.[648]

[643] Stover, note 13, at 78.

[644] Alison Des Forges, Human Rights Watch, Leave None to Tell the Story: Genocide in Rwanda 753–54 (1999) [hereinafter Leave None to Tell the Story].

[645] Rutaganda Transcript, Nov. 24, 1997, at 134. *See also* Paul Willis, *No Lawyers but Rwanda's Village Courts Could Pass Death Sentence*, Daily Telegraph (London), Apr. 9, 2006 ("Human rights groups claim that [*gacaca* is] being hijacked by villagers using the pretence of genocide allegations to settle land disputes and family feuds.").

[646] In 1995, the prosecutor of Kigali estimated that 20 percent of detained persons were innocent. Leave None to Tell the Story, note 644, at 754. That figure was supported by Rwanda's former Minister of Justice Alphonse-Marie Nkubito. Rutaganda Transcript, Nov. 24, 1997, at 134 (testimony of Filip Reyntjens). A Rwandan legal professional acquainted with prison conditions in Rwanda, however, estimated that 60 percent of one prison's detainees were either falsely accused or were guilty only of offenses that do not carry a prison sentence as punishment. Leave None to Tell the Story, note 644, at 754.

[647] Karemera Transcript, Nov. 17, 2006, at 25–31.

[648] Seromba Judgement, note 547, at para. 73. Presumably, FE27 was at the time incarcerated on genocide charges; however, that information does not appear in any of the public case documents.

A final factor motivating many witnesses to perjure themselves is the very ease with which they can do so. For a variety of reasons, even the most basic factual assertions in Rwanda, Sierra Leone, and East Timor are nearly impossible to prove definitively. As a consequence, whereas in a typical Western trial only a few factual issues are in dispute because the remainder cannot be plausibly contested, in international criminal proceedings, virtually every question is open to contest. Even the defendant's very identity can be a matter of dispute. *AFRC* defendant Alex Tamba Brima, for instance, denied that his first name was Alex and maintained that he was a victim of mistaken identity.[649] The other *AFRC* defendants did acknowledge that they were who the prosecution said they were, but they disputed key aspects of their personal histories. For instance, the prosecution and defense disputed whether defendant Brima Bazzy Kamara was born in 1968 or 1970 as well as whether defendant Santigie Borbor Kanu was born in Freetown or in Maforki County in the Port Loko District.[650]

The identities and personal details of witnesses have also been the subjects of conflicting allegations. In the ICTR's *Kamuhanda* case, for instance, the defense alleged that a key witness was not who she said she was,[651] and in the Special Panels' *Los Palos* case, prosecutors did in fact bring the wrong witness to court. The error in *Los Palos* came to light when the witness denied providing a written statement. Only then did it become clear that it was indeed a different person who had given prosecutors the statement, but one who bore the same name as the witness and lived in the same village.[652] In the ICTR's *Simba* case, the prosecution and defense disagreed about whether the defendant's wife and children were Tutsi,[653] whereas in the SCSL's *CDF* case, a dispute arose over whether prosecution witness Albert Nallo was the son or instead the brother of a certain Sierra Leonean chief.[654]

Other factual disputes have concerned not the witnesses' identities but facts that would bear on their credibility and neutrality. *CDF* prosecutors queried, for instance, whether the daughter of a key defense witness was married to the defendant,[655] and the defense in that case asked prosecution witness Albert

[649] AFRC Judgement, note 27, at para. 311. Whereas the prosecution maintained that Brima had been born in the village of Yaryah in the Kono District, Brima claimed to have been born at Wilberforce Village in Freetown. *Id.* at para. 11.

[650] *Id.* at paras. 12–13.

[651] Kamuhanda Judgement, note 38, at para. 251. The defendant did eventually acknowledge that the witness had correctly identified herself. *Id.*

[652] Los Palos Case Notes, Aug. 22, 2001, at 187–88.

[653] Simba Judgement, note 455, at para. 61.

[654] CDF Transcript, Mar. 11, 2005, at 37–38.

[655] CDF Transcript, Feb. 17, 2006, at 44.

Nallo if he had been accused of raping his father's youngest wife.[656] In the *Taylor* case, defense counsel maintained that insider witness Varmuyan Sherif had gone to Mali for treatment of a mental illness that caused Sherif to shout to himself, to walk the streets of Monrovia naked, and to be placed under house arrest by his family.[657] Testimony was heard on these matters, but no conclusive proof was submitted to settle them. In other cases, the very fact of the crime was the subject of dispute. Whereas *CDF* witness TF2-007 provided a detailed eyewitness account of his father's murder at the hands of Kamajors, people in the witness's village told defense counsel that the witness's father was not dead at all but had instead run off with the junta.[658] Likewise, witness TF2-187 described personally witnessing the Kamajors torture and kill her uncle,[659] whereas the defense asserted that the uncle was "very much alive" and living in Gambia.[660] And whereas witness TF2-006 testified that the Kamajors had amputated his fingers, townspeople told defense counsel that the witness had lost his fingers some years before the war in a welding accident.[661] ICTR cases feature similar factual disputes. *Kajelijeli* prosecution witness GDQ testified that "Kanoti's wife" was killed at a roadblock in April 1994, although defense witness MLNL testified that Kanoti's wife was still alive in March 2000.[662] And although *Muhimana* prosecution witness AT testified that the defendant had raped a woman named Mukasine in Ngoma, two defense witnesses – AR1 and TQ28 – testified that Mukasine was a student at Butare University and was not even present in Ngoma during the month in which the rape allegedly took place.[663]

In each of the above factual disputes, one side is almost certainly lying, and they are emboldened to do so by the knowledge that there is virtually no way to detect those lies. For one thing, many ICTR, SCSL, and Special Panels witnesses live in communities that function largely without the widespread use of documentation that can be so useful in proving basic facts. For instance, in no Western trial would there be a dispute about the number of houses in a given town because that fact would be readily ascertainable from government sources.

656 CDF Transcript, Mar. 11, 2005, at 40.

657 Taylor Transcript, Jan. 11, 2008, at 1050–51. *See also* Taylor Transcript, Jan. 16, 2008, at 1394–95 (defense accuses witness of receiving psychiatric treatment); *id.* at 1395–97 (defense accuses witness of being court marshaled for rape).

658 CDF Transcript, Dec. 2, 2004, at 50–59, 82–84.

659 CDF Transcript, June 1, 2005, at 13–14.

660 CDF Transcript, June 2, 2005, at 29.

661 CDF Transcript, Feb. 9, 2005, at 11–13, 53.

662 Kajelijeli Judgement, note 303, at para. 712.

663 Muhimana Judgement, note 363, at para. 268. Similarly, although witness BJ testified that the some of Muhimana's companions raped one Eugenia Murekatete in Ngoma, two defense witnesses testified that Murekatete was in Kigali at the time. *Id.* at para. 287.

Presumably such government sources do not exist in certain parts of Sierra Leone, however, because the *CDF* Trial Chamber heard conflicting eyewitness testimony on just that point.[664] Similarly, Social Security numbers, driver's licenses, and other forms of official identification prevent the occurrence in Western trials of the sort of mistaken identities – or allegations of mistaken identities – that make their way into international tribunal proceedings. International witnesses, by contrast, frequently lack not only birth certificates but also other arguably more probative forms of official identification.[665] Indeed, in the hopes of preventing misidentifications, witnesses are sometimes asked not only their names but whether any other people in their village have the same name.[666]

Lack of documentation stymies efforts to ascertain other basic facts as well. The SCSL noted, for instance, that the CDF "did not keep records of its members like a conventional army would."[667] Neither did the war's other factions, so it was frequently impossible to conclusively determine the rank or affiliation of any given fighter. Similarly, whereas the cause of a Western victim's amputation could be ascertained through a review of the medical treatment he received at the time of his injury, no such records are available to the international tribunals. It may be that treatment was not documented or that no treatment was even obtained. The following section will describe the popularity of alibis at the international tribunals, but suffice it to say here that lack of documentation also allows international defendants to put forth false alibis with much greater ease than would be the case for a Western defendant. An American defendant who claims to have spent six days in Cleveland had better have receipts, ATM statements, or similar documents if his alibi is to be considered plausible. By contrast, because commercial exchanges in many regions of Sierra Leone, Rwanda, and East Timor are carried out by means of cash or goods,[668] a Sierra Leonean, Rwandan, or Timorese defendant truly can

[664] CDF Transcript, Jan. 31, 2006, at 3–7.

[665] Only 48 percent and 53 percent of Sierra Leonean and Timorese births, respectively, are registered. The figure is 83 percent for Rwandan births. *See* UNICEF Statistics Birth Registration, *available at* http://www.childinfo.org/birth_registration_tables.php.

[666] *See, e.g.*, CDF Transcript, Sept. 28, 2006, at 63.

[667] CDF Judgement, note 27, at para. 358.

[668] Many transactions, particularly in rural areas, take the form of barter, *see, e.g.*, Paul Cleary, *It's the Economy Stupid*, Wall Street J., May 23, 2007; The Asia Foundation, *Supporting Economic Growth in East Timor, available at* http://www.asiafoundation.org/pdf/easttimorecon.pdf; Research Institute for Asia and the Pacific (RIAP), the University of Sydney, *The Future of East Timor: Threats and Opportunities for Economic Development of a Small Island State*, Briefing Paper Vol. 3 No. 2 (July 2000), *available at* http://www.usyd.edu.au/riap/about/publications/articles/2000/Future%2520of%2520East%2520Timor.pdf. Cash exchanges are more prevalent in urban areas. *See* U.S. Department of State, Country Specific Information: Sierra Leone, *available at* http://travel.state.gov/travel/cis_pa_tw/cis/cis_

spend considerable time in a particular location and generate no documentary evidence to prove that he was there. Moreover, the fact that the crimes were part of a widespread series of atrocities makes fact verification only that much more difficult, as activities that might be subject to documentary verification during normal times are apt to be suspended during periods of violent turmoil.

Even when evidence to ascertain certain facts does exist, that evidence often will be difficult to obtain for a variety of reasons. For one thing, money is scarce at the international tribunals, and defense counsel have had particular difficulty funding their investigations. SCSL defense counsel initially lacked investigators[669] and still lack sufficient funding, many believe, to conduct thorough investigations.[670] The Special Panels defense was even more constrained by funding shortages; indeed, in the Panels' early days, defense operations were barely funded at all. The Special Panels conducted their work on a meager $6.3 million annual budget, of which $6 million was allocated to the prosecution and virtually all of the remaining $300,000 was spent on the salaries of the international judges.[671] As a result, defense attorneys had no ability to undertake investigations, and, indeed, they called not a single defense witness to testify in the first fourteen Special Panels trials, not even in the massive *Los Palos* case, in which ten defendants were prosecuted for crimes against humanity.[672] As one *Los Palos* defense counsel put it: "We do not have witnesses. We wish we did."[673] He and other defense counsel complained that they lacked both cars and the time to travel to the districts to interview potential witnesses, and they lacked

1016.html ("Sierra Leone is a cash economy."); U.S. Department of State, Country Specific Information: Rwanda, *available at* http://travel.state.gov/travel/cis_pa_tw/cis/cis_1007.html ("Credit cards are accepted at only a few hotels in Kigali and only to settle hotel bills" so "[t]ravelers should expect to handle most expenses, including air tickets, in cash."); U.S. Department of State, Country Specific Information: Timor-Leste, *available at* http://travel.state.gov/travel/cis_pa_tw/cis/cis_1105.html ("Only a few establishments accept credit cards, usually requiring a substantial additional fee, and visitors should be prepared to settle all bills in cash.").

669 Human Rights Watch, *Bringing Justice*, note 614, at 26.

670 Sara Kendall and Michelle Staggs, U.C. Berkeley War Crimes Studies Center, *From Mandate to Legacy: The Special Court for Sierra Leone as a Model for "Hybrid Justice:" Interim Report on the Special Court for Sierra Leone* 14–15 (Apr. 2005).

671 David Cohen, *Seeking Justice on the Cheap: Is the East Timor Tribunal Really a Model for the Future? in* Asia Pacific Issues No. 61, at 5 (East-West Center 2002). As Cohen relates, "[n]o one in either the Public Defenders' office or UNTAET could tell me whether or not the Public Defenders had a budget or, if so, what it was." *Id.*

672 *Id.*; de Bertodano, note 325, at 232; *see also The Los Palos Case Report*, note 281, at § 2.3.2.2; Gonçalves Leto Bere Judgement, note 402, at 4; Prosecutor v. Dos Santos Laku, Case No. 8/2001, Judgement, at 3 (July 25, 2001) [hereinafter Dos Santos Laku Judgement]; Carmona Judgement, note 377, at 2; Prosecutor v. Leke, Case No. 05/2001, Judgement, para. 14 (Sept. 14, 2002).

673 Los Palos Case Notes, Oct. 4, 2001, at 343.

resources to provide witnesses with transportation to the court in Dili and to pay for their food and lodging while there.[674] Defense attorneys themselves were so scarce that one sent a standardized letter to investigators that authorized the investigators to question his clients when he was not present and that included a list of rights to be read to the defendant before the interview.[675]

Lack of funding is not the only factor impeding investigations. With or without money, it is hard to get around in certain parts of Rwanda, Sierra Leone, and East Timor.[676] Whole regions sometimes prove too dangerous for investigators to visit. It was not until the fourth ICTR case that any defense counsel even entered Rwanda; before that, it was considered far too unsafe to go. As a Swiss defense counsel representing a Rwandan defendant in the courts of Switzerland put it: "Better to have two living lawyers in Switzerland than dead ones in Rwanda."[677] And when safety concerns do not stymie investigations, logistical difficulties can. In some areas, roads are poor, impassable, or nonexistent during the rainy season, making travel virtually impossible. SCSL defense counsel described "trek[ing] some six hours to find [a murder victim's] brother... through swamp waters with computers on head [while] strip[ped] down to their underpants."[678] And vehicles were so scarce and travel so difficult in certain regions of East Timor that victims and perpetrators were sometimes transported to court in the same vehicle.[679] Finally, when logistical difficulties, safety concerns, and financial constraints do not impede investigations, political considerations often do. ICTR defense counsel, for instance, have accused the government of Rwanda of placing obstacles in their path. As one defense investigator put it: "Getting witnesses out of Rwanda is virtually impossible.... How are we supposed to conduct a proper defence when investigators are not permitted to work in Rwanda, and when we are not allowed to verify testimony from any of the witnesses presented by the prosecution?"[680] In a number of cases, indeed, defense counsel have maintained that the government of Rwanda has harassed and intimidated defense witnesses to prevent them from testifying.[681]

[674] *The Los Palos Case Report*, note 281, at § 3.2.2.1.

[675] *Id.* at § 3.12.

[676] Eric Stover writes about the difficulties that ICTY investigators confront. Stover, note 13, at 45–46.

[677] Thierry Cruvellier, *Grass-Roots Justice* Int'l Just. Trib., Mar. 29, 1999.

[678] CDF Transcript, Nov. 29, 2006, at 59.

[679] Mearns, note 327, at 41.

[680] Isabel Vincent, *Canadian Lawyers Say Hands Tied in Arusha*, National Post (Canada), July 28, 2001, at B4.

[681] *See, e.g.*, Simba Judgement, note 455, at paras. 41–43; Prosecutor v. Bagosora et al., Case No. ICTR-98-41-T, Defense Motion Concerning Alleged Witness Intimidation, para. 1 (Dec. 28, 2004). *See also* Kai Ambos, *International Criminal Procedure: "Adversarial," "Inquisitorial" or*

The importance of adequate investigations cannot be overestimated. It is no coincidence, I believe, that in three of the five ICTR trials in which defendants were acquitted, the Trial Chambers made on-site visits to the Rwandan crime scenes.[682] By contrast, such on-site visits were made in only four of the eighteen ICTR trials that resulted in convictions,[683] and in one of those trials – *Zigiranyirazo* – the Trial Chamber rigorously scrutinized prosecution witness testimony and rejected the vast bulk of it as unreliable.[684] Furthermore, although the two acquittals in the *Ntagerura* case did not feature an on-site visit by the Trial Chamber, they did feature solid on-site defense investigations. For instance, prosecution witness MZ testified that he was hiding behind a latrine while Ntagerura attended a meeting and addressed a crowd located about ten meters from his hiding place. Defense investigators actually visited the site in question, however, and discovered that the distance was not ten meters, as MZ testified, but forty or fifty meters. With the benefit of this information, the Trial Chamber was able to conclude that "[g]iven the witness's vantage point and the circumstances of the identification," it was doubtful "that the witness could have accurately followed what transpired at the meeting or that he could have positively identified Ntagerura as the speaker."[685]

The bottom line is that international tribunals have considerable difficulty determining even the most basic facts, and that difficulty has broad implications for the incidence of perjury at the tribunals. For whereas this subsection began by delineating various incentives that would tempt international witnesses to lie, the witnesses are not apt to succumb to that temptation – however compelling the incentives – if their lies are likely to be detected. Unfortunately, Rwandan, Sierra Leonean, and East Timorese witnesses can bank on the tribunals' inability to verify the kinds of basic facts that would reveal their lying. This subsection has shown, then, that international witnesses not only have powerful incentives to lie but that they have ample opportunities to do so as well.

Mixed, 3 Int'l Crim. L. Rev. 1, 36 (2003); Frederik Harhoff, *The Role of the Parties Before International Criminal Courts, in* International and National Prosecution of Crimes under International Law 645, 655–56 (Fischer et al. eds., 2001); Stephen Kay & Bert Swart, *The Role of the Defense, in* II The Rome Statute of the International Criminal Court 1421, 1424 (Cassese et al. eds. 2002).

682 *See* Bagilishema Judgement, note 122, at para. 10; Mpambara Judgement, note 471, at Annex 1, para. 4; Rwamakuba Judgement, note 63, at para. 42.

683 The Trial Chambers in *Seromba, Karera, Bikindi,* and *Zigiranyirazo* made on-site visits. *See* Seromba Judgement, note 547, at Annex I, para. 43; Karera Judgement, note 54, at Annex I, para. 7; Prosecutor v. Bikindi, Case No. ICTR-01–72-T, Judgement, paras. 65, n.115, 362, n.817, Annex A, para. 32 (Dec. 2, 2008) [hereinafter Bikindi Judgement]; Zigiranyirazo Judgement, note 498, at Annex I, para. 34.

684 *See* text at notes 1378 to 1387 for a more detailed discussion of the Trial Chamber's treatment of witness testimony in the *Zigiranyirazo* case.

685 Ntagerura Judgement, note 37, at paras. 153–155, 172, 175.

5.C. THE INCIDENCE OF PERJURY AT THE INTERNATIONAL TRIBUNALS

Until now, I have discussed various factors that suggest that perjury is likely to be a significant problem at the international tribunals. The previous sections, for instance, delineate certain financial incentives and ideological commitments that might motivate international witnesses to perjure themselves, and they discuss certain cultural norms that could place perjury in a less negative light than Westerners might expect. The previous sections also suggest that lies are easy to pull off at the international tribunals because basic facts that would serve to reveal those lies are difficult to conclusively establish. But these observations, although provocative, do not speak to the actual incidence of false testimony at the international tribunals. That topic will form the basis for this section. As it happens, we can be sure that a great deal of false testimony is presented to the ICTR and to a lesser extent to the SCSL.[686] How do we know about this false testimony? In rare instances, it can be definitively shown that a particular witness testified falsely.[687] In other instances, the evidence suggesting false testimony, although not conclusive, is nonetheless compelling. Most frequently and most worryingly, however, are instances in which we can be certain that some witness has testified falsely, but we cannot be sure which witness it is.

The primary reason that perjury is so rarely conclusively identified at the international tribunals under study is the same reason that basic facts so rarely can be conclusively established: the oral nature of Rwandan, Sierra Leonean, and East Timorese societies. A prosecution witness may make a claim, for instance, and although that claim will be disputed by defense witnesses or the defendant himself, rarely will there exist documentary or forensic evidence to prove or disprove the claim. Every so often, however, the documentation will exist, and the perjury can be conclusively identified. In the ICTR's *Cyangugu* case, for instance, three witnesses testified that two of the defendants – Ntagerura and Bagambiki – had delivered weapons and made anti-Tutsi speeches at a couple of locations on January 28, 1994.[688] The testimony of these witnesses was unusually clear, detailed, and comprehensible. They provided dates, places, and considerable detail about the weapons that they had seen transported.[689] By ICTR standards in particular, these were strong witnesses indeed. Fortunately for the defendants, one of the men who was implicated in the witnesses' account had been Rwanda's Chief of Military Operations

[686] The Special Panels' judgments are too scant to allow me to assess the incidence of perjury at that body.

[687] False testimony does not necessarily equal perjury. To commit perjury, a witness must willfully testify falsely. *See, e.g.*, 18 U.S.C. § 1621.

[688] Ntagerura Judgement, note 37, at paras. 119–124.

[689] *See, e.g.*, *id.* at para. 123.

and had been sent to Egypt on an official mission on the dates in question. The trip was not only reflected in his diplomatic passport but, on his return home, he submitted a report about the mission to the president of Rwanda.[690] The three prosecution witnesses who provided these false accounts had been housed together in the same Rwandan prison and had apparently collaborated in concocting their stories.

As I note above, although it is exceedingly rare for conclusive proof of false testimony to come to light, it is less rare for there to exist compelling evidence that a witness testified falsely.[691] In some cases, the false testimony can be identified merely through recourse to common sense. Witness TF2-057, for instance, denied knowing another witness who testified by the pseudonym TF2-067. When it later came to light that witness TF2-057 was witness TF2-067's father, witness TF2-057's false testimony became clear.[692] The falsity of witness TF1-033's testimony became apparent when he testified that two attacks occurred simultaneously but later testified that he was present at both.[693] Common sense also revealed the false testimony of Hassan Ngeze, a defendant in the *Media Trial*, who testified that a newspaper photo showed a football match, even though the participants' clothing made it obvious to the Trial Chamber that the photograph showed a political party meeting.[694] In the ICTR's *Rwamakuba* case, witness HF testified that Rwamakuba had selected the witness's sister to be taken from Butare University Hospital to be killed. When testifying in the *Gatera* case in Rwandan courts, however, witness HF told the same story but stated that a Dr. Gatera did the selecting, not Rwamakuba. And in yet another Rwandan case, witness HF testified that her sister was shot by a man named Rurangirwa in a specific *secteur* in Butare prefecture. When confronted with the latter inconsistency, witness HF testified that she had twin sisters with the same Christian name.[695]

The false testimony of ICTR prosecution witness Omar Serushago resembled that of witness HF and became apparent when Serushago testified to the same incident in three trials but changed the facts in each one to implicate the defendant in the particular trial in which he was testifying. Serushago had killed

690 *Id.* at para. 126.

691 In *Rutaganda*, the prosecution charged its own witness with testifying falsely but did not allege that he had the *mens rea* for perjury. Rutaganda Transcript, Oct. 8, 1997, at 19–26.

692 CDF Transcript, Dec. 7, 2004, at 37–38. *See also* Rwamakuba Judgement, note 63, at para. 62 (observing it "interesting" that witness GIT "claimed not to know whether his brother was testifying in this case, although they live near one another and both testified in this case within a short space of time").

693 AFRC Transcript, July 11, 2005, at 86–89.

694 Nahimana Judgement, note 97, at para. 875. One of Ngeze's co-defendants, who was also pictured in the photograph, acknowledged that it showed a political meeting. *Id.*

695 Rwamakuba Judgement, note 63, at para. 189.

the Hutu sister of a Colonel Ngungize, and Ngungize apparently wanted to take revenge for his sister's death on the Hutu militia who had killed her. In the *Media Trial* involving defendant Jean-Bosco Barayagwiza, Serushago testified that Barayagwiza protected him from Ngungize's wrath, saying: "Habyarimana is dead"; "It's not the sister of Nzungize who should be creating disorder by pitting the *Interahamwe* and members of the CDR against one another in Gisenyi town."[696] In the *Karemera* case, however, Serushago described the same incident, but there he placed those same words in the mouth of *Karemera* defendant Joseph Nzirorera. In his sworn statement to the prosecution, Serushago maintained that Nzirorera intervened on his behalf with Colonel Nzungize. According to Serushago: "It was Nzirorera who took the decision. He said even President Habyarimana had died, so why would the death of Nzungize's sister create a problem in Gisenyi?"[697] Finally, in the *Military I* trial prosecuting Anatole Nsengiyumva, Serushago was asked if defendant Nsengiyumva was bothered by the deaths of the people whom Serushago had killed. Serushago replied: "[Anatole Nsengiyumva] himself said that if [Nzungize's sister] was there, it was no problem, because, after all, Habyarimana was dead so we could continue performing our operations as usual."[698] The testimony of witness GAB in the *Rwamakuba* case was disbelieved for the same reason. The *Rwamakuba* Trial Chamber noted the "disturbing similarities" between GAB's testimony in *Rwamakuba* and his testimony in *Kamuhanda*, observing that the witness described Rwamakuba's acts and behavior in the same way that he had described Kamuhanda's criminal acts when he testified in that case. GAB even "attributed much of the same words to Kamuhanda and Rwamakuba."[699] Finally, witness GBV testified about a meeting in both the *Karemera* and *Kajelijeli* trials. The witness's testimony about the meeting was rendered suspect because, although the witness maintained that the meeting was held in the Ruhengeri Stadium, which was filled with people, the only two people who the witness could recall seeing were the two defendants in *Karemera* and *Kajelijeli*.[700]

Sometimes, the witness's account, although not patently ridiculous, proves so implausible that it gives rise to the highest possible suspicion of lying. In discussing genocide trials before Rwandan courts, Alison Des Forges describes witnesses "who recount events that they could not possibly have

[696] Nahimana Transcript, Nov. 16, 2001, at 66.

[697] Karemera Transcript, Nov. 27, 2003, at 42.

[698] Military I Transcript, June 19, 2003, at 6. The judges in the *Media Trial* criticized Serushago's testimony for its many "inconsistencies and contradictions." Nahimana Judgement, note 97, at paras. 817, 824.

[699] Rwamakuba Judgement, note 63, at para. 149.

[700] Karemera Transcript, Dec. 5, 2003, at 54.

seen,"[701] and similarly unlikely testimony is often presented to the international tribunals as well. Some witness accounts, for instance, place witnesses in highly improbable locations. For instance, GAB, the Tutsi witness mentioned above who testified in *Rwamakuba* and *Kamuhanda*, testified that he attended a rally of the Hutu-dominated political party, National Revolutionary Movement for Development (MRND) in August 1993. There, GAB testified, he heard the defendant Kamuhanda make a speech that included ominous anti-Tutsi statements.[702] GAB further testified that some days after the killings had begun, GAB and some friends were playing football in a field when Kamuhanda drove up and began distributing weapons to members of the *Interahamwe* militia. GAB indicated that he was very close to Kamuhanda and his associates; he gave a detailed account of Kamuhanda's actions and testified that Kamuhanda told the *Interahamwe* that "I don't want to hear that any single Tutsi has escaped you."[703] The Trial Chamber found GAB's testimony not credible, stating:

> Considering the dangers, alleged by the Witness, faced by anyone not of Hutu ethnicity attending [the MRND rally], and considering that the Witness is a Tutsi, the Chamber is not convinced that the Witness even attended this rally. Concerning the testimony of the Witness about the distribution of weapons by the Accused..., the Chamber finds it unlikely that Prosecution Witness GAB, a young Tutsi male, would casually have been playing football at such time when tensions between Hutus and Tutsis were high, and the situation was becoming increasingly perilous for the Tutsi population. That he might stand around listening to orders for the massacre of Tutsis, whilst weapons were being distributed, seems improbable.[704]

The testimony of other witnesses has been rejected on similar grounds. Also in *Kamuhanda*, witness GEI testified that he was at the Gikomero Parish along with thousands of other Tutsi who had taken refuge there. According to GEI, when Kamuhanda arrived, Tutsi refugees shouted: "Since Kamuhanda is here, our fate is sealed." Witness GEI testified that, at that point, he moved closer to Kamuhanda – to a distance of about four meters – so that he could overhear Kamuhanda order the killing of Tutsi. The Trial Chamber found it incredible that a Tutsi refugee would move considerably closer to Kamuhanda to eavesdrop when the other refugees had just informed him that the appearance of Kamuhanda had sealed their fates.[705] Similarly, in *Ndindabahizi*, Tutsi witness CGH testified that, during the massacres, he was hiding at the home of Karara,

[701] Leave None to Tell the Story, note 644, at 784.
[702] Kamuhanda Judgement, note 38, at para. 275.
[703] *Id.* at paras. 276–280.
[704] *Id.* at para. 282.
[705] *Id.* at para. 457.

the *bourgmestre* of Gitesi *commune*. CGH testified that he knew the defendant Ndindabahizi because they had been neighbors and had gone to school together, and CGH had seen Ndindabahizi at Ndindabahizi's place of work. CGH further testified that Ndindabahizi had visited Karara's house, and, while CGH was in the room, Ndindabahizi chastised Karara for sparing certain Tutsi women and instructed Karara to make sure that all of these Tutsi were killed.[706] The Trial Chamber found CGH's testimony implausible, concluding that it was highly unlikely that CGH, a Tutsi, who was in hiding from Hutu militias, would remain in a room with Ndindabahizi – who knew CGH and knew that he was a Tutsi – while Ndindabahizi exhorted Karara to stop sheltering Tutsi. The Trial Chamber found it equally unlikely that Karara "would have run the pointless risk of being discovered as a man who sheltered Tutsi."[707] The *Bagilishema* Trial Chamber opined about this problem more generally:

> The Chamber takes this opportunity to note that Witness O, while in hiding or otherwise concealed, surreptitiously was able to observe or overhear a significant number of key events implicating the Accused (among them the meeting with Kayishema, the killing of Karungu, the killing of Muganga, and the preparations for the expedition to Bisesero). This is also true of Prosecution Witness AB. The Chamber is naturally heedful of witnesses who, while purportedly in hiding and in fear of their lives, nonetheless are able to move around from one crime scene to the next, gathering intelligence along the way.[708]

In the examples given above, the Trial Chambers were not only certain or very nearly certain that false testimony had been presented, but they also knew which witness had testified falsely and which statements were false. That is not true for most instances of false testimony, however. Rather, in most cases, the Trial Chambers can be certain that false testimony has been presented, but they will be entirely uncertain about who testified falsely or which statements were false. In numerous ICTR cases, for instance, allegations of perjury are bandied about. Sometimes the witnesses themselves will admit to testifying falsely.[709]

[706] Ndindabahizi Judgement, note 56, at paras. 183–185.

[707] *Id.* at para. 192. For other examples of Tutsi witnesses alleging to have witnessed events after voluntarily placing themselves in dangerous locations, see Bagilishema Judgement, note 122, at paras. 381–386; Kajelijeli Judgement, note 303, at paras. 222–223.

[708] Bagilishema Judgement, note 122, at para. 860. Similarly, cross-examination in *Ntakirutimana* revealed witness UU "as the Zelig of the Rwandan genocide: someone who managed to cross paths with – and provide evidence against – a suspiciously large number of people who have been in the Tribunal's custody." Lars Waldorf, *Remembrance of Things Past*, INT'L JUST. TRIB., Oct. 31, 2001.

[709] Sometimes, however, a witness will indicate that he will recant his testimony but later ends up affirming it. *See* Prosecutor v. Rukundo, Case No. ICTR-2001-70-T, Decision on the Motions Relating to the Scheduled Appearances of Witness BLP and the Defense Investigator, July 4,

Karemera witness BTH, for instance, recanted the inculpatory testimony he provided in that case and three other cases.[710] *Government II* witness GFA admitted that he falsely inculpated ICTR defendants in exchange for being allowed to leave a Rwandan prison.[711] And, as noted above, *Karemera* witness HH and *Seromba* witness FE27 admitted to falsely accusing the defendants in those cases. Similarly, during Kamuhanda's appeal, witness GAA recanted his trial testimony. At trial, GAA testified that he had seen Kamuhanda at the Gikomero Parish Compound inciting a massacre there.[712] When the case was before the Appeals Chamber, however, GAA testified that he had lied at trial: He stated that he had never even been to the Gikomero Parish Compound. GAA further asserted that other prosecution witnesses also had presented false testimony and that they had collaborated before trial in order to avoid presenting contradictory accounts.[713]

In these instances, the Trial Chamber can be sure that the witness committed perjury, but it cannot be sure whether it was the initial testimony that was perjurious, as the witness claimed, or the witness's later recantation. Prosecutors so disbelieved GAA's recantation that they indicted him on six counts of providing false testimony and bribery. The indictment charged GAA with accepting money from Kamuhanda's family in exchange for his recantation and with attempting to persuade other witnesses likewise to recant.[714] What is particularly notable about the indictment is that its allegations are based solely on information provided by the witnesses GAA allegedly asked to recant; that is, the witnesses that GAA accused of lying in their trial testimony. GAA eventually pled guilty to one count of giving false testimony,[715] though, indicating that a witness's claims to perjury might themselves be perjurious.

Sometimes, witnesses will assert that they lied in their statements, and these assertions prove just as difficult to assess. *Karera* prosecution witness BMH, for instance, testified that she lied when she made her statement because she wanted investigators to leave quickly because she thought that they represented

2007, at paras. 2, 5. Witness recantations are a problem not only at the ICTR. For a discussion of a witness recantation at the International Criminal Court, see Mike Corder, *Former Congolese Child Soldier Recants Testimony, Throws Trial of Warlord into Confusion*, A. P., Jan. 28, 2009.

710 Karemera Transcript, Apr. 10, 2008, at 18–60.

711 Thijs Bouwknegt, *Rwanda's Genocide Tribunal's Witness 'Hiding,'* Radio Netherlands Worldwide, Oct. 2, 2008.

712 Kamuhanda Judgement, note 38, at paras. 330–332.

713 Kamuhanda v. Prosecutor, Case No. ICTR-99–54A-A, Appeals Judgement, paras. 212–213 (Sept. 19, 2005) [hereinafter Kamuhanda Appeals Judgement].

714 Prosecutor v. GAA, Case No. ICTR-07–90-R77, Indictment, Mar, 23, 2007.

715 ICTR Press Release, *ICTR Witness Pleas Guilty to Giving False Testimony*, ICTR/INFO-9–2-529.EN, Sept. 19, 2007, *available at* http://69.94.11.53/ENGLISH/PRESSREL/2007/528.htm.

the defendant.[716] *Karemera* witness AWB, for his part, had attested in his statement that he had seen defendant Mathieu Ngirumpatse arrive at his roadblock and encourage the killing of Tutsi there. AWB was scheduled to testify for the prosecution, but when he got on the stand, he informed the Chamber that he had lied when incriminating Ngirumpatse. A number of witnesses at the ICTR's *Media Trial* likewise provided ICTR prosecutors with incriminating information in their sworn statements but ended up recanting those statements and testifying for the defense at trial. Witness RM14, for instance, testified that he falsely claimed in his statement to have attended a meeting during which two of the defendants had incited the audience to kill Tutsi.[717] Witness RM10 similarly switched from the prosecution witness list to the defense witness list, after maintaining that she provided false information to the prosecution about certain ICTR defendants.[718] Other examples appear in the notes.[719] As with the witnesses who recanted their testimony, these witnesses clearly lied at some point during the proceedings, either in their statements or in their subsequent testimony, but it is difficult to determine which allegation is the lie and which is the truth.

Even less easy to assess is the testimony of those witnesses who assert that they were asked to give the ICTR false testimony but declined to do so[720] or the even more commonplace testimony of those witnesses who accuse other witnesses of lying.[721] Many of these witnesses implicate a Tutsi survivors' group called IBUKA. According to *Media Trial* witness RM113, IBUKA "is a tiny group of

[716] Karera Judgement, note 54, at para. 164.

[717] Nahimana Transcript, Jan. 16, 2003, at 4–7. RM 14 further testified that an IBUKA member had asked him to say that Ngeze had destroyed a victim's house when they all knew that the house had been destroyed by a neighbor. They wanted Ngeze blamed for the damage, however, because Ngeze had the means of paying compensation to the victim. *Id.* at 25.

[718] Nahimana Transcript, Jan. 20, 2003, at 15–21. RM10 maintained that when she told the IBUKA representatives that she had never seen one of the defendants whom she was to implicate, they assured her that they would show her a picture of him. *Id.* at 15.

[719] Niyitegeka Judgement, note 56, at para. 298; Seromba Transcript, Jan. 25, 2005, at 20–22; Taylor Transcript, May 6, 2008, at 9079–80; Taylor Transcript, May 7, 2008, at 9238–39; CDF Transcript, Feb. 10, 2005, at 78–80; RUF Transcript, Apr. 8, 2005, at 40; RUF Transcript, Nov. 22, 2005, at 31–33; AFRC Transcript, July 26, 2005, at 73–76; AFRC Transcript, Sept. 23, 2005, at 34–38, 94–100; Alison Thompson, U.C. Berkeley War Crimes Studies Center, Special Court Monitoring Program, Update No. 80A, June 23, 2006, at 2.

[720] Nahimana Transcript, Mar. 13, 2003, at 60 (Witness RM114 testifying that IBUKA representatives asked him to testify that an ICTR defendant had killed his brother when that was not true); Ndindabahizi Transcript, Oct. 30, 2003, at 16 (Witness DC alleging that witness CGH and the inspector of judicial police offered to pay him $50 if he testified about Ndindabahizi's crimes); Kamuhanda Judgement, note 38, at para. 69.

[721] *See, e.g.*, Ndindabahizi Judgement, note 56, at para. 111; Akayesu Judgement, note 32, at para. 44; Ntagerura Judgement, note 37, at para. 322; Rwamakuba Judgement, note 63, at para. 133; Karemera Transcript, Apr. 10, 2008, at 55–58; Nahimana Transcript, Mar. 14, 2003, at 28; Nahimana Transcript, Mar. 13, 2003, at 34.

Tutsis responsible for bringing false accusations, fabricated accusations against people."[722] IBUKA, it is alleged, offers benefits to those who testify falsely. *Media Trial* witness DM maintained that IBUKA has the resources to distribute food,[723] and witness RM10 alleged that IBUKA members promised her more than $2,000 and benefits related to the criminal case pending against her if she testified falsely at the ICTR.[724] On the one hand, these allegations of witness conspiracies have some credibility. Belgian Professor Filip Reyntjens, a Rwanda expert who has repeatedly testified for the ICTR prosecution, has described IBUKA as a blackmailing syndicate.[725] Similarly, a seasoned ICTR investigator told me in an interview that he "didn't have the time of day" for IBUKA.[726] But even if the Trial Chambers can be sure that IBUKA does produce some false testimony in some cases, they have little way of ascertaining the veracity of individual claims of lying. Perhaps as a consequence, the Trial Chambers fail to credit many claims of perjury. The *Kamuhanda* Appeals Chamber did not believe witness GAA's claim to have lied at trial,[727] and the *Media Trial* Trial Chamber failed to credit the many assertions of perjury that were bandied about in that case.[728] An excerpt from the *Ndindabahizi* judgment likewise shows the kinds of competing claims that the Trial Chambers frequently confront:

> The prosecution argues that Defences [sic] Witnesses DR, DO, DM, and DN are all in Gisovu prison together, along with the Accused's brother, Ezekias Seyeze. They therefore had a motive to lie on behalf of the accused, and an opportunity to coordinate false testimony. For its part, the defence contends that Witnesses CGX, CGE, and CGB all admitted to having been recruited by witness CGH. Witness DF charges that Witness CGH, while working as a prison guard, boasted that he was going to manufacture evidence against the Accused. Witness DC alleges that witness CGH took him to see the inspector

722 Nahimana Transcript, Mar. 13, 2003, at 34. In a similar vein, witness DM testified that IBUKA invents false testimony almost as a rule. Nahimana Transcript, Sept. 11, 2001, at 93–96.

723 Nahimana Transcript, Sept. 11, 2001, at 96.

724 Nahimana Transcript, Jan. 20, 2003, at 15–19.

725 Rutaganda Transcript, Nov. 24, 1997, at 135–36.

726 Interview with KU, former ICTR investigator (by telephone July 7, 2006).

727 The Appeals Chamber's failure to credit GAA's allegations may have stemmed in some part from the many inconsistencies in his account of his perjury. In a written statement, GAA claimed that he colluded with another witness to fabricate a story, yet while testifying before the Appeals Chamber, GAA maintained that he himself had individually invented some of the details of his fabricated story. GAA's accounts of his dealings with another witness – GEK – also varied considerably between his statement and his oral testimony. *See* Kamuhanda Judgement, note 38, at paras. 216–218.

728 Witness RM200, for instance, testified on direct examination that she had spoken to five prosecution witnesses about their perjured testimony, Nahimana Transcript, Mar. 14, 2003, at 28–30, yet it was revealed on cross-examination that with respect to four of those witnesses, she had merely overheard their conversations, Nahimana Judgement, note 97, at para. 869.

of judicial police, who was with two white people. They offered to pay him fifty dollars if he testified about crimes committed by the Accused. When he refused, witness CGH implied that he would be deprived of prison privileges because of his failure to cooperate.[729]

Until now, I have discussed particularized instances or allegations of perjury, but the most compelling evidence regarding the incidence of perjury, particularly at the ICTR and SCSL, derives from the fact that virtually every ICTR and SCSL case has featured either an alibi or some other form of stark contradiction between witnesses for the defense and witnesses for the prosecution. Turning first to the ICTR, my review of ICTR transcripts and judgments revealed that twenty-four of the twenty-six contested cases that have been decided (or 92 percent of those cases) featured at least one example of diametrically opposed testimony between one or more witnesses.[730] Many of these contradictions

[729] Ndindabahizi Judgement, note 56, at para. 111. Other tribunals have faced similar problems. Human Rights Watch described the first trial held by the Iraqi High Court as follows:

> During the course of the defense case, private defense lawyers for Saddam Hussein were accused of procuring the perjury of four defense witnesses.... Two had claimed that the chief prosecutor in the Dujail case had tried to bribe them into giving false testimony against Saddam Hussein. Another claimed that some of the individuals alleged by the prosecution to have been executed were in fact alive and living in Dujail, while the fourth witness claimed that a person whom he believed to be the chief prosecutor had attended a celebration in Dujail marking the anniversary of the assassination attempt against Saddam Hussein and that some attendees at that anniversary celebration had taken responsibility for the assassination attempt. The witnesses were detained after the end of the court hearing on May 31 on suspicion of perjury.... They are alleged to have confessed to having knowingly fabricated their testimony due to threats and inducements by one of Saddam Hussein's defense counsel, who allegedly had coached them on what to say. Defense lawyers for Saddam Hussein claimed that the witnesses had been assaulted and detained incommunicado and that their confessions to perjury were coerced.

Human Rights Watch, *Judging Dujail*, note 25, at 70–71. *See also Four Witnesses in Saddam Trial Held*, A.P., June 1, 2006; Paul Schemm, *Key Saddam Witnesses Say They Were Bribed, Coerced*, Agence France-Presse, June 12, 2006.

[730] Many of the cases contain more than one example of starkly contradictory testimony. For the sake of brevity, however, I list only one for each case. In *Kayishema & Ruzindana*, prosecution witnesses testified that they saw Kayishema order an attack on the Catholic church in Kibuye town on April 17, 1994, Kayishema & Ruzindana Judgement, note 25, at paras. 328–330, while Kayishema's wife testified that Kayishema was in hiding with her from April 16 to April 20, 1994, *id.* at para. 245. In *Musema*, prosecution witness F testified that he saw Musema at Muyira Hill on May 13, 1994, taking part in a large-scale attack on the Tutsi. Musema Judgement, note 112, at para. 404. Defense witness MH, however, testified to having met Musema in Rubona on May 13, 1994. *Id.* at para. 329. In *Ndindabahizi*, both prosecution witness CGH and defense witness DN were hiding in the home of Augustin Karara, *bourgmestre* of Gitesi *commune*. Witness CGH testified that he observed Ndindabahizi come to Karara's house at the end of April and was in the room when Ndindabahizi admonished Karara not to spare any Tutsis, Ndindabahizi Judgement, note 56, at paras. 183–185, witness DN testified

that witness CGH would hide in his room whenever there were visitors, and he testified that Ndindabahizi did not visit Karara's house until June, well after witness CGH had fled, *id.* at para. 199. *Ntakirutimana* featured contradictory testimony with respect to allegations against both defendants accused in that case. Prosecution witness KK testified that he saw Elizaphan Ntakirutimana at the ESI Chapel massacre site on April 16 between 9 a.m. and 9:30 a.m., while prosecution witnesses GG and HH testified that they saw Gérard Ntakirutimana shoot and kill Charles Ukobizaba on April 16 between 12 and 1 p.m. Ntakirutimana Judgement, note 69, at paras. 344–346, 365–366. Defense witness 4, by contrast, testified that he and several others, including Elizaphan and Gérard Ntakirutimana, left for Gishyita before 8 a.m. on April 16. *Id.* at para. 299. In *Kajelijeli*, prosecution witness GDO testified that she witnessed the brutal rape and killing of her daughter. Defense witness RHU30 testified that the witness's daughter had been killed but not raped and that the witness had not been present during the attack on her daughter. Kajelijeli Judgement, note 303, at para. 680. In *Rutaganda*, prosecution witness H testified as to seeing Rutaganda on April 11, 1994 during various episodes of violence. Rutaganda Judgement, note 38, at paras. 276–77. Defense witness DDD testified that she and Rutaganda arrived in Kiyovu at 9 a.m. on April 11, 1994 and stayed with a friend who was living there until about midday on that same day. According to witness DDD, she and Rutaganda then traveled to Masango, arriving there at about 6 p.m. *Id.* at para. 155. In *Semanza*, prosecution witness VF testified seeing Semanza during a massacre in Rugende at 10 a.m. on April 10, 1994. Semanza Judgement, note 31, at para. 150. Defense witness PFM testified, however, that she accompanied Semanza to Gitarama town around 9 or 10 a.m. on April 10 and remained in the market with him every day between April 10 and May 20. She maintained that he never left her except to go to the bathroom. *Id.* at para. 122. *Ntagerura et al.* contains witness contradictions involving all three defendants prosecuted in that case. Prosecution witness MZ testified that while hiding out in his tea plantation in Cyangugu on April 17, he heard Ntagerura give a speech, calling for the extermination of the Tutsi. Ntagerura Judgement, note 37, at paras. 153–154. However, defense witness Nkurunziza testified that Ntagerura was with him on April 16 and 17, attending cabinet meetings on Murambi Hill. *Id.* at para. 162. As for Ntagerura's codefendant, Imanishimwe, prosecution witness LAK testified that Imanishimwe had arrived at a roadblock outside of LAK's workplace on April 9, 1994. Once there, according to LAK, Imanishimwe provided weapons to soldiers at the roadblock. *Id.* at paras. 443–444. Defense witness PCG, who worked at the roadblock, contradicted LAK's testimony, stating that the roadblock was not located in front of LAK's workplace but was a kilometer away. PCG further testified that he and the others manning the roadblock did not receive any weapons or any visits from officials on April 9, 1994. *Id.* at para. 475. Witness contradictions pertaining to the third defendant, Emmanuel Bagambiki, as well as other contradictory allegations pertaining to Ntagerura, are discussed in the text. *See* text at notes 688 to 690 and 1149 to 1151. In *Mpambara*, the testimonies of prosecution witness AHY and defense witness Elizabeth Hardinge conflicted regarding Mpambara's whereabouts on the morning of April 9, 1994. AHY had Mpambara at the Paris Center, distributing weapons and encouraging the killing of Tutsi, while Hardinge had Mpambara at Karubamba and subsequently back at Gahini. Mpambara Judgement, note 471, at paras. 122–123. *Rwamakuba* featured numerous instances of divergent testimonies between prosecution and defense witnesses. As one example, a number of prosecution witness testified that they were at Butare University Hospital when Rwamakuba came in and killed some Tutsi patients. Rwamakuba Judgement, note 63, at para. 163. Defense witnesses 1/1 and 9/1, however, testified that on the dates that prosecution witnesses placed Rwamakuba at the hospital, he was in fact with them at Gisenyi. *Id.* at para. 197. Prosecution witness YH in *Simba* testified that on April 21, 1994, Simba encouraged a crowd of Hutu assailants to kill Tutsi in anticipation of a massacre that occurred in Kaduha Parish. Simba Judgement, note 455, at para. 142. Defense witness AJTI contradicted that testimony by testifying that Simba was with her during the Kaduha Parish massacre. *Id.* at para. 367. Two of the three stem from testimony pertaining to the defendant's alibi. *Kamuhanda* provides a prototypical example. There, prosecution witnesses testified that Kamuhanda

defendants accused in the *Nahimana* case were the subject of contradictory witness testimony. Several prosecution witnesses testified that they saw defendant Ngeze on April 7, 1994, distributing weapons and the like. Nahimana Judgement, note 97, at para. 825. Ngeze maintained that he had been arrested on April 6 and had not been released until April 9, an alibi that was supported by several defense witnesses. *Id.* at paras. 826–828. Prosecution witness AEN testified that Ngeze's co-defendant Nahimana had appeared at a meeting on March 29, 1994, during which he expressed his hatred for Tutsi and called for their extermination. *Id.* at para. 622. Nahimana's wife and doctor, however, testified that Nahimana was home, sick with malaria, on March 29. As a result of this illness, the defense witnesses testified that it would have been impossible for Nahimana to travel anywhere. *Id.* at paras. 628–629. In *Seromba,* Prosecution witness CDL testified that Seromba participated in a security meeting held on April 11, 1994. Seromba Judgement, note 547, at para. 68; Seromba Transcript, Jan. 19, 2005, at 57. Defense witnesses FE27 and CF23 testified, by contrast, that Seromba did not attend the meeting but submitted a letter, which was read at the meeting. Seromba Judgement, note 547, at paras. 70–71. In *Bagilishema,* some contradictory testimony was proffered by two sets of prosecution witnesses. Witnesses A and AC placed the defendant at the Gitwaro Stadium in Kibuye town – where thousands of Tutsi refugees were detained and mistreated – at 9 a.m. on April 14, while two other prosecution witnesses alleged that he was 16 kilometers away in Mabanza *commune* at just that time. Bagilishema Judgement, note 122, at paras. 544–553. In *Muvunyi,* prosecution witness CCR testified that Muvunyi convened meetings at Nyantanga Trade Center on April 20 and 21, 1994, during which he called on the audience to fight the *inyenzi.* Muvunyi Judgement, note 455, at paras. 160–161. A number of defense witnesses who lived and worked at the Nyantanga Trade Center testified that no meeting took place there in April 1994. *Id.* at para. 174. *Muhimana* prosecution witness BC placed Muhimana at the scene of a gruesome attack at Ngendombi Hill on April 10, 1994. She testified that, in addition to launching a grenade that killed a number of Tutsi, Muhimana killed the witness's children and cut off the witness's hand. Muhimana Judgement, note 363, at paras. 57–58. Defense witness TQ1 testified, by contrast, that Muhimana attended his son's funeral on April 10 and remained at his home until April 16. *Id.* at para. 59; Muhimana Transcript, Aug. 23, 2004, at 3–4, 12, 15. In *Gacumbitsi,* prosecution witnesses testified that, on April 13, 1994, Gacumbitsi ordered his tenants to leave the house he owned, and intimated that the house was not meant for Tutsis. Gacumbitsi Judgement, note 364, at para. 179. However, defense witness UPT testified that Gacumbitsi did not expel his tenants. *Id.* at para. 182; Gacumbitsi Transcript, Oct. 16, 2003, at 22–23. In *Karera,* prosecution witnesses placed Karera in Kigali-Ville and Rural Kigali prefectures on various dates in April 1994, whereas defense witnesses testified that he was with them in Ruhengeri prefecture on those dates. Karera Judgement, note 54, at paras. 457–458, 460. Prosecution witness AMA in *Rukundo* testified that the defendant along with several soldiers had removed from the CND compound in a minibus 15 refugees who were never seen again. Prosecutor v. Rukundo, Case No. ICTR-2001–70-T, Judgement, paras. 397–398 (Feb. 27, 2009) [hereinafter Rukundo Judgement]. *Rukundo* defense witness CNB, by contrast, accused witness AMA of "telling lies" and maintained that "he saw every vehicle that came to the CND" and he never saw Rukundo or any blue minibus. *Id.* at paras. 424–425. In *Zigiranyirazo,* prosecution witness AVY testified that he attended a meeting at Umuganda Stadium in the last week of April 1994, during which a helicopter arrived carrying Zigiranyirazo. According to witness AVY, Zigiranyirazo took the podium and encouraged the people to continue killing Tutsi. Zigiranyirazo Judgement, note 498, at paras. 150–151. One prosecution witness and four defense witnesses corroborated AVY's testimony that a meeting had occurred and that certain participated in a massacre on April 12, 1994, at the Gikomero Parish.[731] Defense witnesses, by contrast, testified that Kamuhanda could not have participated in the massacre at Gikomero because Kamuhanda was with them for about ten or twelve days, including on the day of the massacre.[732] Other ICTR cases

of the speakers that AVY mentioned had addressed the crowd, but these five witnesses each testified that Zigiranyirazo had not attended the meeting. *Id.* at para. 156. In *Kalimanzira*, prosecution witness AZT testified that Kalimanzira spoke at a meeting at the market square in Nyirakanywero in Nyabitare *secteur* and instructed the people to fight the "accomplices" with all their energy. Prosecutor v. Kalimanzira, Case No. ICTR-05–88-T, Judgement, paras. 259–261 (June 22, 2009) [hereinafter Kalimanzira Judgement]. Several defense witnesses, by contrast, denied that Kalimanzira was present at the meeting. *Id.* at paras. 273–277. In *Nchamihigo*, prosecution witnesses BRF, LAG, and LDC testified that they witnessed Nchamihigo's involvement in the murder of Father Boneza, whereas defense witnesses who also saw the killing denied that Nchamihigo was present. Prosecutor v. Nchamihigo, Case No. ICTR-01–63-T, Judgement and Sentence, paras. 135–140 (Nov. 12, 2008) [hereinafter Nchamihigo Judgement]. Prosecution witness BKW in *Bikindi* testified that Bikindi had participated in the military training of a selected group of *Interahamwe* by French soldiers in Gabiro, Mutara region, around 1992–1993. However, Defence witness Jean Berchmans Hakorimana, a former Rwandan military member, explained that he had received training at the training center from the French, but he stated that the Gabiro training centre was reserved uniquely for the military and that no *Interahamwe* were trained there. Bikindi Judgement, note 683, at paras. 96–98. *Bagosora et al.*, featured contradictions pertaining to each of the defendants. For instance, prosecution witness LAI testified that he was present when defendant Kabiligi addressed *Interahamwe* youth and helped Kabiligi to offload weapons from a helicopter. Bagosora et al. Judgement, note 484, at paras. 260–262. By contrast, some defense witnesses whom LAI had placed at the same locations denied having been there, and documentary evidence showed Kabiligi to be out of the country at the time LAI placed him at the above events. *Id.* at paras. 265–273. As for defendant Bagosora, prosecution witnesses testified that he encouraged the killing of Tutsi at one or more meetings at the end of May and beginning of June 1994, *id.* at paras. 1680, 1697, while defense witnessed testified that Bagosora was traveling abroad with them during that period, *id.* at paras. 1684, 1949, 1951–1954, 1959. With respect to defendant Nsengiyumva prosecution witness DO testified that he was with Nsengiyumva at the Gisenyi military camp on April 7, 1994, at 8:30 a.m., *id.* at para. 1014, while defense witness LSK-1, a neighbor of witness DO, maintained that he spent the entire morning of April 7 with DO, so that "it was impossible for Witness DO to have attended a meeting at Gisenyi military camp on the morning of 7 April 1994, as he was in his company at this time," *id.* at para. 1031. Finally, prosecution witness AH testified that at about 10 a.m. on April 8, he saw Ntabakuze, accompanied by members of the Para Commando Battalion, driving slowly through the area in a blue Toyota Hilux and supervising the killings. Witness AH testified that he had a conversation with Ntabakuze. *Id.* at para. 912. Defense witness Colonel Dewez, the commander of UNAMIR's Kigali Battalion referred to the Kigali Battalion's *Chronique*, a daily record of the activities of the Belgian UNAMIR contingent from April 6–19, 1994, and it showed that Ntabakuze was with U.N. officers on the morning of April 8. *Id.* at paras. 915–917.

Even international tribunals that adjudicate civil claims arising during warfare receive large quantities of conflicting testimony. The Eritrea-Ethiopia Claims Commission has frequently commented on the "deep and wide-ranging conflicts in the evidence" that bedevil its efforts to determine the truth. *See, e.g.*, Eritrea/Ethiopia, Partial Award, Civilians' Claims, Eritrea's Claims 15, 16, 23, 27–32 (Dec. 17, 2004), *available at* http://www.pca-cpa.org.

[731] *See, e.g.*, Kamuhanda Judgement, note 38, at paras. 306–309, 322, 327.

[732] *See id.* at paras. 105–107, 114.

feature additional contradictions that are unrelated to alibis. A typical example of that sort of contradiction can be found in the *Cyangugu* case, where prosecution witness LAK testified that defendant Samuel Imanishimwe arrived at a roadblock outside of LAK's workplace on April 9, 1994, and provided weapons to soldiers at the roadblock.[733] Defense witness PCG, who worked at the roadblock, contradicted LAK's testimony, stating that the roadblock was not located in front of LAK's workplace but was one kilometer away. PCG further testified that he and the others manning the roadblock did not receive any weapons or any visits from officials on April 9, 1994.[734]

Serious contradictions can appear even among witnesses called by the same side of a case. In the ICTR's *Government I* case, prosecution witness Ahmed Mbonyunkiza testified that one of the defendants, Mathieu Ngirumpatse, had encouraged the killing of Tutsi at a Wednesday MRND meeting in February 1992. He also testified that a defendant in another trial, Simon Bikindi, introduced a song at that meeting entitled "Let Us Exterminate Them."[735] Three subsequent prosecution witnesses, by contrast, testified that no such comments were made or songs sung at an MRND meeting during that time.[736] Indeed, two of the prosecution witnesses observed that it made no sense to allege that an exhortation to kill the Tutsi was made at a 1992 MRND meeting because the Chairman of the MRND at that time and many MRND members were themselves Tutsi.[737] *Bagilishema* provides another example of contradictory testimony emanating from witnesses on the same side of a case, as there, prosecution witnesses A and AC placed the defendant at the Gitwaro Stadium in Kibuye town at 9:00 a.m. on April 14, whereas two other prosecution witnesses alleged that the defendant was sixteen kilometers away in Mabanza *commune* at exactly that time.[738] In the SCSL's *CDF* case, former Sierra Leonean Vice President Albert Demby testified as a defense witness that he had not traveled to Conakry. Yet, by so testifying, Demby contradicted the testimony of defense witness Peter Penfold who maintained that he had participated in a meeting in Conakry with Demby and Sierra Leonean President Kabbah.[739] In like vein, *CDF* defendant Norman testified that Osman Vandy was one of the first commanders of the attack on Koribondo. Although Vandy testified for

[733] Ntagerura Judgement, note 37, at paras. 443–444.

[734] *Id.* at para. 475.

[735] Karemera Transcript, Sept. 20, 2005, at 52, 56.

[736] Karemera Transcript, Oct. 14, 2005, at 15–19; Karemera Transcript, Mar. 1, 2006, at 31–36; Karemera Transcript, May 26, 2006, at 37–38.

[737] Karemera Transcript, Oct. 14, 2005, at 16; Karemera Transcript, Mar. 1, 2006, at 33. Defense counsel also maintained that each of the ten people that Mbonyunkiza identified as also having been present at that meeting had refuted Mbonyunkiza's testimony.

[738] Bagilishema Judgement, note 122, at paras. 544–553.

[739] CDF Transcript, Feb. 13, 2006, at 58–59.

the defense, he denied participating in any way in the attack on Koribondo.[740] Other examples appear in the notes.[741]

As alluded to in the preceding discussion, alibis are tremendously popular at the ICTR, and they constitute a measure of the prevalence of perjury at that institution. A whopping twenty-nine of thirty-six ICTR defendants whose cases were contested and resulted in a public judgment put forth alibis; that is, 81 percent of ICTR defendants proffered alibis.[742] And even that statistic fails to adequately convey the exceptional prevalence of alibis at the ICTR because, in four of the seven cases that did not feature alibis, an alibi would not have been an efficacious defense because the charges brought against the defendants were based primarily on the defendants' official responsibilities, not on particular actions that they were alleged to have taken and that might have been rebutted by an alibi.[743] Thus, only two of forty defendants who might have benefited

[740] CDF Transcript, Feb. 20, 2006, at 5.

[741] AFRC Judgement, note 27, at paras. 387 & n.754, paras. 919–924.

[742] The twenty-nine defendants who proffered an alibi are Imanishimwe, Bagambiki, and Ntagerura, *see* Ntagerura Judgement, note 37, at para. 288; Kajelijeli, *see* Kajelijeli Judgement, note 303, at para. 25; Kamuhanda, *see* Kamuhanda Judgement, note 38, at para. 81; Kayishema and Ruzindana, *see* Kayishema & Ruzindana Judgement, note 25, at para. 232; Muhimana, *see* Muhimana Judgement, note 363, at para. 12; Musema, *see* Musema Judgement, note 112, at para. 317; Ndindabahizi, *see* Ndindabahizi Judgement, note 56, at § 4.6; Niyitegeka, *see* Niyitegeka Judgement, note 56, at para. 67; Elizaphan and Gérard Ntakirutimana, *see* Ntakirutimana Judgement, note 69, at para. 293 and § 3.11.4; Rutaganda, *see* Rutaganda Judgement, note 38, at para. 120; Semanza, *see* Semanza Judgement, note 31, at para. 75; Mpambara, *see* Mpambara Judgement, note 471, at para. 151 n.361; Ngeze and Nahimana, *see* Nahimana Judgement, note 97, at paras. 627, 826; Simba, *see* Simba Judgement, note 455, at para. 9; Karera, *see* Karera Judgement, note 54, at paras. 4, 457–462; Rwamakuba, *see* Rwamakuba Judgement, note 63, at para. 70; Rukundo Judgement, note 730, at paras. 538–539; Kalimanzira, *see* Kalimanzira Judgement, note 730, at para. 100; Nchamihigo, *see* Nchamihigo Judgement, note 730, at para. 20; Zigiranyirazo, *see* Zigiranyirazo Judgement, note 498, at para 9; Bagosora, *see* Bagosora et al. Judgement, note 484, at paras. 1944–1968; Kabiligi, *see* Bagosora et al. Judgement, note 484, at paras. 1969–1986; Ntabakuze, *see* Bagosora et al. Judgement, note 484, at para. 1942 & n.2115; Nsengiyumva, *see* Bagosora et al. Judgement, note 484, at para. 1942 & n.2115.

[743] The seven defendants who did not put forth an alibi are Gacumbitsi, Bagilishema, Seromba, Akayesu, Muvunyi, Bikindi, and Barayagwiza, and it is the latter four who would not have benefited from one. In its indictment against Akayesu, *bourgmestre* of Taba *commune*, the prosecution charged that

> As bourgmestre, Jean Paul Akayesu was responsible for maintaining law and public order in his commune. At least 2000 Tutsis were killed in Taba between April 7 and the end of June, 1994, while he was still in power. The killings in Taba were openly committed and so widespread that, as bourgmestre, Jean Paul Akayesu must have known about them. Although he had the authority and responsibility to do so, Jean Paul Akayesu never attempted to prevent the killing of Tutsis in the commune in any way or called for assistance from regional or national authorities to quell the violence.

Bikindi was acknowledged to have been outside Rwanda during the period of the genocide, and the prosecution did not pursue "any allegations regarding Bikindi's 'physical acts' during from an alibi failed to raise one. The prevalence of alibis at the ICTR stands in stark contrast to their infrequent appearance in domestic criminal cases. The most recent research I could find suggested that American defendants tender alibis in only a small percentage of cases – probably less than 15 percent.[744] Alibis similarly appear only rarely in British courts. The Royal Commission on Criminal Justice's Crown Court Study found that British defendants put forth an alibi in between 9 and 12 percent of contested cases.[745] The significantly greater popularity of alibis at the ICTR probably reflects the general difficulty of verifying facts in such nondocumentary societies as Rwanda, a difficulty I have already detailed. In other words, a fabricated alibi is a more efficacious defense in societies in which facts are not readily verifiable by other sources of evidence.

Alibis might be expected to be slightly less common at the SCSL because most of the charges against SCSL defendants stem from acts taken by their subordinates, which cannot be rebutted by the defendant's alibi.[746] But of the three cases that the SCSL has decided, two featured alibis,[747] and all three cases boast plenty of blatantly contradictory testimony that suggested that one or another witness was lying. A few examples will give the flavor of these SCSL contradictions. *CDF* insider witness Albert Nallo testified, for instance, that the three *CDF* defendants had killed Mustapha Fallon during an initiation ceremony, ate some of his body parts, burned his corpse, and used the ashes for subsequent initiations.[748] Fallon's brother testified by contrast that he saw his brother die at the hands of the AFRC.[749] In addition, other witnesses

that period." Bikindi Judgement, note 683, at para. 10. Muvunyi was the interim Commander of the *Ecole des Sous-officiers* and was the most senior military officer in Butare *prefecture* during the genocide. Muvunyi Judgement, note 455, at paras. 8, 57. The charges in *Muvunyi* stemmed primarily from his responsibility for the actions of the soldiers under his command. Barayagwiza was charged primarily on the basis of his official position in Rwanda's hate-radio station, *Radio Télévision Libre des Mille Collines.*

744 *See* David M. Epstein, *Advance Notice of Alibi*, 55 J. Crim. L. Criminology 29, 37 (1964) (discussing a survey in which 80 percent of prosecutors opined that an alibi defense is offered in 0–15 percent of cases while 16 percent of prosecutors opined that it was offered in 16–30 percent of cases).

745 Michael Zander & Paul Henderson, Crown Court Study, RCCJ Research Study No. 19, at 75 (1993).

746 In addition, ICTR defendants are better able to present alibis because ICTR prosecution witnesses were better able to pinpoint the dates of various events than SCSL witnesses. Whereas the Rwandan genocide was short-lived and had a cataclysmic beginning, the Sierra Leonean violence extended for a much longer period of time and featured few notable dates.

747 *See* AFRC Judgement, note 27, at paras. 346–353; RUF Judgement, note 56, at paras. 502, 611–647.

748 CDF Transcript, Mar. 10, 2005, at 55–57.

749 CDF Transcript, Sept. 27, 2006, at 30–31. Other witnesses likewise contradicted Nallo's testimony. Defense witness M.T. Collier said it never happened, arguing that, as town elder, he

contradicted other aspects of Nallo's testimony. Nallo, for instance, testified that while in Baoma on the day of the trade fair in that village, he and Junisa Conneh killed a rebel.[750] Conneh, however, denied that there even was a trade fair in Baoma and categorically denied participating in any operation with Nallo, let alone committing a murder with him.[751] Nallo likewise testified that, on instructions from defendant Norman to eliminate "infiltrators," he and others traveled to Sorgia Village and, once there, tied up and tortured one Joseph Lansana. Nallo testified in particular that he and another man cut off Lansana's ear and killed Lansana's mother.[752] The defense brought Lansana to the stand, and he testified that the Kamajors did not harm him in any way. Most notably, he showed the court his two intact ears.[753] Nallo also testified that when he learned that a Kamajor named Vanjawai had killed a pregnant woman, Nallo made a recommendation to the War Council that Vanjawai be severely punished. According Nallo, the War Council said they "could not touch that case" because Norman had intimidated them.[754] The defense brought Vanjawai to the stand, and he testified, by contrast, that the Council did handle the matter, first deciding to hang him and then deciding to investigate the allegations. Vanjawai testified that after the Council had investigated, it determined that the crime had been committed by an AFRC soldier, so it released him. According to Vanjawai, Norman played no role in the Council's deliberations; the Council itself had the sole authority to decide his fate.[755]

Similarly divergent accounts appeared in the *AFRC* and *RUF* cases. Whereas *AFRC* prosecution witnesses placed defendant Brima in the Koinadugu and Bombali districts during certain periods in 1998, where they maintained that he was acting as the commander of an advance team to set up a base camp, Brima and several defense witnesses testified that he had been arrested and held in RUF detention for much of that time.[756] Questions concerning the command structure of the advance team also gave rise to conflicting testimony. Whereas three prosecution witnesses maintained that defendant Kamara was

surely would have heard about such an incident if it had happened. CDF Transcript, Feb. 17, 2006, at 21–24. Haroun Aruna denied not only that Mustafa Fallon was killed at Base Zero but that any other killings took place there. CDF Transcript, May 15, 2006, at 26–27.

750 CDF Transcript, Mar. 10, 2005, at 53–54.

751 CDF Transcript, Sept. 28, 2006, at 10–17. Witness Tommy Jabbi likewise testified that there was no trade fair in Baoma. *Id.* at 31.

752 CDF Transcript, Mar. 10, 2005, at 45–49.

753 CDF Transcript, Sept. 28, 2006, at 63–64.

754 CDF Transcript, Mar. 11, 2005, at 21.

755 CDF Transcript, Feb. 17, 2006, at 84–87.

756 AFRC Judgement, note 27, at paras. 346–353.

in charge of the advance team,[757] four defense witnesses testified that Foday Kallay held the position of senior commander.[758] Mutually exclusive accounts also featured in *RUF* testimony. In one particularly striking instance, a prosecution witness's account of his wife's gruesome rape and murder clashed with the account of a defense witness who denied that the wife had been killed. The defense witness's contrary testimony was particularly compelling because the defense witness was the wife herself.[759] Additional conflicting testimony was heard regarding forced farming in Kailahun District. In particular, whereas a prosecution witness described in considerable detail the forced farming that took place from 1997 to 2000, a defense witness denied that any forced farming occurred during that period.[760]

Because Timorese defendants so frequently confessed their wrongdoing, alibis and contradictory testimony were not so prevalent at the Special Panels, but they did arise occasionally even there. A passel of prosecution witnesses in the *Marcelino Soares* case placed Soares at the scene of a beating, for instance, whereas a defense witness testified that Soares was with him at a meeting in Dili.[761] And the Special Panels rejected the testimony of five prosecution witnesses in *Tacaqui*, in part because these witnesses had not mentioned the defendant's involvement in the crime until after the defendant had been arrested. Following the arrest, the prosecution collected a series of statements that, as the Panel described them,

> appear to be only focused on the accused; in them there's no narration of facts, only the indication of the name of Tacaqui and his participation to the crime of Teolassi; there is an appalling uniformity in some details of the narrations like the ground "soaked with blood of the victims" or the chilling silence allegedly kept by Tacaqui while slitting throats or chopping bodies . . . give the impression that there was, on the part of the witnesses the self imposed suggestion to include Tacaqui in the list of the perpetrators present to the crime scene.[762]

Of course, the high incidence of alibis and blatantly contradictory testimony stands as only an imperfect measure of perjury since some of the alibis and contradictions could reflect the witnesses' poor memory and perception, rather than their willfully false testimony. However, particularly at the ICTR, the

[757] *Id.* at paras. 485–487.
[758] *Id.* at para. 497.
[759] RUF Judgement, note 56, at paras. 595–597.
[760] RUF Judgment, note 56, at paras. 569–570, 953–954; RUF Transcript, Nov. 21, 2005, at 64–66.
[761] Prosecution v. Marcelino Soares, Case No. 11/2003, Judgement, at 6 (Dec. 11, 2003).
[762] *See, e.g.*, Tacaqui Judgement, note 36, at 46.

alibis and contradictory testimony are so prevalent that it would seem naïve to dismiss all – or even a significant proportions – as stemming from honest mistakes. Willfully false testimony is, I believe, a common feature of many international trials, and because it is so common it supplies another plausible explanation for the communication difficulties detailed in Chapter 2 and the inconsistencies described in Chapter 4. The sum total of these chapters points to an international criminal justice system that has considerable difficulty carrying out its core function: fact-finding. It is to that difficulty that I turn next.

6

Expectations Unfulfilled

The Consequences of the Fact-Finding Impediments

The foregoing chapters show that international criminal trials at the ICTR, SCSL, and Special Panels are beset by a variety of fact-finding impediments. Virtually the only evidence presented to these bodies takes the form of eyewitness testimony, and this testimony is frequently problematic in numerous regards. Witness accounts routinely fail to include information that is crucial to a defendant's ability to refute the witness's allegations and to a fact finder's ability to ascertain what actually happened. Questions regarding dates, times, distances, numbers, and other key details, for instance, often go unanswered so that witness testimony is rendered vague and difficult to challenge or verify. The information that witnesses do provide frequently contradicts the information previously provided by that witness or by other witnesses, and the Trial Chambers have little basis for deciding between competing accounts. The foregoing chapters also examine various factors that may explain these testimonial deficiencies. They explore the linguistic and cultural divides that impede communication between witnesses and their in-court interlocutors, for instance, and they bring perjury out of the shadows.

As I have discussed in previous chapters, these testimonial deficiencies can gravely impair the fact finder's ability to evaluate the credibility of witness testimony and to find facts generally. It is difficult to ascertain just how grave the impairment is, but I begin this chapter by delineating a number of factors that provide some insight into the question. The first – and most obvious – is the prevalence of the fact-finding impediments; that is, the more impediments there are, the more we must be concerned about their impact on the tribunals' fact-finding competence. The previous chapters have shed some light on this question. They revealed, for instance, that virtually every ICTR and SCSL case features some false testimony. They also revealed that the testimony of a majority of ICTR and SCSL witnesses is at odds in some significant respect with those same witness's previous written statements. These measures are themselves imprecise, and the prevalence of many of the other fact-finding impediments is even less quantifiable. For instance, although we know that the need for language interpretation and the existence of certain cultural beliefs and practices impede clear communication between witnesses and court personnel who speak different languages and subscribe to different cultural norms, we cannot know how prevalent such impediments are because we often will not know when an interpreter has distorted a witness's testimony or when a taboo has prevented the witness from providing a complete account of the events witnessed. At the same time, the voluminous citations appearing in the previous chapters' footnotes – which are by no means comprehensive – constitute convincing evidence that the fact-finding impediments that I have identified pervade ICTR, SCSL, and Special Panels proceedings. Although it is certainly true that some tribunals suffer more from some problems than from others, and certain witnesses provide more clear, consistent, and detailed testimony than others, there is no question that the testimonial deficiencies heretofore described are widespread and common features of ICTR, SCSL, and Special Panels proceedings.

Another factor relevant to the impact of the fact-finding impediments is the ability of defense counsel to test the witnesses' accounts through independent investigations. That is, the fact that prosecution witnesses often fail to convey key details or that they provide contradictory accounts will be of relatively minor significance if defense counsel have the ability to supplement deficient testimony with information obtained through their own investigations. A witness's failure to date an anti-Tutsi rally, for instance, would not be especially problematic if defense counsel could ascertain the date through other means. Similarly, a witness's inability to estimate how far her hiding place was from the crime scene is of little consequence if an investigator can get to the crime scene himself to measure the distance. Finally, even the high incidence of false testimony would be less troubling if we could have some confidence in our ability to ascertain through investigations which of the conflicting testimonies – if any – is truthful.

But we cannot. As Chapter 5 describes, the fact that ICTR, SCSL, and Special Panels witnesses live in oral cultures means that, for many questions, there simply are no definitive answers. The anti-Tutsi rally would not have been the subject of a written advertisement, for instance, so the Trial Chamber cannot know when it occurred – or even if it occurred – unless witnesses provide that information. Occasionally, defense investigators are able to measure distances or investigate other disputed factual issues, and the information derived from such investigations often proves immeasurably valuable for the Trial Chamber's factual determinations. But only rarely can such efforts be undertaken. Sometimes the witness's account is so utterly lacking in detail that the investigator would not know where to begin. More frequently, as noted in Chapter 5, investigations are thwarted by political impediments, or investigators lack the time and resources to conduct thorough investigations, particularly given the logistical difficulties that so complicate such endeavors.

A final factor to consider in assessing the impact of testimonial deficiencies is the number of witnesses testifying about a given factual issue. One could argue, for instance, that the greater the quantity of witness testimony addressing a particular point, the smaller the impact that testimonial deficiencies will have on the tribunals' fact-finding competence. So, for instance, although we might consider it objectionable for a Trial Chamber to find a fact based on a witness's testimony when that testimony is sharply inconsistent with the witness's previous written statement, our objection would lose its force if the Trial Chamber also had before it corroborative, consistent testimony of other witnesses. Alternatively, but more controversially, we might believe that although the vague and inconsistent testimony of one international witness is an inadequate basis for conviction, the vague and inconsistent testimony of three international witnesses that basically corroborate one another does provide sufficient support for a defendant's conviction. In other words, the argument is that even though various aspects of international witness testimony may be problematic, we might nonetheless place confidence in the factual determinations that are predicated on that testimony so long as there is a sufficient quantity of it. Robert Boyle made this argument in the eighteenth century when he observed that

> though the testimony of a single witness shall not suffice to prove the accused party guilty of murder; yet the testimony of two witnesses, though but of equal credit, that is, a second testimony added to the first, though of itself never a wit more credible than the former, shall ordinarily suffice to prove a man guilty; because it is thought reasonable to suppose, that, though each testimony single be but probable, yet a concurrence of such probabilities, (which ought in reason to be attributed to the truth of what they jointly tend to prove) may well amount to a moral certainty, i.e., such a certainty, as may warrant the judge to proceed to the sentence of death against the indicted party.[763]

[763] 3 ROBERT BOYLE, WORKS 530–31 (1772). As Matthew Hale put it about a century before Boyle:

> If to any one quantum of fact there be many but probable evidences, which taken singly have not perchance any full evidence, yet when many of those evidences concur and concenter in the evidence of the same thing, their very multiplicity and consent makes the evidence the stronger; as the concurrent testimonies of many Witnesses make an evidence more concludent. MATTHEW HALE, THE PRIMITIVE ORIGINATION OF MANKIND, CONSIDERED AND EXAMINED ACCORDING TO THE LIGHT OF NATURE 130 (1677).

Although this argument has theoretical appeal, its real-world persuasiveness depends substantially on the nature and severity of the testimonial deficiencies.[764] That is, although more is theoretically "better," it may not begin to approach "good enough" if the fact-finding impediments are especially severe. Moreover, if perjury is our primary concern, then the number of witnesses testifying to a particular event is apt to be irrelevant because international cases frequently feature a cabal of perjuring witnesses who collude about the story they present. Virtually every ICTR defendant has presented not one, but several witnesses to corroborate his alibi, and prosecution witnesses have likewise been known to orchestrate their perjurious tales in advance.[765] These caveats notwithstanding, I will discuss the quantity of witness testimony on the assumption that a larger pool of witness accounts does enhance fact-finding competence, at least in some cases.

My analysis suggests that the quantity of eyewitness testimony supporting the international tribunals' factual findings varies some with the case but mostly with the international tribunal. Among the three tribunals under study, Special Panels proceedings featured the largest number of witnesses per factual finding. Although the occasional factual finding at the Special Panels was based on the testimony of only one witness,[766] most findings were supported by at least two and sometimes many witnesses. This testimonial heft was perhaps least needed at the Special Panels, both because that institution's cases were generally less complex than those heard by the other tribunals and because Special Panels' defendants were peculiarly inclined to confess. Thus, the factual determinations in many Special Panels' cases were supported not only by the testimony of a substantial number of eyewitnesses but also by the self-incriminating testimony of the defendant himself.

The quantity of witness testimony in ICTR and SCSL proceedings has varied considerably from case to case. Some ICTR cases – particularly the early

[764] Even without considering the fact-finding impediments that I have described here, a large pool of witnesses does not necessarily make for accurate fact-finding. A number of American defendants who were wrongfully convicted and later exonerated by DNA evidence had been misidentified by numerous eyewitnesses. *See* Loftus, note 44, at 3, 85.

[765] *See* Ntagerura Judgement, note 37, at paras. 119–132. As described in Chapter 5, the Special Panels in the *Tacaqui* case noted the startling similarities in the statements of five witnesses who had not previously mentioned the defendant in their pretrial statements. Tacaqui Judgement, note 36, at 46. Similarly, during his testimony in *Kayishema & Ruzindana*, Rene Degni-Segui, the Special Rapporteur of the Commission on Human Rights on Rwanda, described a Rwandan case in which fifteen witnesses testified that the defendant had participated in the genocide, but it was later conclusively proved that the defendant was out of the country during the genocide. The fifteen witnesses had colluded ahead of time to present a fabricated story. Kayishema & Ruzindana Transcript, Mar. 9, 1998, at 12–13.

[766] *See, e.g.*, Tacaqui Judgement, note 36, at 26–27 (setting forth the evidence pertaining to the defendant's commission of the act alleged in Count 3).

ones – featured a substantial number of witnesses for each factual finding. Virtually all of the factual findings in the *Rutaganda* and *Kayishema & Ruzindana* cases, for instance, are supported by three or more witnesses. The factual findings of other ICTR cases, by contrast, are not so well supported. Each of the Trial Chamber's factual findings in *Ndindabahizi*, for instance, was supported by only one witness,[767] and virtually every factual finding in *Ntakirutimana* likewise is supported by only one witness.[768] Similarly, in *Simba*, the Trial Chamber found the defendant's involvement in the massacres at Murambi Technical School and Kaduha Parish primarily on the basis of one witness's testimony, though, in each instance, it did take note of the testimony of another, less reliable, witness whose testimony was deemed credible only if corroborated.[769] The *Niyitegeka, Musema*, and *Semanza* cases featured something of a combination: Whereas virtually all of the Trial Chamber's factual findings in those cases were supported by the testimony of only one witness, the defendants' involvement in the large-scale massacre that stood at the center of each case was supported by the testimony of many witnesses. So, Niyitegeka's and Musema's participation in the massacres on Muyira Hill was attested to by a passel of witnesses,[770] but the Trial Chambers' other factual findings were supported by the testimony of only one witness.[771] Likewise, although four witnesses testified to Semanza's participation in the Musha church massacres,[772] the Trial Chamber based its other factual findings on the testimony of only one witness.[773]

Turning to the SCSL, Chapter 7 features a detailed analysis of the *CDF* judgment, so I will say here only that many of its factual findings were based on the testimony of only one witness. As for the *AFRC* case, it was common

[767] The testimony of witness CGY supported the Trial Chamber's finding that Ndindabahizi transported assailants and distributed machetes at a roadblock between Gitwa and Karongi Hills. Ndindabahizi Judgement, note 56, at paras. 129–148. The testimony of witness CGN supported the Trial Chamber's conclusion that Ndindabahizi incited the crowd to attack the Tutsi on Gitwa Hill. *Id.* at paras. 149–181. And witness CGC's testimony supported the Trial Chamber's findings that Ndindabahizi distributed weapons and encouraged killings at the Gaseke roadblock, *id.* at paras. 203–231, whereas witness CGM's testimony supported a finding for similar activity at the Nyabahanga Bridge roadblock, *id.* at paras. 248–264.

[768] Ntakirutimana Judgement, note 69, at paras. 160–161, 536–543, 550–559, 573–579, 580–586, 587–598, 599–608, 609–615, 621–628, 629–636, 637–642, 656–661, 662–669, 670–674.

[769] Simba Judgement, note 455, at paras. 88–121, 139–178.

[770] Niyitegeka Judgement, note 56, at paras. 131–205, 208–215; Musema Judgement, note 112, at paras. 695–717, 746–757. *See* Musema Judgement, note 112, at paras. 758–780 (finding Musema's involvement in a massacre at Nyakavumu cave on the basis of the testimony of four witnesses).

[771] Niyitegeka Judgement, note 56, at paras. 54–66, 69–78, 92–108, 115–116, 117–130, 216–225, 226–229, 230–232, 235–238, 239–252, 253–257, 265–268, 269–272, 292–302, 303–312; Musema Judgement, note 112, at paras. 470–473, 667–693, 753, 755, 805–829, 846–862.

[772] Semanza Judgement, note 31, at paras. 162–213.

[773] *Id.* at paras. 214–244, 252–272.

knowledge that AFRC forces perpetrated atrocities, so it came as no surprise that the Trial Chamber received a substantial quantity of witness testimony pertaining to the occurrence of these atrocities. However, much less testimony was heard about the defendants' involvement in the crimes of the AFRC. Many of the latter factual findings are supported by the testimony of only one witness, and, indeed, the testimony of one witness in particular – witness TF1-334 – was key to a substantial number of the defendants' convictions.[774]

Not surprisingly, at both the ICTR and the SCSL, a larger number of witnesses testify about facts that support a defendant's conviction on a command responsibility theory as compared with the facts necessary to prove the defendant's personal commission of a crime. To convict a defendant on a command responsibility theory, the prosecution must prove (1) that there existed a superior–subordinate relationship between the defendant and the person who committed the criminal act; (2) that the defendant knew or had reason to know that the criminal act was about to be or had been committed; and (3) that the defendant failed to take necessary and reasonable measures to prevent the criminal act or to punish the offender.[775] The subordinates' crimes are typically supported by considerable testimony and may even be uncontested. And although a defendant's official position and relationship to subordinates may be disputed, the Trial Chambers typically receive more and more reliable evidence – sometimes including documentary evidence – on that question than on questions pertaining to the specific criminal acts the defendant personally performed.[776]

An analysis of testimonial quantity reveals, then, something of a mixed bag. Indeed, the foregoing discussion in its entirety suggests that testimonial deficiencies are pervasive and their impact not readily ameliorated by information obtained through independent investigations or by confidence gained through a large quantity of witness accounts. Indeed, the foregoing indicates, in my view, that the testimonial deficiencies plaguing the international tribunals impair their fact-finding competence to such a degree as to render international criminal proceedings a form of show trial.

I am by no means the first scholar to use the term "show trial" in relation to international criminal proceedings, but I use it in a very different way than previous scholars. When the first international criminal trials were held, at Nuremberg and Tokyo, they were labeled "show trials" because they targeted only Axis wrongdoers and because they charged them with forms of wrongdoing that theretofore had not been formally subject to criminal

[774] *See, e.g.*, AFRC Judgement, note 27, at paras. 1703, 1756, 1761, 1765, 1767–1769, 1915, 2050–2052, 2057, 2058, 2061.
[775] CDF Judgement, note 27, at para. 235.
[776] At the ICTR, see for example, the *Muvunyi* case.

prohibitions. More recent scholars who examined the Nuremberg proceedings and the subsequent Holocaust trials have likewise labeled them "show trials," but they see the "show" not as reflecting political manipulation of legal form, but as a method of legal storytelling that can compellingly convey the power of law. Lawrence Douglas, for instance, considers the Holocaust trials show trials because they are "orchestrations designed to show the world the facts of astonishing crimes and to demonstrate the power of law to reintroduce order into a space evacuated of legal and moral sense." Such show trials are, in other words, "dramas of didactic legality."[777] In a similar vein, Mark Osiel asserts that trials of mass atrocity "present moments of transformative opportunity in the lives of individuals and societies."[778] According to Osiel, when trials of mass atrocity are "effective as public spectacle," they can "stimulate public discussion in ways that foster the liberal virtues of toleration, moderation, and civil respect."[779] Osiel consequently urges judges and prosecutors to pay close attention to the "'poetics' of storytelling" during a trial for mass atrocity and indeed advocates employing "the law of evidence, procedure, and professional responsibility to recast the courtroom drama in terms of the 'theatre of ideas.'"[780]

Martti Koskenniemi revived the more negative aspects of the show-trial label when he pointed out the potential of international trials to distort history. Koskenniemi observes that international crimes take place in the context of historical events that often "exceed the intentions or action of particular individuals and can be grasped only by attention to structural causes, such as economic or functional necessities or a broad institutional logic through which the actions by individuals create social effects."[781] International trials focus on the individual acts of individual defendants, a focus that Koskenniemi believes is not neutral in its effects and may even "serve as an alibi for the population at large to relieve itself from responsibility."[782] For that reason, Koskenniemi contends that trials concerning large political events require an interpretation of the context of those events, which is precisely what is disputed in the individual actions that are the object of the trial. Thus, "to accept the terms in which the trial is conducted – what deeds are singled out, who is being accused – is to already accept one interpretation of the context among those between which the political struggle has been waged."[783]

[777] Lawrence Douglas, The Memory of Judgment: Making Law and History in the Trials of the Holocaust 3 (2001).
[778] Mark Osiel, Mass Atrocity, Collective Memory and the Law 2 (1997).
[779] *Id.*
[780] *Id.* at 3.
[781] Koskenniemi, note 12, at 13.
[782] *Id.* at 14.
[783] *Id.* at 16–17.

Although the aforementioned scholars might dispute the desirability of conducting international trials as dramaturgical productions, they take for granted that, however the trials are conducted, they have the capacity to adequately elucidate the facts at issue in the case. Indeed, both Douglas and Osiel make clear their view that a trial's first obligation is to do justice. Although Douglas, for instance, believes that there is value in conducting a trial as a spectacle of didactic legality, he cautions that "the notion that a trial can succeed as pedagogy yet fail to do justice is crucially flawed."[784] Osiel concurs, concluding his study by observing that "the central purpose of criminal prosecution remains the deterrence of, and retribution for serious wrongdoing."[785] Even Koskenniemi, who questions whether large political events can be accurately understood when filtered through the individualistic focus inherent in a criminal trial, does not question that a trial can reveal whether the defendant engaged in the particular acts that comprise the large political events. That is, as Koskenniemi observes, Klaus Barbie's deportation of forty-four Jewish children can be portrayed, in the manner of the prosecution, as a component of the most vicious, brutal, and widespread persecutory scheme ever embarked on or rather, in the defense's view, as "a relatively 'normal' episode in the flow of racist persecutions and suffering of which European history has consisted."[786] But although scholars might argue about the appropriate interpretive framework by which we should evaluate Barbie's deportation of forty-four children, and the way in which the conduct of a criminal trial might enhance or distort our understanding of those deportations, they take for granted that an international criminal trial, like a domestic criminal trial, can adequately elucidate whether Klaus Barbie did in fact deport forty-four children. That is, whatever disputes may have arisen about how the prosecuted acts should be treated in an international courtroom – either legally or dramaturgically – scholars have assumed that an international courtroom was an appropriate forum for elucidating what those acts were.

It is that central assumption that my study calls into question. Unlike the Nuremberg Tribunal, which received from the prosecution reams of documents that proved beyond any shadow of a doubt the defendants' commission of certain acts, the ICTR, SCSL, and Special Panels operate in a fact-finding fog of inconsistent, vague, and sometimes incoherent testimony that leaves them unable to say with any measure of certainty who did what to whom. Perhaps Jean de Dieu Kamuhanda led an attack against the Tutsi at the Gikomero Parish Church, as alleged by the prosecution, but the only evidence that he did comes

784 Douglas, note 777, at 3.
785 Osiel, note 778, at 293.
786 Koskenniemi, note 12, at 31.

from alleged eyewitnesses, and the defense has a passel of its own witnesses who claim that Kamuhanda was with them, far from the massacre site. Perhaps Alex Tamba Brima was commander of the AFRC troops in the Kono district in May 1998, as the prosecution claims, but he and defense witnesses maintain that he was in RUF custody at that time.[787] No forensic evidence is available to inform these questions, and the traditional means that judges employ to evaluate the credibility of witness testimony are unilluminating because they presuppose similarities in language and culture between judges and witnesses that simply do not exist in the international context. Witnesses fail to answer questions, and we cannot know whether it is because they do not know the answers or because they do not wish to provide them. Witnesses testify haltingly and dance around relevant topics, and we cannot know whether they do so because that is their normal pattern of speech, because they do not understand the questions they have been asked, because they have in fact answered directly but a mistranslation has created a seeming divergence between the question and answer, or because the witness purposely wishes to evade the question. And Lord only knows what to make of the many inconsistencies between witness testimony and pretrial statements that pervade international criminal proceedings. Witnesses attribute these inconsistencies to investigators' errors. Defense counsel attribute them to witness mendacity. And each explanation, along with a host of others, is plausible.

The Trial Chambers' inability to ascertain the causes of testimonial deficiencies stands as only one of their fact-finding problems, moreover, for even if the Trial Chambers could be sure in a given case that the problematic features of a witness's testimony stemmed from educational factors, say, and not from a desire to mislead, the deficiency itself may nonetheless leave the Trial Chamber in a poor position to make a factual determination. That is, maybe lack of education accounts for the imprecision in a witness's testimony, or maybe the witness truly cannot understand defense counsel's compound questions and for that reason issues nonresponsive replies. But even when the witness's imprecision and nonresponsiveness stem from "innocent" causes, at the end of the day, the Trial Chamber is left with only imprecise, nonresponsive eyewitness testimony on which to base its determination of whether the defendant is guilty of an international crime. We know from Chapter 1 that basing criminal convictions solely on eyewitness testimony is worrisome enough given the likelihood of honest misidentifications. Basing genocide convictions on eyewitness testimony that is vague, inconsistent, and missing key pieces of information is the highest order of questionable, and that remains true even

[787] AFRC Judgement, note 27, at paras. 335–341.

if we are convinced that the vagueness, inconsistencies, and omissions stem from causes beyond the witnesses' control.

The foregoing suggests that international criminal proceedings are vulnerable to the label "show trial" not only for the positive and negative reasons that other scholars have invoked but because they purport a fact-finding competence that they do not in fact possess. International criminal trials are conducted pursuant to a blend of adversarial and inquisitorial criminal procedures that are drawn from the criminal justice systems of western Europe and North America. Although the procedures vary slightly from one tribunal to the next, and diverge more markedly from domestic procedures that are predominantly adversarial or inquisitorial,[788] international criminal trials, both in their broad structural outlines and in their ostensible commitment in to Western due process norms, very much resemble a domestic criminal trial that might be held in any Western nation. And therein lies the show, for although international criminal trials appear on the surface to be Western-style trials, they in fact constitute a much less reliable fact-finding mechanism.

In making this contention, I do not mean to elide over the significant differences that exist between trials in different Western countries and the impact those differences may have on fact-finding accuracy. Tremendous controversy exists, for instance, over whether truth is more readily discernable in an adversarial or an inquisitorial trial, and I take up some of those controversies in Chapter 9.[789] Moreover, I also do not mean to suggest that Western-style trials – whether adversarial or inquisitorial – always or even usually result in accurate factual determinations. In any criminal case, competing accounts may make reaching accurate factual conclusions a difficult task. Indeed, the DNA exonerations described in Chapter 1 are a testament to the many fact-finding failures that occur during Western-style trials. In addition, adversarial trials in particular make use of procedures that are designed to foster dignitary and participatory goals but that can directly undercut the fact finder's

[788] No domestic system of criminal procedure contains purely adversarial or purely non-adversarial forms; every system is something of a blend. *See, e.g.*, Mirjan Damaška, *Evidentiary Barriers to Conviction and Two Models of Criminal Procedure: A Comparative Study*, 121 U. PA. L. REV. 506, 577 (1973) [hereinafter Damaška, *Evidentiary Barriers to Conviction*]; Richard S. Frase, *Comparative Criminal Justice Policy in Theory and in Practice*, *in* INT'L CONF. FOR THE 25TH ANNIVERSARY OF THE INT'L INST. OF HIGHER STUD. IN CRIM. SCI., COMPARATIVE CRIMINAL JUSTICE SYSTEMS: FROM DIVERSITY TO RAPPROCHEMENT 109, 112–13 (1998). But despite this hybridization, most systems of domestic criminal procedure are predominantly adversarial or nonadversarial.

[789] Most commentators believe that nonadversarial procedures are better suited to ascertaining the truth in a criminal case. *See, e.g.*, Damaška, *Evidentiary Barriers to Conviction*, note 788, at 579, 581–89; Nico Jörg et al., *Are Inquisitorial and Adversarial Systems Converging?*, *in* CRIMINAL JUSTICE IN EUROPE: A COMPARATIVE STUDY 41, 42–43 (Phil Fennell et al., eds., 1995).

ability to reach accurate factual determinations. American exclusionary rules, for instance, sacrifice truth in favor of deterring police misconduct while some constitutional rights – such as the right of self-representation – advance autonomy and participation over factual accuracy. I likewise do not wish to overstate the fact-finding challenges that international tribunals face. Although many of the details that international witnesses fail to provide would assist the Trial Chambers in making informed factual determinations, some details are not especially relevant. Furthermore, although much false testimony is presented to the international tribunal, some is so blatantly and easily identified as such that it fools no one. And although the indirect and circumlocutious answers provided by so many witnesses may have evasion as their purpose, their effect in many instances is only to annoyingly lengthen proceedings. These caveats acknowledged, it remains my view that the Western trial form in which international criminal proceedings cloak themselves embodies certain fact-finding expectations that international criminal proceedings are unable to fulfill.

At the most basic level, it is expected that fact witnesses will recount their firsthand experiences in a way that is comprehensible to fact finders and that provides fact finders sufficient information about the events in question. Speaking in relation to child witnesses, Ingrid Cordon and her coauthors observe that adversarial legal systems, in particular, hold many implicit expectations of witnesses, including that witnesses have "some knowledge of judicial processes [and] can understand the language of the courtroom, particularly attorneys' questions."[790] In addition and even more basically, the Western trial form embodies the assumption that witnesses can tell a reasonably clear and detailed story about what they have witnessed and thereby provide fact finders with the information necessary to evaluate the charges against the defendant. That is not to say that witnesses in Western domestic trials always attend to and convey key details. Nor is it to deny that some international witnesses do provide a clear and reasonably detailed account of the events they witnessed. But a substantial proportion do not, and, on the whole, the Western trial form embodies the expectation that witnesses will provide a more detailed, more thorough account of the events they witnessed than international witnesses routinely are able to deliver.

The use of the Western trial form also conveys the expectation that when called on to decide between competing factual accounts, fact finders will be able to inform their decisions by assessing the credibility of the witnesses who appear before them. Concededly, the value of such credibility assessments is open to question even in the context of domestic trials where fact finders and witnesses share the same culture and language. Recent research suggests, for

[790] Cordon et al., note 188, at 168.

instance, that people are not as good at detecting prevarication as they think they are.[791] At the international tribunals, however, the cultural and linguistic "distance" between fact finders and witnesses is so vast that it leaves fact finders without a meaningful frame of reference. The use of interpreters, for instance, impairs the fact finders' ability even to know *how* the witness is testifying; that is, whether the witness is testifying hesitatingly, for instance, or rather with seeming confidence. And even when that information is known, it is of little value because international fact finders cannot know what to make of it. The problem is theoretically less pronounced at the SCSL and Special Panels given the presence of at least one Sierra Leonean judge at the SCSL and one East Timorese judge at the Special Panels. However, the judgments issued by those tribunals – which are discussed more thoroughly in the next chapter – give us little reason to believe that local judges are providing their international counterparts significant guidance in these matters.

The Western trial form also creates the expectation that pretrial investigations will serve to narrow contested issues both by establishing background facts and by providing an efficacious means of testing witness accounts. Investigations are conducted largely by court officials in inquisitorial legal systems and by the parties in adversarial systems, but in either case investigations are presumed capable of providing fact finders with a degree of certainty about a wide range of issues surrounding those that are disputed at trial. Investigations are assumed to be capable, moreover, of identifying some quantity of witness lying and deterring a great deal more. A witness will not falsely claim that an anti-Tutsi rally took place in a certain stadium, for instance, if she knows that a cursory investigation into the stadium's records will show that no rally occurred. Investigations can rarely perform either of these functions at the international criminal tribunals, however. As explained in Chapter 5, investigations are costly and difficult to conduct in the regions in question, and, even when they are conducted, the fact that so many transactions and interactions are carried out without written documentation means that investigators rarely locate evidence that will conclusively prove a given fact. In most instances, the best that international investigators can hope to find are witnesses who will contradict the testimony of opposing witnesses. In sum, whereas there is an expectation that Western trials will present fact finders with narrow factual disputes and feature concomitantly limited opportunities for perjury, all manner of facts are open to question in international trials, and witnesses can lie about matters great and small with virtual impunity.

The use of the Western trial form does not always result in accurate fact-finding, as I have acknowledged, but Western-style trials are nevertheless

[791] *See* Ekman & O'Sullivan, note 429, at 913.

considered mechanisms that are reasonably well suited to reaching accurate conclusions about disputed facts. By using the Western trial form, international criminal proceedings cloak themselves in the form's garb of fact-finding competence, but it is only a cloak, for many of the key expectations and assumptions that underlie the Western trial form do not exist in the international context. International tribunals hear evidence and make determinations about what a particular defendant did or did not do at a particular place and time on the basis of that evidence, as fact finders in other Western trials do; but, given the quantity and nature of much of the testimony that the tribunals receive and their limited capacity to verify facts, these determinations in many cases constitute little more than guesses.

Moreover, the Trial Chambers enhance the illusion of fact-finding competence by obscuring the uncertain foundations of their factual determinations. Tribunal judgments, for instance, frequently fail to mention testimonial deficiencies. Trial Chambers rarely mention a witness's inability or unwillingness to answer questions,[792] and, when they do mention such difficulties, they

[792] *See* Akayesu Judgement, note 32, at paras. 42, 449 (discussing witness J's testimony without mentioning the witness's difficulty in making distance estimations, as appeared at Akayesu Transcript, Jan. 27, 1997, at 128–29); Kamuhanda Judgement, note 38, at paras. 266–272, 312–315, 438–439, 443, 466 (relying on witness GEK's testimony without mentioning her unwillingness/inability to look at photographs, as appeared at Kamuhanda Transcript, Sept. 4, 2001, at 108); Ndindabahizi Judgement, note 56, at paras. 128, 134–146, 148, 179, 181 (assessing witness CGY's testimony without mentioning the witness's difficulty with date, time, and numerical estimations, as appeared at Ndindabahizi Transcript, Sept. 8, 2003, at 42, 49, 53); Ndindabahizi Judgement, note 56, at paras. 124–125, 248, 253–259, 265 (assessing witness CGM's testimony without mentioning that he was not able to answer questions concerning the make or model of the car Ndindabahizi was driving, as appeared at Ndindabahizi Transcript, Sept. 15, 2003, at 10); Ndindabahizi Judgement, note 56, at paras. 118–128 (assessing witness CGV's testimony without mentioning his difficulty with age, distance, duration, and numerical estimations, as appeared at Ndindabahizi Transcript, Sept. 16, 2003, at 7–9, 20, 22–23, 25–26, 27); Ndindabahizi Judgement, note 56, at paras. 203–206, 215–221, 225–228, 230, 265, 470–471 (discussing witness CGC's testimony without mentioning his refusal to estimate the distance between two secteurs, as appeared at Ndindabahizi Transcript, Sept. 29, 2003, at 22); AFRC Judgement, note 27, at paras. 1089, 1091, 1093–1099, 1184–1185, 1228, 1259–1260, 1377–1378, 1977 (discussing witness TF1-085's testimony without mentioning the witness's difficulty in making duration, numerical, and distance estimations, as appeared at AFRC Transcript, Apr. 7, 2005, at 61, 72–73, 104–05, 112); AFRC Judgement, note 27, at paras. 882–886, 901–903, 954, 1224, 1227, 1252–1255, 1258, 1275, 1277–1278, 1363, 1378, 1559, 1710 & nn. 2206, 2208, 2343, 2351, 2356 (relying on witness TF1-157's testimony without mentioning the witness's inability/unwillingness to say whether he met with the prosecution in Freetown, as appeared at AFRC Transcript, July 25, 2005, at 33–36); AFRC Judgement, note 27, at paras. 901, 911, 914–916, 1043, 1046–1048, 1262, 1377, 1774, 1783 (discussing witness TF1-024's testimony without mentioning the witness's difficulty in making distance estimations, as appeared at AFRC Transcript, Mar. 7, 2005, at 81 and Mar. 8, 2005, at 31); AFRC Judgement, note 27, at paras. 236, 900–901, 936, 1043, 1228, 1420, 1427–1429, 1782 & nn. 455, 1714 (relying on witness TF1-083's testimony without mentioning that the witness was unable/unwilling to describe where he went when

sometimes understate their severity or significance. The *AFRC* Trial Chamber, for instance, acknowledged that witness TF1-209 had "some difficulty in conveying what exactly she meant"[793] and that her testimony "was at times unclear,"[794] but those diplomatic phrases entirely failed to convey just how difficult it was for the lawyers and Trial Chamber to get a straight answer out of the witness. The Trial Chambers sometimes even mischaracterize a witness's answers. In *Ndindabahizi*, for instance, the Trial Chamber reported that witness CGV "gave a clear indication that the distance [between himself and the defendant] was about equal to the width of the courtroom," when he did no such thing. Although he initially tried to estimate from "the wall on the other side" to "the other side of the room," his answer did not make clear to the lawyers or judges which walls he was speaking of, and on further questioning he refused to estimate the distance by use of either meters or courtroom references.[795]

The Trial Chambers do mention a lot of inconsistencies, but they also fail to mention many others, including many serious inconsistencies.[796] For instance,

the rebels came, as appeared at AFRC Transcript, Apr. 8, 2005, at 51); CDF Judgement, note 27, at paras. 622–623, 934–937 (relying on witness TF2-096's testimony without mentioning the Trial Chamber's difficulty even understanding the witness's testimony, as appeared at CDF Transcript, Nov. 8, 2004, at 6, 9, 31–32 and *passim*); CDF Judgement, note 27, at paras. 587–590, 592–594 & nn. 1161, 1171–1174, 1176, 1178, 1185, 1188–1191 (discussing witness TF2-033's testimony without mentioning his difficulty making numerical estimates, as appeared at CDF Transcript, Sept. 20, 2004, at 123); CDF Judgement, note 27, at paras. 586–589, 591, 593 & nn. 1167–1170, 1173, 1175, 1177, 1184, 1189 (relying on witness TF2-040's testimony without mentioning his reluctance to describe the police department's organization or his inability to see the perpetrators of the shooting, as appeared at CDF Transcript, Sept. 21, 2004, at 48–51, 55–57); CDF Judgement, note 27, at paras. 477–478 (relying on TF2-198's testimony without mentioning his inability/unwillingness to answer where and with whom he was living in Koribondo, as appeared at CDF Transcript, June 15, 2004, at 10); CDF Judgement, note 27, at paras. 297, 856 & nn. 406–412, 414–415 (relying on Father Garrick's testimony without mentioning his difficulty estimating dates and distances, as appeared at CDF Transcript, Nov. 11, 2004, at 20, 29); *see generally* CDF Judgement, note 27, *passim* (relying on prosecution witness Albert Nallo's testimony without mentioning his inability to estimate the distance between Koribondo and Base Zero, as appeared at CDF Transcript, Mar. 11, 2005, at 104). *But see* Musema Judgement, note 112, at para. 698; Simba Judgement, note 455, at para. 196; Ndindabahizi Judgement, note 56, at paras. 118, 258; Ntakirutimana Judgement, note 69, at paras. 464–467; AFRC Judgement, note 27, at paras. 914, 1087.

793 AFRC Judgement, note 27, at para. 999.

794 *Id.* at para. 1001.

795 Ndindabahizi Transcript, Sept. 16, 2003, at 22–23.

796 *See, e.g.*, Gacumbitsi Judgement, note 364, at paras. 207–208, 219, 226 (relying on witness TAP's testimony without mentioning discrepancies between her statement and testimony regarding the number of men who raped her and the time of day during which she visited the swamp, as were discussed at Gacumbitsi Transcript, Aug. 6, 2003, at 9, 41, 43); Muhimana Judgement, note 363, at paras. 448, 450 (relying on witness AF's testimony that Muhimana participated in the killing of Kabanda without mentioning that in testimony in another ICTR case AF failed to name Muhimana as participating in the killing, as discussed at Muhimana Transcript, Apr. 29, 2004, at 20–24); Muhimana Judgement, note 363, at paras. 284–292 (relying on

CDF witness TF2-021's testimony was riddled with inconsistencies, which I detail in Chapter 7, yet the Trial Chamber not only said nothing about them but

witness BJ's testimony about her rape by Muhimana without mentioning that her statement reports that the *Interahamwe* broke down the door of the hospital room where she was hiding, whereas she testified that Muhimana opened the door, as was discussed at Muhimana Transcript, Apr. 6, 2004, at 50); Muhimana Judgement, note 363, at paras. 448, 450 (relying on witness AT's testimony without mentioning the discrepancy between his statement and testimony regarding Muhimana's treatment of victim Kabanda, as discussed at Muhimana Transcript, Apr. 20, 2004, at 20); Muhimana Judgement, paras. 22, 23, 31, 326–328, 337–340 (crediting witness AP's inculpatory statements about Muhimana, without mentioning that the witness's early statements did not even mention Muhimana, as discussed at Muhimana Transcript, Mar. 30, 2005, at 55–56); Karera Judgement, note 54, at paras. 94–95 (relying on witness BMG's testimony regarding Karera's instructions to police without mentioning inconsistencies regarding whether the witness actually heard Karera give the instructions or only heard about the instructions afterward, as discussed at Karera Transcript, Jan. 9, 2006, at 36–39); Karera Judgement, note 54, at paras. 331, 366 (relying on witness BMR's testimony regarding Karera's orders about the treatment of detainees at roadblocks without mentioning the discrepancy between the witness's statement and testimony about whether Karera ordered the victims killed or only jailed, as discussed at Karera Transcript, Feb. 1, 2006, at 24); Ndindabahizi Judgement, note 56, at para. 306 (discussing witness CGB's testimony that he hid at the home of a Hutu friend without mentioning that CGB never mentioned this to investigators and at trial maintained that he had been afraid to mention it for fear that he would get his Hutu friend in trouble, a discussion that appeared at Ndindabahizi Transcript, Sept. 22, 2003, at 3); Kajelijeli Judgement, note 303, at paras. 519, 524–526, 529, 708, 712 (relying on witness GDQ's testimony about Kajelijeli's presence during an attack without mentioning that the witness failed to mention Kajelijeli's presence in his statement, as was discussed in Kajelijeli Transcript, Dec. 5, 2001, at 72–96 [French version]); Kajelijeli Judgement, note 303, at paras. 637–651, 680 (discussing and relying on witness GDO's testimony without mentioning discrepancies between her statement and testimony about the number of her children with whom she was hiding, as were discussed at Kajelijeli Transcript, July 19, 2001, at 34–35); Akayesu Judgement, note 32, at paras. 154, 418, 421, 449, 452–453, 692–694, 696 (relying on witness JJ's testimony without mentioning that while her statement reported that five hundred Tutsi were beaten by *Interahamwe*, she testified that only sixty had been beaten, an inconsistency that was discussed at Akayesu Transcript, Oct. 23, 1997, at 102–03); Kamuhanda Judgement, note 38, at paras. 335–339, 453, 467, 483 (relying on witness GEE's testimony without mentioning the discrepancy between his statement and testimony regarding the location of his injury, as was discussed at Kamuhanda Transcript, Sept. 19, 2001, at 75–76); Kamuhanda Judgement, note 38, at paras. 438–439, 443 (relying on witness GEK's testimony that Kamuhanda was present just before the Protestant church massacre, without mentioning that this fact does not appear in the witness's statement, as discussed at Kamuhanda Transcript, Sept. 4, 2001, at 80); Muhimana Judgement, note 363, at paras. 246–247 (relying on witness BI's testimony that Muhimana participated in an attack on Tutsi at the Mugonero Complex and Kanyinya Hill without mentioning that BI's statement reports that he hid under bodies in a church, although he testified that he had not been able to enter the church, and, when describing another scene, witness BI's statement reports that a young girl and the defendant were present, whereas the witness testified that only the girl was present, as discussed at Muhimana Transcript, Apr. 30, 2004, at 47–49, 68–69); CDF Judgement, note 27, at paras. 423–424, 428 (relying on witness TF2-159's testimony regarding various crimes without mentioning numerous discrepancies between the witness's statement and testimony regarding the number of victims, the way in which the victims were killed, the number of houses burned and the witness's own treatment, as were discussed at CDF Transcript, Sept. 9, 2004, at 35–38, 104–09, 126–29, 159–60 and Sept. 10, 2004, lauded the witness's testimony "as highly credible and largely reliable. Clearly," the Trial Chamber asserted, "the intensity of his experience has left him with an

at 5–13); CDF Judgement, note 27, at paras. 477–478 (relying on witness TF2-198's testimony regarding his brother's murder without mentioning various important facts about that murder that the witness failed to report to investigators, as were discussed at CDF Transcript, June 15, 2004, at 25–31); CDF Judgement, note 27, at para. 627 (relying on witness TF2-108's testimony that the Kamajors had killed Baggy Vaiey without mentioning that the witness's statement reports that Vaiey had been killed by one Joe Koi, as discussed at CDF Transcript, May 30, 2005, at 21–22); CDF Judgement, note 27, at para. 472 (relying on witness TF2-006's testimony without mentioning significant discrepancies between the witness's testimony and his statement about the number of victims and the witness's occupation, as mentioned in CDF Transcript, Feb. 9, 2005, at 28, 42–43); AFRC Judgement, note 27, at paras. 1484–1485 (relying on witness TF1-004's testimony without mentioning that he testified inconsistently with his statement about the number of his houses that had been burnt, as appeared at AFRC Transcript, June 23, 2005, at 23–24); AFRC Judgement, note 27, at para. 1331 (relying on witness TF1-198's testimony about her meeting with soldiers without mentioning an inconsistency regarding the soldiers' accents, as discussed at AFRC Transcript, June 28, 2005, at 47–49); AFRC Judgement, note 27, at para. 1328 (relying on witness TF1-217's testimony to find that RUF Captain Bai Bureh abducted the witness's sister, without mentioning that the witness's statement named RUF rebel Lieutenant Jalloh as the abductor, as discussed at AFRC Transcript, Oct. 17, 2005, at 36, 41–47); AFRC Judgement, note 27, at paras. 882–883 & nn. 1679, 1680, 1681 (relying on witness TF1-156's testimony without mentioning that he testified that he hid in a graveyard whereas his statement reported that he hid in his house, as discussed at AFRC Transcript, Sept. 26, 2005, at 35, 54–55); AFRC Judgement, note 27, at para. 837 (relying on witness TF1-122's testimony that a rebel named Mosquito killed a farmer without mentioning that the witness's statement reported that Mosquito had instead killed two boys, as appeared at AFRC Transcript, June 24, 2005, at 111–14); AFRC Judgement, note 27, at para. 956 (relying on witness TF1-253's testimony without mentioning the inconsistency between the witness's testimony and statement about the amount of money that had been stolen from him, as discussed at AFRC Transcript, Apr. 18, 2005, at 38–43, and the number of people who were killed during his abduction, as discussed AFRC Transcript, Apr. 18, 2005, at 60–63); AFRC Judgement, note 27, at para. 1048 (relying on witness TF1-024's testimony without mentioning inconsistencies regarding the number of people killed, as discussed at AFRC Transcript, Mar. 7, 2005, at 98–106 and Mar. 8, 2005, at 3–11); AFRC Judgement, note 27, at para. 1489 (crediting witness TF1-054's testimony about the beating of Chief Demby's wife without mentioning that the witness failed to mention that crime in his statement, as discussed at AFRC Transcript, Apr. 22, 2005, at 32–33); AFRC Judgement, note 27, at para. 1608 (crediting witness TF1-184's testimony that defendant "Kanu distributed petrol for the burning of Freetown," without mentioning that the witness's statement did not contain this allegation, as described at AFRC Transcript, Sept. 30, 2005, at 65–67); RUF Judgement, note 56, at para. 1178 (crediting witness TF1-217's testimony that Captain Bai Bureh took the witness's sister for his wife without mentioning that in his statement TF1-217 reported that it had been Lieutenant Jalloh who had taken his sister for his wife, as described at RUF Transcript, July 22, 2004, at 38–40); RUF Judgement, note 56, at para. 1185 (finding that witness TF1-195 had been raped twice without mentioning that the witness's statement mentions only one rape, as described at RUF Transcript, Feb. 1, 2005, at 29–51); RUF Judgement, note 56, at para. 1556 (finding, based on the testimony of TF1-097, that RUF rebel Captain Blood had amputated the witness's hand without mentioning that the witness's statement had reported that an SLA solider had amputated his hand). *See also* AFRC Judgement, Partially Dissenting Opinion of Justice Doherty on Count 7, para. 44 (finding, on the basis of witness TF1-282's testimony, that she was not forced to do any work for the rebel who enslaved her, without mentioning indelible recollection of the events in question."[797] In other instances, the Trial Chambers gloss over inconsistencies. For instance, when *CDF* witness TF2-152 testified inconsistently from his statement about which organ – the heart or the liver – the Kamajors cut out of his friend,[798] the Trial Chamber bridged the inconsistency by reporting that "various organs were removed from TF2-152's friend's torso."[799] Similarly, when witness TF2-154 testified inconsistently from her statement about the way in which two victims were killed,[800] the Trial Chamber ignored the inconsistency and reported only that the two men "were killed."[801] And although Kamuhanda witness GEI testified inconsistently with his statement about which family members were with him when he fled his home,[802] the Trial Chamber reported only that the witness "fled with his family."[803] Finally, even when the Trial Chambers do mention inconsistencies, they frequently do so with a passing reference that does not convey their nature or seriousness.

The style of the tribunals' judgments can also function to obscure their fact-finding difficulties – when the tribunals issue a judgment, that is. In some Special Panels' cases, the Panel failed to issue a judgment at all and instead drafted a three- or four-page "Disposition of the Decision," which did little more than state the crimes for which the defendant was convicted and the sentences that the Panels had imposed for those crimes.[804] Testimonial deficiencies obviously were not revealed in these summary documents.

Most Special Panels cases and all of the SCSL and ICTR cases did result in judgments, however, and although most of these judgments described the witness testimony that supported the Trial Chamber's factual findings, some declined to articulate the substance of the witnesses' testimony and rather related their factual findings as though recounting a historical narrative.[805]

that the witness's statement reported that she cooked, cleaned, and did laundry for the rebel, as discussed at AFRC Transcript, Apr. 14, 2005, at 37–41).

797 CDF Judgement, note 27, at para. 282.

798 *See* CDF Transcript, Sept. 27, 2004, at 152–54.

799 CDF Judgement, note 27, at para. 606.

800 *See* CDF Transcript, Sept. 27, 2004, at 63–72.

801 CDF Judgement, note 27, at paras. 584–585.

802 Kamuhanda Transcript, Jan. 31, 2002, at 75–77.

803 Kamuhanda Judgement, note 38, at para. 357.

804 *See, e.g.*, Prosecutor v. Abilio Mendes Correia, Case No. 19/2001, Disposition of the Decision (Mar. 3, 2004); Prosecutor v. Benjamin Sarmento et al., Case No. 18/2001, Disposition of the Decision Relating to the Conviction of the Accused Benjamin Sarmento and Romeiro Tilman (July 16, 2003); Prosecutor v. Domingos Mendonça, Case No. 18a/2001, Disposition of the Decision (Oct. 13, 2003).

805 The first two international criminal judgments – handed down by the Nuremberg and Tokyo Tribunals – read as a historical narrative. For more recent examples, see, for example, RUF Judgement, note 56; Prosecution v. Alves, Case No. 1/2002, Judgement (July 8, 2004); Prosecution v. Rudolfo Alves Correia, Case No. 27/2003, Judgement (Apr. 25, 2005).

Two of the SCSL's first three judgments, for instance, are written in this fashion. The Trial Chamber in the SCSL's *CDF* and *RUF* cases decided not to include in the judgment an "evaluation of every piece of evidence in the record" but instead "consciously opted" to present its factual findings in a "comprehensive narrative."[806] Consequently, the *CDF* and *RUF* judgments describe the atrocities that occurred and the defendants' involvement in those atrocities as though they were uncontested historical facts.[807] References to the testimony on which these findings were based appear only in the footnotes to the judgment, and the testimony that contradicted the Chamber's findings is not discussed. The Chamber did assure readers that it "fully considered the evidence of each and every witness" including those whose testimony was at odds with the Chamber's factual findings, but it chose not to describe the latter testimony because it "determined that such evidence did not meet the threshold of reliability and credibility necessary to make a factual conclusion upon it."[808] Although the above assertion would suggest that testimony at odds with the Trial Chamber's factual findings appeared nowhere in the judgment, in fact the Trial Chamber sometimes cited such testimony *in support* of its findings. For instance, the *CDF* Trial Chamber found that defendant "Norman said in the open that 'the attack on Tongo will determine who the winner or the looser [sic] of the war would be' and that 'there is no place to keep captured or war prisoners like the juntas, let alone their collaborators.'"[809] For this proposition, the Chamber cited not only the testimony of prosecution witness TF2-222, who did make these assertions, but also the testimony of Norman himself in a *see also* cite that suggested that Norman's testimony supported the Trial Chamber's factual finding. In fact, Norman flatly denied issuing any instructions for the attack on Tongo, let alone that he made the particular statements that TF2-222 attributed to him.[810]

When presenting their judgments as detailed, historical narratives, the Trial Chambers not only conceal the evidentiary bases for their factual findings and the terrifically problematic features thereof, they also convey a misleading sense of certainty about those factual findings. The *CDF* Trial Chamber enhanced this impression of certainty even further by describing various speeches and

806 CDF Judgement, note 27, at para. 274; RUF Judgement, note 56, at para. 479.

807 The judgments also have a section entitled "Context," which sets out the historical background to the conflict and the involvement of the different warring factions. Although the placement and title of the section suggest that it contains well-established historical facts, the "facts" appearing in the CDF "Context" section are directly derived from the problematic testimony of a few witnesses.

808 CDF Judgement, note 27, at para. 276; *see also* RUF Judgement, note 56, at para. 485.

809 CDF Judgement, note 27, at para. 321.

810 CDF Transcript, Feb. 7, 2006, at 42.

conversations of the defendants as direct quotes from the defendants, even though the quotes in fact stemmed from witness testimony that paraphrased the speeches. For instance, in describing the first meeting at the Koribondo Court *Barri*, the Trial Chamber asserted that "Norman stated":

> Hey Kamajors, I thank you very much, but you people have not done my work which I told you to do. You have not done my work at all. Fellows, what did I tell you to do? That inside Koribondo I only want three houses, only three houses in Koribondo here. Oh, look at all these houses. I told you that I wanted the mosque, the court *barri* and one house where I would have to reside, but look at all this crowd that I am seeing here. You people are afraid of killing. Why? The soldiers killed, nothing happened; Kapras killed, nothing happened; rebels killed, nothing happened. Why are you afraid of killing? Why? Really, you have not done my work, you've disappointed me.[811]

The above quote derives from the testimony of witness TF2-198, who was recalling Norman's speech more than six years after the fact. Although the quote may well reflect the gist of Norman's remarks at the Koribondo Court *Barri*, it did not constitute a verbatim transcript of his words. The Trial Chamber was well aware of this fact because other witnesses had described the same meeting,[812] but each did so using different words. Thus, the Trial Chamber had no basis for privileging TF2-198's account over that of the other witnesses, let alone for placing the remarks in quotes and asserting that "Norman stated" them. The judgment features other examples of this phenomenon[813] and, even more bizarrely, the transcripts reveal that certain judges themselves seemed to consider witness testimony to reflect verbatim quotations. For instance, when witness TF2-008 began describing what General Kohbe of ECOMOG said at a meeting, Judge Thompson interrupted to ask, "what were his *exact* words?" When the testimony subsequently became confused, Judge Thompson reassured himself and the other judges by observing, "[a]t least I've got the exact words."[814] A similar exchange took place later in the witness's testimony. When describing a public speech Norman had made six years before, Judge Thompson instructed the witness to "give us exactly what [Norman] said without paraphrasing anything," as though such a feat were possible. No doubt seeking to please the Judge, the witness acceded to the Judge's request: He prefaced his recitation of Norman's remarks with "[a]nd I quote. . . . "[815]

[811] CDF Judgement, note 27, at para. 434.
[812] CDF Transcript, June 16, 2004, at 20–22; CDF Transcript, June 21, 2004, at 27; CDF Transcript, Sept. 9, 2004, at 53–56; CDF Transcript, Sept. 13, 2004, at 60–62.
[813] *See* CDF Judgement, note 27, at paras. 321, 436.
[814] CDF Transcript, Nov. 16, 2004, at 85–86 (emphasis added).
[815] *Id.* at 117–18.

To sum up, proceedings at the SCSL, the ICTR, and the Special Panels are conducted in a way that creates the illusion that they are routinely capable of reaching reliable factual conclusions on the basis of evidence presented to them, when in fact, they are not. The Trial Chambers are adrift, and they are adrift in a way that calls into question the very foundation of the international criminal justice project. That project has only recently been subject to any serious scholarly critique. After centuries in which mass atrocities were followed only by impunity, the establishment of international tribunals to prosecute the large-scale crimes that had occurred in the former Yugoslavia and Rwanda was understandably met with tremendous fanfare.[816] International trials at these institutions were credited, among other things, with imposing much-needed retribution on monstrous killers, deterring brutal dictators from committing future acts of genocide, and enhancing the prospects for individual healing as well as societywide reconciliation.[817] These were high hopes indeed and somewhat unrealistic ones, so it should come as no surprise that more recent scholars have begun to question the ability of international trials to achieve the far-reaching goals attributed to them.

The ability of international criminal trials to effect deterrence has been called into question both by the atrocities that have been committed after the establishment of these institutions[818] as well as on more theoretical grounds.[819] The ability of international trials to heal broken victims and broken communities has been subject to searching inquiry by the empirical research of Laurel Fletcher, Eric Stover, and Harvey Weinstein, among others, who make use of the theories and practices of anthropologists, social psychologists, political scientists, and forensic scientists to conclude that international criminal trials have far less impact on post-atrocity societies than supporters of these trials have cavalierly assumed. For instance, the studies conducted by Stover, Dembour, and Haslam involving former ICTY witnesses suggest that the healing that is said to result from testifying at an international tribunal stands more as myth than reality.[820] Even more troublingly, Stover found that "there is no direct link between criminal trials and reconciliation." He found, indeed, that "criminal trials – especially those of local perpetrators – often divided small

[816] *See* note 2.
[817] *See* notes 3–8.
[818] The Srebrenica massacres as well as the Kosovo expulsions took place after the ICTY was established, despite the fact that the crimes fell within the tribunal's jurisdiction. And crimes continued to be committed in Darfur long after the ICC indicted Sudanese officials.
[819] *See, e.g.*, Ku & Nzelibe, note 12.
[820] Stover, note 13; Dembour & Haslan, note 13.

multiethnic communities by causing further suspicion and fear."[821] Fletcher and Weinstein's empirical work has similarly revealed the limits of international trials to contribute to the process of social reconstruction. Fletcher consequently cautions that "trials are only one component of an appropriate and necessary response to mass violence."[822]

Pretrial and posttrial processes are also subject to microlevel criticisms. Sometimes, the indictment process can become politicized so that charges are brought only against low-level offenders or members of one side to the conflict. Additional critiques target international criminal sentencing, which may seem to lack consistency and be generally ill advised – too lenient for some commentators and too harsh for others.[823] Even the procedures governing the trial process have sometimes garnered criticism, although most of these critiques have stemmed from dissatisfaction with the length and cost of international trials, not with their accuracy. Larry May and Mark Drumbl add their voices to the discussion with macro analyses and critiques. May searches for normative justifications for international criminal trials, and, although he is able to construct them, he rejects much current practice in the process.[824] Drumbl comprehensively assesses the ability of international trials to achieve their stated goals. After ascertaining that there exists a palpable disconnect between the effects of sentencing and the penological theories that are invoked to justify the punishment imposed, Drumbl concludes that "prosecution and incarceration is not always the best way to promote accountability in all afflicted places and spaces."[825]

These are impressive and important studies, for they begin a much-needed interdisciplinary dialogue that seeks to ascertain the values that we might realistically expect international criminal trials to advance. As Payam Akhavan has put it, international criminal justice scholarship has for too long described

[821] Stover, note 13, at 15.

[822] Laurel Fletcher, *From Indifference to Engagement: Bystanders and International Criminal Justice*, 26 Mich. J. Int'l L. 1013, 1016 (2004–2005).

[823] *See, e.g.*, Olaoluwa Olusanya, Sentencing War Crimes and Crimes Against Humanity Under the International Criminal Tribunal for the Former Yugoslavia (2005); Frederik Harhoff, *Sense and Sensibility in Sentencing – Taking Stock of International Criminal Punishment*, *in* Law at War: The Law as It Was and the Law as It Should Be 121, 138 (Ola Engdahl & Pål Wrange eds., 2008) (mentioning commentators who criticize the tribunals' sentencing); Mark B. Harmon & Fergal Gaynor, *Ordinary Sentences for Extraordinary Crimes*, 5 J. Int'l Crim. Just. 683, 711–12 (2007); Andrea Carcano, *Sentencing and the Gravity of the Offense in International Criminal Law*, 51 Int'l & Comp. L. Q. 583 (2002); Jennifer J. Clark, *Zero to Life: Sentencing Appeals at the International Criminal Tribunals for the Former Yugoslavia and Rwanda*, 96 Geo. L.J. 1685, 1691 (2008).

[824] May, Aggression, note 11, at 319–41.

[825] Drumbl, note 1, at 10.

international trials in "celebratory" tones that do little more than reaffirm the assumptions and principles of international criminal justice.[826] As important as these studies are, however, they assume the foundational inquiry that stands at the heart of my research. When May considers whether international criminal trials are normatively justified, when Drumbl considers whether the punishment imposed on international offenders can advance the penological goals expected to be served, these scholars – and others – assume that international trials, even if they are capable of doing nothing else, are capable of separating the guilty from the innocent a reasonable proportion of the time. That is, although international criminal trials may not serve to reconcile former enemies, may not enhance respect for the rule of law in postconflict societies, and may not deter the next genocide, they at least have been thought to constitute a viable mechanism for determining on whom to visit criminal sanctions. That assumption may be ill founded.

In this chapter I have suggested that international criminal trials purport a fact-finding competence that they do not possess. That is, although judicial fact-finding is not hard science in any criminal justice system, it is expected that the factual determinations made following a trial will be based on a reasonable quantity of reasonably reliable evidence about which the fact finders have a reasonable capacity to assess. As Mirjan Damaška puts it: "One of the working assumptions of the practice of adjudication is that truth is in principle discoverable, and that accuracy in fact-finding constitutes a pre-condition for a just decision."[827] International criminal trials do not – and perhaps cannot – fulfill those expectations. They look like Western trials, but the assumptions on which such trials are based – and from which confidence in those trials emanates – cannot be assumed in the international context. What that means for the accuracy of international criminal judgments depends on the way in which the Trial Chambers respond to the uncertainty inherent in their proceedings. The following chapter turns to that question.

[826] Payam Akhavan, *The International Criminal Court in Context: Mediating the Global and Local in the Age of Accountability*, 97 AM. J. INT'L L. 712, 720 (2003). Jan Klabbers similarly observes that "we have all fallen under the spell of international criminal law and the beauty of bringing an end to the culture of impunity." Jan Klabbers, *Just Revenge? The Deterrence Argument in International Criminal Law*, XII FINNISH Y.B. INT'L L. 249, 250 (2001).

[827] Mirjan Damaška, *Truth in Adjudication*, 49 HASTINGS L. J. 289, 289 (1998).

7

Casual Indifference

The Trial Chambers' Treatment of Testimonial Deficiencies

Although the problems identified in Chapters 2 through 5 are worryingly widespread and not easily remedied through other forms of evidence gathering, they need not impair the integrity of the Trial Chambers' legal judgments, so long as the Trial Chambers recognize the significance of the fact-finding impediments and treat them with the requisite seriousness. However, much of the time, Trial Chambers do neither. Some Trial Chambers fail even to mention serious testimonial deficiencies, as I observe in Chapter 6, and although other Trial Chambers do acknowledge the problems, at least in a general way, they often unquestioningly attribute those problems to innocent causes that do not impact the witness's credibility. Those attributions may be accurate in many cases, but it is by no means clear that they are in keeping with the prosecution's burden of proof. Furthermore, even if the causal attributions are accurate, the Trial Chambers frequently fail to appreciate the potential impact of testimonial deficiencies, whatever their causes. In Section 7.A, I analyze the Trial Chambers' treatment of fact-finding deficiencies, focusing first on their general observations and then on the way in which those observations are implemented in the Trial Chambers' decision making. In Section 7.B, I seek to illustrate these general findings by a comprehensive, in-depth analysis of the evidentiary underpinnings of the SCSL's *CDF* case. These two sections reveal that, in many cases, Trial Chambers adopt a cavalier attitude toward testimonial deficiencies and as a consequence are frequently content to base their convictions on deeply flawed testimony. Finally, Section 7.C considers the way in which the Trial Chambers' treatment of testimonial deficiencies intersects with the standard of proof prevailing in international criminal cases and leads to high rates of conviction.

7.A. THE TRIAL CHAMBERS' LACKADAISICAL ATTITUDE TOWARD TESTIMONIAL DEFICIENCIES

Although most testimonial deficiencies receive no mention in international criminal judgments, some of the early ICTR judgments do contain brief, general discussions of some of the problems. In the ICTR's first judgment in the *Akayesu* case, for instance, the Trial Chamber pointed out "the inexperience of witnesses with maps, film and graphic representations of localities."[828] Similarly, the *Rutaganda* Trial Chamber observed that some witnesses "were farmers and people who did not have a high standard of education." These witnesses, the Trial Chamber noted, not only had trouble making sense of photographs and maps but "also experienced difficulty in testifying as to dates, times, distances, colours and motor vehicles."[829] After acknowledging these limitations, the Trial Chambers announced that they did not negatively assess the witnesses' credibility as a consequence of them. The *Akayesu* Trial Chamber, for instance, stated that, because traditional modes of speech in Rwanda can feature indirectness, it "did not draw any adverse conclusions regarding the credibility of witnesses based only on their reticence and their sometimes circuitous responses to questions."[830] Even more broadly, the *Musema* Trial Chamber announced that it had not drawn any adverse conclusions regarding the credibility of a witness based only on the witness's reticence to respond to questions concerning dates, times, distances, locations, maps, and other graphic representations.[831]

The Trial Chambers have also made similarly general pronouncements about their treatment of witness testimony that is inconsistent with the witness's pre-trial statements. In one of the ICTR's earliest cases – *Kayishema & Ruzindana* – the Trial Chamber indicated that it would take a hard look at such inconsistencies because they "may raise doubt in relation to the particular piece of evidence in question or, where such inconsistencies are found to be material, to the witnesses' evidence as a whole."[832] A witness's explanation of the inconsistency might prove sufficient to remove the doubt, the Trial Chamber went on, but only if the explanation was "of substance rather than mere procedure." In particular, the Trial Chamber observed that the "common explanation provided by witnesses ... that the interviewing investigator did not accurately reflect in the written statement what the witness said ... is generally not enough to

[828] Akayesu Judgement, note 32, at para. 156; *see also* Musema Judgement, note 112, at para. 103.
[829] Rutaganda Judgement, note 38, at para. 23.
[830] Akayesu Judgement, note 32, at para. 156.
[831] Musema Judgement, note 112, at para. 103.
[832] Kayishema & Ruzindana Judgement, note 25, at para. 77.

remove doubt."[833] An explanation "relating to the substance of the investigator's question," by contrast, would be.[834]

The *Kayishema & Ruzindana* Trial Chamber's discussion of inconsistencies suggests that inconsistencies would be carefully examined to ascertain their impact on the witness's credibility. But the *Akayesu* judgment, which was issued at approximately the same time, took a more forgiving approach to witness inconsistencies. The *Akayesu* Trial Chamber noted, for instance, that because it "did not have access to transcripts of the interviews" from which the statements were drafted, it was "unable to consider the nature and form of the questions put to the witnesses, or the accuracy of interpretation at the time." It further pointed to "the time lapse between the statements and the presentation of evidence at trial, the difficulties of recollecting precise details several years after the occurrence of the events, the difficulties of translation, the illiteracy of several witnesses who had not read their written statements," and the fact that "the statements were not made under solemn declaration and were not taken by judicial officers." These factors led the *Akayesu* Trial Chamber to conclude that the probative value attached to the statements is "considerably less than direct sworn testimony before the Chamber, the truth of which has been subjected to the test of cross-examination."[835]

As it happens, the difference between the *Akayesu* and the *Kayishema & Ruzindana* approaches to inconsistencies has proven less substantial in practice than it might initially have seemed on paper. The *Kayishema & Ruzindana* Trial Chamber considered inconsistencies to raise serious doubts, but even it acknowledged that such doubts could be put to rest if the witness provided an explanation of substance, such as one that relates "to the substance of the investigator's question." Perhaps as a consequence of the guidance that the *Kayishema & Ruzindana* Trial Chamber provided, witnesses now routinely

[833] *Id.* at para. 78.
[834] *Id.* at para. 79.
[835] Akayesu Judgement, note 32, at para. 137. The ICTY Appeals Chamber pointed to similar factors in deciding to exclude the written statement of a deceased witness. The Appeals Chamber noted:

> [T]he investigator... did not speak Croatian, the language in which Mr. Haskić spoke, and relied on the interpreter's account of what he was saying. The statement of Mr. Haskić was then written in English by the investigator, whose native tongue is Dutch, and was then translated back into Croatian for the witness to sign it. These multiple translations in an informal setting create a much greater potential for inaccuracy than is the case when both the declarant and the witness speak the same language or when the original statement is given in court with professional, double-checked simultaneous translation. Prosecutor v. Kordić & Čerkez, Decision on Appeal Regarding Statement of a Deceased Witness, para. 27 (July 21, 2000).

explain omissions in their statements and other inconsistencies by claiming that the investigator failed to ask questions that would have elicited the information that the witness later provided at trial.[836] More importantly, it was the more forgiving *Akayesu* view that prevailed in subsequent cases. It is now well established in ICTR jurisprudence that "sworn testimony before the Chamber has considerably more probative value than the witness's declarations in prior written statements."[837] SCSL Trial Chambers also adopted that rule, and the *CDF* and *RUF* Trial Chambers went so far as to articulate a number of speculative and implausible justifications for the rule, including that "many witnesses remember, in court, more details which they had previously forgotten."[838] That position is counterintuitive at best since much less time has elapsed between the crime and the statement than between the crime and the in-court testimony. The SCSL moreover has emphasized that the "mere existence of inconsistencies in the testimony of a witness does not undermine the witness's credibility."[839]

The general pronouncements that I have just described find particularized expression in the Trial Chambers' assessments of individual witnesses' testimonies. As detailed in Chapter 6, the Trial Chambers rarely even mention the vagueness of a particular witness's testimony or an inability to answer date, distance, and place questions,[840] and in the uncommon instances in which they do acknowledge such testimonial deficiencies, they do not consider them to impair the reliability or the usefulness of the testimony. Recall, for instance, witness TF1-209, who the *AFRC* Trial Chamber acknowledged "was at times unclear" and who had "some difficulty in conveying what exactly she meant."[841] The Trial Chamber nonetheless credited her testimony, finding that its deficiencies probably resulted from her lack of education, nervousness, the need for translation, and the difficulty of testifying to such traumatic events.[842] The *Musema* Trial Chamber similarly described the testimony of witness I as "confusing in certain respects, particularly with regard to the details of her

[836] *See, e.g.*, note 569.

[837] Niyitegeka Judgement, note 56, at para. 40; *see also* Rutaganda Judgement, note 38, at para. 19; Musema Judgement, note 112, at para. 86; Muvunyi Judgement, note 455, at para. 14; Ntagerura Judgement, note 37, at para. 26. The *Kajelijeli* Trial Chamber held that it would give "*considerably* more weight" to a witness's in-court testimony when the witness was illiterate. Kajelijeli Judgement, note 303, at para. 522 (emphasis added).

[838] CDF Judgement, note 27, at para. 263; *see also* RUF Judgement, note 56, at para. 491.

[839] Prosecutor v. Brima et al., Case No. SCSL-2004–16-A, Judgement, para. 120 (Feb. 22, 2008) [hereinafter AFRC Appeals Judgement]; RUF Judgement, note 56, at para. 489.

[840] *See* note 792 and accompanying text. The citations in note 792 refer to some of the more notable testimonial deficiencies that the Trial Chambers failed to mention. Numerous other deficiencies also go unmentioned.

[841] AFRC Judgement, note 27, at paras. 999, 1001.

[842] *Id.* at para. 1005.

movement and the chronology of events." However, because the Trial Chamber considered her testimony to be "clear and consistent" about the relevant crime, it accepted it.[843] The *AFRC* Trial Chamber was even more critical of witness TF1-033's testimony as a general matter. It observed that the "evidence of the witness regarding the troop restructure at Mansofinia suffered from the deficiencies typical in his testimony: it was overly general in comparison to the testimony of other witnesses present at the same events, but became specific when the presence or actions of one of the Accused were concerned." Nonetheless, the Trial Chamber deemed itself "satisfied . . . that while the witness appears on occasion to have exaggerated figures and was unclear on dates, he did not fabricate events." The Trial Chamber further found the witness to have been "truthful at trial" and pronounced itself "unwilling to conclude that his evidence overall is not credible or reliable."[844] The vague and confusing features of other witnesses' testimony are treated similarly.[845]

Although the details in a witness's account can prove crucial to the defendant's ability to present a defense, as I describe in Chapter 2, some Trial Chambers have shown surprisingly little patience with defense counsel who press witnesses to provide such details.[846] In the *CDF* case, for instance, defense counsel questioned witness TF2-157 about the starting time and duration of a key meeting. Although the witness professed not to be able to answer such questions as a general matter,[847] defense counsel did manage to elicit an apparent contradiction: At one point the witness said that the meeting "started when the sun has come up and it was almost daylight," but directly thereafter he said that the meeting began "when the sun was really up." When the defense sought to question the witness further on this point, the Trial Chamber became impatient and instructed counsel to "get along" because "[t]his man keeps saying, 'I didn't have a watch,' 'I didn't have this,' I mean, we keep coming back to that."[848] Similarly, after witness TF2-007 refused to give a straight answer about whether his father was buried in the local cemetery, Presiding Judge Itoe cut short the questioning saying, "I'm sure that's the way the Mende. . . . He's a real traditional man. He was born and raised in that village and he has lived through the traditions. So you can see his answers, you know, they're never direct. Yes, Mr. Koppe, you can move along."[849] And although the efforts of an

[843] Musema Judgement, note 112, at para. 823.
[844] AFRC Judgement, note 27, at para. 366.
[845] *See, e.g., id.* at paras. 362, 368, 994–996.
[846] *See, e.g.,* RUF Transcript, July 21, 2004, at 12, 14; CDF Transcript, Nov. 11, 2004, at 20; Semanza Transcript, Dec. 6, 2000, at 96–97; Lolotoe Case Notes, Oct. 23, 2002, at 4. *But see* Ntakirutimana Transcript, Oct. 22, 2001, at 112–16 (Trial Chamber pressing witness on distance estimate).
[847] CDF Transcript, June 17, 2004, at 14, 41.
[848] *Id.* at 41.
[849] CDF Transcript, Dec. 2, 2004, at 80.

ICTR defense counsel to determine a witness's distance from the scene he was describing had obvious relevance to the reliability of the witness's account, the *Semanza* Trial Chamber lost patience with the questioning. After the President admonished counsel "not to continue in that direction," Judge Williams asked pointedly: "Where does this take us? Whether some people were three metres from him or some people were five metres from him or some people were ten metres from him, or some people are right up to him, how does all these help us?... How does all of this little distances [sic] here and little distance there, and who is at the side and who is in front, how does that help us?"[850]

The Trial Chambers are inclined not only to unquestioningly accept that witnesses' testimonial difficulties are the products of educational and experiential limitations, but they sometimes *sua sponte* postulate those difficulties when they may not exist.[851] In the SCSL's *RUF* case, for instance, defense counsel asked witness TF1-214 whether "rebels came from Tokoro, southwards to Kondembaia." The witness said "yes." Inexplicably not satisfied with that answer, the Trial Chamber interjected: "Does she understand southwards?... Southwards is too hard." Defense counsel consequently rephrased the question to omit "southwards" even though the witness gave no indication that she had had any difficulty in understanding the term.[852] Also in the *RUF* case, defense counsel asked a different witness in what year certain killings had taken place. Before the witness could answer, the Trial Chamber interjected to say, "[y]ou expect her to know the year?"[853] Similarly, in the *CDF* case, Judge Boutet admonished counsel to stop using the term "office of the prosecutor" because "maybe [the witness] does not understand what you mean by that."[854] The witness, however, had given no indication that he failed to understand the term. Judge Thompson intervened in the same fashion in the *CDF* case after counsel asked the witness, "do you recall modifying that statement...?" Before the witness had had a chance to respond, Judge Thompson admonished counsel, "[w]hat is modify for him? Can't we be a little clear, otherwise we invite a kind of argumentative response?"[855] And in the ICTR's *Rutaganda* case, the witness was asked, "when you left ET-L school, did you leave towards the north?" He answered: "We went towards Rebero as if we are going to Rebero." The president then interjected

[850] Semanza Transcript, Nov. 14, 2000, at 48–49.

[851] In addition to the examples appearing in the text, see RUF Transcript, July 27, 2004, at 61; RUF Transcript, July 22, 2004, at 53 (judges correct that witness did not understand the term "ECOMOG").

[852] RUF Transcript, July 15, 2004, at 7–8.

[853] RUF Transcript, July 19, 2004, at 74.

[854] CDF Transcript, June 21, 2004, at 9.

[855] CDF Transcript, Sept. 10, 2004, at 35. Very soon thereafter, Judge Itoe admonished counsel for using the word "indicate." *Id.* at 36.

to advise: "Simply ask the question where you going? From what place to what place? Is it the north or the south? I don't think we understanding [sic] what that means."[856]

These interjections – and many others like them – indicate that the Trial Chambers have come to expect that witnesses will not be able to answer simple date, time, distance, and space questions even when the witness himself indicates nothing of the kind. Indeed, the Trial Chambers sometimes make generalized comments about witness capabilities that send the same message. One SCSL judge, for instance, said to a witness: "I know that from your status you may not understand many things."[857] When defense counsel complained that another witness was not answering his questions, the same judge assured counsel that the witness was "coming on" and instructed him to "follow his trend," saying that the witness "is an illiterate, you know, [so] he has his own way of arriving at answers."[858] Finally, after chastising counsel for asking the witness when an event occurred, the judge commented: "This is an illiterate witness and you should try and accommodate them, you know, in their intellectual limitations."[859]

Turning now to inconsistencies, the Trial Chambers' treatment of particular witness inconsistencies is likewise in keeping with their general pronouncement that in-court testimony carries more probative weight than prior written statements. Certainly, the Trial Chambers do pay some attention to inconsistencies and will conclude that a witness lacks credibility when the inconsistencies are especially numerous or severe,[860] but they also overlook or explain away a great number of inconsistencies that would be severe enough to shred a witness's credibility in a domestic courtroom.

The *AFRC* Trial Chamber, for instance, credited Gibril Massaquoi's testimony that Defendant Kanu shot and killed one man near the Freetown State House, even though Massaquoi's statement had asserted that Kanu had not personally killed anyone but had only ordered his men to kill.[861] Similarly, the ICTR's *Akayesu* Trial Chamber credited Ephrem Karangwa's testimony even

[856] Rutaganda Transcript, Mar. 25, 1997, at 7–8.

[857] CDF Transcript, Feb. 25, 2005, at 25.

[858] CDF Transcript, June 18, 2004, at 45–46.

[859] RUF Transcript, July 21, 2004, at 25.

[860] *See, e.g.*, Seromba Judgement, note 547, at para. 237; Ndindabahizi Judgement, note 56, at paras. 99, 193–197, 447–451; Musema Judgement, note 112, at paras. 664–665, 697, 843–44; Simba Judgement, note 455, at paras. 106–112, 269–278; Kamuhanda Judgement, note 38, at paras. 563–565; Muhimana Judgement, note 363, at para. 246; Gacumbitsi Judgement, note 364, at para. 192; Muvunyi Judgement, note 455, at paras. 175 (rejecting testimony partially on the basis of inconsistencies), 251–253; Kajelijeli Judgement, note 303, at para. 680; Karera Judgement, note 54, at para. 53.

[861] AFRC Judgement, note 27, at paras. 907, 908, 910.

though it was riddled with serious inconsistencies. Karangwa testified that he was located about 150 meters away from Akayesu when Akayesu came to his house. In a previous statement, he said was standing about a kilometer away.[862] More seriously, Karangwa testified that Akayesu killed all three of Karangwa's brothers by shooting them. His statement reported, however, that Akayesu had killed only one of his brothers and that his other two brothers had been killed not by Akayesu but by men who were with him, and not by gunshots but by machetes. Finally, when asked on the stand whether he had buried his brothers' bodies, Karangwa said that he had not had time to because he left the area directly after the killings. In his previous statement, however, Karangwa asserted that he had buried his brothers near the house of Laurent Kamondo.[863] When confronted with these inconsistencies, the witness denied making the assertions appearing in his statement, and the Trial Chamber believed his denial. Recalling that "the Chamber places greater reliance on direct testimony rather than untested prior statements made under variable circumstances,"[864] the Trial Chamber concluded that "Karangwa gave a truthful account of events actually witnessed by him and that he did so without exaggeration or hostility."[865] Other examples of the Trial Chamber's crediting inconsistent witness testimony appear in the notes.[866]

The Trial Chambers take a similarly generous view of inconsistencies that result when a witness's statement fails to include key facts that later form the basis for the witness's in-court testimony. When asked to explain these omissions from their statements, witnesses frequently assert that the investigators never asked them about the omitted fact. The Trial Chambers virtually always accept that explanation.[867] Indeed, the Trial Chambers often accept witness testimony about a particular event without even mentioning that the event or the

[862] Akayesu Judgement, note 32, at para. 236.
[863] *Id.* at paras. 237–238.
[864] *Id.* at para. 261.
[865] *Id.* at para. 262.
[866] Simba Judgement, note 455, at paras. 164–168; Muhimana Judgement, note 363, at paras. 27–29, 269–270, 272; Ndindabahizi Judgement, note 56, at para. 120 (witness CGV), para. 140 (witness CGY), para. 216 (witness CGC), paras. 254–255 (witness CGM), paras. 309–311 (witness CGB); Ntakirutimana Judgement, note 69, at paras. 173–180; Muvunyi Judgement, note 455, at paras. 201, 206–211; Kajelijeli Judgement, note 303, at para. 522; Niyitegeka Judgement, note 56, at paras. 303, 306, 310; Gacumbitsi Judgement, note 364, at paras. 54, 83, 86; Karera Judgement, note 54, at para. 164 (witness BMH), para. 116 (witness BMU), paras. 296, 297, 307, 314 (witness BMJ), paras. 258, 294, 299–302, 314 (witness BML), para. 304 (witness BMI), para. 369 (witness BMR); AFRC Judgement, note 27, at para. 869 (witness TF1-209), paras. 364–367 (witness TF1-033), para. 437 (witness TF1-045), paras. 822–823 (witness TF1-054).
[867] *See, e.g.*, Niyitegeka Judgement, note 56, at paras. 101, 108; Musema Judgement, note 112, at para. 706; Akayesu Judgement, note 32, at para. 266; Ntakirutimana Judgement, note 69, at paras. 255, 257, 260, 703; Kajelijeli Judgement, note 303, at para. 467; *but see* AFRC Judgement, note 27, at para. 419.

defendant's involvement therein did not appear in a witness's statement.[868] For instance, the *Kajelijeli* Trial Chamber and the *RUF* Trial Chamber never even mentioned that the statements of witnesses ACM and TF1-064, respectively, contained no reference to their rapes.[869] Similarly, the *AFRC* Trial Chamber relied on George Johnson's testimony that Defendant Kanu had ordered troops at the Kissy Mental Home to amputate the limbs of civilians without mentioning that Johnson had failed to mention Kanu's orders to investigators.[870]

As noted above, Trial Chambers sometimes find the inconsistencies between a witness's statement and her testimony to be so grave as to justify discrediting the witness's testimony. Even then, though, a subsequent Trial Chamber or an Appeals Chamber may reach a different conclusion. In *Musema*, for instance, discrepancies emerged between the witness's testimony and his written statement regarding "the dates during which [the witness] was hiding in the tea plantation, the note allegedly discovered by the witness on Muyira hill after a massacre, and the basis of his remembering important dates." Dissatisfied with the witness's responses to questions concerning these matters, the *Musema* Trial Chamber deemed the testimony insufficiently reliable to be admitted as evidence.[871] The same witness subsequently testified in *Niyitegeka*, however, and although the *Niyitegeka* Trial Chamber acknowledged the *Musema* Trial Chamber's conclusions about the witness's reliability, it chose to rely on the testimony, deeming the inconsistencies to have been "adequately explained."[872]

The Special Panels' *Paulino de Jesus* case played out similarly, though there it was the Appeals Panel that rejected the Panel's conclusions. The Panel determined that the prosecution had not proven its case beyond a reasonable doubt largely because the testimony of the victims' parents featured so many serious inconsistencies. First and foremost, in their pretrial statements, the parents named a different man as their daughter's murderer. It was not until two years later that the parents named the defendant as the culprit, and by then they had changed other key aspects of their story as well. For instance, in her statement, the victim's mother maintained that she had been shot in the leg and had run away before her daughter was killed so that she did not see what had happened to her daughter but learned about her murder only later. At trial, the

[868] *See, e.g.*, Kamuhanda Transcript, Sept. 4, 2001, at 80 (French version) (pointing out omissions) and Kamuhanda Judgement, note 38, at para. 439 (relying on the witness's testimony to find the fact that had been omitted); AFRC Transcript, Apr. 18, 2005, at 62 and AFRC Judgement, note 27, at paras. 954, 960, 963 (relying on the witness TF1-253's testimony to find the omitted fact); Kajelijeli Transcript, Dec. 5, 2001, at 92–93 (pointing out omissions) and Kajelijeli Judgement, note 303, at paras. 529–530, 723 (relying on the witness's testimony to find the omitted fact).

[869] *See* Kajelijeli Judgement, note 303, at para. 679.

[870] *See* AFRC Transcript, Sept. 21, 2005, at 4–5 (pointing out omissions) and AFRC Judgement, note 27, at paras. 1238, 1601, 2060 (relying on Johnson's testimony).

[871] Musema Judgement, note 112, at paras. 663–665.

[872] Niyitegeka Judgement, note 56, at paras. 59–66.

mother maintained that she was shot after her daughter was stabbed, but later in the same testimony she ended up confirming the chronology of events that had appeared in her statement. The victim's father's testimony also diverged from his statement. His statement reported that the defendant had stabbed his daughter with a long knife, whereas at trial he stated that small knives were used. The victim's father likewise testified inconsistently about his distance from the crime. In his first statement, he stated that he was ten meters from the murder site. Later, he stated that he was four meters away from the scene, and at trial he twice stated that he was thirty meters away.[873] Despite these serious discrepancies, the Appeals Chamber reversed the Panel's acquittal, concluding that the parents' testimony was clear and convincing. The Appeals Panel "did not even mention a single one of the contradictions or inconsistencies in the parents' testimony, . . . and it completely ignored the testimony of the four witnesses who stated that the accused was elsewhere." The Appeals Chamber also ignored "the fact that three of the five prosecution witnesses were not present when the victim was murdered and a fourth said that he knew nothing of the accused in relation to the crime."[874]

Trial Chambers rarely provide any meaningful justification for their decisions to credit witnesses' testimony even though it is inconsistent with their previous statements. For instance, a Trial Chamber might assert without explanation that "it does not consider that this discrepancy affects [the witness's] credibility"[875] or it might conclude that "[w]hile the Chamber does not find [the witness's] responses to questions concerning the content of his prior statement entirely satisfactory, those responses are in the Chamber's view not sufficient to cast doubt on his testimony."[876] Sometimes the Trial Chambers point to their positive assessments of the witness's demeanor;[877] other times they minimize the magnitude of the discrepancies,[878] and still other times,

[873] Paulino de Jesus Judgement, note 455, at 9–11.

[874] Cohen, *Indifference*, note 239, at 70. *See generally*, Judicial System Monitoring Program, *The Paulino de Jesus Decision* (Apr. 2005), *available at* http://www.jsmp.minihub.org/Reports/jsmpreports/Paulino%20De%20Jesus/paulino%20de%20jesus%20report%20(e).pdf. The Appeals Court Judgment is not available in English, so I rely on Cohen's and JSMP's description of it.

[875] Niyitegeka Judgement, note 56, at para. 102.

[876] Ntakirutimana Judgement, note 69, at paras. 255–256.

[877] Kajelijeli Judgement, note 303, at para. 522; Ntakirutimana Judgement, note 69, at para. 369 ("In court, the witness distanced himself from his prior statement, saying that it must have been recorded improperly. After having observed the witness giving evidence the Chamber accepts his testimony that he was in the open air when he observed the event and that no one held Ukobizaba before he was killed.").

[878] Niyitegeka Judgement, note 56, at para. 161 ("Upon evaluation of the totality of the evidence, the Chamber considers that apart from minor discrepancies, Witness GGR's testimony was clear and consistent and the Chamber finds him to be a credible witness."); AFRC Judgement,

they decline to opine about specific inconsistencies and decree more generally that "[t]he parties made submissions on alleged discrepancies between the prior written statements of witnesses and testimony before the Chamber. The Chamber has considered these submissions fully in assessing the credibility of witnesses."[879]

The preceding discussion reveals that the Trial Chambers routinely discount the significance and potentially distortive effect of many testimonial deficiencies. Moreover, even when Trial Chambers do recognize that a witness is unquestionably lying or gravely mistaken about one aspect of his testimony, they sometimes credit other aspects of the witness's testimony as though the serious mistake or false testimony is relevant only to the particular issue about which the witness erred or lied. In the *RUF* case, for instance, the Trial Chamber announced that "even if some aspects of a witness's testimony are not believed by the Chamber, the Chamber may still accept other portions of the evidence presented provided they are credible in their context and particularly where they are corroborated."[880] Because the *CDF* and *RUF* judgments do not describe the testimony of the witnesses appearing in those cases, the only way to identify instances in which the Trial Chamber credited one aspect of a witness's testimony while rejecting other aspects as not credible is to carefully comb through all of the transcripts. I did so scrutinize the *CDF* transcripts; and because I discuss my findings at length later in this chapter, I here note only that the Trial Chamber chose to credit insider witness Albert Nallo's highly incriminating testimony about the CDF command structure and the criminal instructions that Nallo allegedly received from the defendants even though the Trial Chamber concluded that his testimony about certain crimes was not to be believed.

In the *AFRC* case, similarly, witness TF1-085 testified that she saw Defendant Kanu lead a group of rebels into Wellington. She repeatedly described Kanu as "huge, fat" and "tall." The Chamber noted that the witness's description of Kanu did not correspond with his physical features since he is "a thin man of medium height," so it did "not rely on her evidence *in this regard*."[881] With respect to the rest of her testimony, however, the Chamber concluded that the witness was "consistent and firm in her evidence" and it "accept[ed] her as a witness of truth."[882] *AFRC* witness TF1-158's testimony provides another

note 27, at para. 368 ("The Trial Chamber finds that inconsistencies between the evidence he gave at trial and his prior statement ... were not of sufficient gravity to cast doubt as to his credibility.").

879 Ndindabahizi Judgement, note 56, at para. 22.

880 RUF Judgement, note 56, at para. 490.

881 AFRC Judgement, note 27, at para. 1089 (emphasis added).

882 *Id.* at para. 1099.

example of this phenomenon. The witness testified that Defendant Brima spoke with a stammer. In Brima's twenty-one days of testimony, however, he displayed no signs of a stammer. Furthermore, the witness repeatedly stated that the commanders of the first group that had abducted him were Defendants Brima and Kanu along with SAJ Musa and a man with the nickname "O-Five." The Chamber noted, however, that "other evidence indicated that SAJ Musa and 'O-Five' were not together with the Accused Brima and Kanu in the Bombali District during this period." Finally, the witness also testified that "Staff Alhaji" had trained child soldiers both at Camp Rosos in the Bombali District, during the witness' first abduction, and at Kamabai in Koinadugu District, during his second abduction. The Trial Chamber deemed this allegation "improbable." Despite this, the Trial Chamber observed that, on cross-examination, "the Witness was not shaken with regards to the description of his treatment in captivity." Therefore, although the Trial Chamber declined to rely on the witness's testimony regarding the AFRC command structure, it found that "in spite of his youth, the witness was credible and reliable with regards to the details of captivity and his treatment in captivity."[883] ICTR Trial Chambers also have adopted this approach.[884]

It is certainly possible for a witness to be mistaken about one issue and correct about others. It is less plausible to think that a witness might lie about the defendant's involvement in one massacre, say, and testify truthfully about his involvement in another, though that too is possible. What is troubling is that the Trial Chambers seemingly presume that this is the case. The Trial Chambers also seemingly fail to recognize that the only reason that certain errors or lies come to light is because countervailing evidence existed and was able to be presented. The *CDF* Trial Chamber learned that Nallo perjured himself when he claimed to have cut off the ear of one Joseph Lansana, for instance, because the defense was able to find Lansana, bring him to court, and show the Trial Chamber his two intact ears. The *AFRC* Trial Chamber learned of TF1-085's and TF1-158's mistakes about the defendants' appearance and stammer because it was able to see and hear for itself what the defendants looked and sounded like. Much of the testimony that the Trial Chambers credit, by contrast, pertains to issues that are not easily verified.

[883] *Id.* at para. 1258.

[884] For some ICTR examples, see Prosecutor v. Gacumbitsi, Case No. ICTR-2001–64-A, Appeals Judgement, para. 94 (July 7, 2006); Niyitegeka Judgement, note 56, at para. 164; Kamuhanda Judgement, note 38, at para. 459; Kamuhanda Appeals Judgement, note 713, at paras. 246–248; Kajelijeli Judgement, note 303, at paras. 591–596. *See also* AFRC Judgement, note 27, at para. 1300. This approach conflicts with the views of seventeenth-century authors who maintained that "testimony should not be accepted if part of it proves to be false." Barbara J. Shapiro, "*Fact" and the Proof of Fact, in* How Law Knows 25, 35 (Austin Sarat et al. eds., 2007).

That testimony, then, may seem true only because it cannot reliably be proven false.

A final gauge of the Trial Chambers' lack of concern about testimonial deficiencies can be derived from its treatment of allegations of perjury. Rule 91 of the ICTR Rules of Procedure and Evidence authorizes a Trial Chamber to direct the prosecution to investigate allegations of witness perjury. Alexander Zahar has compellingly argued that the ICTR misinterpreted Rule 91 in its very first case. In particular, although the rule authorizes the Trial Chamber to order an investigation if the Trial Chamber has "strong grounds for believing that a witness may have knowingly and willfully given false testimony," the Trial Chamber in *Akayesu* placed the "onus . . . on the party pleading the case of false testimony to prove: the falsehood of the witness['s] statements; that these statements were made with a harmful intent, or at least that they were made by a witness who was fully aware that they were false; and the possible bearing of the said statements upon the judge's decision."[885] As Zahar points out, the Trial Chamber's interpretation, which requires the movant to prove both the actus reus and mens rea of the offense, renders meaningless the rule's authorization to order an investigation.[886] In other words, once the movant has proven the actus reus and mens rea of the offense, then there is nothing left to investigate. As it happens, the Trial Chambers have virtually never ordered an investigation despite numerous requests[887] and considerable evidence of false testimony. The

[885] Prosecutor v. Akayesu, Case No. 96–4-T, Decision on Defence Motions to Direct the Prosecutor to Investigate the Matter of False Testimony by Witness "R" (Mar. 9, 1998).

[886] Alexander Zahar, *The* Rwamakuba *Case and the Problem of False Testimony at the International Criminal Tribunal for Rwanda in* ANNOTATED LEADING CASES OF INTERNATIONAL CRIMINAL TRIBUNALS, VOL. 25: INTERNATIONAL CRIMINAL TRIBUNAL FOR RWANDA, 2006–2007 (André Klip & Göran Sluiter eds., forthcoming 2010).

[887] *See, e.g.*, Prosecutor v. Karemera et al., Case No. ICTR-98–44-T, Decision on Defence Motion for Investigation of Prosecution Witness Ahmed Mbonyunkiza for False Testimony (Dec. 29, 2006); Prosecutor v. Karemera et al., Case No. ICTR-98–44-T, Decision on Defence Motion for Investigation of Prosecution Witness HH for False Testimony (Sept. 26, 2007); Prosecutor v. Akayesu, Case No. ICTR-96–4-T, Motion to Request Prosecution for Perjury (Jan. 29, 1997); Prosecutor v. Bagilishema, Case No. ICTR-95–1A-T, Defence Motion Under Rule 73 of the Rules of Procedure and Evidence Requesting the Chamber to Direct the Prosecutor to Investigate a Matter with a View to the Preparation and Submission of an Indictment for False Testimony (June 6, 2000); Prosecutor v. Rutaganda, Case No. ICTR-96–3-T, Defence Motion to Direct the Prosecutor to Investigate False Testimony (Mar. 2, 1998) (witness claimed that he explained to prosecutors that the killings he witnessed occurred during two separate incidents but prosecutors denied that he did so); Prosecutor v. Rutaganda, Case No. ICTR-96–3-T, Decision on the Defence Motion to Direct the Prosecutor to Investigate the Matter of False Testimony by Witness "CC" (Mar. 10, 1998); Prosecutor v. Rutaganda, Case No. ICTR-96–3-T, Decision on the Defence Motion to Direct the Prosecutor to Investigate the Matter of False Testimony by Witness "E" (Mar. 10, 1998); Prosecutor v. Bagosora et al., Case No. ICTR-98–41-T, Decision on Request for an Investigation into Alleged False Testimony of Witness DO (Oct. 3, 2003) (witness almost certainly knowingly testified falsely, but Trial Chamber determined that the

Trial Chambers indeed have found some of these motions so meritless that they have threatened or imposed sanctions on counsel bringing them.[888] Granted, a Trial Chamber might wisely decline to order an investigation if faced only with inconsistencies between different accounts of the same witness or different accounts among witnesses, since these could as easily reflect honest mistakes as knowingly and willfully false testimony. At the same time, it is disappointing that the Trial Chambers have only recently ordered any investigations and only where the witnesses confessed to perjury.[889] In the meanwhile, the vast majority of other instances of confessed perjury have not given rise to Rule 91 investigations,[890] and the only witness ever convicted of perjury was a prosecution witness who had recanted his inculpatory testimony.[891] In other words, the only successful perjury investigation targeted a witness who apparently lied to protect the defendant.

This section has described the Trial Chambers' treatment of fact-finding deficiencies in general terms. For the most part, general terms are the best we can do because it is not feasible to conduct an in-depth examination of the

false testimony did not concern a matter material to the case). Some motions do appear entirely meritless. *See, e.g.*, Prosecutor v. Nahimana et al., Case No. ICTR-96–11-I, Decision on Defence Motion to Direct the Prosecutor to Investigate the Matter of False Testimony by Witness "AEN" in Terms of Rule 91(B) (Feb. 27, 2001) (finding no inconsistency in the witness's testimony); Prosecutor v. Rutaganda, Case No. ICTR-96–3-T, Defence Motion for Orders to Direct the Prosecutor to Investigate a Case of False Testimony (Sept. 10, 1997); Prosecutor v. Rutaganda, Case No. ICTR-96–3-T, Response by the Office of the Prosecutor to the Defence Request for a Direction under Rule 91(B) (Sept. 26, 1997) (pointing out that the defense's motion is based on passage appearing in a Belgian Review summarizing articles appearing in Kinyarwanda in the Rwandan press suggesting that the witness had been involved in embezzlement). *See also* Prosecutor v. Sesay et al., Decision on Sesay Defence Motion to Direct the Prosecutor to Investigate the Matter of False Testimony by Witness TF1-366 (July 26, 2006).

888 *See, e.g.*, Prosecutor v. Karemera et al., Case No. ICTR-98–44-T, Decision on Defence Motion for Investigation of Prosecution Witness HH for False Testimony (Sept. 26, 2007); Prosecutor v. Nyiramasuhuko & Ntahobali, Case No. ICTR-97–21-T, Decision on Arsène Shalom Ntahobali's Motion to Have Perjury Committed by Prosecution Witness QY Investigated, para. 13 (Sept. 23, 2005). In *Muhimana*, the Trial Chamber stopped short of threatening sanctions but did admonish counsel that "allegations of this nature must be founded upon solid ground." Prosecutor v. Muhimana, Case No. ICTR-95–1B-T, Decision on the Defence Motion to Appoint an *Amicus Curiae* in Proceeding Against Investigator Tony Lucassen for False Testimony, para. 6 (May 6, 2004).

889 Prosecutor v. Nyiramasuhuko et al., Case No. ICTR-98-42-T, Decision on Ntahobali's Motion for an Investigation into False Testimony and Kanyabashi's Motion for an Investigation into Contempt of Court Relative to Prosecution Witnesses QY and SJ (Mar. 19, 2009); Prosecutor v. Karemera et al., Case No. 98–44-T, Decision on Prosecutor's Confidential Motion to Investigate BTH for False Testimony, para. 6 (May 14, 2008).

890 Zahar chronicles numerous examples. *See* Zahar, note 886, at n. 100.

891 ICTR Press Release, *Former Witness Sentenced to 9 Months for Contempt*, ICTR/INFO-9–2-541.EN, Dec. 3, 2007.

evidentiary bases for each international criminal conviction. At the same time, I do believe it important to illustrate my general discussion with at least one comprehensive case analysis, which I hope will convey at least some flavor of the quantity and the quality of witness testimony that is deemed sufficient to support a conviction. I selected the SCSL's *CDF* case for this purpose and did so for a number of reasons. First and foremost, the quality and quantity of the testimony presented to the *CDF* Trial Chamber as well as the Trial Chamber's treatment thereof is roughly representative of international criminal cases as a whole. Second, a careful look at the *CDF* judgment is informative because, as noted in Chapter 6, the judgment is written in a narrative style that obscures the quality and quantity of the evidence on which its factual findings are based. Thus, it is a case whose factual underpinnings are in need of explication. Finally, the SCSL has escaped much of the criticism that has plagued the first *ad hoc* criminal tribunals – the ICTY and ICTR. A hybrid tribunal with both domestic and international features, the SCSL was seen to inaugurate a new, more efficiently functioning tribunal and one that has been praised in particular for its greater focus on defense concerns.[892] My analysis provides one small bit of evidence as to whether that assessment is justified. In sum, I engage in this examination both to provide clarity and depth to the foregoing discussion and to inform the question that stands at the heart of this chapter: That is, just how worried should we be about the accuracy of the international tribunals' legal conclusions?

7.B. EVIDENTIARY BASES EXPOSED: THE *CDF* JUDGMENT

7.B.i. *A Brief Summary of the Case*

After the government of Sierra Leonean President Ahmad Tejan Kabbah was ousted in a coup in May 1997, Kabbah established the Civil Defence Forces (CDF) through which he channeled efforts to regain control of the country.[893] The CDF was comprised primarily of "Kamajors" – traditional Sierra Leonean hunters who had in the past been employed by local chiefs to defend villages in rural regions of the country.[894] The nature of the Kamajor society changed once the Kamajors were expected to engage in serious military engagements following the coup. In particular, in retaking control of the government, Kamajor forces committed numerous acts of violence against civilians. As a consequence,

[892] *See, e.g.*, Human Rights Watch, *Bringing Justice*, note 614, at 3–5, 22; Human Rights Watch, *Justice in Motion: The Trial Phase of the Special Court for Sierra Leone*, Vol. 17, No. 14(A) (Nov. 2005), at 3–4, *available at* http://hrw.org/reports/2005/sierraleone1105/.

[893] CDF Judgement, note 27, at para. 80.

[894] *Id.* at paras. 1–2.

the SCSL prosecuted three CDF leaders – Sam Hinga Norman, Moinina Fofana, and Allieu Kondewa – who were, respectively, the CDF's national coordinator, its director of war, and its high priest. Hinga Norman died shortly before the Trial Chamber could issue its judgment, so the Trial Chamber passed judgment on only Fofana and Kondewa. Although the Trial Chamber rejected the prosecution's charges of crimes against humanity, determining that the evidence was insufficient to prove that the civilian population was the primary object of the various attacks,[895] it did convict Fofana and Kondewa of various war crimes charges, including murder, cruel treatment, collective punishment, and pillage. The convictions were not unanimous. Sierra Leonean judge Bankole Thompson voted to acquit the defendants, but he did so only on the ground that their criminal acts were excused by the doctrine of necessity.[896] Judge Thompson expressly stated that he concurred with all of the majority's findings of fact except those involving the Kamajor initiation process.[897] Thus, the Trial Chamber found unanimously the factual determinations that I now discuss.

7.B.ii. *Crimes Committed in the Towns of Tongo Field*

The Trial Chamber convicted Fofana and Kondewa of aiding and abetting the war crimes that took place in the towns of Tongo Field.[898] The Trial Chamber based its convictions on speeches the defendants allegedly made at a "passing out parade" in December 1997 that was held in anticipation of the Tongo operation. The Trial Chamber determined that during that parade Norman had provided the Kamajors instructions for the Tongo operation and had in particular directed the Kamajors to destroy the houses of junta members and to chop off the left hand of any junta members they could capture. Norman, the Trial Chamber found, also told the Kamajors that there was no place to detain captured prisoners. The Trial Chamber found that Fofana and Kondewa addressed the Kamajors after Norman had done so. According to the Trial Chamber, Fofana told the crowd that any Kamajor who failed to perform in accordance with Norman's instructions should kill himself and not report back. Kondewa, the Trial Chamber determined, told the Kamajors that the rebels had been given plenty of time to surrender but that the time for surrender had passed. Consequently, Kondewa allegedly said, the CDF "did not need any surrendered rebels."[899]

[895] *Id.* at para. 693.
[896] CDF Judgement, Justice Thompson's Dissent, note 612, at para. 92.
[897] *Id.* at para. 56.
[898] CDF Judgement, note 27, at paras. 749–764.
[899] *Id.* at para. 721(x).

The Trial Chamber found that Fofana's and Kondewa's speeches constituted encouragement and support for the instructions Norman gave to the Kamajors.[900] The Kamajors did engage in the criminal behavior that Norman had allegedly authorized in his speech, and the Trial Chamber found that Fofana's and Kondewa's speeches had a substantial effect on the perpetration of those criminal acts. As a consequence, the Trial Chamber found Fofana and Kondewa guilty of aiding and abetting in the Kamajors' crimes.[901]

To find Fofana and Kondewa guilty of aiding and abetting of Kamajor crimes in the towns of Tongo Field, the Trial Chamber had to conclude that the prosecution had proved beyond a reasonable doubt that (1) Norman made the speech instructing the Kamajors to engage in illegal activity and that (2) Fofana and Kondewa had followed up Norman's speech with speeches of their own conveying the above-described information. The Trial Chamber based its findings on both of these matters exclusively on the testimony of one witness – witness TF2-222.[902] As a general matter, witness TF2-222's testimony was clear and did not feature many of the problems that plague the testimony of most SCSL witnesses. His testimony did diverge in one significant respect from that of his written statement, however.[903] In court, TF2-222 testified that when he arrived at Base Zero, he was met by Defendant Norman. In his statement, the witness alleged that Norman was visiting neighboring villages when he arrived at Base Zero; consequently, he was met by Pa Collier. Although that point was unrelated to the testimony supporting the defendants' convictions, it was also less susceptible of innocent explanation than many SCSL inconsistencies because witness TF2-222 is well educated, fluent in English, and read his statement before signing it.[904] Thus, he could not plausibly blame investigators or interpreters for the discrepancy and must himself have been either mistaken or lying during the statement taking or in court.

On the one hand, because witness TF2-222's testimony did not feature as many problems as that of the typical SCSL witness, it seems a relatively solid foundation for a conviction. On the other hand, an examination of this particular conviction reveals the slim reeds on which international convictions

[900] *Id.* at paras. 722, 735.
[901] *Id.* at paras. 723, 736.
[902] *Id.* at paras. 320–321 & nn. 484–490. For one proposition, the Trial Chamber included in its footnote a *see also* cite to the testimony of another prosecution witness, TF2-005, who testified in a closed session, and the testimony of Defendant Norman, who directly contradicted the testimony of TF2-222. *See id.* at n.485. Although I was not able to review TF2-005's testimony – because he testified in closed session – the fact that the Trial Chamber included it in the *see also* cite with Norman's contradictory testimony leads me to believe that it was not supportive of TF2-222's testimony.
[903] CDF Transcript, Feb. 17, 2005, at 137–43.
[904] *Id.* at 70, 72, 137.

often are based. For one thing, as with virtually all eyewitness testimony at the international tribunals, witness TF2-222's testimony was sharply contested. Defendant Norman flatly denied giving any orders regarding the attack on Tongo,[905] and other defense witnesses maintained that planning for the Tongo attack was undertaken by local Kamajor commanders, not by the defendants.[906] To convict the defendants, the Trial Chamber had to disbelieve the testimony of Norman and the other defense witnesses. Furthermore, although international witness testimony is frequently vague and undetailed, Fofana's and Kondewa's convictions for aiding and abetting the Tongo crimes highlight the key role that details can play in the Trial Chambers' guilt determinations. The *CDF* Trial Chamber also received testimony about a December 1997 commanders' meeting in preparation for the Tongo attack. At that meeting, Norman was said to have reiterated and clarified his earlier unlawful orders and additionally to have instructed the Kamajors to engage in looting. Although one witness testified that Fofana and Kondewa also had participated in the meeting's discussions, that witness was not able to say what in particular those two defendants had said. Because the Trial Chamber did not hear evidence about the defendants' actual words, it concluded that the prosecution had not proven beyond a reasonable doubt that Fofana and Kondewa had either planned or aided and abetted the additional crime of looting that Norman had allegedly authorized at the meeting.[907] In other words, it was only because TF2-222 could remember – or said he could remember – precisely what the defendants had said at the passing-out parade that the Trial Chamber convicted them. If his memory of those very short addresses was mistaken – as his memory of his arrival at Base Zero apparently was, when he described it either to investigators or to the court – then the Trial Chamber wrongfully convicted the defendants of these crimes.

7.B.iii. *Crimes Committed in Koribondo*

The *CDF* Trial Chamber next convicted Fofana on a command responsibility theory for the murders, cruel treatment, and collective punishments that occurred during the Kamajors' attacks on Koribondo.[908] To find a defendant responsible for a subordinate's crimes on a theory of command responsibility, the Trial Chamber must find:

(1) the existence of a superior–subordinate relationship between the superior and the offender of the criminal act;

905 CDF Transcript, Feb. 7, 2006, at 42.
906 CDF Transcript, May 4, 2006, at 58; CDF Transcript, May 16, 2006, at 37–38.
907 CDF Judgement, note 27, at paras. 322, 725, 738.
908 *Id.* at paras. 785–798.

(2) that the superior knew or had reason to know that the criminal act was about to be or had been committed; and
(3) that the superior failed to take the necessary and reasonable measures to prevent the criminal act or punish the offender thereof.[909]

The Trial Chamber found that there existed a superior–subordinate relationship between Fofana and Albert J. Nallo, who claimed to be CDF's Deputy National Director of Operations and Director of Operations, Southern Region. Nallo, the Trial Chamber found, received orders from Norman and Fofana, among other superiors, and was responsible for implementing those orders with the commanders who were beneath him in the CDF hierarchy.[910] Among these commanders were Joe Tamidey, Bobor Tucker, and Lamin Ngobeh, whom the Trial Chamber found to have led seven hundred Kamajors in their attack on Koribondo.[911] As for the second element, the Trial Chamber's determination that Fofana knew or had reason to know that criminal acts were to be committed in Koribondo was based on its finding that in Fofana's presence, Norman ordered the Kamajors to destroy all but three buildings in Koribondo and to kill everyone they met there.[912] The Trial Chamber failed to point to any evidence supporting its determination that the third element had been satisfied, but it presumably considered the element proven because Fofana presented no evidence to suggest that he had taken steps to prevent or punish the crimes.

Most of the testimony supporting the Trial Chamber's finding on the second element was provided in closed sessions, so I am unable to assess it. My evaluation of Fofana's conviction for the Koribondo crimes centers, then, on the Trial Chamber's conclusions about the first element – that is, that a superior–subordinate relationship existed between Fofana and Nallo. A quick glance at the judgment's footnotes reveals that the Trial Chamber's finding on this point was based entirely on Nallo's testimony.[913] The Trial Chamber deemed Nallo to be "the single most important witness in the Prosecution evidence" on Fofana's superior responsibility,[914] and it was not exaggerating the significance of his testimony. What one can learn only from a comprehensive review of the

[909] *Id.* at para. 235.

[910] Nallo testified that he conveyed Norman's instructions to the commanders on the front lines and information from the front lines back to Norman, through Fofana. He maintained that he also transported arms, ammunition, and other supplies to the front lines. CDF Transcript, Mar. 10, 2005, at 33.

[911] CDF Judgement, note 27, at para. 765.

[912] *Id.* at paras. 765(vii), 777.

[913] Like Nallo, prosecution witness TF2-008 also testified about the CDF's general command structure and maintained that Norman, Fofana, and Kondewa held ultimate authority over all important decisions, *see* CDF Transcript, Nov. 16, 2004, at 39, 46–47, 51, 76–77, but he did not testify about Fofana's superior–subordinate relationship with Nallo.

[914] CDF Judgement, note 27, at para. 279.

transcripts, however, is that Nallo's testimony was problematic in a number of key regards.

Beginning first with style, Nallo frequently jumped from topic to topic in his testimony and recounted events in such a nonlinear, circumlocutious fashion that the judges repeatedly complained that they could not understand him.[915] At one point, even a defense counsel interjected to help the judges figure out what Nallo was trying to convey.[916] At the same time, Nallo seemed to thoroughly enjoy testifying against the defendants. NGO courtroom monitors described Nallo's demeanor as "almost jovial,"[917] and when the Trial Chamber's Presiding Judge asked Nallo if he was alright, he responded that he was "very fine" and "very well" and reminded the Trial Chamber that he had been a "warrior."[918] In a similar vein, when the prosecution objected to a defense line of questioning that the prosecution described as composed of "spurious allegations," Nallo interjected to assure the courtroom that, despite the aggressive questioning, he was nonetheless "well composed."[919] Noticeable to me in addition was Nallo's seeming goal orientation. At times, he appeared driven to convey certain (incriminating) evidence even when it had not been asked for.[920] Furthermore, although it may be an ordinary feature of Sierra Leonean speech with which I am unfamiliar, Nallo's in-court references to Norman seemed to my Western ears excessively, almost condescendingly, deferential. For instance, Nallo referred to Norman almost exclusively by his title of "National Coordinator,"[921] and at times ceremoniously elaborated on that title by referring to him as "our most respectable National Coordinator"[922] or "my National Coordinator, head of the Kamajor movement, retired captain Hinga Norman."[923] His references to Norman consequently seemed designed simultaneously to ridicule Norman and to emphasize his leadership role in the CDF.

These impressionistic views about Nallo's demeanor and testimony are of little consequence. Other, substantive aspects of Nallo's testimony carry more weight, however. First off, Nallo had considerable reason to dislike Norman and

[915] *See, e.g.*, CDF Transcript, Mar. 10, 2005, at 18, 29; CDF Transcript, Mar. 11, 2005, at 21–22.

[916] *See* CDF Transcript, Mar. 10, 2005, at 30.

[917] Michele Staggs, U.C. Berkeley War Crimes Studies Center, Special Court Monitoring Program, Update No. 25, Mar. 11, 2005, at 3.

[918] CDF Transcript, Mar. 10, 2005, at 81.

[919] *See* CDF Transcript, Mar. 11, 2005, at 39.

[920] *See, e.g.*, *id.* at 32.

[921] *See, e.g.*, CDF Transcript, Mar. 10, 2005, at 32, 33, 35, 42, 70, 76, 82, 85, 88; CDF Transcript, Mar. 11, 2005, at 23, 30, 32, 33, 42, 92, 93; CDF Transcript, Mar. 14, 2005, at 42, 43, 44, 50, 54, 60; CDF Transcript, Mar. 15, 2005, at 2, 58.

[922] *See* CDF Transcript, Mar. 11, 2005, at 29.

[923] *See id.* at 95.

to desire revenge against him: After the CDF regained control of Sierra Leone from the AFRC junta, Norman dismissed Nallo from his position.[924] Nallo and Norman disputed the reason for the dismissal. Nallo testified that it resulted from his refusal to participate in Norman's corrupt activities,[925] whereas Norman's defense team alleged that it stemmed from Nallo's excessive looting in the Bo area.[926] Whatever the reason for the dismissal, it unquestionably gave rise to ill will between the men.

Second, Nallo's testimony diverges to some degree from the information he provided in his previous written statements. Nallo admitted on the stand that he did not initially tell investigators everything he knew because he was afraid that he himself would be prosecuted or that he would be subject to violent retaliation from the Kamajors.[927] It is not surprising, then, that defense counsel brought to light a few inconsistencies.[928] Most troubling was an omission regarding Defendant Kondewa's involvement in the conflict. Although, in court, Nallo insisted that Kondewa had been a member of the War Council, his statement does not name Kondewa as a member of that body. This particular omission would not seem to be motivated by any fear of retaliation because Nallo fingered the other two defendants in this statement. Furthermore, the omission is all the more problematic because the list of War Council members that Nallo provided was meant to be exhaustive: During the interview, Nallo was specifically asked whether there were any other War Council members in addition to the eleven he had named, and he responded, "[n]o, there was nobody else."[929] Finally, the interview that was transcribed into the statement was audio recorded, rendering the statement far more reliable than most at the international tribunals. Despite all this, Nallo nonetheless steadfastly maintained on the stand that, whatever the statement might say, he had listed Kondewa as a member of the War Council.[930]

Although the issues that I have identified thus far may give us some cause for concern, I do not believe them to be particularly worrisome, at least not when compared to those that arise in the typical international witness testimony. True, Nallo had an incentive to provide incriminating evidence against Norman, but so do most prosecution witnesses, and defense witnesses are motivated by their own incentives. Granted, there were some inconsistencies between Nallo's in-court testimony and his previous written statements, but

[924] *See id.* at 30.
[925] *See id.* at 64.
[926] *See id.* at 67; *see also id.* at 63.
[927] *See id.* at 33–34.
[928] *See, e.g.*, CDF Transcript, Mar. 15, 2005, at 8–9.
[929] *Id.* at 18.
[930] *Id.* at 13–19.

they were less noteworthy than many of the inconsistencies that I have brought to light in the preceding pages. As it happened, Nallo's testimony did feature serious problems, but those came to light only when the defense presented its witnesses.

Norman, for one, disputed virtually every aspect of Nallo's testimony. Beginning with the most basic issue, Norman even disputed Nallo's claim that he was Deputy Director of Operations. Norman maintained that Nallo had held no official position in the CDF but instead had been hired by a man in charge of operations to assist him in the field. Furthermore, although Nallo testified that he had taken many of his instructions from Norman, Norman denied ever giving Nallo any instructions.[931] More particularly, Norman denied making each and every public and private statement that Nallo attributed to him. Describing them as Nallo's "wild allegations, and imaginations of his own fiction," Norman "categorically" denied ordering murders, house burnings, and looting.[932]

Now, defendants commonly deny incriminating testimony, so the Trial Chamber might have been justified in according Norman's denials little weight. But in addition to Norman, several defense witnesses – who were unquestionably less self-interested than Norman – also contradicted key aspects of Nallo's account. I have summarily described some of these incidents earlier but will provide more detail here. Nallo, for instance, testified that he had witnessed Norman, Fofana, and Kondewa kill a Kamajor named Mustapha Fallon, eat some of his body parts, burn Fallon's corpse, and use the ashes for initiations into the Kamajor society.[933] The defense, however, called Fallon's brother to the stand, and he testified that he witnessed his brother's murder but that it was committed by AFRC forces, not the defendants.[934] In another portion of his testimony, Nallo alleged that, on the orders of Norman and Fofana, he traveled to Baoma on the day of the Baoma trade fair. Once there, Nallo testified, he joined Kamajor Junisa Conneh, and the two men killed a rebel.[935] Defense counsel brought Conneh to the stand, however, and he denied, first, that he committed a murder with Nallo, second, that he participated in any operation

[931] CDF Transcript, Jan. 31, 2006, at 32–33, 38–39.

[932] *Id.* at 39–42.

[933] CDF Transcript, Mar. 10, 2005, at 55–57.

[934] CDF Transcript, Sept. 27, 2006, at 30–31. Other witnesses likewise contradicted Nallo's testimony. Defense witness M.T. Collier said that the murder never took place, arguing that, as town elder, he surely would have heard about such an incident had it happened. CDF Transcript, Feb. 17, 2006, at 21–24. Haroun Aruna went so far as to injudiciously assert that the murder and other similar incidents never happened at any time. Alison Thompson, U.C. Berkeley War Crimes Studies Center, Special Court Monitoring Program, Update No. 76, May 19, 2006, at 2–3.

[935] CDF Transcript, Mar. 10, 2005, at 53–54.

with Nallo, and finally, that there even was a trade fair in Baoma.[936] Nallo also testified that he went on a mission to Dodo village with one Billo Conteh.[937] Conteh, however, was brought to the stand and contradicted Nallo's account by denying that he went on that mission – or any other – with Nallo.[938]

The contradictory testimony just described made fact-finding difficult for the Trial Chamber, but the Trial Chamber could have reasonably concluded that the defense witnesses were lying when they denied committing crimes with Nallo. Not so, however, for defense witness Joseph Lansana, who also contradicted one of Nallo's accounts. Nallo testified that after receiving instructions from Norman to eliminate "infiltrators," he and others had traveled to Sorgia Village and, once there, had tied up and tortured one Joseph Lansana, who was said to be a rebel. Nallo recounted in particular that he and another Kamajor cut off Lansana's ear, dripped burning plastic on him, and killed his mother.[939] Nallo acknowledged that he and the other Kamajor had not killed Lansana, and he informed the Court that "if you go to Sorgia village you would find him there."[940] Defense counsel did just that, much to the detriment of Nallo's credibility. Brought to the stand, Lansana testified, first, that his mother had been killed years before the date of Nallo's account. More importantly, Lansana denied that the Kamajors had mistreated him in any way. To prove his point, Lansana dramatically displayed for the court his two intact ears.[941]

Thus, even if the testimony of Fallon, Conneh, and Conteh were not enough to call Nallo's testimony into question, the two-eared Lansana conclusively proved Nallo either to have perjured himself or to have been grossly mistaken about a significant matter. The Trial Chamber did recognize some of the problems with Nallo's testimony. For instance, the Trial Chamber did acknowledge that Nallo occasionally "appeared equivocal or exaggerated in his response to questions," and the Trial Chamber consequently rejected those portions of his evidence.[942] It also rejected Nallo's claims about the crimes allegedly involving Lansana, Conneh, and Conteh "for reasons of reliability."[943] The Trial Chamber noted as an example of these "reasons of reliability" that Lansana's testimony *about his mother's death* engendered in the Trial Chamber "[d]oubts as to Nallo's accurate recollection" about this and other incidents.[944] The Trial

[936] CDF Transcript, Sept. 28, 2006, at 10–17.
[937] CDF Transcript, Mar. 10, 2005, at 45–46.
[938] CDF Transcript, Sept. 28, 2006, at 41–42, 45.
[939] CDF Transcript, Mar. 10, 2005, at 45–49.
[940] *Id.* at 48.
[941] CDF Transcript, Sept. 28, 2006, at 62–64.
[942] CDF Judgement, note 27, at para. 280.
[943] *Id.* at para. 281.
[944] *Id.*

Chamber failed to explain why its doubts would center on "Nallo's accurate recollection" rather than Nallo's willingness to testify truthfully. It likewise failed to explain why, despite its concerns about Nallo's recollection, it chose to believe his account of Fallon's death rather than the contradictory account provided by Fallon's brother.[945] Finally, and most importantly, the Trial Chamber failed to explain why it would see fit to rely – as the sole basis for conviction – on certain claims appearing in a witness's testimony when other claims in that testimony had been shown to be grossly inaccurate. In other words, the Trial Chamber did not explain why, if it knew that Nallo had lied (or at the least had been wildly mistaken) about some events, it would consider his testimony on other points a reliable basis for conviction. The Trial Chamber indeed mentioned none of these difficulties but rather lauded Nallo for his "frank and public admission of his personal role in the war" and for testifying "without hesitation, unambiguously, and, ... through a genuine desire that the truth be known."[946] Sierra Leonean Judge Thompson went so far as to commend Nallo for coming to testify "in order to ensure that there is ... lasting peace in this country."[947]

7.B.iv. *Crimes Committed in the Bo District*

The Trial Chamber next convicted Fofana on a command responsibility theory for the murders, cruel treatment, and collective punishments that occurred during the Kamajors' attacks on Bo. The evidence supporting these convictions is virtually the same as the evidence supporting Fofana's convictions for the crimes in Koribondo. As with Koribondo, it is impossible to assess the evidence supporting the Trial Chamber's conclusion that Fofana knew or had reason to know that crimes would be committed in Bo because virtually all of the testimony on that point was given in closed sessions. To find the first element of command responsibility – that a superior–subordinate relationship existed between Fofana and Nallo – the Trial Chamber again relied exclusively on Nallo's testimony.[948]

7.B.v. *Crimes Committed in the Bonthe District*

The Trial Chamber convicted Kondewa on a command responsibility theory for the crimes that took place in the Bonthe District. With respect to

[945] The Trial Chamber deemed Fallon's brother "not ... a credible witness" but gave no reason for that finding. My review of Fallon's testimony reveals nothing that would explain the Trial Chamber's conclusion.

[946] CDF Judgement, note 27, at para. 280.

[947] CDF Transcript, Mar. 15, 2005, at 70–71.

[948] However, the Trial Chamber did apparently have the benefit of TF2-017's testimony – which was given in closed session – to find that Nallo commanded the Bo attacks.

the first element necessary to prove command responsibility liability, the Trial Chamber found that there existed a superior–subordinate relationship between Kondewa and CDF commanders Morie Jusu Kamara, Julius Squire, and Kamajor Baigeh.[949] The witnesses that the Trial Chamber relied on to support this finding certainly appeared more reliable than Nallo. The problem here is that none of them testified directly about the superior–subordinate relationship. Rather, the Trial Chamber seems to have inferred the relationship from bits and pieces of witness testimony.

The Trial Chamber appeared to rely on three facts to support its finding of a superior–subordinate relationship. First, it found that "Kondewa had exercised effective control over Kamajors in Bonthe District since before the establishment of [CDF Headquarters] Base Zero, as early as August 1997."[950] For this finding, the Trial Chamber relied on the testimony of Father John Emmanuel William Garrick. Garrick testified that, after Kamajors mistreated some civilians in August 1997, a civilian delegation from the Bonthe District traveled to Tihun Sogbini to meet with Kondewa – whom Garrick described as the "supreme head of the Kamajors"[951] – and to appeal to him to prevent further Kamajor harassment of civilians. Garrick's account of his observations during this visit led the Trial Chamber to conclude that Kondewa "had authority and power to issue oral and written directives to the Kamajors in that area, order investigations for misconduct and hold court hearings."[952] Although my review of Garrick's testimony reveals no serious problems, I am not convinced that the testimony is relevant to the question at issue because the events Garrick recounted occurred six months before the crimes for which Kondewa was convicted. Given the rapid developments and continually shifting alliances that characterized the Sierra Leonean conflict, Father Garrick's account of Kondewa's authority in August 1997 may not be especially probative of Kondewa's authority over the commanders of the Bonthe attack, which took place in February 1998.

The second fact that the Trial Chamber invoked pertained to the assistance that Kondewa provided to one Lahai Kndokoi Koroma, a Chiefdom Speaker who had been accused of being a junta collaborator. According both to Father Garrick and witness TF2-071, the Kamajors had initially mistreated Koroma but had then sought Kondewa's advice on Koroma's ultimate fate. These witnesses testified that Kondewa came to Bonthe and spirited Koroma away. According to the Trial Chamber, that action proved that "only Kondewa had authority

949 CDF Judgement, note 27, at paras. 868–871.
950 *Id.* at para. 869.
951 CDF Transcript, Nov. 10, 2004, at 11.
952 CDF Judgement, note 27, at para. 869.

to release Lahai Koroma."[953] The problem with that reasoning is that the Trial Chamber failed to mention the events that preceded Kondewa's rescue of Koroma, which undercut the notion that Kondewa was in a superior–subordinate relationship with Kamajor commanders in Bonthe. In particular, prior to rescuing Koroma, Kondewa had assured a civilian delegation that the Kamajors would not enter Bonthe at all. Despite these assurances, Kamajors did enter Bonthe, and they committed crimes there. When Kondewa came to Bonthe to rescue Koroma, he apologized to the people of Bonthe for the Kamajors' actions and told them that he had not "allowed his men to enter Bonthe" but that they had failed to heed his advice.[954] The Trial Chamber had previously defined a superior as "someone who possesses the power or authority in either a *de jure* or *de facto* capacity to prevent the commission of a crime by a subordinate or to punish the offender of the crime after the crime has been committed." The Trial Chamber had noted moreover that it is "this power or authority of the superior to control the actions of his subordinates which forms the basis for the superior–subordinate relationship."[955] A man whose "subordinates" launch an attack in contravention of his instructions would not seem to be a superior under the Trial Chamber's definition of the term.

As final support for its finding of a superior–subordinate relationship, the Trial Chamber pointed to an incident involving Commander Morie Jusu Kamara and his second-in-command Julius Squire during which the men were presented with a letter from Sierra Leone's Attorney General, Solomon Berewa. The letter asked CDF members not to inflict punishment on suspected AFRC collaborators but to leave such sanctions to appropriate law enforcement agencies. Both Father Garrick and witness TF2-071 testified about obtaining and disseminating the letter, but it was only TF2-071 who testified that, when the letter was presented to Kamara and Squire, they "refused to listen to the letter," saying that if the letter had come from Norman or Kondewa, then they would have paid attention to it.[956] Garrick related nothing of the kind, however, and instead testified that the situation in Bonthe "dramatically improved" after the Kamajors received the letter.[957]

7.B.vi. *Crimes Committed at Talia*

The Trial Chamber convicted Kondewa of murder as a war crime for his alleged killing of a Talia town commander who had had some affiliation with

[953] *Id.* at para. 553.
[954] *Id.*
[955] *Id.* at para. 236.
[956] CDF Transcript, Nov. 11, 2004, at 90.
[957] *Id.* at 43.

the rebels.[958] This conviction, like most of the others previously discussed, was based on the testimony of just one witness – TF2-096 – who claimed to have seen the murder. Despite the fact that witness TF2-096 had had several years of schooling,[959] her testimony was *extremely* difficult to understand even on direct examination (when witnesses tend to be clearer). The judges complained of having "difficulty following the logic of [the witness's] evidence,"[960] and they, as well as the lawyers, had to repeatedly ask the witness to clarify her testimony.[961] It took numerous questions to elicit from the witness clear answers to such relatively simple questions as (1) who was the witness referring to as being angry when she testified that she had been told that "those guys were angry";[962] (2) how much time had elapsed between the time the rebels brought the witness to Talia and the time the Kamajors came;[963] and (3) where was the witness when Jahman said he was going to report the incident to Kondewa.[964] In addition, the witness disavowed considerable portions of her early statements. The prosecution recognized before trial that the witness would testify inconsistently with her statement, so it subsequently obtained from her a revised statement that would be in keeping with her in-court testimony.[965] The Trial Chamber's judgment, however, makes no reference to any of these issues.

7.B.vii. *Crimes Committed in the Moyamba District*

The Trial Chamber found that the Kamajors committed a series of crimes in the Moyamba District; and, for some of these crimes, the Trial Chamber based its findings only on hearsay evidence. The Trial Chamber, for instance, found that Kamajors stole the vehicles of Nbada Fofana and Mrs. Gorvie, solely on the basis of the testimony of witness TF2-073, who stated that Mr. Fofana and Mrs. Gorvie had told him of these events.[966] The Trial Chamber did not convict the defendants of these crimes because it determined either that they were not charged in the indictment, they fell outside the time frame of the indictment, or there was no indication that the defendants were involved in

[958] CDF Judgement, note 27, at paras. 622–623, 934–937.
[959] CDF Transcript, Nov. 8, 2004, at 3.
[960] *Id.* at 9. *See also id.* at 31–32 (Judge Boutet reporting that he was unable to understand the witness's testimony).
[961] *Id.* at 6.
[962] *Id.* at 10.
[963] *Id.* at 9–10.
[964] *Id.* at 33.
[965] *Id.* at 44.
[966] *See* CDF Judgement, note 27, at paras. 642–643.

the crimes.[967] But even to have found that the crimes took place solely on the basis of one witness's hearsay evidence is indicative of the Trial Chamber's less-than-rigorous approach to evidentiary matters.

The Trial Chamber did convict Kondewa of one act of pillage in Moyamba on a command responsibility theory: Witness TF2-073 testified that Kamajors stole his Mercedes Benz and that he later saw Kondewa in the backseat of the car.[968] According to TF2-073, the Kamajors who were engaged in looting in Moyamba had identified themselves as Kondewa's Kamajors;[969] thus, the Trial Chamber concluded that "the looting was done by the Kamajors who operated under the direct orders of Kondewa" and that "Kondewa's knowledge that his subordinates committed crimes of pillage can be established on the basis that the looted car was then given to him to be driven around."[970] Although the Trial Chamber's conclusions are reasonable under the circumstances, they are notable again for being based on the testimony of only one witness. Furthermore, the Trial Chamber failed to report on an aspect of TF2-073's testimony that undercut its finding of command responsibility. TF2-073 testified that he found it surprising the Kamajors under Kondewa's command were looting because he himself had heard Kondewa warn a parade of Kamajor recruits not to harass and loot civilians, telling them that, if they did so, they would "perish with the war."[971] That the Kamajors did engage in looting and harassment in contravention of Kondewa's instructions is an indication that Kondewa did not have effective control over them.

7.B.viii. *The Enlistment or Use of Child Soldiers*

The Trial Chamber heard a great deal of testimony regarding the CDF's use of child soldiers. It heard from three witnesses who themselves had been child soldiers; they testified about the fighting in which they had been engaged, and they testified about the activities of other child soldiers.[972] The Trial Chamber also heard from witnesses who saw children fighting in CDF forces.[973] Despite this plethora of testimony regarding the CDF's use of child combatants, however, the Trial Chamber heard very little testimony that connected the enlistment or use of those children to particular acts of Fofana and Kondewa. Indeed,

[967] *See id.* para. 956.
[968] *See id.* paras. 645–648, 951.
[969] CDF Transcript, Mar. 2, 2005, at 34.
[970] CDF Judgement, note 27, at para. 954.
[971] CDF Transcript, Mar. 2, 2005, at 37; CDF Transcript, Mar. 3, 2005, at 26.
[972] These are witnesses TF2-140, who testified on September 14, 2004; TF2-021, who testified on November 2–4, 2004; and TF2-004, who testified on November 9, 2004.
[973] *See* CDF Judgement, note 27, at para. 688.

the Trial Chamber received no evidence linking the enlistment or use of child soldiers to Fofana, so it acquitted him of all such charges.

The Trial Chamber did convict Kondewa, however, and it did so on the basis of one witness's testimony – TF2-021. Witness TF2-021 testified that RUF rebels had abducted him when he was nine years old and that CDF forces had captured him when he was eleven. TF2-021 further testified that, soon after his capture by the CDF, Kondewa had initiated him and about twenty other young boys into the Kamajor Society, telling them that the initiation process would make them powerful for fighting. When he was thirteen years old, TF2-021 attested, Kondewa initiated him into Kondewa's own group of Kamajors – the Avondo Society.[974] The Trial Chamber acknowledged that initiation into the Kamajor Society did not necessarily amount to enlistment in an armed force, but it relied on TF2-021's testimony about Kondewa's statement during TF2-021's first initiation – that the initiation would make the boys powerful for fighting – along with other details provided by TF2-021 – to conclude that TF2-021 and the others initiated at that time had in fact been enlisted for active military service.[975]

Unfortunately, TF2-021's testimony was problematic in numerous regards. Most importantly, his testimony was sharply inconsistent with the assertions he made in his previous statements. A few examples will suffice to show the quantity and severity of these inconsistencies. In his statement, TF2-021 said that when he and the other Kamajors had arrived in Kenema, "the policemen had already been killed." At trial, he said that he killed at least one of the police officers.[976] In his statement, he said that no one was forced to join the Kamajors; at trial, he testified that he and others were forced to join.[977] In his statement, TF2-021 said that rebels had captured him when he was five years old; at trial he said that he had been nine years old when captured by rebels.[978] In his statement, he said that the RUF had given him a gun; at trial, he denied that he had been given a gun.[979] In his statement he said that SAJ Musa had told a man named Savage not to shoot an old woman. At trial, he denied saying that and maintained that he never saw SAJ Musa.[980] This list is but a sampling. TF2-021's testimony is filled with many more such inconsistencies.[981] Indeed, the inconsistencies were so numerous and so substantial that, on a motion

[974] *Id.* at paras. 674–675, 682.
[975] *Id.* at paras. 968–970.
[976] CDF Transcript, Nov. 3, 2004, at 59.
[977] CDF Transcript, Nov. 4, 2004, at 13.
[978] CDF Transcript, Nov. 2, 2004, at 125–30.
[979] CDF Transcript, Nov. 3, 2004, at 53.
[980] *Id.* at 55.
[981] *See id.* at 54, 57; CDF Transcript, Nov. 4, 2004, at 4–5, 12.

from the defense, the Trial Chamber called as witnesses one of the investigators who had interviewed TF2-021 for one of his statements and an interpreter who translated a different interview. Both the interpreter and the investigator insisted that TF2-021 conveyed the information that appeared in his statements, and both attested that his statements were read back to him and that he accepted them to be true and correct before he put his thumbprint on them.[982] TF2-021, by contrast, insisted that he never said what had been attributed to him in the statements.[983]

TF2-021's testimony was also just plain wrong at times. For instance, he testified that he walked the distance between two towns in one and a half days. Although TF2-021 was not able to estimate the distance between the towns, defense counsel submitted a map showing that they stood 163 miles apart[984] – that is, far too great a distance to walk in one and a half days. In addition to these problems, defense counsel highlighted TF2-021's incentive to lie: TF2-021 received substantial financial support from the SCSL during the four months that he was in Freetown at the behest of the tribunal. He received $24 per week for the first few weeks, and his weekly payments soon rose to $39.[985] As already noted, the average weekly earnings in Sierra Leone stand at less than $4, so these were princely sums indeed. TF2-021 himself acknowledged that he received far more money from the SCSL than he would otherwise have earned.[986] Finally, TF2-021's credibility was impaired to some degree by his drug use. In his statement, he asserted that he could not remember all of his bad acts because he was frequently under the influence of drugs when he performed them.[987]

The Trial Chamber not only relied on TF2-021's testimony and not only relied on it as the exclusive evidence on which to base its conviction of Kondewa; the Trial Chamber did not even mention the foregoing problems. Its failure to mention the witness's inconsistencies is particularly troubling given the conflicting testimony on that subject from the witness and the SCSL staff who took his statements. Indeed, because the SCSL investigator and interpreter insisted that witness TF2-021 made the representations appearing in his statement and witness TF2-021 insisted that he did not, then one of three scenarios must be true: Witness TF2-021 was lying at various points in his testimony or during his statement-taking; witness TF2-021 has an abysmal memory about the events in question; or SCSL investigators fabricated evidence out of whole cloth. None of

[982] CDF Transcript, Mar. 2, 2005, at 9–21; CDF Transcript, May 31, 2005, at 2–9.
[983] CDF Transcript, Nov. 3, 2004, at 53–55, 57–59.
[984] CDF Transcript, Nov. 4, 2004, at 17.
[985] CDF Transcript, Nov. 2, 2004, at 108–11.
[986] *Id.* at 111–12.
[987] CDF Transcript, Nov. 3, 2004, at 53.

these scenarios should inspire confidence in the Trial Chamber's conviction of Kondewa. But the Trial Chamber acknowledged neither the problems nor their troubling implications. Rather, it deemed TF2-021's testimony "pivotal" to its factual findings and observed that, although the events in question occurred when the witness "was very young, and his testimony comes many years after the events in question," the Trial Chamber nonetheless "found his testimony highly credible and largely reliable. Clearly," the Trial Chamber asserted, "the intensity of his experience has left him with an indelible recollection of the events in question."[988]

7.B.ix. *The Underlying Crimes*

As noted above, some of Kondewa's and Fofana's convictions were for directly participating in certain crimes, and others were on a command responsibility theory. For each of the regions delineated above, then, the Trial Chamber made factual findings about the CDF crimes that occurred in that region. The Trial Chamber held the defendants criminally responsible for more than fifty crimes, so I will not carefully examine the quality of the eyewitness testimony supporting each of those factual findings. I will note, however, that for virtually every one of those findings, the Trial Chamber relied on the testimony of just one witness.[989] Sometimes, the Trial Chamber cited more than one witness to support a finding about a crime, but typically the second witness testified about some matter tangential to the commission of the crime[990] or did not himself witness the crime but testified only about what he had heard from others.[991] Not only were virtually all of the Trial Chamber's factual findings based on the testimony of just one witness, but many of the crimes were attested to by the

[988] CDF Judgement, note 27, at para. 282.

[989] The only crimes that were supported by a more substantial quantity of witness testimony concerned the burning of houses in Koribondo. *See* CDF Judgement, note 27, at para. 427 & nn. 824–826, para. 428, & nn. 827–830. Even with respect to the Koribondo house burnings, though, most of the witnesses did not see CDF forces set fire to the houses. They saw only that the houses were on fire. *See, e.g.*, CDF Transcript, June 15, 2004, at 32, 49; CDF Transcript, June 16, 2004, at 14; CDF Transcript, June 17, 2004, at 37; CDF Transcript, Sept. 14, 2004, at 81–82.

[990] In a section of the judgment describing the looting of various locations in Bonthe Town, for instance, the Trial Chamber cited the testimony of witness TF2-071 for the following proposition appearing in the judgment: "At the Fisheries Department Building, Father Garrick pleaded with a young Kamajor called Commander Rambo Conteh to have his Kamajors leave things intact. Rambo answered that they only wanted to take the fuel and then they would leave." TF2-071 testified only that the Kamajors came to Bonthe Town and perhaps that they engaged in some general looting. *See* CDF Transcript, Nov. 11, 2004, at 77 (testimony that the Trial Chamber cited).

[991] *See, e.g.*, CDF Transcript, June 15, 2004, at 33; CDF Transcript, Nov. 9, 2004, at 24–26, 46; CDF Transcript, Nov. 11, 2004, at 75–76; CDF Transcript, Mar. 1, 2005, at 89.

same witness. So, for instance, of the eight crimes that the Trial Chamber found to have been committed in Bo District, witness TF2-017 testified about four of them and witness TF2-001 testified about the other four. Similarly, the thirteen crimes found to have been committed in Bonthe District were based on the testimony of five witnesses. Thus, to the extent that one witness's testimony is problematic, then it calls into question the existence of not one, but several crimes.

7.B.x. *Summary*

By providing an in-depth examination of the *CDF* judgment, this section has sought to concretize the more general discussion that has preceded it, both in this chapter and in previous chapters. It is one thing to read that many convictions are based on the testimony of only one witness, that many witnesses have difficulty providing a minimally detailed and consistent account of the events they witnessed, and that, in most instances, the Trial Chambers do not much seem to care. It is another thing, I believe, to see how those factors can coalesce in a real case, involving real defendants who are facing real jail time. By highlighting the meager quantity of evidence supporting many *CDF* charges and its frequently problematic character, I do not mean to suggest that the *CDF* defendants were innocent of the charges for which they were convicted. Quite the contrary, as I explain in the following chapters, I believe that most of the international criminal convictions are justified but on grounds different from those invoked in the Trial Chambers' judgments. I do suggest here, however, that the Trial Chambers' willingness to overlook the problematic features of witness testimony in *CDF* and other cases is key to their decisions to convict on many of the charges. That is, I believe that the Trial Chambers' attitude toward testimonial deficiencies is a crucial aspect of its determination of reasonable doubt, an issue that I turn to next.

7.C. SUMMARY AND STATISTICS: INTERNATIONAL CRIMINAL TRIALS AND THE CULTURE OF CONVICTION

Given the vague, inconsistent testimony that is the standard fare at the international tribunals, the high incidence of perjury, and the difficulty in verifying even the most basic facts, one might have thought before reading this chapter that Trial Chambers would rarely be able to conclude that the prosecution had proven its allegations beyond a reasonable doubt. The foregoing sections of this chapter show, however, that the Trial Chambers take a cavalier attitude toward the fact-finding impediments just described. They invoke educational or experiential deficiencies to explain the failure of many witnesses to provide relevant details or to answer certain questions, and, because they apparently consider it unfair to hold such deficiencies against the witnesses, the Trial Chambers overlook the potential impact of vague and undetailed testimony on the defendant's ability to present a defense. When it comes to inconsistencies between witnesses' testimony and their previous statements, the Trial Chambers explain these away as products of the passage of time, the frailty of memory, and errors introduced by investigators and interpreters. Inconsistencies between different witness testimonies are assumed to stem from lapses due to the passage of time,[992] from the witnesses' different vantage points,[993] from the witnesses' different levels of familiarity with the locations in question, or from the danger and stress inherent in the events that were witnessed.[994] As a general matter, then, the Trial Chambers give the prosecution witnesses the benefit of the doubt and explain away many problematic features of their testimony on the basis of innocent factors that are beyond the witnesses' control. Indeed, even when it has been proven that a witness lied or was mistaken about one matter, some Trial Chambers nonetheless credit their testimony about other matters. Consequently, although we might have expected that the prevalence and severity of testimonial deficiencies during international criminal trials would lead Trial Chambers to acquit a substantial proportion of defendants, in fact, quite the opposite is true: The international tribunals convict the vast majority of defendants who come before them of at least one of the crimes for which they are charged.

The SCSL is running a 100 percent conviction rate at present, having convicted all eight of the defendants whose cases have thus far been decided. The Special Panels is not far behind with a 97 percent conviction rate. The Special Panels acquitted a paltry three defendants of the eighty-seven whom it tried,[995] and even those figures understate the true acquittal rate because, in two of the three acquittals, prosecutors themselves recognized that there was insufficient evidence on which to base a conviction and sought to withdraw the indictments. In the *Aparicio Guterres* case, prosecutors were so keenly aware that they had no evidence against the defendant that they sought to withdraw the indictment *before* trial.[996] The Panel refused to permit the withdrawal, so the case went to trial, but because the prosecutor presented no inculpatory evidence against the defendant, the Panel had no choice but to acquit him. In the *Florindo Morreira* case, prosecution testimony was likewise so problematic

992 Muhimana Judgement, note 363, at para. 65; Gacumbitsi Judgement, note 364, at para. 83.
993 Gacumbitsi Judgement, note 364, at paras. 83, 159.
994 Kajelijeli Judgement, note 303, at para. 595.
995 U.N. Security Council, *End of Mandate Report of the Secretary-General on the United Nations Mission of Support in East Timor*, para. 20 U.N. Doc. S/2005/310 (May 12, 2005).
996 Guterres Judgement, note 478, at 1.

that the prosecution itself acknowledged that it was not sufficient to support a conviction, and it moved to withdraw the indictment during trial.[997] The last acquittal – in the *Carlos Ena* case – did feature some testimony against the defendant, but the Panel reasonably concluded that it was the product of a mistaken identity.[998] In other words, in only one case out of eighty-seven did the Panels acquit a defendant in a contested trial.

The ICTR's conviction rate – at 85 percent – is lower than the other two tribunals. Three of the six ICTR acquittals featured little or no credible evidence, so those acquittals were all but assured. The acquittals in the other three cases were more surprising and seemed to stem less from real differences in the quality and quantity of the testimony presented, as compared with the testimony in cases that resulted in convictions, than from the Trial Chamber's attitude toward the quality and quantity of that evidence. An examination of these cases is undertaken in Chapter 8 as a part of that chapter's consideration of the motivations underlying the Trial Chambers' factual determinations.

Suffice it to say at this point that the Trial Chambers' lackadaisical attitude toward testimonial deficiencies appears to reflect a proconviction bias that ultimately results in the Tribunals' exceptionally high conviction rates. Now, let me be clear that when I maintain that the Tribunals' fact-finding embodies a proconviction bias, I am not suggesting that the Trial Chambers are convicting innocent defendants. Far from it, as I will discuss in subsequent chapters. What I am suggesting, however, is that the Trial Chambers' cavalier attitude toward fact-finding impediments is inconsistent with the beyond-a-reasonable-doubt standard of proof as that standard is traditionally understood. As I have noted, many cases of problematic testimony feature uncertain causes. Circuitous answers could reflect culturally influenced patterns of speech or efforts to evade. Inconsistencies could signify an investigator's error or a witness's desire to frame the defendant. Because there do exist persuasive reasons in most instances for overlooking discrepancies and explaining them and other problematic features of witness testimony on the basis of "innocent" explanations, the Trial Chambers' inclination to do so would be unproblematic *if* they were deciding cases on a preponderance of the evidence standard; that is, if they had only to decide which account of events – the prosecution's or the defense's – was more likely than not to be the accurate one. The Trial Chambers are not so charged, however. They are required to acquit the defendant unless the prosecution has proven its allegations *beyond a reasonable doubt*.[999]

[997] Prosecution v. Morreira, Case No. 29/2003, Judgement, at 2 (May 19, 2004).

[998] Ena Judgement, note 564, at 11–15.

[999] *See* ICTR RPE, note 607, Rule 87; SCSL RPE, note 607, Rule 87. The Special Panels' procedural rules fail to specify a standard of proof, but the Panels apply a beyond-a-reasonable-doubt-standard. *See, e.g.*, Prosecutor v. Julio Fernandez, Case No. 2/2000, Judgement, at 9

The question, then, is not whether a particular testimonial deficiency can be plausibly explained away: Most of them can. The question is rather whether the existence of that deficiency in testimony that is sharply contested by defense witnesses and cannot be objectively informed by documentary or forensic evidence should be considered to give rise to a reasonable doubt. Considered in isolation, I believe that the answer to that question in most cases is yes. The Trial Chambers do not consider the question in isolation, however, and that fact goes some way toward explaining why the Trial Chambers so rarely reach that answer. Chapter 8 turns to that question in more detail and in the process constructs a fact-finding model that I believe more accurately reflects the process in which the Trial Chambers are actually engaged.

(Feb. 27, 2001); Joseph Leki Judgement, note 402, at 10; Prosecutor v. Joni Marquez et al., Case No. 9/2000, Judgement, para. 976, (Dec. 11, 2001); Carlos Soares Judgement, note 402, at 10; Prosecutor v. Augusto Asameta Tavares, Case No. 02/2001, Judgement, para. 54 (Sept. 28, 2001); Prosecutor v. Jose Cardoso, Case No. 4c/2001, Judgement, para. 462 (Apr. 5, 2003); Dos Santos Laku Judgement, note 672, at 11–12.

8

Organizational Liability Revived

The Pro-Conviction Bias Explained

Chapter 7 reveals that Trial Chambers take a cavalier attitude toward the testimonial deficiencies described in earlier chapters. Although Trial Chambers do discredit witness testimony that is hopelessly vague or inconsistent, they ignore many severe testimonial deficiencies, they minimize the effect of others, and they explain away still others on the basis of innocent causes. In sum, Trial Chambers often seem content to base convictions on highly problematic witness testimony. As a result of these practices, the Trial Chambers under study fail to find reasonable doubt in some of the most doubtful instances and, as a consequence, convict just about every defendant who comes before them. Indeed, a close examination of tribunal judgments and the testimony on which those judgments are said to be based appears to reveal a troubling proconviction bias.

This chapter explores the factors that contribute to that ostensible proconviction bias. I begin in Section 8.A with a discussion of politics. International criminal tribunals are intensely political institutions. From the very fact of their creation to their budgets, their estimated life spans, the targets of their investigations, and the selection of defendants over which they gain custody, global politics plays a role. Political considerations rarely appear to govern the disposition of particular cases; but, as I discuss in Section 8.A, they do operate indirectly to bias the Trial Chambers in favor of conviction. In Section 8.B, I turn to the backgrounds of the judges and explore the ways in which they might contribute to the proconviction bias.

Although these two factors do some work in explaining the Trial Chambers' willingness to base convictions on questionable testimony, they go only so far. That willingness stems more fundamentally, I believe, from commonsense assessments of culpability that derive from the defendant's official position or membership in particular groups or organizations. This chapter suggests, indeed, that doctrines of organizational liability that seemed to be thoroughly discredited following the Nuremberg and Tokyo trials exert continuing influence over the factual determinations of the present-day international tribunals. These principles exert such a powerful influence, in fact, that they help to bridge the gap between the problematic testimony presented to the Trial Chambers and the convictions that the Trial Chambers almost invariably impose. The final section of this chapter, then, maintains in particular that international criminal fact-finding is not what it seems to be. Although the Trial Chambers appear to be evaluating whether a defendant performed X act at Y location on Z date and to be grounding their determination of that fact on the testimony of witnesses who say they saw the defendant do so, in fact the Trial Chambers make much broader and less precise assessments of the defendant's likely involvement in the atrocities. In doing so, this chapter argues, the Trial Chambers engage in a different method of fact-finding than they publicly acknowledge.

8.A. THE POLITICS OF ACQUITTALS

Former ICTR spokesperson Kingsley Moghalu has described international criminal tribunals as pursuing "political justice."[1000] Although "political justice" is a term that can bear different meanings in different contexts, it signifies at the most general level that political considerations influence key aspects of the tribunals' operations. First and foremost, it is politics that drives the very decision to create an international tribunal. It is no coincidence, for instance, that the international community saw fit to establish *ad hoc* tribunals to prosecute the crimes that have taken place in such small, globally unimportant states as Bosnia and Rwanda and not in international powerhouses such as Russia and China.[1001] Likewise, the jurisdictional parameters of these bodies are driven not by an apolitical assessment of how much "justice" is necessary to obtain optimal levels of deterrence, retribution, and reconciliation but largely by an evaluation of how much justice the international community is willing to pay for. When it turned out that the international community was not willing to pay for ICTY and ICTR trials that continued into the indefinite future, for instance, the next wave of *ad hoc* tribunals was created with much more

[1000] Kingsley Chiedu Moghalu, Rwanda's Genocide: The Politics of Global Justice 2 (2005).

[1001] I do not mean to suggest any equivalence in criminality. The magnitude and intensity of the Rwandan atrocities arguably have not been seen since the Holocaust. The point remains, however, that atrocities committed at the behest of powerful states will not be made the subject of international prosecutions.

limited jurisdictional mandates that were designed to ensure that the tribunals completed their work in a discrete, relatively brief period of time.

Crucial aspects of the tribunals' operations – including investigations and arrests – also are influenced by political considerations. For instance, when ICTR Prosecutor Carla del Ponte announced that her office would begin investigating the war crimes and crimes against humanity allegedly committed by soldiers of the current Rwandan government, Rwanda retaliated by preventing ICTR witnesses from traveling to Arusha. Trials stalled,[1002] Del Ponte was eventually removed from her position at least in part as a consequence,[1003] and Del Ponte's replacement abandoned all efforts to investigate the soldiers.[1004] Political considerations also were widely suspected of influencing the ICTY's decision not to investigate possible NATO crimes that took place during its bombing mission in Kosovo.[1005]

Once investigations are undertaken and result in indictments, political considerations also play a role in determining who in fact will be apprehended. Slobodan Milošević was sent to The Hague only after the United States threatened to withhold $500 million in United States and International Monetary Fund aid to Yugoslavia,[1006] and several high-ranking Rwandan offenders were arrested only after the United States offered a $5 million reward for information leading to their arrests.[1007] Conversely, after the Special Panels indicted the former Commander of the Indonesian military, General Wiranto, both East Timor and the United Nations sought to distance themselves from the indictment.[1008] East Timor was particularly disinclined to pursue justice against high-ranking Indonesian officials, apparently believing that the wiser course lay in pursuing friendship with Indonesia, not prosecutions. Thus, when a Special Panels judge issued an arrest warrant against Wiranto in May 2004, the Timorese government categorically opposed the move and refused to ask INTERPOL

[1002] Moghalu, note 1000, at 140; *ICTR/Prosecution – Synthesis: Prosecutors at the ICTR*, Hirondelle News Agency, Oct. 28, 2003, *available at* www.hirondellenews.com/content/view/43/310; *ICTR/Rusatira – General Rusatira's Release Heightens Tension Between Rwanda and the ICTR*, Hirondelle News Agency, Oct. 29, 2003.

[1003] Moghalu, note 1000, at 127, 136–37, 145; Florence Hartmann, Paix et Châtiment 273 (2007).

[1004] Moghalu, note 1000, at 149.

[1005] *See, e.g.*, Pierre Hazan, Justice in a Time of War: The True Story Behind the International Criminal Tribunal for the former Yugoslavia 131–39 (James Thomas Snyder trans., 2004).

[1006] Jack Goldsmith, *The Self-Defeating International Criminal Court*, 70 U. Chi. L. Rev. 89, 93 (2003). Diplomatic and political pressure were also instrumental in convincing Kenya to arrest seven ICTR indictees. The biggest fish – Felicien Kabuga – remains at large, however, allegedly still residing in Kenya. Moghalu, note 1000, at 166–74.

[1007] Thierry Cruvellier, *Angolan Capture*, Int'l Just. Trib., Aug. 13, 2002.

[1008] Othman, note 35, at 126.

to issue an international arrest warrant. East Timor's opposition effectively ended the Special Panels' efforts to impose accountability on Wiranto and other high-level Indonesian offenders.[1009]

The decisions I have just described concern macroelements of the tribunals' operations. Rarely do political considerations overtly influence decisions in particular cases once the cases are under consideration, though that too does occasionally occur. In 1999, for instance, the ICTR Appeals Chamber dismissed with prejudice the indictment of Jean-Bosco Barayagwiza and ordered him released after determining that the prosecution had violated Barayagwiza's right to be brought promptly before a judge following arrest.[1010] Barayagwiza was considered a "kingpin in the planning and execution of the genocide,"[1011] and the decision to free him so outraged Rwanda that it suspended all dealings with the ICTR and refused to issue a visa to the tribunal's chief prosecutor, Carla Del Ponte.[1012] When asking the Appeals Chamber to reconsider its decision, Del Ponte acknowledged Rwanda's power over the tribunal; she observed: "If I don't get cooperation from Rwanda, ... I can first open the door at the detention center and set them all free and then second I can close the door to my office because without them I cannot do anything at all."[1013] Following Del Ponte's plea, the Appeals Chamber reinstated Barayagwiza's indictment, and relations between the ICTR and Rwanda returned to normal.[1014]

1009 *See* JSMP Press Release, *The Wiranto Warrant Political Interference in the Serious Crimes Process* June 22, 2004, *available at* http://www.jsmp.minihub.org/News/2004/June/22jun04_jsmp_wirantowarrant_eng.htm.

1010 Prosecutor v. Barayagwiza, Case No. ICTR-97-17-AR72, Decision (Nov. 3, 1999).

1011 Moghalu, note 1000, at 102.

1012 Franck Petit, *Cameroonian Intrigues*, Int'l Just. Trib., Mar. 5, 2001; *ICTR/Prosecution – Synthesis: Prosecutors at the ICTR*, Hirondelle News Agency, Oct. 28, 2003.

1013 J. Coll Metcalf, *An Interview with United Nations' Chief War Crimes Prosecutor, Carla del Ponte*, Internews, Feb. 15, 2000.

1014 Prosecutor v. Barayagwiza, Case No. ICTR-97-17-AR72, Decision on Prosecutor's Request for Review or Reconsideration (Mar. 31, 2000). For an insider's account of the crisis, see Moghalu, note 1000, at 101–23; *see also* Megan Fairlie, *The Marriage of Common and Continental Law at the ICTY and Its Progeny*, 4 Int'l Crim. L. Rev. 243, 295 (2004). The ostensible basis for the Appeals Chambers' decision to reinstate the indictment was "new facts" that the prosecution brought to light, but few would maintain that Rwanda's hardball tactics did not influence the Appeals Chamber's decision.

The ICTR's *Bagaragaza* case and the ICTY's *Todorović* case also may have been influenced by political factors, though the evidence for this proposition is murkier. Bagaragaza and the ICTR prosecution entered into an agreement in which Bagaragaza promised to provide an extensive statement in which he would incriminate himself and other high-level Rwandan officials while the prosecution promised to seek the transfer of Bagaragaza's case to a national court. Prosecutor v. Bagaragaza, Case No. ICTR-2005–86-R11*bis*, Decision on the Prosecution Motion for Referral to the Kingdom of Norway, para. 2 (May 19, 2006). True to their word, prosecutors requested that the Trial Chamber transfer Bagaragaza's case to the courts of Norway. *Id.* at para. 3. Because Norwegian courts do not have jurisdiction over genocide,

Such overt political interference in the resolution of particular cases is unusual, but I do believe that political considerations indirectly influence the Trial Chambers' general approach to fact-finding in the following way: International judges at some level recognize that if they were to carefully scrutinize testimonial deficiencies and honestly acknowledge the capacity of these deficiencies to undermine the prosecution's case, then they would be forced to acquit a far greater proportion of defendants. Acquittals are very costly to the international tribunals for reasons I will explain below, and consequently they would undermine the value and viability of international trials as a centerpiece response to mass atrocities. International judges are, by and large, committed

Bagaragaza was to be prosecuted there on charges of domestic homicide, for which the maximum sentence is twenty-one years. *Id.* at para. 9. Although prosecutors did not say so, one has to assume that the lenient maximum sentence that Norwegian courts could have imposed on Bagaragaza and Norway's practice of releasing prisoners after they have served only half of their sentences, Penrose, note 9, at 382 n.225, made Norway a particularly attractive trial location for prosecutors seeking to induce Bagaragaza to provide them with information. Norway, indeed, was such an attractive trial location that the government of Rwanda vehemently opposed Bagaragaza's transfer there. *Tribunal Throws out Motion to Have Bagaragaza's Transfer to Norway*, HIRONDELLE NEWS AGENCY, May 23, 2006. Whether influenced by Rwanda's opposition or not, the Trial Chamber denied the prosecution's request for transfer on the ground that because Norwegian courts do not have jurisdiction over the crimes for which Bagaragaza was charged, "Bagaragaza's alleged criminal acts cannot be given their full legal qualification." Prosecutor v. Bagaragaza, Case No. ICTR-2005–86-R11*bis*, Decision on the Prosecution Motion for Referral to the Kingdom of Norway, para. 16 (May 19, 2006).

Political considerations arguably entered the ICTY's *Todorović* case as a consequence of his arrest. Todorović had been captured by four bounty hunters while in his home in the Federal Republic of Yugoslavia. *See* Major Christopher M. Supernor, *International Bounty Hunters for War Criminals: Privatizing the Enforcement of Justice*, 50 A.F. L. REV. 215, 217 n.11 (2001); Marlise Simons, *War Crimes Court Takes It Easy on a Cooperative Bosnian Serb*, N.Y. TIMES, Aug. 1, 2001, at A4. He was allegedly dealt a heavy blow to the head, while being transported to Bosnia-Herzegovina and into the hands of the NATO forces deployed there. *See* Susan Lamb, *Illegal Arrest and the Jurisdiction of the ICTY*, *in* ESSAYS ON ICTY PROCEDURE AND EVIDENCE IN HONOUR OF GABRIELLE KIRK MCDONALD 27, 35 n.33 (Richard May et al. eds., 2001). Upon his arrival at the ICTY, Todorović challenged his arrest and asked the Trial Chamber to order "NATO/SFOR or [] other military and security forces operating in Bosnia to provide documents and witnesses regarding Todorović's detention" and transfer to Bosnia. Sean D. Murphy ed., *Contemporary Practice of the United States Relating to International Law*, 95 AM. J. INT'L L. 387, 401 (2001). The Trial Chamber granted Todorović's motion, over SFOR's vehement objections, and ordered SFOR and the States participating in SFOR to provide Todorović a passel of documents and other forms of information. Prosecutor v. Simić, Case No. IT-95–9-PT, Decision on Motion for Judicial Assistance to Be Provided by SFOR and Others (Oct. 18, 2000). NATO, the United States, and several other NATO States appealed, and while the case was pending before the Appeals Chamber, Todorović and the prosecution negotiated a plea agreement that was very favorable to Todorović. *See* Nancy Amoury Combs, *Copping a Plea to Genocide: The Plea Bargaining of International Crimes*, 151 U. PA. L. REV. 1, 120–22 (2002). Todorović's guilty plea not only disposed of his case, but also eliminated his potentially embarrassing challenge to his arrest.

to the success of international criminal justice and consequently seek to avoid, perhaps even unconsciously, actions that will diminish the role and value of international trials.

Let me unpack these claims and seek to support them. First, I assert that careful judicial scrutiny of testimonial deficiencies would lead to a substantial increase in acquittals. But is this necessarily so? Prosecutors typically charge international defendants with a multitude of crimes. Although careful scrutiny of fact-finding deficiencies would certainly lead Trial Chambers to acquit defendants of some of the charges for which they are now being convicted, such scrutiny may not lead to acquittals on all of the charges. In other words, although the testimony in international cases typically features widespread and pervasive problems that, if carefully considered, would give rise to reasonable doubt about many of the facts that the prosecution seeks to prove, the evidence – even after such careful consideration – still may prove sufficiently reliable to support a conviction for at least one of the crimes for which the defendant is charged.

Although this question is ultimately unanswerable with any measure of certainty, I believe that if Trial Chambers began to take fact-finding impediments seriously, then they would end up acquitting a much greater proportion of defendants of all charges. I base this conclusion first on the prevalence and severity of the fact-finding impediments, factors that I have already discussed. Furthermore, because many charges are supported by only one or two witnesses and the same (problematic) witnesses are frequently relied on to prove many of the facts at issue in a case, we can expect that a change in judicial attitudes toward testimonial deficiencies would have a significant impact on the Tribunals' conviction rates. As we will see in the *Ntagerura* case, which I discuss in Section 8.C, once the defense was able to prove the perjury of a few witnesses, the prosecution's case collapsed because it had based virtually all of its allegations on the testimony of these few witnesses. Similarly, the *Mpambara* prosecution relied on the testimony of witness AVK for a substantial number of its factual allegations[1015] and was able to prove none of them because the Trial Chamber "entertain[ed] significant doubts about Witness AVK's veracity."[1016] Indeed, several ICTR acquittals appeared to result from just the sort of scrutiny under discussion, as I describe in the following pages.

Second, I have asserted that an increase in the tribunals' acquittal rate would have serious consequences for the long-term prospects of international criminal trials. There is no question that international criminal tribunals can withstand some increase in their acquittal rates. Indeed, many believe that

[1015] *See* Mpambara Judgement, note 471, at paras. 50, 54, 60, 64.
[1016] *Id.* at paras. 59, 63, 70, 107.

a respectable number of acquittals enhances the perceived legitimacy of a criminal justice system. But not only do I forecast that the tribunals would see a larger than incidental increase in their acquittal rates if Trial Chambers were to carefully scrutinize testimonial deficiencies, but I believe that acquittals for international crimes are apt to prove particularly costly. They are costly, first of all, in terms of victim reaction. Victims – whether of domestic crimes or international crimes – rarely approve of acquittals. Indeed, Uli Orth's study of secondary victimization shows that victims of domestic crimes frequently suffer significant psychological harm even when the perpetrators of their crimes are convicted but receive lower-than-expected sentences.[1017] The outrage and sense of betrayal that attends a complete acquittal and an acquittal for an international crime, no less, is apt to be all the more intense.[1018]

International crimes typically target victims on the basis of their group identities, such as their race, their religion, or their tribe. The crimes are perpetrated against individual members of these groups but as a means of pursuing broader, ideological goals. In prosecuting these crimes, international criminal trials not only bring to light the specific events that constitute the specific crimes for which the defendants are charged, but they also situate those events in a larger narrative that seeks to define both the broader contours of the conflict as well as the victim and victimizer roles played therein.[1019] As a result both of the group-based nature of international crimes and the tribunals' understandable desire to place those crimes in their broader, historical framework, victims frequently view acquittals for international crimes not in narrow legal terms – that is, not merely as a finding that the evidence presented to the Trial Chamber was not sufficient to establish the elements of the crime beyond a reasonable doubt. Instead, they view acquittals more expansively as repudiating their status as victims in the larger narrative of the conflict that the prosecution advanced. As the Rwandan genocide survivor group IBUKA put it: "Acquitting the planners of the genocide is to deny the genocide of the Tutsis in Rwanda."[1020] Similarly, Tokyo Tribunal prosecutors elected not to indict a particular businessman in order to avoid just that reaction: Because they feared that if the businessman should be acquitted, that acquittal would be interpreted as "a blanket approval of all Japanese industry and industrialists."[1021] Moreover,

[1017] *See* Uli Orth, *Secondary Victimization of Crime Victims by Criminal Proceedings*, 15 Soc. Just. Res. 313 (2002).

[1018] *See, e.g.*, Paul Ntambara, *Jean Mpambara's Acquittal Enrages Residents*, The New Times, Sept. 16, 2006.

[1019] The Tokyo Tribunal's judgment, for instance, comprised 1,218 pages, and the vast bulk of them – 1,050 pages – presented a comprehensive historical survey of Japan that began with the founding of Japan in 660 and centered on the period from 1928 to 1945.

[1020] *New Tensions Between the ICTR and Kigali*, Int'l Just. Trib., Mar. 15, 2004.

[1021] Solis Horwitz, *The Tokyo Trial*, 28 Int'l Conciliation 473, 498 (1950).

because international criminal tribunals are political institutions on so many levels, victims often view acquittals through a political lens; in particular, they see acquittals as calling into serious question the tribunals' integrity and impartiality – indeed, their very legitimacy. After the ICTR acquitted Ntagerura and Bagambiki, for instance, thousands of Rwandans marched through the streets of Cyangugu province bearing placards that read "ICTR Revisionists" and "UN Useless."[1022]

Acquittals at the ICTY have provoked similar reactions.[1023] When the ICTY acquitted one defendant of involvement in the Vukovar massacre and imposed light sentences on two other defendants, Croatian victims were outraged, and Croatian Prime Minister Ivo Sanader called the viability of the ICTY into question, stating: "[T]his is a defeat of the idea of the Hague Tribunal."[1024] Serb officials reacted similarly after the ICTY entered two acquittals against Kosovar Albanian defendants who had been accused of doing violence to Serb civilians. Serb officials called the *Limaj* acquittals "a judicial disgrace" and accused the ICTY of being biased against Serbs.[1025] The *Haradinaj* acquittal gave rise to even more intense recriminations: Serbian Prime Minister Vojislav Kostunica called the verdict a "mockery of justice," and Serbian President Boris Tadić declared that it "degrad[ed] the credibility of the court."[1026] And the ICTY Appeals Chambers' acquittal of three *Kupreškić* defendants gave rise to particular anguish in Bosnian Muslim victims in the town of Ahmići. When Nurija Ahmić, a Bosnian Muslim survivor of the Ahmići atrocities, learned of the acquittals, she "broke down in tears, gasping for breath." Telling a reporter that the defendants' house was just down the street from hers, she asked in a desperate voice: "Am I expected to see them every day on return from work? I do not know how I could survive this."[1027]

In describing these intense and tragic victim reactions, I do not mean to give them undue weight. It may be that no court would ever acquit any defendants if victims had a say in the matter. At the same time, there is no denying that the

[1022] *Thousands Demonstrate Against the UN Tribunal*, Hirondelle News Agency, Feb. 29, 2004.

[1023] *See, e.g.*, Zoran Radosavljević, *Croats Call U.N. War Crimes Verdict "Shameful,"* Reuters, Sept. 28, 2007.

[1024] Government of the Republic of Croatia, News and Announcements, *Prime Minister, Associations of Homeland War Veterans and Victims Slam ICTY Verdict, available at* http://www.vlada.hr/en/naslovnica/novosti_i_najave/2007/rujan/izjava_predsjednika_vlade_o_presudi_haaskog_suda_vukovarskoj_trojci.

[1025] Alexandra Hudson, *U.N. Tribunal Upholds Acquittal of Kosovo Ex-Rebels*, Reuters, Sept. 27, 2007, *available at* http://in.reuters.com/article/worldNews/idINIndia-29747620070927?pageNumber=2&virtualBrandChannel=0&sp=true.

[1026] *Officials: Scandalous Mockery of Justice*, RTV B92 News, Apr. 3, 2008.

[1027] *Ahmići Muslims Shocked by UN Acquittal of War Crimes Suspects*, Agence France-Presse, Oct. 23, 2001. Witnesses who testify against defendants who are later acquitted are apt to be even more profoundly affected, as Eric Stover's research revealed. *See* Stover, note 13, at 106–07.

widespread and intense victim outrage that attends international acquittals causes the tribunals some reputational damage and probably impairs their ability to advance reconciliation between formerly warring parties – a goal that is considered key to the tribunals' mandate.[1028] After the ICTY Appeals Chamber acquitted the Kupreškićs, for instance, the defendants made a heroes' return to their hometown of Ahmići. The defendants, their friends, and their families engaged in raucous partying while Bosnian Croats in the area extended the celebration by organizing a parade: Croats "came with cars, buses, flags, playing loud music and making the victory sign." Ahmići's Bosnian Muslim victims reacted to these public displays of jubilation with predictable distress, a fact that proved to be of no concern to the defendants' supporters. As the sister of one of the Kupreškićs put it: "We feel great and are celebrating and I could not care less . . . about how they (Muslims) feel."[1029] Stories such as these suggest that when it comes to international crimes, reconciliation may be better advanced by no prosecutions than by prosecutions that end in acquittals.

Acquittals can also cost the tribunals some of the support they would otherwise receive from the nations on which they depend most heavily and from the international community as a whole. As discussed above, Rwanda has not hesitated to retaliate against the ICTR when it has disapproved of tribunal decisions. Although I am not aware that Rwanda has retaliated as a result of an ICTR acquittal, that may be because there have been few acquittals. Rwanda has certainly denounced the acquittals,[1030] and the ICTR's acquittal of Bagambiki so disturbed Rwanda, in fact, that it proceeded to prosecute – and convict – Bagambiki on rape charges that the ICTR had not pursued.[1031] If acquittals became more prevalent, then, I would expect Rwanda to take stronger measures.

More importantly, a significant increase in the acquittal rate is apt to play poorly in the North American and Western European countries that provide the bulk of the tribunals' financial and enforcement support. The ICTY's

[1028] *See* S.C. Res. 955, U.N. SCOR, 49th Sess., 3453d mtg. at 1, U.N. Doc. S/RES/955 & Annex (1994).

[1029] *Ahmići Muslims Shocked by UN Acquittal of War Crimes Suspects*, Agence France-Presse, Oct. 23, 2001. *See also U.N. Acquits Top Kosovo Rebel*, BBC News, Nov. 30, 2005, *available at* http://news.bbc.co.uk/2/hi/europe/4485658.stm (describing the street celebrations complete with gunfire and horn honking that greeted the ICTY acquittals of Kosovar rebels).

[1030] Moghalu, note 1000, at 121. Rwandan officials labeled the acquittals of *Cyangugu* defendants Ntagerura and Bagambiki, for instance, "a big joke," *Acquittals of Former Government Officials Raises Mixed Reactions*, Hirondelle News Agency, Feb. 26, 2004, "shocking," and constituting "a miscarriage of international justice," *Rwanda Furious Over Acquittal of Two Suspects*, The East African, Mar. 1, 2004; *see also Kigali Denounces Acquittals at UN Tribunal*, UN Integrated Regional Information Networks, Feb. 26, 2004.

[1031] *Rwandan Court Convicts Genocide Suspect Acquitted by ICTR*, Agence France-Presse, Oct. 11, 2007.

Vukovar acquittal led not only to explicit protests from Croatia but also to a resolution by Christian Democrats in the European Union parliament and a letter of protest signed by more than twenty high-profile Western diplomats, academics, and other legal experts.[1032] The letter labeled the *Vukovar* case "a disturbing example of [the ICTY] failing to entirely serve the interests of justice." Calling themselves "depressed" by the verdicts, the letter's authors observe that the Vukovar crimes were exceptionally public and that "they have not only traumatised the Croatian public, but have shocked the world's conscious [sic] as well." The letter was sent both to the U.N. under secretary-general and the ICTY's Appeals Chamber, which was considering a challenge to the acquittal, and the authors consequently urged the Appeals Chamber to re-examine the case fully.[1033] More broadly, in recent years, the international community has shown a growing reluctance to continue footing the costly bill for international trials,[1034] even though virtually all of the trials result in convictions. Again, a slight increase in the acquittal rate is not likely to diminish the international community's financial or moral commitment to trials, but a greater-than-slight increase almost certainly will have a deleterious effect. It is hard enough to obtain custody over offenders. It is harder still to justify spending millions of dollars per trial – even when virtually all of the trials end in convictions – because the benefits of these convictions are uncertain and the money might be better spent on other post-atrocity measures. If a non-trivial proportion of these tremendously lengthy and costly trials ends in acquittal, the expenditures become virtually impossible to justify. Indeed, I believe that the international community's continued support for international criminal trials is predicated on those trials resulting in convictions most of the time.

To sum up, I have argued that careful judicial scrutiny of testimonial deficiencies would lead to a significant increase in the number of acquittals, and a significant increase in the number of acquittals would seriously undermine

1032 Heikelina Verrijn Stuart, *ICTY, Justice Against All*, Int'l Just. Trib., Dec. 3, 2007.

1033 *Former Diplomats Stress Hague Tribunal Failure*, Javno, Nov. 20, 2007, *available at* http://www.javno.com/en/croatia/clanak.php?id=99813.

1034 During the ICTR's first ten years, it spent more than $800 million, Coalition for International Criminal Justice, Frequently Asked Questions-ICTR, *available at* http://www.cij.org/index.cfm?fuseaction=faqs&tribunalID=2#q7, to dispose of nineteen cases, of which four involved guilty pleas. *Report of the International Criminal Tribunal for the Prosecution of Persons Responsible for Genocide and Other Serious Violations of International Humanitarian Law Committed in the Territory of Rwanda and Rwandan Citizens Responsible for Genocide and Other Such Violations Committed in the Territory of Neighbouring States between 1 January and 31 December 1994*, at summary, U.N. Doc. A/60/229-S/2005/534 (Aug. 15, 2005). Seeking to reduce costs, in 2003, the U.N. Security Council began pressuring the tribunals to adopt a completion strategy that would enable them to close their doors by 2010. *See* S.C. Res. 1503, U.N. Doc. S/RES/1503 (Aug. 28, 2003); S.C. Res. 1534, U.N. Doc. S/RES/1534 (Mar. 26, 2004).

the viability of international trials as a centerpiece response to mass atrocity. I suggest finally that these are facts that may subtly influence the Trial Chambers' treatment of testimonial deficiencies. Now, I do not mean to suggest that international judges convict defendants whom they believe to be innocent in order to advance international criminal justice as an abstract principle. I do believe, however, that most international judges are deeply committed to the ideals of international criminal justice and firmly believe in the power of international criminal trials to deter crimes, to visit much-deserved retribution, to enhance the prospects for reconciliation, and to benefit war-torn societies in a host of other, more amorphous ways. I think former ICTY President Antonio Cassese spoke for most international judges when he extolled international criminal trials for, among other things, establishing "individual responsibility over collective assignation of guilt" and "dissipat[ing] the call for revenge."[1035] International judges, in other words, believe in the value of international trials,[1036] and because they do, they are less likely to take actions that would diminish the long-term prospects of those trials. I do not maintain that any of these considerations rise to the conscious level; I maintain only that the international criminal tribunals' current precarious position, coupled with their noble purposes, may create incentives among those who are committed to advancing those noble purposes to view evidence in the light most favorable to the needs of the Tribunals.

8.B. JUDICIAL BACKGROUNDS

Other factors in addition to political considerations likely are also at work in creating the tribunals' proconviction bias. Perhaps the most obvious and mundane is the professional backgrounds of the tribunal judges. Many ICTR, SCSL, and Special Panels' judges are former academics and or government

[1035] Weinstein & Stover, note 5, at 3–4. For other examples in which international criminal judges extol the value of international criminal trials, see Theodor Meron, *Procedure Evolution in the ICTY*, 2 J. INT'L CRIM. JUST. 520, 520 (2004); Richard May, *Gabrielle Kirk McDonald: A Biographical Note, in* ESSAYS ON ICTY PROCEDURE AND EVIDENCE IN HONOUR OF GABRIELLE KIRK MCDONALD 3, 3 (Richard May et al. eds., 2001) (quoting former ICTY President Gabrielle Kirk McDonald); May & Wierda, note 7, at 252–53; Cassese, *On the Current Trends*, note 4, at 9–10; Cassese, *Reflections*, note 7, at 6–9; Phillip Rapoza, The Serious Crimes Process in Timor-Leste: Accomplishments, Challenges and Lessons Learned, Speech at the International Symposium on UN Peacekeeping Operations in Post-Conflict Timor-Leste: Accomplishments and Lessons Learned, Apr. 28, 2005, *available at* http://www.etan.org/et2005/may/08/28judge.htm; *Court Quashes Appeal*, INT'L JUST. TRIB., June 8, 1998.

[1036] And the few who do not so believe likely see value in international trials as a means of advancing (or at least maintaining) their careers. *Cf.* Mark Osiel, *The Banality of Good: Aligning Incentives Against Mass Atrocity*, 105 COLUM. L. REV. 1751, 1822–29 (2005) (discussing career incentives of international prosecutors).

officials who have no courtroom experience. Harkening back to the points I have just made, Alison Des Forges and Timothy Longman point out that tribunal "judges often appear to pay more attention to political concerns than to experience or competence in judicial matters."[1037] In addition, many judges hail from new democracies and developing nations that do not boast centuries of commitment to due process norms in general and to the beyond-a-reasonable-doubt standard in particular. Although the criminal procedure codes of these States may proudly proclaim all of the prodefendant procedural guarantees required by international human rights treaties, including stringent standards of proof, because these norms have shallow roots in the relevant legal culture they may not exercise much sway in guiding actual evidentiary assessments. Thus, even if a judge arrives at the tribunal armed with considerable judicial experience, if that experience was gained in a criminal justice system that embodies a proconviction bias, we can expect that bias to be replicated in the factual assessments that the judge makes in his or her tribunal cases. In other words, if, in the judge's previous experience, the beyond-a-reasonable-doubt standard is a standard that is applied in name only, then we should not be surprised when the judge fails to consider the testimonial deficiencies that I have described as creating reasonable doubt.

8.C. THE LURE OF ORGANIZATIONAL LIABILITY

The foregoing discussion identifies the professional backgrounds of judges and their ideological commitments as factors that may partially account for the Trial Chambers' failure to take testimonial deficiencies as seriously as we might expect them to be taken. Although I believe that these factors carry some weight, I think that another, still more influential factor is primarily at work. As noted, Trial Chambers are presented with conflicting and frequently problematic testimony for virtually every fact at issue in a case. In many instances, defense and prosecution accounts are both plausible on their face, and a Trial Chamber can have little real confidence in the facts it finds if those findings are based solely on the testimony presented at trial. I do not believe that they are, however. Rather, although Trial Chambers appear to be convicting the defendants solely for the acts charged in the indictments and basing their factual findings about those acts solely on the witness testimony that has been presented to them, I believe that they often supplement that testimony with inferences that they draw from the defendant's official position or institutional affiliation in the context of the international crimes that have been committed. In other words, I believe that the Trial Chambers are inclined

[1037] Des Forges and Longman, note 37, at 49, 53.

to overlook the problematic features of prosecution testimony in many cases because of their commonsense belief that any person who held the position that this defendant held must have done something for which he should be held criminally responsible.

8.C.i. *Organizational Liability as an Evidentiary Proxy*

The reasoning I just articulated finds voice in Article 9 of the Nuremberg Charter. Article 9 authorized the tribunal to declare an organization of which a defendant was a member to be a criminal organization. Once the organization was declared criminal, then its members could be convicted in subsequent trials solely on the basis of their membership in the organization. As a logistical matter, the plan had much to recommend it. Nazi offenders numbered in the seven figures,[1038] so there did not exist the resources to provide each a trial. In addition, the difficulty of obtaining probative evidence of guilt threatened to derail the prosecutions that could be undertaken. In a statement that could have been written about the challenges involved in trying today's war criminals, Nuremberg Chief Prosecutor Robert Jackson bemoaned the evidentiary obstacles facing Nazi prosecutors: "You cannot get witnesses . . . to prove where each was at all times and to prove what he did. It is very hard to identify persons who are in uniform and to get accounts of their part in acts of the organized military or paramilitary units."[1039] Article 9's imposition of organizational liability was intended to enable prosecutors to surmount these evidentiary challenges. The plan, as Jackson described it, would allow prosecutors "to show what offenses were committed and then every person who was part of the general plan, whether he actually held the gun that shot the hostages or whether he sat at a desk somewhere and managed the accounting, would be responsible for the acts of the organization."[1040]

Although the organizational liability provided for in Article 9 was controversial, it constituted a lenient option compared with some proposals that were under consideration. Some thought that all members of the SS should be put to death, for instance, while U.S. Treasury Secretary Henry Morgenthau and his staff had proposed permanent exile for all members of the SS and their

[1038] Herbert Weschler estimates that two million people were included within the scope of the criminal charges, Herbert Weschler, *The Issues of the Nuremberg Trial*, 62 Pol. Sci. Q. 11, 21 (1947), whereas Robert Conot put the number at four million. Robert E. Conot, Justice at Nuremberg 455 (1983).

[1039] Minutes of Conference Session of July 2, 1945 (Document XX), in Report of Robert H. Jackson, Representative to the International Conference on Military Trials 129, 138 [hereinafter Jackson Report].

[1040] *Id.* at 138–39.

families.[1041] Although the Nuremberg Charter provisions on organizational criminality were moderate compared with these options, they nonetheless were recognized to contravene cherished principles of individual criminal responsibility and personal culpability. Prosecutors subsequently introduced some limiting principles into the vague and undetailed provisions that appear in the Charter,[1042] but the very concept of organizational criminal liability nonetheless gave rise to fears of blanket condemnations and guilt by association. The Nuremberg Tribunal's American judge, Francis Biddle, deemed it "shocking" to "convict men without a trial."[1043]

Biddle's view was apparently shared by the other judges, for the tribunal limited the reach of Article 9 so substantially that it effectively gutted the prosecution's plan to expeditiously convict large numbers of Nazis through summary proceedings. Reaffirming that one of the most important and well-settled legal principles is that "criminal guilt is personal, and that mass punishments should be avoided," the tribunal determined that "[m]embership alone is not enough to come within the scope of these declarations." Rather, the tribunal excluded from its finding of criminality those members of indicted groups who "had no knowledge of the criminal purposes or acts of the organization and those who were drafted by the State for membership, unless they were personally implicated in the commission of [criminal] acts."[1044] In most of the subsequent trials of Nazis held pursuant to Control Council Law No. 10, then, the prosecution was required to prove not only that a defendant was a member of the criminal organization in question but that he had voluntarily joined and knew of its criminal purposes.[1045] The imposition of these proof requirements substantially diminished the logistical advantages that Article 9 was intended to deliver, so it was not surprising that the charge of membership in a criminal organization played a relatively minor role in the subsequent trials of Nazis held pursuant to Control Council Law No. 10. A meager eighty-seven defendants were charged and tried on this ground, and of the seventy-four who were convicted only ten were convicted on the membership charge alone.[1046]

The story of organizational liability, then, is a story of principle prevailing over expedience. Those seeking to impose criminal liability on defendants on

[1041] Taylor, note 19, at 42.

[1042] *See, e.g.*, 8 Trial of the Major War Criminals before the International Military Tribunal 367–68 (1947).

[1043] Taylor, note 19, at 556.

[1044] 1 Trial of the Major War Criminals before the International Military Tribunal 256 (1947).

[1045] Trial of Ulrich Greifelt and Others, *in* XIII Law Reports of Trials of the War Criminals 1, 58–59 (UN War Crimes Commission ed., 1949).

[1046] Telford Taylor, *Final Report to the Secretary of the Army on the Nuernberg War Crimes Trials Under Control Council Law No. 10*, at 93 (1949).

the basis of their organizational affiliations did so for understandable reasons. Everyone knew that the Gestapo and the SS were organizations committed to criminal purposes, and everyone knew that the vast majority of the members of those and other Nazi organizations deserved serious criminal punishment. But it was not feasible to prosecute each one of them for specific crimes: There were too many of them, for one thing, and it was too difficult to obtain evidence about the particular acts they had performed. Those good reasons notwithstanding, the Nuremberg Tribunal affirmed the principle of individual guilt assessments for individual defendants. The proof requirements that the Nuremberg Tribunal read into Article 9 meant that fewer Nazis would suffer criminal sanctions, but the tribunal was willing to forego deserved punishment for a large number of individuals in order to safeguard the principle that no one receives criminal sanctions unless that person's guilt has been individually determined.

That principle has seemingly become only more entrenched in international criminal law since the Nuremberg Judgment. Only a few years after the conclusion of the Nuremberg trials, the International Law Commission drafted a Code of Offenses against the Peace and Security of Mankind,[1047] and, with seemingly no discussion, the drafters excluded the possibility of criminal liability for individuals on the basis of group membership.[1048] Forty years later, the drafters of the ICTY Statute considered Nuremberg-style mass liability but rejected it. The U.N. Secretary-General announced his belief "that this concept should not be retained.... The criminal acts set out in this statute are carried out by natural persons," and it is they who should be subject to the jurisdiction of the ICTY irrespective of their membership in organizations.[1049] Those who created the ICTY's progeny came to the same conclusion. Indeed, the possibility of organizational liability is no longer even debated when an international

[1047] International Law Commission, *Report of the International Law Commission on the Work of Its Sixth Session*, U.N. Doc. A/2693 (June 3–July 28, 1954), *reprinted in* [1954] 2 Y.B. Int'l L. Comm'n 140, U.N. Doc. A/CN.4/SER.A/1954.

[1048] The members of the International Law Commission did briefly debate whether organizations could be the subjects of penal responsibility. As they recognized, however, such liability differed from that envisaged by the Nuremberg Charter because at Nuremberg "the effect of the declaration of criminality of an organization was only to make individual members of the organization responsible for its reprehensible activity. No responsibility of the organization as such was established." International Law Commission, *Documents of the Second Session, including the Report of the Commission to the General Assembly*, U.N. Doc. A/CN.4/25 (Apr. 26, 1950), *reprinted in* 2 Benjamin B. Ferencz, An International Criminal Court: A Step Toward World Peace 188 (1980).

[1049] *Secretary-General's Report on Aspects of Establishing an International Tribunal for the Prosecution of Persons Responsible for Serious Violations of International Humanitarian Law Committed in the Territory of the former Yugoslavia*, U.N. SCOR, 48th Sess., Annex, U.N. Doc. S/25704 (1993), para. 51, *reprinted in* 32 I.L.M. 1159 (1993).

tribunal is established. One recent observer of the Iraqi High Tribunal noted, for instance, that because the Ba'athification of all aspects of Iraqi life was partially responsible for the "violent repression in all fields of society and government during the reign of Saddam Hussein," one would have expected the tribunal to have included a provision similar to Article 9 of the Nuremberg Charter.[1050] But, although the Iraqi High Tribunal has numerous controversial features,[1051] even it is authorized to impose liability only on individuals and only for their individual acts or omissions.

Although the specific form of liability envisaged in Article 9 of the Nuremberg Charter no longer has any overt purchase, I believe that organizational liability principles continue to exert a profound influence over international criminal trials. Mark Osiel has observed that organizational liability "may rule us surreptitiously from the grave" through its enduring but unacknowledged influence on the conspiracy-like doctrine of joint criminal enterprise.[1052] I agree with that position and discuss the use of the joint criminal enterprise doctrine more thoroughly in Chapter 9. Here, I extend Osiel's insights by maintaining that not only do the Nuremberg Charter's organizational liability principles inform legal doctrines, such as joint criminal enterprise, they also exert a continued and powerful influence over the way in which current international tribunals select their defendants, conduct their investigations, and, most relevantly, find facts at trial.

I will begin with the targeting of defendants and investigations. In recent years, international criminal investigations have focused almost exclusively on the "big fish" – that is, on the high-level architects and organizers of the atrocities. The SCSL has jurisdiction only over those offenders who "bear the greatest responsibility" for the crimes,[1053] so that the tribunal's focus on high-level offenders was fixed at the outset of its operations. Investigations at the ICTR and the Special Panels, by contrast, were initially more haphazard, but they too soon turned their exclusive gaze to the atrocities' "leaders, policy makers, and senior executors."[1054] As a result of this understandable targeting of high-level offenders, a defendant's official position has frequently served to guide the tribunals' investigations; that is, tribunal investigators targeted their

[1050] Ilias Bantekas, *The Iraqi Special Tribunal for Crimes Against Humanity*, 54 INT'L & COMP. L. Q. 237, 245 (2005).

[1051] The domestic crimes over which the Iraqi High Tribunal has jurisdiction, for instance, are undefined and are so broad, vague, and "susceptible to politicized interpretation and application" that they might be regarded as "political offenses." Human Rights Watch, *Judging Dujail*, note 25, at 8.

[1052] Osiel, note 1036, at 1792.

[1053] Statute of the Special Court for Sierra Leone, art. 1 (Jan. 16, 2002) [hereinafter SCSL Statute].

[1054] OTHMAN, note 35, at 160. For a discussion of the evolution in the ICTR's and Special Panels' investigations strategies, see *id.* at 100–02, 119–28, 171–75.

initial investigations on those bearing authoritative positions in the group or organizations that were seen to be responsible for the atrocities in question. As the ICTR put it in its 2000 Annual Report, its strategy consisted of investigating "persons wielding authority of State during the genocide – more precisely, targeting political and military officials at the highest levels and attempting to elicit proof that they conspired among themselves to organize and execute the genocide."[1055] A similar investigative strategy was employed at the SCSL, and it consequently came as no surprise that the SCSL's initial eight indictments were brought against the high-level leaders of the three parties to the Sierra Leonean conflict as well as against Liberian President Charles Taylor,[1056] who was commonly believed to have played a crucial role in instigating the conflict.

One wonders in fact whether in some cases a suspect's official position is so influential during the investigations that it might substitute for evidence gathering. One indication that it does derives from the fact that, in virtually every ICTR case, prosecutors submit no evidence whatsoever to support some of the counts charged in the indictment.[1057] Similar indications exist at the SCSL[1058]

[1055] *Report of the International Criminal Tribunal for the Prosecution of Persons Responsible for Genocide and Other Serious Violations of International Humanitarian Law Committed in the Territory of Rwanda and Rwandan Citizens Responsible for Genocide and Other Such Violations Committed in the Territory of Neighbouring States between 1 January and 31 December 1994*, U.N. Doc. A/55/435, S/2000/927, para. 120 (Oct. 2, 2000).

[1056] *First Annual Report of the President of the Special Court for Sierra Leone for the Period 2 December 2002 to 1 December 2003*, at 7, *available at* http://www.sc-sl.org/LinkClick.aspx?fileticket=NRhDcbHrcSs%3d&tabid=176.

[1057] *See, e.g.*, Gacumbitsi Judgement, note 364, at paras. 37, 177; Ntagerura Judgement, note 37, at para. 40; Kajelijeli Judgement, note 303, at para. 926; Kamuhanda Judgement, note 38, at paras. 245–246; Muhimana Judgement, note 363, at paras. 9, 61, 62, 158; Ndindabahizi Judgement, note 56, at para. 27; Niyitegeka Judgement, note 56, at para. 468; Rutaganda Judgement, note 38, at para. 314; Semanza Judgement, note 31, at para. 250; Bagilishema Judgement, note 122, at para. 354; Mpambara Judgement, note 471, at para. 119; Rwamakuba Judgement, note 63, at para. 153; Simba Judgement, note 455, at para. 13; Nahimana Judgement, note 97, at para. 12; Muvunyi Judgement, note 455, at para. 18; Karera Judgement, note 54, at para. 83; Bagosora et al. Judgement, note 484, at paras. 1747, 1749; Bikindi Judgement, note 730, at paras. 11, 95; Rukundo Judgement, note 730, at paras. 49, 55, 134; Nchamihigo Judgement, note 730, at para. 229; Zigiranyirazo Judgement, note 498, at paras. 13-15, 233; Kalimanzira Judgement, note 730, at para. 27. ICTR judge Ostrovsky criticized prosecutors for "not even bother[ing] to provide evidence on a number of counts." *See* Thierry Cruvellier *Judge Ostrovsky Speaks Out*, INT'L JUST. TRIB., Apr. 23, 2002.

[1058] *See* RUF Judgement, note 56, at paras. 213 n.383, 236 n.423, 1017, 1026, 1135, 1268, 1284, 1332, 1497, 1692, 1885; AFRC Judgement, note 27, at paras. 807, 842, 866, 881, 953, 970, 983, 1028, 1101, 1111, 1135, 1199, 1215, 1220, 1226, 1311, 1335, 1376, 1402, 1404, 1411, 1646, 1647, 1649, 1650, 1668, 1678, 1679, 1690, 1696, 1720, 1784, 1814, 1847, 1861, 1897, 1906, 1920, 1955a, 1987, 1989, 1990, 1991, 2000, 2009, 2018, 2028, 2029, 2030, 2031, 2062, 2064, 2084. In the *AFRC* case, prosecutors initially failed to provide any particulars about the time or location of the crimes or the identities of the victims. The prosecution's pretrial brief and opening statement were similarly vague. The prosecution did present a great deal of detailed evidence about the crimes during the and the ICTY, which led ICTY Appeals Judge Wolfgang Schomburg to observe that "one can't help getting the impression that an arrest warrant is issued first, and only afterwards do the actual investigations begin."[1059] It is of course possible that at the time they issue the indictments, prosecutors believe that they have reliable witnesses who will testify in support of a given allegation, and they learn only later that the expected testimony will not be forthcoming.[1060] But the phenomenon is so prevalent that one cannot escape the assumption that prosecutors regularly level allegations for which they have no reliable evidence. Indeed, former ICTR Special Counsel and Spokesman Kingsley Moghalu diplomatically conceded that the "tribunal's prosecution . . . was frequently not 'trial-ready' before obtaining arrest warrants."[1061]

Even when it is clear that indictments are issued on the basis of something other than a sufficient quantity of trial-ready evidence, it is not always clear what that something is. The Special Panels, for instance, were initially forced to issue hastily prepared indictments charging Indonesian domestic crimes, rather than international crimes, because they inherited a passel of detainees who had been arrested by U.N. forces before Special Panels investigations could even commence.[1062] Similarly, the ICTR ended up indicting a number of offenders because Rwanda had sought their extradition, but the extraditing State was not willing to transfer them to Rwanda and instead transferred them to the ICTR.[1063] These unusual cases notwithstanding, one has to believe that inferences drawn from a suspect's official position contributed to many instances of insufficiently supported or ill-planned indictments. One such instance may have been the indictment of Leonidas Rusatira, a well-known colonel of the Rwandan army and a commander of the High Military School. It is reasonable to assume that Rusatira's official position played a substantial

course of the trial, however, which suggests that the bulk of the prosecution's investigations occurred after the indictments had been issued.

[1059] Renate Flottau, *Fragwürdige Abmachungen*, Der Spiegel, Jan. 17, 2005. Former ICTY Judge Patricia Wald likewise commented on the notable vagueness of early ICTY indictments. Patricia Wald, *General Radislav Krstić: A War Crimes Case Study*, 16 Geo. J. Legal Ethics 445, 450 n.15 (2003).

[1060] For an example of this occurring in East Timor, see Othman, note 35, at 118. Othman also discusses some ICTY indictments that were withdrawn because they "had rested on a small number of witnesses [who] were in fact unlikely to hold in Court." *Id.* at 170.

[1061] Moghalu, note 1000, at 193.

[1062] Othman, note 35, at 109–113; Suzannah Linton, *Correspondents' Reports*, 2 Y.B. of Int'l Hum. L. 471, 477 (2000). Indeed, when the court asked the prosecutor in the *João Fernandes* case "why the accused is charged with one murder since the evidences [*sic*] in the file show that there were more victims," the prosecutor responded, among other things, that the accused was already detained, and the prosecutor needed to seek "quick justice." Prosecutor v. João Fernandes, Case No. 01/00.C.G.2000, Judgement, at para. 5 (Jan. 25, 2001).

[1063] Othman, note 35, at 171–72.

role in his indictment, for although that position would suggest his involvement in the various crimes for which he was charged, the evidence showed that he opposed a military takeover of the government, that he called for an end to the anti-Tutsi violence, and that he personally saved dozens of Tutsis from death.[1064] Four months after the indictment was issued, Chief Prosecutor Carla Del Ponte was forced to request its withdrawal, on the ground that "the evidence obtained in the course of further investigation of the Accused has been found to be insufficient.[1065] The *Rusatira* "fiasco," one commentator maintained, "raises serious questions about the basis on which ICTR indictments are drawn up."[1066]

Whether or not a defendant's official position does sometimes substitute for evidence gathering at the investigations stage, the more relevant question for my study is whether that official position sometimes substitutes for evidence at the guilt-determination stage. Prosecutors occasionally urge that it should. Although, in most instances, the prosecution presents testimony (however problematic) that directly supports their factual allegations, they sometimes fail to do so and instead ask Trial Chambers to impose just the sort of liability embodied in Article 9 of the Nuremberg Charter. When ICTR prosecutors in *Bagilishema*, for instance, realized that they had presented little evidence showing Bagilishema's commission of the specific criminal acts charged in the indictment, they harkened back to principles of organizational liability and endorsed the position of their expert witness, who had opined that "all those who held political office during the genocide could not remove themselves from responsibility, disclaim responsibility."[1067] Prosecutors further maintained that "remaining as *bourgmestre*, with the full knowledge of the interim government's criminal objectives, gives rise to personal liability."[1068] This sort of overt appeal to rejected Nuremberg principles typically fails. The *Bagilishema* Trial Chamber, for instance, held that it was not enough that a defendant is found to have knowingly been part of an organization with criminal objectives. Rather, the prosecution must prove that the defendant "positively participated in the group's crimes by substantially contributing to the crimes or by influencing the course of related events; alternatively there must have been personal dereliction."[1069] SCSL Justice Thompson made a similar point in the *CDF* case when he took pains to reject "one rather disturbing

[1064] *See* Leave None to Tell the Story, note 644, at 204; Othman, note 35, at 186; Thierry Cruvellier, *Shocking Arrest of Rusatira*, Int'l Just. Trib., May 17, 2002.

[1065] Prosecutor v. Rusatira, Case No., ICTR-2002-80-I, Decision on the Prosecutor's *Ex Parte* Application for Leave to Withdraw the Indictment (Aug. 14, 2002).

[1066] Thierry Cruvellier, *The Error*, Int'l Just. Trib., Aug. 13, 2002.

[1067] Bagilishema Judgement, note 122, at para. 139.

[1068] *Id.* at para. 142; *see also id.* at para. 129.

[1069] *Id.* at para. 144.

feature of the Prosecution's evidence as it unfolded:" the fact that it was "based on an extended version of joint criminal enterprise that approximated the doctrine of guilt by association."[1070]

These examples prove – if such proof is needed – that Article 9 liability truly is no longer a viable basis for conviction. However, sometimes prosecutors invoke a defendant's official position in a far more compelling and justifiable way. In particular, instead of asking Trial Chambers to impose liability merely *because* the defendant held a particular position, prosecutors sometimes ask Trial Chambers to infer from the defendant's position his involvement in the crimes charged in the indictment. Inferences such as these are nothing new. In medieval and early modern times, probabilities were drawn from the sex, age, education, and status of a defendant. Children were thought to be much like their parents, so a family's lifestyle might be invoked to prove a defendant's dishonesty or scandalous behavior. Men were thought more likely to be robbers and women poisoners, whereas well-bred men of professional classes were considered more likely to be innocent of the charges than men of more modest occupations or slaves.[1071] Modern-day fact finders are just as likely to draw inferences from various aspects of a defendant's life, and that reality drives certain evidentiary exclusions. In the United States, for instance, evidence of a defendant's gang membership is frequently excluded because it "creates a risk the jury will improperly infer the defendant has a criminal disposition and is therefore guilty of the offense charged."[1072]

Inferences drawn from official position are apt to be all the more influential in the context of international crimes. First, the fact that the international tribunals face such daunting evidentiary challenges raises the value of such indirect evidence as official position. Moreover, given the nature of international crimes, a defendant's official position truly does provide useful information about the defendant's likely culpability in many cases. International crimes typically involve large-scale violence perpetrated by large numbers of offenders.[1073] Because the crimes are so widespread and systematic, they are

[1070] CDF Judgement, Justice Thompson's Dissent, note 612, at para. 99.

[1071] Barbara J. Shapiro, "Beyond Reasonable Doubt" and "Probable Cause:" Historical Perspectives on the Anglo-American Law of Evidence 117 (1991); *see also* Shapiro, note 884, at 29; Thomas Andrew Green, Verdict According to Conscience: Perspectives on the English Criminal Trial Jury 1200–1800, 17 (1985).

[1072] People v. Williams, 940 P.2d 710, 738 (Cal. 1997); *see also* United States v. Butler, 71 F.3d 243, 251 (7th Cir. 1995); People v. Cardenas, 647 P.2d 569, 572–73 (Cal. 1982); People v. Perez, 114 Cal. App. 3d. 470, 477 (1981); People v. Avitia, 127 Cal. App. 4th 185, 191–96 (2005); People v. Luparello, 187 Cal. App. 3d. 410, 422–27 (1986); People v. Smith, 565 N.E.2d 900, 907–08 (1991).

[1073] Some estimate that as many as one million Rwandans perpetrated international crimes during that country's genocide. William A. Schabas, *Genocide Trials and Gacaca Courts*, 3 J. Int'l Crim. Just. 879, 881 (2005).

self-evidently the products of careful advance planning and mobilization. These are crimes that are orchestrated by the state or by statelike entities that carry out their activities through more or less well-organized sub bodies. Thus, once it is established that a particular group is responsible for the atrocities, then the defendant's official position in that group is unquestionably probative of that individual's involvement in the atrocities. Say, for instance, that the prosecution charges the defendant with ordering civilian killings during a particular attack. As former ICTY and ICTR Chief Prosecutor Carla Del Ponte has observed: "Where large-scale crimes are carried out systematically by military, police or quasi military organs requiring communication and coordination it is logical to infer that criminal activity must have been the result of orders."[1074] And if the defendant was the commander of that attack, it is equally logical to infer that the orders were given *by the defendant.* For that reason, even if the prosecution's direct evidence that the defendant ordered the killings is only meager and problematic witness testimony, the fact that the defendant was the commander of an attack that featured the widespread and systematic killing of civilians is a fact that can compellingly supplement the meager and problematic witness testimony about the orders the defendant gave.

In cases such as these, official position or group membership is probative of the specific crimes or defenses that are at issue in the case. The *Ndindabahizi* Trial Chamber, for instance, considered Ndindabahizi's membership in Rwanda's Interim Government to be relevant to the indictment because "whether the Accused had the ability to lead, incite or otherwise encourage killings of Tutsi is directly relevant to charges throughout the Indictment that he did so."[1075] Similarly, in assessing defendant Florencio Tacaqui's claim to have been forced to join the Sakunar military, the Special Panels pointed to Tacaqui's family as a piece of evidence that the Panel could not "neglect to consider." In particular, because several members of Tacaqui's family held leadership positions in the Sakunar militia,[1076] the Panel concluded that "it can hardly be believed that Tacaqui's membership to [sic] the militia was a forced one."[1077]

Often, however, the relationship between the official position and the crime derives not so much from the specific facts of the crimes or the precise contours of the defendant's official duties but rather from a more amorphous, commonsense understanding that the defendant could not have held the position she did without playing *some* role in the atrocities. Consider Adolf Eichmann,

[1074] Carla Del Ponte, *Investigation and Prosecution of Large-Scale Crimes at the International Level: The Experience of the ICTY*, 4 J. INT'L CRIM. JUST. 539, 548 (2006).
[1075] Ndindabahizi Judgement, note 56, at para. 48.
[1076] Tacaqui Judgement, note 36, at 1.
[1077] *Id.* at 11.

who was head of the Gestapo's Office of Jewish Affairs. Merely to recognize his title is to presume his involvement in Nazi atrocities against the Jews given what we know about Holocaust crimes. Happily, the Nuremberg Tribunal did not need to presume the involvement of Nazi offenders because it was presented documentation that proved their crimes, but the Tokyo Tribunal was not so fortunate. Tokyo Tribunal prosecutors – like their contemporary counterparts – faced daunting evidentiary challenges, not least because Japanese militarists had destroyed inculpatory documents "by the warehouseful."[1078] Perhaps as a consequence, the Tokyo Tribunal did appear to base a number of its convictions on inferences drawn from the defendants' official positions.

Tokyo Tribunal prosecutors had argued that the very nature and scope of the crimes proved that the defendants had ordered them. As lead prosecutor Joseph Keenan put it: "These murders followed such a wide range of territory and covered such a long period of time, and so many were committed after protests had been registered by neutral nations, that we must assume only positive orders from above."[1079] The Tribunal accepted this argument, concluding that the evidence showed the crimes to be so vast and to follow such a common pattern that they must have been "either secretly ordered or willfully permitted by the Japanese Government or members thereof and the leaders of the armed forces."[1080] This finding seemed to underlie several Tokyo Tribunal convictions that were not supported by evidence of the defendants' actual criminal behavior or guilty mindset. Indeed, in exploring the principle of individual responsibility in international criminal law, David Cohen took a hard look at the reasoning underlying certain Tokyo Tribunal convictions and discovered that, at the same time that the Nuremberg Tribunal was proclaiming the crucial need for individualized guilt assessments prior to conviction, the Tokyo Tribunal and other Allied Tribunals were convicting high-level Japanese defendants for engaging in a conspiracy to wage a war of aggression when the only relationship between some of the defendants and the conspiracy stemmed from the defendant's official military or governmental position.

[1078] Brackman, note 221, at 40 (emphasis in original). *See also* Piccigallo, note 274, at 10 ("Rapid demobilization and repatriation of ex-POWs, witnesses and evidence scattered literally throughout the world, wholesale destruction of key documents by Japanese, incredible difficulties in identifying, locating and apprehending suspects in Japan proper and East Asia and other factors combined to render nearly impossible the tasks given to Allied prosecutors.").

[1079] Kenzo Takayanagi, The Tokio Trials and International Law 57 (1948).

[1080] The Tokyo Judgment: The International Military Tribunal for the Far East 385 (B.V.A. Roling & C.F. Ruter eds., 1977) [hereinafter Tokyo Tribunal Judgement].

Hirota Koki, for instance, was convicted of participating in a common plan or conspiracy to wage aggressive wars.[1081] Between 1933 and 1938, Hirota had twice served as Japan's foreign minister and for eleven months had served as her prime minister. Cohen observes that, in convicting Hirota, the Tokyo Tribunal "appears to rely on the connection between Hirota's *position* as foreign minister and briefly, as prime minister and the actions taken by the cabinet and the military leadership." Cohen points out that the tribunal did not focus on Hirota's "actual words and deeds" but instead "repeatedly phrase[d] its narrative in terms of what happened 'during Hirota's term of office.'"[1082] As a consequence, the Tokyo Tribunal judgment, though having "nominally committed itself to basing its verdict on an analysis of individual responsibility, [instead] grounded its judgment on the presumed link between the defendant's formal position and the actual actions of the Japanese military."[1083] The official positions of other Tokyo Tribunal defendants proved equally crucial to their convictions. Although former Japanese Ambassador Shigemitsu Mamoru strongly opposed military expansion, he was held to have played a "principal part" in waging war once he became foreign minister in 1943. In light of the evidence presented, Cohen concludes that "the tribunal can only mean that his formal position alone meant that he 'played a principal part' in a war that he had not helped to initiate and which was surely beyond the scope of his authority to stop."[1084] In a similar vein is the conviction of General Muto Akira for atrocities that occurred in the Philippines. The Tokyo Tribunal judgment does not point to any action or omission that would connect Muto to the atrocities but noted only that "[d]uring his tenure as Chief-of-Staff, a campaign . . . was waged by the troops under . . . Muto."[1085] The tribunal categorically rejected Muto's defense that he knew nothing of the atrocities, though it pointed to no evidence suggesting that Muto did know of the atrocities and was lying in his denials.[1086]

I believe that similar reasoning prevails in many cases at the ICTR, SCSL, and Special Panels. The contours and implementation mechanisms of modern-day massacres in Rwanda, Sierra Leone, and East Timor are not especially well known to Western audiences, but they too can feature Eichmann-like analogues. For instance, Foday Sankoh's position as the leader of the RUF – the Sierra Leonean rebel force that is widely blamed for having amputated the

[1081] *Id.* at 447.
[1082] David Cohen, *Beyond Nuremburg: Individual Responsibility for War Crimes, in* HUMAN RIGHTS IN POLITICAL TRANSITIONS: GETTYSBURG TO BOSNIA 53, 64 (Carla Hesse & Robert Post eds., 1999) (quoting Tokyo Tribunal Judgement).
[1083] *Id.* at 64.
[1084] *Id.* at 65–66.
[1085] Tokyo Tribunal Judgement, note 1080, at 430.
[1086] Cohen, *Beyond Nuremburg*, note 1082, at 68.

limbs of thousands of civilians – creates the strong inference of his involvement in the violence. The leadership of the Rwandan genocide is less clear-cut, but even there, some positions appear patently pertinent to the defendant's likely culpability. For instance, the *Interahamwe* – which was the youth wing of the MRND political party – has been widely blamed for zealously implementing the genocide throughout Rwanda. As a consequence, the fact that ICTR defendant Georges Rutaganda was vice president of the National Committee of the *Interahamwe* has to be relevant – at least in a gestalt sort of way – to the Trial Chamber's assessment of the testimony that placed Rutaganda at various massacre sites. The inference to be drawn from *Interahamwe* leadership is obvious as a result of the *Interahamwe's* high-profile involvement in the genocide, but other positions may be equally informative to those familiar with the relevant sociopolitical structures. Rwanda expert André Guichaoua, for instance, testified against ICTR defendant Alfred Musema, who had been director of the government-owned Gisovu Tea Factory during the genocide. To the uninformed, the position of public tea company director does not suggest a link to the Rwandan crimes, but Guichaoua drew this link by opining that it would have been "impossible for a person who has lived in a prefecture such as the Kibuye prefecture not to have in one way or the other, participate [sic] in the decision making process being in a position such as the one Mr. Musema was occupying."[1087]

However persuasive a defendant's official position might be in suggesting that the defendant played some – if an undefined – role in the atrocities, those suggestions rarely come to the fore in current international trials because prosecutors typically charge defendants with performing specific criminal acts, and they present direct evidence of the defendant's commission of those acts. So, although Rutaganda's position as vice president of the National Committee of the *Interahamwe* is in and of itself damning given the *Interahamwe's* well-established role in the Rwandan genocide, the prosecution sought to prove that Rutaganda personally distributed weapons, hunted down Tutsi, and participated in massacres,[1088] and it presented witnesses who testified that he had. Even the highest-level ICTR defendants are frequently alleged to have physically participated in the crimes – at the least to have distributed weapons to the killers[1089] if not to have personally joined in the killings[1090] – and those who are

[1087] Musema Transcript, May 7, 1999, at 63–64.

[1088] Prosecutor v. Rutaganda, Case No. ICTR-96-3-I, Indictment (Feb. 13, 1996).

[1089] *See, e.g.*, Prosecutor v. Bagosora, Case No. ICTR-96–7-I, Indictment, paras. 5.28–5.31 (Aug. 12, 1999); Prosecutor v. Bizimungu et al., Case No. ICTR-2000–56-I, Indictment, paras. 27, 41 (Aug. 23, 2004).

[1090] Prosecutor v. Bizimungu et al., Case No. ICTR-2000–56-I, Indictment, para. 38 (Aug. 23, 2004).

not are charged with planning the genocide during particular meetings[1091] or inciting the genocide during particular speeches and rallies;[1092] that is, events that the prosecution must prove beyond a reasonable doubt. Consequently, it is these allegations that appear in the indictments, these allegations that prosecutors seek to prove by means of the problematic witness testimony described in Chapters 2 through 5, and these allegations that ostensibly underlie the convictions that are the end result of virtually every case. The problem, of course, is that it is these allegations that are so difficult to prove beyond a reasonable doubt for all the reasons heretofore discussed. Of course, as Chapter 7 details, the Trial Chambers routinely find them proven beyond a reasonable doubt despite deficiencies in the witnesses' testimony, despite the alibis proffered by virtually every defendant, and despite the lack of any nontestimonial evidence that might assist the Trial Chamber in deciding between competing accounts. But this is where the defendant's official position becomes relevant, for the Trial Chambers find these allegations proved beyond a reasonable doubt, I believe, in large part because the Chambers supplement the very muddy evidentiary picture that is presented to them at trial with commonsense inferences that they draw from the defendant's official position. These commonsense inferences, indeed, can be seen as bridging the gap between the prosecution's poorly supported factual allegations about specific acts and events and the Trial Chambers' convictions.

Reliance on such inferences, in fact, helps both to explain and to justify factual findings that seem questionable on their face. Consider, for instance, the *CDF* case. There, prosecutors urged the Trial Chamber to infer that the defendants had ordered CDF forces (the Kamajors) to commit crimes. Prosecutors acknowledged that they were not "in a position to say that [a] Kamajor received a direct order from someone" to engage in a particular killing,[1093] yet they pointed out that "an objective observer watching over Sierra Leone . . . would see the CDF arriving at the same place, at the same time, in large numbers and attacking and often defeating an armed enemy." As a consequence, the prosecution maintained, "the only reasonable inference that can be drawn was that there was a central command unit. Combatants did not turn up randomly hoping that other combatants would be there . . . with the same goal in mind."[1094] Prosecutors accordingly urged the Trial Chamber to "look at the breadth of the offences, . . . the manner in which they occurred, . . . people

[1091] *See, e.g.*, Prosecutor v. Karemera et al., Case No. ICTR-98–44-I, Indictment, paras. 28.1, 38, 40, 47 (Aug. 24, 2005).
[1092] *See, e.g.*, Prosecutor v. Casimir Bizimungu et al., Case No. ICTR-99–50-I, Indictment, paras. 5.3–5.10 (May 7, 1999).
[1093] CDF Transcript, Nov. 28, 2006, at 63–64.
[1094] *Id.* at 79.

being killed in public, no attempt to disguise what was going on, no attempt to camouflage their face." Given the quantity and nature of the Kamajors' criminality, prosecutors maintained that the "only inference one can draw is that the Kamajors were committing acts which were within the framework created by" the defendants.[1095] In convicting the three CDF defendants, the Trial Chamber did not expressly invoke this reasoning; indeed, it instead identified specific criminal acts that it found the defendants had engaged in. But given the meager, problematic testimony that supported the defendants' commission of those specific criminal acts, there is every reason to believe that it was the prosecution's reasoning that drove the Trial Chamber's factual determinations.

To recap the discussion in Chapter 7, the *CDF* Trial Chamber convicted Moinina Fofana on a command responsibility theory for the crimes that occurred during the Kamajors' attacks on Koribondo and Bo. The testimony of Albert Nallo was the sole support for one element of the command responsibility theory – that there existed a superior–subordinate relationship between Fofana and Nallo, who claimed to be the CDF's deputy national director of operations and director of operations, southern region. Reliance on Nallo's testimony was questionable because Nallo also claimed that he committed certain offenses pursuant to the defendants' instructions, and some of these claims were certainly mistaken and probably perjured. Fofana's conviction for aiding and abetting the Kamajors' crimes in the towns of Tongo Field was similarly questionable but for a different reason. There, too, the Trial Chamber convicted Fofana after relying on the testimony of only one witness – this time, TF2-222. That witness had testified that, during a "passing out parade" held in anticipation of the Tongo operation, Norman had instructed the Kamajors to commit crimes. After Norman's address, TF2-222 alleged, Fofana had told the Kamajors that any Kamajor who failed to perform in accordance with Norman's instructions should kill himself. The Trial Chamber held that Fofana's words constituted encouragement and support for Norman's instructions and consequently convicted him of aiding and abetting. As I note in Chapter 7, the testimony of witness TF2-222 was clearer and featured fewer inconsistencies than the testimony of many SCSL witnesses, yet it nonetheless remains a slender reed on which to base a conviction, especially because TF2-222 was the only witness to have testified about Fofana's speech, he testified about it more

[1095] *Id.* at 66. In a similar vein, the prosecution argued that "[o]ne only has to look at the consistency of behaviour by the Kamajors in different areas and at different times to be satisfied there was a pattern of conduct." *Id.* at 77; *see also id.* at 83 (The Kamajors "would not have committed these offences unless the accused men had implemented a policy of win at all costs, had allowed them, had given them the imprimatur to commit offences that are now before you on the indictment.").

than seven years after it took place, and the specific words that Fofana allegedly uttered were crucial to the Trial Chamber's conviction.

Fofana's convictions, then, appear weakly supported if one views them only in light of the evidence on which they are ostensibly based. Fofana's official position in the CDF, however, serves to bridge the gap between the meager, problematic testimony that the Trial Chamber invoked and the Chamber's conclusions about Fofana's involvement in the crimes. There is no question that CDF forces committed atrocities in Bo, Koribondo, and the towns of Tongo Field. The Trial Chamber heard numerous witnesses attesting to the atrocities,[1096] and they also have been the subject of considerable NGO reporting.[1097] There is likewise no question that Fofana was the CDF's second-in-command and its director of war. Although the *CDF* defendants sought to portray the CDF War Council as primarily responsible for determining the conduct of the war,[1098] that claim was subject to conflicting testimony;[1099] and, even if the War Council did play a significant decision-making role, Fofana's high-ranking position nonetheless creates a persuasive inference that he too was substantially involved in the crimes. Thus, although the testimony that the Trial Chamber ostensibly relied on constitutes a weak foundation for a finding that Fofana uttered a particular sentence at a passing-out parade or that he issued particular instructions to Albert Nallo, when that testimony is viewed in the context of Fofana's official position it provides a much firmer foundation for the Trial Chamber's factual findings and its ultimate decision to convict Fofana.

Kondewa's conviction for enlisting child soldiers can be explained and justified similarly. The Trial Chamber received considerable evidence pertaining to the CDF's use of child soldiers, but only one witness linked Kondewa to

[1096] For testimony about crimes in Bo, see CDF Transcript, June 15, 2004, at 20–25, 31–32; CDF Transcript, Nov. 23, 2004, at 93–103, 111–127; CDF Transcript, Nov. 29, 2004, at 114–123; CDF Transcript, Nov. 30, 2004, at 1–20, 86–100; CDF Transcript, Dec. 1, 2004, at 1–14; CDF Transcript, Dec. 2, 2004, at 49–64; Michele Staggs, U.C. Berkeley War Crimes Studies Center, Special Court Monitoring Program, Update No. 14, Nov. 26, 2004, at 1–3, 5. For testimony about Koribondo, see CDF Transcript, June 15, 2004, at 18–19, 32–33; CDF Transcript, June 16, 2004, at 14–22; CDF Transcript, June 17, 2004, at 79–83; CDF Transcript, June 21, 2004, at 23–24; CDF Transcript, Sept. 8, 2004, at 12–31; CDF Transcript, Sept. 9, 2004, at 24–41, 48–49; CDF Transcript, Sept. 13, 2004, at 47–50, 52–54. For testimony about the towns of Tongo Field, see CDF Transcript, Feb. 11, 2005, at 6–17; CDF Transcript, Feb. 11, 2005, at 37–66; CDF Transcript, Feb. 14, 2005, at 11–28; CDF Transcript, Feb. 22, 2005, at 2–5.

[1097] Amnesty International, *Sierra Leone: 1998 – A Year of Atrocities Against Civilians* 33–34, AI Index AFR 51/022/1998, Nov. 1, 1998; Human Rights Watch, *We'll Kill You if You Cry: Sexual Violence in the Sierra Leone Conflict*, Vol. 15, No. 1(A), at 48 (Jan. 15, 2003).

[1098] CDF Transcript, Jan. 30, 2006, at 57–58; CDF Transcript, Jan. 31, 2006, at 43–46; CDF Transcript, Feb. 2, 2006, at 26–27.

[1099] CDF Transcript, Feb. 17, 2005, at 101–02; CDF Transcript, May 26, 2005, at 45–49; CDF Judgement, note 27, at paras. 304–306.

them. Witness TF2-021, a former child soldier, testified that that Kondewa had initiated him and other minors into the Kamajor Society. The Trial Chamber noted that the mere act of initiating minors into the Kamajor Society did not necessarily amount to enlistment into an armed force because many parents asked for their children to be initiated because they believed it would protect them from the violence that was occurring all around them.[1100] In determining that Kondewa's initiation did in fact constitute enlistment, the Trial Chamber considered the circumstances surrounding the initiation and relied, among other things, on witness TF2-021's testimony that Kondewa had told the minors that the initiation process would make them powerful for fighting. The problem with the Trial Chamber's finding was that TF2-021's testimony differed sharply and in numerous respects from the accounts he provided in pretrial statements, so that it constituted an extremely weak basis for a conviction. But that gap between the evidence and the conviction can be bridged by Kondewa's position and its significance in light of the crimes that we know were committed. Kondewa was unquestionably the Kamajors' high priest, and in that position, Kondewa unquestionably initiated civilians and fighters into the Kamajor society, telling them that initiation would protect them from bullets. The CDF unquestionably included minors in its fighting forces. The Trial Chamber heard a great deal of witness testimony on that point,[1101] and it too has been well documented in NGO reports.[1102] Thus, although as a formal matter, the Trial Chamber based Kondewa's conviction exclusively on the testimony of witness TF2-021, that reliance was purely formal. For one thing, it is difficult to imagine the Trial Chamber placing significant weight on testimony that contradicted past statements in so many key respects. And more importantly, the Trial Chamber did not need to rely on that testimony. With or without TF2-021's testimony, the information the Trial Chamber had about the crimes and about Kondewa's role and functions in the CDF created a compelling picture of Kondewa's liability for the enlistment of child soldiers.

[1100] CDF Judgement, note 27, at para. 969.

[1101] CDF Judgement, note 27, at paras. 667–689. Even Norman testified that he "knew that children were involved in the war," but he said that they were because their chiefs would send them to be initiated and immunized so that they could help to defend their country. CDF Transcript, Jan. 31, 2006, at 53–54.

[1102] Amnesty International, *Sierra Leone: 1998 – A Year of Atrocities against Civilians* 28–30, AI Index AFR 51/022/1998, Nov. 1, 1998; Amnesty International, *Sierra Leone: Childhood: A Casualty of Conflict*, AI Index AFR 51/069/2000, Aug. 31, 2000; The Secretary-General, *Fourth Report of the Secretary-General on the United Nations Mission in Sierra Leone*, para. 49, *delivered to the Security Council*, U.N. Doc. S/2000/455 (May 19, 2000); Human Rights Watch, *Sowing Terror: Atrocities Against Civilians in Sierra Leone*, Vol. 10, No. 3(A), section III (July 1998), *available at* http://www.hrw.org/reports98/sierra/.

The foregoing discussion suggests that Fofana's and Kondewa's official positions played a key role in the Trial Chamber's decision to convict them of certain crimes. With respect to other cases, my claim is not so broad. Indeed, as a general matter, my claim is not that most international criminal convictions are founded primarily on inferences drawn from official position instead of on the evidence presented at trial. That may be true in some cases, but whether it is true in a given case depends on the quantity and quality of evidence supporting the Trial Chambers' factual findings as well as on the salience of the defendant's official position vis-à-vis the crimes he is charged with committing. My more modest claim, rather, is that inferences drawn from official position shape the Trial Chambers' treatment of testimonial deficiencies and in particular help to explain – and to some measure justify – the Trial Chambers' seemingly lackadaisical attitude toward those deficiencies.

As I have noted heretofore, testimonial deficiencies can derive from innocent or not-so-innocent causes. Nonresponsive testimony may reflect culturally driven indirectness or a desire to evade. Testimony that contradicts previous statements may reflect interpretation errors or bald-faced lies. The cause of any given testimonial deficiency is key to a Trial Chamber's assessment of the witness's credibility, but in the abstract Trial Chambers have little basis for choosing between causes. Inferences drawn from a defendant's official position create such a basis. Inferences drawn from official position, in fact, simultaneously enhance the apparent reliability of prosecution witness testimony in spite of its deficiencies while minimizing the overall importance of that testimony to the Trial Chamber's fact-finding. On this theory, then, international criminal fact-finding is not nearly as adrift as it appears from reading the transcripts. It remains true that virtually every ICTR case, for instance, features an alibi or some other irreconcilable contradiction between prosecution witness and defense witness testimony. It likewise remains true that in virtually every ICTR case, the Trial Chamber receives no documentary or forensic evidence that would assist it in deciding between competing accounts. But in many cases, the defendant's official position provides such useful information that, although the Trial Chamber is just as uncertain about whether the defendant was in fact participating in a massacre on Bisesero Hill on April 16, 1994 – the particular allegation charged in the indictment – that uncertainty recedes in importance because the defendant's position suggests that even if he was not, he was almost certainly involved in the genocide in some other significant way.

Although reliance on a defendant's official position provides a compelling explanation for many of the Trial Chamber's questionable factual findings, I neither wish to overstate that influence nor to understate the role of direct evidence in shaping the particular convictions that the Trial Chambers eventually impose. Certainly, official position, no matter how compelling, is not alone a sufficient basis for a conviction. Trial Chambers need some evidence on which to publicly base their convictions,[1103] and they need to ensure that the convictions conform to that evidence. So, for instance, because *CDF* witness TF2-222 testified that Fofana told the Kamajors only that they should kill themselves if they failed to carry out Norman's orders, Fofana was convicted of aiding and abetting Norman's instructions to commit war crimes, rather than ordering the war crimes himself. Similarly, because Nallo's testimony involving Fofana primarily centered on their relationship and not on particular orders that Fofana issued to Nallo,[1104] Fofana was convicted on a command responsibility theory for the Kamajors' crimes in Koribondo and Bo rather than for ordering those crimes.

Finally, when the Trial Chambers receive no testimony directly linking the defendant to the crime, then they acquit the defendant of that crime regardless of the salience of his official position. So, for instance, although Fofana was probably just as responsible for the Kamajors' looting of the towns of Tongo Field as he was for the other crimes that the Kamajors committed in those towns, he was not convicted of looting because, according to TF2-222's recounting of Norman's address at the December 1997 passing out parade, Norman had not specifically mentioned looting in the litany of crimes he authorized CDF forces to commit. Another witness testified that Norman did authorize the looting, but during another meeting – a December 1997 commanders' meeting. That witness testified that Fofana also spoke at that meeting, but the witness was unable to remember what Fofana had said, and without some evidence – any evidence – on which to base a finding that Fofana's speech constituted encouragement to Norman's looting instructions, the Trial Chamber was forced to acquit Fofana of looting. Finally, as problematic as witness TF2-021's testimony was, it at least provided the Trial Chamber with some evidence linking Kondewa with the enlistment of child soldiers. Given the CDF's widespread use of child soldiers and Fofana's high leadership position in the CDF, it is reasonable to infer that Fofana also bore some criminal responsibility for the enlistment of child soldiers, but because the prosecution failed to

[1103] At least in most cases, they do. In the *Da Costa and Punef* case, the Special Panels convicted defendants of the murders of eighteen people although it conceded that "not a single direct testimony has been heard in this trial in relation to the murders." The Panel assumed the existence of the murders, reasoning "that this episode is the basis from which all counts of the indictment originate. It is the single most severe criminal event in the history of East Timor. Ceremonies are held each year to commemorate the events.... It would unduly limit the Court to ignore these events and their relevance to this case. Based on the stated magnitude of the facts, the Court finds it impossible not to take them into consideration." Da Costa & Punef Judgement, note 355, at 8.

[1104] Nallo did testify at length, however, about orders he received from Norman. *See, e.g.*, CDF Transcript, Mar. 10, 2005, at 33–35.

present *any* direct evidence of that involvement the Trial Chamber acquitted Fofana of those charges.

In a context in which objective or reliable evidence is so hard to come by, Trial Chambers rely on official position as a proxy, an indicator, if you will, of the defendant's involvement in the atrocities. Prosecutors must still present some evidence to support the specific allegations appearing in the indictment, but the stronger the inferences that can reasonably be drawn from official position, the more that Trial Chambers are willing to ignore problematic features of prosecution witness testimony or attribute them to innocent causes. But just as a defendant's official position can suggest that person's involvement in the atrocities and by doing so can lead Trial Chambers to take a cavalier attitude toward testimonial deficiencies, other proxies can motivate Trial Chambers to scrutinize testimonial deficiencies more carefully. Indeed, although I show in Chapter 7 that Trial Chambers are generally inclined to ignore or explain away testimonial deficiencies, a careful examination of the ICTR's acquittals reveals that that is not always the case, as the following subsection shows.

8.C.ii. *Explaining the Acquittals by Evidentiary Proxies*

In three of the ICTR's six acquittals, the evidence supporting the prosecution's allegations was similar in quality and quantity to the evidence supporting most ICTR convictions. The cases resulted in acquittals rather than convictions, however, and this section suggests that the different result stemmed from the different treatment given to the testimonial deficiencies. In particular, in these acquittal cases, the Trial Chambers appeared to make far more searching inquiries into testimonial deficiencies than is the norm at the ICTR. They scrutinized identifications more carefully, they discredited testimony on the basis of vagueness or inconsistencies of the sort that are routinely overlooked or explained away in other cases, and they seemed, in general, to apply the beyond-a-reasonable-doubt standard with far greater rigor. Although one can hypothesize numerous factors that might explain this enhanced scrutiny – from the temperament of the judges on the panel to the demeanor of witnesses on the stand – a careful examination of the cases suggests that the inclination of these Trial Chambers to conduct a more searching inquiry into testimonial deficiencies was driven primarily by their sense that the defendant did not generally support the genocide. In other words, just as the Trial Chambers' general sense that the defendant was involved in the genocide in some way – that he was one of the bad guys, as it were – inclines it to accept problematic inculpatory testimony about the specific acts that the defendant is charged with performing, the Trial Chamber's general sense that the defendant did not support the genocide – that he was one of the good guys, as it were – inclines it to reject problematic inculpatory testimony about those same sorts of acts. And because any given testimonial deficiency can be plausibly explained on the basis of innocent and not-innocent grounds, the Trial Chamber can choose from an array of rationales to justify its factual determinations.

Consider, for instance, the ICTR prosecution of Ignace Bagilishema, the *bourgmestre* of Mabanza *commune*. The prosecution presented numerous witnesses who claimed to have seen Bagilishema participate in the genocide in various ways and at various times, and Bagilishema presented no particularly strong evidence to rebut that witness testimony. What Bagilishema did present, however, was several pieces of documentary evidence that suggested that he had sought to protect Tutsi and to generally maintain security in his *commune* in spite of the violence that was taking place. Bagilishema appeared unable to stem the anti-Tutsi violence that racked Mabanza *commune* and the surrounding areas in the weeks following President Habyarimana's April 6, 1994, assassination, but Mabanza's register of outgoing mail showed that, from about April 27, Bagilishema made efforts to punish those who had committed crimes against Tutsi and to protect those who were threatened with violence for sheltering Tutsi.[1105] Many Tutsi in Mabanza were killed at roadblocks, which were set up to identify Tutsi and prevent their passage. Although Bagilishema acknowledged that he had authorized the creation of one "official" roadblock, he presented to the Trial Chamber a June 3, 1994, letter in which he asked roadblock guards "not to ill-treat passersby, as some already have done." In that letter, Bagilishema also notified guards that he was establishing a five-member commission to monitor, among other things, "whether passersby have been maltreated."[1106] Finally, and perhaps most notably, the Trial Chamber received into evidence a June 1994 letter that Bagilishema had written to the Prefect; in it, Bagilishema told the Prefect that he had been labeled an RPF "accomplice" by people who claimed that his wife was a Tutsi. Bagilishema also asked the Prefect's assistance in repelling attacks that were being planned against alleged RFP "accomplices" in Mabanza, who Bagilishema claimed, did not exist.[1107]

It is not unusual for ICTR defendants – and particularly those who held regional positions of authority – to assert that they opposed the massacres and did what they could to prevent the anti-Tutsi violence.[1108] What was unusual about Bagilishema's assertions was that they were backed up with documentary evidence. Whereas most defendants who make such assertions support

[1105] Bagilishema Judgement, note 122, at paras. 258–259.
[1106] *Id.* at para. 909.
[1107] *Id.* at para. 323.
[1108] *See, e.g.*, Gacumbitsi Judgement, note 364, at paras. 48, 56, 61, 64, 133–135; Karera Judgement, note 54, at paras. 4, 343, 347, 402, 415; Kajelijeli Judgement, note 303, at para. 262.

them only with their own testimony or the testimony of family members and other Hutu, Bagilishema was able to present contemporaneous documentation that confirmed his efforts to maintain security in the *commune*. Consequently, although the documentary evidence that I have just described did not rebut any of the prosecution's testimony about the specific acts that Bagilishema was alleged to have committed, it provided a context in which to view that testimony. In particular, it created a general sense that Bagilishema was not one of the local officials driving the genocide. And I believe that general sense influenced the Trial Chamber's assessment of the testimony supporting the prosecution's particular allegations. Indeed, whereas Trial Chambers seem relatively unconcerned about the quality and quantity of the testimony supporting the prosecution's charges when the defendant's official position strongly suggests his involvement in the genocide, the *Bagilishema* Trial Chamber turned a searching gaze on the quality and quantity of the testimony supporting the particular charges against Bagilishema and rejected the testimony of numerous prosecution witnesses, pointing to vagueness and inconsistencies – the very testimonial deficiencies that ICTR Trial Chambers routinely overlook.

The *Bagilishema* Trial Chamber, for instance, rejected prosecution witness AC's account largely because her testimony and statements diverged as to the date on which she saw Bagilishema at the Kibuye Stadium; that is, on April 14, 15, or 16. The Trial Chamber also invoked inconsistencies to explain its refusal to credit the testimony of witness O, who had testified that she had overheard Bagilishema planning genocidal acts with Prefect Clement Kayishema. The Trial Chamber pointed in particular to the following inconsistencies between witness O's testimony and her two previous written statements: In both statements, witness O had dated the conversation she overheard as occurring on April 11, 1994, whereas in testimony she placed it on April 12. In her initial statement, the witness failed to mention any derogatory comments made by Prefect Kayishema, whereas those appear in her second statement and in her testimony. Furthermore, in her initial statement, witness O stated that the conversation between Bagilishema and Kayishema had occurred in front of three *gendarmes*, not one, as she stated in testimony, and she placed the conversation as occurring in Bagilishema's office, not in the IGA building, which was 150 to 200 meters away. Her second statement and her testimony placed the event in the IGA building.

The Trial Chamber also pointed to inconsistencies between witness O's testimony in *Bagilishema* and her previous testimony in *Kayishema & Ruzindana*. First, in her *Kayishema & Ruzindana* testimony, witness O was not able to describe the color of one vehicle, maintaining that she did not remember its color because "[w]e were so afraid. We did not have time to pay attention to vehicles." In *Bagilishema*, by contrast, she described the vehicle as a "blue Hilux belonging to Mabanza *commune*."[1109] Second, in *Kayishema & Ruzindana*, witness O described the window where she stood as having had no curtains. In *Bagilishema*, she said that the window had had curtains but that the curtains were not fully drawn and that the window was open. Finally, in *Kayishema & Ruzindana*, the witness described the conversation between Kayishema and Bagilishema as lasting about ten or fifteen minutes, whereas in *Bagilishema* she placed its duration at two to three minutes.[1110] To be sure, the Trial Chamber's careful attention to these inconsistencies is appropriate as such inconsistencies frequently signal false accusations. What careful attention to such inconsistencies is not, however, is standard operating procedure at the Tribunals. Indeed, witness O's inconsistencies are nothing short of trivial when compared to the kinds of inconsistencies that ICTR Trial Chambers routinely overlook. And the Trial Chamber's careful scrutiny of witness O's testimony was not an isolated occurrence. The Chamber likewise rejected the testimony of other witnesses on the basis of similar inconsistencies.[1111]

Finally, the *Bagilishema* Trial Chamber expressed significant concern about vagueness in witness testimony. In one set of allegations, for instance, the prosecutor maintained that Bagilishema had "held a number of meetings during which he encouraged the local population to kill the Tutsi."[1112] Witnesses H and K testified in support of this allegation, but the Trial Chamber found it to be unproven because the testimonies of these witnesses lacked detail. Witness H testified that Bagilishema had "held a meeting in the Gacaca commune and he said all Tutsi houses which were destroyed and which were close to the road, should be cleared off completely because apparently there was a commission of white men which was to come and gather information on the owners of these houses."[1113] This testimony the Trial Chamber deemed "uncorroborated and sketchy" because it was "unclear when the meeting occurred, whether [the witness] was present at the meeting or whether his evidence is hearsay."[1114] Witness K's testimony made out no better. She testified that Bagilishema had conducted a meeting at a clinic, during which he made various anti-Tutsi statements and told the population to destroy Tutsi houses because white people would soon arrive to investigate the events that had taken place

[1109] Bagilishema Judgement, note 122, at para. 392.
[1110] For a discussion of all of the inconsistencies, see *id.* at paras. 387–393, 410–414.
[1111] *See, e.g., id.* at paras. 607–637, 691–700.
[1112] *Id.* at para. 266.
[1113] Bagilishema Transcript, Nov. 19, 1999, at 62.
[1114] Bagilishema Judgement, note 122, at para. 270.

in the *commune*.[1115] Mirroring its treatment of witness H's testimony, the Trial Chamber also deemed witness K's testimony "uncorroborated and sketchy," noting that the witness was "unable to remember in which month the meeting she attended occurred, despite stating it was in June in her witness statement." In addition, the witness "did not know whether, apart from the Accused, other authorities were present."[1116] Juxtaposing this "uncorroborated and sketchy" testimony with the testimony of a number of defense witnesses, who testified that Bagilishema had convened meetings to encourage the population to resist the violence and protect the Tutsi, the Chamber determined that the prosecution had not proven beyond a reasonable doubt that Bagilishema had held meetings to encourage the population to kill Tutsi.

Similarly, the Trial Chamber rejected other testimony at least in part on vagueness grounds. For instance, the Trial Chamber noted that witness A's testimony that he saw Bagilishema at the Kibuye Stadium on April 13 "was recounted with the minimum amount of information." The Trial Chamber noted in particular that the witness "did not mention what the Accused was doing, whether he was accompanied or alone, whether he was standing or sitting in a vehicle, whether he was armed or unarmed."[1117] Witness AC's corroborating testimony – that he too saw Bagilishema at the Stadium on April 13 – was similarly deemed "a bare sketch."[1118] Finally, the Trial Chamber rejected on vagueness grounds witness A's testimony that he saw Bagilishema again at the Stadium on April 14. The Trial Chamber noted, for instance, that it was not clear where in the Stadium witness A was standing when he saw Bagilishema, and witness A's testimony about the defendant's "conduct and other details concerning the course of his visit" was also "very limited."[1119]

As these examples show, the *Bagilishema* Trial Chamber adopted a very different attitude toward fact-finding than is typical for the ICTR, and its divergence from the norm did not go unnoticed. Judge Güney dissented from Bagilishema's acquittal, and in doing so he criticized the "strict assessment standards" that the majority applied to the evidence, maintaining that they were inconsistent with the evidentiary assessment standards articulated in ICTR precedents. Judge Güney pointed in particular to the ICTR's first case – *Akayesu* – where the Trial Chamber had declined to draw adverse inferences from a witness's failure "to be specific as to dates, times, distances and locations" because that failure was attributed to "cultural constraints." As noted in Chapter 7, the *Akayesu* Trial Chamber also adopted a forgiving attitude

[1115] *Id.* at paras. 281–282.
[1116] *Id.* at para. 303.
[1117] *Id.* at para. 537.
[1118] *Id.* at para. 541.
[1119] *Id.* at paras. 547–548.

toward inconsistencies, which Judge Güney likewise cited with approval.[1120] Indeed, in comparison with *Akayesu* and other ICTR precedents, Judge Güney deemed the *Bagilishema* majority's evidentiary approach to be "artificial and far-fetched."[1121]

The *Mpambara* case, another ICTR acquittal, also featured a *bourgmestre* – this time Jean Mpambara – who alleged that he sought to protect Tutsi from the bloodthirsty hordes who eventually massacred thousands of them. Unlike *Bagilishema*, Mpambara presented no documentary evidence to support his claims, but he did present the testimony of a British physiotherapist and a Spanish priest, and that testimony created a compelling picture of Mpambara as a *bourgmestre* who did everything he could to protect the Tutsi in his *commune*. Although defendants in other cases present witnesses who make similar claims, their witnesses are Rwandan. Mpambara's witnesses were not, and the Trial Chamber seemed to give their testimony greater weight presumably because the testimony was not so apt to be colored by the incentives or biases that can prove influential to Rwandan witnesses. Indeed, the *Mpambara* Trial Chamber gave the defense testimony such weight that it reversed what had been a *de facto* presumption: Whereas Trial Chambers typically disbelieve defense witness testimony when it contradicts the testimony of prosecution witnesses,[1122] the *Mpambara* Trial Chamber discredited prosecution witness testimony that contradicted the accounts provided by the British physiotherapist and the Spanish priest. And in justifying its rejection of such prosecution testimony, the *Mpambara* Trial Chamber, like the *Bagilishema* Trial Chamber, pointed to the kinds of testimonial deficiencies that Trial Chambers typically overlook.

For instance, like the *Bagilishema* Trial Chamber, the *Mpambara* Trial Chamber expressed considerable concern about inconsistencies between witnesses' testimony and their pretrial statements. Witness LED, for instance, testified that Mpambara had delivered quartzite stones to *Interahamwe* militia members located outside of the Rukara Parish church to use against Tutsi refugees sheltering inside the church. The Trial Chamber rejected LED's testimony, noting that it was inconsistent in some respects with his prior statement. In

[1120] Prosecutor v. Bagilishema, Case No. ICTR-95-1A-T, Separate and Dissenting Opinion of Judge Mehmet Güney, paras. 28–29 (June 7, 2001) [hereinafter Judge Güney Dissent] (quoting Akayesu Judgement, note 32, at para. 156).

[1121] Judge Güney Dissent, note 1120, at para. 27.

[1122] *See, e.g.*, Kajelijeli Judgement, note 303, at paras. 524–530, 680; Ntakirutimana Judgement, note 69, at paras. 293–302, 375–384; Gacumbitsi Judgement, note 364, at paras. 89, 153; Karera Judgement, note 54, at paras. 119, 309–313, 372–373, 499, 525; Kayishema & Ruzindana Judgement, note 25, at paras. 244–255, 266–271, 394; Simba Judgement, note 455, at paras. 177, 279–295, 381; Semanza Judgement, note 31, at paras. 91–93; Muhimana Judgement, note 363, at paras. 134–155, 250–251; Ndindabahizi Judgement, note 56, at paras. 384–396.

particular, LED's statement reported that Mpambara had come to the church three times, rather than just once, and had deposited the stones at various locations outside of the church.[1123] LED asserted on cross-examination that there must have been a translation error, for he had said "that the offloading took place in three different locations and he moved from one corner to another and to another," not that the vehicle had come three times.[1124] The Trial Chamber's judgment fails even to mention LED's explanation, and although it is just the sort of explanation that Trial Chambers usually credit, particularly given their stated preference for oral testimony, the *Mpambara* Trial Chamber summarily concluded that the "discrepancy is not easily explained as a transcription or translation error."[1125] The Trial Chamber's rejection of LED's testimony is likewise not easily explained by a general concern about inconsistencies. More important no doubt was the fact that two defense witnesses – one of whom was the Spanish priest – had been inside the church when Mpambara was alleged to have delivered the rocks, but neither had seen the delivery. Trial Chambers usually dismiss that sort of testimony, pointing out that just because a witness did not see an event does not mean that the event did not occur.[1126] Here, however, it was a particularly credible defense witness who failed to see an event, and that failure formed part of a larger narrative that presented Mpambara as uninvolved in the atrocities.

The Trial Chamber similarly pointed to discrepancies between the accounts of witnesses AVK and LEF to justify its refusal to credit their testimony.[1127] Both witnesses testified that Mpambara had come to the Akabeza Center on the morning of April 7, 1994, and had met with certain individuals – Gacumbitsi, Gasana, and Butera – who later led attacks against the *commune*'s Tutsi. According to witness AVK, Mpambara had arrived at about 11:00 a.m.; had entered a shop with Gacumbitsi, Gasana, and Butera; and had emerged from the shop with the same three individuals about twenty minutes after he had arrived. Gacumbitsi then addressed the crowd, telling it to avenge the death of President Habyarimana by killing Tutsi. Witness AVK maintained that Mpambara was present when Gacumbitsi made this particular statement but left soon after, while Gacumbitsi was still speaking. LEF, by contrast, placed Mpambara's arrival at the Center between 9 and 10 a.m. LEF testified that as soon as Mpambara exited his truck, he made a loud anti-Tutsi statement. According

[1123] Mpambara Judgement, note 471, at para. 151.
[1124] Prosecutor v. Mpambara, Case No. ICTR-01–65-T, Transcript, Sept. 26, 2005, at 36.
[1125] Mpambara Judgement, note 471, at para. 151.
[1126] *See, e.g.*, Gacumbitsi Judgement, note 364, at para. 223; Karera Judgement, note 54, at para. 525; Ndindabahizi Judgement, note 56, at para. 169; Muhimana Judgement, note 363, at paras. 25, 104, 161, 162, 201, 250, 342, 343, 373, 374.
[1127] Mpambara Judgement, note 471, at paras. 58–59.

to LEF, Mpambara went indoors for his meeting, but Butera stayed outside exhorting the crowd to avenge the president's death.[1128] The Trial Chamber concluded that the discrepancies between the two witnesses' accounts could not be explained by their different vantage points and that the discrepancies were "significant enough" that they raised "a reasonable doubt as to the reliability of both witnesses in respect of this event."[1129]

In recounting the Trial Chamber's treatment of AVK's and LEF's testimony, I do not mean to suggest that I consider the discrepancies between their accounts to be trivial. Far from it. I do suggest, however, that they are precisely the sort of discrepancies that Trial Chambers frequently encounter and just as frequently overlook. In *Kajelijeli*, for instance, witnesses GBG and ACM both described an attack at Munyemvano's compound. Both witnesses claimed that Kajelijeli had led the attack, but that was the only commonality in their testimony. Whereas witness GBG gave the number of *Interahamwe* participating in the attack as around a hundred, ACM put the number at about thirty. Whereas witness GBG testified that Kajelijeli wore no uniform, witness ACM maintained that he wore the same uniform as the *Interahamwe*. Finally, and most importantly, whereas witness GBG claimed that Kajelijeli had killed one Gateyiteyi, the son of Munyemvano, witness ACM testified that Gateyiteyi was killed by a man named Felix Ndayambaje.[1130] Although the Trial Chamber acknowledged these many discrepancies, it dismissed them as unimportant, determining that it was appropriate to "make an allowance" because "both Witnesses were in fear of their lives, and the Witnesses' attention would have been otherwise focused than paying attention to details."[1131] Although the *Kajelijeli* Trial Chamber was not willing to find that Kajelijeli had killed Gateyiteyi because witness ACM had identified another man as his killer, it did find it proven beyond a reasonable doubt that Kajelijeli had commanded and supervised the attack at Munyemvano's compound.[1132] It did so, moreover, in spite of defense witnesses who testified that no attack had occurred at Munyemvano's compound. Although the Trial Chamber was in possession of no forensic evidence proving that an attack had occurred, it nonetheless summarily labeled the defense testimony "unpersuasive" and concluded that it was "not inclined to believe their testimonies."[1133] In a similar vein, *AFRC* witnesses TF1-334 and TF1-033 testified about certain instructions that defendant Brima gave to his troops. The *AFRC* Trial Chamber determined that the two witnesses were speaking of the

[1128] *Id.* at paras. 55–56.
[1129] *Id.* at para. 59.
[1130] Kajelijeli Judgement, note 303, at paras. 592–594.
[1131] *Id.* at para. 595.
[1132] *Id.* at para. 597.
[1133] *Id.* at para. 596.

same event even though they placed it in different cities and gave substantially different accounts of the content of the instructions.[1134] For better or worse, the treatment of witness discrepancies appearing in *Kajelijeli* and *AFRC* stands as the norm.[1135]

The *Mpambara* Trial Chamber diverged from that norm in one final respect: its careful scrutiny of time discrepancies, which mirrored the *Bagilishema* Trial Chamber's careful scrutiny of date discrepancies. Prosecution witness AHY testified that Mpambara had arrived at the Paris Center sometime between 9 and 10 a.m. on April 9, 1994, and made statements inciting anti-Tutsi violence.[1136] The timing of Mpambara's arrival at the Paris Center was important because defense witness Elizabeth Hardinge – the British physio-therapist – testified that Mpambara was with her that day from about 9:30 a.m. onward. Mpambara could have visited both the Paris Center and Ms. Hardinge, because witness AHY testified that Mpambara's stop at the Paris Center lasted only ten to fifteen minutes, the two locations were only three kilometers apart, and Ms. Hardinge was not sure of the exact time that Mpambara came to her. The Trial Chamber nonetheless rejected witness AHY's testimony, ostensibly because he reported in a statement given two weeks before he testified that Mpambara had arrived at the Paris Center at 11 a.m. The witness's assertion that the time was written incorrectly in the statement "due to a translation error" was summarily deemed "not . . . plausible."[1137]

Although, on the surface, the ICTR's acquittal of Emmanuel Bagambiki, the former prefect of Cyangugu, differed to some degree from the *Bagilishema* and *Mpambara* acquittals, a closer look suggests that it was driven by the same factors; that is, by the Trial Chamber's overall sense that Bagambiki did not support the genocide. Unlike Bagilishema and Mpambara, Bagambiki did not present particularly credible evidence suggesting that he had no involvement in the violence. Indeed, Bagambiki admitted engaging in much of the conduct the prosecution attributed to him, and the question for the Trial Chamber was what legal conclusions could be drawn from that conduct.[1138] Bagambiki admitted, for instance, that he had removed sixteen refugees who were accused of having RPF ties from the Cyangugu Cathedral and the Kamarampaka Stadium and

1134 *Compare* AFRC Transcript, May 23, 2005, at 15–17 *with* AFRC Transcript, July 11, 2005, at 13–15. *See also* AFRC Judgement, note 27, at paras. 1691, 1693.

1135 And this norm diverges from early Roman and English law, which provided that "when two accusers or witnesses varied in their testimony, neither was to be credited." Shapiro, note 884, at 30.

1136 Mpambara Judgement, note 471, at para. 122.

1137 *Id.* at para. 123.

1138 Although a few witnesses claimed that Bagambiki distributed weapons or made anti-Tutsi statements, the testimony of these witnesses was so problematic that the Trial Chamber had no choice but to discredit it.

that he had handed them over to soldiers for questioning.[1139] The refugees were killed later that day, and the prosecution, along with Judge Williams in dissent, argued that Bagambiki had aided and abetted in their murders, not least because he publicly denounced the refugees as RPF associates and turned them over to soldiers whom he knew had engaged in previous, public anti-Tutsi massacres.[1140] Although that conclusion seemed well supported by the facts, the majority determined that the Trial Chamber lacked "sufficient reliable evidence" to conclude that Bagambiki bore any criminal responsibility for the deaths of the refugees.[1141]

The majority reached a similar conclusion about the death of Côme Simugomwa, an opposition party member. The majority determined that Bagambiki and others had removed Simugomwa from a crowd of refugees at the Gashirabwoba football field, after announcing that Simugomwa had been summoned to discuss party affairs. Simugomwa was found dead later that day. Although given the violence prevailing at the time, it again would have been reasonable to infer that Bagambiki knew of the harm that would likely befall Simugomwa when he removed him from the football field, the majority concluded that it lacked "sufficient evidence to determine what role" Bagambiki played in Simugomwa's death.[1142] Finally, in a similar vein, two prosecution witnesses testified that Bagambiki had chastised certain *gendarmes* for killing some *Interahamwe* militia members. Bagambiki and a defense witness provided different accounts of Bagambiki's treatment of the *gendarmes*, however, and the Trial Chamber concluded that it lacked sufficient reliable evidence to conclude that Bagambiki had chastised the *gendarmes*.[1143]

By reaching these conclusions, the Trial Chamber put real teeth into the beyond-a-reasonable-doubt standard, unprecedented teeth, in fact. The Trial Chamber's failure to find that Bagambiki had chastised the *gendarmes* who had killed the *Interahamwe* members was particularly surprising because the Trial Chamber pointed to no defects in the testimony of the prosecution witnesses, and all things being equal, Trial Chambers typically do not view defense witness testimony that contradicts prosecution witness testimony as creating reasonable doubt. Why the Trial Chamber applied the reasonable doubt standard with such uncharacteristic rigor in this case and not in others cannot be conclusively determined, but my analysis suggests that the Trial Chamber's conclusions stemmed not from any real doubt, for instance, that Bagambiki knew and indeed probably intended the fate that befell the particular

[1139] Ntagerura Judgement, note 37, at paras. 279–281.
[1140] *Id.* at Dissenting Opinion of Judge Williams, at paras. 9–15.
[1141] *Id.* at paras. 337, 674.
[1142] *Id.* at paras. 435–442.
[1143] *Id.* at paras. 552, 559, 566, 574, 582.

Tutsi refugees whom he delivered to soldiers but because his actions with respect to those Tutsi did not bespeak his support for or his involvement in the larger genocidal project.

As noted, Bagambiki admitted to removing the sixteen refugees from the Cyangugu Cathedral and Kamarampaka Stadium, but he did so, he maintained, for a good reason: to prevent a large-scale attack against the entire lot of refugees who were taking shelter at the stadium. Bagambiki testified that the assailants had provided him a list of refugees, who, they alleged, were armed, were communicating with the RPF via radio, and who were planning to attack their neighbors. Bagambiki believed, he said, that removing these people from the stadium would forestall an attack against all of the refugees, and he maintained that the refugees agreed with his reasoning. Bagambiki testified that when he went to the stadium and explained the situation to the refugees, "they applauded the decision to remove the sixteen or seventeen listed persons in order to ensure the safety of the stadium."[1144] Bagambiki's contentions were plausible because the prosecution presented no credible evidence that Bagambiki was involved in any large-scale massacre. The picture created in *Bagambiki*, then, is not of the entirely innocent public servant who opposed the massacres and who had absolutely no involvement in them, which was the picture depicted in *Bagilishema* and *Mpambara*. Bagambiki, by contrast, almost certainly had blood on his hands. But that blood got there from Bagambiki's efforts to minimize the harm that would otherwise have been done to the Tutsi. Bagambiki decided to sacrifice the few for the benefit of the many, and, in doing so, he probably satisfied the elements of aiding and abetting murder as a crime against humanity. But the Trial Chamber did not convict him of that crime, I suspect, not because it reasonably doubted his commission of it but because Bagambiki did not appear to be a *genocidaire*.

An examination of ICTR cases – both the many convictions and the occasional acquittals – shows that when the Trial Chambers assess prosecution witness testimony concerning the specific acts or events that the witness allegedly witnessed, their assessments of that testimony are substantially influenced by the Trial Chambers' overall views about the defendant's likely support for the genocide. That overall view derives in large measure from the defendant's official position but can also stem from particularly credible evidence that shows the defendant to have resisted the violence or, if he participated in it, to have participated without genocidal intent. Thus, because a defendant's official position so often gives Trial Chambers strong reason to believe that the defendant played some substantial role in the genocide, Trial Chambers typically proclaim their preference for oral testimony and dismiss inconsistencies between

[1144] *Id.* at para. 281.

that testimony and a witness's previous statements as stemming from innocent causes. Yet, Trial Chambers will invoke those same sorts of inconsistencies to discredit prosecution testimony when their overall sense is that the defendant was not driving the genocidal violence in that region. Similarly, divergences in the accounts of prosecution witnesses that Trial Chambers usually explain away as resulting from different vantage points or an understandable failure to attend to details given the stresses of the situation will be seen to fundamentally undermine the prosecution's allegations, when those allegations fail to conform to the Trial Chamber's overall assessment of the defendant's culpability. And in those cases reasonable doubt, which so rarely makes an appearance in international criminal cases, can unexpectedly materialize to derail prosecution allegations.

I have explained the Trial Chambers' more rigorous scrutiny of testimonial deficiencies in *Bagilishema*, *Mpambara*, and *Bagambiki* as deriving from the Chambers' overall sense that those defendants did not support the genocide. That overall sense, particularly in *Bagilishema* and *Mpambara*, was created by defense evidence that was more credible and reliable than the norm. However, because official position stands as such a probative indicator of a defendant's participation in the atrocities, I believe that it was not coincidental to their acquittals that the three defendants held positions that did not necessarily give rise to inculpatory inferences. Bagilishema and Mpambara were *bourgmestres*, and Bagambiki was a *prefet*, which positions can be roughly analogized to a mayor and a governor, respectively. Certainly many *bourgmestres* and *prefets* enthusiastically participated in the violence in their regions. Indeed, the Rwandan government classified eighty-six of the approximately 140 *bourgmestres* who were in office while the genocide took place – or 61 percent – as Category 1 offenders who planned, instigated, or organized the genocide.[1145] But even that statistic, which may be inflated given the Rwandan government's well-known tendency to overcharge, still acknowledges that a substantial minority of *bourgmestres* were not driving local violence. After Bagambiki was acquitted, his lawyers stated: "We had feared that he would be judged for the position he held and not for his personal responsibility."[1146] Fortunately for Bagambiki, the "position he held" did not create as strong a presumption of guilt as many positions do.

The final three defendants to be acquitted by the ICTR did hold positions that create a strong presumption of guilt. Gratien Kabiligi held a high-level position in the Rwandan army at the time of the genocide, and André Ntagerura and

[1145] Othman, note 35, at 175.
[1146] *Acquittals of Former Government Officials Raises Mixed Reactions*, Hirondelle News Agency, Feb. 26, 2004.

André Rwamakuba were in Rwanda's Interim Government. Rwandan Colonel Théoneste Bagosora – the man who is widely believed to have masterminded the genocide – handpicked the ministers of the Interim Government, all of whom were members of the "Hutu Power" factions of their parties.[1147] Thus, although the Ministers "nominally came from a range of political parties, . . . in reality they either represented hardliner factions within their respective parties or were malleable."[1148] Because the official positions of Kabiligi, Ntagerura, and Rwamakuba strongly suggested their involvement in the genocide, it came as something of a surprise when the ICTR acquitted them. A closer look at the cases, however, reveals that the prosecution's evidence was terrifically problematic even by international tribunal standards. *Ntagerura, Rwamakuba,* and *Kabiligi,* then, are not cases like *Bagilishema* and *Mpambara,* where the Trial Chambers rejected prosecution testimony of the sort Trial Chambers routinely accept. Rather, as one would expect in cases involving defendants who held high-level positions in a government that carried out a genocide, the prosecution testimony that the Trial Chambers rejected in acquitting Ntagerura, Kabiligi, and Rwamakuba was either proven to be perjured or was otherwise patently unreliable.

It was perjured testimony that predominated in the trial of André Ntagerura, who had been Minister of Transport and Communications in the Interim Government and who was tried together with Bagambiki and a third defendant, Samuel Imanishimwe. In particular, virtually all of the allegations against Ntagerura derived from the testimony of three witnesses who were shown to have perjured themselves and a fourth witness who was accused of testifying falsely in a criminal case in Rwanda. The three perjuring witnesses were LAI, LAP, and LAB, whose perjury was discussed in Chapter 5. In sum, these witnesses accused Ntagerura, Bagambiki, and Gratian Kabiligi, – who was tried in a different case – of distributing weapons to *Interahamwe* militia at the Bugarama football field on January 28, 1994, and of encouraging the *Interahamwe* to commit violence against the Tutsi. Kabiligi's passport showed him to have been in Egypt on that day, however, so it came as no surprise when the Trial Chamber determined that the "events did not occur in the manner alleged by witnesses LAI and LAP."[1149] Witness LAB, for his part, was shown to have

[1147] Leave None to Tell the Story, note 644, at 196–98; Linda Melvern, Conspiracy to Murder: The Rwandan Genocide 173 (2004).

[1148] Scott Straus, The Order of Genocide: Race, Power and War in Rwanda 47 (2006). After the Ministers in the Interim Government had been appointed, their names "were read over the radio by Hutu Power hardliners Valérie Bemeriki and Noël Hitimana. After Bemeriki read out the names of the ministers she began to giggle and told her listeners the opposition members in the previous government could not be found." Melvern, note 1147, at 172.

[1149] Ntagerura Judgement, note 37, at para. 129.

lied when he accused Ntagerura of engaging in criminal activities in Rwanda during the end of April and beginning of May because Ntagerura's passport showed him to have been out of the country during that time.[1150] After determining that the witnesses' testimony on these matters was not to be believed, the Trial Chamber declined to credit other aspects of their testimony, which the prosecution had relied on to support most of its remaining allegations.[1151]

The Trial Chamber had no direct proof that the fourth witness – witness LAH – perjured himself, but a defense witness alleged that LAH had made and then recanted false testimony about that witness in Rwandan courts, and the defense substantiated that allegation by introducing letters allegedly written by LAH in which he admitted the perjury before the Rwandan courts. The Trial Chamber found these allegations sufficient to call witness LAH's credibility into serious question.[1152] Virtually all of the allegations against Ntagerura were made by the four witnesses just described; the few remaining allegations were made by witness LAJ and witness MZ. Witness LAJ's testimony overlapped with and corroborated witnesses LAI and LAP's perjured testimony regarding the weapons distribution at the Bugarama football field. Because witness LAJ did not implicate Kabiligi, as LAI and LAP had, the Trial Chamber had no direct proof that his testimony was perjured, although it would be reasonable to suspect that it was. Witness LAJ's testimony did, however, sharply diverge from his previous statement; in particular, whereas witness LAJ testified that he had participated with Ntagerura in the weapons distribution on January 28, 2004, his statement reported that he had remained at home between January and April 1994 as a result of an injury. The Trial Chamber consequently invoked this inconsistency when it declined to credit his testimony.[1153] The only prosecution witness for whom there was no substantial evidence of perjury was witness MZ, who testified that while hiding behind a latrine in a tea plantation, he heard Ntagerura encourage a crowd to attack Tutsi. Witness MZ testified that he was about ten meters away from Ntagerura when Ntagerura made this speech, but a defense investigator visited the site and determined that the latrine was located between forty and fifty meters from Ntagerura's alleged position. Because the distance between the two men was great, the Trial Chamber determined that the witness could not have identified Ntagerura or accurately followed what was taking place at the meeting.[1154] Ntagerura's acquittal shows, then, that Trial Chambers might be willing to explain away some serious inconsistencies and to give prosecution witnesses the benefit of the doubt in some questionable

[1150] *Id.* at para. 176.
[1151] *Id.* at paras. 92, 108, 113, 174.
[1152] *Id.* at para. 118.
[1153] *Id.* at para. 130.
[1154] *Id.* at para. 175.

circumstances where the defendant's official position is strongly suggestive of his guilt, but they will not base a conviction on the testimony of proven perjurers.

Although Kabiligi was tried with a different set of co-defendants, some of the charges against Kabiligi concerned the same incidents featured in *Ntagerura*. With respect to these charges, as just noted, Kabiligi presented several alibis that placed him outside of Rwanda during key events;[1155] these alibis, consequently, contradicted the testimony of numerous prosecution witnesses. The Trial Chamber accepted Kabiligi's alibis because they were confirmed by documentary evidence and the testimony of UN officials and foreign diplomats.[1156] The prosecution also included Kabiligi in many of the charges that it leveled against his codefendants, but with respect to a large proportion of those charges, the prosecution failed to present any evidence implicating Kabiligi.[1157] Finally, for each of the remainder of the charges for which the prosecution did present some testimony against Kabiligi, it relied on the testimony of only one witness,[1158] and the testimony of most of these witnesses was plagued by serious credibility problems. Thus, each of the prosecution's charges against Kabiligi failed: some because they were supported by no evidence;[1159] some because they conflicted with one of Kabiligi's well-proven alibis;[1160] some because they were based on only the hearsay testimony of one witness; and some because they were based on the testimony of only one witness who was almost certainly lying or fundamentally mistaken.[1161] Indeed, most of the claims suffered from a combination of these defects,[1162] and the defects were so obviously fatal to the prosecution's case that the prosecution declined even to appeal Kabiligi's acquittal.[1163]

Even more severe problems bedeviled the testimony supporting the prosecution's allegations against André Rwamakuba, a medical doctor who had served as minister of primary and secondary education in the Interim Government. At the very start of its judgment, the Trial Chamber intimated that the prosecution had not put together a very strong case. Of eighteen prosecution

1155 Bagosora et al. Judgement, note 484, at paras. 1969–1986.
1156 *Id.* at paras. 1970, 1976, 1981, 1986.
1157 *Id.* at paras. 383, 410, 425, 580-581, 619, 648, 724, 753, 891, 1429.
1158 *Id.* at para. 33.
1159 *See* sources cited in note 1157.
1160 Bagosora et al. Judgement, note 484, at paras. 270, 281, 298, 503, 794, 906, 927, 939, 972, 989, 1361, 1382, 1521, 1529, 1629, 1749, 1776, 1928.
1161 *Id.* at paras. 271, 1521, 1567, 1785–1788.
1162 *See, e.g., id.* at paras. 268–274, 515–1521, 1528–1530, 1881, 1895.
1163 Prosecution v. Bagosora et al., Case No. ICTR-98-41-T, Decision on Prosecution Motion Requesting the Trial Chamber to Lift Restrictions on Gratien Kabiligi's Liberty, para. 2 (Mar. 24, 2009).

witnesses, only five claimed to have direct knowledge of Rwamakuba, leading the Trial Chamber to observe that "the Prosecution's evidence consisted mainly of hearsay evidence."[1164] Moreover, a number of those witnesses almost certainly perjured themselves. For instance, a passel of prosecution witnesses testified that Rwamakuba had called for anti-Tutsi violence at a number of rallies during the end of 1993 and the beginning of 1994, but Rwamakuba was studying at the Prince Leopold Institute in Antwerp, Belgium, between September 1993 and March 1994, and his passport showed that he did not enter Rwanda during those months.[1165] The prosecution's other allegations against Rwamakuba were also supported only by highly problematic witness testimony. For example, although six witnesses attested to Rwamakuba's substantial involvement in the massacres at Butare University Hospital, five failed even to mention Rwamakuba in their statements to investigators or in their testimony in other cases. Witness XV, indeed, gave prosecutors *seven* prior statements, and he testified in *three* cases in Rwanda, yet in none of these did he make any mention of Rwamakuba.[1166] Other witnesses struggled even to identify Rwamakuba. Only one of the six witnesses – witness XV – claimed to have known Rwamakuba before the events at issue, and XV's claim itself proved questionable; whereas XV said that he had gotten to know Rwamakuba when Rwamakuba was attending the Faculty of Medicine of Butare University during 1973 and 1974, Rwamakuba was in fact in Belgium during those years.[1167] The Trial Chamber noted in addition that witness XV "did not appear to know what André Rwamakuba looked like." He first "confused Rwamakuba with one Rekeraho. Then, when shown a picture in court, he confused Rwamakuba with a priest."[1168] Witness GIO's identification was not much better, as he also identified the man named Rekeraho "as probably being Rwamakuba."[1169] And several other witnesses said that they had not known Rwamakuba before the events in question but had only been told that it was he by XV – whose identification was seemingly faulty – or by people who had since died.[1170]

Numerous and severe inconsistencies also served to discredit the testimony of these witnesses. The "core element" in witness GIO's testimony, for instance, concerned an attack on her brother at Butare University Hospital. At trial, witness GIO testified that Rwamakuba and other Hutu doctors had checked the identity cards of patients in the surgical ward and had identified her

1164 Rwamakuba Judgement, note 63, at para. 36.
1165 *Id.* at paras. 70–83.
1166 *Id.* at para. 172.
1167 *Id.* at para. 171.
1168 *Id.* at para. 174.
1169 *Id.* at para. 176.
1170 *Id.*

brother as a Tutsi. Immediately thereafter, witness GIO maintained, one of the doctors – Dr. Gatera – killed her brother with an axe. Then, Rwamakuba, Dr. Gatera, and the *Interahamwe* put her brother's corpse into a pickup truck, along with the corpses of other Tutsi whom they had killed. However, prior to her testimony in *Rwamakuba*, witness GIO had testified in another ICTR case and had given ICTR prosecutors several statements; in each one, her account of her brother's death changed. In some statements, she asserted that she had not seen her brother's killing but that he had been driven away, while still alive, in the pickup truck. In another statement, she attested that she had witnessed Dr. Gatera kill her brother with an axe, but in that account Rwamakuba was not present. And in yet another statement, witness GIO claimed that Dr. Gatera ordered a man named Athanas to kill her brother, which he did.[1171]

The inconsistencies pervading the testimony of witness HF were just as striking. Witness HF testified that she was at the Butare University Hospital visiting her sister, who had just given birth. Witness HF asserted that over a period of days, she saw Rwamakuba doing violence to Tutsi patients; and, on one of these days, Rwamakuba took the witness's sister away. This account differs from the accounts witness HF provided to ICTR investigators, which themselves diverge from one another. In some accounts, the witness's brother was also at the hospital and was also taken away, whereas in other accounts the sister and brother were killed while lying in their hospital beds. Witness HF's testimony in the *Rwamakuba* trial differed also from her testimony in two cases that were brought in Rwandan courts. In one case, the witness gave a different name for her sister than the name she provided in *Rwamakuba*. In the other case, she testified that one of her sisters had been shot by one Rurangirwa in a specific *secteur* in Butare *prefecture*. The name she gave for the sister who had been shot by Rurangirwa was the same as the name she gave for the sister she claimed had been killed at Butare University Hospital. And if these inconsistencies were not enough, HF's testimony contradicted other prosecution evidence.[1172]

The testimony supporting the few remaining allegations against Rwamakuba was equally problematic.[1173] It came as no surprise, therefore, when the Trial

[1171] *Id.* at para. 186.

[1172] *Id.* at paras. 187–190.

[1173] Because Rwamakuba refused to attend his trial, *id.* at para. 9, many witnesses "were not able to offer any physical description of the person they claim[ed] to be Rwamakuba," *id.* at para. 94. In addition, the allegations that Rwamakuba distributed machetes to the home of Etienne Kamanzi, for instance, or that he participated in a massacre at the Kayanga Health Center were attested to by the same witnesses who placed Rwamakuba at Rwandan rallies when he was in fact in Belgium. Moreover, the testimony of these witnesses was problematic even without regard to their testimony about the rallies. For instance, two of the witnesses – GAC and GAB – had testified for the prosecution in the *Kamuhanda* case, but had been found

Chamber acquitted Rwamakuba despite his high-level position in the Rwandan government.

8.C.iii. *Summary*

In this section, I have argued that the factors that drove the drafters of the Nuremberg Charter to provide for organizational liability remain at work today at the international tribunals under study, and they provide an especially compelling explanation for the Trial Chambers' cavalier treatment of testimonial deficiencies. The Charter's drafters provided for organizational liability because they did not have the resources to try each offender individually, and, even if they did, they would not have been able to obtain evidence of the defendants' criminal acts. New and unusual methods for ascribing liability were therefore necessary because, as Article 9's drafter Murray Bernays put it: "It will never be possible to catch and convict every Axis war criminal, or even any great number of them, under the old concepts and procedures."[1174]

The foregoing chapters show that it may not be possible to "catch and convict" even a relatively small number of high level international offenders "under the old concepts and procedures" given the difficulties of obtaining credible, reliable evidence of their criminal acts. In the typical ICTR case, for instance, prosecutors seek to prove that the defendant has engaged in X, Y, or Z acts which satisfy the actus reus and mens rea elements of genocide. But because the testimony supporting these allegations is so frequently problematic, group membership, or even more specifically official position, continues to be a salient factor in a Trial Chamber's decision whether to convict or acquit a defendant. It is not the only factor, as the drafters of the Nuremberg Charter envisioned that it would be. But it is a highly influential factor in many cases, and in these cases it serves to explain the Trial Chambers' willingness to base convictions on questionable prosecution testimony. In many cases, indeed, the inferences that can reasonably be drawn from the defendant's official position so strongly indicate his involvement in the crimes that the particular testimony placing the defendant at particular locations and engaged in particular acts recedes substantially in importance.

I contended in Chapter 6 that international trials purport a fact-finding competence that they do not possess. The Trial Chambers, I argued, were adrift.

to be unreliable by the *Kamuhanda* Trial Chamber, and one of them indeed had "described André Rwamakuba's behaviour and the account of events in the same way as he described Kamuhanda's criminal acts when testifying as a Prosecution witness in that case; he also attributed much of the same words to Kamuhanda and Rwamakuba." *Id.* at para. 149.

[1174] Bradley F. Smith, The American Road to Nuremberg: The Documentary Record 1944–1945, at 35 (1982).

This chapter has suggested that although the Trial Chambers' fact-finding is adrift when it comes to the specific allegations that appear in the indictments, that fact is not so troubling as it might appear because the Trial Chambers' determinations about those specific allegations often do not drive their decisions to convict or acquit defendants. At the same time, my analysis suggests that the show trial elements of international criminal trials may be more extensive than initially apprehended precisely because these trials purport to center themselves around testimony that in many cases plays only a supporting role in the Trial Chamber's decision to convict or acquit the defendant. Although the prosecution presents witness testimony, the Trial Chambers assess this testimony, and the Trial Chambers' assessments ostensibly form the bases of the Trial Chambers' legal conclusions, my analysis suggests that Tribunal fact-finding is broader and less focused on specific acts than it appears. Rather than focusing exclusively on whether a defendant transported armed *Interahamwe* members to a massacre site on April 12, 1994, for instance – a question that the Trial Chamber will not be able to answer with any certainty in any event – the Trial Chambers instead are engaging in a more comprehensive and holistic process that seeks to determine beyond a reasonable doubt whether the defendant was involved in the violence in some substantial way.

In discussing the American practice of charge bargaining, Mirjan Damaška wrote that the American criminal justice system "often seems satisfied with establishing merely a rough basis for punishment – sometimes a mere torso of actual wrongdoing – leaving the more precise delineation of factual parameters to the initiative of the parties."[1175] It is this same "rough basis for punishment," this "torso of actual wrongdoing" that frequently must suffice even after a lengthy, costly international trial has been conducted. Precision about acts and events is not attainable at the international tribunals under study, and the best that we can hope for in many cases is a finding beyond a reasonable doubt that the defendant played some role – or did not – in the relevant atrocities. That is not a palatable truth, however, so the Trial Chambers invoke only the specific testimony that they receive about the specific acts the defendant engaged in. As a consequence, however, the stated justifications for many international criminal convictions markedly diverge from their actual ones.

[1175] Mirjan Damaška, The Faces of Justice and State Authority: A Comparative Approach to the Legal Process 112 (1986) [hereinafter Damaška, Faces of Justice].

9

Help Needed

Practical Suggestions and Procedural Reforms to Improve Fact-Finding Accuracy

The foregoing chapters have sought to analyze and explain international criminal fact-finding as it is carried out by the ICTR, SCSL, and Special Panels. That analysis and explanation give rise to a series of normative questions, which I consider in this chapter and the next. This chapter explores various reforms that might be undertaken to improve the accuracy of international criminal fact-finding. Now that we know what sort of fact-finding impediments exist at the international tribunals, we can consider proposals to ameliorate the effects of those impediments. Section 9.A begins that discussion by considering various adaptations to the pretrial, trial, and posttrial processes that currently exist at the international tribunals. Section 9.B explores more radical reforms; it considers whether international trial procedures should be fundamentally reformulated, as a means of enhancing fact-finding accuracy. Before launching into my suggestions for improvement, I wish to frame them with the recognition that the evidentiary problems that I have heretofore identified permit no easy resolution. Western criminal procedures presuppose the existence of witnesses who are willing and able to convey – in a way understandable to the fact-finder – certain information about the events that they have witnessed. To the extent that witnesses are unwilling or unable to perform these tasks, factual accuracy will suffer. How much factual accuracy will suffer is, I believe, influenced to some degree by the criminal procedures that I discuss in the following pages, but the problems I have identified are sufficiently severe, pervasive, and intractable that no combination of reforms is likely to entirely eliminate their distortive effect. Thus, I take as my goal a modest improvement in factual accuracy, and I explore in this section the ways in which international procedures and liability doctrines can be adapted to achieve that end.

Because I do not know that the procedural reforms I advocate will be adopted, and, even if they are adopted, I do not expect them to wholly eliminate the tribunals' fact-finding impediments, the final section of this chapter, along with the whole of Chapter 10, assumes either a fact-finding status quo or a marginal improvement. Given that assumption, I advocate in Section 9.C that prosecutors make greater use of controversial association doctrines such as joint criminal enterprise as a means both of reducing the impact of testimonial deficiencies and of more closely aligning the Trial Chambers' actual justifications for their judgments with their stated justifications.

A final preparatory note concerns the coverage of this chapter and Chapter 10. Up until this point, this book has focused on identifying and analyzing the fact-finding impediments at the international criminal tribunals. I have centered that discussion on the trials of the ICTR, SCSL, and Special Panels both because those tribunals had had a sufficient number of trials for me to analyze and because the problems appearing in those trials seemed likely also to appear in the trials of the ICC and in the newer wave of *ad hoc* tribunals, which include the Extraordinary Chambers in the Courts of Cambodia and the Special Tribunal for Lebanon. This chapter and the next, in contrast to all that has come before them, consider future reforms that might be undertaken to ameliorate the fact-finding impediments heretofore described. For that reason, I broaden my gaze to include consideration of the ICC and other *ad hoc* tribunals for they are most apt to benefit from such reforms.

9.A. IMPROVING THAT WHICH ALREADY EXISTS: SMALL-SCALE ADAPTATIONS TO EXISTING PROCEDURES

I begin this section with an acknowledgment. Although in the following pages I suggest improvements that might be made to certain aspects of tribunal proceedings, I wish expressly to recognize the difficulties inherent in establishing and running international criminal tribunals. Some of the tribunals' first employees have detailed the tremendously challenging circumstances they faced at the tribunals' outsets when funding was scarce[1176] and chaos plentiful.

[1176] Lawyers Committee for Human Rights, *Prosecuting Genocide in Rwanda: A Lawyers Committee Report on the ICTR and National Trials*, at VI(B) (1997) (describing the ICTR's funding as "inadequate and unpredictable since its inception"); THEODOR MERON, WAR CRIMES LAW COMES OF AGE 281 (1998); Payam Akhavan, *Justice in The Hague, Peace in the Former Yugoslavia? A Commentary on the United Nations War Crimes Tribunal*, 20 HUM. RTS. Q. 737, 280 (1998) (mentioning the ICTY's "budgetary difficulties"); STEVEN S. RATNER & JASON S. ABRAMS, ACCOUNTABILITY FOR HUMAN RIGHTS ATROCITIES IN INTERNATIONAL LAW: BEYOND THE NUREMBERG LEGACY 188 (1997) (noting both tribunals' "resource problems"); MICHAEL P. SCHARF, BALKAN JUSTICE 79–84 (1997) (detailing the ICTY's funding difficulties); Catherine Cissé, *The International Tribunals for the Former Yugoslavia and Rwanda: Some Elements of Comparison*, 7 TRANSNAT'L L. & CONTEMP. PROBS. 103, 115 (1997) (stating that the ICTR's "inadequate budget" led to inefficient work); Bernard D. Meltzer, *War Crimes: The Nuremberg Trial and the Tribunal for the Former Yugoslavia*, 30 VAL. U. L. REV. 895, 908 (1996) (noting the ICTY's "serious underfunding and understaffing").

ICTR prosecutor Sara Darehshori, for instance, reported that when she and her twelve office mates first arrived in Arusha, they "fought over garbage cans, which [they] used as chairs," they made "makeshift desks by removing doors from their hinges and placing them on crates," and they shared one telephone line, which "was erratic."[1177] Circumstances were worse still in East Timor at the start of the Special Panels. Indonesian forces had conducted a "scorched earth" campaign that resulted in unparalleled property destruction. Entire villages were razed, and virtually every aspect of East Timor's infrastructure was destroyed.[1178] Of particular relevance to the Special Panels was the fact that virtually all court buildings were in rubble, and all court equipment, furniture, registers, records, and archives as well as law books and case files were lost or burned.[1179] Despite the chaos, Special Panels prosecutors had to quickly issue indictments because suspects had already been arrested and detained.[1180] Special Panels funding was also notoriously inadequate.[1181] At their inceptions, the Special Panels did not possess the resources to employ secretaries, court reporters, stenographers, or law clerks. The absence of support staff meant that judges had to answer their own phones and even move their own furniture.[1182]

Even the Special Court for Sierra Leone has had to contend with significant logistical difficulties. Although the Berkeley War Crimes Study Center sometimes has been critical of certain decisions made by David Crane, the SCSL's first head prosecutor, the War Crimes Study Center acknowledged that

[1177] Sara Darehshori, *Inching Toward Justice in Rwanda*, N.Y. Times, Sept. 8, 1998, at A25.

[1178] "The damage to private and public property ranges from 60 to 80 per cent in the whole country. Even more serious is the fact that most hospitals and health centres have been destroyed, as well as school buildings. The destruction includes damage to public utilities, such as water and power." *Report of the International Commission of Inquiry on East Timor to the Secretary-General*, U.N. Doc. A/54/726-S/2000/59, para. 130 (Jan. 31, 2000).

[1179] Hansjörg Strohmeyer, *Policing the Peace: Post Conflict Judicial System Reconstruction in East Timor*, 24 U. New S. Wales L.J. 171, 172 (2001).

[1180] Linton, note 1062, at 481.

[1181] *See generally* Cohen, *Seeking Justice*, note 671. After the prosecutorial arm of the Special Panels – the Serious Crimes Unit – was established by UNTAET Regulation 2000/11, no budget was prepared, and the Serious Crimes Unit had to borrow personnel and equipment from other departments, Suzannah Linton, *Cambodia, East Timor and Sierra Leone: Experiments in International Justice*, 12 Crim. L. F. 185, 215 (2001) [hereinafter Linton, *Experiments*]; *see also id.* at 206 n.70 (quoting *Estafeta*, the newsletter of the East Timor Action/Network/US, April 2001, stating that the Serious Crimes Unit is "inadequately funded and staffed"). Laura Dickinson stated in 2003 that the Serious Crimes Unit "continues to be hampered by lack of funding, inexperienced personnel, and vacancies in key positions," and she reported that "the appellate panel currently cannot function because too few judges have been hired, and the trial courts have also been forced to suspend proceedings periodically because of lack of personnel." Laura A. Dickinson, *The Promise of Hybrid Courts*, 97 Am. J. Int'l L. 295, 299 (2003).

[1182] Cohen, *Seeking Justice*, note 671, at 5.

Crane was "essentially responsible for 'creating a new organization out of whole cloth' – a formidable task under any circumstances, but particularly so in a post-conflict society, on a tight budget, under tremendous pressure to work fast." In particular,

> Crane had to execute his prosecutorial plans amidst rapid, phased institutional growth and in a manner responsive to the conditions on the ground as he found them. The former chief Prosecutor described working seven days a week, 12 hours a day for his first six months in Sierra Leone, overseeing investigations and developing the indictments while dealing with a long list of logistical hurdles. Physically, the OTP had to set up temporary functioning offices while awaiting construction of the permanent court facility. Staff needed to be hired, and newly arrived personnel needed help adjusting to the difficult conditions of life in Freetown. Energy also had to be devoted to developing internal procedures, including security protocol and information management systems, as well as fostering productive working relationships with the diplomatic corps, civil society, and non-governmental organizations (NGOs) in Sierra Leone.[1183]

As time has passed, the number of problems facing the tribunals has declined and their functioning has improved, but funding at many tribunals remains inadequate and uncertain, and consequently hard choices frequently must be made. I highlight these challenges here both to put into perspective the shortcomings that I discuss in the coming pages and to acknowledge that addressing these shortcomings may prove challenging. That said, I now consider improvements that might be made in the areas of language interpretation, investigations, and trial procedures.

9.A.i. *Language Interpretation*

As I discuss in Chapter 3, many of the distortions caused by the need for language interpretation are not amenable to substantial improvement. Distortions will necessarily occur when interpretation must be made between wildly divergent languages that are spoken by people from substantially different cultures. At the same time, many of the colossal interpretation failures that I have recounted stemmed not from intractable linguistic or cultural divergences but from resource constraints. Indeed, the interpretation difficulties experienced by the woefully underresourced Special Panels prove this point beyond question. Certainly the other tribunals under study seem to have experienced fewer interpretation difficulties than the Special Panels, but it is a concern that, to this day, ICTR interpretation from Kinyarwanda to English must proceed through

[1183] van Tuyl, note 563, at 6.

a French relay. That is, the ICTR has virtually no Kinyarwanda–English interpreters, so interpretation proceeds first from Kinyarwanda to French and then from French to English. Similarly, the ICC must use a French relay when interpreting between Swahili and English and Lingala and English.

Distortions are prevalent enough when a language such as Kinyarwanda must be interpreted into a very different language such as French. The potential for miscommunication increases considerably when every word in a trial must proceed through yet another round of interpretation. Perhaps interpreters of certain languages are truly so scarce that multiple interpretations are simply unavoidable. That seems more likely to be the case at the ICC, which only just began its proceedings, than at the ICTR, which is coming to the end of its life after operating for more than fifteen years. During that time, one might have expected the ICTR to have been able to engage Kinyarwanda–English interpreters, if doing so had been a high priority. Indeed, even if such interpreters could not be engaged, if the broader goal of minimizing interpretation distortion had been a high priority, we might have expected the ICTR to have minimized the importance of English interpretation by focusing its hiring efforts on French speakers. In fact, however, most ICTR judges, prosecutors, and other staff members listen to the English interpretation. As I said at the outset, substantial distortion is apt to pervade the interpretation of international criminal proceedings even if the tribunals were making their best efforts to ameliorate that distortion. However, because it is not clear that such best efforts have been made, making them would be the natural first step.

Once we have confidence that an adequate number of properly trained interpreters have been employed, we can focus on more tangible steps to improve interpretation. Joshua Karton, for instance, suggests certain straightforward measures that judges can undertake, such as insisting that litigants and witnesses speak slowly and use simple sentences and ensuring that interpreters are provided adequate breaks between interpretation stints.[1184] More fundamentally, Karton considers it imperative that judges "remain actively aware of the effects of interpretation" as a means of making them "more sensitive to inconsistent testimony and more likely to think twice in the face of vague or ambiguous statements, rather than making a snap judgment."[1185]

9.A.ii. *Investigations*

Chapter 4 details the numerous and severe inconsistencies that pervade international criminal proceedings. As discussed there, a substantial proportion of

[1184] Karton, note 270, at 49.
[1185] *Id.* at 48–49.

international witnesses provide testimony that contradicts or is inconsistent with the representations that appear in their pretrial statements. That fact should be worrisome enough because, when a witness's courtroom testimony differs from her previous representations, fact finders must assess the likelihood of lying, misperception, or memory failure. The inconsistencies that appear during international criminal proceedings are even more troubling because most international witnesses lay them at the feet of investigators. According to most international witnesses, their stories have remained the same throughout their interviews and testimony; thus, any inconsistencies that have appeared have stemmed from the mistakes or the malfeasance of investigators and interpreters. Witnesses similarly blame investigators when their statements fail to contain crucial facts about which they later testify at trial. That is, when witnesses are asked why they failed to convey to investigators such key information, they typically maintain that it is because investigators failed to ask the questions that would have elicited the information.

Unfortunately, such allegations have plausibility. As I note in Chapter 4, interviews with ICTR and SCSL investigators generate off-the-record stories of lazy and incompetent investigators. At the Special Panels, moreover, concerns about investigator incompetence and dishonesty made it into the court records. For instance, Special Panels Judge Samith da Silva noted that "the investigators may have influenced answers or tried to make them 'look nicer.'" Da Silva found it revealing that many investigators provide only the translations of the statements they collect and fail to include the originals.[1186] Similarly, former Special Panels' General Prosecutor Mohamed Othman confirmed that concerns about investigator competence were well founded when he opined that out of 1,485 investigators who were deployed in East Timor, only ten or twelve had the skills necessary for the position.[1187]

Although the unusually severe resource and staffing shortages that plagued the Special Panels no doubt played a significant role in that tribunal's investigations difficulties, other tribunals have suffered similar, if slightly less severe, problems. A report by the U.C. Berkeley War Crimes Studies Center, for instance, identifies serious deficiencies in the SCSL's investigations practices. The report reveals that SCSL investigations were not conducted pursuant to formal standard operating procedures and were not subject to virtually any oversight.[1188] In addition, investigator training proved inadequate as many

[1186] Cohen, *Indifference*, note 239, at 27. SCSL defense counsel likewise have sometimes had difficulty obtaining the original, untranslated witness statements. van Tuyl, note 563, at 44–45.
[1187] Othman, note 35, at 100.
[1188] van Tuyl, note 563, at 15, 34, 46.

investigators understood little about the history of the Sierra Leonean conflict or its finer points. Sierra Leone specialist Corinne Dufka was hired to educate investigators about such matters, but many had little interest in being educated. According to Dufka, "certain crucial briefing materials received very little notice – such as an atrocity-mapping project she completed to assist investigators with the geographic and temporal distribution of various incidents that occurred during the lengthy civil war." Indeed, many early investigators "remained unfamiliar with the basic geographical lay of the land in Sierra Leone, and never quite mastered the political power divisions and nature of the conflict between the RUF, the AFRC and the CDF." Although Dufka was available to personally assist investigators, she noted that many lacked "enthusiasm for familiarizing themselves with the historical elements of the conflict, and they lacked management from above to ensure that they were equipped with the proper contextual information."[1189]

Not surprisingly, the SCSL investigators who did not thoroughly understand the conflict also did not know what questions to ask and what leads to pursue. As a consequence, prosecutors who later reviewed witness statements were often unpleasantly surprised by their inadequacies. Senior Trial Attorney Kevin Tavener reported, for instance, that the quality of the *CDF* witness statements was so poor that the *CDF* trial team was forced to reinterview nearly every witness they presented at trial. These reinterviews often generated witness statements that were inconsistent with the witnesses' initial statements. Thus, some of the inconsistencies detailed in Chapter 4 and in my in-depth description of the *CDF* case in Chapter 7 likely sprang from these investigative deficiencies.

Improving fact-finding at the international tribunals, then, requires that more attention be paid to investigations practices. Improving investigations practices will almost certainly reduce omissions and inconsistencies because at least some of the glaring omissions and startling inconsistencies that I have detailed must have stemmed from the failure of investigators to ask key questions the first time around. Furthermore, even if improved investigations practices do not substantially reduce the quantity of omissions and inconsistencies, they can better equip fact finders to evaluate their significance. Consider, for instance, that at present many witness statements are not transcripts of the witnesses' interviews but rather mere summaries of the information that the witnesses ostensibly conveyed to the investigators. When such statements fail to contain a critical piece of information about which the witness later testifies, she can plausibly claim that the statement does not contain the information because she was never asked about it. For this reason, it is crucial that statements contain not only the answers that witnesses provide but also the

[1189] *Id.* at 43.

questions that they are asked. Taping the interviews would be optimal,[1190] but even a written transcript of the interview would elucidate matters significantly.

The ICTR Appeals Chamber in *Niyitegeka* made just this point in 2004 when it described an "ideal" record of a witness interview as containing "all the questions that were put to a witness and all of the answers given by the witness."[1191] The Appeals Chamber considered it "necessary to disclose the questions put to the witness in order to make the statement intelligible" and in order to enable the defense "to prepare for cross-examination properly." Indeed, the Chamber went so far as to assert that "it may be impossible to assess the probative value of the witness's answer without juxtaposing it with the relevant question."[1192] That said, most ICTR statements before *Niyitegeka* failed to include the questions asked of the witness,[1193] and the prosecution has not changed the format for its witness statements since the *Niyitegeka* decision. Thus, the vast majority of ICTR statements remain merely a summary of the information the witness has provided. Only for important insider witnesses has the prosecution audiotaped the interviews and then transcribed them, thereby providing the Chamber the questions as well as the answers.[1194]

Whatever the specific reforms undertaken, the more general point is that Trial Chambers must have confidence in the investigators' competence and professionalism because, without that confidence, a Trial Chamber is in no position to assess the significance of inconsistencies between witness testimony and pretrial statements. The current practice of the Trial Chambers is to place little weight on witness statements and to explain away all but the most serious discrepancies between their statements and their subsequent testimony. One can understand the Trial Chambers' inclination to minimize the significance of pretrial statements given the shoddy nature of some statement taking, but,

[1190] The drafters of the procedural rules for Extraordinary Chambers in the Courts of Cambodia recognized the value of taped interviews and consequently provided in Rule 25(1) that "[w]henever possible, when the Co-Prosecutors or Co-Investigating Judges question a Suspect or Charged Person, in addition to the written record of the interview, it shall be audio or video-recorded" pursuant to a detailed procedure. Although Rule 25(1) stands as a welcome development, it requires taping only "whenever possible," and its value as a precedent is limited because Extraordinary Chambers' proceedings are largely nonadversarial and consequently diverge markedly from the procedures employed by the other international tribunals.

[1191] Prosecutor v. Niyitegeka, Case No. ICTR-96–14-A, Judgement, para. 31 (July 9, 2004). The Appeals Chamber went on to say that in an ideal record of a witness interview, "[t]he time of the beginning and the end of an interview, specific events such as requests for breaks, offering and accepting of cigarettes, coffee, and other events that could have an impact on the statement or its assessment should be recorded as well." *Id.*

[1192] *Id.* at para. 33.

[1193] *Id.* at paras. 35–36.

[1194] Interview with Peter Robinson, ICTR defense counsel, Aug. 2, 2009 (by e-mail).

by doing so, the Trial Chambers eliminate a valuable mechanism for assessing witness credibility, and they substantially disadvantage defendants; that is, although some inconsistencies stem from the failure of investigators to record the witness's statement accurately, other inconsistencies appear because the witness really did tell different stories on different occasions. By placing little weight on witness statements, the Trial Chambers effectively adopt the former explanation in all but the most egregious instances and thereby impair the defendant's ability to cast doubt on the witness's credibility. Improving investigations practices will neither entirely eliminate inconsistencies nor entirely eliminate the uncertainty surrounding the causes of inconsistencies, but it may enable the Trial Chambers to make a more informed assessment of the significance of the inconsistencies.

9.A.iii. *On-Site Visits*

Another way that Trial Chambers can enhance their fact-finding capacity is by regularly making visits to crime sites.[1195] Such visits would be particularly cost effective in cases that center on one massacre or several massacres that occurred in a small geographical radius, and their potential benefits are many. For one thing, an on-site visit could be considered a valuable form of outreach. The ICTR has been criticized for failing to adequately publicize the work of the tribunal in Rwanda, so sending judges to view massacre sites is an efficient way to increase the tribunal's profile locally.[1196] Indeed, the government of Rwanda lauded the tribunal's first on-site visit, which occurred in the *Bagilishema* case. After the Trial Chamber's visit, Rwanda's representative to the ICTR expressed appreciation, stating that "many things have been put right as far as the workings of the Tribunal and its relationship with Rwanda." [1197]

More relevantly to my study, on-site visits can help Trial Chambers to fill informational gaps that were created from unclear or undetailed witness testimony. If a witness cannot estimate the distance between his hiding place in a latrine and the massacre site, an on-site visit can shed light on the matter. During an on-site visit in the ICTY's *Blagojević* and *Jokić* case, for instance, the judges confirmed a witness's estimate that the distance between a particular school and two execution sites was eight hundred meters.[1198] Indeed, the

[1195] Such visits are frequently undertaken in criminal trials in Continental European countries. *See* Damaška, Faces of Justice, note 1175, at 137.

[1196] Maury D. Shenk et al., *International Criminal Tribunals for the Former Yugoslavia and for Rwanda*, 35 Int'l L. 622, 628 n.76 (2001).

[1197] Coalition for International Justice, *ICTR Judges to Visit Crime Scenes*, Aug. 16, 2000, *available at* http://web.archive.org/web/20001010003755/http://www.cij.org/.

[1198] Prosecutor v. Blagojević & Jokić, Case No. IT-02–60-T, Judgement, para. 316 n.1159 (Jan. 17, 2005).

value of on-site visits is apparent from the fact that when tribunal judges do make such visits, they frequently cite them in their factual findings.[1199] At the ICTR, for instance, the *Karera* Trial Chamber made clear that its site visit was instrumental to its conclusion that the prosecution had not proven beyond a reasonable doubt that the defendant watched a certain attack take place.[1200] Although in that way, the on-site visit undermined the prosecution's case, the visit also assisted the prosecution by satisfactorily explaining what appeared to be a damaging inconsistency in the prosecution's case.[1201] Similarly, when a Swiss court tried Rwandan mayor Fulgence Niyonteze for his role in the 1994 violence, it visited the crime scene and even climbed Mount Mushubati, a key location in the trial. Based on its observations about the mountain and its surrounding areas, the court found many of Niyonteze's claims about his activities to be not credible.[1202]

Finally, on-site visits are apt to enhance fact-finding accuracy most profoundly in ways that are least able to be verifiable: by deterring witnesses from lying. If on-site visits were a customary practice, witnesses would know that at least some portion of their stories would be personally verified. Such verification will not be capable of deterring all forms of lying, but it will deter some.

9.B. PUBLICIZING AND PUNISHING PERJURY

False testimony is pervasive at least at some of the international tribunals, and the Trial Chambers could help to reduce it both by publicizing it and by sanctioning it. Turning first to its sanctioning power, Chapter 7 observes that, pursuant to Rule 91 of the Rules of Procedure and Evidence of the ICTY, the ICTR, and the SCSL, a Trial Chamber that has "strong grounds for believing that a witness has knowingly and wilfully given false testimony" may

[1199] *See, e.g.*, Prosecutor v. Blagojević & Jokić, Case No. IT-02–60-T, Judgement, para. 265, nn. 118, 164, 195, 212, 213, 265, 1158, 1159, 1333 (Jan. 17, 2005); Prosecutor v. Brđanin, Case No. IT-99–36-T, Judgement, para. 614, n.1556 (Sept. 1, 2004); Prosecutor v. Strugar, Case No. IT-01–42-T, Judgement, para. 316 (Jan. 31, 2005).

[1200] Karera Judgement, note 54, at paras. 130–135.

[1201] In particular, the testimony of *Karera* prosecution witnesses BME, BMF, and BMH seemed inconsistent because BME testified that she had hidden in "a space under the bridge," whereas BMF and BMH testified that there was no bridge in the area. However, the Chamber's on-site visit revealed the existence of a small gutter under the road near Karera's house. Although witnesses BMH and BMF did not recall a bridge, they both described this ditch and after viewing it, the Trial Chamber concluded that a "small person could hide in this gutter and perceive the road above it as a 'bridge.'" Karera Judgement, note 54, at para. 161.

[1202] *See* Public Prosecutor v. Niyonteze (Trib. Militaire de division 2, Aug. 26, 1999), at 101–04 (Switzerland); Niyonteze v. Public Prosecutor (Trib. Militaire d'appel 1A, May 26, 2000), at 14, 17–18 (Switzerland).

direct the prosecutor to investigate the matter with a view to preparing and submitting an indictment for false testimony.[1203] At the outset of the tribunals, it looked as though Rule 91 would prove a potent weapon for addressing false testimony. A witness in the ICTY's very first case – *Tadić* – admitted to lying under oath, and the Trial Chamber consequently directed the prosecution to undertake an investigation pursuant to Rule 91.[1204] However, after conducting its investigation, the prosecution declined to issue an indictment because it concluded, among other things, that the false testimony was not sufficiently material to justify prosecution and that "such collateral prosecution" would have a minimal deterrent effect and would contribute very little to the tribunal's overall objectives.[1205] Since that time, the Trial Chambers at the ICTY and ICTR have virtually never directed the prosecution to conduct another perjury investigation.

Concededly, this book has amply demonstrated the difficulty inherent in determining when a witness has "*knowingly*" given false testimony. In addition, there is also no gainsaying that the tribunals already have their hands full in prosecuting mass atrocities expeditiously without diverting substantial time and resources to perjury investigations. At the same time, in many cases there do exist "strong grounds" for believing that a witness knowingly presented false testimony – sometimes because the witness himself admitted to doing so[1206] – and in such cases, action should be taken. Although the prosecution's decision in *Tadić* was understandable, it was nevertheless misguided because it failed to recognize that the overall objectives of the tribunal can be advanced only through proceedings that place the highest possible value on truthfulness.

"Strong grounds for believing that a witness has knowingly and wilfully given false testimony" is a stringent standard, and one that most instances of questionable testimony will not meet. But even where that standard has not been met, the Trial Chambers can advance the value of truth telling by ordering an investigation or, at the least, by highlighting in their judgments testimony that appears suspicious. The ICTR's *Rwamakuba* case stands as a model for this latter mechanism. There, the Trial Chamber began its judgment

[1203] The Rules of Procedure and Evidence of other international tribunals feature a similar rule. *See, e.g.*, ECCC Internal Rules, Rule 36 (2009), *available at* http://www.eccc.gov.kh/english/cabinet/fileUpload/121/IRv3-EN.pdf.

[1204] Prosecutor v. Tadić, Case No. IT-94–1-T, Order for the Prosecution to Investigate the False Testimony of Dragan Opacić (Dec. 10, 1996).

[1205] Gabriël Oosthuizen, *Of Misconduct, Contempt, False Testimony, Rule Mutations and Other Interesting Powers: A Potpourri of Questions and Notes, in* Essays on ICTY Procedure and Evidence in Honour of Gabrielle Kirk McDonald 387, 395–96 (Richard May et al. eds., 2001).

[1206] *See, e.g.*, the cases discussed at notes 709 to 713.

by highlighting the overall deficiencies in the prosecution's evidence,[1207] and it went on to describe forthrightly and unsparingly the problematic features of specific witness testimony.[1208] At one level, the Trial Chamber's unfavorable description of prosecution witness testimony should surprise no one given that the Trial Chamber acquitted Rwamakuba of all charges. Indeed, in a realm in which acquittals are so rare and so unpopular, we would expect Trial Chambers to take extra efforts to justify them with a strong critique of the prosecution's evidence. I believe it advisable, however, for Trial Chambers to engage in a similarly forthright treatment of questionable testimony even on charges on which the Trial Chambers will ultimately convict.

It is advisable not only for the obvious reason that it – along with regular recourse to Rule 91 – may help to deter witnesses from providing false testimony, but also for the less obvious and arguably more important reason that such efforts will affirm and enhance the tribunals' culture of truthfulness. The importance of truthfulness at the tribunals may seem hardly in need of affirming. Tribunal judges, prosecutors, and defense counsel are certainly aware of the importance of truthful witness testimony, and the witnesses themselves are made aware of that fact – if it previously escaped them – when they are required to solemnly declare that they will tell the truth.[1209] But although the tribunals manifest a formal commitment to the value of truth telling, the very fact that questionable testimony is so pervasive at the international tribunals and yet admonished so infrequently may serve to undercut the tribunals' actual commitment to truthfulness. Indeed, the sense I have gained through interviews with prosecutors and defense counsel is that false testimony forms part of the landscape of international criminal trials. Everyone knows about it; little is done about it. Consequently, although I have no reason to believe that prosecutors or defense counsel would knowingly put on testimony they believed to be false, I do fear that their attitude about false testimony may be more cavalier than would be optimal. Increased use of Rule 91 along with a willingness to publicize and criticize problematic testimony could

[1207] In the first paragraph of its factual findings, the *Rwamakuba* Trial Chamber reported that the prosecution's evidence consisted mainly of hearsay evidence concerning both the content of the allegations and also the identification of André Rwamakuba. Five of the eighteen prosecution witnesses claimed to have direct knowledge of Rwamakuba. Two witnesses gave uncorroborated evidence to support specific allegations in the Indictment. The prosecution did not specify why this was the case and it must be presumed that this was the best evidence available. The defense called witnesses who had both direct and indirect knowledge of Rwamakuba and many of them claimed to have been eyewitnesses to events alleged in the indictment. Rwamakuba Judgement, note 63, at para. 36.

[1208] *Id.* at paras. 60–84, 94, 171–176, 178–193.

[1209] *See, e.g.*, ICTR RPE, note 607, Rule 90(B).

motivate lawyers to exercise greater caution when putting witnesses on the stand.

9.C. LARGE-SCALE PROCEDURAL REFORMS

The previous section advocates certain adaptations to existing procedures at the international tribunals. This section considers whether broader, more structural procedural changes will enhance fact-finding. In subsection 9.C.i, I discuss the way in which sociopolitical and cultural elements have shaped the rise and fall of various past and present domestic procedures. Because the optimal set of criminal procedures depends on a complex set of sociopolitical, cultural, and structural factors, it is unrealistic to expect that any one set of criminal procedures will well serve different sets of populations. The international tribunals, however, seem to have developed their procedures with just those unrealistic expectations in mind. Indeed, although the procedures of the different tribunals diverge in some ways, in their broad outlines they are cut from the same cloth, as subsection 9.C.ii details, and the differences that do exist arose as a consequence of factors unrelated to concerns about fact-finding accuracy. I recognize that international procedures cannot develop in the organic, contextual way that domestic procedures do, but if we truly care about enhancing fact-finding accuracy at the international tribunals, then I believe that we must pay closer attention to the particular fact-finding impediments at play at a tribunal, for it is only through an understanding of the particular evidentiary problems that an international tribunal is likely to confront that we can craft optimal procedures for that institution.

With that attention in mind, I advocate in subsection 9.C.iii creative thinking and an expansion of the kinds of procedures and methods of fact-finding that might be used in international tribunals. In particular, I urge a greater openness to integrating local criminal procedures and a greater willingness to borrow recent, creative innovations, such as the intermediary. Finally, I consider in subsection 9.C.iv the broader question of whether adversarial or nonadversarial trial procedures are better suited to ameliorating the tribunals' fact-finding impediments. Again, I begin by urging a contextual approach because I believe that some fact-finding impediments would respond better to nonadversarial trial procedures, whereas other impediments would be better addressed through adversarial procedures. Unfortunately, even though a contextual approach would be best able to meet the particular needs of a particular tribunal, the assessments that would have to be undertaken to make the determinations inherent in a contextual approach are apt to prove diplomatically and politically problematic. In recognition of that fact, I propose a set of uniform trial procedures that I believe have the greatest potential to address the tribunals' fact-finding challenges.

9.C.i. *The Case for Contextualization*

Domestic criminal procedures are both driven by and reflect the prevailing social and political conditions of the society in which the procedures function.[1210] Throughout the centuries, criminal procedures – from compurgation to race-based peremptory challenges – have risen and fallen as a result of a complex set of economic, social, political, and structural factors. One only has to look at the multifarious factors contributing to the Warren Court's procedural revolution of the 1960s to see that criminal procedures are deeply embedded in a State's social and political life.[1211]

The lens of history allows us to view with even greater clarity the influential role that existing social and political conditions play in the development of criminal procedures. Take, for instance, the procedural transformations that occurred in England on the one hand and the Continent on the other following the abolition of the ordeal. Although ordeals had been widely used both in England and on the Continent to decide criminal cases for which insufficient proof otherwise existed,[1212] their abolition in 1215 led to the emergence of two very different methods of fact-finding – the trial jury in England and the inquisitorial process on the Continent. Presentment juries – bodies tasked with identifying those who were suspected of crimes – had long existed in England.[1213] By 1215, presentment juries had also developed an adjudicatory

[1210] *See, e.g.*, Peter J. van Koppen & Steven D. Penrod, *The John Wayne and Judge Dee Versions of Justice, in* ADVERSARIAL VERSUS INQUISITORIAL JUSTICE: PSYCHOLOGICAL PERSPECTIVES ON CRIMINAL JUSTICE SYSTEMS 347, 349–54, (Peter J. van Koppen & Steven D. Penrod eds., 2003) (describing the socio-political roots of Dutch and American criminal justice systems).

[1211] *See, e.g.*, ARCHIBALD COX, THE WARREN COURT: CONSTITUTIONAL DECISION AS AN INSTRUMENT OF REFORM 85–88 (1968); ED CRAY, CHIEF JUSTICE: A BIOGRAPHY OF EARL WARREN 459 (1997).

[1212] ROBERT BARTLETT, TRIAL BY FIRE AND WATER: THE MEDIEVAL JUDICIAL ORDEAL 42–69 (1986) (describing the continuing popularity of the ordeal in England and throughout England and western Europe); RAOUL C. VAN CAENEGEM, THE BIRTH OF THE COMMON LAW 64–65 (2d ed. 1988) (describing the prevalence of ordeals in twelfth-century England); ADHEMAR ESMEIN, A HISTORY OF CONTINENTAL CRIMINAL PROCEDURE 57–58 (1913, reprinted 1968).

[1213] *See* THOMAS ANDREW GREEN, VERDICT ACCORDING TO CONSCIENCE: PERSPECTIVES ON THE ENGLISH CRIMINAL TRIAL JURY 1200–1800, 7–8; BARTLETT, note 1212, at 137. Presentment juries are conventionally dated to the 1166 Assize of Clarendon. For the view that jury accusations predated 1166, see Naomi D. Hurnard, *The Jury of Presentment and the Assize of Clarendon*, 56 ENG. HIST. REV. 374 (1941). For skepticism about that view, see Raoul C. Van Caenegem, *Public Prosecution of Crime in Twelfth-Century England, in* CHURCH AND GOVERNMENT IN THE MIDDLE AGES 41, 44–49 (C.N.L. Brooke et al. eds., 1976).

power by which they would make a preliminary assessment of a suspect's guilt or innocence as a means of deciding which suspects should be forced to undergo ordeals.[1214] The abandonment of ordeals in 1215, then, naturally led to the emergence of the trial jury, which constituted merely a slight alteration on the presentment jury as it had evolved.[1215] Continental procedures might have developed in a similar fashion because juries were also prevalent throughout northern Europe in the early medieval period,[1216] but by the time ordeals were abolished, Continental authorities were heavily influenced by the principles contained in ecclesiastical procedure and Roman law.[1217] Consequently, on the Continent, ordeals were replaced by the Roman-canon law of proof, which included official judicial torture to obtain the confessions that were necessary to satisfy that law of proof.[1218] Thus, although criminal procedures in England and on the Continent bore considerable resemblance before the demise of the ordeal, they diverged sharply thereafter as a consequence of particular local circumstances prevailing in the different locations.

The influence of local conditions can also be seen in the development of criminal procedures in the European colonies. Although colonial administrators introduced the criminal procedures of their home countries into their various colonies, those procedures were adapted as a consequence of their interaction with local laws and local conditions.[1219] East Cameroonian courts, for instance, ostensibly applied French criminal procedure law, but, whereas in France three different people would serve in the roles of magistrate (judge), *procureur de la république* (prosecutor), and *juge d'instruction* (investigating judge), in Cameroon, there were so few legal professionals that all three

[1214] Roger D. Groot, *The Jury of Presentment before 1215*, 26 AM. J. LEGAL HIST. 1, 1–2 (1982).

[1215] As historian Thomas Green put it: "It was not so much that the trial jury was adopted as that the ordeal was dispensed with." GREEN, note 1213, at 4. Presentment juries were used in cases of public prosecutions. For a discussion of the pre-1215 use of juries in cases of private prosecutions, see Roger D. Groot, *The Jury in Private Criminal Prosecutions before 1215*, 25 AM. J. LEGAL HIST. 113 (1983).

[1216] Raoul C. Van Caenegem, *The Law of Evidence in the Twelfth Century: European Perspectives and Intellectual Background, in* PROCEEDINGS OF THE SECOND INTERNATIONAL CONGRESS OF MEDIEVAL CANON LAW 298 (Stephan Kuttner & J. Joseph Ryan eds., 1965) [hereinafter Van Caenegem, *The Law of Evidence*]; *see also* JOHN PROFFATT, A TREATISE ON TRIAL BY JURY 11–14 (1877) (describing early Scandinavian juries); WILLIAM FORSYTH, HISTORY OF TRIAL BY JURY 13–44 (1875) (describing early Scandinavian and German juries).

[1217] Morris Ploscowe, *The Development of Present-Day Criminal Procedures in Europe and America*, 48 HARV. L. REV. 433, 446–47 (1935). *See also* ESMEIN, note 1212, at 78–79; JOHN H. LANGBEIN, PROSECUTING CRIME IN THE RENAISSANCE 133, 137 (1974).

[1218] JOHN LANGBEIN, TORTURE AND THE LAW OF PROOF 4–8 (1976); BARTLETT, note 1212, at 139–43; ESMEIN, note 1212, at 91.

[1219] Anne Griffiths, for instance, describes the relationship between common law and customary law as "symbiotic" and involving "a process of mutual adaptation." Anne Griffiths, *Legal Duality: Conflict or Concord in Botswana*, 27 J. AFRICAN L. 150, 150 (1983).

positions were held by one person.[1220] For the same reason, East Cameroonian courts were forced to modify French rules on the qualifications for judges.[1221] Similarly, the structure of British colonial courts and the powers given to court officials varied according to local circumstances.[1222] More or less authority was bestowed on magistrates, for instance, depending on their need to exercise control in the location in question. And few Anglophone colonies adopted the hallmark of the English criminal trial – the jury[1223] – possibly because the more heterogeneous nature of some African communities would generate a suspicion of jury prejudice. Instead, many colonies adapted the jury concept and provided for three lay assessors who, like the English jury, opine as to the defendant's guilt or innocence, but whose opinions the judge can ignore.[1224]

Not only do criminal procedures emerge as a result of particular social and political factors, but efforts to transplant procedures often fail, despite considerable effort, when the appropriate conditions are not in place. For instance, some of the United States' efforts to promote adversarial procedures in Latin American countries and elsewhere failed because American promoters of these procedures did not take account of local conditions.[1225] The Guatemalan government, for instance, acceded to USAID pressure to adopt a new criminal procedure code that provided for due process protections, but those protections were not implemented because no one had persuaded Guatemalan judges and prosecutors of their legitimacy.[1226]

Although a variety of factors influence the way in which new criminal procedures develop, a primary reason that new procedures emerge in the first place is the perceived inefficacy of existing procedures. Even procedures that are abandoned primarily for nonfunctional reasons are typically also considered inefficacious at the time they are eliminated. For instance, although a primary cause of the abolition of ordeals was their uncanonical status,[1227] ecclesiastical elites had also increasingly come to question their efficacy in separating the

[1220] Peter Bringer, *The Abiding Influence of English and French Criminal Law in One African Country: Some Remarks Regarding the Machinery of Criminal Justice in Cameroon*, 25 J. African L. 1, 3–4 (1981).

[1221] *Id.* at 4 (reporting that in the years following independence, court secretaries, clerks, and registrars were welcomed into the ranks of the judiciary).

[1222] J. H. Jearey, *The Structure, Composition and Jurisdiction of Courts and Authorities Enforcing the Criminal Law in British African Territories*, 9 Int'l & Comp. L. Q. 396, 402, 403 (1960).

[1223] *Id.* at 398; Kenneth Roberts Wray, *The Adaptation of Imported Law in Africa*, 4 J. African L. 66, 73 (1960).

[1224] Wray, note 1223, at 73.

[1225] *See* Richard Vogler, A World View of Criminal Justice 174 (2005).

[1226] *See* Thomas Carothers, Aiding Democracy Abroad: The Learning Curve 172 (1999).

[1227] By the early thirteenth century, ordeals were also considered an illegitimate tempting of God. Bartlett, note 1212, at 81–86. For additional discussions of the demise of the ordeal, see *Paul Hyams, Trial by Ordeal: The Key to Proof in the Early Common Law, in* On the Laws and Customs of England, Essays in Honor of Samuel E. Thorne 90 (Morris S. Arnold et al.

guilty from the innocent.[1228] And many procedural revolutions spring entirely from the bottom up; that is, from the recognition that existing procedures were simply not working in the way in which they were intended. American pretrial procedures in the middle of the twentieth century, for instance, were widely understood to operate in a discriminatory manner that disadvantaged the poor and racial minorities, and the due process revolution wrought by the Warren Court was in large measure an effort to remedy this inequality.[1229]

It is with these recent and historical precedents in mind that I consider revisions to international criminal procedures to remedy some of the fact-finding impediments detailed earlier. Although my survey of the rise and fall of various procedures is exceedingly brief and selective, it should suffice to establish two uncontroversial points. The first is that the optimal set of criminal procedures for any given place and time is highly contextual and dependent on a complex set of social, political, and structural factors. In other words, it is unrealistic to expect that one set of criminal procedures will well serve different sets of populations. Second, and even less controversially, assessing the appropriateness of a given set of procedures requires an examination of the way in which those procedures actually function in the relevant context. That is, procedures that appear in the abstract to be well designed to promote a fair and accurate determination of facts may fail miserably at achieving those ends when employed under particular conditions. These lessons – though largely self-evident – have for the most part been lost on the international tribunals, a topic I turn to next.

9.C.ii. *International Criminal Procedures: Uniformity in the Face of Diversity*

Although some of the tribunals' provisions on subject-matter jurisdiction were crafted with an eye toward the particulars of the relevant conflict,[1230] the

eds., 1981); Peter Brown, *Society and the Supernatural: A Medieval Change*, 104 DÆDALUS, 133 (1975); Van Caenegem, *The Law of Evidence*, note 1216, at 306–10.

[1228] As Belgian historian Raoul van Caenegem put it: "Once people were convinced that to win in a judicial combat was a question of paying for the best champion, that being successful in a cold water ordeal was a question of breathing control, that success in the ordeal of the hot iron depended on calloused hands or tricks such as having a holy host in one's hand or blessed ointment in it, then the days of the old system were numbered." Van Caenegem, *The Law of Evidence*, note 1216, at 307. Doubts about the efficacy of ordeals were expressed as early as the ninth century, BARTLETT, note 1212, at 72–75, but these gained fuller expression in the twelfth century, as ecclesiastical elites maintained that the miracles required for the ordeals could not be guaranteed, BARTLETT, note 1212, at 86–89.

[1229] LUCAS A. POWE, JR., THE WARREN COURT AND AMERICAN POLITICS 386 (2000); CRAY, note 1211, at 459.

[1230] For instance, although the Statutes of the ICTR and the ICTY are very similar and their procedural rules were initially identical, their provisions on subject-matter jurisdiction differed because the Rwandan conflict was considered to be a noninternational armed conflict, procedures adopted to prosecute these crimes were chosen seemingly without reference to the nature of the conflict that gave rise to the tribunal or to the capacity of the witnesses who would be heard there. That is, the international tribunals seemingly selected their initial procedures with little or no appreciation for the way in which those procedures were apt to function in the actual contexts in which they would operate. As I explain in more detail below, the early tribunals initially adopted procedures that were primarily adversarial in nature, but they have introduced more nonadversarial elements to their procedural rules as time has passed. More recent tribunals have included some nonadversarial features at the outset and thus have created a more "mixed" procedural system. But either in establishing or amending their procedural systems, none of the tribunals appeared to take account of specific circumstances that might render one set of procedures more efficacious than another in eliciting clear and accurate testimony from international witnesses.

Before delving into the tribunals' current procedural systems, a brief description of adversarial and nonadversarial procedures[1231] is required.[1232] Adversarial and nonadversarial procedural systems diverge from the time an investigation is launched, but, given the problems I seek to ameliorate, my focus here is

whereas the Yugoslavian war could be considered an international armed conflict. As a consequence of these different characterizations, the ICTR has jurisdiction over violations of Common Article 3 and Protocol II, S.C. Res. 955, U.N. SCOR, 49th Sess., 3453d mtg. at art. 4, U.N. Doc. S/RES/955 & Annex (1994) [hereinafter ICTR Statute], while the ICTY has jurisdiction over violations of the grave breaches provisions of the Geneva Conventions and over other provisions understood to apply in an international armed conflict. S.C. Res. 827, U.N. SCOR, 48th Sess., 3217th mtg. at 28, U.N. Doc. S/RES/827 arts. 2–3 (1993) [hereinafter ICTY Statute]. Likewise, because the Sierra Leonean conflict was considered to be largely noninternational, the Statute of the SCSL conferred on that court jurisdiction over violations occurring during a noninternational armed conflict, SCSL Statute, note 1053, at art. 3, and it also conferred jurisdiction over the conscription of child soldiers and over attacks on U.N. peacekeeping operations. SCSL Statute, note 1053, at art. 4 (b) & (c). The latter crimes were widely believed to have taken place in Sierra Leone and for that reason they were included within the jurisdiction of the SCSL but not the other tribunals.

1231 Continental criminal procedures are frequently termed "inquisitorial," but that term, particularly in the past, "conjure[d] up the excesses of the Star Chamber or the haunting memories of the Spanish Inquisition." G.E.P. Brouwer, *Inquisitorial and Adversary Procedures–A Comparative Analysis*, 55 Australian L.J. 207, 208 (1981); *see also* David Luban, Lawyers and Justice: An Ethical Study 93–94 (1988) (remarking that the label "inquisitorial" "evokes images of the auto-da-fé and the Iron Maiden, the Pit and the Pendulum"); Damaška, *Evidentiary Barriers to Conviction*, note 788, at 556–58. To avoid these connotations, I will use the term "nonadversarial."

1232 For more detailed (yet still summary) comparisons of the two systems, see Alphons Orie, *Accusatorial v. Inquisitorial Approach in International Criminal Proceedings Prior to the Establishment of the ICC and in the Proceedings before the ICC, in* 2 The Rome Statute of the International Criminal Court: A Commentary 1439, 1442–56 (Antonio Cassese et al. eds., 2002); Fairlie, note 1014, at 246–60.

on the presentation of witness testimony at trial. Whereas proceedings in an adversarial system are structured in the form of a contest, featuring two opposing litigants who present their best evidence and arguments to a neutral and largely passive fact finder, proceedings in a nonadversarial system are structured more in the form of an inquiry,[1233] directed by a judge,[1234] on the basis of a *dossier*, that is, a collection of written materials compiled by government officials who have investigated the case.[1235] As that short description of the two sets of trial procedures indicates, the primary difference between evidence presentation in adversarial and nonadversarial systems relates to who is driving the process. Trials in adversarial systems are driven by the parties. Each party calls her own witnesses and seeks to elicit from them information favorable to her case. Opposing parties also have their chance to question the witnesses, and through cross-examination they seek to undermine the witnesses' testimony in one fashion or another. Judges in adversarial systems stay largely above the fray. Not only is judicial intervention considered inappropriate, it is also unlikely to be meaningful because judges in adversarial systems come to the trial knowing virtually nothing about the case. They thus have little ability to ask useful questions.[1236]

By contrast, the presentation of witness testimony in nonadversarial systems is judge driven. Through his reading of the *dossier*, the judge is well informed about the case prior to trial and takes the lead in questioning witnesses. Thus, in nonadversarial trials, witnesses are not considered defense witnesses or prosecution witnesses. They are witnesses for the court, and it is the judge who has the primary duty to obtain information from them.[1237] The judge typically begins by asking the witness to provide a narrative account of what the witness knows about the case. This narrative takes place largely without interruption,

[1233] See DAMAŠKA, FACES OF JUSTICE, note 1175, at 3.

[1234] See Mary C. Daly, *Some Thoughts on the Differences in Criminal Trials in the Civil and Common Law Legal Systems*, 2 J. INST. STUDY LEGAL ETHICS 65, 67–68 (1999); Gordon van Kessel, *Adversary Excesses in the American Criminal Trial*, 67 NOTRE DAME L. REV. 403, 431 (1992) (contrasting the judge's role at trial in each type of system).

[1235] See Daly, note 1234, at 67–68; Jörg et al., note 789, at 47 (stating that in The Netherlands, the *dossier* "reports every step in the procedure" and "not only forms the basis for the trial, but also a coherent system of supervision and control"); Bron McKillop, *Anatomy of a French Murder Case*, 45 AM. J. COMP. L. 527, 544–46 (1997) (providing a detailed description of the *dossier* in a French murder case).

[1236] Mirjan Damaška, *Presentation of Evidence and Factfinding Precision*, 123 UNIV. PA. L. REV. 1083, 1090–91 (1975).

[1237] *Id.* at 1088; GERHARD ROBBERS, AN INTRODUCTION TO GERMAN LAW 189 (1998); Daly, note 1234, at 70; Edward A. Tomlinson, *Nonadversarial Justice: The French Experience*, 42 MD. L. REV. 131, 143 (1983); Christine Van Den Wyngaert, *Belgium, in* CRIMINAL PROCEDURE SYSTEMS IN THE EUROPEAN COMMUNITY 1, 33 (Van Den Wyngaert et al. eds., 1993) [hereinafter Van Den Wyngaert, *Belgium*].

and when it is complete, the judge begins the questioning. It is only when the judge's interrogation is finished that the two parties are permitted to pose questions to the witness.[1238] By then, few questions remain to be asked,[1239] and, in some systems, the parties are discouraged from asking anything at all because to do so suggests that the judge's interrogation had not been sufficiently thorough.[1240]

Turning back now to the international tribunals, the first of them – at Nuremberg and Tokyo – featured procedural systems that were almost exclusively adversarial. Half-hearted efforts to create a system that more closely resembled the criminal procedure codes of France or Russia were defeated,[1241] and the resulting procedural rules of the Nuremberg and Tokyo Tribunals contained only a few nonadversarial features.[1242] Approximately fifty years elapsed before the ICTY was established, and its procedural rules were similarly adversarial; indeed, the ICTY's initial set of procedural rules were taken almost verbatim from a draft provided by the U.S. Department of Justice.[1243] As a consequence, the ICTY's procedural system bore no resemblance to the inquisitorial procedures prevailing in the State where the war took place – the former Yugoslavia – and it took no particular account of the fact-finding challenges that an international tribunal examining Yugoslavian witnesses would confront. A year later, the judges of the ICTR adopted for that tribunal procedures virtually identical to those of the ICTY, despite the manifest differences in the victim and offender populations and in the patterns of violence that characterized the Rwandan and Yugoslavian conflicts. And the international community continued the pattern in 2002 when it adopted for the SCSL the procedural rules of the ICTR.[1244]

[1238] Mirjan Damaška, *Of Hearsay and Its Analogues*, 76 Minn. L. Rev. 425, 433 (1992); *see also* Damaška, *Presentation of Evidence and Factfinding Precision*, note 1236, at 1089.

[1239] *See* Luban, note 1231, at 94–95; Tomlinson, note 1237, at 143 (observing that, in French trials in the assize courts, the "number of questions proposed by the other participants is usually quite limited").

[1240] Luban, note 1231, at 94–95 (1988); Hein Kotz, *Civil Justice Systems in Europe and the United States*, 13 Duke J. Comp. & Int'l L. 61, 62 (2003); Oscar G. Chase, *Legal Processes and National Culture*, 5 Cardozo J. Int'l & Comp. L. 1, 4–5 (1997) ("For the lawyer to examine at length after the court seemingly has exhausted the witness is to imply that the court has not done a satisfactory job – a risky stratagem.").

[1241] Antonio Cassese, International Criminal Law 376–81 (2003).

[1242] These included the tribunals' simple evidentiary rules, the authority conferred on the judges to play an active role in the trial by questioning and calling witnesses, and the right conferred on the defendants to make unsworn statements at the end of the trial. *See id.* at 381–82.

[1243] 1 Virginia Morris & Michael Scharf, An Insider's Guide to the International Criminal Tribunal for the Former Yugoslavia 176–77 (1995); Theodor Meron, *Procedural Evolution in the ICTY*, 2 J. Int'l Crim. Just. 520, 522 (2004).

[1244] SCSL Statute, note 1053, at art. 14.

The initial procedural rules of the ICTY, the ICTR, and the SCSL, then, were virtually identical and primarily adversarial. Tribunal judges have seen fit to amend the rules numerous times,[1245] often to introduce nonadversarial features, but the introduction of those features was aimed primarily at enhancing the tribunals' efficiency, not its fact-finding accuracy. Early tribunal trials were criticized for their extraordinarily slow pace, so tribunal judges replaced a number of adversarial procedures with nonadversarial procedures in the hope that shorter trials would result.[1246] The ICTY removed a presumption in favor of oral testimony, for instance, to permit more evidence to be presented in documentary form.[1247] Additionally, judges were given greater control over case management in order to expedite proceedings. For instance, an early round of amendments authorized tribunal judges to ask the parties to reduce the number of witnesses they intended to call and to reduce the amount of time they intended to take for case presentation when such reductions were appropriate.[1248] In 2001, the ICTY went even further by authorizing the judges themselves to set the number of witnesses, the length of time for case presentation, and even to "fix a number of crime sites or incidents comprised in one or more of the charges."[1249]

The procedural rules of some of the more recent tribunals have diverged somewhat from those of the ICTY, the ICTR, and the SCSL, but in some cases the divergences are more apparent than real, and – more to the point for present purposes – the divergences for the most part were not driven by context-specific features of the Tribunals. The procedures of the ICC, for instance, feature more nonadversarial elements, including a pretrial Chamber that has significant oversight powers and that, among other things, issues

[1245] As of July 2009, the ICTY had revised its rules more than forty times, whereas the ICTR and SCSL have revised their rules seventeen and eleven times, respectively.

[1246] Initial assessments suggest that these hopes were not realized. See Máximo Langer & Joseph W. Doherty, *A Sisyphean Task? An Empirical Assessment of the Managerial Judging Reforms to Expedite the Procedure of the International Criminal Tribunal for the Former Yugoslavia*, 14 U.C.L.A J. Int'l L. & Foreign Aff. (forthcoming 2010).

[1247] The ICTY's procedural rules initially provided for the principle of orality, with Rule 90(A) stating that "witnesses shall, in principle, be heard directly by the Chambers." The provision was later removed, however, and Rule 89(F) was added to provide that "[a] Chamber may receive the evidence of a witness orally or, where the interests of justice allow, in written form."

[1248] *See* Máximo Langer, *The Rise of Managerial Judging in International Criminal Law*, 53 Am. J. Comp. L. 835, 886 (2005) ("The driving force behind these reforms has . . . [been] the criticisms and problems about the pace of proceedings. . . . ICTY judges have aimed to expedite the docket, not only to reduce the length of pre-trial detention, but also to defend ICTY's legitimacy and international support.").

[1249] ICTY Rules of Procedure and Evidence, Rules 73*bis* (B), (C), (D) and 73*ter* (B), (C), *available at* http://www.icty.org/x/file/Legal%20Library/Rules_procedure_evidence/IT032_Rev43_en .pdf [hereinafter ICTY R.P.E.]

arrest warrants,[1250] confirms charges,[1251] and can play some role in authorizing and carrying out investigations.[1252] Further and more relevantly to this study, the presiding judge of an ICC Trial Chamber has considerable discretion in structuring the presentation of evidence at trial,[1253] a point I address in more detail in the following discussion. The inclusion of these features, however, like the nonadversarial additions to the *ad hoc* tribunals' procedures, were driven by concerns unrelated to enhancing accuracy. The desire to avoid some of the most time-consuming elements of the *ad hoc* tribunals' trials played some role in the adoption of certain nonadversarial procedures[1254] as did political considerations[1255] and the desire to better represent the procedures of civil law countries,[1256] many of whom were among the ICC's staunchest supporters. The ICC's practice, moreover, has in many regards hewed closely to that of its more adversarial predecessors. Thus, although the Rome Statute permits the Presiding Judge to structure the presentation of evidence in a nonadversarial way, the ICC's subsequently adopted Rules of Procedure put some limits on the Presiding Judge's discretion,[1257] and the Trial Chamber in the ICC's first case structured the presentation of evidence along adversarial lines.[1258]

The Special Panels also relied heavily on its predecessors for procedural inspiration. The Special Panels modeled many of its provisions on those of

[1250] Rome Statute of the International Criminal Court, United Nations Diplomatic Conference of Plenipotentiaries on the Establishment of an International Criminal Court, U.N. Doc. A/CONF.183/9 (1998), art. 58, *reprinted in* 37 I.L.M. 999 (1998) [hereinafter Rome Statute].

[1251] *Id.* at art. 61.

[1252] *See id.* at arts. 15, 56, 57(d). *See also id.* at arts. 53(3) (pretrial Chamber's authority to review the prosecution's decision not to proceed with an investigation). Leila Sadat and Richard Carden describe the pretrial Chamber as representing "a victory for countries in the civil law tradition who felt that the court, as originally conceived, tracked a common law model too closely." Leila Nadya Sadat & S. Richard Carden, *The New International Criminal Court: An Uneasy Revolution*, 88 Geo. L.J. 381, 399 (2000).

[1253] Article 64(8)(b) of Rome Statute provides that "the presiding judge may give directions for the conduct of proceedings."

[1254] *See, e.g.*, Gilbert Bitti, *Two Bones of Contention Between Civil and Common Law: The Record of the Proceedings and the Treatment of a Concursus Delictorum, in* International and National Prosecution of Crimes Under International Law 273, 276 (Horst Fischer et al. eds., 2001).

[1255] Ambos, note 681, at 7–9 (arguing that the pretrial Chamber's powers derive less from a particular legal system and more from a political compromise).

[1256] Silvia A. Fernández de Gurmendi, *International Criminal Law Procedures, in* The International Criminal Court: The Making of the Rome Statute 217, 220 (Roy S. Lee ed., 1999).

[1257] *See* ICC Rules of Procedure and Evidence, Rule 140(2) (Sept. 9, 2002) (permitting parties to question the witnesses they call and the witnesses called by their opponents and encouraging judges to conduct their questioning either before or after questioning by a party so as to prevent judges from interfering in a party's cross-examination of a witness).

[1258] *See* Prosecutor v. Lubanga, Case No. ICC-01/04–01/06-T-104-ENG, Transcript, Jan. 16, 2009, at 37–38 [hereinafter Lubanga Transcript].

the ICC, and it adopted a hybrid set of procedural rules that draw from both civil-law and common-law traditions. Commentators have noted, however, that the drafters of the Special Panels' rules failed to adequately consider the difficulties of implementing such a regime in East Timor.[1259] Suzannah Linton observes, for instance, that "by adopting provisions meant for the International Criminal Court, UNTAET may have been overambitious and bound itself to completing an extremely costly and complex process that would seem to be beyond its capacity."[1260] Only the most recent tribunals to be established – the Special Tribunal for Lebanon and the Extraordinary Chambers in the courts of Cambodia have significantly diverged from their predecessors. The Extraordinary Chambers adopted nonadversarial procedures derived primarily from Cambodian law,[1261] but commentators have questioned the efficacy of these procedures in the international context[1262] and have criticized the procedural scheme because it contains "elements that are wholly alien to lawyers from a common law system," as well as elements "which have since been abandoned by other civil law systems."[1263] The Special Tribunal for Lebanon adopted procedural rules that in the main bear considerable resemblance to those of the ICTY, except for the provisions concerning evidence presentation, which I consider in more detail in the following discussion.

[1259] Linton, *Experiments*, note 1181, at 211–13. At a broader level, Linton queries "why UNTAET decided the Cambodian model of mixed panels within the existing criminal justice system was appropriate for East Timor, with its destroyed infrastructure, dysfunctional criminal justice system with novice legal personnel . . . shell-shocked society and atrocities committed over a brutal twenty-four-year long occupation." *Id.* at 213.

[1260] *Id.* at 205.

[1261] Article 12, section 1 of the agreement establishing the ECCC states: "The procedure shall be in accordance with Cambodian law." ECCC may seek international guidance regarding its procedural rules only in those instances where (1) Cambodian law does not deal with a particular matter, or (2) where there is uncertainty regarding the interpretation or application of a relevant rule of Cambodian law, or (3) where there is a question regarding the consistency of such a rule with international standards. Agreement Between the United Nations and the Royal Government of Cambodia Concerning the Prosecution Under Cambodian Law of Crimes Committed During the Period of Democratic Kampuchea, art. 12(1), June 6, 2003, *available at* http://www.eccc.gov.kh/english/agreement.list.aspx. Cambodian criminal procedure itself was not concretely established at the time of the agreement, as the Cambodian National Assembly did not establish its own uniform Criminal Procedure Code until late 2007. Rupert Skilbeck, *Defending the Khmer Rouge*, 8 Int'l Crim. L. Rev. 423, 430 (2008). Due to the confusion that could arise from the variety of legal standards, the ECCC adopted the Internal Rules that seek to "integrate Cambodian criminal procedure provisions and relevant international standards." Jenia Iontcheva Turner, *Civil Party Participation in Provisional Detention Appeals: Extraordinary Chambers in the Courts of Cambodia*, 103 Am. J. Int'l L. 116, 117, 120 (2009).

[1262] Göran Sluiter, *Due Process and Criminal Procedures in the Cambodian Extraordinary Chambers*, 4 J. Int'l Crim. Just. 314, 322–26 (2006); Skilbeck, note 1261, at 431.

[1263] Skilbeck, note 1261, at 431.

Given the controversy and political sparring that often surround the establishment of an international tribunal and that give rise to more pressing problems than the niceties of procedure, it is not surprising that one tribunal's procedures would substantially resemble another's and that both would be crafted without reference to the contextual elements that might bear on their effectiveness. Moreover, as Mirjan Damaška has shown us, adversarial and nonadversarial systems of criminal procedure are driven by different values and flourish in different structures of state authority, all of which develop over time. International criminal procedures, which contain hurriedly cobbled together elements of both adversarial and nonadversarial systems, do not form fully integrated, philosophically coherent systems and cannot be expected to. These realities acknowledged, it is nonetheless true that a procedural system that sought to minimize serious fact-finding impediments would take account of a number of factors, including the nature of the atrocities; the linguistic, educational, and cultural attributes of the victims and witnesses; and the various geopolitical factors that might affect the tribunal's ability to obtain evidence of the crimes.

The fact is, optimal procedures for eliciting clear, truthful testimony from Yugoslavian witnesses are not likely to be optimal procedures for eliciting clear, truthful testimony from East Timorese witnesses. The vast majority of the Yugoslavian witnesses appearing before the ICTY, for instance, are literate, have received at least a primary-school education,[1264] and have some familiarity with Western-style criminal trials. The vast majority of East Timorese witnesses appearing before the Special Panels, by contrast, are illiterate, have never before left their regions, and are accustomed to adjudicating criminal offenses through informal local justice mechanisms. Given these circumstances, we should not be surprised when trial procedures that may be well calculated to elicit clear and truthful testimony from Yugoslav witnesses lead only to confusion when used with the East Timorese. Similarly, we can expect that different procedures will be optimal to elicit testimony concerning the systematic, carefully planned, large-scale attacks that, in three-months' time, killed approximately eight hundred thousand members of an ethnic group in Rwanda than would be

[1264] U.S. Department of State, *Background Note: Bosnia and Herzegovina, available at* http://www.state.gov/r/pa/ei/bgn/2868.htm (the literacy rate of Bosnia in 2007 was 94.1 percent.); Cent. Intelligence Agency, The World Factbook, *Croatia, available at* https://www.cia.gov/library/publications/the-world-factbook/geos/HR.html (the literacy rate of the population of Croatians over fifteen years of age is 98.1 percent.); Cent. Intelligence Agency, The World Factbook, *Serbia, available at* https://www.cia.gov/library/publications/the-world-factbook/geos/RI.html (the literacy rate of population of Serbians over fifteen years of age is 96.4 percent.); Cent. Intelligence Agency, The World Factbook, *Yugoslavia* 2002, *available at* http://www.umsl.edu/services/govdocs/wofact2002/geos/yi.html#People.

optimal to elicit evidence concerning either an eleven-year war in Sierra Leone that featured chaotic attacks and seemingly mindless violence or an isolated political assassination in Lebanon that resulted in the deaths of a former prime minister and twenty-two others.

Indeed, as I have mentioned before, although the fact-finding impediments that I identify in Chapters 2 through 5 appear to some degree in each of the tribunals under study, they are unevenly distributed throughout those institutions. That is, different clusters of problems predominate in different tribunals. For instance, although SCSL testimony is occasionally distorted as a result of language interpretation, the problem is not severe. Some Sierra Leonean witnesses testify in English,[1265] and a good proportion of the rest testify in Krio, a language that is derived from English. By contrast, Special Panels', processes were plagued by interpretation difficulties, as an inadequate number of untrained interpreters struggled to do the impossible: to translate Portuguese legalese into simple, tribal languages. Similarly, although the ICTR has been the target of widespread and persistent allegations of witness lying, some of which have been conclusively proved, lying did not seem nearly so prevalent at the Special Panels. Indeed, although it appeared that some Special Panels witnesses did perjure themselves, most Special Panels defendants not only seemed disinclined to lie but were eager to confess their crimes during their first interactions with the prosecution. Differences such as these matter. Indeed, I maintain that if procedures are to be used to enhance fact-finding accuracy at a particular tribunal, then they must be crafted with an understanding of the particular evidentiary difficulties that that international tribunal is likely to confront.

9.C.iii. *Considering Context through the Importation of Domestic Procedures*

To take into account some of the contextual features described above, we might consider adopting for a given tribunal the trial procedures of the State where the atrocities took place. After all, local procedures should be best suited to meet local needs and expectations. But local procedures are not necessarily better suited to eliciting clear, accurate testimony in *international* criminal trials, and, even if they were, other factors might counsel against their adoption. For one thing, it may be difficult even to identify the relevant domestic criminal procedures because the laws of many of the states where atrocities take place

[1265] *See, e.g.*, AFRC Transcript, Apr. 12, 2005, at 6–7; AFRC Transcript, Sept. 15, 2005, at 4; RUF Transcript, Oct. 4, 2004, at 44–45; RUF Transcript, Oct. 7, 2004, at 64; RUF Transcript, Oct. 14, 2004, at 21; Taylor Transcript, Apr. 7, 2008, at 6801.

are not set out clearly or authoritatively.[1266] Furthermore, even if the relevant procedures are clear and well established, they may not conform to prevailing human rights standards.[1267] Finally, and most importantly, the adoption of a particular set of domestic procedures at an international tribunal may prove ill advised even if none of the above countervailing factors exists simply because procedures that function beautifully for run-of-the-mill domestic crimes may prove a functional disaster in the context of international crimes. International criminal prosecutions typically feature dramatically more legal and factual complexity than domestic criminal prosecutions. International crimes often span vast distances and lengthy time periods. International prosecutors consequently must adduce larger quantities and different sorts of evidence that often pertain to numerous crime sites. Because trials of this scope are rare in domestic courts, domestic procedures may not be well suited to process them. Finally, as I discuss in this book's conclusion, many of the fact-finding impediments that are so prevalent at the international tribunals do not appear in domestic criminal prosecutions, so the relevant domestic procedures may not be equipped to address them.[1268]

But just because we may not find the adoption of an entire set of domestic procedures to be an efficacious means of ameliorating fact-finding impediments at the international tribunals does not mean that these procedures have nothing to offer. Quite the contrary; in many cases domestic procedures can usefully inform the development of international criminal procedures. Indeed, although many of the fact-finding impediments that international tribunals confront do not appear in the domestic trials of the States where the conflict took place, a few do. These should be identified and the domestic response to them studied. Likewise, we should be open to borrowing court procedures from Western criminal justice systems that have the potential to enhance factual accuracy at the international tribunals. In particular, many Western criminal justice systems feature isolated fact-finding impediments that resemble those

[1266] On the difficulty of identifying Cambodian law, see Sluiter, *Due Process*, note 1262, at 319; Skilbeck, note 1262, at 430. Sierra Leonean law is likewise opaque. *See* Hanatu Kabbah, *Sierra Leone Legal System and Legal Research*, GLOBAL LEX, *available at* http://www.nyulawglobal.org/Globalex/Sierra_Leone1.htm (observing that the last Sierra Leonean law reports were published in 1973); *see also* Chandra Lekha Sriram, *Revolutions in Accountability: New Approaches to Past Abuses*, 19 AM. U. INT'L L. REV. 301, 304 (2003).

[1267] *See* Sluiter, *Due Process*, note 1262, at 315.

[1268] Some studies find, for instance, that nearly 90 percent of criminal cases are "clear cut in terms of evidence." Peter J. van Koppen & Steven D. Penrod, *Adversarial or Inquisitorial: Comparing Systems, in* ADVERSARIAL VERSUS INQUISITORIAL JUSTICE: PSYCHOLOGICAL PERSPECTIVES ON CRIMINAL JUSTICE SYSTEMS 1, 16 (Peter J. van Koppen & Steven D. Penrod eds., 2003). Thus, domestic procedures that work well for these evidentiarily easy cases may have little to recommend them when it comes to large-scale, complex international cases, of which few are "clear cut in terms of evidence."

appearing (with much greater frequency) at the international tribunals. As I mention in Chapter 3, for instance, some Canadian and Australian criminal trials feature Aboriginal witnesses or defendants whose cultural attributes and communication style differ sharply from those of courtroom personnel. As a consequence, judges in these countries are required to attend classes that will educate them about the relevant cultural differences.[1269] Such training should likewise be required of international judges. Cultural training is no panacea, I acknowledge,[1270] but it can help judges to place witness demeanor into an appropriate context and enable them to better assess testimonial deficiencies.

Efforts taken by the United Kingdom, Australia, and South Africa to improve the quality of evidence received from vulnerable witnesses also could prove relevant to the international tribunals. Studies have shown that child witnesses and witnesses who have comparatively unsophisticated language skills have particular difficulty answering questions during cross-examination because lawyers rarely modify the format and vocabulary of their cross-examination to take account of the witnesses' language abilities.[1271] Not only do lawyers frequently use language that is inappropriate to the age or linguistic capacity of a witness, but a study by Mark and Roslin Brennan identified thirteen frequently used language devices and questioning styles that serve to confuse child witnesses and destroy their credibility.[1272] These include "the use of negatives, double negatives, multi-part questions, complex syntax, and difficult vocabulary."[1273] Other studies have similarly revealed that traditional cross-examination techniques including "the technique of juxtaposing unrelated topics, the use of complex sentence structure, and the use of difficult and specific vocabulary" prove particularly confusing when used on child witnesses.[1274] To better equip

[1269] *See, e.g.*, Courts Administration Authority, South Australia District Court Judicial Officers, *available at* http://www.courts.sa.gov.au/courts/district/judicial_officers.html.

[1270] The SCSL hired Sierra Leone specialist Corinne Dufka, among other reasons, to "educate investigators on the basic history of the conflict and orient them to Sierra Leonean society," but it is likely that many investigators failed to utilize the information they were given to the greatest possible degree. War Crimes Studies Center, *Effective, Efficient, and Fair?: An Inquiry into the Investigative Practices of the Office of the Prosecutor at the Special Court for Sierra Leone* 43 (Sept. 2008). Judges, however, as fact-finders, arguably are in even greater need of such training.

[1271] Anne Graffam Walker, Handbook on Questioning Children: A Linguistic Perspective 37, 50 (1994); Anne Graffam Walker, *Questioning Young Children in Court: A Linguistic Case Study*, 17 L. & Hum. Behav. 59, 62–66 (1993).

[1272] Mark Brennan & Roslin E. Brennan, Strange Language: Child Victims Under Cross-examination 62 (1998).

[1273] *Id.* at 62–77. *See also* Cordon et al., note 188, at 171.

[1274] Louise Ellison, *The Mosaic Art: Cross-Examination and the Vulnerable Witness*, 21 Legal Studies 353, 356 (2001); *see also* David Carson, *Regulating the Examination of Children*, 4(1) Expert Evidence 2 (1995); Nancy W. Perry et al., *When Lawyers Question Children, Is Justice Served?*, 19 L. & Hum. Behav. 609 (1995).

vulnerable witnesses to provide clear and elucidating testimony, some domestic criminal justice systems have introduced intermediaries.[1275] The function of an intermediary is to assist in the communication between courtroom participants and the witness. Intermediaries act as passive translators, "reinterpreting lawyers' complex language in a more developmentally appropriate and therefore accessible form as well as explaining a witness's answers where necessary, for the benefit of the court."[1276]

Although the differences distinguishing international witnesses from vulnerable witnesses in domestic courts are greater than the similarities between the two groups, the difficulty some international witnesses experience in understanding unfamiliar legal terminology or complex compound sentences suggests that intermediaries could assist both in improving communication in some international trials and in identifying instances where communication is not the problem. For instance, as noted in Chapter 2, international witnesses frequently provide unresponsive answers to the questions posed of them. In most cases, the witness's failure to respond appropriately stems from a genuine failure to understand the question, so the efforts of an intermediary to "translate," as it were, would advance communication between the lawyer and the witness. Moreover, in the cases in which the witness's nonresponsiveness instead stems from a desire to evade, the presence of an intermediary might make such evasion harder to carry out.

Although intermediaries may help to facilitate communication and identify, if not thwart, efforts to evade, considering the introduction of intermediaries into international criminal processes also shows the difficulty of transplanting domestic procedures into the international realm. Intermediaries are intended to "translate" complex questions into phrasing that is more understandable to witnesses, but, in the domestic courtrooms in which intermediaries are used, all of the participants speak the same language. The fact that in an international courtroom questions and answers must be translated (at times through multiple rounds) into different languages would seem to limit to some degree the clarification that intermediaries can provide. Furthermore, determining which witnesses in an international trial would benefit from an intermediary would prove a difficult, potentially sensitive task because the determination would not be based on objective criteria such as the witness's age or established clinical disability, as it is in a domestic context, but on more

[1275] *See* Youth Justice and Criminal Evidence Act § 29 (United Kingdom); Criminal Procedure Act 1977, § 170A (South Africa); Evidence Act 1906 § 106(F)(2) (Western Australia).

[1276] Ellison, note 188, at 126. *See also* Louise Ellison, *Cross Examination and the Intermediary: Bridging the Language Divide*, Crim. L. Rev. 14, 16 (Feb. 2002); Jenny McEwan, *In Defense of Vulnerable Witnesses: The Youth Justice and Criminal Evidence Act 1999*, 4 Int'l J. Evid. & Proof 1, 1 (2000).

amorphous factors relating to the witness's seeming ability to understand and answer questions.[1277]

Introducing intermediaries into the international tribunals may also prove unworkable for the simple fact that so many intermediaries would be needed. Whereas the average domestic trial that makes use of an intermediary makes use of that intermediary for one witness, an international trial may require the services of several intermediaries to assist a significant proportion of the large numbers of witnesses who are typically called in an international trial. Frequent use of intermediaries not only gives rise to cost concerns but also to concerns about fundamentally altering the nature of the evidence presentation at trial. In an adversarial trial, lawyers carefully consider what questions to ask and how precisely to phrase those questions, particularly on cross-examination. Although the task of an intermediary is merely to translate the communication between the lawyer and the witness and back again, no one can doubt that such "translation" substantially impairs the lawyer's ability to conduct the case as he considers most advantageous. Manuals on trial advocacy give precise instructions on the sorts of questions that a lawyer should and should not ask on cross-examination. Lawyers should ask only leading questions,[1278] for instance, and should never ask a "why" or "how" question that would allow the witness to explain.[1279] Although intermediaries might be instructed to retain, as much as possible, the interrogator's sentence structure and to alter only that which absolutely must be altered to enable the witness to comprehend the question, there is no doubt that the intervention of the intermediary will significantly reduce the lawyers' ability to control the testimony that is heard. To the extent, then, that a criminal justice system – through the use of intermediaries – prevents a lawyer from asking the relevant questions the lawyer wishes to ask, it moves toward a nonadversarial system.[1280] Interjecting an occasional intermediary into the occasional trial for the occasional vulnerable witness would not substantially alter the nature of the evidence presentation in a given

[1277] Objective criteria relating to a witness's education level or literacy skills could be developed, but these may not be optimal to predict which witnesses would most benefit from intermediaries.

[1278] Steven Lubet, Modern Trial Advocacy: Analysis and Practice 117 (1997). Thomas A. Mauet, Trial Techniques 254–55 (6th ed. 2002); Irving Younger, The Art of Cross-Examination 22–23 (1976).

[1279] Mauet, note 1278, at 253.

[1280] Of course, even in an adversarial system, lawyers are not given completely free rein with their questioning. The U.S. Federal Rules of Evidence authorizes the court to "exercise reasonable control over the mode and order of interrogating witnesses and presenting evidence so as to (1) make the interrogation and presentation effective for the ascertainment of the truth, (2) avoid needless consumption of time, and (3) protect witnesses from harassment or undue embarrassment." Fed. R. Evid. 611(a).

criminal justice system. But if intermediaries were used in the international realm, they would be used in such greater numbers that they could undermine the adversarial system of evidence presentation that currently prevails at most international tribunals.

Borrowing a few – or even more than a few – procedures from the domestic courts where the conflict took place or from other domestic courts may improve testimonial quality at the margins, but the discussion of intermediaries shows that such improvement may give rise to costs in other areas and may have knock-on effects on the procedural system as a whole. The next obvious topic for discussion, then, is the system as a whole, and it is to that topic that I turn next.

9.C.iv. *The Choice between Adversarial and Nonadversarial Methods of Evidence Presentation*

The discussion of intermediaries in the previous section – and in particular the concern that the introduction of intermediaries would lead to a less adversarial evidence presentation at the trial – takes us to the broadest question that this section must address, namely: Which sort of evidence presentation – adversarial or nonadversarial – is better suited to ameliorate the fact-finding impediments that I have previously described? Before I begin this discussion, however, let me be clear about what I do not explore. Mirjan Damaška has rightly observed that adversarial and nonadversarial systems are oriented toward different values.[1281] In particular, Damaška has shown that nonadversarial systems of procedure are more committed to the search for truth. By contrast, adversarial systems, though also concerned with establishing truth, manifest a greater willingness to sacrifice that value in order to advance other values, such as individual autonomy and the prevention of governmental abuse.[1282] Given these different orientations, one might ask which would better reflect and advance the complex, multifaceted goals of international criminal trials as they are conducted in the complex, messy world of interstate relations and global politics. Although that is a vitally important question, it is not one that I set out to consider here. Rather, I confine my discussion primarily to the presentation of evidence at trial. Although I must also discuss some pretrial features that affect evidence presentation, I do not purport to opine on the relative merits of a tribunal's entire set of procedures. Second, I confine my assessment to one – albeit one important – variable. That is, I seek to evaluate adversarial and nonadversarial methods of evidence presentation only in terms

[1281] Damaška, *Evidentiary Barriers to Conviction*, note 788, at 578–80.
[1282] *Id.* at 583–84.

of their ability to elicit clear, accurate testimony at trial from such witnesses as those appearing before the ICTR, the SCSL, and the Special Panels.

As noted, Damaška, along with other scholars of domestic criminal procedures, believes that nonadversarial procedures are better suited to ascertaining the truth,[1283] and that opinion, if correct, might seem at first glance to answer the question that I am asking. It does not, however, for the same reason that it would not be useful to blindly adopt the domestic procedures of the state where the crime took place. Although nonadversarial procedures might be extraordinarily efficacious in elucidating truth in the domestic context, that context does not require them to confront the multifarious fact-finding impediments that render fact-finding far more complex in the international realm. Indeed, I began this chapter by observing the way in which contextual factors can help to shape a criminal procedure system, and I opined that, to enhance fact-finding accuracy at the international tribunals, international criminal procedures must be crafted with an understanding of the particular evidentiary difficulties that a tribunal is likely to confront. It is to that idea that I now return in considering the merits of adversarial or nonadversarial procedures for eliciting clear, truthful testimony from international witnesses. In particular, whether adversarial or nonadversarial procedures would better advance this goal likely depends on which set of problems predominate at the tribunal in question. If the primary impediment to clear, accurate testimony at a particular tribunal stems from the witnesses' inability to convey clear and accurate testimony, then I believe that nonadversarial procedures are better suited to improving the quality of the testimony. By contrast, if testimonial deficiencies at a given tribunal stem primarily from witnesses' unwillingness to provide clear, accurate testimony – that is, from their desire to evade, obfuscate, or downright lie – then adversarial procedures will probably do a better job of identifying that behavior and deterring it.

My first proposition is that nonadversarial evidence presentation at trial is apt to be more efficacious at ameliorating the testimonial deficiencies that arise when witnesses find it difficult to provide the information expected of them. To see why, we must consider the two key differences between adversarial and nonadversarial evidence presentation: the style of the questioning and the role of the questioner. Turning first to style: Whereas, in an adversarial system, testimony is elicited through a formal interrogation, in a nonadversarial trial, witnesses convey their testimony through exchanges that bear greater

[1283] *Id.* at 579, 581–89; Jörg et al., note 789, at 42–43 (concluding that, in the inquisitorial system used on the Continent, "priority is given to truth-finding"). For instance, the German Code of Criminal Procedure imposes an express legal duty on judges to find the truth. Richard S. Frase, *The Search for the Whole Truth About American and European Criminal Justice*, 3 Buff. Crim. L. Rev. 785, 820 (2000).

resemblance to a informal conversation than a judicial interrogation.[1284] For one thing, witnesses are usually permitted to begin their testimony in narrative form; that is, they begin by telling their stories largely without any interruptions.[1285] Damaška observes that the only questions a judge might ask during the witness's narrative are those designed "to help the witness express himself, to clarify a point, or to steer the witness back from the labyrinth of utter irrelevancy."[1286] Moreover, even when judges do begin their questioning, the resulting exchanges take on a conversational tone.

To the extent that this more relaxed, informal method of communication will put the witness at ease,[1287] then we can expect it to enhance the accuracy of the witness's testimony because psychological studies show "a negative correlation between high levels of stress and the ability of observers to recall and relay information accurately and effectively."[1288] Certainly, that research could also raise concerns about the effects of adversarial questioning in domestic cases because even a well-prepared witness in a domestic court is apt to be nervous on the witness stand. However, it raises particularly compelling concerns about the results of adversarial questioning during international trials because the average international witness is apt to suffer particularly intense stress while testifying both as a result of the subject matter of the witness's testimony and the circumstances under which it is given. International witnesses have typically seen or been subject to almost inconceivable violence. They have seen or been the victims of amputations, decapitations, cannibalism, and repeated rapes, sometimes with implements. They have seen their children, parents, spouses, and other close members of their families murdered, mutilated, and sexually assaulted. It is not surprising, therefore, that international witnesses frequently break down on the witness stand when trying to describe their experiences.

In addition to the stress inherent in remembering and recounting such ghastly scenes, the very act of testifying before an international tribunal is

[1284] Damaška, *Presentation of Evidence*, note 1236, at 1089.

[1285] *Id.*; van Kessel, note 1234, at 433; Brouwer, note 1231, at 218.

[1286] Damaška, *Presentation of Evidence*, note 1236, at 1089.

[1287] Renée Lettow Lerner's study of a French trial suggests that we can expect nonadversarial questioning to be more likely to put witnesses at ease. Lerner reported that during questioning in the French trial, "witnesses were relatively relaxed and often more forthcoming with information." Renée Lettow Lerner, *The Intersection of Two Systems: An American on Trial for an American Murder in the French Cour D'assises*, 2001 U. Ill. L. Rev. 791, 818 (2001).

[1288] Ellison, note 188, at 12. *See also* R. Edward Geiselman et al., *Enhancement of Eyewitness Memory with the Cognitive Interview*, 99 Am. J. of Psychol. 385 (1986); Stephen Moston & Terry Engelberg, *The Effects of Social Support on Children's Eyewitness Testimony*, 6 Applied Cognitive Psychol. 61 (1992); Helen R. Dent, *Stress as a Factor in Influencing Person Recognition in Identification Parades*, 30 Bull. of the Brit. Psychol. Soc. 339, 339–340 (1977); Cathleen A. Carter et al., *Linguistic and Socioemotional Influences on the Accuracy of Children's Reports*, 20 Human Behavior 335 (1996).

itself likely to be intensely stress inducing. Most international witnesses have no experience with any formal court procedures, let alone with the unfamiliar procedures of an international tribunal that operates in a foreign language and that is located many hundreds, if not thousands, of miles from their homes. Many international witnesses have never flown on an airplane or even left the region in which they were born. Thus, given the subject matter of their testimony and the unfamiliarity of everything related to testifying, international witnesses are apt to be extremely nervous indeed when on the witness stand, and if informal, conversational questioning is more conducive to putting such witnesses at ease than the highly regulated, formal interrogations that characterize an adversarial presentation of evidence, then the former should enhance fact-finding accuracy for this reason alone.[1289]

But this is not the only reason. Rather, the narrative nature of much witness testimony in nonadversarial trials is also likely to enrich communication and enhance understanding. Some commentators believe that allowing a witness to begin her testimony with an uninterrupted narrative leads to "more evidence go[ing] to the factfinder than that elicited from 'yes' or 'no' responses to attorney questions."[1290] William Pizzi and other commentators report, moreover, that "[s]tudies suggest that witnesses who are permitted to give evidence in an uninterrupted narrative are able to remember more about events and to remember things more accurately than are witnesses who have to break up their recollection to fit a tight question-and-answer format."[1291] That research pertains to domestic witnesses, but it suggests that narrative testimony would prove an especially valuable mechanism for eliciting useful testimony from

[1289] An isolated example supporting this position can be found in Francis Pakes's study of two ICTY trials, one presided over by a judge from the United States – a country that uses adversarial procedures – and the other presided over by a judge from France – a country that uses nonadversarial procedures. Although both trials were conducted pursuant to the predominantly adversarial procedures of the ICTY, Pakes found that the French judge intervened in the questioning far more frequently – as is customary in France, but that in doing so "showed great awareness for the distress" that the court appearance might have caused a young witness who was describing crimes that had occurred when he was fourteen. Francis J. Pakes, *Styles of Trial Procedure at the International Criminal Tribunal for the Former Yugoslavia, in* ADVERSARIAL VERSUS INQUISITORIAL JUSTICE: PSYCHOLOGICAL PERSPECTIVES ON CRIMINAL JUSTICE SYSTEMS 309, 315–16 (Peter J. van Koppen & Steven D. Penrod eds., 2003).

[1290] *See* Franklin D. Strier, *Major Problems Endemic to the Adversary System and Proposed Reforms,* 19 WESTERN ST. U. L. REV. 463, 491 (1992).

[1291] WILLIAM PIZZI, TRIALS WITHOUT TRUTH: WHY OUR SYSTEM OF CRIMINAL TRIALS HAS BECOME AN EXPENSIVE FAILURE AND WHAT WE NEED TO DO TO REBUILD IT 198 (1999). *See also* Pasi Pölönen, *Witness Examination in Finnish Criminal Trials, in* 51 SCANDINAVIAN STUDIES IN LAW: PROCEDURAL LAW 437, 445 (2007) ("[W]itness psychological research indicates that a freely given testimony has high probative value as it is likely to contain authentic and reliable information more often than answers to questions, which may be misleading in some way.").

international witnesses who have difficulty answering the questions asked of them. In addition, I believe that a narrative presentation has the potential to enhance understanding amongst individuals who use different patterns of communication. When witnesses are questioned – even on direct examination – they are required to present the aspects of their experience that the lawyer wishes the court to hear in the order in which the lawyer wishes the court to hear them. Concededly, in most cases, the pieces of information that lawyers want conveyed are the legally relevant pieces of information, and the sequence in which they wish them conveyed is the logical sequence from a Western point of view. What the questioning of witnesses acts to conceal, however, is the witness's own understanding of what is important in his story and the witness's method of communicating that story. And that information can be highly probative to fact finders when the witnesses' cultural traits and communication style differ sharply from their own.

Having said this, I recognize that the kind of witness narratives that regularly occur in domestic courts in continental European countries are not apt to be replicated in an international courtroom. For one thing, the fact that many international witnesses are so entirely unfamiliar with courtroom processes and so nervous about testifying suggests that an open invitation to tell their stories may prove too boundary-less. In such cases, questioning can be necessary to guide the witness and provide him reassurance that he is assisting the court as he should. Furthermore, even if an international witness is sufficiently familiar with court processes and sufficiently confident about testifying, the very breadth of his experiences could give rise to a need for questioning. A witness to a domestic armed robbery knows that the purpose of her testimony is to convey what she saw during the robbery, and she will convey that information when asked to testify in a narrative form. Most international witnesses, by contrast, have witnessed or been the victims of numerous crimes, sometimes over lengthy periods of time. As a consequence, without the guidance provided by questions, international witnesses may have no way of knowing which aspects of their experience they should recount. These differences suggest that the narrative portion of a witness's testimony may not be as lengthy or as informative in international trials as it is in continental European trials. But despite these limitations, narrative testimony at the international tribunals is apt to provide fact finders with, if nothing else, a frame of reference regarding the witness's communication style and the key aspects of her experiences.[1292] In particular, fact finders will be better able to evaluate the witness's credibility

[1292] Permitting some narrative testimony is also likely to make a difficult experience somewhat easier for the witness. Although that benefit is not relevant to my focus here, it should carry some weight.

center.[1345] Witnesses further testified that, after this Serb offensive, they found the bodies of five local men who had been shot to death. Although several witnesses saw Tadić beating various men and leading them away, none of the witnesses saw him or anyone else kill the five murder victims. As a consequence, the Trial Chamber found that, although the prosecution had proved beyond a reasonable doubt that Tadić had entered Jaskići with the armed men and had taken part in removing the male villagers to the Keraterm detention center,[1346] the prosecution had not proven beyond a reasonable doubt that Tadić had played any part in killing any or all of the five men.[1347] It consequently acquitted Tadić of that crime.

The Appeals Chamber reversed Tadić's acquittal. Although it acknowledged that the prosecution had presented no evidence suggesting that Tadić had personally participated in any of the murders,[1348] the Appeals Chamber held that Tadić could nonetheless be held responsible for the murders by virtue of his involvement in the common plan to carry out criminal activity. Scrutinizing World War II cases, the Appeals Chamber determined that many of them were prosecuted on a "common purpose" theory that held that a person who acts with others to further a common criminal purpose may be held liable for crimes committed by the other members of the group. *Tadić* held that that theory of liability – now called joint criminal enterprise – "encompasses three distinct categories of collective criminality."[1349] The first category arises when all of the codefendants act pursuant to a common design and possess the same criminal intention. This sort of JCE would arise, for instance, if a group of defendants determined to kill someone and each defendant played a different role in the murder scheme. The second category of JCE derives from World War II concentration camp cases; there, liability arises as a result of the defendant's participation in an institutionalized system of ill treatment. Finally, the third category of JCE – the so-called "extended JCE" – comes into play when a group of people enter into a common design to pursue one course of criminal conduct and one of the perpetrators commits an act that falls outside of the common design but that was nevertheless a natural and foreseeable consequence of the common design.[1350] The Appeals Chamber's description of an extended JCE reflects the facts of *Tadić*: Tadić actively took part in "the common purpose to rid the Prijedor region of the non-Serb population by committing inhumane acts." Although the common purpose of the plan did not encompass

[1345] Prosecutor v. Tadić, Case No. IT-94-T, Judgement, paras. 345–347 (May 7, 1997).
[1346] *Id.* at para. 369.
[1347] *Id.* at para. 373.
[1348] Prosecution v. Tadić, Case No. IT-94-1-A, Judgement, para. 185 (July 15, 1999).
[1349] *Id.* at para. 195.
[1350] *Id.* at paras. 196–204.

killing the non-Serb men, Tadić was aware that killings often accompanied the inhumane acts, making the murders foreseeable. Consequently, the Appeals Chamber held Tadić to have participated – through an extended JCE – in the killings of the five men in Jaskići.[1351]

In *Tadić*, the ICTY confronted a scenario well known to readers of this book: The evidence presented to the *Tadić* Trial Chamber created a strong suspicion of Tadić's guilt but did not prove that guilt beyond a reasonable doubt. Concededly, the *Tadić* scenario differed from the cases canvassed here most notably in that the *Tadić* prosecutors did not present *any* witnesses who could attest to Tadić's responsibility for the murders. In the cases studied here, by contrast, prosecutors do typically present *some* testimony regarding the defendant's commission of a specific act, but the testimony is riddled with difficulties and consequently is inadequate to prove the defendant's guilt beyond a reasonable doubt. But although the nature and causes of *Tadić's* evidentiary deficiency may differ from those of the cases that I have described, the resulting predicament they present is the same.

The ICTY chose to remedy the evidentiary deficiency that it confronted in *Tadić* by constructing an expansive legal doctrine that permits the imposition of criminal liability on defendants who did not themselves personally commit the crimes in question or intend that such crimes be committed. That is, under an extended JCE theory, the fact that the Trial Chamber has received no evidence that a defendant had anything whatever to do with a particular crime need not be dispositive of the defendant's liability for that crime if prosecutors can prove that the defendant entered into a common plan to commit other crimes and the crime in question was a foreseeable consequence of the common plan. It should come as no surprise that such a broad imposition of liability has provoked severe criticism. For instance, Allison Danner and Jenny Martinez cynically opine that "[t]here is little explanation for the result in *Tadić* other than the Appeals Chamber's conviction that Tadić was guilty of killing the villagers in Jaskići despite the prosecution's inability to produce evidence of Tadić's participation – and, indeed, in spite of the Trial Chamber's conclusion that there was not enough evidence that the group in which Tadić acted had committed the killings."[1352] Other commentators view the joint criminal enterprise doctrine more positively, as a means of presenting "a more accurate account of the criminal activities" of individuals and the groups to which they

[1351] *Id.* at paras. 230–233.

[1352] Allison Marston Danner & Jenny S. Martinez, *Guilty Associations: Joint Criminal Enterprise, Command Responsibility, and the Development of International Criminal Law*, 93 Cal. L. Rev. 75, 133 (2005).

belong than other more conventional forms of criminal liability.[1353] Even those who approve of the doctrine, however, acknowledge that its potential breadth and elasticity – particularly in its extended manifestation – are worrisome. Tribunal precedents neither require that a defendant substantially contribute to the joint criminal enterprise before he can be held liable, nor do they restrict the prosecutor's discretion in defining the enterprise.[1354] Thus, as Danner and Martinez point out, JCE liability "poses significant challenges to the criminal law paradigm"[1355] by permitting "any member of an armed force or paramilitary group that engages in widespread or widely-known violations" to be held "guilty for all crimes committed by that organization if that individual engages in any wrongdoing criminal under international criminal law, no matter how minor or isolated."[1356]

Perhaps JCE liability does raise "the specter of guilt by association," as Danner and Martinez claim,[1357] but, even if does, at least it does so openly. Prosecutors alleging an extended joint criminal enterprise do not claim to have evidence of the defendant's personal perpetration of the crime in question. Certainly, one might think that a defendant should be required to make a substantial contribution to the common design before joint criminal enterprise liability attaches.[1358] Or one might believe that a defendant should have to have a subjective awareness of the crime's foreseeability.[1359] Or one might conclude that the extended JCE doctrine should be abolished entirely because it inappropriately imposes the same criminal liability on the defendant who actually committed the murder as it does on the defendant who not only did not

[1353] Katrina Gustafson, *The Requirement of an 'Express Agreement' for Joint Criminal Liability: A Critique of Brđanin*, 5 J. INT'L CRIM. JUST. 134, 139 (2007). For other (mostly) positive assessments of the JCE doctrine, see Antonio Cassese, *The Proper Limits of Individual Responsibility Under the Doctrine of Joint Criminal Enterprise*, 5 J. INT'L CRIM. JUST. 109 (2007); Elies van Sliedregt, *Joint Criminal Enterprise as a Pathway to Convicting Individuals for Genocide*, 5 J. INT'L CRIM. JUST. 184 (2007); Rebecca L. Haffajee, Note, *Prosecuting Crimes of Rape and Sexual Violence at the ICTR: The Application of Joint Criminal Enterprise Theory*, 29 HARV. J. L. GENDER 201 (2006); Allen O'Rourke, Recent Development, *Joint Criminal Enterprise and* Brđanin: *Misguided Overcorrection*, 47 HARV. INT'L L. J. 307 (2006).

[1354] *See* Allison Marston Danner, *Joint Criminal Enterprise, in* INTERNATIONAL CRIMINAL LAW 483, 487–89 (M. Cherif Bassiouni ed., 2008).

[1355] Danner & Martinez, note 1352, at 134.

[1356] *Id.* at 137.

[1357] *Id.*

[1358] *See, e.g., id.* at 150; Jacob A. Ramer, *Hate by Association: Joint Criminal Enterprise Liability for Persecution*, 7 CHI.-KENT J. INT'L & COMP. L. 31, 33, 110–12 (2007).

[1359] For a discussion of the foreseeability questions to which JCE liability gives rise, see Kai Ambos, *Joint Criminal Enterprise and Command Responsibility*, 5 J. INT'L CRIM. JUST. 159 (2007); Jens David Ohlin, *Three Conceptual Problems with the Doctrine of Joint Criminal Enterprise*, 5 J. INT'L CRIM. JUST. 69, 81–85 (2007).

commit the murder but did not even intend that the murder be committed.[1360] Whatever one's position on these and other questions, however, the benefit of using a JCE theory is that it permits such positions to be openly debated and assessed. We can evaluate whether the ICTY was justified in convicting Tadić of participating in the murders of the five men from Jaskići because the ICTY clearly and candidly acknowledged that it had no evidence of Tadić's personal perpetration of the crime, and it clearly and candidly set forth the actual grounds for its conviction.

It is this clear and candid acknowledgement of the grounds for conviction that is often missing from the cases examined here. In those cases, Trial Chambers purport to convict defendants for their personal acts, but, because those acts are so difficult to prove by means of the witness testimony that is presented, the Trial Chambers are frequently forced to supplement that testimony with common sense inferences drawn from the nature of the crimes and the defendant's membership in groups known to have participated in the crimes. Although, in most of the cases I have examined, the Trial Chambers do not conduct a JCE analysis, they do, I believe, rely on many of the same factors that would support a conviction under a JCE theory. I have argued, for instance, that in assessing whether a defendant performed a particular genocidal act, ICTR Trial Chambers find relevant not only the testimony of eyewitnesses who claim to have seen him perform that act but also the defendant's membership in Rwanda's Interim Government, which was well known to have played a key role in implementing the genocide. Likewise, I have maintained that an SCSL defendant's high-level position in a faction that is well known to have committed atrocities against civilians strongly influences the Trial Chamber's assessment of the testimony it hears about that defendant's personal involvement in those atrocities. Under a JCE theory of liability, these factors would also prove relevant but more openly so. Instead of relying on vague suspicions to bolster the value of problematic witness testimony, Trial Chambers that consider a defendant's liability on a JCE theory openly ask whether the defendant, as a minister in the Interim Government or as the director of war for the CDF, was part of a common plan to commit international crimes with other such Ministers or high-level officials.

For one reason or another, the tribunals under study have made little use of JCE.[1361] The Special Panels had little need to rely on JCE theories because the

[1360] For a discussion of this objection to JCE liability, see Antonio Cassese, *The Proper Limits of Individual Responsibility Under the Doctrine of Joint Criminal Enterprise*, 5 J. Int'l Crim. Just. 109, 117–23 (2007); Ohlin, note 1359, at 85–88.

[1361] Contrast those tribunals with the ICTY, which has relied heavily on the doctrine. For statistics regarding the ICTY's use of JCE, see Danner, note 1354, at 485–86.

only defendants over which the Panels were able to obtain custody were low-level offenders who themselves had participated in discrete, local episodes of violence.[1362] JCE has likewise played little role in ICTR convictions. Rarely have prosecutors charged that mode of liability, and, when they have, they sometimes have not proved it[1363] and sometimes have not set it forth sufficiently clearly in the indictment.[1364] Indeed, only two ICTR defendants have been convicted on a JCE theory, and one of those defendants was convicted of JCE in name only, for JCE in fact played no role in shaping the defendant's convictions.[1365] Like their counterparts at the Special Panels, ICTR prosecutors have charged most defendants with having perpetrated specific acts of violence. Such charges made sense because the prosecution had witnesses who were willing to testify about specific acts, and a prosecution based on discrete acts of violence perpetrated by the defendant is likely to be quicker, more streamlined, and less controversial than a JCE prosecution. For instance, former ICTR Chief of Prosecutions Stephen Rapp reported that Eliezer Niyitegeka was initially charged with genocide crimes that stemmed from his affiliation with Radio Rwanda and its virulent anti-Tutsi broadcasts. However, because considerable time and

[1362] Additionally, Timorese offenders were so likely to confess that the Panels had little difficulty justifying their convictions, even though witness testimony was often woefully deficient.

[1363] *See* Bikindi Judgement, note 683, at paras. 400–402.

[1364] *See* Nchamihigo Judgement, note 730, at para. 328; Rukundo Judgement, note 730, at para. 35.

[1365] The prosecution alleged that defendant Aloys Simba had engaged in a Category I joint criminal enterprise, the purpose of which was to kill Tutsi at five locations in Gikongoro and Butare Prefectures. Simba Judgement, note 455, at para. 394. The Trial Chamber concluded that a JCE existed, finding that the massacres at the Murambi Technical School, the Kaduha Parish and the Cyanika Parish were so highly coordinated that "the only reasonable inference from the evidence is that a common criminal purpose existed to kill Tutsi at those three sites." *Id.* at para. 402. The Trial Chamber further found that Simba had contributed to the JCE by his personal involvement in the massacres at the Murambi Technical School and Kaduha Parish, *id.* at paras. 117–118, 174–175, and that he shared the common purpose of killing Tutsi at these two locations, *id.* at paras. 403, 406. But because the Trial Chamber determined that the prosecution had not proven that Simba was personally involved in the Cyanika Parish massacre, it held that there was not sufficient evidence to prove that Simba shared the common purpose to kill Tutsi at Cyanika Parish. *Id.* at para. 407. In other words, the Trial Chamber defined the joint criminal enterprise as including a massacre in which Simba did not participate, and because Simba did not participate in that massacre, the Trial Chamber was unwilling to find that Simba shared the common purpose as it applied to that massacre. In reaching these conclusions, the *Simba* Trial Chamber interpreted the JCE doctrine in a particularly narrow way. The benefit to prosecutors of JCE liability is that it permits a defendant to be convicted for *all* of the crimes that form part of the common purpose, and – if they are foreseeable – even the crimes that extend outside of it. Certainly, Simba could have been convicted of crimes stemming from the Cyanika Parish massacre on an extended JCE theory and, given the Trial Chamber's findings regarding Simba's involvement in the massacres at the Kaduha Parish and Murambi Technical School, he also could have been convicted of Cyanika Parish crimes on a Category I JCE theory.

resources would have been required to prove Niyitegeka's responsibility for the broadcasts, and there was in any event "strong evidence that Niyitegeka had personally led killing expeditions to the Bisesero Hills, . . . a case was developed focusing only on the latter activity." Rapp endorsed the prosecution's strategy, noting that because its case was so narrowly focused, the prosecution was able to present its evidence in only eighteen days, yet Niyitegeka was nonetheless convicted of genocide, and he received the maximum sentence, life in prison.[1366]

SCSL prosecutors have charged JCE liability in each of the SCSL's four cases, but the Trial Chambers initially proved reluctant to convict on that theory.[1367] In the *AFRC* case, for instance, prosecutors charged defendants with engaging with RUF leaders in a wide-ranging joint criminal enterprise "to take any actions in order to gain and exercise political power and control over the territory of Sierra Leone."[1368] The *AFRC* Trial Chamber rejected this charge because the common purpose of the purported JCE did not encompass a crime within the SCSL's jurisdiction.[1369] However, it is useful to examine the attempted use of JCE liability in the *AFRC* case as well as the successful use of JCE liability in the ICTR's *Zigiranyirazo* case because doing so demonstrates the way in which the doctrine can reduce reliance on questionable witness testimony and better reflect a Trial Chamber's actual conclusions about criminal liability.

The most obvious consequence of the Trial Chamber's rejection of JCE liability in the *AFRC* case was the defendants' acquittals on several charges. Had JCE liability been available, the defendants would have been linked to atrocities in which they played no personal role but which formed part of the common purpose of the joint criminal enterprise or a foreseeable consequence thereof. Instead, because the *AFRC* Trial Chamber rejected the prosecutor's JCE submissions, the Trial Chamber was forced to find that the defendants bore no responsibility for many of the atrocities at issue in the case.[1370] The prosecution had submitted no evidence to prove the defendants' personal

[1366] Rapp, note 299, at 283.

[1367] In the *CDF* case, the Trial Chamber found that the prosecution had not proven JCE liability. CDF Judgement, note 27, at paras. 732, 770, 803, 850, 863. There, the prosecution's JCE theory was substantially undercut when the most high-level and seemingly most culpable defendant in the *CDF* case – Sam Hinga Norman – died before the Trial Chamber could issue its judgment. A great deal of trial testimony had centered on Norman's crimes, and one can plausibly hypothesize that the Trial Chamber would have reached a different conclusion on JCE liability had it been passing on Norman's liability.

[1368] AFRC Judgement, note 27, at para. 18.

[1369] *Id.* at paras. 67–85. This holding was reversed on appeal. *See* AFRC Appeals Judgement, note 839, at paras. 66–87.

[1370] *See* AFRC Judgement, note 27, at paras. 1646–1650, 1664, 1668, 1673, 1678–1679, 1685, 1814, 1819, 1847, 1855, 1861, 1897, 1903, 1906a, 1910, 1955a, 1987–1991, 1996, 2000, 2005, 2009, 2014, 2018, 2024, 2028–2031, 2049, 2084, 2088.

involvement in these crimes, so without a JCE theory the Trial Chamber had no basis for a conviction.

To some, these acquittals might stand as a positive consequence of the Trial Chamber's rejection of JCE liability in the *AFRC* case. A negative consequence can be found through a comparison of the evidence supporting the actual convictions and the evidence that would have been invoked to support convictions on a JCE theory. In sum, JCE convictions would likely have been based on a different and potentially more reliable set of evidence. Without the JCE theory, the *AFRC* Trial Chamber had to rely on particular eyewitnesses who said that they saw the defendants committing specific acts; that they saw defendant Kanu amputate an arm,[1371] for instance, or heard defendant Brima order the killing of ECOMOG soldiers.[1372] That is, the Trial Chamber did convict the defendants of various crimes, finding them liable both for personally perpetrating some of the crimes as well as on a superior liability theory, but the Trial Chamber had to base many of these convictions on the testimony of only one or two witnesses.[1373] The testimony of these witnesses was sharply contradicted by the testimony of defense witnesses, and some of the former was marred by severe inconsistencies. The Trial Chamber, for instance, relied on the testimony of witness TF1-033 for a considerable number of its findings despite the fact that the witness testified inconsistently about whether the AFRC defeated the RUF at Tombodu,[1374] whether TF1-033 personally witnessed any rapes in Mandaya,[1375] and whether a certain commander had acted under the orders of the defendant,[1376] among many other inconsistencies.[1377]

The *Zigiranyirazo* Trial Chamber, by contrast, did base the defendant's conviction on the JCE doctrine and thereby showed the way in which the doctrine can be used to reduce reliance on questionable eyewitness testimony. The *Zigiranyirazo* Trial Chamber indeed relied on very little witness testimony because it found virtually all of it unreliable, citing the witnesses' inconsistencies,[1378]

[1371] *Id.* at paras. 2050–2052.

[1372] *Id.* at para. 1779.

[1373] Many of Brima's convictions for the personal commission of criminal acts were supported by the testimony of only one witness. *See, e.g., id.* at paras. 1703, 1756–1764, 1768, 1777.

[1374] AFRC Transcript, July 11, 2005, at 84–85.

[1375] AFRC Transcript, July 12, 2005, at 7–8.

[1376] AFRC Transcript, July 11, 2005, at 145–48.

[1377] *See also id.* at 141–42, 150, 151, 152; AFRC Transcript, July 12, 2005, at 13–14, 20–21. The Trial Chamber also relied heavily on the testimony of witness TF1-184, and although his testimony featured only a few, relatively minor inconsistencies in the *AFRC* case, *see, e.g.*, AFRC Transcript, Sept. 29, 2005, at 69–70; AFRC Transcript, Sept. 30, 2005, at 65–67, he also testified in the *RUF* case, and there his testimony was riddled with serious inconsistencies, *see, e.g.*, RUF Transcript, Dec. 5, 2005, at 79, 83–93; RUF Transcript, Dec. 8, 2005, at 43–50.

[1378] Zigiranyirazo Judgement, note 498, at paras. 116, 155, 165, 171–175, 177, 180, 201, 305.

vagueness,[1379] previous lies,[1380] incentives to lie,[1381] and other deficiencies.[1382] Because it declined to credit the testimony of so many witnesses, the Trial Chamber rejected virtually all of the charges that the prosecutor had leveled against Zigiranyirazo.[1383] The Trial Chamber did find proven, however, a portion of the prosecution's allegations regarding Zigiranyirazo's involvement in the attack on Kesho Hill. In particular, the Trial Chamber found that, following an earlier unsuccessful attack on Tutsi refugees, Zigiranyirazo arrived at Kesho Hill as part of a convoy of presidential guard soldiers, *gendarmes*, and *Interahamwe* militia. Once there, Zigiranyirazo addressed the group of assailants; the assailants applauded his address and then immediately attacked the Tutsi refugees. Although some witnesses had testified that they were able to hear the content of Zigiranyirazo's speech and that he had called for the Tutsi to be killed, the Trial Chamber found that testimony unreliable.

Because the Trial Chamber was able to find beyond a reasonable doubt only that Zigiranyirazo had addressed the assailants and not that his address had called for the extermination of the Tutsi, the Trial Chamber was unable to convict Zigiranyirazo of ordering or instigating the crime of genocide.[1384] It did, nonetheless, find him guilty of genocide, but on a JCE theory. In particular, the Trial Chamber found the existence of a common criminal purpose to kill the Tutsi in the fact that the attack on Kesho Hill was a "coordinated operation backed by Presidential Guards, soldiers, *Interahamwe*, and civilians, armed with guns, grenades and traditional weapons, with organisational support from prominent personalities."[1385] The Trial Chamber found that Zigiranyirazo shared the common criminal purpose in the fact that he arrived at the massacre site with the assailants, addressed the assailants, was applauded for his address, and did not leave the massacre site until the attack had commenced.[1386] Finally, the Trial Chamber found that Zigiranyirazo's speech significantly contributed to the execution of the JCE.[1387]

One might believe that a genocide conviction should be based on something more than a speech whose content cannot be ascertained. If so, one might place the blame on the JCE doctrine or on the *Zigiranyirazo* Trial Chamber's application of that doctrine. But whatever one's views on the merits of the *Zigiranyirazo* decision, one should at least admire its transparency. Zigiranyirazo's

[1379] *Id.* at para. 180.
[1380] *Id.* at para. 221.
[1381] *Id.* at paras. 138–140, 154, 164.
[1382] *Id.* at paras. 135, 137, 147, 177, 310, 312.
[1383] *See id.*, at paras. 126, 141, 149, 157, 166, 175, 177, 180, 213, 344, 361, 379.
[1384] *Id.*, at paras. 404–405.
[1385] *Id.* at para. 407.
[1386] *Id.* at para. 408.
[1387] *Id.* at para. 409.

genocide conviction unquestionably would have seemed more satisfying and less controversial had the Trial Chamber based it on the testimony of witnesses who said they heard Zigiranyirazo call for the Tutsi killings. And the Trial Chamber could have reached that conclusion. Plenty of genocide convictions at the ICTR are based on just the sort of testimony presented to the *Zigiranyirazo* Trial Chamber. But to base Zigiranyirazo's genocide conviction on this testimony, the Trial Chamber would have had to ignore its many problematic features. Instead, because it unflinchingly scrutinized the testimony, the Trial Chamber was forced to reject it and was forced to decide the much more difficult question of whether a speech of unascertained content delivered to an enthusiastic group of assailants who immediately thereafter commenced an attack suffices to support a genocide conviction. That is a far more controversial question to answer, but in most international cases it will be just the sort of question that needs to be answered because in most international cases the eyewitness testimony that prosecutors present to prove genocide more directly is deficient in one way or another. That is, in most cases genocidal actions and intentions – if they exist – must be inferred from just the sort of evidence that the *Zigiranyirazo* Trial Chamber relied on. And whether such evidence is or is not sufficient to support a genocide conviction can be excruciatingly difficult to decide, but it is a question that should be confronted, not sidestepped.

Admittedly, the use of the JCE doctrine does not entirely eliminate the need for witness testimony. To convict *Zigiranyirazo*, the Trial Chamber did not need to receive evidence regarding the content of Zigiranyirazo's speech to the assailants, but it did need evidence that Zigiranyirazo delivered some speech to the assailants. Likewise, when the ICTY found Tadić guilty on a JCE theory for the Jaskići murders, it did not need to receive evidence of Tadić's personal commission of the murders, but it did need to receive evidence that Tadić had entered Jaskići with the armed Serb soldiers, rounded up the Jaskići men, and ill treated them. The evidence the Trial Chambers received on these issues took the form of eyewitness testimony, and, if that body of testimony was unreliable, then Zigiranyirazo's and Tadić's convictions on the JCE theory were just as questionable as they would have been on a direct commission theory. At the same time, the JCE doctrine can function to reduce the Trial Chamber's reliance on witness testimony, first of all because, on a JCE theory, the prosecution need not present witness testimony to prove the defendant's participation in each and every massacre. It can obtain a conviction for all of them nonetheless merely by proving that the whole lot of massacres really formed the component parts of a single plan and that the defendant participated in some aspect of that plan. The need for witness testimony would be reduced, in addition, because the inquiries relevant to JCE liability are more likely to be the subject of documentary evidence. The *AFRC* Trial Chamber,

for instance, received very little documentary evidence, but what documentary evidence it did receive was submitted to support the prosecution's claim that the defendants were high-ranking members of the AFRC's governance bodies.[1388] These allegations were sharply contested and would have been highly relevant to a JCE analysis. Indeed, a conviction under a JCE theory would have focused less on the specific details of the specific crimes and more on the larger patterns of violence and the defendants' likely involvement therein, given their overall roles in the AFRC's military and governance structures.

Finally, and most importantly, the factors that the Trial Chambers must consider in assessing a JCE allegation are apt to correspond more closely to the factors that actually guide tribunal decision making, whether they are articulated or not. As I indicate in previous chapters, I am skeptical that the problematic witness testimony that is the standard fare of international criminal trials can convince Trial Chambers beyond a reasonable doubt of many of the facts on which the Trial Chambers routinely base their convictions. I argue indeed that the Trial Chambers engage in a less rigorous, less precise form of fact-finding than they publicly acknowledge – one that relies to some degree on witness testimony but one that is also substantially informed by such factors as the nature and pattern of the crimes and the defendants' membership in groups that are well established to have committed large numbers of the crimes. Reliance on such imprecise, amorphous factors more closely resembles a JCE analysis than an effort to determine the precise contours of the defendant's specific acts. The very existence of a common plan, for instance, frequently must be inferred from such circumstantial evidence as the large-scale, coordinated nature of the crimes,[1389] and the defendant's intentions with respect to the common plan are likewise typically proven by circumstantial and not direct evidence. Concededly, the prosecution does need to prove the defendant's participation in the common plan, and proof of this element will typically come in the form of eyewitness testimony, but because the prosecution needs to prove only that the defendant participated in one aspect of the common plan, the Trial Chamber has a greater ability to reject problematic witness testimony and base its finding of the defendant's participation on the one or two allegations that are the best supported.

International prosecutors, like their domestic counterparts, have at their disposal not only JCE but other liability doctrines that permit the

[1388] AFRC Judgement, note 27, at paras. 264–325; *see also* Karera Judgement, note 54, at paras. 60–78 (discussing letters bearing on whether the defendant held the position of acting Prefect of Kigali-Rural prefecture).

[1389] *See* Prosecutor v. Vasiljević, ICTY Case No. IT-98-32-A, Appeals Judgement, para. 100 (Feb. 25, 2004) ("There is no necessity for this purpose to have been previously arranged or formulated. It may materialise extemporaneously and be inferred from the facts.").

conviction of defendants who did not themselves physically perpetrate the crimes. For instance, under principles of accomplice liability, a defendant may be convicted of aiding and abetting an international crime when she knowingly makes a substantial contribution to the crime.[1390] In addition and even more relevantly, international crimes are often perpetrated by members of hierarchical organizations, and under the doctrine of superior responsibility a commander may be convicted of crimes committed by his subordinates when the commander knew or had reason to know that the subordinate was about to commit a crime and failed to prevent that crime or punish the person responsible.[1391] These theories of liability can be broad and amorphous and are sometimes subject to some of the same criticisms that are leveled at JCE.[1392] Because they often can be satisfied without eyewitness testimony regarding particular acts performed by defendants, they also may give rise to the same benefits. My discussion here has focused on JCE, however, because that doctrine is the most expansive, and it is that very expansiveness that makes it so useful for cases featuring problematic eyewitness testimony that is insufficient to support a conviction on a direct commission theory.

Critics of the JCE doctrine presuppose that there is a better way – that we could make use of traditional doctrines of criminal liability that reflect cherished notions of individual responsibility and that, by resorting to JCE liability, we take an expedient and unfortunate shortcut so as to convict those for whom we have insufficient evidence of criminality. My study, however, calls that presupposition into question. The fact-finding challenges identified in the foregoing chapters should cause us to question whether in fact we *could* use traditional doctrines of criminal liability in a great number of international criminal cases. No one would deny that it is better to ground criminal convictions on reliable evidence of the defendant's personal commission of criminal acts or omissions. But if such evidence does not exist in the vast run of cases, and if we have not decided to abandon international trials altogether, then it may be more normatively justified to respond to those evidentiary deficiencies by candidly expanding criminal liability doctrines than by ignoring those deficiencies and purporting to base convictions on traditional doctrines. Thus, my point in discussing JCE liability is not to opine about its desirability as an abstract matter. It is rather to suggest that, whether desirable in the abstract or not, the use of a JCE theory of liability provides Trial Chambers with a more transparent vehicle for taking account of many of the factors that actually drive their factual determinations.

[1390] Prosecution v. Kvočka, Case No. IT-98–30/1, Appeals Judgement, para. 90 (Feb. 28, 2005).
[1391] Prosecutor v. Blagojević & Jokić, No. IT-02–60-T, Judgement, para. 790 (Jan. 17, 2005).
[1392] *See, e.g.*, Mirjan Damaška, *The Shadow Side of Command Responsibility*, 49 Am. J. Comp. L. 455 (2001).

10

Assessing the Status Quo

They Are Not Doing What They Say They Are Doing, but Is What They Are Doing Worth Doing?

The previous chapter considers ways of improving fact-finding accuracy at the international tribunals. The first two sections of Chapter 9 explore large and small procedural reforms to improve testimonial quality. Assuming those reforms would be insufficient to the task at hand, the final section considers, as a less desirable alternative the increased use of associational doctrines. These doctrines not only can be satisfied with less testimonial evidence, they are more easily satisfied than doctrines of direct liability by the kinds of evidence presented to the international tribunals. The goal of Chapter 9, then, is to improve fact-finding accuracy preferably by improving the quality of the evidence that fact-finders receive but, failing that, then by making more accurate, transparent use of the suboptimal evidence that fact finders receive.

This final chapter, by contrast, assumes the status quo and assesses it. That is, in this chapter, I assume that the tribunals' fact-finding deficiencies have not been ameliorated by the reforms advocated in Chapter 9, and I consider the normative implications of these deficiencies. In particular, I consider different theories by which we might justify the tribunals' current method of fact-finding. To recap, I previously asserted that in many cases Trial Chambers supplement the problematic testimony they receive with inferences that they draw from the defendants' official position or institutional affiliation in the context of the international crimes that have been committed. So, in section 10.A, I consider the adequacy of those inferences in satisfying the prosecution's burden of proof. I conclude that in many cases inferences drawn from official position create such a compelling picture of criminal liability as to easily satisfy the beyond-a-reasonable-doubt standard. In other cases, however, they provide far less useful information. In the latter cases, the Trial Chambers are left only with problematic witness testimony on which to base their factual determinations. Because such testimony frequently proves an uncertain basis at best, I evaluate in section 10.B the fact-finding theory implicitly advanced in the SCSL Appeals Chamber's first judgment. That theory reduces the importance

of witness testimony, but it too proves deficient in ways that I delineate. The final section of this chapter, then, goes to the heart of the matter by considering the way in which the evidence presented at the international tribunals interacts with the standard of proof. In particular, I explore the work of modern scholars and researchers who view the beyond-a-reasonable-doubt standard as a variable standard that signifies (and should signify) different levels of certainty in different cases. These views not only afford us an alternative explanation for international criminal fact-finding but also provide a compelling justification for it.

10.A. THE ADEQUACY OF INFERENCES

Chapter 8 suggests that Trial Chambers rely on institutional affiliation and official position to supplement the problematic witness testimony they receive. Occasionally, institutional affiliation and official position suggest the defendant's commission of the specific crime or series of crimes for which he is charged. For instance, as I observe in Chapter 8, if the prosecution charges the defendant with ordering civilian killings during an attack in which civilians were killed in a systematic manner, the fact that the defendant was the commander of the forces that carried out that attack is in itself compelling evidence that the defendant did in fact order the killings. Frequently, however, a defendant's official position creates a strong suspicion of criminal culpability but of a general, undefined sort. The issue in these cases is whether convictions based on such imprecise factors are defensible convictions. From a doctrinal standpoint, the answer is clearly no. International human rights treaties require prosecutors to charge defendants with specific criminal acts and to provide defendants with sufficient information about those alleged acts to enable them to mount an effective defense.[1393] Thus, if the indictment charges the defendant with participating in a massacre at the Kaduha Parish on April 12, 1994, and the testimony presented is not sufficient to convince the Trial Chamber beyond a reasonable doubt that the defendant did in fact participate in that particular massacre, then the Trial Chamber must find that fact not proved and acquit the defendant.

Fact-finding in many domestic criminal justice systems is not as precise as international human rights treaties contemplate, and these precedents may serve to ameliorate some of our qualms about the fact-finding that currently takes place at the international tribunals. Studies of American trials,

[1393] International Covenant on Civil and Political Rights, art. 14, Dec. 16, 1966, 999 U.N.T.S. 171; Manfred Nowak, U.N. Covenant on Civil and Political Rights: CCPR Commentary 255 (1993).

for instance, have shown that jurors' decisions to convict or acquit a defendant are frequently influenced by considerations that are not legally or factually relevant to the precise allegations that comprise the prosecution's case. Such extralegal factors – which often include the defendant's sex, race, socioeconomic status, and even physical attractiveness[1394] – have been found to be particularly influential in cases where the evidence of the defendant's guilt is inconclusive.[1395] In other cases, jurors reach questionable conclusions not because they inappropriately consider extralegal factors but because they base their verdicts on their misapprehensions of the law. One prominent example of that phenomenon comes from the prosecution of the notorious New York subway vigilante Bernie Goetz. George Fletcher's study of the Goetz trial showed that jurors rejected both prosecution and defense theories and based their decision to acquit Goetz on their own legally erroneous conception of "intent."[1396] Although I by no means hold up these precedents as models or suggest that they justify inappropriate international tribunal fact-finding, one could reason that if a well-resourced, sophisticated criminal justice system such as that of the United States permits convictions to be entered on the basis of legally or factually irrelevant factors, then we should not be too surprised – or too disturbed – to learn that international tribunals do likewise.

An examination of other aspects of international criminal proceedings also can help to place the tribunals' fact-finding impediments in a useful perspective. International criminal justice is a new phenomenon, and many of its features bear the marks of an immature and weak criminal justice system. Victors' justice still sometimes reigns at the international tribunals;[1397] prosecutorial

[1394] For a careful review of these studies, see Dennis J. Devine et al., *Jury Decision Making: 45 Years of Empirical Research on Deliberating Groups*, 7 Psychiatry, Pub. Policy & L. 622, 678–84 (2001). *See also* Harry Kalven, Jr. & Hans Zeisel, The American Jury 301–47, 395–410 (1966).

[1395] *See* Kalven & Zeisel, note 1394, at 164–67; Barbara F. Reskin & Christy A. Visher, *The Impacts of Evidence and Extralegal Factors in Jurors' Decisions*, 20 L. & Soc'y Rev. 423, 436 (1986).

[1396] Both the prosecution and the defense in *Goetz* had agreed that Goetz's actions satisfied the elements of attempted murder: that is, that Goetz had intended to kill the young men whom he shot. The defense sought Goetz's acquittal, however, on the ground that Goetz's actions were taken in justifiable self-defense. The jurors acquitted Goetz but not because they accepted the Goetz's self-defense argument. The jurors never even got to the question of self-defense, in fact, because they determined that Goetz had not "intended" to kill the men. In reaching this conclusion, the jurors viewed intent not in the way that it is legally defined – as a "cold factual judgment that an actor sought to bring about a particular result" – but as including a motive component. And because the jurors determined that Goetz had no motive to kill, they acquitted him of attempted murder. George P. Fletcher, A Crime of Self-Defense: Bernhard Goetz and the Law on Trial 185–87 (1988).

[1397] The ICTR has been able to prosecute only those offenders who committed violent acts against the Tutsi. Rwanda has thwarted its efforts to prosecute RPF soldiers who committed atrocities against Hutu.

selection processes are still sometimes driven more by political considerations than legal considerations; and, although international tribunals trumpet their steadfast commitment to international human rights norms, they sometimes breach those norms in gross and glaring ways.[1398] Although these failings are well known and lamentable, commentators have not considered them to fundamentally undercut the international criminal justice mission. Indeed, when ICTY defendant Dragan Nikolić challenged the legality of his arrest – which had been carried out by means of an abduction – the Appeals Chamber acknowledged that the abduction violated principles of state sovereignty but nonetheless rejected Nikolić's challenge, emphasizing the importance of achieving accountability for "Universally Condemned Offences." As the Appeals Chamber put it:

> [T]he damage caused to international justice by not apprehending fugitives accused of serious violations of international humanitarian law is comparatively higher than the injury, if any, caused to the sovereignty of a State by the limited intrusion into his territory, particularly when the intrusion occurs in default of the State's cooperation. Therefore, the Appeals Chamber does not consider that in cases of universally condemned offences, jurisdiction should be set aside on the ground that there was a violation of the sovereignty of a State when the violation is brought about by the apprehension of fugitives from international justice, whatever the consequences for the international responsibility of the State or organization involved.[1399]

Commenting on this decision, Robert Currie observed that the Appeals Chamber promoted the idea that "the interest in effectively prosecuting the core international crimes outweighs any messiness left behind."[1400]

Unfortunately, fact-finding "messiness" is a different and more worrisome sort of messiness than that at issue in *Nikolić* because fact-finding accuracy – or at least good-faith efforts to achieve fact-finding accuracy – constitutes an essential component of a fair criminal trial. Furthermore, even if we could somehow justify "messy" factual findings that are not based exclusively on the specific evidence presented but that are in addition substantially informed by other contextual factors, we must have confidence that those factors are in fact informative. For one thing, although it may seem reasonable to draw inferences

[1398] For instance, the lengthy pretrial detention in which many international defendants are held is commonly said to violate the defendants' right to an expeditious trial. *See, e.g.*, Hafida Lahiouel, *The Right of the Accused to an Expeditious Trial, in* Essays on ICTY Procedure and Evidence in Honour of Gabrielle Kirk McDonald 197, 197–98 (Richard May et al. eds., 2001). *See also* Harhoff, note 823, at 140.

[1399] *The Prosecutor v. Dragan Nikolić*, Case No IT-94-2-AR73, Decision on Interlocutory Appeal Concerning Legality of Arrest, para. 26 (June 5, 2003).

[1400] Robert J. Currie, *Abducted Fugitives Before the International Criminal Court: Problems and Prospects*, 18 Crim. L. Forum 349, 370 (2007).

from a defendant's official position, it is so only if those inferences are solidly grounded on a sophisticated and nuanced understanding of the way in which the violence was carried out in the region in question. Although some positions appear self-evidently integral to the orchestration or implementation of the atrocities, others are not so informative. For instance, it had been commonly thought that *bourgmestres* and other local leaders in Rwanda often led the violence in their communities. However, Scott Straus's recent research into the Rwandan genocide suggests that, whereas the massacres in some regions were indeed driven by local leaders, in other regions, local leaders opposed the violence but their opposition was overcome by military elites, by national or regional political figures, and even by the local population, which was in many cases hell bent on eliminating "the enemy."[1401] And the controversial research of Christian Davenport and Alan Stam tells an even more unconventional story, as those scholars maintain that the majority of Rwandan victims were Hutu.[1402] These works show that if Trial Chambers are going to use official position as a proxy for clear, consistent witness testimony, then the inferences they draw from that position must have a solid grounding in the nature of the crimes in question. Unfortunately, it is not easy for Trial Chambers to obtain that grounding. For one thing, many key facts are unknowable; even social scientists who spend their entire careers studying such events often disagree about fundamental aspects of them. Moreover, Trial Chambers typically fail to receive what useful information is available because the inquiries that would generate that information are not seen as relevant to the prosecution's specific allegations.

Finally, it should go without saying that if we are to rely on official position as a means of enhancing the accuracy of international criminal fact-finding, then prosecutors must indict those individuals whose official positions provide useful information about the individual's likely involvement in the atrocities. SCSL prosecutors arguably did so; all of the SCSL defendants held high-level positions in one of the three warring factions, although some of those positions seemed more relevant to the faction's military operations than others. By contrast, although many ICTR defendants held political or military positions, some were only at the local level, and other ICTR defendants held no such positions and were merely elite members of the community who were alleged to have instigated the violence or participated in it. ICTR defendants Elizaphan Ntakirutimana and Athanase Seromba, for instance, were religious

[1401] Straus, note 1148, at 65–94.

[1402] Kroc Institute for International Peace Studies, Research Sheds New Light on Rwanda Killings, *available at* http://kroc.nd.edu/newsevents/news/research-sheds-new-light-rwandakillings-512; Christian Davenport, Professor of Peace Studies, Political Science, and Sociology, University of Notre Dame, Speech at The College of William and Mary (Apr. 11, 2008).

leaders, Gérard Ntakirutimana was a doctor, and Aloys Simba and Laurent Semanza had formerly held important military and governmental positions.[1403] Although these defendants had no official governmental or military affiliations, their status as leaders in the community may have enabled them to influence the course of the violence or facilitate its commission. At the same time, their generalized status as important members of the community provides us no real insights into whether they in fact did influence the course of the violence or facilitate its commission. These considerations suggest, indeed, that official position can prove a useful source of information only in a select group of cases. It is one thing for Eichmann's position as Head of the Gestapo's Office of Jewish Affairs to influence a Trial Chamber's factual determinations of Eichmann's alleged acts; it is quite another for a defendant's position in local government or status as an elite member of the community to prove influential. In particular, if we are to ameliorate the fact-finding difficulties I have heretofore described by reasoning from official position or institutional affiliation, then prosecutors must begin their investigations with the realistic awareness that the witness testimony that they will eventually present to the Trial Chambers is apt to suffer from deficiencies that may well render it an insufficient basis for a conviction. Knowing that, prosecutors should focus their investigations on those defendants whose official positions truly would provide the Trial Chambers with meaningful information about the defendant's likely commission of the crimes. Stated more bluntly, prosecutors should consider limiting their indictments to those defendants whose official positions go a long way toward suggesting their guilt before witness testimony is even heard.

10.B. THE CLOSE-ENOUGH APPROACH TO FACT-FINDING

Because a defendant's status or position has not always provided useful information, I next consider what I have labeled the "close-enough" approach to fact-finding that the SCSL Appeals Chamber implicitly adopted in the *AFRC* case. There, the Appeals Chamber accepted several of the prosecution's challenges to the Trial Chamber's factual and legal findings, but it refused to alter the defendants' convictions or sentences. For instance, the Appeals Chamber agreed with the prosecution that the Trial Chamber had erred in dismissing the counts alleging a joint criminal enterprise. As a result of that dismissal, the Trial Chamber had absolved the defendants of responsibility for many of

[1403] Semanza had been bourgmestre of Bikumbi *commune* for more than twenty years and had left that position only one year before the genocide. Semanza Judgement, note 31, at para. 15. Simba had held high-level military positions for many years preceding the genocide. Simba Judgement, note 455, at para. 56.

the atrocities committed by AFRC forces. The Appeals Chamber's reversal of that dismissal consequently had the potential to radically alter the nature and quantity of the defendants' convictions. However, instead of seizing the opportunity to revise the convictions, as Appeals Chambers of other tribunals have done, the SCSL Appeals Chamber held that there was "no need to make further factual findings or to remit the case to the Trial Chamber for that purpose, having regard to the interest of justice."[1404]

What the Appeals Chamber meant by its enigmatic reference to the "interest of justice" became clear through its treatment of other alleged Trial Chamber errors. The Appeals Chamber, for instance, refused even to address the prosecution's first and third grounds for appeal, in which the prosecution claimed that the Trial Chamber had erroneously failed to enter certain convictions. Pointing out that the defendants had already been convicted and sentenced to forty-five-and fifty-year terms of imprisonment, the Appeals Chamber asserted that, "taking all the circumstances into consideration, particularly having regard to the length of the sentences imposed," it would become "an academic exercise and also pointless to adjudicate further on minute details raised in Grounds One and Three of the Prosecution's Appeal."[1405] The Appeals Chamber likewise refused to consider the prosecution's claim that the Trial Chamber had erred in holding that three enslavement crimes were not acts of terrorism or collective punishment. The Appeals Chamber "exercise[d] its discretion not to entertain" that ground for appeal,[1406] it said, because "the Prosecution's attempt to search for further acts of terrorism by adding the three enslavement crimes to this list is an unnecessary exercise since the Appellants have already been convicted of acts of terrorism and an adequate sentence has been imposed."[1407] Finally, even though the Appeals Chamber did adjudicate and uphold the prosecution's claim that the Trial Chamber had erred in its treatment of cumulative convictions, it held that "no useful purpose will be served by the Appeals Chamber now entering convictions on the basis of such findings," given "the adequate global sentence imposed on each Appellant."[1408]

By refusing even to address many of the prosecution's claims and refusing to alter the defendants' convictions when it did reverse the Trial Chamber's legal conclusions, the *AFRC* Appeals Chamber took a pragmatic approach to fact-finding. International tribunals have been lauded in some quarters for their capacity to create a historical record of the conflict,[1409] but the *AFRC*

[1404] AFRC Appeals Judgement, note 839, at para. 87.
[1405] *Id.* at para. 169.
[1406] *Id.* at para. 174.
[1407] *Id.* at para. 172.
[1408] *Id.* at para. 216.
[1409] *See* authorities cited in note 7.

Appeals Chamber eschewed that role. Concededly, some of the prosecution's grounds for appeal would have, if accepted, resulted in only minor additions to the defendants' list of convictions. But the Appeals Chamber's decision on JCE liability had the potential to radically alter the picture that the SCSL presented of the defendants' criminality. Whereas the Trial Chamber held the defendants responsible only for the specific acts that they or their direct subordinates had performed, the Appeals Chamber's decision subjected the defendants to liability for all of the criminal acts that were encompassed in the common plan to "take any action necessary to gain and exercise political power and control over the territory of Sierra Leone." Clearly, the Appeals Chamber's decision had the potential to dramatically redefine the nature of the crimes at issue in the case and to result in criminal liability of a substantially broader scope.

The *AFRC* Appeals Chamber chose, however, not to go there. It chose, by contrast, to be satisfied, in Damaška's words, with "a mere torso of actual wrongdoing."[1410] The defendants had already been convicted of many serious crimes. The sentences they had received could hardly have been longer. Consequently, the Appeals Chamber concluded that it was not in the "interest of justice" to augment the incomplete picture of criminal liability that the Trial Chamber had drawn. Although the Appeals Chamber's lack of concern about factual completeness is particularly patent and stark in the *AFRC* case, it is by no means unprecedented. Charge bargaining, although previously rare at the international tribunals, is now practiced increasingly often at the ICTR and has led the prosecution to withdraw provable charges in exchange for a defendant's guilty plea.[1411] Furthermore, even when not angling for a guilty plea, prosecutors have been known to charge a defendant with a subset of the crimes that he likely committed in order to expedite proceedings. Stephen Rapp described taking just such an approach in the *Niyitegeka* case,[1412] and ICTY prosecutor Mark Harmon made similar representations about the *Deronjić* case. When Presiding Judge Wolfgang Schomburg asked Harmon why the prosecution had indicted Deronjić only for his involvement in the crimes that had been committed during one day in the one town of Glogova, when the evidence suggested Deronjić's involvement in the larger ethnic cleansing campaign that was conducted throughout the municipality of Bratunac, Harmon responded that, because ICTY trials can take more than two years to complete, the prosecutor had purposely chosen to limit the indictment "for purposes of resolving this case quickly in order to fulfill the mandate of" the tribunal.[1413]

[1410] Damaška, Faces of Justice, note 1175, at 112.

[1411] *See* Nancy Amoury Combs, Guilty Pleas in International Criminal Law: Constructing a Restorative Justice Approach 97–108 (2007).

[1412] *See* text at note 1366.

[1413] Prosecutor v. Deronjić, Case No. IT-02-61-S, Transcript, Mar. 5, 2004, at 314.

These precedents reflect the view that so long as the defendant has been rightfully convicted of some serious crime and has received an appropriately lengthy sentence therefor, then the remaining details need not be trifled over. This view has much to recommend it. Money is scarce, and international criminal trials are lengthy, costly affairs – even at their most efficient. Consequently, prosecuting one defendant for all of the crimes for which he might reasonably be charged will necessarily prevent an international tribunal from prosecuting other defendants. There are real costs to completeness, therefore, and its benefits are at best unclear. Although as I mentioned, in the initial enthusiasm for international trials, some commentators credited them with the capacity to craft a historical record of the conflict, it is now acknowledged that their jurisdictional confines and adversarial procedures render them largely unsuitable for that task.[1414] Consequently, whether a given defendant is convicted for all five of his crimes or only two of the five is likely to have no broad or long-term impact so long as his sentence is appropriately long.

The "close-enough" approach to fact-finding that is exemplified in the *AFRC* Appeals judgment is relevant to my study because under that approach the testimonial deficiencies identified in previous chapters lose some of their significance. One could argue, for instance, that it is not terrifically important if some of a Trial Chamber's factual determinations are erroneous so long as some of the Trial Chamber's factual determinations are not erroneous and these nonerroneous factual determinations justify the defendant's conviction and the sentence he received. Lengthy sentences are likely to be justified because virtually all of the allegations in international criminal cases involve serious wrongdoing. Thus, it may be that the defendant did not personally participate in a massacre or call for the extermination of the Tutsi at a large rally, as the Trial Chamber found, but so long as he did distribute weapons to killers or transport killers to a massacre site, then he is guilty of aiding and abetting genocide at a minimum, and he should be subject to a lengthy prison sentence as a consequence.

Such an approach is deeply unsatisfying, however. It is one thing to realistically acknowledge that fact finders are fallible and will of necessity make some mistakes in some of their factual determinations. It is quite another to suppose that such mistakes do not really matter very much. Certainly,

[1414] *See, e.g.*, Minow, note 3, at 58–60; Charles S. Maier, *Doing History, Doing Justice: The Narrative of the Historian and of the Truth Commission*, *in* Truth v. Justice 261, 265–66 (Robert I. Rotberg & Dennis Thompson eds., 1999); Sierra Leone Truth and Reconciliation Commission Report, *available at* http://www.nuigalway.ie/human_rights/publishing.html, Vol. Two, Ch. Two, paras. 576–577 ("Criminal prosecutions deliver justice on specifically framed charges by attempting to meet the burden of proof on each element of the charge.... Accordingly, courts are limited in their ability to reach the broader truth.").

criminal punishment is the most obvious and significant consequence of a criminal conviction, so if a wrongful conviction does not result in additional and inappropriate punishment, then that is some comfort. But wrongful criminal convictions also impose dignitary harms, and a defendant suffers these regardless of whether or not he is appropriately convicted of other crimes. Furthermore, even if we were comfortable with a close-enough approach to fact-finding on a theoretical level, a key practical problem remains: namely, that the testimonial deficiencies that pervade international criminal cases may leave us unable to place sufficient confidence in even one conviction. I raised this issue in Chapter 8 when I considered whether more careful scrutiny of testimonial deficiencies would lead Trial Chambers to acquit defendants of all the crimes for which they have been charged or only a subset thereof. As I indicated there, I have not researched this question and consequently cannot offer an informed opinion. Certainly, in most cases, international prosecutors seek to prove numerous facts, and most any one of them would support a conviction for crimes against humanity or genocide. At the same time, prosecutors frequently rely on the same witnesses to prove a whole series of allegations, so if a Trial Chamber were to find a particular witness's testimony unreliable, then many of the prosecution's allegations would fail as a result.

10.C. RECONCEPTUALIZING THE STANDARD OF PROOF

The foregoing sections consider ways in which we might justify and make more justifiable the international criminal fact-finding that I describe in previous chapters. In section 10.A I conclude that, although official position is so highly informative in some cases that it can appropriately supplement trial testimony and convince Trial Chambers beyond a reasonable doubt of the defendant's guilt, in other cases it is not so enlightening. Prosecutors can do a better job of targeting their indictments against individuals whose official positions more clearly indicate their guilt, but, assuming that they will not always do so, I considered in section 10.B the *AFRC* Appeals Chamber's approach to fact-finding. With respect to it, I concluded that although many cases feature at least one well-supported conviction that would justify the Trial Chamber's imposition of a lengthy prison sentence, others probably do not, and, even if they do, we may believe that poorly supported international criminal convictions can never be justified, even if they do not result in the imposition of additional punishment. If, then, no improvement is made to international criminal fact-finding, the legitimacy of international criminal convictions would seem to be put into question for I have suggested in Chapter 7 that the Tribunal's cavalier treatment of fact-finding deficiencies is, in many cases, inconsistent with the beyond-a-reasonable-doubt standard of proof. Although I stand by that assertion, I do not consider it to fatally undermine the legitimacy of international criminal convictions because my assertion assumes a traditional conception of "beyond a reasonable doubt." More recently, judges, scholars, and empirical researchers have begun to reconceptualize "beyond a reasonable doubt," and this reconceptualization has dramatic, positive implications for the legitimacy of international criminal convictions.

The traditional view of the beyond-a-reasonable-doubt standard conceives of it as a fixed and unchanging standard that reflects a high level of certainty.[1415] That view has been called into question, however, by scholars and researchers who have compellingly shown that any given standard of proof is necessarily variable and can encompass a relatively broad probability range. These insights are important because, when we conceive of "beyond a reasonable doubt" as accommodating a variable range of certainty, we find both an alternative explanation for the international tribunals' cavalier treatment of fact-finding deficiencies as well as a convincing justification for the convictions that follow. Indeed, in the pages that follow, I argue that reconceptualizing "beyond a reasonable doubt" as a variable standard of proof provides us both the most

[1415] I recognize that considerable controversy surrounds the precise meaning of the beyond-a-reasonable-doubt standard. For a compelling account of the disagreement, see LARRY LAUDAN, TRUTH, ERROR, AND CRIMINAL LAW: AN ESSAY IN LEGAL EPISTEMOLOGY 32–51 (2006). Laudan points out that, until recent decades, the most common method informed jurors that proof beyond a reasonable doubt meant "belief to a moral certainty," *id.* at 35, but that phrasing has lately fallen out of favor, *see United States v. Indorato*, 628 F.2d 711, 720–21 (1st Cir.), *cert. denied*, 449 U.S. 1016 (1980); *United States v. Byrd*, 352 F.2d. 570, 575 (2d. Cir. 1965). Now, jurors are sometimes instructed that proof beyond a reasonable doubt is "proof of such a convincing character" that jurors would be "willing to rely and act upon it without hesitation" in the most important affairs of their own lives. Fifth Circuit District Judges Association, *Pattern Jury Instructions (Criminal Cases)* (2001), *available at* www.lb5.uscourts.gov/juryinstructions/crim2001.pdf. In other cases, jurors are told that a defendant has been proven guilty beyond a reasonable doubt when the jurors have "an abiding conviction that the defendant is guilty." Federal Judicial Center, PATTERN CRIMINAL JURY INSTRUCTIONS, 28–29 (1988). Trial courts sometimes take a different tack and define for jurors the meaning of "reasonable doubt." Some courts, for instance, instruct that a reasonable doubt is "the kind of doubt that would make a reasonable person hesitate to act." Edward J. Devitt et al., FEDERAL JURY PRACTICE AND INSTRUCTIONS § 12.10, at 354 (4th ed. 1987). The problem here, as Laudan points out, is not just that these different definitions encompass different meanings for the standards but that some courts have held unconstitutional instructions that other courts consider exemplary. LAUDAN, *supra* at 47. In response, some appellate courts instruct their trial courts to provide jurors no definition of beyond a reasonable doubt, *id.* at 47–48, a policy that Australian courts have also adopted, *see* Australian Law Reform Commission, *Evidence Reference Research Paper No. 14: Aspects of Proof*, para. 38 (1983) [hereinafter Australian Law Reform Commission Report]; *Green v. The Queen*, (1971) 126 C.L.R. 28 (Australia); *Brown v. The King*, (1913) 17 C.L.R. 570, 584 (Australia); *Thomas v. The Queen*, (1960) 102 C.L.R. 584, 595, 604–05 (Australia).

accurate and the most satisfying way of understanding international criminal convictions.

Let me begin this discussion with a few words about the nature and function of any standard of proof. As Larry Laudan has explained, a standard of proof "specifies a *minimum* threshold for asserting as proven some hypothesis."[1416] Raising a standard of proof will not reduce the number of erroneous decisions that fact finders will make,[1417] but it will allocate those erroneous decisions differently. For instance, if we believe that errors against the plaintiff are equal in societal cost to errors against the defendant, then we would set our standard of proof at 51 percent or a preponderance of the evidence. Because the cost of errors against each party is equal, then the party with the best case should win, even if that party's case is only just slightly better than the case of her opponent. Thus, as Laudan and other scholars have observed, the only reason to set a legal standard of proof higher than a preponderance of the evidence is that we believe one sort of mistake is a worse, or more costly, mistake than another sort of mistake. In the context of criminal cases, for instance, we believe that the conviction of an innocent person is more costly than the acquittal of a guilty person. Were it not for that belief, we would instruct fact finders to convict a defendant if they think it more likely than not that he committed the crime.

How much worse is it, we might ask, to convict an innocent person than to acquit a guilty person? The great thinkers of the past, speaking rhetorically, reached different conclusions: Matthew Hale opined that "[i]t is better that five guilty persons should escape punishment than one person should die."[1418] William Blackstone put the ratio at ten guilty persons to one innocent person.[1419] Benjamin Franklin, for his part, was willing to acquit one hundred guilty persons to save one innocent,[1420] and Moses Maimonides would have

[1416] LAUDAN, note 1415, at 64.

[1417] Indeed, as Erik Lillquist has pointed out, raising the standard of proof can result in an *increase* in the overall number of errors depending on the ratio of guilty to innocent defendants in the pool of defendants to be prosecuted. *See* Erik Lillquist, *Recasting Reasonable Doubt: Decision Theory and the Virtues of Variability*, 36 U. C. DAVIS L. REV. 85, 102 (2002).

[1418] 2 SIR MATTHEW HALE, HISTORIA PLACITORUM CORONÆ [THE HISTORY OF THE PLEAS OF THE CROWN] 289 (P. R. Glazebrook ed., London Prof'l Books 1971) (1736).

[1419] WILLIAM BLACKSTONE, 4 COMMENTARIES ON THE LAWS OF ENGLAND 352 (1769); William O. Douglas, *Foreword* to JEROME FRANK & BARBARA FRANK, NOT GUILTY 11 (1971); Bunnell v. Sullivan, 947 F.2d 341, 352 (9th Cir. 1991) (en banc) (Kozinski, J., concurring); United States v. Greer, 538 F.2d 437, 441 (D.C. Cir. 1976).

[1420] Letter from Benjamin Franklin to Benjamin Vaughan (Mar. 14, 1785) *in* XI THE WORKS OF BENJAMIN FRANKLIN 11, 13 (John Bigelow, ed., Fed. Ed., 1904). Thomas Starkie concurred, asserting that the "maxim of the law is. . . . that it is better that ninety-nine . . . offenders shall escape than that one innocent man be condemned." 9 JOHN WIGMORE, EVIDENCE IN TRIALS AT COMMON LAW § 2497 at 409–10 (Chadbourn rev. 1981).

acquitted one thousand.[1421] Even if we could obtain societal consensus on the optimal ratio between wrongful convictions and wrongful acquittals, that ratio would not dictate the standard of proof as a probabilistic measure because the relationship between standards of proof and ratios of error also depends on the accuracy with which juries discriminate among truly innocent and truly guilty defendants and the proportion of guilty versus innocent defendants in the defendant pool.[1422] But although we cannot derive a standard of proof as a specific probabilistic measure from our assessment of the optimal ratio between wrongful convictions and wrongful acquittals, we can know that that ratio influences the probabilistic measure because – all things being equal – higher standards of proof result in more erroneous acquittals and fewer erroneous convictions.[1423] That is, the more we wish to prevent wrongful convictions, the higher we should set the standard of proof. The more we wish to prevent wrongful acquittals, the lower the standard of proof should go.

In the context of domestic crimes, we have traditionally considered it a far graver mistake to convict the innocent than to acquit the guilty, and this view is reflected in the high standard of proof that must be met before a defendant can be convicted of a domestic crime. Many countries of the world, for instance, employ the demanding beyond-a-reasonable-doubt standard,[1424] which, when quantified, is often said to signify a 90 or 95 percent probability level.[1425]

[1421] 2 Moses Maimonides, The Commandments 270 (Charles B. Chavel trans., 1967).

[1422] Michael DeKay, *The Difference Between Blackstone-Like Error Ratios and Probabilistic Standards of Proof*, 21 L. & Soc. Inquiry 95, 99 (1996); Lillquist, note 1417, at 105.

[1423] *See, e.g.*, DeKay, note 1422, at 97; Ronald J. Allen, *The Restoration of* In Re Winship: *A Comment on Burdens of Persuasion in Criminal Cases After* Patterson v. New York, 76 Mich. L. Rev. 30, 47 n.65 (1977).

[1424] The following countries, among others, employ the beyond-a-reasonable doubt standard: The United States, *In re Winship*, 397 U.S. 358 (1970); England and Wales, John Hatchard, *Criminal Procedure in England and Wales, in* Comparative Criminal Procedure 176, 187 (John Hatchard et al. eds., 1996); Australia, *Legal Services Commission of South Australia, Law Handbook, available at* www.lawhandbook.sa.gov.au (2007); South Africa, P.J. Schwikkard & W.E. van der Merwe, *South Africa, in* Criminal Procedure: A Worldwide Study 319, 349 (Craig Bradley ed., 1999); Ireland, McAuley & O'Dowd, note 1302, at 193; Canada, *R. v. Lifchus*, 3 S.C.R. 320 (1997); Israel, Eliahu Harnon & Alex Stein, *Israel, in* Criminal Procedure: A Worldwide Study 217, 240–241 (Craig Bradley ed., 1999); Denmark, Vagn Greve, *Denmark, in* Criminal Procedure Systems in the European Community 51, 62 (Christine Van Den Wyngaert et al. eds., 1993); Belgium, Van Den Wyngaert, *Belgium*, note 1237, at 21; Italy, Piermaria Corso, *Italy, in* Criminal Procedure Systems in the European Community 223, 238 (Christine Van Den Wyngaert et al. eds., 1993); The Netherlands, A.H.J. Swart, *The Netherlands, in* Criminal Procedure Systems in the European Community 279, 296 (Christine Van Den Wyngaert et al. eds., 1993).

[1425] Laudan, note 1415, at 44; Ronald J. Allen, *Factual Ambiguity and a Theory of Evidence*, 88 N.W. U. L. Rev. 604, 604 (1994); *see also* Dale A. Nance, *Naturalized Epistemology and the Critique of Evidence Theory*, 87 Va. L. Rev. 1551, 1594 (2001).

Thus, the traditional view of the beyond-a-reasonable-doubt standard conceives of it as a fixed and unchanging standard that signifies a particularly high level of certainty. However, modern scholars, researchers, and increasingly judges now consider the traditional account of standards of proof to be "psychologically naïve."[1426] According to Mirjan Damaška, for instance, it is inconsistent with "the psychological realities of adjudicative factfinding" to assume that sufficiency of proof requirements do not change from case to case.[1427] Damaška thus contends that "tolerable doubt appears more as a sliding point along a continuum than a fixed entity."[1428] Erik Lillquist has developed this argument further, contending that the notion of a fixed standard of proof wrongly assumes that we know how to weigh the various costs and benefits that make up a standard of proof. Relying on insights drawn from behavioral economics and social norms literature, Lillquist argues that "there is no existing theory that can explain what the relative costs and benefits of the various verdict possibilities ought to be across all cases." Because the costs of erroneous verdicts and the benefits of accurate verdicts will necessarily fluctuate as a consequence of various factors, Lillquist argues that the standard of proof will also necessarily fluctuate accordingly.[1429] John Kaplan, for his part, applies decision theory to the fact-finding process and observes that

> in any rational system the utilities (or disutilities) that determine the necessary probability of guilt will vary with the crime for which the defendant is being tried, and indeed with the particular defendant. In a criminal trial, as in any decision process, we must consider the utilities associated with differing decisions of the particular case at issue – not just the average utilities over many disparate types of criminal cases. Thus the rational fact-finder should consider the disadvantages of convicting *this* defendant of *this* crime if he

Significant controversy, of course, surrounds formal attempts to equate probabilities with legal standards. *See, e.g.*, Michael Finkelstein & William Fairley, *A Bayesian Approach to Identification Evidence*, 83 HARV. L. REV. 489 (1970) (defending use of formal, sophisticated probability theory to make legal determinations); Laurence Tribe, *Trial by Mathematics: Precision & Ritual in the Legal Process*, 84 HARV. L. REV. 1329 (1971) (contesting Finkelstein & Fairley); Finkelstein and Fairley reply at 84 HARV. L. REV. 1801 (1971); Lea Brilmayer & Lewis Kornhauser, *Quantitative Methods and Legal Decisions*, 46 U. CHI. L. REV. 116 (1978). For a helpful overview of the issues, see David Kaye, *The Law of Probability and the Law of the Land*, 47 U. CHI. L. REV. 34 (1979); David Kaye, *The Limits of the Preponderance of the Evidence of the Evidence Standard: Justifiably Naked Statistical Evidence and Multiple Causation*, 2 ABA FOUNDATION RESEARCH J. 487 (1982). For a book-length treatment on the role of probability and proof, see L. JONATHAN COHEN, THE PROBABLE AND THE PROVABLE (1978).

1426 Damaška, *Evidentiary Barriers to Conviction*, note 788, at 543. *See also* Richard O. Lempert, *Modeling Relevance*, 75 MICH. L. REV. 1021, 1036 (1977).

1427 Damaška, *Evidentiary Barriers to Conviction*, note 788, at 543; *See also* Lempert, note 1426, at 1036.

1428 Damaška, *Evidentiary Barriers to Conviction*, note 788, at 543.

1429 Lillquist, note 1417, at 91.

> is innocent as compared with those of acquitting him if he is guilty. It is obviously less serious to society, for instance, to acquit an embezzler, who, in any event, may find it very difficult to be placed again in a position of trust, than it would be to acquit a child molester, since the latter crime tends to be repeated.[1430]

Judges, particularly in England and Australia, sometimes agree and find that standards of proof necessarily vary. These judges usually make this pronouncement in civil cases where they hold that the gravity of the issue influences the level of certainty required to find that issue proved.[1431] But judges sometimes acknowledge the variability of the criminal standard as well. As L. J. Denning put it in the Australian case of *Bater v. Bater*:

> It is of course true that by our law a higher standard of proof is required in criminal cases than in civil cases. But this is subject to the qualification that there is no absolute standard in either Case. In criminal cases the charge must be proved beyond reasonable doubt, but there may be degrees of proof within that standard.[1432]

This view has been adopted by the Australian Law Reform Commission,[1433] and some Australian commentators go so far as to argue that it is unnecessary to have two standards of proof – one for civil and another for criminal

[1430] John Kaplan, *Decision Theory and the Factfinding Process*, 20 STAN. L. REV. 1065, 1073–74 (1968).

[1431] *See, e.g.*, Briginshaw v. Briginshaw (1938) 60 C.L.R. 336, 361–62 (Australia); Peter Williamson Pty. Ltd. v. Capitol Motors Ltd. (1982) 41 A.L.R. 613, 619–20 (Australia); Hardcastle v. Commissioner of Australian Federal Police and Another (1984) 53 A.L.R. 593, 603 (Australia); M. v. M (1988) 166 C.L.R. 69, 76–77 (Australia); Helton v. Allen (1940) 63 C.L.R. 691, 701 (Australia); Rejfek v. McElroy (1965) 112 C.L.R. 517, 521 (Australia); Trade Practices Commission v. Nicholas Enterprises Pty Ltd [No. 2], 40 F.L.R. 83, 105 (Australia); Smith & Co Ltd v. Westralian Farmers Co-operative Ltd (1979) V.L.R. 129, 147 (Australia); In Re Fagan (1980) 23 S.A. St. R. 454, 465 (Australia); Nixon v. Comm'r of Taxation (1979) 36 F.L.R. 172, 177 (Australia); Blyth v. Blyth (1966) A.C. 643, 668 n.56 (United Kingdom). But courts also "accept that the cogency of the evidence required to satisfy the criminal standard may vary depending on the nature of the case." Australian Law Reform Commission Report, note 1415, at para. 36; *see also* Bater v. Bater (1951) P35, 36–37 (Australia); Hornal v. Neuberger Products Ltd (1957) 1 Q.B. 247, 263–64 (United Kingdom).

Some judges assert that "it is not so much that a different standard of proof is required in different circumstances varying according to the gravity of the issue, but . . . that the gravity of the issue becomes part of the circumstances which the court has to take into consideration in deciding whether or not the burden of proof has been discharged," but even these judges recognize that this distinction is "academic," Re Dellow's Will Trusts (1964) 1 All E.R. 771, 773 (United Kingdom), and that "the more serious the allegation the higher degree of probability that is required," Hornal v. Neuberger Products Ltd (1957) 1 Q.B. 247, 258 (United Kingdom).

[1432] Bater v. Bater, (1951) P35, 36–37 (Australia).

[1433] Australian Law Reform Commission Report, note 1415, at para. 6.

cases – because once "it is accepted that the standard of proof is variable depending on the nature of the case, only one variable standard is required."[1434]

Recognizing the variable nature of standards of proof allows us to see how different factors can influence the level of tolerable doubt in a particular case. In the excerpt above, Kaplan notes the salience of the likelihood of recidivism and elsewhere points to the defendant's reputation.[1435] Damaška, for his part, refers to a series of "sometimes imponderable factors," including "the magnitude of punishment, prior inquiries into guilt, [and the] dichotomy between physical facts and 'inner' facts relating to mental state."[1436] And Richard Lempert develops a "regret matrix"[1437] that postulates that decision makers seek to minimize the expected regret that they will feel as a result of their decisions.[1438] He concludes that although "[a]t law the burden of proof needed to sustain a conviction is the same for all defendants: good or evil, young or old, attractive or unattractive, dangerous or nonthreatening," in practice, the ideal of an unvarying standard is not achieved. Rather, jurors are likely to "regret the mistake of convicting basically good people more than the mistake of convicting the basically evil," and these preferences effectively change the standard of proof from one case to another.[1439]

The insights of these theorists are supported by a spate of empirical studies that likewise suggest that fact finders alter their understanding of the beyond-a-reasonable-doubt standard from case to case.[1440] A study by Rita Simon and Linda Mahan, for example, indicated that jurors would require substantially different levels of certainty to convict depending on the crime charged.[1441]

1434 *Id.* at para. 47. Some British commentators have taken the same view. *See* David A. Hamer, *The Presumption of Innocence and Reverse Burdens: A Balancing Act*, 66 CAMBRIDGE L. J. 142, 149 (2007).

1435 Kaplan observes that "[t]he better the reputation of the defendant, the greater the tragedy of his fall from grace, and hence perhaps the greater disutility of convicting him should he be innocent." Conversely, fact finders might reason from a defendant's previous convictions not only that he is more likely to be guilty of this offense but also that because he has been convicted several times before, "it is not very important to him or society that he is convicted one more time." Kaplan, note 1430, at 1074.

1436 Damaška, *Evidentiary Barriers to Conviction*, note 788, at 542. With respect to the dichotomy between physical facts and "inner" facts relating to mental state, Damaška notes that "very demanding proof requirements will in actual practice be set concerning the question whether the defendant has fired a shot at the decedent. Much less proof will be required to become 'convinced' of the intent to injure or kill, although there is no legal presumption of intent stemming from the act of the shooting." *Id.* at 542, n.82.

1437 Lempert observes that what he refers to as a "regret matrix" is commonly called a "utility matrix" in decision theory literature. Lempert, note 1426, at 1032.

1438 *Id.*

1439 *Id.* at 1034.

1440 Lillquist, note 1417, at 115–17.

1441 Rita James Simon & Linda Mahan, *Quantifying Burdens of Proof: A View from the Bench, the Jury and the Classroom*, 5 LAW & SOC'Y REV. 319, 325, 329 & table 10 (1971).

Studies by Stuart Nagel and Marian Neef further showed that some of these divergences are gender specific. For instance, although there were no substantial differences between the level of certainty required by men and women across all classes of cases, substantial differences can arise with respect to certain crimes. For instance, Nagel's and Neef's studies indicated that male study participants were considerably more concerned than female study participants about the wrongful conviction of rape; hence, the male study participants required higher probability levels to convict on rape charges.[1442] Other factors influencing the level of certainty required for a conviction include the severity of the threatened punishment and the punishment that the defendant has already suffered along with the evidence about the defendant's character and any past convictions.[1443]

These studies comport with related research that suggests that American lay fact finders routinely convict defendants on much lower levels of certainty than that embodied in the traditional understanding of "beyond a reasonable doubt." Recall that the beyond-a-reasonable-doubt standard is typically considered to require a certainty level of 90 or 95 percent. However, a study by Rita Simon indicated that jurors voted to convict when they thought the probability of guilt was a mere 74 percent.[1444] Francis Dane's study reproduced that finding for jurors who made their assessments before deliberating with one another. After they deliberated, the level of certainty required to convict dropped to 52.5 percent.[1445] Dane's latter finding was replicated in a similar study conducted by Robert MacCoun, which found that a reasonable doubt instruction yielded a 56 percent decision criterion.[1446] A study of Florida jurors is even more unsettling: It revealed that nearly 25 percent of the jurors believed that when the weight of evidence was equally balanced between the prosecution and defense, they should find the defendant guilty. Moreover, only half of the jurors realized that the defendant did not have to present any evidence establishing her innocence.[1447]

Given this research, the notion that standards of proof are variable seems virtually immune from serious challenge as a descriptive account. In the context of international criminal prosecutions, this account also provides a compelling alternative explanation for the Trial Chambers' willingness to convict

[1442] Stuart S. Nagel & Marian G. Neef, Decision Theory and the Legal Process 197 (1979).

[1443] Lillquist, note 1417, at 117.

[1444] Rita James Simon, *"Beyond a Reasonable Doubt" – An Experimental Attempt at Quantification*, 6 J. Applied Behav. Sci. 203, 207 (No. 2, 1970).

[1445] Francis C. Dane, *In Search of Reasonable Doubt: A Systematic Examination of Selected Quantification Approaches*, 9 L. & Hum. Behav. 141, 150 (1985).

[1446] Lillquist, note 1417, at 114–15 (describing unpublished PhD dissertation of Robert J. MacCoun).

[1447] David Strawn & Raymond Buchanan, *Jury Confusion: A Threat to Justice*, 59 Judicature 478, 480–81 (1976).

defendants on the basis of seemingly questionable evidence. If standards of proof are inherently variable, and if the characteristics of the defendant are highly relevant to a fact finder's understanding of reasonable doubt in a particular case, then the Trial Chambers' willingness to convict international defendants despite the apparent presence of considerable doubt is wholly to be expected. Indeed, in Chapter 8 I maintain that the Trial Chambers relied on a series of factors – the most prominent of which is the defendant's institutional affiliation – to supplement inadequate testimony and find the defendant guilty beyond a reasonable doubt. Specifically, because an international defendant's official position or institutional affiliation often suggests either that he committed *some* crime, or more broadly – in Lempert's words – that he is evil, fact finders are apt to undervalue the harm associated with his wrongful conviction and overvalue the harm associated with his wrongful acquittal. As a consequence of those assessments, fact finders will require less certainty to satisfy the beyond-a-reasonable-doubt standard in the case of that defendant.

Conceptualizing beyond a reasonable doubt as a variable standard that can encompass less certainty in certain cases not only provides an alternative descriptive account of international criminal fact-finding but also locates convictions pronounced by international tribunals within the mainstream of criminal convictions. Admittedly, the fact that American jurors routinely vary the standard of proof from case to case and routinely convict defendants on a lower probability assessment than that which we have traditionally understood "beyond a reasonable doubt" to signify is not a normative argument in favor of international judges doing likewise. But it might nonetheless reassure us to know that the practice is widespread even in mature criminal justice systems that do not confront severe fact-finding impediments. Indeed, the fact that domestic fact finders routinely require less certainty to convict even in a context where greater certainty is achievable suggests that efforts to adhere to a very high standard of proof in the international context will prove unavailing.

As noted, however, the fact that fact finders in both domestic and international courts *do* treat beyond a reasonable doubt as a variable standard does not mean that they *should*; thus, if we aim to justify the international criminal convictions that do not appear to meet the traditional, fixed conception of "beyond a reasonable doubt," then we must have a normative basis for believing that it is appropriate to vary the standard of proof from case to case. Lillquist's treatment of the question provides such a basis. As mentioned earlier, Lillquist critiques the traditional decision theory model of the beyond-a-reasonable-doubt standard for failing to provide any method by which to determine the various utilities it considers.[1448] He contends that "despite our articulated preference for a fixed, high level of certainty before convicting in criminal cases overall,

[1448] Lillquist, note 1417, at 131.

the traditional view cannot provide a normative justification for that result. The model fails because existing justifications for the substantive criminal law cannot lead to a fixed decision standard of proof."[1449] Through a detailed analysis, Lillquist convincingly argues that seeking to obtain a consensus over the possible utilities for all criminal cases is a hopeless endeavor. Consequently, Lillquist maintains, because there presently is no clear way to determine the relevant utility functions, "we cannot, with any true confidence, generate a normatively preferable standard of proof to apply to all cases."[1450]

What we can do, according to Lillquist, is to set relative utilities across classes of cases. Providing numerous examples, Lillquist analyzes the utilities and disutilities across different types of crimes and defendants to show that they do and should vary markedly from case to case. According to Lillquist, the different utilities in the hypothetical cases that he examined are sufficiently great "that we would expect society to prefer different proof standards in those cases."[1451] As a consequence, "the law appropriately leaves the amount of certainty unstated, so that jurors can make the final decision on the proper level. This is because the optimal level of certainty in any particular case is both crime and defendant-specific – some particular types of crime and some particular defendants might optimally require very high levels of certainty, whereas other crimes and defendants might optimally require much lower levels of certainty. The use of a flexible standard allows the decision maker to apply the level of certainty that is most appropriate to a particular case."[1452]

Lillquist provides a compelling normative justification for a variable standard of proof, and, although his focus is on domestic prosecutions, his conclusions apply to international prosecutions as well. Indeed, a brief comparison of the costs of wrongful convictions and acquittals in the domestic and international spheres shows why fact finders might justifiably conceive beyond a reasonable doubt as signifying a higher probability level in the domestic context than in the international. Recall that the function of a standard of proof is to allocate errors. Consequently, the more we wish to prevent wrongful convictions, the more certainty we should require in our standard of proof. By contrast, the more we wish to prevent wrongful acquittals, the less certainty we should require. In comparing the optimal level of certainty for domestic convictions with that of international convictions, then, we must ask whether, as a general matter, we might be justifiably less concerned about convicting innocent defendants accused of international crimes than about convicting innocent defendants accused of domestic crimes. Also, we must

[1449] *Id.* at 146.
[1450] *Id.* at 148.
[1451] *Id.* at 159.
[1452] *Id.* at 92.

ask whether we might be justifiably more concerned about acquitting guilty defendants accused of international crimes than about acquitting guilty defendants accused of committing domestic crimes. I believe that the answer to both questions is yes.

We may be justifiably less concerned about preventing the wrongful conviction of a defendant accused of an international crime because the nature of international crimes, their perpetration, and their subsequent investigation are apt to put the defendant's innocence in a different light from the innocence of a typical domestic defendant. Consider, for instance, the O. J. Simpson case. If O. J. did not kill his ex-wife and her companion, then we have no reason to believe that he committed any other serious moral or legal wrong. Thus, convicting O. J. of a murder that he did not commit would prove a highly costly mistake that we should take great pains to avoid – by conceptualizing "beyond a reasonable doubt" as requiring near certainty. By contrast, if the evidence presented in an international trial along with whatever inferences we can reasonably draw from the defendant's official position do not provide us near certainty of the defendant's guilt, we nonetheless might be justifiably willing to convict him for the following four reasons.

First, there is a greater likelihood in an international case featuring reasonable doubt than in a domestic case featuring reasonable doubt that the reasonable doubt arose as a consequence of investigatory failures rather than as a consequence of true evidentiary insufficiency. Without denying that some domestic investigations are difficult to conduct, the fact remains that international investigations must contend with a host of problems that are virtually unknown in the domestic realm. Some of these I already mentioned in Chapter 5. Logistical difficulties can substantially impede international investigations, for instance, as whole regions in even a relatively stable country such as Rwanda sometimes prove too dangerous for investigators to visit. In those cases, investigators typically ask victims' groups to identify and transport potential witnesses to the investigators. If the victims' group does a poor job of locating witnesses, though, then the prosecution's case will suffer accordingly. Investigators must also contend with the same fact-finding impediments that will later bedevil the Trial Chambers. For instance, for every aspect of their work, investigators must rely on interpreters who not only might make mistakes but who also might distort the translations to further their own interests.[1453]

In addition, international investigators often have difficulty persuading witnesses to testify. They must convince victims of sexual violence to report the crimes perpetrated against them, even though to do so is to buck cultural norms and risk societal condemnation. And they must convince victims and witnesses to testify against potentially dangerous defendants when doing so could prove

[1453] *See* Overdulve, note 583, at 279.

fatal to them.[1454] The ICTY prosecution's case in *Haradinaj* was dealt a serious blow after several prosecution witnesses refused to testify, claiming that they had been threatened and that others who had given evidence to the ICTY had already been murdered.[1455] Likewise, many *CDF* witnesses were reluctant to discuss the crimes with investigators because they feared retaliation, not from their compatriots, but from supernatural forces. Tamba Gbeki, the SCSL's Assistant to the Head of Investigations, reported that he had to "break down [witnesses'] deep reluctance" to reveal the secrets of the Kamajors because the witnesses feared that their revelations would cause their stomachs to "swell until they died" or cause them to "turn . . . to ash."[1456] Domestic investigators and prosecutors can face similar problems in gang or organized crime cases, where witness intimidation can also derail an investigation.[1457] But, at least in most of those cases, prosecutors can engage in extensive wiretapping to gain evidence before issuing their indictments.[1458] Besides, such cases constitute only a small

[1454] *See, e.g.*, Joe Bavier, *Congo Ministers Attacked in Bemba Trial "Warning,"* Reuters, Aug. 31, 2009.

[1455] Prosecutor v. Haradinaj, Case No. IT-04-84-T, Transcript, Sept. 16, 2005, at 124; *id.* Mar. 5, 2007, at 359–61; *id.*, June 5, 2007, at 5439–5440; Sara Goodman, *Albanian Witness Refuses to Testify in Haradinaj Trial*, 505 Int'l War & Peace Reporting, June 8, 2007, *available at* http://listserv.acsu.buffalo.edu/cgi-bin/wa?A2=ind0706&L=JUSTWATCH-L&P=R10424&I=-3; *Witness Refuses to Testify Because Witnesses Get Killed in Kosovo*, SENSE News Agency, June 5, 2007, *available at* http://www.sense-agency.com/en/stream.php?sta=3&pid=9776&kat=3; *Problems With Prosecution Witnesses*, SENSE News Agency, June 29, 2007, *available at* http://www.sense-agency.com/en/stream.php?sta=3&pid=9930&kat=3. After Haradinaj was acquitted, ICTY prosecutors indicted two Kosovar Albanian government officials for contempt of court, alleging that they had tried to persuade a protected witness not to testify against Haradinaj. ICTY Press Release, *Astrit Haraqija and Bajrush Morina Indicted for Contempt Of Court*, CVO/MOW/1244e, Apr. 25, 2008, *available at* http://www.icty.org/sid/9898.

[1456] Kelsall, note 142, at 180.

[1457] *See, e.g.*, David Kocieniewski, *A Little Girl Shot, and a Crowd That Didn't See*, N.Y. Times, July 9, 2007, at A1; Tara C. Kowalski, Note, Alvarado v. Superior Court: *A Death Sentence for Government Witnesses*, 35 U. C. Davis L. Rev. 207, 208–10, 223–24 (2001); Stuart Mass, Note, *The Dilemma of the Intimidated Witness in Federal Organized Crime Prosecutions: Choosing Among the Fear of Reprisals, the Contempt Powers of the Court, and the Witness Protection Program*, 50 Fordham L. Rev. 582, 582–88 (1982); Ronald Goldstock and Dan T. Coenen, *Controlling the Contemporary Loanshark: The Law of Illicit Lending and the Problem of Witness Fear*, 65 Cornell L. Rev. 127, 206–08 (1980).

These problems also arise in domestic prosecutions of crimes that could be characterized as war crimes and crimes against humanity. *See Another Dirty War Witness Goes Missing*, A.P., Apr. 30, 2008.

[1458] Former ICTY and ICTR Chief Prosecutor Carla Del Ponte expounded on the difficulty of gathering evidence of large-scale crimes without the use of contemporaneous wiretaps or surveillance in Carla Del Ponte, *Investigation and Prosecution of Large-Scale Crimes at the International Level: The Experience of the ICTY*, 4 J. Int'l Crim. Just. 539, 552 (2006). Del Ponte had prosecuted money laundering, drug trafficking, and organized crime cases in her native Switzerland, so she knew how useful these investigatory methods can be.

fraction of all domestic criminal cases, whereas investigator impediments are intense and pervasive in every international criminal proceeding.[1459] The bottom line, then, is that we can have much greater confidence in a domestic case than in an international case that the evidence the prosecution presents is the best evidence available. Consequently, when the evidence in a domestic case leaves any quantity of doubt in the mind of the fact finder, that doubt is more indicative that the defendant is in fact innocent.

Second, even if the evidence is insufficient to prove that an international defendant committed a particular crime in the particular way alleged in the indictment, there is a greater likelihood that he (as opposed to a domestic defendant) committed the same crime but in a different way. So, perhaps Simba did not personally distribute weapons during the Kaduha parish massacre, as alleged in his indictment,[1460] but given the widespread nature of the massacres, it is far more likely that he committed other acts of genocide than that O. J. committed a different set of murders than the one for which he was charged. Third, even if the international defendant did not commit genocide – either through the acts alleged in the indictment or through other acts, there is a greater likelihood than in the domestic context that he committed some other crime. He may have committed a similarly serious crime such as a crime against humanity, or he may have committed a relatively trivial crime, such as one of the many thousands of property offenses that took place during the Rwandan genocide. Finally, even if the international defendant committed no crime during the genocide, he may bear some moral culpability for acquiescing in it. As Mark Drumbl has pointed out, large groups of persons in addition to actual perpetrators typically bear responsibility for mass atrocities, even though they have not, strictly speaking, committed any international crimes. "This group comprises bystanders: those multitudes who comply with the violence, who acquiesce in it, or who idle while it unfolds around them." Drumbl points out that most bystanders of atrocity are also beneficiaries of atrocity, both ideologically, as they "feel part of a grand social project without bloodying their own hands," and materially, as they are frequently able to capitalize on the misfortunes of the victims.[1461]

Many of these factors may seem familiar because they are just the factors that incline the Trial Chambers to determine that the prosecution has met the beyond-a-reasonable-doubt standard as traditionally conceived. They also function, however, to suggest that more doubt is tolerable in the context of

[1459] Defense witnesses also face intimidation. *See* Simba Judgement, note 455, at paras. 41–42.

[1460] *See* Prosecutor v. Simba, Case No. ICTR-2001-76-1, Amended Indictment, paras. 29–34 (May 10, 2004).

[1461] Drumbl, note 1, at 25.

international convictions than domestic convictions. Indeed, I invoke these factors to show that the line between guilty and innocent, which is typically quite distinct in the context of domestic crimes,[1462] blurs when it comes to mass atrocity. It blurs as a moral matter, given the presence of both morally culpable bystanders as well as morally innocent offenders, who committed the crimes under compulsion. And it blurs as an evidentiary matter, as I have spent most of this book describing. As many as one million Hutu committed genocide and other serious crimes during 1994.[1463] Our hypothetical international defendant may not have been one of them, but he is more likely to be guilty of something – even if he is not guilty of the specific crime for which he has been charged – than is the average domestic defendant who is not guilty of the specific crimes for which he has been charged. Domestic crimes prove exceptions to the norm of lawfulness; international crimes, by contrast, take place in a context in which violence is so widespread, officially approved, and socially accepted that it cannot be considered deviant. Journalist Philip Gourevitch has observed of the Rwandan genocide that "the work of the killers was not regarded as a crime . . . ; it was effectively the law of the land."[1464] In such a context – where so many are guilty – heightened concern about preventing the wrongful conviction of innocents that a particularly stringent conception of the beyond-a-reasonable-doubt standard instantiates may not be necessary.

That said, I wish to be clear that I am not suggesting that we convict international defendants on the basis of speculation. Perhaps our hypothetical international defendant did commit genocide in a way different from that alleged in his indictment or perhaps he committed some other crime. Plenty of Rwandans did. But assuming that we have no evidence that he did, such speculations should not form the basis for his conviction. What I am suggesting, however, is that the factual context surrounding the crimes for which a defendant is charged may legitimately inform our views about how much doubt is tolerable in a given case. To reiterate, any standard of proof higher than a preponderance-of-the-evidence standard reflects our view that convicting the innocent is a more costly mistake than acquitting the guilty. And a very stringent conception of the beyond-a-reasonable-doubt standard reflects our belief that convicting the innocent is much, much more costly than acquitting the guilty. The foregoing analysis suggests, however, that it may not be as costly

[1462] The line between the guilty and the innocent is not always distinct even in the context of domestic crimes because domestic defendants who are members of large-scale drug conspiracies, white-collar criminal syndicates, and organized crime networks resemble international criminals in many ways.

[1463] William A. Schabas, *Genocide Trials and Gacaca Courts*, 3 J. Int'l Crim. Just. 879, 881 (2005).

[1464] Philip Gourevitch, We Wish to Inform You That Tomorrow We Will Be Killed with Our Families: Stories from Rwanda 123 (1998).

to wrongfully convict a defendant of one crime when there is a not trivial likelihood that he is guilty of another crime than it is to wrongfully convict a defendant who, if he did not commit the crime for which he has been charged, is entirely innocent. Thus, although we may not want to convict O. J. Simpson on an 85 percent probability because if we are wrong about his guilt we have made a very grave mistake indeed, we may feel more comfortable convicting an international defendant on an 85 percent probability because our mistake in doing so may not be quite so costly.

Up until now, I have considered whether we might be justifiably less concerned about convicting defendants who are innocent of the specific international crimes for which they are charged than we would be about convicting defendants who are innocent of the specific domestic crimes for which they are charged. A standard of proof reflects not only our views about the costs of wrongful convictions but also the costs of wrongful acquittals. As noted above, at the same time that a high standard of proof decreases the likelihood of wrongful convictions, it increases the likelihood of wrongful acquittals. Although wrongful acquittals are less costly than wrongful convictions in both the international and the domestic contexts, I believe that wrongful acquittals of international defendants cost more than wrongful acquittals of domestic defendants. The cost-benefit comparison is a difficult one to make because the costs of wrongful acquittals are very different for domestic crimes than they are for international crimes. Although both the domestic and the international criminal go free when wrongfully acquitted and both fail to receive deserved punishment, the effects of those consequences vary considerably between the domestic and international contexts. For instance, in both contexts, the unpunished defendant remains free to commit subsequent crimes, but the international defendant rarely does. Whereas recidivism is common for those who commit domestic crimes, most people who commit international crimes have committed no previous crimes and will commit no future crimes. Most international criminals are not violent individuals but rather are individuals who became violent because of the violence that ripped through their regions. Once the large-scale contextual violence ceases, so too does their individual violence.

The deterrence implications of wrongful acquittals also differ between the international and domestic contexts. When a defendant is wrongfully acquitted of a domestic crime "[t]he message is sent to prospective criminals that they too may be able to avoid prosecution for their crimes."[1465] Sadly, deterrence is

[1465] *See* Laudan, note 1415, at 69. For a summary discussion of the other costs of wrongful acquittals, see Rinat Kitai, *Protecting the Guilty*, 6 Buff. Crim. L. Rev. 1163, 1166–67 (2003).

far less potent in the international realm; indeed, because we have considerable reason to fear that international criminals are not in fact deterred by the rightful imposition of criminal punishment, then wrongful acquittals of international defendants are not apt to significantly reduce deterrence effects.

Although these considerations might suggest that wrongful acquittals of domestic defendants are costlier than wrongful acquittals of international defendants, other considerations cut in the opposite direction. First off, as noted in Chapter 8, international acquittals are likely to affect victims more profoundly because international victims so often view acquittals through an ideological lens. International acquittals are also more likely to impair the reputation of the international tribunal because they are seen as undermining the tribunal's very mission. That is, whereas domestic victims may bemoan a criminal justice system that they believe is "too soft on crime" or that frees defendants "on technicalities," they do not call into serious question the neutrality of the court that issued the acquittal in the way that international victims do.

The cost of international acquittals is particularly high, most importantly, because international criminals are so difficult to apprehend. Concededly, international enforcement mechanisms have improved in recent years. The international community did eventually persuade Nigeria to hand over Charles Taylor and Serbia to hand over Slobodan Milošević and Radovan Karadžić. But the international community's enforcement failures remain legion. The Special Panels never did get its hands on any high-level offenders, and the ICC has obtained custody over fewer than half of its current indictees. In addition, when political and diplomatic constraints do not impede arrests, financial constraints often do. ICTY and ICTR prosecutors were not initially limited in the number of indictments that they could issue, but the high costs of proceedings at those tribunals soon convinced the international community to require them to adopt completion strategies and to severely limit the jurisdictional mandates of subsequent international tribunals.[1466] As a consequence, ICTY and ICTR prosecutors were forced to abandon some investigations[1467] and

[1466] *See generally* Langer, note 1248, at 835 (describing the procedural changes that these pressures brought about).

[1467] Press Release, ICTY, *Address by the Prosecutor of the International Criminal Tribunals for the Former Yugoslavia and Rwanda, Mrs. Carla del Ponte, to the United Nations Security Council*, JJJ/P.I.S/.709-e (Oct. 30, 2002) *available at* http://www.un.org/icty/pressreal/p709-e.htm. For a discussion of the ICTR's reduction in investigations, see Letter dated 30 April 2004, from the president of the International Criminal Tribunal for the Prosecution of Persons Responsible for Genocide and Other Serious Violations of International Humanitarian Law Committed in the Territory of Rwanda and Rwandan Citizens Responsible for Genocide and Other Such Violations Committed in the Territory of Neighbouring States between 1 January and 31 December 1994 addressed to the president of the Security Council, paras. 6, 30, U.N. Doc. S/2004/341 (May 3, 2004).

withdraw some indictments;[1468] the Special Panels were forced to close prematurely; and prosecutors at the SCSL and the Extraordinary Chambers in Cambodia are authorized to indict only those "persons who bear *the greatest responsibility*" for the atrocities.[1469] As a result of these limited mandates, the SCSL and the Extraordinary Chambers each will prosecute only about ten individuals.[1470]

In sum, it requires a tremendous expenditure of financial, diplomatic, and political capital merely to get a defendant into an international courtroom, and with the mandates of the international tribunals rapidly shrinking, few defendants are even sought. Because it is so difficult and rare even to bring an international defendant to trial, the cost of wrongfully acquitting one is high indeed. In fact, as discussed in Chapter 8, a substantial number of international acquittals – whether rightful or wrongful – could doom international criminal justice entirely. The ICC is still struggling to prove that it can flourish without the support of the United States, the SCSL is still begging for voluntary donations so it can complete its cases, and the Extraordinary Chambers are still trying desperately to get on with their prosecutions before all of their indictees die of old age. With these daunting challenges forming the backdrop for every international criminal trial, wrongful acquittals of guilty defendants must be considered to impose very high costs indeed on the international criminal justice system.

Just as I wished to make clear in my discussion of the costs of wrongful convictions that I am not arguing that international defendants should be convicted on the basis of speculation that they committed some other crime, I likewise here want to emphasize that I am not suggesting that because international criminal justice faces considerable challenges merely to prosecute defendants that means that those defendants who are prosecuted must be convicted. I am suggesting, however, that these considerable challenges raise the cost of wrongful international acquittals. Indeed, the foregoing is intended to suggest that although a substantial cost disparity exists between wrongful convictions and wrongful acquittals of domestic crimes and that disparity supports conceiving of "beyond a reasonable doubt" in particularly exacting terms, the

1468 ICTY Bull., No. 21, July 27, 1998, at 4; *see also* Sean D. Murphy, *Progress and Jurisprudence of the International Criminal Tribunal for the Former Yugoslavia*, 93 Am. J. Int'l L. 57, 74–75 (1999) (describing the withdrawn indictments).

1469 Statute of the Special Court for Sierra Leone, art. 1 (Jan. 16, 2002); Agreement between the United Nations and the Royal Government of Cambodia Concerning the Prosecution Under Cambodian Law of Crimes Committed during the Period of Democratic Kampuchea, arts. 1, 5(3), 6(3) (June 6, 2003).

1470 David Scheffer, *A Rare Chance to Try These Architects of Atrocity*, Financial Times (London), Aug. 16, 2004; Richard Woodd & Vong Sokheng, *US Senate Moves to Block KR Trial Funds*, Phnom Penh Post, Oct. 8, 2004.

cost disparity between wrongful convictions and wrongful acquittals of international crimes may not be so great. It is that cost disparity that drives the stringency of the standard of proof, so less disparity justifies an understanding of "beyond a reasonable doubt" that legitimately encompasses more doubt.

Although the factors just described suggest that fact finders applying the beyond-a-reasonable-doubt standard in international criminal prosecutions will and arguably should require comparatively less certainty to find that standard satisfied, other factors appear to cut in the opposite direction. For instance, many of the scholars and judges who advocate the use of a variable standard of proof assume that higher levels of certainty will be required for more serious crimes that elicit the most severe punishments.[1471] Larry Laudan, for instance, notes that the beyond-a-reasonable-doubt standard was developed at a time when all felonies were punished by death. Today, criminal punishments vary considerably; consequently, Laudan suggests that the cost of a wrongful conviction for a minor crime may not warrant the rigorous standard of proof that we desire when we prosecute more serious crimes.[1472] Similarly, in discussing the rigor with which trial and appellate courts should enforce the beyond-a-reasonable-doubt standard, Judge Jon Newman suggests that cases involving particularly serious crimes deserve heightened scrutiny.[1473] Although these scholars accept the principle that one size need not fit all when it comes to standards of proof in criminal cases, the criteria by which they would vary the standards can be seen to cut against a lower standard for international crimes. This is because Professors Laudan and Lillquist along with Judge Newman each maintain that prosecutions involving the risk for severe punishment – and capital cases especially – warrant a particularly high standard of proof given the particularly severe harm that would result from a wrongful conviction.[1474] Shari'a law likewise embodies this reasoning: Although it requires the testimony of two eyewitnesses to prove most serious crimes, to prove adultery – a crime that results in particularly harsh punishment – four eyewitnesses are needed.[1475] This makes sense. The more serious the crime and the harsher the

[1471] *See, e.g.*, Briginshaw v. Briginshaw, (1938) 60 C.L.R. 336, 361–62 (Australia) ("The seriousness of an allegation made, the inherent unlikelihood of an occurrence of a given description, or the gravity of the consequences flowing from a particular finding are considerations which must affect the answer to the question whether the issue has been proved to the reasonable satisfaction of the tribunal.").

[1472] LAUDAN, note 1415, at 55–61.

[1473] Jon O. Newman, *Beyond "Reasonable Doubt,"* 68 N.Y.U. L. REV. 979, 998–1000 (1993).

[1474] *Id.* at 999–1000; Lillquist, note 1417, at 91; LAUDAN, note 1415, at 55–61.

[1475] Ma'amoun M. Salama, *General Principles of Criminal Evidence in Islamic Jurisprudence, in* THE ISLAMIC CRIMINAL JUSTICE SYSTEM 109, 118–19 (M. Cherif Bassiouni ed., 1988); Hisham M. Ramadan, *On Islamic Punishment, in* UNDERSTANDING ISLAMIC LAW: FROM CLASSICAL TO CONTEMPORARY 43, 44–45 (Hisham M. Ramadan ed., 2006); Abdel Salam Sidahmed, *Problems in Contemporary Applications of Islamic Criminal Sanctions: The Penalty for Adultery in Relation to Women*, 28 BRIT. J. MIDDLE EASTERN STUDIES 187, 203 (2001). Married persons penalties, the greater the harm wrought by a wrongful conviction and the more rigorous the standard of proof should be to try to prevent that harm.

The crimes and punishments at issue in international criminal trials are particularly grave and severe. Genocide, the crime for which most ICTR defendants have been convicted, has been labeled the "crime of crimes,"[1476] and it along with crimes against humanity and war crimes are considered humankind's most heinous offenses. As for the likely punishment, although the international tribunals cannot impose death penalty, most of the tribunals can and have imposed life sentences,[1477] and the SCSL, which cannot, has imposed the effective equivalent in two of the three cases that it has decided.[1478] Given the gravity of the crimes charged and the severity of the penalties imposed, we might well conclude that the beyond-a-reasonable-doubt standard in the international context should signify a particularly high level of certainty. That is, we might conclude that before labeling someone a *genocidaire*, we should be as certain as we can possibly be that the label fits.

Although the gravity of the crime and the severity of the punishments do caution in favor of a high proof standard, other factors may prove more influential. One such factor is the nature of the criminal activity under consideration, a point that Lillquist made in the context of domestic prosecutions. Lillquist argues that the utility of an accurate acquittal might be quite low in cases where the evidence clearly establishes that the defendant is participating, for instance, in the drug trade or in a car theft ring or even a terrorist network but fails to support a beyond-a-reasonable-doubt finding of guilt for a particular crime. As Lillquist puts it:

> Consider, for instance, a case involving an individual linked to al-Qaeda. The person is arrested and the evidence of a link to the organization is strong but

who are convicted of adultery are subject to the sanction of death by stoning. Aly Aly Mansour, Hudud *Crimes, in General Principles of Criminal Evidence in Islamic Jurisprudence, in* The Islamic Criminal Justice System 195, 199 (M. Cherif Bassiouni ed., 1988).

1476 *See, e.g.*, Prosecutor v. Akayesu, Case No. ICTR-96-4-T, Sentence, para. 8 (Oct. 2, 1998); Serushago Judgement, note 607, at para. 15.

1477 Virtually all of the ICTR defendants convicted of genocide have received life sentences, including the following: Jean-Paul Akayesu, Théoneste Bagosora, Juvénal Kajelijeli, Jean Kambanda, Jean de Dieu Kamuhanda, Clément Kayishema, Alfred Musema, Ferdinand Nahimana, Siméon Nchamihigo, Hassan Ngeze, Eliezer Niyitegeka, Anatole Nsengiyumva, Aloys Ntabakuze, and Georges Rutaganda. Jean-Bosco Barayagwiza would have received a life sentence, but the Trial Chamber reduced his sentence to thirty-five years' imprisonment to remedy the prosecution's violation of his procedural rights. Nahimana Judgement, note 97, at para. 1106.

1478 The *AFRC* Trial Chamber sentenced the *AFRC* defendants to forty-five-and fifty-year terms of imprisonment, Prosecutor v. Brima et al., Case No. SCSL-04-16-T, Sentencing Judgement, at Disposition (July 19, 2007), and the *RUF* Trial Chamber sentenced two of its defendants to forty- and fifty-two–year terms of imprisonment, Prosecutor v. Sesay et al., Case No. SCSL-04-15-T, Sentencing Judgement, at Disposition (Apr. 8, 2009).

> the evidence of specific criminal wrongdoing is weak. In such a case, there is a risk of an erroneous conviction: the defendant may not have committed the specific crime with which he is charged. Nonetheless, the actual harm that flows from such an erroneous conviction would be low, because of the risk that the defendant would commit other terrorist acts. Accordingly, it would make sense for a juror to require less proof in such a case before convicting.[1479]

Indeed, Lillquist argues that the rightful acquittal of such persons, even though merited on the evidence and ordinarily considered desirable, might "have disutilities associated with it, because it would free the defendant to continue his wrongful conduct."[1480]

Lillquist's analysis of the beyond-a-reasonable-doubt standard as applied to members of drug rings or terrorist networks mirrors my own analysis largely because of the organizational similarities between drug rings and terrorist networks on the one hand and groups that commit international crimes on the other. In both cases, a defendant's membership in a particular group can create a compelling suspicion that the defendant is guilty of some crime even if it provides few details about the defendant's specific criminal acts. Indeed, although I have contrasted international crimes with domestic crimes and have suggested that the beyond-a-reasonable-doubt standard might justifiably permit less certainty for the former than the latter, I invoked, for purposes of that contrast, the typical domestic crime; that is, the crime that involves one perpetrator or a small number of perpetrators who engage in a discrete set of criminal acts. To the extent that certain domestic crimes and criminals resemble international crimes and criminals, then the conception of "beyond a reasonable doubt" that applies in the international context would also apply to these domestic crimes. Moreover, the fact that "beyond a reasonable doubt" is likely to be satisfied with a lower level of certainty in some international prosecutions than it has traditionally been thought to require in domestic prosecutions does not mean that the certainty level will be lower in every international prosecution. Indeed, ICTR Trial Chambers applied an especially stringent understanding of "beyond a reasonable doubt" in some of their cases that resulted in acquittals. That they did should come as no surprise, as my examination of these cases in Chapter 8 revealed the defendants to be sympathetic characters whose wrongful conviction would be seen as especially costly. These cases demonstrate that standards of proof vary not only between different categories of crimes but also within them. Thus, to the extent that a wrongful conviction in any given international prosecution would give rise

[1479] Lillquist, note 1417, at 162.
[1480] *Id.* at 161.

to comparatively high costs, then we can expect the Trial Chamber to require considerably greater certainty before convicting the defendant.

To recap, I have shown that, although standards of proof have traditionally been conceived as signifying fixed, unchanging probability levels, compelling theoretical and empirical research has shown them instead to be variable. Multifarious factors influence the way in which a standard of proof will vary across and throughout different sets of cases, and a consideration of these factors suggests that fact finders will (and perhaps should) find more doubt tolerable in the average international prosecution than they will in the average domestic prosecution. Having provided this summary, I will now address a potential objection to the foregoing analysis, namely that it is grounded in utilitarianism and pays insufficient attention to deontological considerations that support a stringent understanding of "beyond a reasonable doubt" in every criminal case.[1481] Kant instructs that the defendant should be a subject in a criminal trial and should never serve as its object.[1482] Many believe that reducing the standard of proof to lower than "beyond a reasonable doubt" would violate this principle. As Rinat Kitai put it: "Exposing the individual to a concrete, calculated risk by lowering the standard of proof, thereby enabling conviction despite reasonable doubt as to his guilt, is the conscious sacrifice of that individual for the sake of the common interest."[1483] Similarly, Laurence Tribe asserted that to intentionally punish a man of whose guilt we feel unsure is wrong:

> Whatever the resulting social gain, such action is morally and constitutionally reprehensible. Given a system known to contain imperfections, there is a qualitative difference between the outcome of erroneously convicting a man when the trier has been fully convinced of his guilt and the outcome of erroneously convicting a man when the trier has reason to believe that he may be innocent. In the first of these situations, the trier is not called upon to make an explicit decision to risk morally condemning and punishing an innocent man. In the second situation, such a decision is required; it cannot be made without greatly undermining society's commitment to the dignity of the individual as an end in himself.[1484]

Although I have not suggested lowering the standard of proof, it could be argued that recognizing and accepting "beyond-a-reasonable-doubt" as a

[1481] For a well-known deontological justification for the beyond-a-reasonable-doubt standard of proof, see Ronald Dworkin, A Matter of Principle 79–89 (1986).
[1482] Immanuel Kant, The Metaphysical Elements of Justice 100 (John Ladd trans., 1965).
[1483] Kitai, note 1465, at 1186.
[1484] Laurence H. Tribe, *An Ounce of Detention: Preventative Justice in the World of John Mitchell*, 56 Va. L. Rev. 371, 386 (1970).

variable standard is the effective equivalent. In particular, if a deontological understanding of the standard of proof provides that it is simply wrong to allow a conviction on anything less than the highest level of certainty,[1485] then a variable standard of proof that fluctuates according to all manner of utilitarian considerations could be seen as violating this principle.

The fact is, however, reasonable doubt will vary from case to case not only for the reasons that Lillquist, Damaška, Kaplan, and other scholars identify but also because "the highest level of certainty" will necessarily vary over space and time. For instance, the evidence that might have easily satisfied the beyond-a-reasonable-doubt standard for a rape conviction thirty years ago may no longer be sufficient now that DNA testing is available. Similarly, because international criminal cases are prosecuted under very different circumstances than domestic cases, we can expect that the "highest level of certainty" will vary between the two contexts. In particular, fact finders in domestic trials who are required to pass on a few discrete criminal acts that occurred recently, that are the subject of detailed forensic testimony, and that were committed in the same community in which the courtroom is located will be able to have higher levels of certainty about the facts of their cases than will fact finders in international trials featuring large numbers of criminal acts, none of which is the subject of forensic evidence, but all of which occurred years if not decades before, in the context of a brutal war that took place hundreds if not thousands of miles from the courtroom. Laurence Tribe deemed the beyond-a-reasonable-doubt standard to be a "standard that seeks to come as close to certainty as human knowledge allows."[1486] The problem is that human knowledge allows for markedly different levels of certainty for different facts and different situations. Given the fact-finding impediments I have described, it is my belief that most international criminal facts simply cannot be known with anything near to the level of certainty that we consider optimal. It might nonetheless "come as close to certainty as human knowledge allows." When it comes to international trials, we arguably have, in the words of Robert Bartlett, a situation in which "certain knowledge [i]s impossible but uncertainty [i]s intolerable."[1487]

1485 Talia Fisher, *The Boundaries of Plea Bargaining: Negotiating the Standard of Proof*, 97 J. Crim. L. & Criminology 943, 976–77 (2007).
1486 Tribe, note 1484, at 388.
1487 Bartlett, note 1212, at 33.

Conclusion

Although this book has presented a troubling picture of international criminal fact-finding, it is largely a retrospective picture. I have closely examined the work of three international tribunals – the ICTR, the SCSL, and the Special Panels. One of those tribunals – the Special Panels – closed its doors in 2005 and was never taken very seriously even during its short lifetime. The other two tribunals are still in existence, having been afforded longer life spans and more plausible resources, but their prosecutions also are coming to an end. Certainly, it is useful to know about the fact-finding challenges that a subset of international tribunals have had to confront, but the findings and recommendations appearing in this book will be of lasting consequence only if those challenges will also afflict the ICC and the new generation of *ad hoc* tribunals. Sadly, early indications suggest that the ICC and Extraordinary Chambers in the Courts of Cambodia (ECCC) are already contending with just the sort of fact-finding impediments that have plagued their predecessors. Indeed, the very first witnesses in the ICC's and ECCC's very first trials have had difficulty understanding compound questions[1488] and basic terminology[1489] and have had difficulty answering questions seeking dates,[1490] duration,[1491] distance,[1492] numerical estimations,[1493] and other details about the crimes[1494] and their subsequent

[1488] Prosecutor v. Kaing Guek Eav "Duch," Case No. 001/18-07-2007-ECCC/TC, Transcript, June 9, 2009, at 2 [hereinafter Duch Transcript].

[1489] Lubanga Transcript, Feb. 23, 2009, at 10–11; Duch Transcript, Aug. 3, 2009, at 4, 42–44.

[1490] Lubanga Transcript, Feb. 20, 2009, at 11, 23; Lubanga Transcript, Feb. 23, 2009, at 72, 77; Lubanga Transcript, Feb. 27, 2009, at 7; Duch Transcript, July 14, 2009, at 50–51; Duch Transcript, Aug. 3, 2009, at 41; Duch Transcript, Aug. 5, 2009, at 23–24.

[1491] Lubanga Transcript, Feb. 20, 2009, at 28, 38, 43, 46; Lubanga Transcript, Feb. 23, 2009, at 66, 77; Lubanga Transcript, Mar. 5, 2009, at 21; Lubanga Transcript, Mar. 6, 2009, at 52; Duch Transcript, Aug. 5, 2009, at 24–25; Duch Transcript, Aug. 4, 2009, at 105.

[1492] Lubanga Transcript, Feb. 23, 2009, at 65; Lubanga Transcript, Mar. 4, 2009, at 22–23.

[1493] Lubanga Transcript, Feb. 20, 2009, at 12, 50; Lubanga Transcript, Feb. 23, 2009, at 4.

[1494] Lubanga Transcript, Feb. 20, 2009, at 12, 16, 26, 27, 42, 45; Lubanga Transcript, Feb. 23, 2009, at 76; Lubanga Transcript, Feb. 27, 2009, at 60–61.

investigations.[1495] These very early transcripts have also featured serious inconsistencies between testimony and pretrial statements[1496] and even perjury.[1497]

Although I have endeavored through this study to illuminate the evidentiary challenges facing international criminal tribunals, I recognize that my research is preliminary and that much more needs to be done both to quantify my findings and to understand their impact. My primary aim in this book has been to shine a spotlight on a previously unilluminated aspect of international criminal justice. With copious citations to support my findings, I believe I have proved that various fact-finding impediments are widespread and that they present substantial challenges to the tribunals under study, but, with respect to most of those impediments, I have not sought to quantify them precisely. I did quantify the percentage of witnesses whose testimony had serious inconsistencies with their pretrial statements, and I also provided an in-depth study of the testimony supporting all of the convictions in the *CDF* case. But I could do no more within the confines of this work because I was also committed to providing analytical and normative accounts of international criminal fact-finding.

Of course, my analytical and normative accounts are based on my empirical research, and additional quantification could require me to alter my conclusions. For instance, although the abundant citations that I have provided prove, I am confident, that the problems I identify are legion, it is also true that international trials are so long and international witnesses so plentiful that it is possible that the actual incidence of fact-finding deficiencies is not as high as I believe it to be. Furthermore, international trials feature different types of witnesses; some witnesses provide crime-based evidence and evidence that is intended to prove the contextual elements of the international crime, whereas others testify as to the role of the defendant in the crime. Although deficiencies appearing in the testimony of crime-based witnesses is regrettable, it is not catastrophic because no one seriously questions that large-scale atrocities took place. Thus, if the testimony of a few crime-based witnesses was not sufficiently reliable to establish the large-scale atrocities, other witnesses could be identified and deployed. Witnesses who have relevant information about the defendant's role in the crime, by contrast, are harder to come by and consequently more valuable. Accordingly, deficiencies in the testimony of these witnesses

[1495] Duch Transcript, Aug. 4, 2009, at 16.

[1496] Lubanga Transcript, Feb. 27, 2009, at 5; Lubanga Transcript, Mar. 4, 2009, at 7, 8–16, 18, 19, 30–32, 38–40, 49, 56–59; Duch Transcript, July 7, 2009, at 79–81; Duch Transcript, July 8, 2009, at 35–39; Duch Transcript, July 13, 2009, at 2–3, 61–62, 73–75; Duch Transcript, Aug. 4, 2009, at 49; Duch Transcript, Aug. 11, 2009, at 9–10; *see also* Seth Mydans, *Torture and Death Recounted at Cambodian Trial*, N.Y. Times, July 14, 2009.

[1497] Lubanga Transcript, Jan. 28, 2009, at 39–42.

will have a far greater impact on fact-finding accuracy at the tribunals. My strong sense is that testimonial deficiencies are not only widespread but occur at least proportionally between the different types of witnesses, if not with a greater frequency amongst witnesses testifying about the defendant's specific acts. Certainly, many of the most serious inconsistencies that I described in Chapter 4 occurred during the testimony of insider witnesses or witnesses who were describing the defendant's actions. But, although I feel relatively confident about these assessments, more quantification would certainly be valuable.

More quantification may in fact prove difficult to obtain because many fact-finding impediments are difficult to identify. We may never know, for instance, that a witness provided an inaccurate answer because an interpreter translated the question inaccurately or because a cultural divergence caused her to misunderstand the question. Serious efforts to quantify will also prove challenging because a great deal of information is unavailable. Some transcripts are not posted to the Internet, and much testimony within the transcripts that are posted is held in closed sessions. Despite these difficulties, quantification efforts should be undertaken, as they will provide the tribunals valuable information about what is of most concern and where they should deploy their resources.

The final issue with which I conclude this study involves alternatives to international criminal trials. Even if "certain knowledge [i]s impossible" at the international tribunals, the resulting uncertainty may not be intolerable if we are able to look to domestic courts to provide a viable alternative forum. In other words, some of the proposals that I have put forth in the preceding chapters have been suboptimal at best, and although they can be defended, they can be defended only if there do not exist alternative fora that are better placed to accurately find facts. It is useful, then, to conclude with a brief look at the capacity of domestic criminal justice systems to prosecute international crimes.

Certainly domestic prosecutions of international crimes provide some comparative advantages over international prosecutions, particularly in the realm of outreach and sensitivity to local concerns.[1498] Moreover, when we specifically

[1498] The Commission of Experts that examined the Rwandan atrocities opined, for instance, that municipal courts might be more attuned to the needs of the local community, could investigate the crimes more easily because they would be in-country, and could issue judgments that may have "greater and more immediate symbolic force" because they were rendered by courts familiar to the local community." Letter Dated 1 Oct. 1994 From the Secretary-General Addressed to the president of the Security Council, U.N. Doc. S/1994/1125, para. 134 (Oct. 4, 1994). Scholars have expanded upon these themes. *See, e.g.*, José E. Alvarez, *Crimes of State/Crimes of Hate: Lessons from Rwanda*, 24 Yale J. Int'l L. 365 (1999).

consider the fact-finding impediments that I have detailed in previous chapters, we see that, although domestic courts would also confront some of these impediments, many would disappear or at least cause considerably less distortion. Consider, for instance, the distortion caused by language interpretation. There is no need for language translation in Rwanda's genocide trials, for instance, because Rwandans speak one language – Kinyarwanda. Domestic trials in other countries, such as Sierra Leone or East Timor, might necessitate some language interpretation because some witnesses speak only tribal languages, but the quantity of language interpretation in these domestic courts would be greatly reduced and its quality apt to be significantly improved. Interpretation would not substantially impede communication in an East Timorese court if the court had only to interpret the testimony of the occasional Bunak-speaking witness into Tetum, the lingua franca of East Timor. Most witnesses who speak Bunak or other tribal languages also speak Tetum, and for those who do not, interpretation proves not to be so problematic because Bunak and Tetum bear some relationship to one another,[1499] and interpreters proficient in Bunak–Tetum interpretation are reasonably easy to procure. Interpretation impeded communication so profoundly at the Special Panels, by contrast, because the Panels needed to put the testimony of *every* witness through *several* translations to allow the Timorese witnesses to communicate with their English- or Portuguese-speaking interlocutors.

Similarly, in domestic prosecutions of international crimes, cultural divergences would create only a small portion of the confusion and uncertainty that they currently sow in international tribunal trials. Concededly, cultural practices can vary throughout the different regions in which atrocities take place, so that domestic courts may receive testimony that touches on beliefs or practices that are unfamiliar to domestic fact finders. But, in the main, domestic courts receive testimony from local witnesses. Besides, even fact finders who hail from a country's capital are likely to have some familiarity with the taboos that guide behavior in more remote regions as well as with the patterns of speech and worldviews that so influence the manner and content of witness testimony. Fact-finding at the SCSL and Special Panels has benefited from a bit of this cultural knowledge because some SCSL and Special Panels defendants have been represented by Sierra Leonean and Timorese defense counsel, and the SCSL and Special Panels have each employed a Sierra Leonean and

[1499] Marian Klamer, *Typical Features of Austronesian Languages in Central/Eastern Indonesia*, 41 Oceanic Linguistics 363, 365 (Dec. 2002); Geoffrey Hull, *The Languages of East Timor: Some Basic Facts, available at* http://www.portphillip.vic.gov.au/default/CommunityGovernanceDocuments/The_Languages_of_East_Timor_Some_Basic_Facts.pdf.

Timorese judge, respectively. Indeed, it is not surprising that invocations of cultural norms appear most prevalent and most confounding at the ICTR, which uses no Rwandan judges, prosecutors, or defense counsel. Local judges and lawyers, although they too can be fooled, at least bring to the table a basic understanding of the culture that renders them more willing – and more able – to reject implausible cultural invocations.

A domestic criminal justice system's improved ability to conduct investigations would also ameliorate much of the uncertainty that pervades international criminal fact-finding. Local investigators have a better sense of where to go and what to ask; and, given their proximity to witnesses and crime sites, they have an enhanced ability to actually get the job done. Concededly, even under the best of investigatory circumstances, many facts at issue in an international trial are not subject to conclusive determination because the only evidence available regarding those facts will be conflicting eyewitness accounts. But local investigators can better inform domestic fact finders even on these issues because they can more easily visit the relevant locations and interview a wider range of witnesses. That is, although it may be that no evidence exists to conclusively determine the cause of witness TF2-006's finger amputation, local investigators will be able to interview a larger proportion of TF2-006's neighbors to determine what they know about the injury. More importantly, TF2-006 is less likely to claim that the amputation occurred during the war when it was in fact a welding injury if TF2-006 appears before a domestic court.

Indeed, following on that point, perjury admittedly occurs in both domestic and international tribunals; Rwanda's domestic courts have certainly seen their fair share of false accusations. But witnesses are less likely to lie when their lies are more likely to be detected, and domestic courts have a greater ability to detect lies. Consequently, we can expect that domestic trials would feature fewer factual disputes. Whereas international investigations often leave the Trial Chambers uncertain about even the most basic matters – whether an anti-Tutsi rally was even held or whether a given roadblock even existed – domestic investigations could probably settle more of those matters, so that due attention could be paid to the key questions in the case.

The foregoing suggests that the fact-finding impediments that plague international proceedings are not so apt to distort fact-finding in domestic proceedings. The problem is that other factors will. Political considerations are particularly likely to prove distortive. Rwanda, for instance, has shown an admirable commitment to prosecuting international crimes, but that commitment extends only to prosecuting Hutu accused of perpetrating violence against Tutsi. Rwanda's Tutsi-led government has rendered the Tutsi RPF soldiers who committed retaliation crimes against Hutu civilians functionally immune from prosecution. Similarly, Croatia's early prosecutions targeted almost exclusively Serb defendants accused of committing war crimes against Croats. Croatian courts convicted the vast majority of these Serb defendants *in absentia*,[1500] whereas they acquitted most of the few Croatian defendants who were prosecuted.[1501] The problem in other States, by contrast, has been less the imposition of victors' justice and more the reluctance to pursue any justice at all. Government officials in Latin American countries such as Chile and Argentina committed thousands of forced disappearances and then followed up those crimes by enacting broad-based, retroactive amnesties that prevented prosecutions for decades. In more recent times, Sudan has promised to prosecute the perpetrators of crimes in Darfur, but its Special Criminal Court on the Events in Darfur has heard virtually no cases.[1502] Similarly, Indonesia has conducted only a few prosecutions of Indonesians accused of perpetrating violence in East Timor, and these have been dismissed as shams designed to shield offenders from punishment.[1503]

Finally, although domestic criminal justice systems possess the potential to find facts more accurately if the criminal justice systems are functioning as they should, most are not functioning as they should after a mass atrocity. The sheer number of individuals who perpetrate a mass atrocity would overwhelm the world's most well-resourced, technologically sophisticated criminal justice systems, and the criminal justice systems of States that suffer mass atrocities are typically neither well resourced nor technologically sophisticated. Sierra Leone has five million people but only 125 lawyers, and 95 percent of them are based in the capital, Freetown.[1504] A Commonwealth Human Rights Initiative report observed that despite the existence of "an elaborate judicial structure,

[1500] Organization for Security and Co-Operation in Europe, Mission to Croatia, *Background Report: Domestic War Crime Trials 2003*, at 6–7 (June 22, 2004) (reporting, among other things, that 90 percent of Serbs were convicted *in absentia*). The percentage of Serb defendants convicted is also considerably higher than the percentage of Croat defendants convicted. *Id.* at 7.

[1501] *See Croatia's Top Court Orders War Crimes Retrial*, REUTERS, Aug. 19, 2004; Human Rights Watch, *Croatia: Conviction Spotlights Justice Failings*, at 1 (July 19, 2004), *available at* http://hrw.org/english/docs/2004/07/19/croati.9083.htm.

[1502] Human Rights Watch, *Sudan: National Courts Have Done Nothing on Darfur*, June 11, 2004, *available at* http://hrw.org/english/docs/2007/06/11/sudan16110.htm; *see also* Human Rights Watch, *Darfur: No Redress for Rape*, Apr. 7, 2008, *available at* http://hrw.org/english/docs/2008/04/03/darfur18424.htm.

[1503] *See, e.g.*, Amnesty International & Judicial System Monitoring Programme, *Indonesia & Timor-Leste, Justice for Timor-Leste: The Way Forward*, §§ 5–9, AI Index: ASA 21/006/2004 (Apr. 1, 2004).

[1504] Paul James-Allen, *Accessing Justice in Rural Sierra Leone: A Civil Society Response*, JUSTICE INITIATIVES 57, 57 (Feb. 2004).

Sierra Leone's judicial system can barely function – even in Freetown."[1505] Sierra Leone's formal judicial system had "ceased to function years before the war," and a decade of civil war left "this already compromised edifice a hollow shell."[1506]

East Timor's post-atrocity judicial system was equally inadequate. Indonesia had installed its own judges, lawyers, and prosecutors during its twenty-four-year occupation of East Timor, and all of them returned to Indonesia following East Timor's independence referendum. Consequently, after the violence, it was estimated that fewer than ten very inexperienced lawyers remained in East Timor. In addition, virtually all of the court buildings were in rubble, and the equipment, furniture, registers, records, and archives as well as law books and case files had been lost or burned during the violence.[1507] Even the Rwandan criminal justice system, which seemed to function at a higher level than Sierra Leone's or East Timor's before their respective atrocities, was nearly crushed under the weight of the genocide cases. Within two years of the genocide, Rwanda had arrested and imprisoned approximately 130,000 people.[1508] Many of these defendants were detained for years in overcrowded prisons without access to legal counsel. Some were never formally charged or even verbally informed of their alleged crimes.[1509] By 2001, the Rwandan criminal justice system's complete inability to process these genocide cases was apparent and led to the establishment of informal community tribunals, called *gacaca*. Although the use of *gacaca* has helped Rwanda to process genocide cases more rapidly, it has not substantially ameliorated the fact-finding difficulties plaguing those proceedings. G*acaca* judges are regularly accused of accepting bribes to influence their legal determinations,[1510] *gacaca* witnesses are regularly subject to violent retaliation for their testimony,[1511] and

1505 Niobe Thompson, *In Pursuit of Justice: A Report on the Judiciary in Sierra Leone*, COMMONWEALTH HUMAN RIGHTS INITIATIVE 10 (2002).

1506 Zainab Hawa Bangura, *Sierra Leone: Ordinary Courts and the Special Court*, JUSTICE INITIATIVES 54, 55 (Feb. 2005).

1507 Strohmeyer, note 1179, at 172; *see also* Dionísio Babo-Soares, *Law and Order: Judiciary Development in East Timor*, at 9, CONFERENCE PAPER FOR CONFERENCE ON COMPARING EXPERIENCES WITH POST-CONFLICT STATE BUILDING IN ASIA AND EUROPE, Denpasar, Bali-Indonesia, Oct. 15–17, 2001 (on file with author).

1508 Drumbl, *Rule of Law Amid Lawlessness*, note 9, at 571; Penal Reform International, *PRI Research Team on Gacaca: Report IV* (Jan. 2003), at 3 [hereinafter *PRI Research Team on Gacaca*]; Michael T. Johnson et al., *American Lawyers In Rwanda Offer Tools to Tame Chaos*, 16 CRIM. JUST. 34, 34 (2001).

1509 *See generally* Amnesty International, *Rwanda: The Troubled Course of Justice*, AI-index AFR 47/010/2000 (Apr. 4, 2000).

1510 Christopher J. Le Mon, *Rwanda's Troubled Gacaca Courts*, 14 HUM. RTS. BRIEF 16, 17 (2007).

1511 *See* Karen McVeigh, *Spate of Killings Obstructs Rwanda's Quest for Justice*, THE OBSERVER (London), Dec. 3, 2006; *Gacaca Witness' House Set Ablaze*, THE NEW TIMES (Kigali), Oct. 22, eyewitness accusations and denials are bandied about before *gacaca* judges who have no ability to investigate the allegations.[1512] Although this is not the forum to engage in a comprehensive comparison between domestic and international trial mechanisms, the foregoing suggests that there is little reason to believe that recourse to domestic mechanisms will substantially enhance fact-finding accuracy.

Determining that domestic prosecutions constitute no ready alternative to international prosecutions forces us to confront head-on the most difficult question of all: Are we better off conducting international trials, with all their flaws, than conducting no trials at all? Unfortunately, the fact-finding flaws that I have identified are not international criminal justice's only flaws. Indeed, as I note in Chapter 6, various scholars have begun to question whether international criminal justice can advance many of the goals that it purports to advance. These studies raise worrisome questions, and they did not even contemplate the fact-finding deficiencies that form the subject of this work. That is, it is troubling enough if international criminal punishment cannot meet its penological goals when we have confidence that punishment is being imposed on the correct individuals. To the extent we have reason to question whether the recipients of that punishment should be receiving it, then the value of international trials declines further still. To put it another way, although I have recommended various substantive and procedural adaptations in Chapters 9 and 10, I recognize that some stand as still more distasteful compromises that international criminal justice must embrace if it is to survive. At their core, the work of such scholars as Martti Koskenniemi and Mark Drumbl question whether international criminal justice should survive. That is a much broader question than I can contemplate in this work, but what I can say is that my conclusions impact the answer that one gives to that question just as the critiques of other scholars impact my view of the normative effect of fact-finding deficiencies. Indeed, just as past scholars have delivered their critiques all the while assuming a fact-finding competence that international tribunals do not possess, my normative assessment of the tribunals' fact-finding deficiencies assumes that international criminal trials are valuable endeavors. But just how valuable and for what purposes are questions that I believe to be unanswerable at present. In his careful and sophisticated response to the critiques of Drumbl and Koskenniemi, Larry May points out both the limits of our current knowledge of the efficacy of international criminal punishment and the

2006; Steven Baguma, *Genocide Survivor Boycotts Gacaca, Cites Harassment*, The New Times (Kigali), Nov. 16, 2006; Steven Baguma, *Gacaca Witnesses Attacked*, The New Times (Kigali), Dec. 18, 2006.

[1512] *PRI Research Team on Gacaca*, at 8–10 (noting that *gacaca* does not have the resources to verify or investigate defendants' confessions).

lack of viable alternatives thereto.[1513] In my view, these factors together make a compelling case for the international criminal justice project persevering at least for the time being. And although the problems discussed in this book by no means enhance prospects for the long-term success of the international criminal justice project, I also do not believe them to doom the endeavor to failure.

[1513] MAY, AGGRESSION, note 11, at 319–41.

Bibliography

ARTICLES

Akhavan, Payam, *Justice and Reconciliation in the Great Lakes Region of Africa: The Contribution of the International Criminal Tribunal for Rwanda*, 7 Duke J. Comp. & Int'l L. 325 (1997)

Akhavan, Payam, *Justice in The Hague, Peace in the Former Yugoslavia? A Commentary on the United Nations War Crimes Tribunal*, 20 Hum. Rts. Q. 737 (1998)

Akhavan, Payam, *The International Criminal Court in Context: Mediating the Global and Local in the Age of Accountability*, 97 Am. J. Int'l L. 712 (2003)

Allen, Ronald J., *The Restoration of* In Re Winship: *A Comment on Burdens of Persuasion in Criminal Cases After* Patterson v. New York, 76 Mich. L. Rev. 30 (1977)

Allen, Ronald J., *Factual Ambiguity and a Theory of Evidence*, 88 N.W. U. L. Rev. 604 (1994)

Alvarez, José E., *Crimes of State/Crimes of Hate: Lessons from Rwanda*, 24 Yale J. Int'l L. 365 (1999)

Ambos, Kai, *International Criminal Procedure: "Adversarial," "Inquisitorial" or Mixed*, 3 Int'l Crim. L. Rev. 1 (2003)

Ambos, Kai, *Joint Criminal Enterprise and Command Responsibility*, 5 J. Int'l Crim. Just. 159 (2007)

Babo-Soares, Dionísio, *Law and Order: Judiciary Development in East Timor*, Conference Paper for Conference on Comparing Experiences with Post-Conflict State Building in Asia and Europe, Denpasar, Bali-Indonesia, Oct. 15–17, 2001

Babo-Soares, Dionísio, Nahe Biti: *The Philosophy and Process of Grassroots Reconciliation (and Justice) in East Timor*, 5 Asia Pacific J. Anthropology 15 (2004)

Bangura, Zainab H., *Sierra Leone: Ordinary Courts and the Special Court*, Justice Initiatives 54 (Feb. 2005)

Bantekas, Ilias, *The Iraqi Special Tribunal for Crimes Against Humanity*, 54 Int'l & Comp. L. Q. 237 (2005)

Bassiouni, M. *Cherif, Justice and Peace: The Importance of Choosing Accountability over Realpolitik*, 35 Case W. Res. J. Int'l L. 191 (2003)

Blakey, G. Robert, *The RICO Civil Fraud Action in Context: Reflections on* Bennett v. Berg, 58 Notre Dame L. Rev. 237 (1982)

Brigham, John C., et al., *The Effect of Arousal on Facial Recognition*, 4 Bas. Applied Soc. Psychol. 279 (1983)

Brilmayer, Lea, & Lewis Kornhauser, *Quantitative Methods and Legal Decisions*, 46 U. Chi. L. Rev. 116 (1978)
Bringer, Peter, *The Abiding Influence of English and French Criminal Law in One African Country: Some Remarks Regarding the Machinery of Criminal Justice in Cameroon*, 25 J. African L. 1 (1981)
Brouwer, G. E. P., *Inquisitorial and Adversary Procedures–A Comparative Analysis*, 55 Australian L.J. 207 (1981)
Brown, Peter, *Society and the Supernatural: A Medieval Change*, 104 Dædalus 133 (1975)
Carcano, Andrea, *Sentencing and the Gravity of the Offense in International Criminal Law*, 51 Int'l & Comp. L. Q. 583 (2002)
Carson, David, *Regulating the Examination of Children*, 4(1) Expert Evidence 2 (1995)
Carter, Cathleen A., et al., *Linguistic and Socioemotional Influences on the Accuracy of Children's Reports*, 20 Human Behavior 335 (1996)
Cassese, Antonio, *On the Current Trends Towards Criminal Prosecution and Punishment of Breaches of International Humanitarian Law*, 9 Eur. J. Int'l L. 2 (1998)
Cassese, Antonio, *Reflections on International Criminal Justice*, 61 Mod. L. Rev. 1 (1998)
Cassese, Antonio, *The Proper Limits of Individual Responsibility Under the Doctrine of Joint Criminal Enterprise*, 5 J. Int'l Crim. Just. 109 (2007)
Chase, Oscar G., *Legal Processes and National Culture*, 5 Cardozo J. Int'l & Comp. L. 1 (1997)
Chin, William Y., *Multiple Cultures, One Criminal Justice System: The Need for a "Cultural Ombudsman" in the Courtroom*, 53 Drake L. Rev. 651 (2005)
Christianson, Sven-Ake, & Elizabeth F. Loftus, *Memory for Traumatic Events*, 1 Applied Cogn. Psychol. 225 (1987)
Cissé, Catherine, *The International Tribunals for the Former Yugoslavia and Rwanda: Some Elements of Comparison*, 7 Transnat'l L. & Contemp. Probs. 105 (1997)
Clark, Jennifer J., *Zero to Life: Sentencing Appeals at the International Criminal Tribunals for the Former Yugoslavia and Rwanda*, 96 Geo. L.J. 1685 (2008)
Clifford, Brian R., & Clive R. Hollin, *Effects of Type of Incident and the Number of Perpetrators on Eyewitness Memory*, 66 J. Applied Psychol. 364 (1981)
Cohen, David, *Seeking Justice on the Cheap: Is the East Timor Tribunal Really a Model for the Future?* Asia Pacific Issues No. 61 (East-West Center, 2002)
Cohen, David, *Indifference and Accountability: The United Nations and the Politics of International Justice in East Timor*, East-West Center Special Reports, No. 9 (June 2006)
Cole, Richard W., & Laura Maslow-Armand, *The Role of Counsel and the Courts in Addressing Foreign Language and Cultural Barriers at Different Stages of a Criminal Proceeding*, 19 W. New Eng. L. Rev. 193 (1997)
Combs, Nancy Amoury, *Copping a Plea to Genocide: The Plea Bargaining of International Crimes*, 151 U. Pa. L. Rev. 1 (2002)
Conley, John M., et al., *The Power of Language: Presentation Style in the Courtroom*, 1978 Duke L. J. 1375 (1978)
Cooke, Michael, *Interpreting in a Cross-Cultural Examination: An Aboriginal Case Study*, 113 Int'l J. of the Soc. of Language 99 (1995)
Currie, Robert J., *Abducted Fugitives Before the International Criminal Court: Problems and Prospects*, 18 Crim. L. Forum 349 (2007)

Curtin, Phillip J., *Comment, Genocide in East Timor? Calling for an International Criminal Tribunal for East Timor in Light of Akayesu*, 19 Dick. J. Int'l L. 181 (2000)
Daly, Mary C., *Some Thoughts on the Differences in Criminal Trials in the Civil and Common Law Legal Systems*, 2 J. Inst. Study Legal Ethics 65 (1999)
Damaška, Mirjan, *Evidentiary Barriers to Conviction and Two Models of Criminal Procedure: A Comparative Study*, 121 U. Pa. L. Rev. 506 (1973)
Damaška, Mirjan, *Presentation of Evidence and Factfinding Precision*, 123 U. Pa. L. Rev. 1083 (1975)
Damaška, Mirjan, *Of Hearsay and Its Analogues*, 76 Minn. L. Rev. 425 (1992)
Damaška, Mirjan, *Truth in Adjudication*, 49 Hastings L. J. 289 (1998)
D'Amato, Anthony, *Peace vs. Accountability in Bosnia*, 88 Am. J. Int'l L. 500 (1994)
Dane, Francis C., *In Search of Reasonable Doubt: A Systematic Examination of Selected Quantification Approaches*, 9 L. & Hum. Behav. 141 (1985)
Danner, Allison M., & Jenny S. Martinez, *Guilty Associations: Joint Criminal Enterprise, Command Responsibility, and the Development of International Criminal Law*, 93 Cal. L. Rev. 75 (2005)
de Bertodano, Sylvia, *Current Developments in Internationalized Courts*, 1 J. Int'l Crim. Just. 226 (2003)
DeKay, Michael, *The Difference Between Blackstone-Like Error Ratios and Probabilistic Standards of Proof*, 21 L. & Soc. Inquiry 95 (1996)
Del Ponte, Carla, *Investigation and Prosecution of Large-Scale Crimes at the International Level: The Experience of the ICTY*, 4 J. Int'l Crim. Just. 539 (2006)
Dembour, Marie-Benedicte, & Emily Haslan, *Silencing Hearings? Victim-Witnesses at War Crimes Trials*, 15 Eur. J. Int'l L. 151 (2004)
Dent, Helen R., *Stress as a Factor in Influencing Person Recognition in Identification Parades*, 30 Bull. of the Brit. Psychol. Soc. 339 (1977)
De Turck, Mark A., & Gerald R. Miller, *Training Observers to Detect Deception: Effects of Self-Monitoring and Rehearsal*, 16 Hum. Comm. Q. 420 (1990)
Devine, Dennis J., et al., *Jury Decision Making: 45 Years of Empirical Research on Deliberating Groups*, 7 Psychiatry, Pub. Policy & L. 622 (2001)
Dickinson, Laura A., *The Promise of Hybrid Courts*, 97 Am. J. Int'l L. 295 (2003)
Drumbl, Mark A., *Rule of Law Amid Lawlessness: Counseling the Accused in Rwanda's Domestic Genocide Trials*, 29 Colum. Hum. Rts. L. Rev. 545 (1998)
Eades, Diana, *Legal Recognition of Cultural Differences in Communication: The Case of Robyn Kina*, 16 Language & Communication 215 (1996)
Eaton, Shana, *Sierra Leone: The Proving Ground for Prosecuting Rape as a War Crime*, 35 Geo. J. Int'l L. 873 (2004)
Ekman, Paul, & Maureen O'Sullivan, *Who Can Catch a Liar?*, 46 Am. Psychologist 913 (1991)
Ellison, Louise, *The Mosaic Art: Cross-Examination and the Vulnerable Witness*, 21 Legal Studies 353 (2001)
Ellison, Louise, *Cross Examination and the Intermediary: Bridging the Language Divide*, Crim. L. Rev. 14 (Feb. 2002)
Epstein, David M., *Advance Notice of Alibi*, 55 J. Crim. L. Criminology 29 (1964)
Erny, Pierre, *L'esprit de l'éducation au Rwanda ou le "caractère national" décrit par un groupe d'étudiants*, Geneve-Afrique, vol. XXI no.1, 25 (Michele Slachetka trans., 1983)

Fairlie, Megan, *The Marriage of Common and Continental Law at the ICTY and Its Progeny*, 4 INT'L CRIM. L. REV. 243 (2004)
Fisher, Talia, *The Boundaries of Plea Bargaining: Negotiating the Standard of Proof*, 97 J. CRIM. L. & CRIMINOLOGY 943 (2007)
Fletcher, Laurel, *From Indifference to Engagement: Bystanders and International Criminal Justice*, 26 MICH. J. INT'L L. 1013 (2004–2005)
Fletcher, Laurel, & Harvey Weinstein, *Violence and Social Repair: Rethinking the Contribution of Justice to Reconciliation*, 24 HUM. RTS. Q. 573 (2002)
Frase, Richard S., *The Search for the Whole Truth About American and European Criminal Justice*, 3 BUFF. CRIM. L. REV. 785 (2000)
Frase, Richard S., *Comparative Criminal Justice as a Guide to American Law Reform: How Do the French Do It, How Can We Find Out, and Why Should We Care?*, 78 CAL. L. REV. 539 (1990)
Frase, Richard S., & Thomas Weigend, *German Criminal Justice as a Guide to American Law Reform: Similar Problems, Better Solutions?*, 18 B.C. INT'L & COMP. L. REV. 317 (1995)
Freedman, Monroe H., *Professional Responsibility of the Criminal Defense Lawyer: The Three Hardest Questions*, 64 MICH. L. REV. 1469 (1966)
Fyle, C. M., & Isabella Heroe, *Krio Traditional Beliefs*, 7 AFRICANA RESEARCH BULL. 3 (1977)
Garrett, Brandon L., *Judging Innocence*, 108 COLUM. L. REV. 55 (2008)
Garro, Alejandro Miguel, & Enrique Dahl, *Legal Accountability for Human Rights Violations in Argentina: One Step Forward and Two Steps Backward*, 8 HUM. RTS. L.J. 283 (1987)
Gee, James Paul, *The Narrativization of Experience in the Oral Style*, 167 J. EDUC. 9 (1985)
Geiselman, R. E., et al., *Enhancement of Eyewitness Memory with the Cognitive Interview*, 99 AM. J. OF PSYCHOL. 385 (1986)
Goldsmith, Jack, *The Self-Defeating International Criminal Court*, 70 U. CHI. L. REV. 89 (2003)
Goldsmith, Jack, & Stephen Krasner, *The Limits of Idealism*, DÆDALUS, 47 Winter 2003
Goldstock, Ronald, and Dan T. Coenen, *Controlling the Contemporary Loanshark: The Law of Illicit Lending and the Problem of Witness Fear*, 65 CORNELL L. REV. 127 (1980)
Goldstone, Richard, *Conference Luncheon Address*, 7 TRANSNAT'L L. & CONTEMP. PROBS. 1 (1997)
Goodman, Gail S., et al., *Face-to Face Confrontation: Effects of Closed-Circuit Technology on Children's Eyewitness Testimony and Juror's Decisions*, 22 L. & HUMAN BEHAVIOR 165 (1998)
Griffiths, Anne, *Legal Duality: Conflict or Concord in Botswana*, 27 J. AFRICAN L. 150 (1983)
Groot, Roger D., *The Jury of Presentment Before 1215*, 26 AM. J. LEGAL HIST. 1 (1982)
Gustafson, Katrina, *The Requirement of an "Express Agreement" for Joint Criminal Liability: A Critique of Brđanin*, 5 J. INT'L CRIM. JUST. 134 (2007)
Haffajee, Rebecca L., *Note, Prosecuting Crimes of Rape and Sexual Violence at the ICTR: The Application of Joint Criminal Enterprise Theory*, 29 HARV. J. L. GENDER 201 (2006)
Hamer, David A., *The Presumption of Innocence and Reverse Burdens: A Balancing Act*, 66 CAMBRIDGE L. J. 142 (2007)

Harmon, Mark B., & Fergal Gaynor, *Ordinary Sentences for Extraordinary Crimes*, 5 J. INT'L CRIM. JUST. 683 (2007)

Herrmann, Joachim, *Bargaining Justice – A Bargain for German Criminal Justice?*, 53 U. PITT. L. REV. 755 (1992)

Hohe, Tanja, & Rod Nixon, *Reconciling Justice: "Traditional" Law and State Judiciary in East Timor, Paper prepared for the United States Institute of Peace and delivered at the workshop on the Working of Non-State Justice Systems, held at the Development Institute*, Brighton U.K. (Mar. 6–7, 2003)

Horwitz, Solis, *The Tokyo Trial*, 28 INT'L CONCILIATION 473 (1950)

Hurnard, Naomi D., *The Jury of Presentment and the Assize of Clarendon*, 56 ENG. HIST. REV. 374 (1941)

Jackson, Michael D., *Structure and Event: Witchcraft Confession Among the Kuranko*, 10 J. ROYAL ANTHROPOL. INST. (MAN) 387 (1975)

James-Allen, Paul, *Accessing Justice in Rural Sierra Leone: A Civil Society Response*, JUSTICE INITIATIVES 57 (Feb. 2004)

Jearey, J. H., *The Structure, Composition and Jurisdiction of Courts and Authorities Enforcing the Criminal Law in British African Territories*, 9 INT'L & COMP. L. Q. 396 (1960)

Johnson, Michael T., et al., *American Lawyers in Rwanda Offer Tools to Tame Chaos*, 16 CRIM. JUST. 34 (2001)

Kabbah, Hanatu, *Sierra Leone Legal System and Legal Research*, GLOBAL LEX, *available at*: www.nyulawglobal.org/Globalex/Sierra_Leone1.htm

Kaplan, John, *Decision Theory and the Factfinding Process*, 20 STAN. L. REV. 1065 (1968)

Karton, Joshua, *Lost in Translation: International Criminal Tribunals and the Legal Implications of Interpreted Testimony*, 65 VAND. J. TRANSNAT'L L. 1 (2008)

Kassin, Saul M., *Eyewitness Identification: Victims Versus Bystanders*, 14 J. APPLIED SOC. PSYCHOL. 519 (1984)

Katzenstein, Suzanne, *Note, Hybrid Tribunals: Searching for Justice in East Timor*, 16 HARV. HUM. RTS. J. 245 (2003)

Kitai, Rinat, *Protecting the Guilty*, 6 BUFF. CRIM. L. REV. 1163 (2003)

Klabbers, Jan, *Just Revenge? The Deterrence Argument in International Criminal Law*, XII FINNISH Y.B. INT'L L. 249 (2001)

Klamer, Marian, *Typical Features of Austronesian Languages in Central/Eastern Indonesia*, 41 OCEANIC LINGUISTICS 363 (Dec. 2002)

Koskenniemi, Martti, *Between Impunity and Show Trials*, 6 MAX PLANCK Y.B. U.N. L. 1 (2002)

Kotz, Hein, *Civil Justice Systems In Europe and the United States*, 13 DUKE J. COMP. & INT'L L. 61 (2003)

Kowalski, Tara C., Note, *Alvarado v. Superior Court: A Death Sentence for Government Witnesses*, 35 U. C. DAVIS L. REV. 207 (2001)

Ku, Julian, & Jide Nzelibe, *Do International Criminal Tribunals Deter or Exacerbate Humanitarian Atrocities?*, 84 WASH. U. L. REV. 777 (2007)

Lakoff, Robin Tolmach, *Women's Language*, 10 LANGUAGE & STYLE 222 (1977)

Landsman, Stephan, *Alternative Responses to Serious Human Rights Abuses: Of Prosecution and Truth Commissions*, 59 L. & CONTEMP. PROBS. 81 (1996)

Langbein, John H., *The Criminal Trial Before the Lawyers*, 45 UNIV. CHI. L. REV 263 (1978)

Langer, Máximo, *The Rise of Managerial Judging in International Criminal Law*, 53 AM. J. COMP. L. 835 (2005)
Langer, Máximo, & Joseph W. Doherty, *A Sisyphean Task? An Empirical Assessment of the Managerial Judging Reforms to Expedite the Procedure of the International Criminal Tribunal for the Former Yugoslavia* (forthcoming 2010)
Lempert, Richard O., *Modeling Relevance*, 75 MICH. L. REV. 1021 (1977)
Le Mon, Christopher J., *Rwanda's Troubled Gacaca Courts*, 14 HUM. RTS. BRIEF 16 (2007)
Lerner, Renée L., *The Intersection of Two Systems: An American on Trial for an American Murder in the French Cour D'Assises*, 2001 U. ILL. L. REV. 791 (2001)
Leventhal, Harold, et al., *The Nuernberg Verdict*, 60 HARV. L. REV. 857 (1947)
Lillquist, Erik, *Recasting Reasonable Doubt: Decision Theory and the Virtues of Variability*, 36 U. C. DAVIS L. REV. 85 (2002)
Linton, Suzannah, *Correspondents' Reports*, 2 Y.B. OF INT'L HUM. L. 471 (2000)
Linton, Suzannah, *Cambodia, East Timor and Sierra Leone: Experiments in International Justice*, 12 CRIM. L. F. 185 (2001)
Linton, Suzannah, & Caitlin Reiger, *The Evolving Jurisprudence and Practice of East Timor's Special Panels for Serious Crimes on Admissions of Guilt, Duress and Superior Orders*, 4 Y.B. OF INT'L HUM. L. 1 (2001)
Littlejohn, James, *Temne Space*, 36 ANTHROPOLOGICAL Q. 1 (1963)
Mack, Kathy, *An Australian Perspective on Feminism, Race and Evidence*, 28 S.W. U. L. REV. 367 (1999)
Malamud-Goti, Jaime, *Transitional Governments in the Breach: Why Punish State Criminals?* 12 HUM. RTS. Q. 1 (1990)
Mass, Stuart, Note, *The Dilemma of the Intimidated Witness in Federal Organized Crime Prosecutions: Choosing Among the Fear of Reprisals, The Contempt Powers of the Court, and the Witness Protection Program*, 50 FORDHAM L. REV. 582 (1982)
McEwan, Jenny, *In Defense of Vulnerable Witnesses: The Youth Justice and Criminal Evidence Act* 1999, 4 INT'L J. EVID. & PROOF 1 (2000)
McKillop, Bron, *Anatomy of a French Murder Case*, 45 AM. J. COMP. L. 527 (1997)
Mearns, David, *Looking Both Ways: Models for Justice in East Timor*, AUSTRALIAN LEGAL RESOURCES INTERNATIONAL PUBLICATION (Nov. 2002)
Meltzer, Bernard D., *War Crimes: The Nuremberg Trial and the Tribunal for the Former Yugoslavia*, 30 VAL. U. L. REV. 895 (1996)
Meron, Theodor, *Procedure Evolution in the ICTY*, 2 J. INT'L CRIM. JUST. 520 (2004)
Mikkelson, Holly, *Towards a Redefinition of the Role of the Court Interpreter*, 3 INTERPRETING 21 (1998)
Mikkelson, Holly, *Verbatim Interpretation: an Oxymoron, available at*: www.acebo.com/papers/verbatim.htm
Morano, Anthony, *A Re-examination of the Development of the Reasonable Doubt Rule*, 55 B.U. L. REV. 507 (1975)
Morgan, Charles A. III, et al., *Accuracy of Eyewitness Memory for Persons Encountered During Exposure to Highly Intense Stress*, 27 INT'L J. L. & PSYCHIATRY 265 (2004)
Moston, Stephen, & Terry Engelberg, *The Effects of Social Support on Children's Eyewitness Testimony*, 6 APPLIED COGNITIVE PSYCHOL. 61 (1992)
Mundis, Daryl A., *Improving the Operation and Functioning of the International Criminal Tribunals*, 94 AM. J. INT'L L. 759 (2000)

Murphy, Sean D., *Progress and Jurisprudence of the International Criminal Tribunal for the Former Yugoslavia*, 93 AM. J. INT'L L. 57 (1999)
Murphy, Sean D., ed., *Contemporary Practice of the United States Relating to International Law*, 95 AM. J. INT'L L. 387 (2001)
Nance, Dale A., *Naturalized Epistemology and the Critique of Evidence Theory*, 87 VA. L. REV. 1551 (2001)
Newman, Jon O., *Beyond "Reasonable Doubt,"* 68 N.Y.U. L. REV. 979 (1993)
Nice, Geoffrey, & Philippe Vallières-Roland, *Procedural Innovations in War Crime Trials*, 3 J. INT'L CRIM. JUST. 354 (2005)
Nishimuko, Mikako, *Access to Primary Education in Sierra Leone, the Perceived Gap Between Policy and Practice and the Role of Religious Affiliation and British Aid*, 6 EDUCATE 32 (2006)
Norman, Steve, *Assessing the Credibility of Refugee Applicants: A Judicial Perspective*, 19 INT'L J. REFUGEE L. 273 (2007)
Ohlin, Jens D., *Three Conceptual Problems with the Doctrine of Joint Criminal Enterprise*, 5 J. INT'L CRIM. JUST. 69 (2007)
Orentlicher, Diane F., *Settling Accounts: The Duty to Prosecute Human Rights Violations of a Prior Regime*, 100 YALE L.J. 2537 (1991)
O'Rourke, Allen, *Recent Development, Joint Criminal Enterprise and Brđanin: Misguided Overcorrection*, 47 HARV. INT'L L. J. 307 (2006)
Orth, Uli, *Secondary Victimization of Crime Victims by Criminal Proceedings*, 15 SOC. JUST. RES. 313 (2002)
Osiel, Mark, *The Banality of Good: Aligning Incentives Against Mass Atrocity*, 105 COLUM. L. REV. 1751 (2005)
Overdulve, C. M., *Fonction de la langue et de la communication au Rwanda*, 53 NOUVELLE REVUE DE SCIENCE MISSIONNAIRE, 271 (Michele Slachetka trans., 1997)
Penrose, Mary Margaret, *Lest We Fail: The Importance of Enforcement in International Criminal Law*, 15 AM. U. INT'L L. Rev. 321 (1999)
Perry, Nancy W., et al., *When Lawyers Question Children, Is Justice Served?*, 19 L. & HUM. BEHAV. 609 (1995)
Ploscowe, Morris, *The Development of Present-Day Criminal Procedures in Europe and America*, 48 HARV. L. REV. 433 (1935)
Posner, Richard A., *An Economic Approach to the Law of Evidence*, 51 STAN. L. REV. 1477 (1999)
Rand, Joseph W., *The Demeanor Gap: Race, Lie Detection, and the Jury*, 33 CONN. L. REV. 1 (2000)
Ramer, Jacob A., *Hate by Association: Joint Criminal Enterprise Liability for Persecution*, 7 CHI.-KENT J. INT'L & COMP. L. 31 (2007)
Rapp, Stephen J., *Achieving Accountability for the Greatest Crimes: The Legacy of the International Tribunals*, 55 DRAKE L. REV. 259 (2007)
Reskin, Barbara F., & Christy A. Visher, *The Impacts of Evidence and Extralegal Factors in Jurors' Decisions*, 20 L. & SOC'Y REV. 423 (1986)
Reydams, Luc, *International Decision:* Niyonteze v. Public Prosecutor, 96 AM. J. INT'L L. 231 (2002)
Rigney, Azucena C., *Questioning in Interpreted Testimony*, 6 FORENSIC LINGUISTICS 83 (1999)
Rimmer, Susan Harris, *"Orphans" or Veterans?: Justice for Children Born of War in East Timor*, 42 TEX. INT'L L.J. 323 (2007)

Robinson, Patrick L., *Ensuring Fair and Expeditious Trials at the International Criminal Tribunal for the Former Yugoslavia*, 11 Eur. J. Int'l L. 569 (2000)

Rukebesha, Aloys, *Esotérisme et Communication Sociale au Rwanda: Rukebesha nous parle de son ouvrage*, 35 La Relève 3 (Michele Slachetka trans., 1985)

Ruppel, Joanna, *The Need for a Benefit of the Doubt Standard in Credibility Evaluation of Asylum Applicants*, 23 Colum. Hum. Rts. L. Rev. 1 (1992)

Sadat, Leila N., & S. Richard Carden, *The New International Criminal Court: An Uneasy Revolution*, 88 Geo. L.J. 381 (2000)

Schabas, William A., *Genocide Trials and Gacaca Courts*, 3 J. Int'l Crim. Just. 879 (2005)

Shenk, Maury D., et al., *International Criminal Tribunals for the Former Yugoslavia and for Rwanda*, 35 Int'l L. 622 (2001)

Sholar, Monica Hersh Khetarpal, *Jurors' Perceptions of Gender-Based Linguistic Differences*, 10 Wm & Mary J. of Women & L. 91 (2003)

Sidahmed, Abdel S., *Problems in Contemporary Applications of Islamic Criminal Sanctions: The Penalty for Adultery in Relation to Women*, 28 Brit. J. Middle Eastern Studies 187 (2001)

Simon, Rita J., *Judges' Translations of Burdens of Proof into Statements of Probability*, 1969 Trial Law. Guide 103

Simon, Rita J., *"Beyond a Reasonable Doubt" – An Experimental Attempt at Quantification*, 6 J. Applied Behav. Sci. 203 (No. 2, 1970)

Simon, Rita James, & Linda Mahan, *Quantifying Burdens of Proof: A View from the Bench, the Jury and the Classroom*, 5 Law & Soc'y Rev. 319 (1971)

Simonović, Ivan, *Dealing with the Legacy of Past War Crimes and Human Rights Abuses*, 2 J. Int'l Crim. Just. 701 (2004)

Skilbeck, Rupert, *Defending the Khmer Rouge*, 8 Int. Crim. L. Rev. 423 (2008)

Sluiter, Goran, *Due Process and Criminal Procedures in the Cambodian Extraordinary Chambers*, 4 J. Int'l Crim. Just. 314 (2006)

Sriram, Chandra L., *Revolutions in Accountability: New Approaches to Past Abuses*, 19 Am. U. Int'l L. Rev. 301 (2003)

Strawn, David, & Raymond Buchanan, *Jury Confusion: A Threat to Justice*, 59 Judicature 478 (1976)

Strier, Franklin D., *Major Problems Endemic to the Adversary System and Proposed Reforms*, 19 Western St. U. L. Rev. 463 (1992)

Strohmeyer, Hansjörg, *Policing the Peace: Post Conflict Judicial System Reconstruction in East Timor*, 24 U. New S. Wales L.J. 171 (2001)

Supernor, Major Christopher M., *International Bounty Hunters for War Criminals: Privatizing the Enforcement of Justice*, 50 A.F. L. Rev. 215 (2001)

Sward, Ellen E., *Values, Ideology, and the Evolution of the Adversary System*, 64 Ind. L.J. 301 (1989)

Taylor, Telford, *The Nuremberg Trials*, 55 Colum. L. Rev. 488 (1955)

Tomlinson, Edward A., *Nonadversarial Justice: The French Experience*, 42 Md. L. Rev. 131 (1983)

Tremblay, Paul R., *Interviewing and Counseling Across Cultures: Heuristics and Biases*, 9 Clinical L. Rev. 373 (2002)

Tribe, Laurence H., *An Ounce of Detention: Preventative Justice in the World of John Mitchell*, 56 Va. L. Rev. 371 (1970)

Turner, Jenia I., *Civil Party Participation in Provisional Detention Appeals: Extraordinary Chambers in the Courts of Cambodia*, 103 AM. J. INT'L L. 116 (2009)
van Kessel, Gordon, *Adversary Excesses in the American Criminal Trial*, 67 NOTRE DAME L. REV. 403 (1992)
van Sliedregt, Elies, *Joint Criminal Enterprise as a Pathway to Convicting Individuals for Genocide*, 5 J. INT'L CRIM. JUST. 184 (2007)
Wald, Patricia, *General Radislav Krstić: A War Crimes Case Study*, 16 GEO. J. LEGAL ETHICS 445 (2003)
Wald, Patricia, *Running the Trial of the Century: The Nuremberg Legacy*, 7 CARDOZO L. REV. 1559 (2006)
Wald, Patricia M., *To "Establish Incredible Events by Credible Evidence:" The Use of Affidavit Testimony in Yugoslavia War Crimes Tribunal Proceedings*, 42 HARV. INT'L L.J. 535 (2001)
Waldorf, Lars, *Mass Justice for Mass Atrocity: Rethinking Local Justice as Transitional Justice*, 79 TEMPLE L. REV. 1 (2006)
Walker, Anne G., *Questioning Young Children in Court: A Linguistic Case Study*, 17 L. & HUM. BEHAV. 59 (1993)
Wellborn, Olin Guy III, *Demeanor*, 76 CORNELL L. REV. 1075 (1991)
Weschler, Herbert, *The Issues of the Nuremberg Trial*, 62 POL. SCI. Q. 11 (1947)
Wise, Edward M., *RICO and Its Analogues: Some Comparative Considerations*, 27 SYRACUSE J. INT'L L. & COM. 303 (2000)
Wray, Kenneth R., *The Adaptation of Imported Law in Africa*, 4 J. AFRICAN L. 66 (1960)
Zahar, Alexander, *The ICTR's Media Judgement and the Reinvention of Direct and Public Incitement to Genocide*, 16 CRIM. L. FORUM 33 (2005)

BOOKS

BARTLETT, ROBERT, TRIAL BY FIRE AND WATER: THE MEDIEVAL JUDICIAL ORDEAL (1986)
BELLMAN, BERYL L., THE LANGUAGE OF SECRECY: SYMBOLS AND METAPHORS IN PORO RITUAL (1984)
BERK-SELIGSON, SUSAN, THE BILINGUAL COURTROOM: COURT INTERPRETERS IN THE JUDICIAL PROCESS (2002)
BLACKSTONE, WILLIAM, 4 COMMENTARIES ON THE LAWS OF ENGLAND (1769)
BOYLE, ROBERT, WORKS (1772)
BRACKMAN, ARNOLD C., THE OTHER NUREMBERG (1987)
BRENNAN, MARK, & ROSLIN E. BRENNAN, STRANGE LANGUAGE: CHILD VICTIMS UNDER CROSS-EXAMINATION (1998)
CASSESE, ANTONIO, INTERNATIONAL CRIMINAL LAW (2003)
CAROTHERS, THOMAS, AIDING DEMOCRACY ABROAD: THE LEARNING CURVE (1999)
COHEN, JOHN, & IAN CHRISTIANSEN, INFORMATION AND CHOICE (1970)
COMBS, NANCY A., GUILTY PLEAS IN INTERNATIONAL CRIMINAL LAW: CONSTRUCTING A RESTORATIVE JUSTICE APPROACH (2007)
CONOT, ROBERT E., JUSTICE AT NUREMBERG (1983)
COX, ARCHIBALD, THE WARREN COURT: CONSTITUTIONAL DECISION AS AN INSTRUMENT OF REFORM (1968)
CRAY, ED, CHIEF JUSTICE: A BIOGRAPHY OF EARL WARREN (1997)

Crepeau, Pierre, Parole et Sagesse: Valeurs Sociales dans les Proverbes du Rwanda (Michele Slachetka trans., 1985)
Cutler, Brian L., & Steven D. Penrod, Mistaken Identification: The Eyewitness, Psychology, and the Law (1995)
Damaška, Mirjan, The Faces of Justice and State Authority: A Comparative Approach to the Legal Process (1986)
Damaška, Mirjan, Evidence Law Adrift (1997)
Davidson, Eugene, The Trial of the Germans (1994)
Des Forges, Alison, Human Rights Watch, Leave None to Tell the Story: Genocide in Rwanda (1999)
de Lame, Danielle, A Hill Among a Thousand (2005)
The Demjanjuk Trial (Alex Felix Landau, ed., 1991)
Devitt, Edward J., et al., Federal Jury Practice and Instructions (4th ed. 1987)
Douglas, Lawrence, The Memory of Judgment: Making Law and History in the Trials of the Holocaust (2001)
Drumbl, Mark A., Atrocity, Punishment, and International Law (2007)
Dworkin, Ronald, A Matter of Principle (1986)
Ellison, Louise, The Adversarial Process and the Vulnerable Witness (2001)
Esmein, Adhemar, A History of Continental Criminal Procedure (1913, reprinted 1968)
Federal Judicial Center, Pattern Criminal Jury Instructions (1988)
Ferme, Mariane, The Underneath of Things: Violence, History, and the Everyday in Sierra Leone (2001)
Fletcher, George P., A Crime of Self-Defense: Bernhard Goetz and the Law on Trial (1988)
Forsyth, William, History of Trial by Jury (1875)
Freedman, Monroe H., Lawyers' Ethics in an Adversary System (1975)
Gaiba, Francesca, The Origins of Simultaneous Interpretation: The Nuremberg Trial (1998)
Gaskin, Hilary, Eyewitnesses at Nuremberg (1990)
Ginn, John L., Sugamo Prison, Tokyo: An Account of the Trial and Sentencing of Japanese War Criminals in 1948, by a U.S. Participant (1992)
Gittins, Anthony J., Mende Religion (1987)
Gourevitch, Philip, We Wish to Inform You That Tomorrow We Will Be Killed with Our Families: Stories from Rwanda (1998)
Green, Thomas A., Verdict According to Conscience: Perspectives on the English Criminal Trial Jury 1200–1800 (1985)
Hale, Matthew, The Primitive Origination of Mankind, Considered and Examined According to the Light of Nature (1677)
Hale, Matthew, Historia Placitorum Coronæ [The History of the Pleas of the Crown] (P. R. Glazebrook, ed., London: Prof'l Books 1971) (1736)
Hamilton, Alvin C., A Feather and Not a Gavel: Working Towards Aboriginal Justice (2001)
Hartmann, Florence, Paix et Châtiment (2007)
Hayner, Priscilla B., Unspeakable Truths (2001)

HAZAN, PIERRE, JUSTICE IN A TIME OF WAR: THE TRUE STORY BEHIND THE INTERNATIONAL CRIMINAL TRIBUNAL FOR THE FORMER YUGOSLAVIA (James Thomas Snyder, trans., 2004)

HUMAN RIGHTS WATCH, SHATTERED LIVES: SEXUAL VIOLENCE DURING THE RWANDAN GENOCIDE AND ITS AFTERMATH (1996)

JACKSON, ROBERT, THE NURNBERG CASE (1947)

JACQUEMET, MARCO, CREDIBILITY IN COURT: COMMUNICATIVE PRACTICES IN THE CAMORRA TRIAL (1996)

KALVEN, HARRY JR., & HANS ZEISEL, THE AMERICAN JURY (1966)

KANT, IMMANUEL, THE METAPHYSICAL ELEMENTS OF JUSTICE (John Ladd trans., 1965)

KELSALL, TIM, CULTURE UNDER CROSS-EXAMINATION: INTERNATIONAL JUSTICE AND THE SPECIAL COURT FOR SIERRA LEONE (2009)

LAFAVE, WAYNE R., ET AL., CRIMINAL PROCEDURE (4th ed., 2004)

LAKOFF, ROBIN, LANGUAGE AND WOMEN'S PLACE (1975)

LANDSMAN, STEPHAN, THE ADVERSARY SYSTEM: A DESCRIPTION AND DEFENSE (1984)

LANGBEIN, JOHN H., PROSECUTING CRIME IN THE RENAISSANCE (1974)

LANGBEIN, JOHN H., TORTURE AND THE LAW OF PROOF (1976)

LANGBEIN, JOHN H., THE ORIGINS OF THE ADVERSARY CRIMINAL TRIAL (2003)

LAUDAN, LARRY, TRUTH, ERROR, AND CRIMINAL LAW: AN ESSAY IN LEGAL EPISTEMOLOGY (2006)

LOFTUS, ELIZABETH, ET AL., EYEWITNESS TESTIMONY: CIVIL AND CRIMINAL (2007)

LUBAN, DAVID, LAWYERS AND JUSTICE: AN ETHICAL STUDY (1988)

LUBET, STEVEN, MODERN TRIAL ADVOCACY: ANALYSIS AND PRACTICE (1997)

MAGA, TIM, JUDGMENT AT TOKYO: THE JAPANESE WAR CRIMES TRIAL (2001)

MAIMONIDES, MOSES, THE COMMANDMENTS 270 (Charles B. Chavel, trans., 1967) (vol. 2)

MAUET, THOMAS A., TRIAL TECHNIQUES (6th ed., 2002)

MAY, LARRY, AGGRESSION AND CRIMES AGAINST PEACE (2008)

MAY, LARRY, CRIMES AGAINST HUMANITY: A NORMATIVE ACCOUNT (2005)

MAY, LARRY, WAR CRIMES AND JUST WAR (2007)

MCNALLY, RICHARD J., REMEMBERING TRAUMA (2003)

MELVERN, LINDA, CONSPIRACY TO MURDER: THE RWANDAN GENOCIDE (2004)

MERON, THEODOR, WAR CRIMES LAW COMES OF AGE (1998)

MINOW, MARTHA, BETWEEN VENGEANCE AND FORGIVENESS: FACING HISTORY AFTER GENOCIDE AND MASS VIOLENCE (1998)

MOGHALU, KINGSLEY CHIEDU, RWANDA'S GENOCIDE: THE POLITICS OF GLOBAL JUSTICE (2005)

MORRIS, VIRGINIA, & MICHAEL SCHARF, AN INSIDER'S GUIDE TO THE INTERNATIONAL CRIMINAL TRIBUNAL FOR THE FORMER YUGOSLAVIA (1995)

MORTON, JAMES C., & HUTCHISON, SCOTT C., THE PRESUMPTION OF INNOCENCE (1987)

NAGEL, STUART S., & MARIAN G. NEEF, DECISION THEORY AND THE LEGAL PROCESS (1979)

NOWAK, MANFRED, U.N. COVENANT ON CIVIL AND POLITICAL RIGHTS: CCPR COMMENTARY 255 (1993)

OSIEL, MARK, MASS ATROCITY, COLLECTIVE MEMORY AND THE LAW (1997)

OTHMAN, MOHAMED C., ACCOUNTABILITY FOR INTERNATIONAL HUMANITARIAN LAW VIOLATIONS: THE CASE OF RWANDA AND EAST TIMOR (2005)

Olusanya, Olaoluwa, Sentencing War Crimes and Crimes Against Humanity Under the International Criminal Tribunal for the Former Yugoslavia (2005)

Persico, Joseph E., Nuremberg: Infamy on Trial (1994)

Piccigallo, Philip R., The Japanese on Trial: Allied War Crimes Operations in the East 1945–1951 (1980)

Pizzi, William, Trials Without Truth: Why Our System of Criminal Trials Has Become an Expensive Failure and What We Need to Do to Rebuild It (1999)

Powe, Lucas, A. Jr., The Warren Court and American Politics (2000)

Proffatt, John, A Treatise on Trial by Jury (1877)

Ratner, Steven S., & Jason S. Abrams, Accountability for Human Rights Atrocities in International Law: Beyond the Nuremberg Legacy (1997)

Gerhard Robbers, An Introduction to German Law (1998)

The Tokyo Judgment: The International Military Tribunal for the Far East (B.V. A. Roling, & C. F. Ruter, eds., 1977)

Ross, Fiona C., Bearing Witness: Women and the Truth and Reconciliation Commission in South Africa (2003)

Rukebesha, Aloys, Ésotérisme et Communication Sociale (Michele Slachetka trans., 1985)

Scharf, Michael P., Balkan Justice (1997)

Shapiro, Barbara J., "Beyond Reasonable Doubt" and "Probable Cause": Historical Perspectives on the Anglo-American Law of Evidence (1991)

Shaw, Rosalind, Memories of the Slave Trade: Ritual and the Historical Imagination in Sierra Leone (2002)

Shepherd, John W., et al., Identification Evidence: A Psychological Evaluation (1982)

Smith, Bradley F., The American Road to Nuremberg: The Documentary Record 1944–1945 (1982)

Stover, Eric, The Witnesses: War Crimes and the Promise of Justice in The Hague (2005)

Straus, Scott, The Order of Genocide: Race, Power and War in Rwanda (2006)

Takayanagi, Kenzo, The Tokio Trials and International Law (1948)

Taylor, Telford, The Anatomy of the Nuremberg Trials (1992)

Teitel, Ruti G., Transitional Justice (2000)

Trial of the Major War Criminals Before the International Military Tribunal (1947)

Tusa, Ann, & John Tusa, The Nuremberg Trial (1983)

Van Caenegem, Raoul C., The Birth of the Common Law (2nd ed. 1988)

Vogler, Richard, A World View of Criminal Justice (2005)

Wagenaar, Willem A., et al., Anchored Narratives: The Psychology of Criminal Evidence (1993)

Walker, Anne G., Handbook on Questioning Children: A Linguistic Perspective (1994)

Wigmore, John, Evidence in Trials at Common Law (Chadbourn rev. 1981)

Younger, Irving, The Art of Cross-Examination (1976)

Zander, Michael, & Paul Henderson, Crown Court Study, RCCJ Research Study No. 19 (1993)

BOOK CHAPTERS

Ackerman, John E., *Assignment of Defense Counsel at the ICTY, in* ESSAYS ON ICTY PROCEDURE AND EVIDENCE IN HONOR OF GABRIELLE KIRK MCDONALD 167 (Richard May et al. eds., 2001)

Andenaes, Johannes, *The Scandinavian Countries, in* CHILDREN'S EVIDENCE IN LEGAL PROCEEDINGS: AN INTERNATIONAL PERSPECTIVE 9 (J. R. Spencer et al. eds. 1989)

Bitti, Gilbert, *Two Bones of Contention Between Civil and Common Law: The Record of the Proceedings and the Treatment of a Concursus Delictorum, in* INTERNATIONAL AND NATIONAL PROSECUTION OF CRIMES UNDER INTERNATIONAL LAW 273 (Horst Fischer et al. eds., 2001)

Bitti, Gilbert, *Functions and Powers of the Trial Chamber, in* 2 COMMENTARY ON THE ROME STATUTE OF THE INTERNATIONAL CRIMINAL COURT 1215 (Otto Triffterer ed., 2008)

Bradley, Craig, *United States, in* CRIMINAL PROCEDURE: A WORLDWIDE STUDY 395 (Craig M. Bradley, ed., 1999)

Burns, Robert P., *How Law Knows in the American Trial Court, in* HOW LAW KNOWS 126 (Austin Sarat et al. eds., 2007)

Cohen, David, *Beyond Nuremburg: Individual Responsibility for War Crimes, in* HUMAN RIGHTS IN POLITICAL TRANSITIONS: GETTYSBURG TO BOSNIA 53 (Carla Hesse & Robert Post eds., 1999)

Cooke, Michael, *Aboriginal Evidence in the Cross-Cultural Courtroom, in* LANGUAGE IN EVIDENCE: ISSUES CONFRONTING ABORIGINAL AND MULTICULTURAL AUSTRALIA 55 (Diana Eades ed., 1995)

Cooke, Michael, *Understood by All Concerned?: Anglo/Aboriginal Legal Translation, in* TRANSLATION AND THE LAW 37 (Marshall Morris ed., 1995)

Cordon, Ingrid M., et al., *Children in Court, in* ADVERSARIAL VERSUS INQUISITORIAL JUSTICE: PSYCHOLOGICAL PERSPECTIVES ON CRIMINAL JUSTICE SYSTEMS 167 (Peter J. van Koppen & Steven D. Penrod eds., 2003)

Corso, Piermaria, *Italy, in* CRIMINAL PROCEDURE SYSTEMS IN THE EUROPEAN COMMUNITY 223 (Christine Van Den Wyngaert et al. eds., 1993)

Cutler, Brian L., et al., *Conceptual, Practical, and Empirical Issues Associated with Eyewitness Identification Test Media, in* ADULT EYEWITNESS TESTIMONY: CURRENT TRENDS AND DEVELOPMENTS 163 (David F. Ross et al. eds., 1994)

Danner, Allison M., *Joint Criminal Enterprise, in* INTERNATIONAL CRIMINAL LAW 483 (M. Cherif Bassiouni ed., 2008)

Des Forges, Alison, & Timothy Longman, *Legal Responses to Genocide in Rwanda, in* MY NEIGHBOR, MY ENEMY: JUSTICE AND COMMUNITY IN THE AFTERMATH OF MASS ATROCITY 49 (Eric Stover & Harvey Weinstein eds., 2004)

de Gurmendi, Silvia A. F., *International Criminal Law Procedures, in* THE INTERNATIONAL CRIMINAL COURT: THE MAKING OF THE ROME STATUTE 217 (Roy S. Lee ed., 1999)

de León, Lourdes, *The Mixtecs' Annual 3000-Mile Journey, in* NOSOTROS, THE HISPANIC PEOPLE OF OREGON, ESSAYS AND RECOLLECTIONS 119 (Erasmo Gamboa & Carolyn M. Buan eds., 1995)

DeMuniz, Paul J., *Introduction to* IMMIGRANTS IN COURTS 3 (Joanne I. Moore ed., 1999)

Douglas, William O., *Foreword to* JEROME FRANK & BARBARA FRANK, NOT GUILTY 11 (1971)

Dunnigan, Timothy, & Bruce T. Downing, *Legal Interpreting on Trial: A Case Study, in* TRANSLATION AND THE LAW 93 (Marshall Morris ed., 1996)

Ellis, Hadyn D., *Practical Aspects of Face Memory, in* EYEWITNESS TESTIMONY: PSYCHOLOGICAL PERSPECTIVES 12 (Gary L. Wells & Elizabeth F. Loftus eds., 1984)

Feeley, Malcolm, *The Adversary System, in* 2 ENCYCLOPEDIA OF THE AMERICAN JUDICIAL SYSTEM 753 (Robert J. Janosik ed., 1987)

Feldman, David J., *England and Wales, in* CRIMINAL PROCEDURE: A WORLDWIDE STUDY 91 (Craig M. Bradley ed., 1999)

Fox, James J., *Tracing the Path, Recounting the Path: Historical Perspectives on Timor, in* OUT OF THE ASHES: DESTRUCTION AND RECONSTRUCTION OF EAST TIMOR 8 (James J. Fox & Dionísio Babo-Soares eds., 2003)

Franklin, Benjamin, *Letter from Benjamin Franklin to Benjamin Vaughan (Mar. 14, 1785), in* XI THE WORKS OF BENJAMIN FRANKLIN 11 (John Bigelow ed., Fed. Ed., 1904)

Frase, Richard S., *Comparative Criminal Justice Policy, in Theory and in Practice, in Int'l Conf. for the 25th Anniversary of the Int'l Inst. of Higher Stud. in* CRIM. SCI., COMPARATIVE CRIMINAL JUSTICE SYSTEMS: FROM DIVERSITY TO RAPPROCHEMENT 109 (1998)

Fuller, Lon L., *The Adversary System, in* TALKS ON AMERICAN LAW 30 (Harold J. Berman ed., 1962)

Goldstone, Richard J., *50 Years After Nuremberg: A New International Criminal Tribunal for Human Rights Criminals, in* CONTEMPORARY GENOCIDES: CAUSES, CASES, CONSEQUENCES 215 (Albert J. Jongman ed., 1996)

Greve, Vagn, *Denmark, in* CRIMINAL PROCEDURE SYSTEMS IN THE EUROPEAN COMMUNITY 51 (Christine Van Den Wyngaert et al. eds., 1993)

Gumperz, John J., *Contextualization and Ideology in Intercultural Communication, in* CULTURE OF COMMUNICATION: ANALYSES OF INTERCULTURAL SITUATIONS 35 (Aldo Di Luzio et al. eds., 2001)

Hall, David F., et al., *Postevent Information and Changes in Recollection for a Natural Event, in* EYEWITNESS TESTIMONY: PSYCHOLOGICAL PERSPECTIVES 124 (Gary L. Wells & Elizabeth F. Loftus eds., 1984)

Harhoff, Frederik, *The Role of the Parties Before International Criminal Courts, in* INTERNATIONAL AND NATIONAL PROSECUTION OF CRIMES UNDER INTERNATIONAL LAW 645 (Horst Fischer et al. eds., 2001)

Harhoff, Frederik, *Sense and Sensibility in Sentencing: Taking Stock of International Criminal Punishment, in* LAW AT WAR: THE LAW AS IT WAS AND THE LAW AS IT SHOULD BE 121 (Ola Engdahl & Pål Wrange eds., 2008)

Harnon, Eliahu, & Alex Stein, *Israel, in* CRIMINAL PROCEDURE: A WORLDWIDE STUDY 217 (Craig Bradley ed., 1999)

Hatchard, John, *Criminal Procedure in England and Wales, in* COMPARATIVE CRIMINAL PROCEDURE 176 (John Hatchard et al. eds., 1996)

Henige, David, *Oral Tradition as a Means of Constructing the Past, in* WRITING AFRICAN HISTORY 176 (John Edward Philips ed., 2005)

Hyams, Paul, *Trial by Ordeal: The Key to Proof in the Early Common Law, in* ON THE LAWS AND CUSTOMS OF ENGLAND, ESSAYS IN HONOR OF SAMUEL E. THORNE 90 (Morris S. Arnold et al. eds., 1981)

Jebens, Sverre E., *The Right to Fair Trial in Norway, in* THE RIGHT TO A FAIR TRIAL 584 (David Weissbrodt & Rüdiger Wolfrum eds., 1997)

Jörg, Nico, et al., *Are Inquisitorial and Adversarial Systems Converging? in* CRIMINAL JUSTICE IN EUROPE: A COMPARATIVE STUDY 41 (Phil Fennell et al. eds., 1995)

Kay, Stephen, & Bert Swart, *The Role of the Defense, in* II THE ROME STATUTE OF THE INTERNATIONAL CRIMINAL COURT 1421 (Antonio Cassese et al. eds. 2002)

Lahiouel, Hafida, *The Right of the Accused to an Expeditious Trial, in* ESSAYS ON ICTY PROCEDURE AND EVIDENCE IN HONOUR OF GABRIELLE KIRK MCDONALD 197 (Richard May et al. eds., 2001)

Lamb, Susan, *Illegal Arrest and the Jurisdiction of the ICTY, in* ESSAYS ON ICTY PROCEDURE AND EVIDENCE IN HONOUR OF GABRIELLE KIRK MCDONALD 27 (Richard May et al. eds., 2001)

Lewis, Peter, *Trial Procedure, in* THE INTERNATIONAL CRIMINAL COURT: ELEMENTS OF CRIMES AND RULES OF PROCEDURE AND EVIDENCE 539 (Roy S. Lee et al. eds. 2001)

Longman, Timothy, & Théonèste Rutagengwa, *Memory, Identity and Community in Rwanda, in* MY NEIGHBOR, MY ENEMY: JUSTICE AND COMMUNITY IN THE AFTERMATH OF MASS ATROCITY 162 (Eric Stover & Harvey Weinstein eds., 2004)

Maier, Charles S., *Doing History, Doing Justice: The Narrative of the Historian and of the Truth Commission, in* TRUTH V. JUSTICE 261 (Robert I. Rotberg & Dennis Thompson eds., 1999)

Mansour, Aly A., *Hudud Crimes, in General Principles of Criminal Evidence in Islamic Jurisprudence, in* THE ISLAMIC CRIMINAL JUSTICE SYSTEM 195 (M. Cherif Bassiouni ed., 1988)

May, Richard, & Marieke Wierda, *Evidence Before the ICTY, in* ESSAYS ON ICTY PROCEDURE AND EVIDENCE IN HONOUR OF GABRIELLE KIRK MCDONALD 249 (Richard May et al. eds., 2001)

May, Richard, *Gabrielle Kirk McDonald: A Biographical Note, in* ESSAYS ON ICTY PROCEDURE AND EVIDENCE IN HONOUR OF GABRIELLE KIRK MCDONALD 3 (Richard May et al. eds., 2001)

McAuley, Finbarr, & John O'Dowd, *Ireland, in* CRIMINAL PROCEDURE SYSTEMS IN THE EUROPEAN COMMUNITY 185 (Christine Van den Wyngaert et al. eds., 1993)

Mikkelson, Holly, & Hanne Mintz, *Orientation Workshops for Interpreters of All Languages: How to Strike a Balance Between the Ideal World and Reality, in* THE CRITICAL LINK: INTERPRETERS IN THE COMMUNITY 55 (Silvana E. Carr et al. eds., 1995)

Moore, Joanne I., & Ron A. Mamiya, *Interpreters, in Court Proceedings, in* IMMIGRANTS IN COURTS 29 (Joanne I. Moore ed., 1999)

Narby, Douglas J., et al., *The Effects of Witness, Target, and Situational Factors on Eyewitness Identifications, in* PSYCHOLOGICAL ISSUES IN EYEWITNESS IDENTIFICATION 23 (Siegfried L. Sporer et al. eds. 1996)

Oosthuizen, Gabriël, *Of Misconduct, Contempt, False Testimony, Rule Mutations and Other Interesting Powers: A Potpourri of Questions and Notes, in* ESSAYS ON ICTY PROCEDURE AND EVIDENCE IN HONOUR OF GABRIELLE KIRK MCDONALD 387 (Richard May et al. eds., 2001)

Orie, Alphons, *Accusatorial v. Inquisitorial Approach in International Criminal Proceedings Prior to the Establishment of the ICC and in the Proceedings before the ICC, in* 2 THE ROME STATUTE OF THE INTERNATIONAL CRIMINAL COURT: A COMMENTARY 1439 (Cassese et al. eds., 2002)

Pakes, Francis J., *Styles of Trial Procedure at the International Criminal Tribunal for the Former Yugoslavia, in* Adversarial Versus Inquisitorial Justice: Psychological Perspectives on Criminal Justice Systems 309 (Peter J. van Koppen & Steven D. Penrod eds., 2003)

Palerm, Juan-Vicente, et al., *Mexican Immigrants in Courts, in* Immigrants in Courts 73 (Joanne I. Moore ed., 1999)

Park, Roger, *Adversarial Influences on the Interrogation of Trial Witnesses, in* Adversarial Versus Inquisitorial Justice: Psychological Perspectives on Criminal Justice Systems 131 (Peter J. van Koppen & Steven D. Penrod eds., 2003)

Peters, Douglas P., *Eyewitness Memory and Arousal in a Natural Setting, in* 1 Practical Aspects of Memory: Current Research and Issues: Memory in Everyday Life 89 (Michael M. Gruneberg et al. eds., 1988)

Pölönen, Pasi, *Witness Examination in Finnish Criminal Trials, in* 51 Scandinavian Studies in Law: Procedural Law 437 (2007)

Ramadan, Hisham M., *On Islamic Punishment, in* Understanding Islamic Law: From Classical to Contemporary 43 (Hisham M. Ramadan ed., 2006)

Salama, Ma'amoun M., *General Principles of Criminal Evidence in* Islamic Jurisprudence, in The Islamic Criminal Justice System 109 (M. Cherif Bassiouni ed., 1988)

Salas, Denis, *The Role of the Judge, in* European Criminal Procedures 488 (Mireille Delmas-Marty & J. R. Spencer eds., 2002)

Schwikkard, P. J., & W. E. van der Merwe, *South Africa, in* Criminal Procedure: A Worldwide Study 319 (Craig Bradley ed., 1999)

Shapiro, Barbara J., *"Fact" and the Proof of Fact, in* How Law Knows 25 (Austin Sarat et al. eds., 2007)

Shaw, Rosalind, *Cannibal Transformations: Colonialism and Commodification in the Sierra Leone Hinterland, in* Magical Interpretations, Material Realities: Modernity, Witchcraft and the Occult in Post-Colonial Africa 50 (Henrietta L. Moore & Todd Sanders eds., 2001)

Shaw, Rosalind, *Robert Kaplan and "Juju Journalism" in Sierra Leone's Rebel War: The Primitivizing of an African Conflict, in* Magic and Modernity: Interfaces of Revelation and Concealment 81 (Birgit Meyer & Peter Pels eds., 2003)

Shaw, Rosalind, *"Tok Af, Lef Af": A Political Economy of Temne Techniques of Secrecy and Self, in* African Philosophy as Cultural Inquiry 25 (Ivan Karp & D. A. Masolo eds., 2000)

Swart, A. H. J., *The Netherlands, in Criminal Procedure Systems in* The European Community 279 (Christine Van Den Wyngaert et al. eds., 1993)

Ta, Tai Van, *Vietnamese Immigrants in American Courts, in* Immigrants in Courts 140 (Joanne I. Moore ed., 1999)

Trial of Ulrich Greifelt and Others, in XIII Law Reports of Trials of the War Criminals 1 (U. N. War Crimes Commission ed., 1949)

van Caenegem, Raoul C., *The Law of Evidence in the Twelfth Century: European Perspectives and Intellectual Background, in* Proceedings of the Second International Congress of Medieval Canon Law 298 (Stephan Kuttner & J. Joseph Ryan eds., 1965)

van Caenegem, Raoul C., *Public Prosecution of Crime in Twelfth-Century England, in* Church and Government in the Middle Ages, 41 (C. N. L. Brooke et al. eds., 1976)

Van Den Wyngaert, Christine, *Belgium*, *in* Criminal Procedure Systems in the European Community 1 (Van Den Wyngaert et al. eds., 1993)
van Koppen, Peter J., & Steven D. Penrod, *The John Wayne and Judge Dee Versions of Justice*, *in* Adversarial Versus Inquisitorial Justice: Psychological Perspectives on Criminal Justice Systems 347 (Peter J. van Koppen & Steven D. Penrod eds., 2003)
van Koppen, Peter J., & Steven D. Penrod, *Adversarial or Inquisitorial: Comparing Systems*, *in* Adversarial Versus Inquisitorial Justice: Psychological Perspectives on Criminal Justice Systems 1 (Peter J. van Koppen & Steven D. Penrod eds., 2003)
Vogler, Richard, *Criminal Procedure in France*, *in* Comparative Criminal Procedure 14 (John Hatchard et al. eds., 1996)
Walsh, Michael, *Interactional Styles in the Courtroom: An Example from Northern Australia*, *in* Language and the Law 217 (John Gibbons ed., 1994)
Weinstein, Harvey M., & Eric Stover, *Introduction: Conflict, Justice and Reclamation*, *in* My Neighbor, My Enemy: Justice and Community in the Aftermath of Mass Atrocity 1 (Harvey M. Weinstein & Eric Stover eds., 2004)
Zahar, Alexander, *The Rwamakuba Case and the Problem of False Testimony at the International Criminal Tribunal for Rwanda*, *in* Annotated Leading Cases of International Criminal Tribunals, Vol. 25: International Criminal Tribunal for Rwanda, 2006–2007 (André Klip & Göran Sluiter eds., forthcoming 2010)

CASES AND CASE DOCUMENTS

Prosecutor v. Akayesu, Case No. ICTR-96-4-T, Motion to Request Prosecution for Perjury (Jan. 29, 1997)
Prosecutor v. Akayesu, Case No. ICTR-96–4, Transcript (various dates)
Prosecutor v. Akayesu, Case No. ICTR-96-4-T, Judgement (Sept. 2, 1998)
Prosecutor v. Akayesu, Case No. ICTR-96-4-T, Sentence (Oct. 2, 1998)
Prosecution v. Alves, Case No. 1/2002, Judgement (July 8, 2004)
People v. Avitia, 127 Cal. App. 4th 185 (2005)
Prosecutor v. Bagaragaza, Case No. ICTR-2005-86-R11*bis*, Decision on the Prosecution Motion for Referral to the Kingdom of Norway (May 19, 2006)
Prosecutor v. Bagilishema, Case No. ICTR-95-1A-T, Transcript (various dates)
Prosecutor v. Bagilishema, Case No. ICTR-95-1A-T, Defence Motion Under Rule 73 of the Rules of Procedure and Evidence Requesting the Chamber to Direct the Prosecutor to Investigate a Matter with a View to the Preparation and Submission of an Indictment for False Testimony (June 6, 2000)
Prosecutor v. Bagilishema, Case No. ICTR-95-1A-T, Judgement (June 7, 2001)
Prosecutor v. Bagilishema, Case No. ICTR-95-1A-T, Separate and Dissenting Opinion of Judge Mehmet Güney (June 7, 2001)
Prosecutor v. Bagosora, Case No. ICTR-96-7-I, Indictment (Aug. 12, 1999)
Prosecutor v. Bagosora et al., Case No. ICTR-98-41-T, Transcript (various dates)
Prosecutor v. Bagosora et al., Case No. ICTR-98-41-T, Decision on Request for an Investigation into Alleged False Testimony of Witness DO (Oct. 3, 2003)
Prosecutor v. Bagosora et al., Case No. ICTR-98-41-T, Defense Motion Concerning Alleged Witness Intimidation (Dec. 28, 2004)

Prosecutor v. Bagosora et al., Case No. ICTR-98-41-T, Judgement and Sentence (Dec. 18, 2008)
Prosecutor v. Barayagwiza, Case No. ICTR-97-17-AR72, Decision (Nov. 3, 1999)
Prosecutor v. Barayagwiza, Case No. ICTR-97-17-AR72, Decision on Prosecutor's Request for Review or Reconsideration (Mar. 31, 2000)
Bater v. Bater, [1951] P35 (Australia)
Briginshaw v. Briginshaw, [1938] 60 CLR 336 (Australia)
Prosecutor v. Bikindi, Case No. ICTR-01-72-T, Judgement (Dec. 2, 2008)
Prosecutor v. Bisengimana, Case No. ICTR-2002-60-I, Decision on Bisengimana's Motion for Complete and Accurate Translation into Working Languages of the Tribunal and Respect for the Rights of the Accused (Mar. 7, 2003)
Prosecutor v. Casimir Bizimungu et al., Case No. ICTR-99-50-I, Indictment (May 7, 1999)
Prosecutor v. Bizimungu et al., Case No. ICTR-99-50-I, Transcript (various dates)
Prosecutor v. Augustin Bizimungu et al., Case No. ICTR-2000-56-I, Indictment (Aug. 23, 2004)
Prosecutor v. Blagojević & Jokić, Case No. IT-02-60-T, Judgement (Jan. 17, 2005)
Prosecutor v. Blaškić, Case No. IT-94-14-AR108*bis*, Judgement on the Request of the Republic of Croatia for Review of the Decision of Trial Chamber II of 18 July 1997 (Oct. 29, 1997)
In Kwan Fai Mak v. Blodgett, 754 F. Supp. 1490 (W.D. Wash. 1991, *aff'd per curiam and remanded* 970 F.2d 614 (9th Cir. 1992))
Blyth v. Blyth [1966] AC 643 (United Kingdom)
Prosecutor v. Brđanin, Case No. IT-99-36-T, Judgement (Sept. 1, 2004)
Prosecutor v. Brima et al., Case No. SCSL-2004-16, Transcript (various dates)
Prosecutor v. Brima et al., Case No. SCSL-2004-16-T, Judgement (June 20, 2007)
Prosecutor v. Brima et al., Case No. SCSL-04-16-T, Sentencing Judgement, at Disposition (July 19, 2007)
Prosecutor v. Brima et al., Case No. SCSL-2004-16-A, Judgement (Feb. 22, 2008)
Brown v. The King [1913] 17 CLR 570 (Australia)
United States v. Butler, 71 F.3d 243 (7th Cir. 1995)
United States v. Byrd, 352 F.2d. 570 (2d. Cir. 1965)
People v. Cardenas, 647 P.2d 569 (Cal. 1982)
Prosecutor v. Jose Cardoso, Case No. 4c/2001, Judgement (Apr. 5, 2003)
Prosecutor v. Carlos Soares Carmona, Case No. 03C.G.2000, Judgement (Apr. 25, 2001)
Lino de Carvalho v. Prosecutor General, Court of Appeal of East Timor, Criminal Appeal No. 25 of 2001, Judgement of Fredrick Egonda-Ntende (Oct. 29, 2001)
Prosecutor v. Abilio Mendes Correia, Case No. 19/2001, Disposition of the Decision (Mar. 3, 2004)
Prosecution v. Correia, Case No. 27/2003, Judgement (Apr. 25, 2005)
Prosecution v. Rudolfo Alves Correia, Case No. 27/2003, Judgement (Apr. 25, 2005)
Prosecutor v. Agustinho da Costa, Case No. 07/2000, Judgement (Oct. 11, 2001)
Prosecutor v. Da Costa & Punef, Case No. 22/2003, Judgement (Apr. 25, 2005)
Prosecutor v. Joao Franca da Silva et al., Judicial System Monitoring Programme, Case Notes (various dates)
Re Dellow's Will Trusts [1964] 1 All ER 771 (United Kingdom)
Prosecutor v. Deronjić, Case No. IT-02-61-S, Transcript (Mar. 5, 2004)

Prosecution v. Kaing Guek Eav "Duch," Case No. 001/18-07-2007-ECCC/TC, Transcript (various dates)
Prosecutor v. Ena, Case No. 05/2002, Judicial System Monitoring Programme, Preliminary Hearing Case Notes (Feb. 14, 2003)
Prosecution v. Ena & Ena, Case No. 05/2002, Judgement (Mar. 23, 2004)
Eritrea/Ethiopia Claims Commission, Partial Award, Civilians' Claims, Eritrea's Claims 15, 16, 23, & 27–32 (Dec. 17, 2004), *available at*: www.pca-cpa.org
In Re Fagan [1980] 23 SASR 454, 465 (Australia)
Prosecutor v. João Fernandes, Case No. 01/00.C.G.2000, Judgement (Jan. 25, 2001)
Prosecutor v. Julio Fernandez, Case No. 02 C.G.2000, Judgement (Mar. 1, 2000)
Prosecutor v. Julio Fernandez, Case No. 2/2000, Judgement (Feb. 27, 2001)
Julio Fernandes v. Prosecutor General, Court of Appeal of East Timor, Criminal Appeal No. 7 of 2001, Judgement of Fredrick Egonda-Ntende (June 29, 2001)
Prosecutor v. Fofana & Kondewa, Case No. SCSL-04-14-T, Judgement (Aug. 2, 2007)
Prosecutor v. Fofana & Kondewa, Case No. SCSL-04-14-T, Judgement (Aug. 2, 2007) Annex C, Separate Concurring and Partially Dissenting Opinion of Hon. Justice Bankole Thompson Filed Pursuant to Article 18 of the Statute
Prosecutor v. GAA, Case No. ICTR-07-90-R77, Indictment (Mar. 23, 2007)
Prosecutor v. Gacumbitsi, Case No. ICTR-01-64-T, Transcript (various dates)
Prosecutor v. Gacumbitsi, Case No. ICTR-2001-64-T, Judgement (June 17, 2004)
Prosecutor v. Gacumbitsi, Case No. ICTR-2001-64-T, Appeals Judgement (July 7, 2006)
Green v. The Queen, [1971] 126 CLR 28 (Australia)
Prosecutor v. Gonçalves Leto Bere, Case No. 10/2000, Judgement (May 15, 2001)
United States v. Greer, 538 F.2d 437 (D.C. Cir. 1976)
Prosecution v. Aparicio Guterres, Case No. 18a/2003, Judgement (Feb. 28, 2005)
Prosecutor v. Haradinaj, Case No. IT 04-84-T, Transcript (various dates)
Hardcastle v. Commissioner of Australian Federal Police and Another [1984] 53 A.L.R. 593 (Australia)
Helton v. Allen [1940] 63 C.L.R. 691 (Australia)
Hornal v. Neuberger Products Ltd [1957] 1 Q.B. 247 (United Kingdom)
United States v. Indorato, 628 F.2d 711 (1st Cir.), *cert. denied*, 449 U.S. 1016 (1980)
Prosecutor v. Paulino de Jesus, Case No. 6/2002, Judgement (Jan. 28, 2004)
Prosecutor v. Kajelijeli, Case No. ICTR-98-44A-T, Transcript (various dates)
Prosecutor v. Kajelijeli, Case No. ICTR-99-44A-T, Decision on Kajelijeli's Request to Admit into Evidence the Statements of GAO (July 1, 2003)
Prosecutor v. Kajelijeli, Case No. ICTR-98-44A-T, Judgement and Sentence (Dec. 1, 2003)
Prosecutor v. Kalimanzira, Case No. ICTR-05-88-T, Judgement (June 22, 2009)
Prosecutor v. Kambanda, Case No. ICTR-97-23-1, Joint Motion for Consideration of Plea Agreement Between Jean Kambanda and the Office of the Prosecutor, Annexure A Plea Agreement Between Jean Kambanda and the Office of the Prosecutor (Apr. 30, 1998)
Prosecutor v. Kamuhanda, Case No. ICTR-95-54A-T, Transcript, (various dates)
Prosecutor v. Kamuhanda, Case No. ICTR-95-54A-T, Judgement (Jan. 22, 2004)
Prosecutor v. Kamuhanda, Case No. ICTR-95-54A-T, Appeal Judgement (Sept. 19, 2005)
Prosecutor v. Karemera et al., Case No. ICTR-98-44-I, Indictment (Aug. 24, 2005)
Prosecutor v. Karemera et al., Case No. ICTR-98-44-T, Transcript (various dates)

Prosecutor v. Karemera et al., Case No. ICTR-98-44-AR73(C), Decision on Prosecutor's Interlocutory Appeal of Decision on Judicial Notice (June 16, 2006)
Prosecutor v. Karemera et al., Case No. ICTR-98-44-T, Decision on Defence Motion for Investigation of Prosecution Witness Ahmed Mbonyunkiza for False Testimony (Dec. 29, 2006)
Prosecutor v. Karemera et al., Case No. ICTR-98-44-T, Decision on Defence Motion for Investigation of Prosecution Witness HH for False Testimony (Sept. 26, 2007)
Prosecutor v. Karemera et al., Case No. 98-44-T, Decision on Prosecutor's Confidential Motion to Investigate BTH for False Testimony (May 14, 2008)
Prosecutor v. Karera, Case No. ICTR-01-74-T, Transcript (various dates)
Prosecutor v. Karera, Case No. ICTR-01-74-T, Judgement (Dec. 7, 2007)
Prosecutor v. Kayishema & Ruzindana, Case No. ICTR-95-1-T, Transcript (various dates)
Prosecutor v. Kayishema & Ruzindana, Case No. ICTR-95-1-T, Judgement (May 21, 1999)
Prosecutor v. Kordić and Čerkez, Decision on Appeal Regarding Statement of a Deceased Witness (July 21, 2000)
Prosecutor v. Kupreškić et al., Case No. IT-95-16-A, Appeals Judgement (Oct. 23, 2001)
Prosecution v. Kvočka, Case No. IT-98-30/1, Appeals Judgement (Feb. 28, 2005)
Prosecutor v. Dos Santos Laku, Case No. 8/2001, Judgement (July 25, 2001)
Prosecutor v. Leke, Case No. 05/2001, Judgement (Sept. 14, 2002)
Prosecutor v. Gaspar Leki, Judicial System Monitoring Programme, Case Notes (Apr. 4, 2002)
Prosecutor v. Joseph Leki, Case No. 5/2000, Judgement (June 11, 2001)
R. v. Lifchus, 3 S.C.R. 320 (1997)
Prosecutor v. Limaj, Case No. IT-03-66-T, Judgement and Sentence (Nov. 30, 2005)
Prosecutor v. Thomas Lubanga Dyilo, Case No. ICC-01/04-01/06, Transcript (various dates)
People v. Luparello, 187 Cal. App. 3d. 410 (1986)
M. v. M, [1988] 166 C.L.R. 69 (Australia)
Prosecutor v. Joni Marques et al., Judicial System Monitoring Programme, Case Notes, (various dates)
Prosecutor v. Joni Marques et al., Case No. 9/2000, Judgement (Dec. 11, 2001)
Prosecutor v. Domingos Mendonça, Case No. 18a/2001, Disposition of the Decision (Oct. 13, 2003)
Prosecution v. Mesquita et al., Case No. 28/2003, Judgement (Dec. 6, 2004)
Prosecution v. Morreira, Case No. 29/2003, Judgement (May 19, 2004)
Prosecutor v. Mpambara, Case No. ICTR-01-65-T, Judgement (Sept. 11, 2006)
Prosecutor v. Mucić et al., Case No. IT-96–21, Transcript (Sept. 4, 1997)
Prosecutor v. Muhimana, Case No. ICTR-95-1B-T, Transcript (various dates)
Prosecutor v. Muhimana, Case No. ICTR-95-1B-T, Decision on the Defence Motion to Appoint an *Amicus Curiae* in Proceeding Against Investigator Tony Lucassen for False Testimony (May 6, 2004)
Prosecutor v. Muhimana, Case No. ICTR-95-1B-T, Judgement and Sentence (Apr. 28, 2005)
Prosecutor v. Musema, Case No. ICTR-96-13-T, Transcript (various dates)
Prosecutor v. Musema, Case No. ICTR-96-13-A, Judgement and Sentence (Jan. 27, 2000)

Prosecutor v. Muvunyi, Case No. ICTR-2000-55A-T, Judgement and Sentence (Sept. 12, 2006)
Prosecutor v. Nahimana et al., Case No. ICTR-99-52-T, Transcript (various dates)
Prosecutor v. Nahimana et al., Case No. ICTR-96-11-I, Decision on Defence Motion to Direct the Prosecutor to Investigate the Matter of False Testimony by Witness "AEN" in Terms of Rule 91(B) (Feb. 27, 2001)
Prosecutor v. Nahimana et al., Case No. ICTR-99-52-T, Judgement and Sentence (Dec. 3, 2003)
Prosecutor v. Nahimana et al., Case No. ICTR-99-52-A, Appeals Judgement (Nov. 28, 2007)
Prosecutor v. Nchamihigo, Case No. ICTR-01-63-T, Judgement and Sentence (Nov. 12, 2008)
Prosecutor v. Ndindabahizi, Case No. ICTR-01-71-T, Transcript (various dates)
Prosecutor v. Ndindabahizi, Case No. ICTR-2001-71-I, Judgement and Sentence (July 15, 2004)
Prosecutor v. Ngeze, Case No. ICTR-97-27-I, Decision on the Defence's Motion to Suppress the Identification of Hassan Ngeze (Oct. 12, 2000)
Prosecutor v. Dragan Nikolić, Case No IT-94-2-AR73, Decision on Interlocutory Appeal Concerning Legality of Arrest (June 5, 2003)
Nixon v. Comm'r of Taxation [1979] 36 F.L.R. 172 (Australia)
Prosecutor v. Niyitegeka, Case No. ICTR-96-14-T, Transcript (various dates)
Prosecutor v. Niyitegeka, Case No. ICTR-96-14-T, Judgement (May 16, 2003)
Prosecutor v. Niyitegeka, Case No. ICTR-96-14-A, Judgement (July 9, 2004)
Public Prosecutor v. Niyonteze (Trib. Militaire de division 2 Aug. 26, 1999) (Switzerland)
Niyonteze v. Public Prosecutor (Trib. Militaire d'appel 1A May 26, 2000) (Switzerland)
Prosecutor v. Sam Hinga Norman et al., Case No. SCSL-2004-14-T, Transcript (various dates)
Prosecutor v. Ntagerura et al., Case No. ICTR-99-46-T, Transcript (various dates)
Prosecutor v. Ntagerura et al., Case No. ICTR-99-46-T, Judgement and Sentence (Feb. 25, 2004)
Prosecutor v. Elizaphan & Gerald Ntakirutimana, Case No. ICTR-96-17-T, Transcript (various dates)
Prosecutor v. Elizaphan & Gérard Ntakirutimana, Case No. ICTR-96-17-T, Judgement and Sentence (Feb. 21, 2003)
Prosecutor v. Nyiramasuhuko et al., Case No. ICTR-98-42-T, Transcript (various dates)
Prosecutor v. Nyiramasuhuko & Ntahobali, Case No. ICTR-97-21-T, Decision on Arsène Shalom Ntahobali's Motion to Have Perjury Committed by Prosecution Witness QY Investigated (Sept. 23, 2005)
Prosecutor v. Nyiramasuhuko et al., Decision on Ntahobali's Motion for an Investigation into False Testimony and Kanyabashi's Motion for an Investigation into Contempt of Court Relative to Prosecution Witnesses QY and SJ (Mar. 19, 2009)
Prosecutor v. Nzirorera, Case No. ICTR-98-44-T, Motion to Compel Full Disclosure of ICTR Payments for the Benefit of Witnesses G and T (Apr. 21, 2006)
People v. Perez, 114 Cal. App. 3d. 470 (1981)
Prosecutor v. Francisco Perreira, Case No. 34/2003, Judgement (Apr. 27, 2005)
Rejfek v. McElroy [1965] 112 C.L.R. 517 (Australia)
Prosecutor v. Ruggiu, Case No. ICTR-97-32-DP, Plea Agreement Between Georges Ruggiu and the Office of the Prosecutor (Apr. 11, 2000)

Prosecutor v. Ruggiu, Case No. ICTR-97-32-I, Judgement and Sentence (June 1, 2000)
Prosecutor v. Rukundo, Case No. ICTR-2001-70-T, Decision on the Motions Relating to the Scheduled Appearances of Witness BLP and the Defense Investigator (July 4, 2007)
Prosecutor v. Rukundo, Case No. ICTR-2001-70-T, Judgement (Feb. 27, 2009)
Prosecutor v. Rusatira, Case No., ICTR-2002-80-I, Decision on the Prosecutor's *Ex Parte* Application for Leave to Withdraw the Indictment (Aug. 14, 2002)
Prosecutor v. Rutaganda, Case No. ICTR-96-3-I, Indictment (Feb. 13, 1996)
Prosecutor v. Rutaganda, Case No. ICTR-96-3-T, Transcript (various dates)
Prosecutor v. Rutaganda, Case No. ICTR-96-3-T, Defence Motion for Orders to Direct the Prosecutor to Investigate a Case of False Testimony (Sept. 10, 1997)
Prosecutor v. Rutaganda, Case No. ICTR-96-3-T, Response by the Office of the Prosecutor to the Defence Request for a Direction Under Rule 91(B) (Sept. 26, 1997)
Prosecutor v. Rutaganda, Case No. ICTR-96-3-T, Defence Motion to Direct the Prosecutor to Investigate a Case of False Testimony (Mar. 2, 1998)
Prosecutor v. Rutaganda, Case No. ICTR-96-3-T, Decision on the Defence Motion to Direct the Prosecutor to Investigate the Matter of False Testimony by Witness "CC" (Mar. 10, 1998)
Prosecutor v. Rutaganda, Case No. ICTR-96-3-T, Decision on the Defence Motion to Direct the Prosecutor to Investigate the Matter of False Testimony by Witness "E" (Mar. 10, 1998)
Prosecutor v. Rutaganda, Case No. ICTR-96-3, Judgement (Dec. 6, 1999)
Prosecutor v. Rwamakuba, Case No. ICTR-98-44C-T, Judgement (Sept. 20, 2006)
Public Prosecutor v. Sarmento, Special Panel for Serious Crimes, Court Record at 10 (June 30, 2003)
Prosecutor v. Benjamin Sarmento et al., Case No. 18/2001, Disposition of the Decision Relating to the Conviction of the Accused Benjamin Sarmento and Romeiro Tilman (July 16, 2003)
Prosecution v. Semanza, Case No. ICTR-97-20-T, Transcript (various dates)
Prosecutor v. Semanza, Case No. ICTR-97-20-T, Judgement (May 15, 2003)
Prosecutor v. Seromba, Case No. ICTR-01-66-T, Transcript (various dates)
Prosecutor v. Seromba, Case No. ICTR-2001-66-I, Judgement (Dec. 13, 2006)
Prosecutor v. Serushago, Case No. ICTR-98-37, Plea Agreement Between Omar Serushago and the Office of the Prosecutor (Dec. 4, 1998)
Prosecutor v. Serushago, Case No. ICTR-98-39-S, Sentence (Feb. 5, 1999)
Prosecution v. Sesay et al., SCSL-04-15-T, Transcript (various dates)
Prosecutor v. Sesay et al., Decision on Sesay Defence Motion to Direct the Prosecutor to Investigate the Matter of False Testimony by Witness TF1-366 (July 26, 2006)
Prosecutor v. Sesay et al., Case No. SCSL-04-15-T, Judgement (Mar. 2, 2009)
Prosecutor v. Sesay et al., Case No. SCSL-04-15-T, Sentencing Judgement, at Disposition (Apr. 8, 2009)
Prosecutor v. Simba, Case No. ICTR-2001-76-1, Amended Indictment (May 10, 2004)
Prosecution v. Simba, Case No. ICTR-01-76-T, Judgement and Sentence (Dec. 13, 2005)
Prosecutor v. Simić, Case No. IT-95-9-PT, Decision on Motion for Judicial Assistance to Be Provided by SFOR and Others (Oct. 18. 2000)
People v. Smith, 565 N.E.2d 900 (Ill. 1991)
Smith & Co. Ltd v. Westralian Farmers Co-Operative Ltd, [1979] V.R. 129 (Australia)
Prosecution v. Marcelino Soares, Case No. 11/2003, Judgement (Dec. 11, 2003)

Prosecutor v. Carlos Soares, Case No. 12/2000, Judgement (May 31, 2001)
Prosecutor v. Strugar, Case No. IT-01-42-T, Judgement (Jan. 31, 2005)
Bunnell v. Sullivan, 947 F.2d 341 (9th Cir. 1991) (en banc) (Kozinski, J., concurring)
People v. Superior Court (Soon Ja Du), 7 Cal. Rptr. 2d 177, 181 (Cal. Dist. Ct. App. 1992)
Prosecution v. Tacaqui, Case No. 20/2001, Judgement (Dec. 9, 2004)
Prosecutor v. Tadić, Case No. IT-94-I-T, Transcript (May 7, 1996)
Prosecutor v. Tadić, Case No. IT-94-1-T, Order for the Prosecution to Investigate the False Testimony of Dragan Opacić (Dec. 10, 1996)
Prosecutor v. Tadić, Case No. IT-94-I-T, Judgement (May 7, 1997)
Prosecutor v. Tadić, Case No. IT-94-I-T, Appeals Judgement (July 15, 1999)
Prosecutor v. Augusto Asameta Tavares, Case No. 02/2001, Judgement (Sept. 28, 2001)
Prosecutor v. Taylor, Case No. SCSL-2003-01-T, Transcript (various dates)
Thomas v. The Queen, [1960] 102 C.L.R. 584 (Australia)
Trade Practices Commission v. Nicholas Enterprises Pty Ltd [No 2], 40 F.L.R. 83 (Australia)
Prosecutor v. Jose Valente, Case No. 3/2001, Judgement (June 19, 2001)
Prosecutor v. Vasiljević, Case No. IT-98-32-T, Judgement (Nov. 29, 2002)
Prosecutor v. Vasiljević, ICTY Case No. IT-98-32-A, Appeals Judgement (Feb. 25, 2004)
People v. Williams, 940 P. 2d. 710 (Cal. 1997)
Peter Williamson Pty. Ltd. v. Capitol Motors Ltd., [1982] 41 A.L.R. 613 (Australia)
In re Winship, 397 U.S. 358 (1970)
Prosecutor v. Zigiranyirazo, Case No. ICTR-01-73-T, Judgement (Dec. 18, 2008)

INTERVIEWS

Telephone interview with DD, former SCSL investigator (Sept. 26, 2006)
Telephone interview with FL, former ICTR prosecutor (July 10, 2006)
Telephone interview with Leopold Furufuru, ICTR translator (Mar. 13, 2006)
Telephone interview with KJ, former ICTR investigator (July 7, 2006)
Telephone Interview with Nicholas Koumjian, Deputy Prosecutor for Serious Crimes, Special Panels for Serious Crimes (July 29, 2004)
Telephone interview with KU, former ICTR investigator (July 7, 2006)
Telephone interview with Howard Morrison, former ICTY and ICTR defense counsel (May 22, 2006)
Interview with NE, ICTR Defense Investigator (May 31, 2006)
Telephone interview with Michiel Pestman, SCSL Defense Counsel (May 19, 2006)
Telephone interview with Peter Robinson, ICTR Defense Counsel (May 9, 2006)
Email interview with Peter Robinson, ICTR Defense Counsel (Aug. 2, 2009)
Telephone interview with SS, SCSL Defense Section (May 24, 2006)

NEWSPAPER ARTICLES

Acquittals of Former Government Officials Raises Mixed Reactions, HIRONDELLE NEWS AGENCY, Feb. 26, 2004.
Ahmići Muslims Shocked by UN Acquittal of War Crimes Suspects, AGENCE FRANCE-PRESSE, Oct. 23, 2001
Another Dirty War Witness Goes Missing, A.P., Apr. 30, 2008.

Baguma, Steven, *Genocide Survivor Boycotts Gacaca, Cites Harassment*, The New Times (Kigali), Nov. 16, 2006
Baguma, Steven, *Gacaca Witnesses Attacked*, The New Times (Kigali), Dec. 18, 2006
Bavier, Joe, *Congo Ministers Attacked in Bemba trial "Warning,"* Reuters, Aug. 31, 2009
Bennett, Jessica, *Not Above the Law*, Newsweek, June 12, 2007
Bouwknegt, Thijs, *Rwanda's Genocide Tribunal's Witness "Hiding,"* Radio Netherlands Worldwide, Oct. 2, 2008
Carlin, Peter, *What Becomes of the Resurrected?*, Los Angeles Times Magazine, Mar. 8, 1992, at 22
Cleary, Paul, *It's the Economy Stupid*, Wall St. J., May 23, 2007
Coalition for International Justice, *ICTR Judges to Visit Crime Scenes*, Aug. 16, 2000, *available at* http://web.archive.org/web/20001010003755/http://www.cij.org/
Corder, Mike, *Former Congolese Child Soldier Recants Testimony, Throws Trial of Warlord into Confusion*, A. P., Jan. 28, 2009
Court Quashes Appeal, Int'l Just. Trib., June 8, 1998
Croatia's Top Court Orders War Crimes Retrial, Reuters, Aug. 19, 2004
Cruvellier, Thierry, *Grass-Roots Justice*, Int'l Just. Trib., Mar. 29, 1999
Cruvellier, Thierry, *Shocking Arrest of Rusatira*, Int'l Just. Trib., May 17, 2002
Cruvellier, Thierry, *Judge Ostrovsky Speaks Out*, Int'l Just. Trib., Apr. 23, 2002
Cruvellier, Thierry, *Angolan Capture*, Int'l Just. Trib., Aug. 13, 2002
Cruvellier, Thierry, *The Error*, Int'l Just. Trib., Aug. 13, 2002
Darehshori, Sara, *Inching Toward Justice in Rwanda*, N.Y. Times, Sept. 8, 1998
Ega-Musa, Nasser, *Another Failure of Justice in Africa*, Wash. Post, Mar. 6, 1997
Finn, Peter, *Lawyers Criticize Quality of Guantanamo Interpreters*, Wash. Post, Oct. 14, 2008
Flottau, Renate, *Fragwürdige Abmachungen*, Der Spiegel, Jan. 17, 2005
Four Witnesses in Saddam Trial Held, A.P., June 1, 2006
Gacaca Witness' House Set Ablaze, The New Times (Kigali), Oct. 22, 2006
Genocide Survivors in Danger, Says IBUKA, Hirondelle News Agency, Nov. 16, 2005
Glassborow, Katy, *ICC Investigative Strategy Under Fire*, Int'l War & Peace Reporting, Oct. 17, 2008
Goldberg, Jeffrey, *A Continent's Chaos: Why Do Americans Find It Intolerable in Europe but Inevitable in Africa?* N.Y. Times Mag., May 21, 2000
Goodman, Sara, *Albanian Witness Refuses to Testify in Haradinaj Trial*, 505 Int'l War & Peace Reporting, June 8, 2007
Gosnell, Christopher M., *A Court Too Far*, Int'l Herald Trib., Mar. 28, 2008
Hudson, Alexandra, *U.N. Tribunal Upholds Acquittal of Kosovo Ex-Rebels*, Reuters, Sept. 27, 2007
ICTR/Prosecution – Synthesis: Prosecutors at the ICTR, Hirondelle News Agency, Oct. 28, 2003
ICTR/Rusatira – General Rusatira's Release Heightens Tension Between Rwanda and the ICTR, Hirondelle News Agency, Oct. 29, 2003
ICTR/Zigiranyirazo-Bagaragaza Press Release, *Witness Gives the Defense a Hard Time*, Hirondelle News Agency, June 15, 2006.
Indonesia Colluded with Timor Militia Terror: Gusmao Wife, Agence France-Presse, Nov. 9, 2000
"Intuitive' Identification," Sense News Agency, June 25, 2007
It's a Lying Shame, South China Morning Post, Mar. 22, 2006

Kessy, Modestus, *Genocide Witness Killed After Testifying*, THE GUARDIAN (Dar es Salam), Oct. 22, 2004

Kigali Denounces Acquittals at UN Tribunal, UN INTEGRATED REGIONAL INFORMATION NETWORKS, Feb. 26, 2004

Kocieniewski, David, *A Little Girl Shot, and a Crowd That Didn't See*, N.Y. TIMES, July 9, 2007

Kolker, Ken, *Trial and Errors*, GRAND RAPIDS PRESS, Feb. 21, 1993

Kosovo Journalist Indicted by UN Court, BALKAN INSIGHT, May 20, 2008

Metcalf, J. Coll, *An Interview with United Nations' Chief War Crimes Prosecutor, Carla del Ponte*, INTERNEWS, Feb. 15, 2000

Mydans, Seth, *Sexual Violence as Tool of War: Pattern Emerging in East Timor*, N.Y. TIMES, Mar. 1, 2001

Mydans, Seth, *Torture and Death Recounted at Cambodian Trial*, N.Y. TIMES, July 14, 2009

New Tensions Between the ICTR and Kigali, INT'L JUSTICE TRIB., Mar. 15, 2004

Ntambara, Paul, *Jean Mpambara's Acquittal Enrages Residents*, THE NEW TIMES (Sept. 16, 2006)

Officials: Scandalous Mockery of Justice, RTV B92 NEWS, Apr. 3, 2008.

Petit, Franck, *Cameroonian Intrigues*, INT'L JUST. TRIB., MAR. 5, 2001

Power, Samantha, *Rwanda: The Two Faces of Justice*, 50 N.Y. REVIEW OF BOOKS, Jan. 16, 2003

Problems with Prosecution Witnesses, SENSE NEWS AGENCY, June 29, 2007, *available at* www.sense-agency.com/en/stream.php?sta=3&pid=9930&kat=3

Prosecution Witness Assassinated in Rwanda, HIRONDELLE NEWS AGENCY, Oct. 20, 2004

Radosavljević, Zoran, *Croats Call U.N. War Crimes Verdict "Shameful,"* REUTERS, Sept. 28, 2007

Rwanda Furious over Acquittal of Two Suspects, THE EAST AFRICAN, Mar. 1, 2004

Rwandan Court Convicts Genocide Suspect Acquitted by ICTR, AGENCE FRANCE-PRESSE, Oct. 11, 2007

Scheffer, David, *A Rare Chance to Try These Architects of Atrocity*, FINANCIAL TIMES (London), Aug. 16, 2004

Schemm, Paul, *Key Saddam Witnesses Say They Were Bribed, Coerced*, AGENCE FRANCE-PRESSE, June 12, 2006

Simons, Marlise, *War Crimes Court Takes It Easy on a Cooperative Bosnian Serb*, N.Y. TIMES, Aug. 1, 2001

Stuart, Heikelina V., *ICTY, Justice Against All*, INT'L JUST. TRIB., DEC. 3, 2007

Thousands Demonstrate Against the UN Tribunal, HIRONDELLE NEWS AGENCY, Feb. 29, 2004

Tribunal Throws out Motion to Have Bagaragaza's Transfer to Norway, HIRONDELLE NEWS AGENCY, May 23, 2006

U.N. Acquits Top Kosovo Rebel, BBC NEWS, Nov. 30, 2005, *available at* http://news.bbc.co.uk/2/hi/europe/4485658.stm

Waldorf, Lars, *Silent Partner*, DIPLOMATIE JUDICIAIRE, Nov. 27, 2001

Waldorf, Lars, *Remembrance of Things Past*, INT'L JUSTICE TRIB., Oct. 31, 2001

Willis, Paul, *No Lawyers but Rwanda's Village Courts Could Pass Death Sentence*, DAILY TELEGRAPH (London), Apr. 9, 2006

Woodd, Richard & Vong Sokheng, *US Senate Moves to Block KR Trial Funds*, PHNOM PENH POST, Oct. 8, 2004

McVeigh, Karen, *Spate of Killings Obstructs Rwanda's Quest for Justice*, The Observer (London) Dec. 3, 2006

Vincent, Isabel, *Canadian Lawyers Say Hands Tied in Arusha*, National Post (Canada), July 28, 2001

Witness Refuses to Testify Because Witnesses Get Killed in Kosovo, SENSE News Agency, June 5, 2007, *available at* www.sense-agency.com/en/stream.php?sta=3&pid=9776&kat=3

PRESS RELEASES AND PRESS BRIEFINGS

ICTR Press Release, *ICTR Witness Pleas Guilty to Giving False Testimony*, ICTR/INFO-9-2-529.EN, Sept. 19, 2007

ICTR Press Release, *Former Witness Sentenced to 9 Months for Contempt*, ICTR/INFO-9-2-541.EN, Dec. 3, 2007

ICTY Press Release, *Astrit Haraqija and Bajrush Morina Indicted for Contempt Of Court*, CVO/MOW/1244e, Apr. 25, 2008, *available at* http://www.icty.org/sid/9898

ICTY Bull., No. 21, July 27, 1998

JSMP Press Release, *The Wiranto Warrant Political Interference in the Serious Crimes Process* June 22, 2004, *available at* www.jsmp.minihub.org/News/2004/June/22jun04_jsmp_wirantowarrant_eng.htm

Prosecutor's Statement Regarding the Death of ICTR Indictee Juvénal Uwilingiyimana, ICTR Newsletter, December 2005–January 2006, *available at* http://69.94.11.53/ENGLISH/newsletter/dec05-jan06/dec05-jan06.pdf

REPORTS

Amnesty International, *Sierra Leone: 1998- A Year of Atrocities Against Civilians 33-34*, AI Index AFR 51/022/1998 (Nov. 1, 1998)

Amnesty International, *Rwanda: The Troubled Course of Justice*, AI-index AFR 47/010/2000 (Apr. 4, 2000)

Amnesty International, *Sierra Leone: Childhood: A Casualty of Conflict*, AI Index AFR 51/069/2000 (Aug. 31, 2000)

Amnesty International & Judicial System Monitoring Programme, *Indonesia & Timor-Leste. Justice for Timor-Leste: The Way Forward*, AI Index: ASA 21/006/2004 (Apr. 1, 2004)

Amnesty International, *Sierra Leone: Getting Reparations Rights for Survivors of Sexual Violence*, AI Index: AFR 51/005/2007 (Nov. 1, 2007)

The Asia Foundation, *Supporting Economic Growth in East Timor, available at* www.asiafoundation.org/pdf/easttimorecon.pdf

Australian Law Reform Commission, *Evidence Reference Research Paper No. 14: Aspects of Proof* (1983)

Bambrick, Kati, *Silent Victims, Young Girls at Risk: An Evaluation of Post-War Rape and Response to Rape in the Provinces of Sierra Leone* (Campaign for Good Governance, 2004), *available at* www.peacewomen.org/resources/Sierra_Leone/GoodGovernanceSilentVictims.pdf

Commission for Reception Truth and Reconciliation in East Timor, *Chega! The Report of the Commission for Reception Truth and Reconciliation in Timor-Leste* (2005)

Courts Administration Authority, South Australia District Court Judicial Officers, *available at* www.courts.sa.gov.au/courts/district/judicial_officers.html

Human Rights Watch, *Sowing Terror: Atrocities Against Civilians in Sierra Leone*, July 1998, Vol. 10, No. 3(A), *available at* www.hrw.org/reports98/sierra/

Human Rights Watch, *We'll Kill You if You Cry: Sexual Violence in the Sierra Leone Conflict*, Vol. 15, No. 1(A) (Jan. 15, 2003)

Human Rights Watch, *Sudan: National Courts Have Done Nothing on Darfur* (June 11, 2004), *available at* http://hrw.org/english/docs/2007/06/11/sudan16110.htm

Human Rights Watch, *Croatia: Conviction Spotlights Justice Failings*, July 19, 2004, *available at* http://hrw.org/english/docs/2004/07/19/croati.9083.htm.

Human Rights Watch, *Bringing Justice: the Special Court for Sierra Leone Accomplishments, Shortcomings, and Needed Support*, Vol. 16, No. 8A (Sept. 2004)

Human Rights Watch, *Struggling to Survive: Barriers to Justice for Rape Victims in Rwanda* (Sept. 29, 2004)

Human Rights Watch, *Justice in Motion: The Trial Phase of the Special Court for Sierra Leone*, Vol. 17, No. 14(A) (Nov. 2005), *available at* http://hrw.org/reports/2005/sierraleone1105/

Human Rights Watch, *Judging Dujail: The First Trial Before the Iraqi High Tribunal* (Nov. 2006)

Human Rights Watch, *Darfur: No Redress for Rape* (Apr. 7, 2008), *available at* http://hrw.org/english/docs/2008/04/03/darfur18424.htm

Jackson, Robert H., Minutes of Conference Session of July 2, 1945 (Document XX), International Conference on Military Trials 129

The Innocence Project, 2006 *Annual Report*, *available at* www.innocenceproject.org/Images/437/ip_annual_report_06_final.pdf

International Crisis Group, *The International Criminal Tribunal for Rwanda: Justice Delayed*, June 7, 2001

Judicial System Monitoring Programme, *Special Panels for Serious Cases – Weekly Report 27–31 January 2003* (Jan. 27–31, 2003) *available at* www.jsmp.minihub.org/Reports/spscweeksumm/SPSC27-31Jan03jr10feb03.pdf

Judicial System Monitoring Programme, *The General Prosecutor v. Joni Marques and 9 Others (The Los Palos Case): A JSMP Trial Report* (Mar. 2002)

Judicial System Monitoring Programme, *The Lolotoe Case: A Small Step Forward* (July 2004)

Judicial System Monitoring Program, *The Paulino de Jesus Decision* (Apr. 2005), *available at* www.jsmp.minihub.org/Reports/jsmpreports/Paulino%20De%20Jesus/paulino%20de%20jesus%20report%20(e).pdf

Lawyers Committee for Human Rights, *Prosecuting Genocide in Rwanda: A Lawyers Committee Report on the ICTR and National Trials* (1997)

Organization for Security and Co-Operation in Europe, *Mission to Croatia, Background Report: Domestic War Crime Trials 2003* (June 22, 2004)

Penal Reform International, *PRI Research Team on Gacaca: Report IV* (January 2003)

Research Institute for Asia and the Pacific (RIAP), the University of Sydney, *The Future of East Timor: Threats and Opportunities for Economic Development of a Small Island State*, Briefing Paper Vol. 3 No. 2 (July 2000), *available at*: www.usyd.edu.au/riap/about/publications/articles/2000/Future%2520of%2520East%2520Timor.pdf.

Shaw, Rosalind, *Rethinking Truth and Reconciliation Commissions: Lessons from Sierra Leone, United States Institute of Peace Special Report* (Feb. 2005), *available at* http://www.usip.org/files/resources/sr130.pdf.

Sierra Leone Truth and Reconciliation Commission Report, available at http://www.nuigalway.ie/human_rights/publishing.html

Special Court for Sierra Leone, First Annual Report of the President of the Special Court for Sierra Leone for the Period 2 December 2002 to 1 December 2003, *available at* http://www.sc-sl.org/LinkClick.aspx?fileticket=NRhDcbHrcSs%3d&tabid=176

Special Court for Sierra Leone, Second Annual Report of the President of the Special Court for Sierra Leone for the Period 1 January 2004–17 January 2005, *available at* www.sc-sl.org/Documents/specialcourtannualreport2004–2005.pdf

Taylor, Telford, *Final Report to the Secretary of the Army on the Nuernberg War Crimes Trials Under Control Council Law No. 10* (1949)

Thompson, Niobe, *In Pursuit of Justice: A Report on the Judiciary in Sierra Leone*, Commonwealth Human Rights Initiative (2002)

U.C. Berkeley War Crimes Studies Center, Michelle Staggs and Sara Kendall, Special Court Monitoring Program, Update No. 4 (Sept. 17, 2004)

U.C. Berkeley War Crimes Studies Center, Michele Staggs, Special Court Monitoring Program, Update No. 14 (Nov. 26, 2004)

U.C. Berkeley War Crimes Studies Center, Michele Staggs, Special Court Monitoring Program, Update No. 20 (Feb. 4, 2005)

U.C. Berkeley War Crimes Studies Center, Michele Staggs, Special Court Monitoring Program, Update No. 25 (Mar. 11, 2005)

U.C. Berkeley War Crimes Studies Center, Michele Staggs, Special Court Monitoring Program Update No. 28 (Mar. 25, 2005)

U.C. Berkeley War Crimes Studies Center, Sara Kendall and Michelle Staggs, *From Mandate to Legacy: The Special Court for Sierra Leone as a Model for "Hybrid Justice:" Interim Report on the Special Court for Sierra Leone* (Apr. 2005)

U.C. Berkeley War Crimes Studies Center, Kyra Sanin, Special Court Monitoring Program Update No. 56 (Sept. 23, 2005)

U.C. Berkeley War Crimes Studies Center, Kyra Sanin, Special Court Monitoring Program, Update No. 57 (Oct. 5, 2005)

U.C. Berkeley War Crimes Studies Center, Kyra Sanin, Special Court Monitoring Program, Update No. 58 (Oct. 10, 2005)

U.C. Berkeley War Crimes Study Center, Kyra Sanin and Anna Stirnemann, Child Witnesses at the Special Court for Sierra Leone 23–24 (March 2006), *available at* http://socrates.berkeley.edu/~warcrime/ChildWitnessReport_000.pdf.pdf

U.C. Berkeley War Crimes Studies Center, Alison Thompson, Special Court Monitoring Program, Update No. 70 (Feb. 24, 2006)

U.C. Berkeley War Crimes Studies Center, Alison Thompson, Special Court Monitoring Program, Update No. 71 (Mar. 3, 2006)

U.C. Berkeley War Crimes Studies Center, Alison Thompson, Special Court Monitoring Program, Update No. 72 (Mar. 10, 2006)

U.C. Berkeley War Crimes Studies Center, Alison Thompson, Special Court Monitoring Program, Update No. 76 (May 19, 2006)

U.C. Berkeley War Crimes Studies Center, Alison Thompson, Special Court Monitoring Program, Update No. 80a (June 23, 2006)

U.C. Berkeley War Crimes Studies Center, Penelope van Tuyl, *Effective, Efficient, and Fair? An Inquiry into the Investigative Practices of the Office of the Prosecutor at the Special Court for Sierra Leone* (Sept. 2008)

United Nations Development Programme, *Timor-Leste Faces Development Challenges, available at* http://content.undp.org/go/newsroom/march-2006/timor-leste-hdr20060309.en?g11n.enc=ISO-8859–1

United Nations Development Programme, Report, *The Community Reconciliation Process of the Commission for Reception, Truth and Reconciliation* (April 2004), *available at* www.undp.easttimor.org/documentsreports/governance_capacity development/Piers%20report%20Final.pdf

Washington State Court Interpreter Task Force, Evaluation of Spanish Interpreters in Washington Courts, *Final Report, 1988, Annex to Final Report of the Court Interpreter Task Force* (1989)

STATUTES, STATUTORY MATERIALS, AND CONSTITUTIONS

Code of Ethics for Interpreters and Translators Employed by the Special Court for Sierra Leone, art. 7(c) (May 25, 2004)

Criminal Procedure Act 1977, § 170A (South Africa)

ECCC Internal Rules, Rule 25(1) (2009)

ECCC Internal Rules, Rule 36 (2009)

Evidence Act 1906 § 106(F)(2) (Western Australia)

Finland Code of Judicial Procedure, 4/1734, Amendments up to 259/2002, Chapter 17 § 33(1) (690/1998)

ICC Rules of Procedure and Evidence, Rule 140(2) (Sept. 9, 2002)

ICTR Rules of Procedure and Evidence, Rule 66(A)(i)-(ii) (2008)

ICTR Rules of Procedure and Evidence, Rule 67(A)(ii)(a)-(b) (2008)

ICTR Rules of Procedure and Evidence, Rule 68 (2008)

ICTR Rules of Procedure and Evidence, Rule 73*bis* (2008)

ICTR Rules of Procedure and Evidence, Rule 74*ter*(B) (2008)

ICTR Rules of Procedure and Evidence, Rule 87 (2008)

ICTR Rules of Procedure and Evidence, Rule 90(b) (2008)

ICTR Rules of Procedure and Evidence, Rule 101(b)(ii) (2008)

ICTR Statute, S.C. Res. 955, U.N. SCOR, 49th Sess., 3453d mtg. at 15, U.N. Doc. S/RES/955 & Annex (1994)

ICTY Rules of Procedure and Evidence, Rule 65 *ter*

ICTY Rules of Procedure and Evidence, Rule 66(A)(i)-(ii)

ICTY Rules of Procedure and Evidence, Rule 67(B)(i)(a)-(b)

ICTY Rules of Procedure and Evidence, Rule 68

ICTY Rules of Procedure and Evidence, Rule 73*bis* (B), (C), (D)

ICTY Rules of Procedure and Evidence, Rule 73*ter* (B), (C)

ICTY Rules of Procedure and Evidence, Rule 89F

ICTY Rules of Procedure and Evidence, Rule 90(A),

ICTY Statute, S.C. Res. 827, U.N. SCOR, 48th Sess., 3217th mtg. at 28, U.N. Doc. S/RES/827 (1993)

Norway Criminal Procedure Act, § 133, Act of 22 May 1981 No. 25, amended 17 July 1998 No. 56

Organized Crime Control Act of 1970, Pub. L. No. 91–452, 84 Stat. 922 (1970)
Rome Statute of the International Criminal Court, United Nations Diplomatic Conference of Plenipotentiaries on the Establishment of an International Criminal Court, U.N. Doc. A/CONF.183/9 (1998), *reprinted in* 37 I.L.M. 999 (1998), arts. 15, 56, 57(D), 58, 61, 64(8)
SCSL Rules of Procedure and Evidence, Rule 67(A)(ii)(a)-(b)
SCSL Rules of Procedure and Evidence, Rule 68
SCSL Rules of Procedure and Evidence, Rule 73*bis*
SCSL Rules of Procedure and Evidence, Rule 73*ter* (B)
SCSL Rules of Procedure and Evidence, Rule 87
SCSL Rules of Procedure and Evidence, Rule 101(b)(ii) (2008)
Statute of the Special Court for Sierra Leone (Jan. 16, 2002)
Statute of the Special Tribunal for Lebanon, S/RES/1757, Attachment, art. 30(2), May 30, 2007
Special Tribunal for Lebanon Rules of Procedure and Evidence, Rule 145(A) (Mar. 20, 2009)
Swedish Code of Criminal Procedure, DS 1998:000, Chapter 36, § 17
United States Code, 18 U.S.C. 1621
United States Rule of Evidence, Fed. R. Evid. 611(a)
UNTAET Regulation No. 2000/30 on Transitional Rules of Criminal Procedure, UNTAET/REG/2000/30 (as amended by Regulation 2001/25 of September 14, 2001)
Youth Justice and Criminal Evidence Act § 29 (United Kingdom)

SPEECHES

Davenport, Christian, College of William and Mary, April 11, 2008
Del Ponte, Carla, Address by the Prosecutor of the International Criminal Tribunals for the Former Yugoslavia and Rwanda, Mrs. Carla del Ponte, to the United Nations Security Council, JJJ/P.I.S/.709-e (Oct. 30, 2002) *available at* www.un.org/icty/pressreal/p709-e.htm
Rapoza, Phillip, The Serious Crimes Process in Timor-Leste: Accomplishments, Challenges and Lessons Learned, Speech at the International Symposium on UN Peacekeeping Operations in Post-Conflict Timor-Leste: Accomplishments and Lessons Learned (Apr. 28, 2005)

TREATIES AND SIMILAR AGREEMENTS

Agreement Between the United Nations and the Royal Government of Cambodia Concerning the Prosecution Under Cambodian Law of Crimes Committed During the Period of Democratic Kampuchea, June 6, 2003, *available at* www.eccc.gov.kh/english/agreement.list.aspx.
International Covenant on Civil and Political Rights, Dec. 16, 1966, 999 U.N.T.S. 171

UN DOCUMENTS

ICTR, *Report of the International Criminal Tribunal for the Prosecution of Persons Responsible for Genocide and Other Serious Violations of International Humanitarian Law Committed in the Territory of Rwanda and Rwandan Citizens Responsible for*

Genocide and Other Such Violations Committed in the Territory of Neighbouring States between 1 January and 31 December 1994, U.N. Doc. A/55/435, S/2000/927 (Oct. 2, 2000)

ICTR, *Report of the International Criminal Tribunal for the Prosecution of Persons Responsible for Genocide and Other Serious Violations of International Humanitarian Law Committed in the Territory of Rwanda and Rwandan Citizens Responsible for Genocide and Other Such Violations Committed in the Territory of Neighbouring States between 1 January and 31 December 1994*, U.N. Doc. A/60/229-S/2005/534 (Aug. 15, 2005)

ICTY, *Report of the International Tribunal for the Prosecution of Persons Responsible for Serious Violations of International Humanitarian Law Committed in the Territory of the Former Yugoslavia since 1991*, 49th Sess., U.N. Doc. A/49/150 (Aug. 29, 1994)

International Law Commission, *Documents of the Second Session, including the Report of the Commission to the General Assembly*, U.N. Doc. A/CN.4/25 (Apr. 26, 1950), *reprinted in* 2, Benjamin B. Ferencz, An International Criminal Court: A Step Toward World Peace, 188 (1980)

International Law Commission, *Report of the International Law Commission on the Work of its Sixth Session*, U.N. Doc. A/2693 (June 3-July 28, 1954), *reprinted in* [1954] 2, Y.B. Int'l L. Comm'n 140, U.N. Doc. A/CN.4/SER.A/1954.

Human Rights Committee, *General Comment No. 13.7*, U.N. Doc. CCPR General Comment No. 13 (Apr. 13, 1984)

Letter dated 1 Oct. 1994 from the Secretary-General Addressed to the President of the Security Council, U.N. Doc. S/1994/1125 (Oct. 4, 1994)

Letter dated 30 April 2004, from the President of the International Criminal Tribunal for the Prosecution of Persons Responsible for Genocide and Other Serious Violations of International Humanitarian Law Committed in the Territory of Rwanda and Rwandan Citizens Responsible for Genocide and Other Such Violations Committed in the Territory of Neighbouring States Between 1 January and 31 December 1994 addressed to the President of the Security Council, paras. 6, 30, U.N. Doc. S/2004/341, (May 3, 2004)

Report of the International Commission of Inquiry on East Timor to the Secretary-General, U.N. Doc. A/54/726-S/2000/59 (Jan. 31, 2000)

The Secretary General, *The Rule of Law and Transitional Justice in Conflict and Post-Conflict Societies, delivered to the Security Council*, U.N. Doc. S/2004/616 (Aug. 23, 2004)

S.C. Res. 955, U.N. SCOR, 49th Sess., 3453d mtg. at 1, U.N. Doc. S/RES/955 & Annex (1994)

S.C. Res. 1503, U.N. Doc. S/RES/1503 (Aug. 28, 2003)

S.C. Res. 1534, U.N. Doc. S/RES/1534 (Mar. 26, 2004)

Secretary-General's Report on Aspects of Establishing an International Tribunal for the Prosecution of Persons Responsible for Serious Violations of International Humanitarian Law Committed in the Territory of the former Yugoslavia, U.N. SCOR, 48th Sess., Annex, U.N. Doc. S/25704 (1993), *reprinted in* 32 I.L.M. 1159 (1993)

The Secretary-General, *Fourth Report of the Secretary-General on the United Nations Mission in Sierra Leone, delivered to the Security Council*, U.N. Doc. S/2000/455 (May 19, 2000)

United Nations, *End of Mandate Report of the Secretary-General on the United Nations Mission of Support in East Timor*, S/2005/310 (May 12, 2005)

WEB SITES

Central Intelligence Agency, The World Factbook, *Croatia, available at* www.cia.gov/library/publications/the-world-factbook/geos/HR.html

Central Intelligence Agency, The World Factbook, *Serbia, available at* www.cia.gov/library/publications/the-world-factbook/geos/RI.html

Coalition for International Criminal Justice, *Frequently Asked Questions – ICTR, available at* www.cij.org/index.cfm?fuseaction=faqs&tribunalID=2#q7

Fifth Circuit District Judges Association, *Pattern Jury Instructions (Criminal Cases)* (2001), *available at* www.lb5.uscourts.gov/juryinstructions/crim2001.pdf

Former Diplomats Stress Hague Tribunal Failure, JAVNO, Nov. 20, 2007, *available at* www.javno.com/en/croatia/clanak.php?id=99813

Government of the Republic of Croatia, News and Announcements, *Prime Minister, Associations of Homeland War Veterans and Victims Slam ICTY Verdict, available at* www.vlada.hr/en/naslovnica/novosti_i_najave/2007/rujan/izjava_predsjednika_vlade_o_presudi_haaskog_suda_vukovarskoj_trojci

Helping Hand to ICTR Witnesses, Internews, *available at* www.internews.org.rw/articles5.htm#helping

Hull, Geoffrey, *The Languages of East Timor: Some Basic Facts, available at* http://www.portphillip.vic.gov.au/default/CommunityGovernanceDocuments/The_Languages_of_East_Timor_Some_Basic_Facts.pdf

Jallow, Hassan B., *The OTP-ICTR: Ongoing Challenges of Completion*, GUEST LECTURE SERIES OF THE OFFICE OF THE PROSECUTOR, Nov. 1, 2004, *available at* http://69.94.11.53/ENGLISH/colloquium06/ictr_completion.pdf

Kroc Institute for International Peace Studies, Research Sheds New Light on Rwanda Killings, *available at* http://kroc.nd.edu/newsevents/news/research-sheds-new-light-rwanda-killings-512

Legal Services Commission of South Australia, Law Handbook, available at www.lawhandbook.sa.gov.au (2007)

The Trial of Charles Taylor, *Prosecution Witness "Zigzag" Marzah Finishes Testimony, says Taylor Ate Human Hearts*, Mar. 14, 2008, *available at* http://charlestaylortrial.org/

United Nations Development Programme, *Timor-Leste Faces Development Challenges, available at* http://content.undp.org/go/newsroom/march-2006/timor-leste-hdr20060309.en?g11n.enc=ISO-8859–1

UNICEF, *Rwanda, available at* www.unicef.org/infobycountry/rwanda_1717.html

UNICEF, *At a Glance: Sierra Leone, available at* www.unicef.org/infobycountry/sierraleone_statistics.html

UNICEF Statistics Birth Registration, *available at* www.childinfo.org/birth_registration_tables.php

UN Office for the Coordination of Humanitarian Affairs, *Rwanda Humanitarian Country Profile, available at* www.irinnews.org/country.aspx?CountryCode=RW&RegionCode =GL;

UN Office for the Coordination of Humanitarian Affairs, *Sierra Leone Humanitarian Country Profile, available at* www.irinnews.org/country.aspx?CountryCode=SL&RegionCode=WA

US AID Country Profile, *Rwanda, available at* www.usaid.gov/locations/sub-saharan_africa/countries/rwanda/rwanda_profile.pdf